Combating Trafficking in Human Beings for Labour Exploitation

Conny Rijken (ed.)

Combating Trafficking in Human Beings for Labour Exploitation
C. Rijken (ed.)

ISBN 978-90-5850-653-5

2011

Cover:
Slavernij monument, Amsterdam
Slavery monument

Editor

Wolf Legal Publishers/WLP
POB 31051
6503 CB Nijmegen
The Netherlands
Info@wolfpublishers.nl

"With the financial support from the Prevention of and Fight against Crime Programme of the European Union
European Commission - Directorate-General Home Affairs.
This publication reflects the views only of the authors, and the European Commission cannot be held responsible for any use which may be made of the information contained therein",

Introduction

In this book, the results of the project 'Combating THB for Labour Exploitation' funded by the European Commission and commissioned to Tilburg University are presented.[1] The research started in April 2010, and was concluded with a closing seminar on 8 April 2011. Researchers with different legal backgrounds from five countries; Austria, the Netherlands, Romania, Serbia and Spain[2], participated in the project.

When combating trafficking in human beings (THB) in general, a comprehensive approach based on human rights to combat it is advocated at an EU level. The prosecution of traffickers and the protection of victims of THB are two of the main features of this approach. The overall aim of the project was to bring together the prosecution of traffickers and the protection of victims of THB as two aspects of the human rights based approach to THB for labour exploitation in an integrated and interrelated way, and to strengthen the operational response to this form of THB. Based on this aim the following research question was drawn:

> What obstacles and best practices can be identified (in police and judicial cooperation) in the participating States when identifying victims and when investigating and prosecuting (cross-border) THB for labour exploitation?

Based on the Palermo Protocol[3], the extension of the definition of THB to labour exploitation requires additional skills, knowledge and awareness for effective investigation and prosecution, and for the identification and assistance of victims of this form of THB. Actors (such as labour inspectorates, social investigation services and municipalities) other than the police and the prosecution services have also become involved in these activities. It is unclear which role these actors can have in identifying victims and in investigating and

---

[1] Full title of the project: ' Improving the investigation and prosecution of THB for labour exploitation. Identifying problems and best practices' number Project JLS/2009/ISEC/AG/176.

[2] See Appendix 1 for a list of the participants in the project.

[3] Protocol to the United Nations Convention against Transnational Organised Crime to Prevent, Suppress and Punish Trafficking in Persons, Especially Women and Children, 15 November 2000 A/RES/55/25.

prosecuting (cross-border) THB for labour exploitation and which improvements are needed. They are often unfamiliar with, for instance, the specific needs of victims, how trafficking networks operate, and how to cooperate with colleagues abroad. These problems obviously hamper the combating of THB for labour exploitation. In addition, difficulties in defining THB for labour exploitation still exist. Labour exploitation, as such, is not a term used in the Palermo Protocol or the EU Directive on Preventing and Combating THB and Protecting Victims. When considering the explanation of exploitation given in the Palermo Protocol, one can make the distinction between THB for the purpose of sexual exploitation, labour exploitation (including forced and compulsory labour and services, slavery and slavery-like practices) and the removal of organs. It is in this way that the term labour exploitation in this research must be understood, although this does not solve the problems encountered in defining the crime.

In this book, these problems, as well as the challenges of dealing with these problems, are identified. To this end, research took place in the five participating countries and the EU legal framework was analysed. The results thereof formed the basis of further reflections and recommendations. The country reports are based on information derived from three main sources; 1) an analysis of the legal framework, relevant policy and case law, 2) semi-structured interviews with at least ten experts involved in the investigation and prosecution of (cross-border) THB for labour exploitation, and the protection and assistance of victims of THB for labour exploitation, and 3) the study of two (transnational) cases of THB for labour exploitation. Terms of reference for the country reports, questionnaires for the semi-structured interviews and the case studies were drafted beforehand in order to be able to conduct the analysis of the reports. Based on the terms of reference, the reports are divided into five parts: the legal framework, cooperation in the investigation and prosecution (national and international), victim protection and assistance, case studies, and recommendations. These reports, and the analysis thereof, were discussed during a meeting with invited experts in February 2011, when distinguished specialists made valuable contributions to various aspects of the reports, which were gratefully used to further improve them.

The book contains the results of the country studies in separate chapters, a chapter on the EU legal framework and a chapter on the results of the analysis of the country studies. Furthermore, four chapters are included in which experts in the field of THB for labour exploitation reflect on some of the findings of the project.

Planitzer and Sax, start with an analysis of the situation in Austria and point out that there is still a lack of attention to THB for labour exploitation, which is reflected in the low number of prosecutions and convictions. They furthermore focus on the difficult overlap in the crime of THB for labour exploitation and the exploitation of foreigners, which is defined as a separate crime in Austria. In the next chapter, the situation in the Netherlands is reflected upon by Heemskerk and Rijken. The Netherlands is the only country in this research that has a Social Security Intelligence and Investigation Service specialised in, among other things, labour law issues. Although this service is not used to its full potential, cases of THB for labour exploitation do require specific expertise and therefore it is good to have such a specialised service. In the Netherlands, there is also a great struggle in relation to the definition of THB for labour exploitation. After five years of irresolution by the judiciary to qualify situations as being THB for labour exploitation, a development has now taken place in the opposite direction. In his analysis of the Romanian situation, Zaharia draws our attention to a specific aspect of Romanian law that qualifies the violation of labour laws as a form of THB for labour exploitation when it was preceded by acts and means. Furthermore, he explains the paradoxical situation in Romania in which some situations where exploitation did not take place are punished more severely than situations where exploitation did indeed take place. Copic and Nikolić-Ristanović, in their contribution on Serbia, make us aware that the problems in Serbia are different because Serbia is primarily a country of transit and origin. When law enforcement officers take action in cases of THB for labour exploitation, the cases are often difficult to qualify as such because the exploitation has not actually taken place and the intent of the suspect to exploit the person is difficult to prove. In addition, the researchers give valuable insight into the needs and problems that are specific to victims of THB for labour exploitation. The way that support and assistance is organised in Serbia, with a central role for the Agency for the Coordination of Protection of Victims of Trafficking in Human Beings, a State service from the Ministry of Labour and Social Policy, is different from the other States and makes victim support and assistance less dependent on law enforcement, although Copic and Nikolić-Ristanović have some critical observations as to its functioning. Arrieta Idiakez, Manrique López and Manrique Rojo explain the newly adopted legislation in Spain. It is interesting to note that apart from a provision for THB for labour exploitation, they also have a separate section in the criminal code dealing with Criminal Labour Law. The authors analyse the link between these two areas of crime in Spanish law. In their research, they show that Spain has recently taken some important steps to combat THB for labour exploitation in which cooperation between various actors is specifically addressed. Furthermore, they point out the specific position of Spain as an EU Member State that receives a high number of Third Country Nationals and how this relates to the problems of THB for labour exploitation. In order to be able to place the country studies in the EU environment, Middelburg and Rijken give an analysis of the EU legal framework as far as is relevant for the contribution to a human rights based approach. In the chapter on pitfalls and challenges to combat THB for labour exploitation, Rijken points out the main problems and good practices that can be derived from the country studies. She places these in a broader perspective, including the current debates on the relevant matters. She finally draws conclusions and makes recommendations that might support the EU to further operationalise a comprehensive approach based on human rights for THB for labour exploitation.

Further in the book, distinguished experts in the field reflect on some of the outcomes of the project. Van der Leun, in her contribution, centralises the relation between migration and THB on the punitive and protective perspectives of THB for labour exploitation, and concludes that organisations seem to be divided between those looking at labour issues and migration control on the one hand, and those aiming at combating THB on the other. She furthermore pleads for an increase in the possibilities for people to work legally in the EU. Van Dijk and Vonk give their reflections on a broad spectrum of issues, including areas that are normally not linked with THB for labour exploitation. By doing so, they implicitly show that THB for labour exploitation affects many more aspects of our daily life than law enforcement, victim protection and labour law. They finally focus on the role Europol can play in combating THB for labour exploitation. Beirnaert focuses on international discussions in relation to labour exploitation and shows the important role that the ILO had and still has in this field. He highlights the role that trade unions play or must play in the agency of workers, which is considered key in effectively combating THB for labour exploitation. The last chapter, by van Krimpen, gives a detailed insight into the whimsical developments in Dutch case law in relation to defining THB for labour exploitation. She makes some critical remarks about the latest developments in which convictions for THB took place in relation to the purchase of telephone contracts, which were considered as a service in relation to THB.

Considering this short overview of the content of the book, it is clear that concerted action to combat THB for labour exploitation must be taken in various areas, rather than being limited to merely legal or repressive measures. With this book, we hope to contribute some guidance for such action not only on an EU level but on a national level as well.

I would like to express my gratitude to the European Commission as well as the institutions the researchers work at, for (co-)funding this project. I am furthermore thankful to our experts in the project (Bärbel Uhl and Floris van Dijk) for the valuable discussions and contributions throughout the project. Last but not least I want to thank the researchers for their dedication to the project and the inspiring cooperation. I hope that the outcome of the project will stimulate all of us to bring the comprehensive approach based on human rights a step closer.

Conny Rijken
Tilburg, March 2011

TABLE OF CONTENTS

Abbreviations

ADAPRE	Association for the Development of Alternative Practices of Reintegration and Education
AECID	Spanish International Co-operation for Development Agency
AEL	Alien Employment Law
AI	AI *Arbeidsinspectie*
AMF	Directie Arbeidsmarktfraude van de Arbeidsinspectie *(Directorate Market Fraud of the Labour Inspectorate)*
APA	Aliens' Police Act
Arbo	Directie Arbeidsomstandigheden *(Directorate Labour Conditions of the Labour Inspectorate)*
art	Article
AWR	Algemene Wet Rijksbelastingen *(General Act on Royal Taxes)*
B9 procedure	Chapter B9 of the Immigration Circular part B
BDTRATA	Data-Management System regarding Trafficking in Human Beings.
BNRM	Bureau Nationaal Rapporteur Mensenhandel *(Bureau National Rapporteur Trafficking in Human Beings)*
CC	Criminal Code
CCP	Code on Criminal Procedure
CCLA	Corporate Criminal Liability Act
cf.	compare
CIE	Criminele Inlichtingen Eenheid *(Criminal Intelligence Unit)*
CJIB	Centraal Justitieel Incassobureau *(Central Fines Collection Agency)*
CoMensha	Coordinatiecentrum Mensenhandel *(Coordination Center THB)*
COMMCA	Council of Ministers of Women's Affairs of Central America.
COS	Comprehensive Operational Strategic Planning for the Police
CPS:	Country Strategy Papers.
CV:	Curriculum Vitae.
DIOCT	Department for Investigating Organised Crime and Terrorism

DNR	Dienst Nationale Recherche van de Korps Landelijke Politie Diensten *(National Investigation Team of the National Police Services Brigade)*
DPC	Wetboek van Strafrecht *(Dutch Penal Code)*
DPPC	Wetboek van Strafvordering *(Dutch Penal Procedure Code)*
DSO	Dienst Stedelijke Ontwikkeling *(Service Urban Development)*
eds	editors
eg	for example
EJN	European Judicial Network
EMM	Expertise Centrum Mensenhandel Mensensmokkel *(Expertise Center Human Trafficking Human Smuggling)*
ESBC:	Eastern Sea Borders Centre.
EU	European Union
EUBAM	European Union Border Assistance Mission
EU-JZG	Bundesgesetz über die justizielle Zusammenarbeit in Strafsachen mit den Mitgliedstaaten der Europäischen Union
EU-PolKG	EU-Polizeikooperationsgesetz
FATF	Financial Action Task Force
FIOD	Fiscale Inlichtingen- en Opsporingsdienst *(Fiscal Intelligence and Investigation Department)*
FMEIA	Federal Ministry for European and International Affairs
Functional Office	Functioneel Parket van het OM *(Functional Office of the national prosecution service)*
G.D.	Government Decision
G.E.O.	Government Emergency Ordinance
G.O.	Government Ordinance
JIT	Joint Investigation Team
IBF	Interventionsstelle für Betroffene des Frauenhandels
ID	Identity
ILO	International Labour Organisation
IND	Immigratie en Naturalisatiedienst *(Immigration and Naturalization Service)*
KLPD	Korps Landelijke Politiedienesten *(National Police Services Brigade)*
SIVE	Integrated Border Patrol System
SIS	Schengen Information System
SPA	Security Police Act

SRA	Settlement and Residence Act
SVB	Sociale Verzekeringsbank *(Social Security Bank)*
SZW	Ministerie van Sociale Zaken en Werkgelegenheid *(Ministry Social Affairs and Employment)*
THB	Trafficking in Human Beings
TRLET	Royal Decree 1/1995 of 24 March, which approves the consolidated text of the Law of the Statute of Workers.
TRLISOS	Royal Legislative Decree 5/2000, of 4th August, which approves the 'Consolidated Law on Offenses and Penalties in the Social Order'.
UNODC	United Nations Office on Drugs and Crime
UN	United Nations
UNGA	United Nations General Assembly
UWV	Uitvoeringsinstituut Werknemers Verzekeringen *(Employee Insurance Agency)*
VCA	Victims of Crime Act
VIS	Visa Information System
WAV	Wet Arbeid Vreemdelingen *(Aliens Employment Act)*
WML	Wet Minimum Loon en Minimum Vakantietoeslag *(Act Minimum Wage and Minimum Holiday Allowance)*
WSBC	Western Sea Borders Centre

Chapter 1
Combating Trafficking in Human Beings for Labour Exploitation in Austria

Julia Planitzer and Helmut Sax[1]

Part I
The legal framework on defining Trafficking in Human Beings for labour exploitation and the dimensions of this crime

1.1 The definition of Trafficking in Human Beings for labour exploitation in Austria

Trafficking in human beings (THB) is legally defined in the Criminal Code[2] and follows in general the definition given in Art. 3(a) of the Protocol to Prevent, Suppress and Punish Trafficking in Persons, especially Women and Children, supplementing the United Nations Convention against Transnational Organized Crime[3] of *trafficking in persons*.

The forms of *exploitation* provided for in Criminal Code s. 104a (1) are: sexual exploitation, the removal of organs and labour exploitation.

For various reasons, CC s. 104a does not list all forms of exploitation as given in the Palermo Protocol. Forms of exploitation such as slavery or forms similar to slavery would be covered by the offence 'trafficking in slaves' of CC s. 104[4] and therefore CC s. 104a speaks only about 'labour exploitation'. The term 'trafficking in slaves' can, however, be misleading since the offence includes (since 2009) also slavery in itself, and treating a person like a slave.[5] In particular, CC s. 104 includes deprivation of liberty of a person through slavery and slavery-like practices. The central characteristic of slavery is the fact that a person is seen as an object and as property which can be used at will and arbitrarily. Slavery-like practices include debt bondage and serfdom.[6]

---

[1] Julia Planitzer is researcher at Group on Women's Rights, Child Rights and Human Trafficking, Ludwig Boltzmann Institute of Human Rights, Vienna, Austria. Helmut Sax is researcher and team-leader of this Group.

[2] Criminal Code (Federal Law Gazette No. 60/1974), s. 104(a).

[3] UNGA Res 55/25 (15 November 2000), Annex II, hereinafter 'Palermo Protocol'.

[4] For a long time hardly not used, the offence 'trafficking in slaves' gained a lot of publicity since in the famous case 'F.' the perpetrator was accused of slavery for having locked the victim for 24 years in a cellar.

[5] K. Schwaighofer, in Frank Höpfel and Eckart Ratz (eds), *Commentary of the Criminal Code* (2nd edn, Manz, Vienna 2006) CC s. 104(2)(a).

[6] K. Schwaighofer, in Frank Höpfel and Eckart Ratz (eds), *Commentary of the Criminal Code* (2nd edn, Manz, Vienna 2006) CC s. 104(4).

Practices which do not fulfil all criteria of slavery and acts similar to slavery would be caught by the offence of trafficking in human beings (CC s. 104a).

Exploitation within the meaning of CC s. 104a includes the ruthless and lasting oppression of vital interests. The perpetrator has to intend to oppress the vital interests in the longer term. It is irrelevant whether the perpetrator or a third person is the beneficiary of the exploitation. An additional important element of exploitation is the significant disproportionality between 'services' delivered by the victim and the reward for them.[7] Since the offence 'pimping' (CC s. 216) includes the term exploitation and exists longer than the offence 'trafficking in human beings' in the Austrian CC, relevant case law regarding 'exploitation' exists within 'pimping' The interpretation of 'sexual exploitation' as well as 'labour exploitation' is influenced by the case law on 'pimping'. Under this offence, exploitation occurs when the majority of payments are taken away ruthlessly. Consequently, vital interests of the victim are infringed.[8] Sexual exploitation within THB occurs when the victim has to conduct sexual services and the full or predominant parts of payments are held back. Not only can lack of payments amount to exploitation, but working conditions can also lead to an infringement of vital interests. Exploitation is not foreseen when difficult working conditions are compensated with higher payments.[9]

However, the term 'labour exploitation' within the provision on 'trafficking in human beings' would include a ruthless exploitation of vital interests of the victim. This would include *inter alia* circumstances in which the victim either does not receive any, or receives entirely inadequate, remuneration for his or her work for a lengthy period of time. Exploitation also includes instances where regular working hours are excessively exceeded or when working conditions are unacceptable. Payments falling slightly under the minimum wage, foreseen in collective agreements, as well as the occasional exceeding of average working hours, will not amount to exploitation.[10] CC s. 104a also covers begging as a possible form of labour exploitation.[11]

Trafficking for the purpose of exploitation in respect of *prostitution* is not mentioned explicitly in CC s. 104a - it speaks only about *sexual exploitation*. The reason for this phrasing can be found in the historical development of CC

---

[7] K. Schwaighofer, in Frank Höpfel and Eckart Ratz (eds), *Commentary of the Criminal Code* (2nd edn, Manz, Vienna 2006) CC s. 104(a)(8).

[8] Supreme Court (OGH), 12 Os 73/81, 16 July 1981 see also Supreme Court (OGH), 12 Os 17/85, 9 May 1985.

[9] K. Schwaighofer, in Frank Höpfel and Eckart Ratz (eds), *Commentary of the Criminal Code* (2nd edn, Manz, Vienna 2006) s. 104(a)(9).

[10] Materials regarding the Law on amending the CC 2004 (Federal Law Gazette No. 15/2004) p. 12.
<http://www.parlament.gv.at/PAKT/VHG/XXII/I/I_00294/fname_010159.pdf> accessed 17 November 2010.

[11] Interview with a public prosecutor (November 2010).

s. 104a, as this particular provision was only implemented in 2004.[12] Until 2004, trafficking in human beings only covered trafficking in prostitution, which no longer fulfilled the requirements of the Palermo Protocol. Although a new section on trafficking in human beings was implemented, the former version remained in the CC and has the title 'transnational prostitution trade' (CC s. 217).

Summarised as *action* within the definition of the Palermo Protocol, the Criminal Code lists recruitment, harbouring or receipt of persons, transportation, offering and passing on. *Means* include deceit, abuse of power, exploitation of situations of distress or of mental illness or any condition rendering the person defenceless as well as giving or receiving of payments or benefits to achieve the consent of a person having control over another person. In the case of child trafficking, the use of 'means' is not an essential requirement.

There are different levels of sanctions foreseen. The usual penalty for THB can be up to a maximum of three years imprisonment. In cases where the perpetrator used threat or force, the penalty is between six months and 5 years. Aggravating circumstances include trafficking in children below the age of 14, committing the crime within the activities of an organised criminal group, causing particularly serious harm to the victim, or the use of severe force, which will lead to sanctions of between one and ten years imprisonment.

CC s. 104a does not provide, as foreseen in the Palermo Protocol, for a specific clause dealing with the consent of the victim. It is assumed by the Austrian legislator that the usage of '(unfair) means' constitutes an impaired free will.[13] Consequently, a specific clause was not deemed necessary.

1.2 Other legislation and policies relevant for Trafficking in Human Beings for labour exploitation

1.2.1 Criminal law

Transnational prostitution trade

Closely linked to CC s. 104a is the offence covering the 'transnational prostitution trade', which – as mentioned above - used to be *the* offence on trafficking in human beings until 2004. CC s. 217 is usually also mentioned along with 'trafficking in human beings' as the relevant provision regarding

---

[12] Law on amending the CC 2004 (Federal Law Gazette No. 15/2004).

[13] Materials regarding the Law on amending the CC 2004 (Federal Law Gazette No. 15/2004) p. 13 <http://www.parlament.gv.at/PAKT/VHG/XXII/I/I_00294/fname_010159.pdf> accessed 22 November 2010.

trafficking in human beings in general.[14] CC s. 217 punishes the recruitment or procurement of a person into prostitution in another country. If the perpetrator seeks regular profits from these criminal acts, the punishment is between one and ten years imprisonment. CC s. 217 (2) foresees the same punishment in cases where the perpetrator uses force or deceit regarding the work to be done in the other country. The title of this offence might be misleading, since the actual definition of 'trafficking in human beings' does not have to be necessarily fulfilled.[15]

Firstly, CC s. 217 (2) can be applied for cases of trafficking in human beings for the purpose of sexual exploitation only. Offences covering trafficking in women for the purpose of exploitation in prostitution can fall under CC s. 104a or CC s. 217 as well. In order to apply CC s. 217, an additional special intent to exploit has to be proven. If this is the case, the application of CC s. 217 prevails over CC s. 104a due to its higher punishment. If both would be applicable, CC s. 217 (2) and CC s. 104a, then 'transnational prostitution trade' is used.

The second difference between 'trafficking in human beings' and 'transnational prostitution trade' is the fact that a border needs to be crossed in order to apply CC s. 217. The victim is brought from one State to another. The victim does not have the citizenship of this State and does not permanently reside there. Also, movements between EU Member States are covered by CC s. 217.[16]

The available statistics show that 'transnational prostitution trade' is applied rather often compared to the application of CC s. 104a ('trafficking in human beings').[17] Since 'transnational prostitution trade' prevails in cases of trafficking in women for the purpose of exploitation in prostitution, it can be assumed that a major part of Austria's cases on trafficking in women are dealt with under CC s. 217.[18] In conclusion, the offence 'trafficking in human beings' is

---

[14] Cf. Austrian Task Force on Combating Human Trafficking, *First Austrian Report on Combating Human Trafficking* (2008) p. 25.

[15] T. Philipp, in Frank Höpfel and Eckart Ratz (eds), *Commentary of the Criminal Code* (2nd edn, Manz, Vienna 2006) s. 217(1).

[16] T. Philipp, in Frank Höpfel and Eckart Ratz (eds), *Commentary of the Criminal Code* (2nd edn, Manz, Vienna 2006) s. 217 (12) (emphasis added).

[17] Convictions regarding CC s. 217: 85 in 2007, 18 in 2008 and 30 in 2009. Judicial criminal statistics 2007, 2008 and 2009 of Statistics Austria <http://www.statistik.at/web_de/dynamic/statistiken/soziales/kriminalitaet/verurteilungen_gerichtliche_kriminalstatistik/publikationen?id=6&webcat=176&nodeId=333&frag=3&listid=176> accessed 18 November 2010.

[18] Generally, next to CC s. 104a ('trafficking in human beings') and CC s. 217 ('transnational prostitution trade') further provisions of the CC are mentioned being relevant for trafficking in human beings for the purpose of sexual exploitation: These are CC s. 214 ('paid negotiation of sexual contacts with minors'), CC s. 207 (b) ('sexual abuse of minors'), CC s. 215 ('leading persons towards prostitution') and CC s. 215 (a)

regulated in CC s. 104a, which covers all forms of exploitation. Nevertheless this offence is accompanied by 'transnational prostitution trade', which can also cover cases of trafficking in women for the purpose of exploitation in prostitution.

Corporate liability

As well as establishing the criminal liability of individuals, Austria is also obliged to establish the criminal liability of legal persons with regard to trafficking in human beings.[19] The Austrian Corporate Criminal Liability Act[20] implements these obligations and States that all criminal offences are covered by the Act, including trafficking in human beings.[21] When cases of trafficking in human beings are committed for the benefit of a legal person, the CCLA would be applicable. Since entering into force in 2006, the CCLA has not been applied very often and no specific case on trafficking in human beings has been dealt with. In the years 2006 and 2007, no convictions of legal persons based on the CCLA were registered. The comparably low number of cases lodged under the CCLA has also not met the expectations of the implementing Ministry of Justice; however the number of cases increased significantly in the year 2007.[22] The Ministry of Justice currently evaluates the application of the CCLA and has been asked to help increase the number of applications by offering guidelines for public prosecutors.[23] But given the low numbers of cases under the CCLA, combined with the low numbers of cases before courts dealing with THB in general, it might be concluded that it will take further time until the CCLA can be applied effectively against THB for the purpose of labour exploitation in business.

('promoting prostitution and pornographic actions of minors'). Since the report focuses on trafficking for the purpose of labour exploitations, these provisions are not further discussed.

[19] Cf. Council of Europe Convention on Action against Trafficking in Human Beings (No. 197, adopted 16 May 2005, entered into force 1 February 2008) art 22 and Council Framework Decision 2002/629/JHA on combating trafficking in human beings [2002] OJ L203/1 art 4.

[20] Federal Law Gazette I No. 151/2005 as amended by Federal Law Gazette I No. 112/2007.

[21] Cf. CCLA s. 1(1).

[22] National Council of the Parliament, Answer to parliamentarian question 4398/J-NR/2008 (14 July 2008) <http://www.parlament.gv.at/PAKT/VHG/XXIII/AB/AB_04399/fnameorig_116474.html> accessed 18 November 2010.

[23] Council of Europe, Group of states against corruption, *Joint First and Second Round Evaluation Compliance Report on Austria* (Report) (11 June 2010) paras 105-107 <http://www.coe.int/t/dghl/monitoring/greco/evaluations/round2/GrecoRC1&2%28 2010%291_Austria_EN.pdf> accessed 18 November 2010.

The principle of extraterritoriality
CC s. 64 contains a catalogue of offences which can be prosecuted when committed by Austrians abroad. All offences listed in CC s. 64 can be prosecuted irrespective of the criminal law of the country where the offence was committed. This catalogue contains *inter alia* 'trafficking in slaves', 'trafficking in human beings' and 'transnational prostitution trade'.

1.2.2 Labour law

An employee is one who obligates him/herself to work for an employer based on a written or oral employment contract. Main characteristics of an employment relationship are the personal dependency and the economic dependency of the employee. Employees enjoy the full protection of labour laws. The labour contract contains obligations for employers and employees. It includes the obligation to pay wages for the employer and the obligation on the part of the employee to fulfil his/her duties.[24]

Austria does not have a legally-based minimum wage. Collective agreements settle for every labour sector specific levels of income, which are not allowed to be undermined.[25] Collective agreements are adopted by unions or associations representing the employers' interests and unions representing employees and should ensure a balance of interests.[26]

Protection of employees can be divided into three areas: protection against risks at the work place, protection regarding working time and protection regarding the form of required work. This encompasses, for example, restrictions for pregnant workers or forms of work adequate for children and adolescents.[27] Regulations regarding protection against risks are controlled by labour inspectorates according to the Act on the Protection of Employees[28].[29] Based on a law on working time, the usual daily working time is eight hours; the weekly working time of 40 hours may not be exceeded. It is possible to work ten hours a day, but the weekly limit of 40 hours must not be

[24] H. Krejci, in Peter Rummel, *Commentary of the Civil Code* (3rd edn, Manz, Vienna, 2007) s. 1151(6).
[25] W. Brodil, M. Risak and C. Wolf, *Arbeitsrecht in Grundzügen* (6th edn, LexisNexis, Vienna 2010)(248).
[26] W. Brodil, M. Risak and C. Wolf, *Arbeitsrecht in Grundzügen* (6th edn, LexisNexis, Vienna 2010)(113).
[27] W. Brodil, M. Risak and C. Wolf, *Arbeitsrecht in Grundzügen* (6th edn, LexisNexis, Vienna 2010)(310).
[28] Federal Law Gazette I No. 450/1994 as amended by Federal Law Gazette II No. 221/2010.
[29] W. Brodil, M. Risak and C. Wolf, *Arbeitsrecht in Grundzügen* (6th edn. LexisNexis, Vienna 2010)(315).

exceeded.[30]

Participation of non-nationals in the Austrian labour market

Austrian laws on migration classify migrants in different categories and distinguish between EU citizens, Convention refugees who have been granted asylum, migrants from countries with bilateral or association agreements with Austria,[31] and other third-country citizens.[32] Entry, residence and settlement in Austria are regulated by the Settlement and Residence Act (SRA)[33] as well as by the Aliens' Police Act (APA).[34] Entry into the labour market by migrants is regulated by the Alien Employment Law (AEL).[35] Within this rather complex system of laws, several intersections, dependencies and also inconsistencies exist. In general, all persons who are non-citizens of Austria or of any other EU Member State need specific permission to enter the labour market.[36]

However, for citizens of new EU Member States, access to the labour market is limited. For these citizens, except Malta and Cyprus, the regulations of the AEL apply in respect of access to the labour market. The AEL was, with some exceptions, applicable for citizens of Hungary, Poland, Czech Republic, Slovakia, Slovenia, Estonia, Lithuania and Latvia until the end of April 2011, and for citizens of Romania and Bulgaria until the end of December 2011.[37]

For third country nationals in general, seven different forms of work permissions exist, which are based on the SRA and the AEL.[38] The first level forms the temporary work permit (*Beschäftigungsbewilligung*) which is requested by the employer at the Austrian Employment Service (AES). It allows

[30] Cf. Act on Working Time, Federal Law Gazette No. 461/1969 as amended by Federal Law Gazette I No. 149/2009, s. 3 and 4.

[31] Eg Turkey.

[32] Forschungs- und Beratungsstelle Arbeitswelt, *Austria Country Report, Undocumented Worker Transitions* (Report) (July 2007) 7.

[33] Federal Law Gazette I No. 100/2005 as amended by Federal Law Gazette I No. 122/2009.

[34] Federal Law Gazette I No. 100/2005 as amended by Federal Law Gazette I No. 135/2009.

[35] Federal Law Gazette I No. 218/1975 as amended by Federal Law Gazete I No. 135/2009.

[36] A. Binder, 'Zirkuläre Migration in die Gemüsebaugebiete Österreichs' (Thesis, University of Vienna 2008) p. 43.

[37] General Information of the Federal Ministry of Labour, Social Affairs and Consumer Protection on employment of EU citizens <http://www.bmask.gv.at/cms/site/attachments/9/8/5/CH0688/CMS1236265784545/2010-07-26_beschaeftigung_von_arbeitskraeften_aus_den_neuen_eu-mitgliedstaaten.pdf> accessed 24 November 2010.

[38] Not all of them are discussed within this report, such as the access to the labour market as key person (*Schlüsselkraft*).

employment with a certain company for a maximum of one year.[39] Several prerequisites, such as the fulfilment of a specific quota for migrant workers allowed in the Austrian labour market, make it especially difficult to obtain a temporary work permit.[40] In addition, the temporary work permit can only be granted after an assessment of the labour market (*Arbeitsmarktprüfung*). This assessment includes questioning whether current developments within the labour market would allow the employment, and whether public interests would oppose employment.[41]

The next level would be the work permit (*Arbeitserlaubnis*), which allows for work in one federal province of Austria for a maximum of two years. The migrant can apply for it her-/himself at the Austria Employment Service. The migrant must have been employed prior in Austria for a specific period of time and needs to lawfully reside in Austria.[42] Following this, a certificate of exemption (*Befreiungsschein*) could be issued to the migrant, which allows work all over Austria for five years. Lawful title to settlement is again a prerequisite, and – among further requirements – a prior legal employment of at least five years in the preceding eight years in Austria is necessary.[43]

AEL s. 29 foresees that migrants who are working but do not fulfil the requirements of the AEL or SRA are entitled to the same claims as persons with a regular working contract. Working contracts between an employer and employee which do not fulfil all criteria of the AEL or SRA are usually considered void. With regard to claims such as wages, the employee has the same status as if she/he had a valid working contract.[44]

The Act on the adaption of employment contract law (*Arbeitsvertragsrechts-Anpassungsgesetz*)[45] states in s. 7b that posted workers coming from abroad and working in Austria have specific minimum claims. These claims encompass a minimum wage, which is usually paid at the place of work, thus in Austria, as well as paid leave and working hours based on collective agreements. This section should prevent dumping of wages due to different levels of average wages.

---

[39] Forschungs- und Beratungsstelle Arbeitswelt, *Austria Country Report, Undocumented Worker Transitions* (Report) (July 2007) p. 8.

[40] D. Einwallner and T. Neugschwendtner, *EU-Recht und ausländische ArbeitnehmerInnen – muss Österreich handeln?* (OEGB Vienna 2009) p. 59.

[41] Cf. AEL s 4(1).

[42] D. Einwallner and T. Neugschwendtner, *EU-Recht und ausländische ArbeitnehmerInnen – muss Österreich handeln?* (OEGB Vienna 2009) pp. 61-62.

[43] D. Einwallner and T. Neugschwendtner, *EU-Recht und ausländische ArbeitnehmerInnen – muss Österreich handeln?* (OEGB Vienna 2009) p. 65.

[44] R. Dittrich and H. Tades, *Arbeitsrecht* (2nd edn, Manz, Vienna 2010) AEL s. 29(E)(8).

[45] Federal Law Gazette No. 459/1993 as amended by Federal Law Gazette I No. 29/2010.

Participation of victims of THB in the Austrian labour market

Improving access to the labour market for victims of THB is part of the National Action Plan and therefore part of discussions.[46] In general, victims of THB who stay longer in Austria and require access to labour market is rather small.

Victims of THB coming from the new EU Member States need to have a specific confirmation of registration (*Anmeldebescheinigung*)[47] regarding their residence and had to obey the AEL until April 2011 or in the case of Romania and Bulgaria have to do so until December 2011. This means that certain quota may not be exceeded and an assessment of the labour market must be enacted before a temporary working permit can be issued.

Third country nationals can after one year get an unlimited authorisation of settlement (*Niederlassungsbewilligung-unbeschränkt*), which is based on certain prerequisites.[48] The unlimited authorisation of settlement allows for unlimited access to the labour market.[49]

As indicated above, access to the labour market is *inter alia* regulated by specific quotas. Under certain circumstances, the maximum numbers of permits can be exceeded, according to a specific regulation (*Bundeshöchstzahlüberziehungsverordnung*). The Task Force suggests amending this regulation to include a specific provision for victims of THB. Experience of LEFOE-IBF shows that obtaining temporary work permits (*Beschäftigungsbewilligungen*) for low-skilled jobs is very difficult.[50] In 2009, only one temporary work permit was issued to a woman supported by LEFOE-IBF.[51] Recently, a draft amendment to the AEL was presented by the Ministry of Labour, Social Affairs and Consumer Protection.[52] This amendment foresees that victims of THB can also get a temporary working permit when quota are exceeded. This measure

---

[46] Cf. National Action Plan against Human Trafficking, IV.3 <http://www.bmeia.gv.at/fileadmin/user_upload/bmeia/media/2-Aussenpolitik_Zentrale/Menschenrechte/TFM_Aktionsplan_engl_V20091007_LAYOUT_FINAL.pdf> accessed 2 February 2011.

[47] For further information see G. Cristinel Zaharia, Combating Trafficking in Human Beings for Labour Exploitation in Romania, Chapter 3, para 2.2 in this book.

[48] For further information see G. Cristinel Zaharia, 'Combating Trafficking in Human Beings for Labour Exploitation in Romania', Chapter 3, paras 2.2 in this book.

[49] Cf. AEL s. 17 and SRA s. 8(2)(3).

[50] Austrian Task Force on Combating Human Trafficking, *First Austrian Report on Combating Human Trafficking* (2008) pp. 11-12.

[51] Cf. LEFOE-IBF, *2009 Annual Report* (Vienna 2010) p. 27.

[52]<http://www.bmask.gv.at/cms/site/dokument.html?channel=CH0175&doc=CMS1291907038590> accessed 2 February 2011.

should ensure that victims of THB have easier access to the labour market with no assessment of the labour market needing to be done.[53]

Regulation of specific sectors

Regarding *seasonal work in tourism and agriculture*, specific work permits are issued in order to be able to answer the higher demand for workers during high seasons in tourism and harvesting times.[54] The quotas for these short-term permits are regulated in decrees for each season.[55] The short-term permit can be issued for a maximum of six months. In exceptional cases, the migrant can get a permit for up to nine months. For harvesting, shorter permits can be issued; harvesting permits are valid for a maximum of six weeks.[56] The harvesting permit can only be issued to citizens of countries who can enter Austria without any further entry permit or visa requirement (*sichtvermerksfreie Einreise*[57]).[58] In 2009, the AES granted in total around 65.000 short term permits for the tourism sector (winter/summer), for harvesting, forestry and agriculture.[59] Wages within these short-term permits are based on collective agreements.[60] For the province of Styria, the monthly wage of an unskilled worker in agriculture would be € 1.109,50 (pre-tax).[61] Since March 2010, a seasonal agricultural worker in the provinces of Vienna, Lower Austria and

---

[53] Amendment to the AEL, introductory and commentary to the amendments, p. 6 <http://www.bmask.gv.at/cms/site/attachments/7/7/9/CH0175/CMS1291907038590/vorblatt_und_erlaeuterungen.pdf> accessed 2 February 2011.

[54] Cf. AEL s. 5(1).

[55] Cf. Decree on employment of migrants in tourism (Federal Law Gazette II 351/2010). It states that in November 2010 for the upcoming winter tourism season 5895 short-term permits can be issued. The quota are divided according to the demand to the provinces of Austria.

[56] General Information of the Federal Ministry of Labour, Social Affairs and Consumer Protection on employment of EU citizens <http://www.bmask.gv.at/cms/site/attachments/9/8/5/CH0688/CMS1236265784545/2010-07-26_beschaeftigung_von_arbeitskraeften_aus_den_neuen_eu-mitgliedstaaten.pdf> accessed 24 November 2010.

[57] This would encompass all EU Member States (including ‚new' Member States) and numerous third states such as Croatia and (under further certain requirements) Serbia, Montenegro and FYROM.

[58] Cf. AEL s. 5(1)(2).

[59] Austrian Employment Service, 2009 Annual Report (Vienna 2010) p. 47 <http://www.ams.at/_docs/Die_Auslaenderbeschaeftigung.pdf> accessed 24 November 2010.

[60] A. Binder, 'Zirkuläre Migration in die Gemüsebaugebiete Österreichs' (Thesis, University of Vienna 2008) p. 50.

[61] Cf. Chamber of workers in forestry and agriculture Styria <http://www .landarbeiterkammer.at/steiermark/_lccms_/_00132/KV-Agrar.htm?VER=100201180547&MID=135&LANG=lak> accessed 24 November 2010.

Burgenland has to receive, according to the collective agreement, a daily wage of € 39,75.[62]

Despite the regulations on working times and collective agreements, working conditions in harvesting are poor. Excessive working hours are reported, living conditions are bad and passports are taken away and locked during the harvest season.[63]

Concerning the social benefits, persons holding a harvesting permit are not protected fully by the social security system (including insurance of sickness, work-related accidents and pensions).[64] Additionally harvest helpers and seasonal workers are not entitled to receive unemployment benefits, since they are not lawfully residing after the time period of the permit.[65] It is shown, that seasonal workers and harvest helpers do not make use in general of the social benefits. In case they would make use of rights such as paid leave or payment during sickness, they would run the risk to lose the job immediately or to not get the job next summer.[66]

In order to reorganise the *care sector* in Austria, a specific Home Care Law (HCL) was introduced in 2007.[67] Before the HCL entered into force, 24 hour-care at home was usually organised by two women alternatively working for two weeks. During the time one of the women works in Austria, the other goes back to her home country. This system worked until 2007 without any legal basis and was illegal. Working without any contract, the women had no possibility to claim for adequate wages or social benefits and faced exploitation.[68] The new HCL seeks to decriminalise the system of 24 hour-care at home. It

---

[62] Collective Agreement between the Trade Union (PRO-GE) and the chamber of employers <http://www.proge.at/servlet/BlobServer?blobcol=urldokument&blobheadername1=content-type&blobheadername2=content-disposition&blobheadervalue1=application%2Fpdf&blobheadervalue2=inline%3B+filename%3D%22Lohntabelle_f%25C3%25BCr_die_landwirtschaftlichen_SaisonarbeiterInnen_in_den_landwirtschaftlichen_Betrieben_der_Bundesl%25C3%25A4nder_Nieder%25C3%25B6sterreich%252C_Burgenland_und_Wien.pdf%22&blobkey=id&root=P01&blobnocache=false&blobtable=Dokument&blobwhere=1257346755789> accessed 24 November 2010.

[63] D. Behr, 'Saisonniers und ErnehelferInnen im Marchfeld' in Gétaz Raymond (ed), *Bittere Ernte* (Europäisches BürgerInnenforum, CEDRI 2004) pp. 73-79.

[64] Cf. General Social Insurance Act s. 5(1)(13) (Federal Law Gazette I No. 189/1955 as amended by Federal Law Gazette I No. 92/2010).

[65] Cf. D. Einwallner and T. Neugschwendtner, *EU-Recht und ausländische Arbeitnehmerinnen – muss Österreich handeln?* (OEGB Vienna 2009) p. 101.

[66] D. Behr, 'Saisonniers und ErnehelferInnen im Marchfeld' in Gétaz Raymond (ed), *Bittere Ernte* (Europäisches BürgerInnenforum, CEDRI 2004) p. 78.

[67] Federal Law Gazette I No. 33/2007 as amended by Federal Law Gazette I No. 57/2008.

[68] F. Drott, 'Pflegerinnen aus Osteuropa gesucht' (Thesis, University of Vienna 2009) pp. 35-36.

enables the employment of a care person and offers also the opportunity to work as a care person self-employed.[69] The possibility to be self-employed was highly criticised and is seen as a form of bogus self-employment since in most cases the women are personally and economically dependent.[70] Self-employment leads to undermining standards of labour law and legitimising precarious and exploitative labour conditions.[71] Figures show that the system of self-employment is more popular than the employment option. In 2007, around 300 employed persons were registered, but in August 2008 around 11.000 self-employed persons are reported.[72] The law foresees exceptions of labour law standards and explicitly takes advantage of differences in wages in Austria and eastern countries and leads to exploitation based on gender and ethnic discrimination.[73]

1.2.3 Migration law

Smuggling

The definition of smuggling can be found in the Aliens' Police Act (APA) s. 114. Smuggling and THB are often discussed in the general THB-discourse as two different offences which need to be clearly distinguished. Looking at the Austrian regulation on smuggling, the wording of the offence precludes confusion.

In short, the perpetrator is punished in cases when the person organises the illegal entry to, or transit through, Member States of the EU and neighbouring countries of Austria. The perpetrator must intend to profit from 'organizing'. Organizing includes every service for the smuggled person which supports the illegal entry or transit. This includes the organisation of forged documents, maps, transportation in cars or providing smuggled persons with basic needs.[74]

Exploitation of a foreigner

A provision which is also closely linked to trafficking in human beings is also dealt with in the APA. The offence punishes the 'exploitation of a foreign person' (APA s. 116). This offence is categorised in the APA because it is argued that this offence can also be closely linked to smuggling (APA s. 114)

---

[69] F. Drott, 'Pflegerinnen aus Osteuropa gesucht' (Thesis, University of Vienna 2009) p. 39.
[70] F. Drott, 'Pflegerinnen aus Osteuropa gesucht' (Thesis, University of Vienna 2009) p. 49.
[71] F. Drott, 'Pflegerinnen aus Osteuropa gesucht' (Thesis, University of Vienna 2009) p. 56.
[72] A. Buchinger, 'Der irreguläre Pflegearbeitsmarkt' (Thesis, University of Vienna 2009) p. 146.
[73] F. Drott, 'Pflegerinnen aus Osteuropa gesucht' (Thesis, University of Vienna 2009) p. 80.
[74] A. Tipold, in Frank Höpfel and Eckart Ratz (eds), *Commentary of the Criminal Code* (2nd edn, Manz, Vienna 2006) APA s. 114(10).

and usually follows smuggling.[75] Nevertheless, it is not necessary that the victim has been smuggled in order to apply APA s. 116.[76]
The perpetrator takes advantage of the victim's specific dependency which is based on the fact that the foreign person is either illegally in the country, does not have a regular working permit or is in any other particular situation of dependency. The dependency of a victim is also apparent in cases where the foreigner can move freely and leave the exploiter, but cannot use this possibility out of fear or threat of being identified by authorities and possibly deported.[77]

The interpretation of exploitation follows established case law on exploitation of victims within the framework of pimping.[78] As elaborated with regard to THB (CC s. 104a) above, the ruthless exploitation of vital interests of the victim is also necessary. Exploitation occurs when the victim receives only as much as being able to cover basic needs or nothing at all in the longer term. Excessive working hours or unacceptable working conditions can amount to exploitation. Taking advantage of the difference between average wages in Austria and the country of origin as such does not qualify as exploitation. *Excessiveness* is important - minor violations of limits (working hours, minimum wages) do not amount to exploitation.[79]

A person who exploits a foreigner in order to receive continuous profits can be punished with a prison sentence of up to three years. The perpetrator can be punished with a prison sentence of six months up to five years in cases when she/he leads the foreigner to a situation of hardship or exploits a larger number of persons. The situation of hardship means that there is a shortage of food, housing, clothing and medical care. The foreigner is not able to provide for goods and services indispensable to life. A 'larger number of persons' means around ten victims.[80] If the exploitation causes the death of the foreigner, the perpetrator faces a minimum of one year up to a maximum of ten years imprisonment.

When directly comparing CC s. 104a and APA s. 116, following the elements of the definition of trafficking in human beings (*action-means-purpose*), it can be seen that only the element of *action* is not required in APA s. 116. All

[75] A. Tipold, in Frank Höpfel and Eckart Ratz (eds), *Commentary of the Criminal Code* (2nd edn, Manz, Vienna 2006) APA s. 116(1).
[76] A. Tipold, in Frank Höpfel and Eckart Ratz (eds), *Commentary of the Criminal Code* (2nd edn, Manz, Vienna 2006) APA s. 116(6).
[77] A. Tipold, in Frank Höpfel and Eckart Ratz (eds), *Commentary of the Criminal Code* (2nd edn, Manz, Vienna 2006) APA s. 116(6).
[78] Cf. CC 216(2), A. Tipold, in Frank Höpfel and Eckart Ratz (eds), *Commentary of the Criminal Code* (2nd edn, Manz, Vienna 2006) APA s. 116(7).
[79] A. Tipold, in Frank Höpfel and Eckart Ratz (eds), *Commentary of the Criminal Code* (2nd edn, Manz, Vienna 2006) APA s. 116(8-9) (emphasis added).
[80] A. Tipold, in Frank Höpfel and Eckart Ratz (eds), *Commentary of the Criminal Code* (2nd edn, Manz, Vienna 2006) APA s. 116 (11-13).

other elements of the definition need to be fulfilled also for APA s. 116. 'Trafficking in human beings' (CC s. 104a) foresees the usage of certain means which includes also the exploitation of situations of distress. These cover also situations of social distress, such as illegal residency.[81] The purpose of APA s. 116 is to combat exploitation, although it is not further defined which forms of exploitation are covered.

Another difference concerns the definition of the victim: An Austrian citizen cannot be a victim of APA s. 116, since this person would not be a foreigner (as defined in APA s. 2 (4) (1)). On the other hand, 'trafficking in human beings' would also cover cases of internal trafficking and cases in which Austrian citizens are victims.

As also shown by interview, it is rather unclear in which cases 'trafficking in human beings' or 'exploitation of a foreigner' might be applied. As discussed above and also affirmed by the interview partner, the distinction between these two offences is rather difficult to define. One interview partner pointed out that in many cases both offences would be applicable. In particular, since both offences have the same levels of punishment, both offences could be applied.[82]

In general, APA s. 116 is applied rather seldom. In recent years, the following numbers have been recorded regarding complaints under APA s. 116[83]:

Year	2008	2009	Jan-Sept 2010
Registered complaints	3	8	2
Clarified complaints[84]	3	7	1

Since the numbers of complaints are low, also convictions of exploitation of a foreigner are rare. In 2007, three convictions were registered regarding the exploitation of a foreigner[85], in 2008 one conviction was registered, and none

[81] K. Schwaighofer, in Frank Höpfel and Eckart Ratz (eds), *Commentary of the Criminal Code* (2nd edn, Manz, Vienna 2006) CC s. 104(a)(6).
[82] Interview with Ministry of Justice (July 2010).
[83] Information provided upon request by the Criminal Intelligence Service (Email correspondence 4 November 2010). The Criminal Intelligence Service publishes annually a report on criminality (including statistics and analysis).
[84] Complaints are clarified when the alleged criminal was caught in the act, or she/he confessed or other evidences lead to assumption that the person is the perpetrator as well as in the case when the alleged criminal cannot be found by the police but the identity is known and evidences lead to the assumption that the person is the perpetrator. Cf. Criminal Intelligence Service, *Report on Criminality 2006* (Report) (2007) A4.
[85] A. Tipold, in Frank Höpfel and Eckart Ratz (eds), *Commentary of the Criminal Code* (2nd edn, Manz, Vienna 2006) APA s. 116(2). The convictions are registered for the provision in place before a major amendment of the APA (APA 1997 s. 105).

were recorded in 2009.[86] However, it has to be pointed out that the judicial criminal statistics only show the conviction of the principal offence in one proceeding.

1.3. The dimensions of Trafficking in Human Beings for labour exploitation in Austria

1.3.1 Characterisation of Trafficking in Human Beings for labour exploitation at the national level

Data on trafficking in human beings can be collected from various sources, but Austria does not collect such data comprehensively, as coordinated by one institution. Data on trafficking in human beings in general, as well as data on trafficking for labour exploitation in particular are scarce. Furthermore, the reports of the Austrian Task Force on Combating Human Trafficking give little information about trafficking for labour exploitation. Information collected in the interviews summarise the available information on both trafficking in human beings and situations in which exploitation and illegal employment take place and have been detected, but which have not necessarily been identified as trafficking in human beings.

Generally speaking, in Austria the most frequent forms of trafficking in human beings are trafficking for the purpose of sexual exploitation, slavery-like situations of domestic servants and child trafficking.[87] With regard to trafficking in children, traffickers exploit children in begging, committing theft and pick pocketing, prostitution and other forms of forced labour. Additionally, cases of trafficking in children linked to illegal adoption as well as for the purpose of marriage are detected.[88]

Based on the available information and interviews, THB for labour exploitation and its forms in Austria can be described as follows:

The most frequently mentioned *sectors* in which THB for labour exploitation occurs are the catering sector, agriculture[89] and the construction sector[90]. Further sectors are exploitation in households, including diplomatic

---

[86] Judicial criminal statistics 2008 and 2009 of Statistics Austria <http://www.statistik.at/web_de/dynamic/statistiken/soziales/kriminalitaet/verurteilungen_gerichtliche_kriminalstatistik/publikationen?id=6&webcat=176&nodeId=333&frag=3&listid=176> accessed 22 November 2010.

[87] Austrian Task Force on Combating Human Trafficking, *First Austrian Report on Combating Human Trafficking* (2008) p. 1.

[88] Austrian Task Force on Combating Human Trafficking, *Report by the Working Group on Child Trafficking* (2008) p. 1.

[89] Interview with NGO (August 2010).

[90] Interview with Ministry of Finance (August 2010).

households, and exploitation through forced begging.[91] The media has reported on cases of THB for the purpose of exploitation in diplomatic households.[92] Very few cases are monitored in the sector of cleaning services at construction sites and dismantling of industrial plants.[93]

The *country of origin* of the victims seems to be linked to the sector in which victims are going to be exploited. Generally speaking, victims of trafficking in human beings for the purpose of labour exploitation seem to be third country nationals or citizens of new EU Member States. Romania is mentioned, for example, as a country of origin in cases of THB for the purpose of exploitation in begging[94] as well as with regard to exploitation in the construction sector.[95] Furthermore, Bulgaria, Slovakia[96], as well as Serbia and Macedonia[97] are mentioned. Countries of origin outside Europe would be Brazil, Columbia and Sri Lanka, Philippines, Thailand[98] and China[99].

The *gender of victims* is clearly linked to the sector in which the exploitation takes place. Most victims of trafficking in human beings are women and children. Areas which are prone to illegal employment and exploitation include the construction sector and the catering sector. Mirroring the classical gender segregation of the labour market, men are largely assumed to be affected within the construction sector, whilst more women than men are exploited in the catering sector.[100] At the same time, it has also been observed that more men are exploited in the catering sector[101], for example in respect of those men who must pay off their smuggling.[102] With regard to cases on exploitation in households, women are mostly affected.

Since documented cases of trafficking for the purpose of labour exploitation are rather scarce, information on the *age of victims* is predominantly based on general observations and the assumptions of the interview partners. Regarding women, it is assumed that the age structure is different for the group of women being exploited for the workforce than for the group of women being exploited sexually. Also, trafficked women around the age of 50 have been

---

[91] Interview with regional Criminal Intelligence Service (November 2010) and interview with a public prosecutor (November 2010).

[92] I. Brickner, 'Hilfe für ausländische 'Haussklavinnen' (Help for foreign 'houseslaves') *Der Standard* (Vienna 2 December 2009).

[93] Interview with Ministry of Finance (August 2010).

[94] Interview with regional Criminal Intelligence Service (November 2010) and interview with a public prosecutor (November 2010).

[95] Interview with Ministry of Finance (August 2010) .

[96] Interview with Criminal Intelligence Service (September 2010).

[97] Interview with Control Unit for Illegal Employment (August 2010).

[98] Interview with Criminal Intelligence Service (September 2010).

[99] Interview with Ministry of Finance (August 2010).

[100] Interview with Ministry of Finance (August 2010).

[101] Interview with Control Unit for Illegal Employment (August 2010).

[102] Interview with regional Criminal Intelligence Service (November 2010).

identified, who have been exploited in households.[103] Persons who are exploited are between 18 or 19 and 50 years old.[104] Regarding trafficking in children, the crisis centre of the Viennese youth welfare authority, called 'Drehscheibe', takes care of trafficked children and such children are in most cases under the age of 14, which is the age of criminal responsibility.[105]

A difference between trafficking for the purpose of sexual exploitation and labour exploitation regarding *recruitment* is that victims of labour exploitation are usually not deceived regarding the form of promised work. When jobs in households are promised, then this is the work the victim is later exploited in.[106] In the case of begging, victims generally know that begging will be a way of earning money. It is understood that payments have to be made for housing, for example.[107] However, the conditions of work in Austria are clearly misrepresented by the traffickers and working hours exceed that promised, earnings are less and services are overcharged. In some cases of trafficking in women who have been exploited in households, double the actual wage received, as well as vocational training, has been promised. Exploitation in households seems to depend a lot on informal contacts among family and friends. Traffickers and exploited persons often come from the same country. Systems of recruitment agencies or labour brokerage are not monitored in Austria regarding domestic work.[108]

Forms of coercion or force in the exploitation of domestic work can be understood in terms of isolation and permanent control. In one case, a woman was permanently observed by the exploiters and could not make a phone call in privacy. In another case, the woman was not allowed to leave the house alone. Generally, a very strong dependency prevents the victim from fleeing: on the one hand, there is the urgent need to earn money, and on the other hand the exploited person does not know whether the exploiter will actually pay. In informal employment, no regulations are provided regarding the day of payment or the amount to be paid. The victim may realise very late that the promised payments will not take place as agreed. Exploitation in domestic work and catering is often linked with sexual violence.[109] But at the same time, if there is a legal working contract this may be used as a pressuring tool. Quitting the contract of foreign workers can lead to the loss of the working

---

[103] Cf. Interview with NGO (August 2010).

[104] Cf. Interview with Criminal Intelligence Service (September 2010).

[105] M. Ammer, M. Nowak, FRA Thematic Study on Child Trafficking, Austria (2008) (34) <http://fra.europa.eu/fraWebsite/attachments/Child-trafficking-09-country-at.pdf> accessed 23 November 2010.

[106] Cf. Interview with NGO (August 2010).

[107] Cf. Interview with a public prosecutor (November 2010).

[108] Cf. Interview with NGO (August 2010).

[109] Cf. Interview with NGO (August 2010).

permit and consequently the right of residence.[110] Another pattern of exploitation concerns the exploitation that occurs when paying off smuggling fees. Cases have been detected in Austria in which persons, predominantly from Asian countries, are forced to work in restaurants in order to pay off the fee, and are exploited at the same time.[111]

1.3.2 Facts and Figures on Trafficking in Human Beings for labour exploitation in Austria

As already mentioned above, Austria does not have a comprehensive data collection system on THB. In general, figures exist regarding the conviction of perpetrators of 'trafficking in human beings' (CC s. 104a), registered by the Ministry of Justice, as well as regarding registered complaints (*Anzeige*) collected by the Federal Criminal Intelligence Service. However, these data do not provide information about the form of exploitation. Based on the information collected in the interviews, it can be assumed that within these numbers a considerable number may be trafficking for the purpose of sexual exploitation.

The criminal court statistics regarding 'trafficking in human beings' show the following:[112]

Year	2005	2006	2007
Total proceedings	16	33	18
Sentence	1	9	2
Dismissal of case	12	11	9
Acquittal	0	5	1
Pending proceedings	3	8	6

In the year 2009, two convicted perpetrators were registered.[113]
In addition to the judicial criminal statistics, the Criminal Intelligence Service provides statistics regarding complaints filed on THB. Four complaints were registered in the year 2008.[114] The victims involved in these complaints were

---

[110] Cf. Interview with Criminal Intelligence Service (September 2010).

[111] Cf. Interview with regional Criminal Intelligence Service (November 2010).

[112] Austrian Task Force on Combating Human Trafficking, *First Austrian Report on Combating Human Trafficking* (2008) p. 25.

[113] Judicial criminal statistics 2008 and 2009 of Statistics Austria <http://www.statistik.at/web_de/dynamic/statistiken/soziales/kriminalitaet/verurteilungen_gerichtliche_kriminalstatistik/publikationen?id=6&webcat=176&nodeId=333&frag=3&listid=176> accessed 22 November 2010 Regarding 2008 no data on CC s. 104(a) are given. Note that within the criminal statistics only the proceedings of the leading provision/gravest crime are given.

[114] Criminal Intelligence Service, *Report on Criminality 2008* (Report) (2009) B2. All 4 complaints have been clarified.

two women and two men.[115] The number rose significantly in 2009, when 32 complaints were registered. Up until September, 13 complaints were reported for 2010.[116]

Additionally, the NGO LEFOE-IBF[117] provides statistics in its annual report about the number of women who received counselling and support. However, giving an impression of the dimension of trafficking in women in general, these numbers do not differentiate between women who have been sexually exploited and those exploited in other sectors of labour. It can be assumed that the vast majority concerns sexually exploited women.

Year	2000	2001	2002	2003	2004	2005	2006	2007	2008	2009
Number of women supported[118]	143	183	208	142	167	151	162	170	203	182

Regarding child trafficking, little reliable comparative data exists.[119] The data above, collected by the Ministry of Justice and the Criminal Intelligence Service, does not indicate whether children have been involved in criminal proceedings. The crisis centre for the Viennese youth welfare authority called 'Drehscheibe' provides data on trafficked children and accompanied minors who have been identified in Vienna and taken care of. The 'Drehscheibe' registers in its statistics all unaccompanied minors without housing who were used for criminal activities in Vienna, identified by the police and then brought to the 'Drehscheibe'. The numbers amounted to 315 in 2004, 701 in 2005, 319 in 2006 and 72 in 2007.[120] According to 'Drehscheibe', the numbers decreased because of the good cooperation between the

[115] Criminal Intelligence Service, *Report on Criminality 2008* (Report) (2009) B 22-23. All victims have been older than 18 years.

[116] Information provided upon request by the Criminal Intelligence Service (E-mail correspondence 24 November 2010).

[117] LEFOE-IBF is an intervention centre for trafficked women based in Vienna and recognised victim protection institution acting on behalf of the Ministry of Interior and the Federal Chancellery of Austria. LEFOE-IBF is mandated by the Ministry of Justice to provide psycho-social and legal assistance to trafficked women.

[118] Information based on the annual reports of LEFOE-IBF. Cf. LEFOE-IBF, *2008 Annual Report* (Vienna 2009) p. 12.

[119] M Ammer, M Nowak, FRA Thematic Study on Child Trafficking, Austria (2008)(32) <http://fra.europa.eu/fraWebsite/attachments/Child-trafficking-09-country-at.pdf> accessed 23 November 2010.

[120] Austrian Task Force on Combating Human Trafficking, *Report by the Working Group on Child Trafficking* (2008) p. 10.

'Drehscheibe' and Bulgarian authorities.[121] Since all children are registered, it is also possible that not all of them are victims of child trafficking.

1.4 Summary of the findings

1.4.1 Identified obstacles

Austria's policies and measures against trafficking in human beings still seem to be driven predominantly by the notion that trafficking in human beings is linked mostly to exploitation of women, predominantly sexual exploitation, and that trafficking in human beings necessarily needs to encompass a certain level of force, threat and confinement of the victim.

In Austria, the main regulation on THB is CC s. 104a. In addition, further offences are relevant with regard to THB. The most relevant offence is CC s. 217, the 'transnational prostitution trade'. Prior to the newly introduced offence on THB (CC s. 104a) in the Criminal Code in 2004, the 'transnational prostitution trade' was used for THB. Since this offence was too narrow according to the Palermo Protocol, a new regulation had to be introduced. Although CC s. 217 does not fall directly within the scope of THB for labour exploitation, it offers the opportunity to show that there are significantly more legal proceedings on 'transnational prostitution trade' than on THB. Clearly, CC s. 217 covers THB for the purpose of sexual exploitation. THB for sexual exploitation is obviously more present in Austria's policies on anti-trafficking than THB for labour exploitation. Whereas – as shown above – in total 18 proceedings on THB were registered in 2007, 524 proceedings were registered regarding 'transnational prostitution trade'.[122]

Cases on THB for labour exploitation are rather rare according to the information gathered. CC s. 104a is not very often applied in cases - as shown above, the numbers are rather low.

Additionally, the official statistics on CC s. 104a give no information on the respective form of exploitation.

Also relevant to THB is the regulation on 'exploitation of a foreign person' (APA s. 116). This offence seems to be of minor importance according to the official numbers and the information gathered in the interviews.

In both cases (CC s. 104a and APA s. 116) it seems that the interpretation of the term 'exploitation' is rather challenging. The application of 'exploitation' in order to be able to file a complaint and then to bring an indictment is seen as difficult. The jurisdiction on exploitation is in general

---

[121] Cf. Austrian Task Force on Combating Human Trafficking, *Report on the Working Group on Child Trafficking* (2008) p. 10.

[122] Austrian Task Force on Combating Human Trafficking, *First Austrian Report on Combating Human Trafficking* (2008) p. 26.

based on the exploitation of victims within pimping. The given case law – as described above – gives specific indicators on when exploitation might have occurred. With regard to APA s. 116, the element of *excessiveness* is important, since minor violations of limits (working hours, minimum wages) do not amount to exploitation. But in practice, the application of both offences is seen as difficult, since the term 'exploitation' is still very vague.[123] The limits of excessiveness are not clear. In cases of 'exploitation of a foreign person' it is difficult to gather the evidence indicating very low wages, for example. Usually, no further information or notes are provided in respect of paid wages.[124] The evidence of the victim is very important in these cases. In one case, the decisive element of exploitation resulted from the fact that the perpetrators charged high fees for services or documents which would have been issued by the public authority to the victims free of charge. The imbalance between fees charged by the perpetrators and the services or housing offered in return to the victims was decisive with regard to the exploitation.[125] The vagueness of the term 'exploitation' might in some cases be combined with a lack of awareness on THB, which can lead consequently to less cases that are assessed as THB.

The CCLA, which regulates the criminal liability of legal persons in Austria, is applied very seldom. Corporate liability can play a very important role in combating THB for labour exploitation.

Within agriculture, the working conditions of migrants are in general described as rather poor. Reports show that seasonal workers and harvest helpers can in practice not make use of their – anyway limited – social benefits. Migrant workers in agriculture are in a situation of dependency due to the residence regulations in this sector. It can be assumed that there are probably more cases of THB within the agricultural sector in Austria than currently reported. Usually, the agricultural sector is prone to conditions of exploitation, but only very few concrete cases are known and documented.[126]

1.4.2 Good practices

The Austrian Task Force on Combating Human Trafficking is the coordinating body for all efforts against THB in Austria and includes all relevant institutions, ministries and NGOs. The regular exchange allows current trends and developments to be discussed.[127] Issues or identified gaps are included in the National Action Plan.

---

[123] Cf. Interview with Criminal Intelligence Service (September 2010).

[124] Cf. Interview with regional Criminal Intelligence Service (November 2010).

[125] Cf. Interview with a public prosecutor (November 2010).

[126] Cf. Case study 2.

[127] For further information on the Task Force see M. Heemskerk and C. Rijken, 'Combating Trafficking in Human Beings for Labour Exploitation in The Netherlands', Chapter 2, para 1 in this book.

The identified obstacles with regard to the application of CC s. 104 a are included in the National Action Plan. The Ministry of Justice, in cooperation with other relevant ministries, reviews all regulations which are relevant for THB with a view defining THB, and elaborates recommendations regarding the application of these regulations.[128]

In order to improve the situation on statistics regarding THB in Austria, a working group was established. Coordinated by the Ministry of Justice, several institutions that are relevant regarding official crime statistics are involved.[129] This measure is based on the National Action Plan, which foresees the improvement of data.[130] In addition, the National Action Plan requires the Ministry of Interior to further improve the collection of data with a view to standardizing the collection of data on THB in the EU.[131]

---

[128] Cf. National Action Plan against Human Trafficking, V.4 <http://www.bmeia.gv.at/fileadmin/user_upload/bmeia/media/2-Aussenpolitik_Zentrale/Menschenrechte/TFM_Aktionsplan_engl_V20091007_LAYOUT_FINAL.pdf> accessed 30 November 2010.

[129] Austrian Task Force on Combating Human Trafficking, *First Austrian Report on Combating Human Trafficking* (2008) p. 26.

[130] Cf. National Action Plan against Human Trafficking, VII.2 <http://www.bmeia.gv.at/fileadmin/user_upload/bmeia/media/2-Aussenpolitik_Zentrale/Menschenrechte/TFM_Aktionsplan_engl_V20091007_LAYOUT_FINAL.pdf> accessed 30 November 2010.

[131] Cf. National Action Plan against Human Trafficking, VII.1<http://www.bmeia.gv.at/fileadmin/user_upload/bmeia/media/2-Aussenpolitik_Zentrale/Menschenrechte/TFM_Aktionsplan_engl_V20091007_LAYOUT_FINAL.pdf> accessed 30 November 2010.

Part II
Cooperation in the investigation and prosecution of cases of Trafficking in Human Beings for labour exploitation

2.1 Actors involved in investigating and prosecuting Trafficking in Human Beings for labour exploitation

Actors who are involved in the investigation and prosecution of cases of THB for labour exploitation may differ from those actors usually involved in cases of THB for sexual exploitation. In Austria, the Task Force on combating human trafficking consists of representatives from all relevant ministries, the federal provinces and non-governmental organisations. The group is headed by the Federal Ministry for European and International Affairs (FMEIA); consequently, the FMEIA coordinates all meetings and tasks. Additionally, the first high-ranking Austrian National Coordinator on Combating Human Trafficking[132] was appointed in 2009 to ensure external visibility and general awareness of the work of the Task Force. The group meets regularly and aims to enhance cooperation between all actors and intensify the measures taken by Austria in order to combat THB. In addition to the regular meetings, the Task Force has also set up two specific working groups; one group deals with trafficking in children, and the other group addresses prostitution.[133] In particular, the tasks of the group are determined by the second National Action Plan against Human Trafficking covering the time between 2009 and 2011, which also includes a section on criminal prosecution. Awareness raising regarding THB for labour exploitation also falls within the activities of the Task Force. Although not one of the first 'core-members' of the Task Force of 2004, the Ministry of Finance has for several years taken part in the meetings of the Task Force, since the ministry has important functions with regard to THB for labour exploitation. The *Control Unit for Illegal Employment*, forms part of the Ministry of Finance, and plays a role in respect of THB for labour exploitation.

The *Federal Criminal Intelligence Service* (*Bundeskriminalamt*) forms part of the Federal Ministry of Interior. Within the division dealing with investigation, organised and general crime, one department is occupied with THB and smuggling.[134] This 'Central Service for Combating Human Smuggling/Human Trafficking' serves *inter alia* as a contact point for THB,

---

[132] Director-General Ambassador Dr. Elisabeth Tichy-Fisslberger.

[133] Cf. <http://www.bmeia.gv.at/fileadmin/user_upload/bmeia/media/2-Aussenpolitik_Zentrale/ menschenrechte/TFM_Aktionsplan_engl_V20091007 _LAYOUT_FINAL.pdf> accessed 30 November 2010.

[134] Cf. Overview of the Federal Criminal Intelligence Service <http://www.bmi.gv.at/cms/BK/wir_ueber_uns/organigramm/files/BK_Organigramm_Juli_2010.pdf > accessed 30 November 2010.

and runs a hotline which operates 24 hours a day. This newly established hotline should not be understood as an emergency hotline; it should rather encourage everyone (also anonymously) to forward information on THB to the police.[135]

At the level of federal provinces the Regional Criminal Police Offices (*Landeskriminalamt*) have a special investigation section (investigation section No 10) for dealing with THB. This section is the central investigation body in each of the nine federal provinces dealing with THB. Every lead received by any police officer has to be forwarded to the specialist criminal officers. In general, the investigation is driven by the general principle that criminal police and the public prosecutor have to examine *ex officio* any crime which comes to their attention.[136]

In order to improve the exchange of information and experiences the Federal Criminal Intelligence Service organises trainings at police stations at the provincial level in order to inform police officers on the ground. The internal rules on training foresee that the investigating officers of the competent special investigation of the individual Regional Criminal Police Office are informed twice a year about new developments in THB, and that legal and tactical aspects of current issues are addressed and pending investigations are discussed. At least once a year, the heads of the special investigation section participate in a comprehensive exchange of information and experiences with *inter alia* non-governmental organisations and representatives of the judiciary.[137] Consequently, possibilities for further training are provided internally. Courses are announced regularly and police officers can apply. Additionally, courses at European level or abroad may be attended. However, specific courses on THB for labour exploitation are not offered.[138]

The Task Force's report indicates several trainings for the judiciary on THB. These trainings include *inter alia* seminars with LEFOE-IBF, held once every two years, as well as a seminar in another province of Austria or a seminar organised with the help of the Council of Europe.[139] So far, no specific seminar on THB for labour exploitation has been conducted. Although there was one planned, the minimum number of participants was not attained. The demand for trainings on THB seems to be rather low, since

---

[135] Cf. Criminal Intelligence Service, News, <http://www.bmi.gv.at/cms/BK/presse/files/18102010_Kampf_gegen_Menschenhandel_Meldestelle_und_Hotline_im_Bundeskriminalamt.pdf> accessed 30 November 2010.

[136] Based on CCP s. 2.

[137] Austrian Task Force on Combating Human Trafficking, *First Austrian Report on Combating Human Trafficking* (2008) p. 18.

[138] Cf. Interview with regional Criminal Intelligence Service (November 2010) and interview with Criminal Intelligence Service (September 2010).

[139] Cf. Austrian Task Force on Combating Human Trafficking, *First Austrian Report on Combating Human Trafficking* (2008) p. 18.

the number of cases of THB within the judiciary is in general low. THB plays only a minor role in the daily work life of public prosecutors and judges. Demanding workloads and the low level of importance given to THB cases mean there is little demand for seminars on THB.[140]

The *Control Unit for Illegal Employment* was established in the early 1990s and has since been reorganised several times. It is under the supervision of the custom authorities at the Federal Ministry of Finance. In recent years, the Control Unit has expanded.[141] Around 300 persons are currently working for the Control Unit. In comparison with Germany, this figure is rather low, since the density of control in Germany is twice that of Austria.[142] The recently adopted Act on Anti-Fraud 2010 (*Betrugsbekämpfungsgesetz*)[143] foresees a major amendment to the function of the Control Unit. The unit will be further enlarged and will soon be part of a special Financial Police Force (*Finanzpolizei*). The Financial Police Force will basically have the same competences to enter premises as the Control Unit now has.[144] Compared to the Control Unit, which mainly deals with illegal employment, the Financial Police Force will have these competences for all purposes of taxation. Additionally, the force's competences are not limited to districts of the specific tax authorities; controls can, for example, be conducted all over Austria.[145]

The Control Unit has several functions that have their basis in different legal acts. Within the framework of THB for labour exploitation, the following seem to be the most important: control of compliance with the AEL and the Act on the adaptation of employment contract law (*Arbeitsvertragsrechts-Anpassungsgesetz*), combating social insurance fraud[146] as well as support and participation in criminal proceedings as a witness or as an informant.[147] The main act is the AEL which provided for the Control Unit as the principal organ for the investigation of violations of the AEL. Other organs have the duty to support the Control Unit in its tasks within the AEL.[148] The control unit is, on the one hand, dealing with the AEL, whilst on the other with the control of fiscal law. Due to the different functions of the Control Unit,

---

140 Interview with a public prosecutor (November 2010).

141 M. Jandl and others, *Migration and Irregular Work in Austria* (Amsterdam University Press, Amsterdam 2009) p. 56.

142 H. Houf, W. Lehner, Handbuch KIAB –Kontrollen (Manz, Vienna 2008)(4).

143 Federal Law Gazette I No. 105/2010 adopted on 14 December 2010.

144 Cf. Explanatory Notes 875 d.B. XXIV. GP 8 (government bill regarding the Act on Anti-Fraud 2010).

145 HP. Lehofer, 'Die Finanzpolizei kommt', OEJZ 2010/78.

146 This includes for example 'fraudulent withholding of social security duties' CC s 153(d) (Betrügerisches Vorenthalten von Sozialversicherungsbeiträgen und Zuschlägen nach dem Bauarbeiter-Urlaubs- und Abfertigungsgesetz).

147 H. Houf, W. Lehner, Handbuch KIAB –Kontrollen (Manz, Vienna 2008) p. 2.

148 H. Houf, W. Lehner, Handbuch KIAB –Kontrollen (Manz, Vienna 2008) p. 18.

different procedural regulations have to be obeyed. This complicated situation can sometimes lead to uncertainty within an inspection for the employer, as well as for the inspectors themselves.[149]

For the inspection itself, the unit is allowed to enter business premises and all rooms in which employees might work. This may also include the private home of the employer where there is a possibility that employees work there. Accommodation facilities for employees do not fall within the scope of the unit.[150] Employers also have to unlock specific rooms. Additionally, the number and names of foreigners being employed in the business by the employer can be requested.[151] The assumption that a person is a foreigner allows the Control Unit to request the name, date of birth and address of the person. Before the inspection starts, the unit has to inform the employee.[152] Most inspections are carried out when the Control Unit receives certain information beforehand. This information can come from private persons (e.g. neighbours) or unsuccessful bidders in tenders who lost because the successful bidder employs low-cost irregular workers. Additionally, information can also come from other authorities such as health and sanitary inspectors. As well as previously received information, the Control Unit also follows specific strategies and inspects all businesses of a certain branch in one area in a specific time period.[153] Controls have to be conducted in accordance with the protected right to privacy. Inspections of private homes in which employees work therefore raise several questions and the requirements are in general rather high in order for it to be permissible to enter a private home. Anonymous tips, for example, would not provide sufficient justification.[154] Irregular work in private households such as cleaning or caretaking is usually not inspected, since the Control Unit does not usually have access to private homes due to the high level of conditions. In the construction sector, common forms of irregularities include bogus self-employment while in the catering sector the underreporting of the extent of employment is also commonplace.[155]

Since 2006, the Ministry of Finance has been organising seminars for the Control Unit specifically on trafficking in human beings, and has included the topic in its annual meeting of team leaders.[156] The seminars are seen as very

---

[149] H. Houf, 'Was steckt dahinter?' (2009) persaldo H1, p. 17.

[150] These can only be controlled by the labour inspections.

[151] H Houf, W Lehner, Handbuch KIAB –Kontrollen (Manz, Vienna 2008) pp. 202-203.

[152] H. Houf, W. Lehner, Handbuch KIAB –Kontrollen (Manz, Vienna 2008) pp. 206-207.

[153] M. Jandl and others, *Migration and Irregular Work in Austria* (Amsterdam University Press, Amsterdam 2009) p. 57.

[154] H. Houf, W. Lehner, Handbuch KIAB –Kontrollen (Manz, Vienna 2008) pp. 198-199.

[155] M. Jandl and others, *Migration and Irregular Work in Austria* (Amsterdam University Press, Amsterdam 2009) pp. 60-61.

[156] Cf. Interview with Ministry of Finance (August 2010).

important since they raise awareness about THB and give essential knowledge on the topic for implementation on a day-to-day basis.[157]

The following authorities are also entitled to inspect workplaces and may therefore be relevant. The *Labour Inspectorate* is part of the Federal Ministry of Labour, Social Affairs and Consumer Protection, and encompasses around 500 staff members. The Labour Inspectorate's main mandate is the protection of the life and health of workers.[158] In order to fulfil its functions, the Labour Inspectorate is entitled to enter the premises of employers at any time. Additionally, it can also inspect the accommodation facilities of employees which are provided by the employer.[159] Inspections are conducted without prior notification of the employer, but the inspectors can decide to notify the inspection in advance. In some cases, it seems feasible to inform the employer in order to, for example, have the relevant persons present. But the majority of inspections in the construction sector are conducted without notification. Focusing on the construction sector, around 1000 construction sites are inspected per year.[160] The Labour Inspectorate has a special duty to keep information it receives confidential.[161] THB for labour exploitation is not defined as a task within the scope of the Act on Labour Inspection.

The *District Health Insurance Fund* (Vienna) also includes the Department on Control of Contributions. This department investigates whether employers contribute the necessary payments for social insurance. The health insurance authority looks at specific information, such as whether all employees are registered.[162] Specific attention is given to the question of whether employees are registered at the Health Insurance Fund accordingly.[163] Employers are obliged to provide all necessary information regarding social insurance.[164] The number of inspections has increased significantly this year, and the number of experts in the department has also increased. In the first half of 2010, 20 staff

---

[157] Cf. Interview with Control Unit for Illegal Employment (August 2010).

[158] Federal Ministry of Labour, Social Security and Consumer Protection, *Labour Inspectorate* (2009) <http://www.arbeitsinspektion.gv.at/NR/rdonlyres/F5C28318-D67E-4B52-AF95-12DAB1DF5125/0/arbig_d_gb_2009_Broschuere.pdf> accessed 30 November 2010.

[159] Cf. Act on Labour Inspection (Federal Law Gazette No. 27/1993 as amended by Federal Law Gazette I No. 150/2009) s. 4.

[160] Cf. Act on Labour Inspection s. 18 and interview with Labour Inspectorate (November 2010).

[161] Cf. Act on Labour Inspection s. 3(6) and interview with Labour Inspectorate (November 2010).

[162] Cf. General Social Insurance Act s. 41(a).

[163] Cf. District Health Insurance Fund (Vienna) <http://www.wgkk.at/portal27/portal/wgkkportal/channel_content/cmsWindow?action=2&p_menuid=59454&p_tabid=6> accessed 30 November 2010.

[164] Cf. General Social Insurance Act s. 42.

members conducted around 1.800 on-site inspections. In the catering sector, in construction and in transportation, most of the unregistered employees were found. These sectors are in particular subject to inspections.[165]

The *Construction Workers' Annual Leave and Severance Pay Fund* provides certain services primarily regulated under the Act on Construction Workers' Annual Leave and Severance Pay,[166] as well as further applicable collective agreements. The primary function of the fund is the settlement of annual leave remuneration, severance pay, winter holiday and bad weather compensation for construction workers. The fund receives contributions from employers; consequently the fund administrates the contributions and settles the workers' claims.[167] The claims are paid by the fund and not – as is normally the case – by the employer. Without having an intermediary fund between employer and construction worker, the risk would be too high that construction workers would not receive their claims due to very short periods of employment.[168] Since 2009, the fund has also the competence to undertake inspections at construction sites. The employer has to ensure access to all relevant information. Construction workers are obliged upon request to give their identity cards or passports to the fund while inspecting.[169] The act defines cooperation between the fund and the health insurance fund and states that the health insurance fund has to provide the construction workers' fund with data on employed workers. At the same time, the fund is allowed to use the database[170] of the Control Unit for Illegal Employment.[171]

---

[165] District Health Insurance (Vienna) press release 'District Health Insurance (Vienna) successful in combating illicit work and social fraud' (23 August 2010) <http://www.ots.at/presseaussendung/OTS_20100823_OTS0058/wgkk-erfolgreich-im-kampf-gegen-schwarzarbeit-und-sozialbetrug> accessed 30 November 2010.

[166] Federal Law Gazette No. 414/1972 as amended by Federal Law Gazette I No.59/2010.

[167] <http://www.buak.at/servlet/ContentServer?pagename=BUAK/Page/Index&n=BUAK_71> accessed 1 December 2010.

[168] W. Schramml, *Arbeitsrecht 2* (Braumüller, Vienna 2008) XXVIII 3 A.

[169] Cf. Act on Construction Workers' Annual Leave and Severance Pay, s. 23(a).

[170] This data encompasses data on the employer, the business and name, date of birth and employment period of the worker.

[171] Cf. Act on Construction Workers' Annual Leave and Severance Pay s. 31.

2.2 Cooperation between actors within the country

2.2.1 Legal framework for cooperation

Cooperation between actors

The *Control Unit for Illegal Employment*[172] benefits from the general duty of other public authorities and institutions such as the Health Insurance Funds to support the Control Unit in all its functions in respect of the AEL. At the same time, AEL s. 27 (5) explicitly states that authorities have to inform the control unit in cases where there is reasonable suspicion that the AEL has not been applied. Importantly, the police has to support the Control Unit upon request in conducting inspections.[173] However, the support is mutual since the Control Unit is also obliged to notify other relevant authorities when monitoring any infringements of labour regulations or environmental regulations.[174] The Control Unit is – based on different legal acts – under different obligations to file a complaint. For example, with regard to criminal offences in respect of social fraud, such as fraudulent withholding of social security duties[175], the Control Unit falls under the general duty of all authorities to file a complaint at the police or public prosecutor[176].[177]

The *Labour Inspectorate,* similar to the Control Unit for Illegal Employment, benefits from a general duty to be supported by other public authorities.[178] In order to be able to fulfil its obligations, the Labour Inspectorate is allowed to make use of the data of the Control Unit for Illegal Employment. The data which are allowed to be used are predefined by law and encompass data about the employer such as names, dates of birth, addresses, and places of employment and time periods of employment.[179] Additionally, the health insurance fund also has to support the inspection and provide data, which are stored. With this provision, it is possible for the inspector to find out who the employer is; in some cases, the inspector is only aware of the names of employees.[180] When bigger construction sites are inspected in particular, it is

[172] Regarding the cooperation the focus is laid on the obligations of the Control Unit based on the AEL and does not discuss in detail the obligations based on the Act on income tax or the Gambling Act.

[173] Cf. AEL s. 27(3).

[174] Cf. AEL s. 27(2).

[175] Cf. CC s. 153(d).

[176] CCP s. 78.

[177] Cf. W. Lehner, 'Anzeigerechte und Anzeigepflichten der KIAB' (2009) taxlex, p. 212.

[178] Cf. Act on Labour Inspection s. 20(1).

[179] Cf. Act on Labour Inspection s. 20(7).

[180] Cf. Act on Labour Inspection s. 21(1)(a). G. Ercher, 'Bundesgesetz, mit dem das Arbeitsinspektionsgesetz 1993, das Arbeitsvertragsrechts-Anpassungsgesetz, das Allge-

not easy for the labour inspectorate to identify the employer of the workers, since several companies work together. According to the Act on Labour Inspection s. 21 (1a), the health insurance fund has to provide the labour inspection with this data, which is absolutely necessary for the actual inspection the inspector does.[181] Again similar to the Control Unit for Illegal Employment, the Labour Inspectorate is supported by the police in order to be able to conduct inspections.[182]

The basis of cooperation between *police* and *public prosecutor* lies within the regulation of the investigation procedure based on the Code on Criminal Procedure.[183] After filing a complaint, the formal investigation procedure starts. The investigation procedure in criminal cases is driven by the basic principle that public prosecution and police jointly conduct the investigation. The joint investigation balances the investigative competences of the police with the competence of the public prosecution to bring an indictment.[184] At the same time, the public prosecutor leads the investigation. Public prosecutors give orders to the police and the police must keep them informed. In the end, public prosecutors decide whether the investigation ends, or an indictment is brought.[185] Experiences in actual cooperation between police and public prosecutors in cases on THB vary. In practice, there is variation among individual public prosecutors on how much evidence has, for example, to be gathered by the police. Some public prosecutors may require more evidence than others in order to follow up the investigation. According to one case, there is room for improvement regarding the cooperation. With regard to another case, police and public prosecutors both stated that cooperation was very good. However, a lot of time was invested in this particular case, and unusually high staff costs were borne. In general, the police must act pro-actively in cases of THB in order for the on-going investigation headed by the public prosecutor to be successful.[186]

---

meine Sozialversicherungsgesetz und das Bundesgesetz über Verkehrs-Arbeitsinspektion geändert werden, BGBl I 2009/150' (2010) AsoK, p. 71.

[181] Amendment to the Act on Labour Inspection, introductory and commentary to the amendments <http://www.parlament.gv.at/PAKT/VHG/XXIV/I/I_00490/fnameorig_172256.html> accessed 7 February 2011.

[182] Cf. Act on Labour Inspection s. 20(6).

[183] Federal Law Gazette No. 631/1975 as amended by Federal Law Gazette I No. 64/2010.

[184] M. Vogl, in Frank Höpfel and Eckart Ratz (eds), *Commentary of the Criminal Code (Code on Criminal Procedure)* (2nd edn, Manz, Vienna 2006) CCP s. 98, p. 2.

[185] M. Vogl, in Frank Höpfel and Eckart Ratz (eds), *Commentary of the Criminal Code (Code on Criminal Procedure)* (2nd edn, Manz, Vienna 2006) CCP s. 101, pp. 5-9.

[186] Cf. Interview with Criminal Intelligence Service (September 2010), interview with Control Unit for Illegal Employment (August 2010), interview with Labour Inspectorate (November 2010) and interview with a public prosecutor (November 2010)

Another aspect of cooperation is that between the police and LEFOE-IBF. After identifying a presumed victim, the usual next step for the police is to bring the woman to LEFOE-IBF. The cooperation between police and LEFOE-IBF is based on s. 25 of the Security Police Act[187], which allows the police to involve NGOs which support victims of violence. Since LEFO-IBF supports women, the police and the Federal Chancellery/Women and Equality jointly assign this NGO.[188] The police underlines its well-functioning cooperation with LEFOE-IBF and points out the necessity of the cooperation for a successful and efficient investigation procedure. In 2008, the police referred 58 women to LEFOE-IBF from all over Austria.[189]

Investigation techniques

The investigation techniques used by the police can be divided into three groups regarding their preconditions. There are measures which can be enacted by the police independently. Additionally, there are measures that can only be enacted when so ordered by the public prosecutor. The third group consists of measures which have to be enacted by the public prosecutor after being authorised by the court.[190]

The enquiry *(Erkundigung)*[191] and questioning *(Vernehmung)*[192] are usually the first techniques which are applied in cases of THB. Next step can be the observation, but this is decided on a case-to-case basis and depends also on the cooperation with the public prosecutor.[193]

In general, observation *(Observation)*[194] is permitted if it is necessary to clarify a criminal act or to investigate the whereabouts of the accused. In cases where the observation takes longer than 48 hours, for example, then it is only permitted if *inter alia* the criminal act is sanctioned with more than one year imprisonment.[195] The latter form of observation needs to be ordered by the

---

187 Federal Law Gazette 566/1991 as amended by Federal Law Gazette I No. 133/2009.

188 Additionally, LEFOE-IBF is supported by the Ministry of Justice with regard to psycho-social and legal assistance.

189 Ministry of Interior and Ministry of Justice, *Report on Security 2008,* p. 351 <http://www.parlament.gv.at/PAKT/VHG/XXIV/III/III_00099/imfname_173662.pdf> accessed 1 December 2010.

190 H. Houf, W. Lehner, Handbuch KIAB –Kontrollen (Manz, Vienna 2008)(128).

191 Cf. CCP s. 152.

192 Cf. CCP s. 153.

193 Interview with regional Criminal Intelligence Service (November 2010).

194 Cf. CCP s. 130.

195 Council of Europe, Group of states against corruption, *Joint First and Second Round Evaluation Compliance Report on Austria* (Report) (11 June 2010) para. 44 <http://www.coe.int/t/dghl/monitoring/greco/evaluations/round2/GrecoRC1&2%282010%291_Austria_EN.pdf> accessed 18 November 2010.

public prosecutor; otherwise the police can decide to use it independently.[196] In practice, the observation is used in specific cases of THB.[197]

A usual undercover investigation *(verdeckte Ermittlung)*[198] may be carried out if it appears to be necessary for clarifying a criminal act. Longer or systematic undercover investigations can be conducted in cases in which for example the crime is sentenced with at least one year of imprisonment. Longer undercover investigations have to be ordered by the public prosecutor.[199] Fictitious purchase *(Scheingeschäft)*[200] is allowed if it is necessary for the clarification of a crime or if the seizure of objects or assets that originate or presumably originate from a crime would otherwise be significantly hindered. Both techniques, fictitious purchase and undercover investigation, are rarely or not used at all for cases of THB.[201]

The acoustical and visual observation of person *(optische und akustische Überwachung von Personen)*[202] is a form of secret observation; it includes the observation of actions of a person as well as statements which are private. The observation is supported by technical instruments. In general there are five different forms: three cases of acoustical and visual observation and two different forms of visual observation. Every form has different preconditions.[203] Preconditions are strict and therefore relatively difficult to reach; it is therefore – if applicable at all–used very seldom.[204] Also *recording of telecommunication* is possible, monitoring of communication *(Überwachung von Nachrichten)* includes the analysis of the content of communication. It encompasses every message or information which is distributed by an official telecommunication provider.[205]

The purpose of searching of premises and objects as well as personal search *(Durchsuchung von Orten und Gegenständen sowie von Personen)* is to find a person or specific objects. It is only allowed when for example high probability exists

[196] Cf. CCP s. 133.

[197] Interview with a public prosecutor (November 2010) and interview with regional Criminal Intelligence Service (November 2010).

[198] Cf. CCP s. 131.

[199] Cf. CCP s. 133.

[200] Cf. CCP s. 132.

[201] Interview with regional Criminal Intelligence Service (November 2010) and interview with Criminal Intelligence Service (September 2010).

[202] Cf. CCP s. 136.

[203] S. Reindl-Krauskopf, in Frank Höpfel and Eckart Ratz (eds), *Commentary of the Criminal Code (Code on Criminal Procedure)* (2nd edn, Manz, Vienna 2006) CCP s. 136(1-2).

[204] Interview with regional Criminal Intelligence Service (November 2010).

[205] S. Reindl-Krauskopf, A Tipold, I Zerbes in Frank Höpfel and Eckart Ratz (eds), *Commentary of the Criminal Code (Code on Criminal Procedure)* (2nd edn, Manz, Vienna 2006) CCP s. 134(41-43).

that the searched person will be present before entering premises.[206] This measure is used regularly in cases of THB.[207]
A seizure *(Sicherstellung)*[208] has to be ordered by the public prosecutor and is for example necessary in order to ensure a later forfeiture (*Verfall*)[209] or confiscation (*Einziehung*)[210]. Mostly computers and other data media are seized. Also for cases of THB theses seized assets have been analysed and used as evidence. More important are seizing of mobile phones and other mobile data media.[211]

The next step after a seizure is the sequestration *(Beschlagnahme)* as defined in CCP s. 115. The sequestration is inter alia necessary in cases when seized objects are further used as evidence in the on-going procedure. Upon request of the public prosecutor, the court has to decide on it.

These measures are important in order to support a confiscation of profits (*Abschöpfung der Bereicherung*) at a later stage of the proceedings as well as for evidential purposes. It applies to persons who committed an offense and benefitted from it economically or received any benefit for committing an offense. The Austrian system of confiscation is value-based, so the person receives a court order to pay an amount of money equivalent to the illegal profits received.[212] It seems that confiscation of profits in general and in cases of THB especially could be further enhanced. Enhanced usage of these tools can also support later claims of compensation of trafficked persons.

Police should earlier cooperate with the specialists on confiscation of profits during the investigation in order to ensure the confiscation. Transnational cases in addition lead to the uncertainty which State finally benefits from the confiscation.[213] The Ministry of Justice issued a decree for judges and public prosecutors about practical problems involved in using these tools as well as

---

[206] A. Tipold, I Zerbes, in Frank Höpfel and Eckart Ratz (eds), *Commentary of the Criminal Code (Code on Criminal Procedure)* (2nd edn, Manz, Vienna 2006) CCP s. 119(17).
[207] Interview with regional Criminal Intelligence Service (November 2010).
[208] Cf. CCP s. 110.
[209] Cf. CC s. 20b.
[210] Cf. CC s. 26. It encompasses the confiscation of objects which have been used or have been intended to be used to commit an offense or have been produced by this offense, if this is necessary to counteract the commitment of offenses.
[211] Ministry of Interior and Ministry of Justice, *Report on Security 2008,* pp. 436-437 <http://www.parlament.gv.at/PAKT/VHG/XXIV/III/III_00099/imfname_173662.pdf> accessed 1 December 2010.
[212] FATF/OECD, 'Austria, Mutual Evaluation Report, Anti-Money Laundering and Combating the Financing of Terrorism' (2009)(206) <http://www.fatf-gafi.org/dataoecd/22/50/44146250.pdf> accessed 3 December 2010.
[213] Cf. Interview with Criminal Intelligence Service (September 2010).

possibilities to improve the application. The utilisation of these tools should be increased.[214]

Another investigation technique used in cases of THB is the request for information on bank data *(Auskunft über Bankkonten und Bankgeschäfte)*.[215]

But as stated above, this can only be done upon order of the public prosecutor.

Next to the police, also the *Control Unit for Illegal Employment* has competences to act as police in cases the unit investigates in cases of social insurance fraud. Therefore the unit acts during the investigation in cooperation with the public prosecutor. The unit may apply in these cases all investigation techniques, which are accessible for the police also. As described in the Code on Criminal Procedure, the unit acts either independently, or upon request by the public prosecutor, or requested by the public prosecutor after being authorised by the court.[216]

2.2.2 Application of the legal framework in practice

Cooperation between actors

As shown above the responsibilities of each actor are clearly defined and also the framework for cooperation is elaborated in forms of duties to notify each other or the duty to file a complaint. As shown by interviews, a certain level of cooperation between the actors mentioned above exists. But the intensity of cooperation varies significantly and especially concerning cases of THB, it is not clear how actors are supposed to proceed.

Usually, inspections which are conducted jointly are rather rare or do not happen at all in practice. Due to limited time and staff resources joint inspections of the Control Unit for Illegal Employment and the Labour Inspectorate do not happen. The Control Unit and the Labour Inspectorate notify each other, when situations are monitored during inspections which fall under the responsibility of the other. Although this notification happens, there is no exchange of the follow up. In particular cases only, phone calls are made in order to be informed on the follow-up cases. At the same time, the general cooperation between the Control Unit and the Labour Inspectorate is very good and is supported by exchange meetings, which take place only once in two to three years. However, with regard to specific cases there are only sporadic contacts.

The Control Unit for Illegal Employment and the Labour Inspection can be supported by the police in inspections. Some years ago, the police as well as

---

[214] Council of Europe, Group of states against corruption, *Joint First and Second Round Evaluation Compliance Report on Austria* (Report) (11 June 2010) , para. 58 <http://www.coe.int/t/dghl/monitoring/greco/evaluations/round2/GrecoRC1&2%282010%291_Austria_EN.pdf> accessed 18 November 2010.

[215] Cf. CCP s. 116.

[216] H. Houf, W. Lehner, Handbuch KIAB –Kontrollen (Manz, Vienna 2008)(126-128).

the aliens' police usually accompanied the Control Unit. Now, inspections are rather not done in cooperation with the police. Experience of the Control Unit shows that inspections can be done in a smoother way when police is not involved. There are some reasons for that, for example the officers of the Control Unit do not wear a uniform or police officers attract more attention. Only in exceptional cases police supports the inspections. On the other hand, the Control Unit possesses a rather broad competence to enter premises. This is also used by other actors or authorities, such as the police, which then may profit from entering premises. Also Labour Inspectorate conducts inspections rather without the support of the police since the main responsibility of the Labour Inspectorate is to ensure the safety of the workplace and the inspection does not deal with the status of the worker (e.g. residence status) or with employees him- or herself.

With regard to situations in which exploitation might occur, it is, on the one hand, often not clear what indicators of THB might exist. On the other hand, it is not clear, under which circumstances the police should be contacted, although there is awareness raising.[217] Consequently, two obstacles pave the cooperation between the Control Unit and the police in matters of THB for labour exploitation. First of all, it is not clear which situations might amount to exploitation since indicators on THB for labour exploitation are not defined and trained. Secondly, it is unclear, whom to contact within the police when the unit suspects exploitative situations.

Differently is the cooperation between LEFOE-IBF and the police. The cooperation in cases of THB for sexual exploitation is based on practice of several years. THB for labour exploitation is only in so far covered, as women are victims. The support of two different ministries is laid down in a contract for five years, which includes also regulations on the cooperation. One legal basis for the cooperation between LEFOE-IBF and police can be found in SPA s. 56, which allows the transfer of personal data. The transfer is allowed for the police, as long as it is necessary for the protection of the individual at risk. Additionally, the instrument of legal and psycho-social assistance throughout criminal proceedings, which is also organised by LEFOE-IBF for victims of THB, is financed by another ministry (Ministry of Justice).

Investigation techniques

As indicated above, the application of investigation techniques depends in some cases on an order of the public prosecutor or a decision of the court. Since the investigation procedure should be conducted jointly between public prosecutor and police, under the supervision of the public prosecutor though, individual cooperation influences the work. It might be influenced by the

---

[217] Interview with Labour Inspectorate (November 2010), interview with Control Unit for Illegal Employment (August 2010) and interview with Ministry of Finance (August 2010).

personal relation between public prosecutor and police in a specific case. In some investigations, it seems to work very well; in others cooperation was rather low. Although various techniques can lead to numerous evidences, the evidences are difficult to gather. Interviews showed that consequently the statement of the victim still plays a crucial rule throughout the investigation and proceedings.[218]

One specific case concerning THB and begging as form of exploitation is an example for excellent cooperation between police and public prosecution and usage of investigation techniques. Within the case around 50 to 80 Romanian begging persons have been identified, who faced exploitation in Vienna. For example, the rent for a bed has been excessive. The indictment included18 accused and around 60 victims. The Austrian police got in contact with the Romanian public prosecution and the whole case was further investigated by Romanian authorities. Finally, five arrest warrants have been issued. Police invested an exceptional amount of time and human resources and made use of all possible investigation techniques. It would probably not be possible to invest as much time and resources in every similar case.[219]

2.3 Cooperation between States

2.3.1 Legal framework for cooperation in trans-national Trafficking in Human Beings-cases

Implementation of the EU legal framework

The basis of international cooperation in cases of THB is mainly regulated by the Extradition and Mutual Legal Assistance Act.[220] The act is applicable when no other inter-state treaty exists.[221] The act is based on the principle of reciprocity. Consequently a request of another State can only be supported when this State would also support Austria's requests. In case of uncertainty about the reciprocity, the Ministry of Justice has to be consulted.[222] The act regulates extradition[223], transit of persons through Austria for the purpose of law enforcement[224], legal assistance[225], transfer of proceedings including the

[218] Cf. Interview with Control Unit for Illegal Employment (August 2010), interview with a public prosecutor (November 2010) and interview with Criminal Intelligence Service (September 2010).

[219] Cf. Interview with a public prosecutor (November 2010) and interview with Criminal Intelligence Service (September 2010) .

[220] Federal Law Gazette No. 529/1979 as amended by Federal Law Gazette I No. 112/2007.

[221] Cf. Extradition and Mutual Legal Assistance Act s. 1.

[222] Cf. Extradition and Mutual Legal Assistance Act s. 3.

[223] Cf. Extradition and Mutual Legal Assistance Act s. 10-41.

[224] Cf. Extradition and Mutual Legal Assistance Act s. 42-49.

[225] Cf. Extradition and Mutual Legal Assistance Act s. 50-59(a).

transfer of monitoring of persons who received convictions on probation[226] and transfer of enforcement of foreign convictions.[227]

Legal assistance allows inter alia for the following measures: production, search and seizure of information, documents, or evidence from financial institutions, or other natural or legal persons; taking evidence or statements from persons or sending of relevant documents and records.[228]
The Ministry of Justice is the central authority for mutual legal assistance or extradition and forwards requests to the respective authority. All incoming requests are registered in a database which is accessible for the public prosecution and all courts.[229]

Regarding police cooperation, the Police Cooperation Act (*Polizeikooperationsgesetz, PolKG)*[230] and the Police Cooperation Act on cooperation within the EU *(EU-Polizeikooperationsgesetz, EU-PolKG*[231]*)* are of high importance. The international police cooperation encompasses international assistance in police matters and measures of law enforcement authorities abroad as well as foreign law enforcement authorities in Austria, especially for observation.[232] Law enforcement is obliged to render assistance upon request in case of reciprocity. Even in the case that there is no formal request issued yet, law enforcement is obliged to act.[233] The transfer of personal data to Austrian law enforcement authorities is possible under certain circumstances. At the same time the transfer of personal data to Europol, Interpol or any foreign law enforcement authority is only allowed under certain conditions. These data are not allowed to be used for any other purpose as agreed without the consent of the Austrian authority and, inter alia, the data have to be erased immediately when not needed anymore.[234]

The Police Cooperation Act on cooperation within the EU regulates the cooperation with other law enforcement authorities within the EU and with Europol. Since recently, it is clearly stated, that also the financial authorities

---

[226] Cf. Extradition and Mutual Legal Assistance Act s. 60.

[227] Cf. Extradition and Mutual Legal Assistance Act s. 64.

[228] FATF/OECD, *Austria, Mutual Evaluation Report, Anti-Money Laundering and Combating the Financing of Terrorism* (2009)(1127) <http://www.fatf-gafi.org/dataoecd/22/50/44146250.pdf> accessed 3 December 2010.

[229] FATF/OECD, *Austria, Mutual Evaluation Report, Anti-Money Laundering and Combating the Financing of Terrorism* (2009)(1120-1130) < http://www.fatf-gafi.org/dataoecd/22/50/44146250.pdf> accessed 3 December 2010.

[230] Federal Law Gazette I No. 104/1997 as amended by Federal Law Gazette I No. 132/2009.

[231] Federal Law Gazette I No. 132/2009.

[232] Cf. PolKG s. 1(2).

[233] Cf. PolKG s. 3 (1), (2).

[234] Cf. PolKG s. 8.

can cooperate with Europol.[235] Additionally, it regulates trans-border cooperation, the usage of the Visa Information System (VIS) and Schengen Information System (SIS).

The Federal law on judicial cooperation in criminal matters with the Member States of the European Union *(Bundesgesetz über die justizielle Zusammenarbeit in Strafsachen mit den Mitgliedstaaten der Europäischen Union, EU-JZG)*[236] implements the European Arrest Warrant in the Austrian legislation. The offence has to be punishable by imprisonment or a detention order for a maximum period of at least one year. In addition, the double criminality rule applies, which means that the offence has to be punishable in the requesting State as well as in the executing State. Regarding specific offences including THB this rule does not apply. The Austrian law copied the respective exemptions of the Framework Decision on the European Arrest Warrant verbally in its Annex I.[237]

The same law regulates building Joint Investigation Teams (JITs). In case, investigations in Austria, which have to be supported by police organs of other EU Member States, are needed, the Austrian public prosecutor has to contact the relevant counterpart in other EU Member States directly. The Austrian public prosecutor suggests building a JIT and has to inform the Austrian police as well as the head of public prosecution. If another EU Member State requests a JIT, the Austrian public prosecutor decides upon Austria's participation.[238]

In the field of police cooperation, several bilateral agreements have been concluded; inter alia with Albania (entry into force 1 January 2008) or Bosnia and Herzegovina (entry into force 1 September 2007).[239] Negotiations on agreements regarding police cooperation have been initiated or continued with inter alia Malta, Ukraine, Georgia, Tunisia and Mexico.[240]

The well working net of liaison officers of the Ministry of Interior supports the daily transnational work. The ministry currently employs 23 attachés in

---

[235] Cf. Explanatory Notes 875 d.B. XXIV. GP 8 (government bill regarding the Act on Anti-Fraud 2010).

[236] Federal Law Gazette I No. 36/2004 as amended by Federal Law Gazette I No. 112/2007.

[237] L. Sautner, 'Die Vollstreckung eines Europäischen Haftbefehls nach dem EU-JZG' (2005) ÖJZ 2005/20.

[238] Federal law on judicial cooperation in criminal matters with the Member States of the European Union s. 61.

[239] European Migration Network, NCP Austria, *Annual Policy Report 2009* (Vienna 2010) 31 <http://www.emn.at/emn-reports.html> accessed 30 November 2010.

[240] Ministry of Interior and Ministry of Justice, Report on Security 2008, p. 320 <http://www.parlament.gv.at/PAKT/VHG/XXIV/III/III_00099/imfname_173662.pdf> accessed 1 December 2010

countries such as Bulgaria, Albania, Georgia, Italy, Greece, Jordan and – as of 2011 – also in South-East Asia.[241]

Trans-national cooperation in THB-cases

International cooperation with regard to THB is also part of the Austrian National Action Plan. The plan envisages under chapter VIII, on the one hand, the intensification of cooperation within international bodies and, on the other hand, the improvement of cooperation with Eastern Europe partners in the fields of criminal prosecution. According to the plan, projects should be implemented which focus on training activities for and coordination of actions aimed at officials in the fields of law enforcement and criminal prosecution. Inter alia the Ministry of Interior aims at promoting further activities to enhance police cooperation at the EU and international levels.[242]

Austria is coordinating a COSPOL (Comprehensive Operational Strategic Planning for the Police) project to combat THB. This project is mainly focusing on Romania, in particular on trafficking in children and women for the purpose of sexual exploitation. Aim of the project is to identify and prosecute especially Romanian criminal organisations which are active in the EU. Starting in 2006, the project firstly collected relevant data in 2007. All participating countries were asked to collect the same data. The findings of this first step have been further evaluated by Europol. Reforms and staff changes in the relevant authority in Romania caused some delays, nevertheless the operational investigation started in 2008.[243]

Due to Austria's geographical position, Austria puts a strong focus in police cooperation with countries of the Western Balkans. Austria intends to continue specific projects which support countries in this region in the field of criminal police. COSPOL projects against THB should be continued, also projects against smuggling and on border management.[244]

Within the framework of smuggling and illegal migration, police reports also on cooperation with EUBAM (European Union Border Assistance Mission) in cases on THB. Adolescents between 14 and 18 years from Moldova are

[241] M. Sebanz, 'Säulen der Verbrechensbekämpfung' (Pillars of Combating Crime) *Öffentliche Sicherheit* (Vienna, 9-10/10).

[242] Cf. National Action Plan against Human Trafficking, VIII.7 and VIII.8 <http://www.bmeia.gv.at/fileadmin/user_upload/bmeia/media/2-Aussenpolitik_Zentrale/Menschenrechte/TFM_Aktionsplan_engl_V20091007_LAYOUT_FINAL.pdf> accessed 30 November 2010.

[243] Cf. Austrian Task Force on Combating Human Trafficking, *First Austrian Report on Combating Human Trafficking* (2008) pp. 23-24.

[244] European Migration Network, NCP Austria, *Annual Policy Report 2009* (Vienna 2010) p. 35 <http://www.emn.at/emn-reports.html> accessed 30 November 2010.

trafficked to Austria in order to commit burglaries. Investigations started in cooperation with Slovakia, Italy and EUBAM.[245]

2.3.2 Application of legal framework in practice

Generally, police cooperation in cases of THB can be described as rather well working. Within Austria, regional police turns to the Criminal Intelligence Service, which has the relevant contacts to police departments abroad. Cooperation works very well with specific countries, such as Bulgaria or Romania. Ideal police cooperation requires one single point of contact. Sometimes specific units or departments are labelled as single points of contact for THB matters, but do not have all necessary competences or would not have a good overview of the whole country and the respective regional authorities. Additionally, a common spoken language helps enormously and facilitates communication. Legal barriers, such as significant differences in the legislation, are less within the EU.[246]

During a case on THB for the purpose of exploitation through begging, Romania took over the investigations from Austria and continued the investigation procedure in Romania. The Austrian police initiated the contact with the Romanian public prosecutor. Within this case, a rather organisational obstacle in trans-border cooperation came up, the language barrier. Informally it was agreed which parts of the investigation records need to be translated, usually the full records have to be translated. But this would have taken a very long time, probably up to a year, and meant high translation costs.[247] This language barrier is also mentioned within mutual administrative assistance within the Posting of Workers Directive.[248] Translation costs are usually high, consequently translations are reluctantly done.[249]

Austria had cases on THB which were investigated within a JIT, but JITs are used for more complex cases. However, Austrian experiences with JITs are also gained in the area of smuggling. This is also seen as valuable information for THB, since trends can be detected and some cases of smuggling can turn into THB cases later. In the experience of the police JITs have several advantages. One major advantage is that information can be exchanged much faster and easier. Secondly, JITs offer also some financial support, consequently necessary travels or funding for common operational measures can be secured.

---

245 Cf. Ministry of Interior, *Annual Report on Illegal Migration* (2008) p. 39 <http://www.bmi.gv.at/cms/BK/publikationen/files/JAHRESBERICHT_2008_Final_Version.pdf> accessed 1 December 2010.

246 Cf. Interview with Criminal Intelligence Service (September 2010).

247 Cf. Interview with a public prosecutor (November 2010).

248 Directive 96/71/EC of the European Parliament and of the Council of 16 December 1996 concerning the posting of workers in the framework of the provision of services.

249 Cf. Interview with Ministry of Finance (August 2010).

It is usually not difficult to get the permission to build up a JIT; it depends on the public prosecutor, who decides.[250]

The benefits of the network of liaison officers of the Ministry of Interior are emphasised. The network supports in providing the requested information and is less bureaucratic. The liaison officers are able to receive information faster and have the right contacts to the local police and judiciary. The formal procedure using Interpol or Europol would sometimes cost too much time.[251]

2.4 Summary of findings

2.4.1 Identified obstacles

Actors who are involved in identifying and investigating cases of THB for labour inspection may differ from those authorities, which are usually involved in THB for sexual exploitation. The main, different actor is the Control Unit for Illegal Employment, which is allowed to enter business premises and further rooms – also private homes – in which employees might work. Further authorities, which are also allowed to enter work sites and business premises, are the Labour Inspectorate, the District Health Insurance Fund and the Construction Workers' Annual Leave and Severance Pay Fund. These authorities have specific tasks, such as protecting the security at the work place, but THB is not in their scope of responsibility.

Authorities, which are usually involved in investigating THB, are mainly the police, public prosecution, judges and the Control Unit for Illegal Employment. All these authorities conduct trainings in THB in general. But according to the information received, the trainings are usually not focused on THB for labour exploitation. The authorities do not offer specific courses or trainings on THB for labour exploitation. The trainings for the Control Unit for Illegal Employment deal with THB for labour exploitation and for sexual exploitation. Within the judiciary, the demand for trainings on THB is rather low due to demanding workloads and the low level of importance of THB cases in the daily work of judges or public prosecutors.

As already discussed above, the term exploitation is seen as rather vague by the involved authorities, although case law exists regarding this term. Nevertheless, specific questions are left open, such as the question regarding the excessiveness of working hours. How excessive have the working hours to be in order to amount to exploitation? As shown by interviews, it is unclear in which cases *exploitation* could be involved. Specific indicators or reference points on THB for labour exploitation do not exist, but would be supportive and would help in an assessment.

---

[250] Cf. Interview with Criminal Intelligence Service (September 2010).

[251] Interview with regional Criminal Intelligence Service (November 2010).

After identifying presumed cases of THB, it is shown by interviews, that it is rather unclear how to cooperate in cases of THB for labour exploitation. As indicated in the chapters 2.2.1 and 2.2.2, cooperation between the authorities is regularised, but on a general basis. It is often unclear to the actors, how the case proceeds. The *Control Unit for Illegal Employment* for example does not receive information on further investigations after having filed a complaint at the public prosecutor. Exchange with the public prosecution on the reasons for closing the investigation for example would be helpful for the control unit.[252] At the same time, when forwarding relevant documents or information on inspections by the Control Unit for Illegal Employment to other authorities, it would be useful to have an exchange on the follow-up.[253]

Apart from the general legally defined cooperation, cooperation between the various authorities with regard to THB for labour exploitation is not determined specifically. Cooperation in cases of THB for sexual exploitation is practised since several years and the authorities and NGOs involved are clear. Sharing tasks is, on the one hand, practised and, on the other hand, defined in the basic contract of the relevant ministries with LEFOE-IBF and the contract on the psycho-social and legal assistance between the Ministry of Justice and LEFOE-IBF. With regard to cases falling outside the scope of LEFOE-IBF's tasks, practice exists to a lesser extent with regard to THB for labour exploitation. There is no formalised cooperation between the relevant authorities and institutions regarding THB for labour exploitation. Cooperation with regard to THB for labour exploitation seems in general to be rather low and not elaborated enough.

There is the impression that the statement of a victim is still the most important evidence in cases of trafficking in human beings. The victim acting as witness is essential for the criminal proceedings. This is also shown in the case on exploitative labour conditions in agriculture. The victims did not appear at the court, therefore their testimonial was missing. The alleged perpetrators have been acquitted later on due to a lack of evidence.[254] Additionally the victim's testimonial is essential, since gathering other evidences by using various investigation techniques is very time consuming. As shown in one case concerning THB and begging as form of exploitation, police gathered a lot of evidences, but had to designate a lot of time and staff to this case. This case had been transferred to Romania successfully later on. The vagueness of the term 'exploitation' leads to the fact, that State prosecutors require different standards of evidences in order to proof 'exploitation'.

Linked to this case, one obstacle in trans-national cooperation was discussed, the language barrier in trans-national cases. The Romanian public prosecution took over a case from the Austrian police and further investigated.

---

[252] Cf. Interview with Ministry of Finance (August 2010).

[253] Cf. Interview with Control Unit for Illegal Employment (August 2010).

[254] Cf. Case study 2.

For this transfer it was agreed which parts of the investigation records need to be translated, usually the full records have to be translated. The translation of only parts of the records cost a lot of money. Also within another context it is mentioned that translation costs of documents are rather high and therefore are reluctantly allowed.

Another obstacle in trans-nation cooperation, especially for the investigation, is the necessity of single points of contacts in other countries for cases on THB in general. These contact points need to have sufficient operational competences, in order to ensure also cooperation with police units at provincial level.

The formal cooperation via Interpol and Europol is described as working on a good basis. It is also described, that information gathering is sometimes too slow via Europol or Interpol and other ways are used in order to get information faster.

Using JITs is seen as very conducive in the investigation of trans-national cases. Although it would be in general not very difficult to build up a JIT, the establishment has to be assessed in every relevant case. At the end, not the police, but the public prosecutor decides on the establishment.

2.4.2 Good practices

In order to ensure sufficient awareness regarding THB in general, every police officer receives information on THB in the basic training programme. THB forms part of all further relevant trainings of the Federal Security Academy and of the training of further levels of staff.[255] Additionally trainings at police stations at provincial level are organised. Also, several trainings of public prosecution and judges conducted by the Ministry of Justice are mentioned with regard to THB.[256]

The introduction of trainings on THB for the Control Unit for Illegal Employment is highly appreciated by the staff of the control unit and has a positive impact on the work of the unit. The trainings are conducted in cooperation with the police or LEFOE-IBF. Therefore, the training offers the opportunity to get to know the relevant actors with regard to THB and sustainable cooperation can be established. The importance of these trainings, which have been introduced in 2006, is stressed by several authorities in the interviews. Since receiving the training on THB, this topic would be part of the scope of daily work of the staff.

The net of liaison officers of the Ministry of Interior offers the possibility to get information and support in a less bureaucratic way and usually faster.

---

[255] Cf. Austrian Task Force on Combating Human Trafficking, *First Austrian Report on Combating Human Trafficking* (2008) p. 9-10.

[256] Cf. Austrian Task Force on Combating Human Trafficking, *First Austrian Report on Combating Human Trafficking* (2008) p. 18.

Part III
Victim protection and assistance

3.1 Identification of victims

Identification of victims of THB in general

Usually, police would identify victims of THB and refer them either to the NGO LEFOE-IBF or – in the case of children - to the crisis centre 'Drehscheibe' administered by the Viennese Youth Welfare authority. The police contacts LEFOE-IBF in the case of presumed victims of THB; the NGO can be reached 24/7 by the police. Police start the investigation and LEFOE-IBF or the 'Drehscheibe' continue with the victims' assistance, which includes *inter alia* housing.

As already indicated above[257], the cooperation between police and LEFOE-IBF is considered successful. However, in addition to referring victims from the police to this NGO, victims are also identified by the NGO itself. Victims contact the NGO via friends or a social community. Regarding exploitation in domestic work, church is considered to be a very important factor for a possible identification. Some trafficked women exploited in domestic work are only allowed to leave the house on their own for the service on Sunday. The church then informs the NGO.[258] In 2009, 33% of all supported women at LEFOE-IBF had contacted the NGO via friends, other NGOs or organisations engaged in migration. 68% of the women who have lived in the shelter have been referred to LEFOE-IBF by the police. Only 2% of these women managed to contact the NGO on their own. Victims rarely find out about counselling centres, since they are usually controlled and often speak only very little or no German at all.[259]

The cooperation between LEFOE-IBF and the law enforcement authorities is based on a contract; for several years, the Ministry of Interior has been planning to prepare a nationwide internal decree which would envisage that LEFOE-IBF be responsible for all female victims of human trafficking identified in Austria.[260] This further step towards a more formalised way of cooperation takes time. However, in the meantime other NGOs in Austria have begun to take care of trafficked persons, such as the organisation EXIT in Vienna. EXIT offers counselling though its work is mainly focussed on

---

[257] See chapter 2.2.1.

[258] Cf. Interview with NGO (August 2010).

[259] Cf. LEFOE-IBF, *2009 Annual Report* (Vienna 2010) p. 15.

[260] Cf. Austrian Task Force on Combating Human Trafficking, *First Austrian Report on Combating Human Trafficking* (2008) p. 14.

women being trafficked from Nigeria to Austria for the purpose of sexual exploitation.[261]

Although numerous trainings are conducted for law enforcement,[262] it is assumed that a large number of victims remain unidentified. The reasons why many remain unidentified are manifold. The above described situation of identification and usual way of referral is limited to the identification of women who are in most cases sexually exploited and – in fewer cases – of children. Other forms of THB or cases involving male victims of THB involve bigger obstacles in respect of THB identification.

Only recently, the Federal Criminal Intelligence Service installed a hotline for THB and smuggling.[263] The general public can inform the police about situations which might be linked to THB or smuggling per email or on the phone, and anonymously if wanted. The hotline should support the identification and encourage the general public to report. The hotline does not have a clear focus on THB for the purpose of labour exploitation. According to its description, the hotline seeks information from clients of the sex industry.[264]

Identification of child victims of THB

The identification of child victims of THB is described as rather difficult, since it seems to be very challenging to distinguish between unaccompanied children seeking asylum, trafficked children or children who were smuggled. Additionally, children are usually identified while committing a crime such as pick pocketing; therefore the police has to investigate more deeply in order to come to the conclusion that the child might be presumed trafficked.[265] The problems around identification are, however, paired with a lack of awareness, especially within the youth welfare authorities in other provinces of Austria. Other provinces' authorities are rarely, if at all, aware of any cases of THB involving children.[266] This leads to the conclusion that most children affected by THB are not identified in Austria.

---

[261] Cf. <http://www.adesuwainitiatives.org> accessed 13 December 2010. Additionally CARITAS supports within the project 'Talitha' victims of THB in the province of Carinthia, cf. <http://www.caritas-kaernten.at/index.php> accessed 13 December 2010.

[262] Cf. Austrian Task Force on Combating Human Trafficking, *First Austrian Report on Combating Human Trafficking* (2008) p. 3 and chapter 2.1 above.

[263] Cf. <http://www.bmi.gv.at/cms/BK/meldestellen/menschenhandel/start.aspx> accessed 14 December 2010.

[264] Cf. Federal Ministry of Interior <http://www.bmi.gv.at/cms/BK/ presse/files/ 181020_Kampf_gegen_Menschenhandel_Meldestelle_und_Hotline_im_Bundeskriminal amt.pdf> accessed 14 December 2010.

[265] Cf. Austrian Task Force on Combating Human Trafficking, *Report on the Working Group on Child Trafficking* (2008) p. 11.

[266] Cf. Austrian Task Force on Combating Human Trafficking, *Report on the Working Group on Child Trafficking* (2008) pp. 10-11.

It is therefore suggested that a process on identification is developed which involves several stakeholders, including the youth welfare institutions. At the moment, police identifies most of the children.[267] Additionally, child trafficking is a nationwide problem in Austria, but institutionalised referral only exists in Vienna. A nationwide problem needs nationwide care and support.[268] At the moment, such a National Referral Mechanism focussed on child trafficking does not exist in Austria, though the Austrian Task Force is working on it since the issue is included in the National Action Plan.[269] Currently, other provinces' youth welfare institutions are not able to provide child victims of THB with specialised institutions, therefore children are housed in general youth welfare institutions led by persons who are not specialised in trafficked children either.[270] The lack of awareness can be solved by conducting trainings, but a strategy for multi-stakeholder trainings does not exist.[271] Mostly, multi-stakeholder trainings with regard to child trafficking are conducted by the NGO Ecpat Austria.[272]

Age assessments of children are usually conducted by the aliens' police. If the age of a child cannot be clearly determined by documents, the police has to assess the age medically. In case of doubt about the age of the child, the age has to be assumed.[273]

If a child is identified as a presumed victim of THB and is unaccompanied, the youth welfare authority has to apply for a transfer of custody. A guardian is appointed who has full custody over the child, including legal representation.[274] In Austria, the crisis centre of the Viennese youth welfare authority called 'Drehscheibe' is formally in charge of all children who are identified as victims of THB Vienna. The data of the 'Drehscheibe' do not

---

[267] Cf. Ecpat Austria (ed), *Alternative Report on the Implementation of the Optional Protocol to the Convention on the Rights of the Child on the Sale of Children, Child Prostitution and Child Pornography* (April 2008) p. 30.

[268] Cf. Austrian Task Force on Combating Human Trafficking, *Report on the Working Group on Child Trafficking* (2008) p. 6.

[269] Cf. National Action Plan against Human Trafficking, IV.8 <http://www.bmeia.gv.at/fileadmin/user_upload/bmeia/media/2-Aussenpolitik_Zentrale/Menschenrechte/TFM_Aktionsplan_engl_V20091007_LAYOUT_FINAL.pdf> accessed 30 November 2010.

[270] Ecpat Austria (ed), *Alternative Report on the Implementation of the Optional Protocol to the Convention on the Rights of the Child on the Sale of Children, Child Prostitution and Child Pornography* (April 2008) p. 30.

[271] M. Ammer, M. Nowak, *FRA Thematic Study on Child Trafficking* Austria (2008)(42) <http://fra.europa.eu/fraWebsite/attachments/Child-trafficking-09-country-at.pdf> accessed 23 November 2010.

[272] Cf. <http://www.ecpat.at/index.php?id=48> accessed 14 December 2010.

[273] Cf. APA s. 12(4).

[274] M. Ammer, M Nowak, *FRA Thematic Study on Child Trafficking*, Austria (2008)(65-66) <http://fra.europa.eu/fraWebsite/attachments/Child-trafficking-09-country-at.pdf> accessed 23 November 2010

give further information on how the children have been referred to the 'Drehscheibe'. The police refers almost all children to this place, and only a small percentage are referred by other institutions or organisations.[275] In exceptional cases, LEFOE-IBF takes care of girls under the age of 18.

Identification of victims of THB for the purpose of labour exploitation

In order to tackle the issue of THB for the purpose of labour exploitation, the Ministry of Finance made a first, important step and introduced trainings on a regular basis for staff members of the *Control Unit for Illegal Employment* regarding THB in 2006. The trainings offered have a great impact regarding awareness raising. However, the trainings discuss mainly the topic of THB for the purpose of sexual exploitation, since these are the most important cases in the daily work of the unit. They seem to be rather short and information on how to handle cases of THB is missing.[276]

Female victims of THB for the purpose of labour exploitation have been referred to LEFOE-IBF by the police, and the police is adequately sensitised regarding this form of THB. The police might be informed by private persons or by a hospital. In cases of domestic workers particularly, victims may turn to the embassy which would then inform LEFOE-IBF.[277]

The system of referral with regard to female victims of THB for sexual exploitation is based on experience of cooperation between LEFOE-IBF and the police. This experience does not exist with, on the one hand, male trafficked persons and, on the other hand, other sectors besides exploitation in domestic work or sexual exploitation. New and further modalities of identification need to be found and consequently new systems of referral need to be identified. Police experience shows that cooperation with male victims seems to be rather difficult.[278]

The system of identification should not be entirely based on identification by police. Civil society is mentioned as an important actor with regard to women exploited in households. The cashier at the supermarket or the kindergarten teacher can play important roles in identifying.[279] The newly installed hotline of the police may be a useful tool in the future in order to get more information from the general public.

---

[275] Ecpat Austria (ed), *Alternative Report on the Implementation of the Optional Protocol to the Convention on the Rights of the Child on the Sale of Children, Child Prostitution and Child Pornography* (April 2008) p. 6.

[276] Cf. Interview with Ministry of Finance (August 2010) and interview with Control Unit for Illegal Employment (August 2010).

[277] Cf. Interview with NGO (August 2010).

[278] Cf. Austrian Task Force on Combating Human Trafficking, *First Austrian Report on Combating Human Trafficking* (2008) p. 14.

[279] Cf. Interview with NGO (August 2010).

But in addition to civil society, other public authorities need to be identified which might be supportive with regard to THB for the purpose of labour exploitation.[280]

The role of the Control Unit for Illegal Employment has already been discussed above. It was mentioned that authorities of the asylum system should also be more involved in combating THB and contribute to more identifications. The integration of NGOs into the work of the first reception centres for asylum seekers is planned in order to identify those asylum seekers who are presumed victims of THB. Additionally, organisations and social institutions should be further sensitised with regard to THB, offering for example information on, or provision of, basic care[281] for asylum seekers.

Furthermore, the control units of the District Health Insurance Funds are mentioned as possible further actors.[282] The District Health Insurance Fund has a different view though, and it mentioned that although on-site inspections are conducted, THB is definitely not in their scope of responsibility. For this actor, it is of primary concern whether an employer established working relations with employees and did not register the employees for social security issues at the same time. THB-issues would be out of its scope. Furthermore, it was explained that any action during these inspections with regard to THB would rather be an interference with long-term planned investigations on THB by the police, which would only be jeopardised by the fund.[283]

Additionally, the Labour Inspectorate is also allowed to conduct inspections. But, like the District Health Insurance Funds, the Labour Inspectorate also considers THB issues as outside of its scope of work or legal responsibility. In the case of an inspection, from the perspective of the Labour Inspection, it is only relevant whether a certain person actually works at the inspected work site. In the case that the person might be working illegally, the Control Unit for Illegal Employment is responsible. In the case that the employer might not have registered the person with regard to social security payments, the District Health Insurance Fund is responsible. The Labour Inspectorate is basically not interested in the legal status of a person; the main purpose of the inspections is the protection of employees and the avoidance of accidents. Since THB is not within its competences, no specific trainings are offered.[284]

---

[280] Cf. Interview with NGO (August 2010).

[281] The basic care for asylum seekers is regulated in the Basic Welfare Support Agreement (*Grundversorgungsvereinbarung*) and comprises for example accommodation, board, money, monthly pocket money or medical examination. Cf. <http://www.erso-project.eu/partners/national-asylum-return-policy/austria> accessed 14 December 2010.

[282] Cf. Interview with Criminal Intelligence Service (September 2010) and interview with Labour Inspectorate (November 2010).

[283] Cf. Interview with District Health Insurance Fund Vienna (November 2010).

[284] Interview with Labour Inspectorate (November 2010)

Although sensitised to THB, the Control Unit for Illegal Employment also faces difficulties in the inspection. The primary 'target' of an inspection is first of all the business and the employer, but not the employees. Employees are instructed what to say when asked by any control organ. Employees are usually not able to distinguish between the different control organs that may appear at the work site.[285] It could be the unit of police dealing with foreigners, the Labour Inspectorate or, for example, the control unit of the health insurance. Workers, who know that their status of residence or working permit violates Austrian law, will be rather reluctant to talk to Austrian control organs. Additionally, the fear of losing their job might also be an obstacle to getting more information from the employees.[286] Third country nationals who are illegally in the country are usually referred to the unit of police dealing with foreigners.[287]

As described above[288] after filing a complaint, the formal investigation under the supervision of the public prosecutor starts. Since the public prosecutor decides whether the investigations are closed or an indictment is made, awareness raising of public prosecution is very important. Police needs to act pro-actively in order to be able to 'persuade' public prosecution.[289] As shown above[290], no specific seminar on THB for labour exploitation was conducted with the judiciary. Cooperation with public prosecutors seems in some cases to be rather challenging. As described in case study 2, the Control Unit for Illegal Employment stated that more intense communication and exchange with the public prosecutor during the formal investigation procedure would have been helpful. However, in this case dealing with exploitation in agriculture, the public prosecutor did not close the investigation and issued an indictment. Later on, the persons were acquitted. Since this was the very first case, every actor seemed to have been overburdened with the new, challenging form of cases.[291] Austria does not follow an administrative procedure in order to qualify someone as a victim of trafficking in human beings and there are no formal criteria established. At the same time, victims cannot themselves apply for an official status. Before being assigned with the residence permit for special protection, a person is presumed trafficked. LEFOE-IBF's support is not limited to presumed trafficked women referred by the police; it also offers support to women who were referred by other organisations.

---

[285] Interview with Ministry of Finance (August 2010).

[286] Interview with Ministry of Finance (August 2010).

[287] Interview with Control Unit for Illegal Employment (August 2010).

[288] Cf. M. Heemskerk and C. Rijken, 'Combating Trafficking in Human Beings for Labour Exploitation in The Netherlands', Chapter 2, para 2.1 in this book.

[289] Cf. Interview with Criminal Intelligence Service (September 2010).

[290] Cf. M. Heemskerk and C. Rijken, 'Combating Trafficking in Human Beings for Labour Exploitation in The Netherlands', Chapter 2, para 1 in this book.

[291] Cf. Interview with Control Unit for Illegal Employment (August 2010).

3.2 Legal framework for the protection of the rights of victims of Trafficking in Human Beings for labour exploitation

3.2.1 Assistance to victims

As already described above[292], with regard to female victims of THB, LEFOE-IBF plays a central role. In general, LEFOE-IBF offers counselling and housing to trafficked women and girls above the age of 14, and the majority are transferred to them by the police. LEFOE-IBF also gives counselling to women who do not live in an apartment of LEFOE-IBF. Women can live in an apartment together with other clients of LEFOE-IBF. The women are supported 24 hours a day there, the place is safe and the address is kept secret. The apartment offers space for ten women on a long term basis, while there is space for two for use in exceptional cases. In the year 2009, 49 women were living in the apartment, and in total LEFOE-IBF supported 182 women in the same year. Additionally LEFOE-IBF introduced a system of a 'transfer-apartment' which should support the women in their independent reintegration into society. Counsellors come to this apartment three times a week, and women self-organise living in this apartment. This apartment offers space for six.[293]

With regard to children, the crisis centre of the Viennese youth welfare authority called 'Drehscheibe' offers housing to trafficked children. As described above,[294] the 'Drehscheibe' is only responsible for children identified in Vienna, in other provinces of Austria the general youth welfare authorities take care of children. The majority of the children housed by the 'Drehscheibe' are below the age of 14 and are therefore under the age of criminal responsibility.[295] Generally, 'Drehscheibe' needs more funding for its activities.[296] The 'Drehscheibe' set up cooperation agreements with youth welfare institutions in Bulgaria and Romania. Staff in specific crisis centres in these two countries is trained by 'Drehscheibe' and should take care of the

---

[292] Cf. G. Cristinel ZAHARIA, 'Combating Trafficking in Human Beings for Labour Exploitation in Romania', Chapter 3, para 1 in this book.
[293] Cf. LEFOE-IBF, *2009 Annual Report* (Vienna 2010) pp. 11-12.
[294] Cf. G. Cristinel ZAHARIA, 'Combating Trafficking in Human Beings for Labour Exploitation in Romania', Chapter 3, para 1 in this book.
[295] Cf. Ecpat Austria (ed), *Alternative Report on the Implementation of the Optional Protocol to the Convention on the Rights of the Child on the Sale of Children, Child Prostitution and Child Pornography* (April 2008) p. 8.
[296] Cf. Ecpat Austria (ed), *Alternative Report on the Implementation of the Optional Protocol to the Convention on the Rights of the Child on the Sale of Children, Child Prostitution and Child Pornography* (April 2008) p. 32.

trafficked children coming back from Austria.[297] 'Drehscheibe's approach is to return the trafficked children to the country of origin as soon as possible[298], consequently it can be assumed that these children do not spend much longer in Austria after being identified as trafficked. This short period of residence in Austria makes it difficult to establish long-term perspectives for trafficked children, which would *inter alia* include access to education or vocational training in Austria.

The Austrian framework on victim assistance does not provide for shelter or counselling services to male victims of THB. Although this issue was already part of the first, and still is part of the second, National Action Plan, no further progress on the topic can be identified. The very low numbers of identified male victims renders the instalment of a counselling centre unnecessary. Interestingly, the Task Force states that there is currently no need to set-up a facility for trafficked males.[299]

Medical support in the case of emergency is ensured by law in Austria for victims of THB. Until women coming from EU Member States receive the residence permit *for special protection,* they are not protected by health insurance. Until the issue of the residence permit, women only have access to emergency care. LEFOE-IBF can provide the trafficked women with medical support only based on informal contacts and networks of medical doctors who offer treatments for free. By law, the residence permit has to be issued after six weeks.[300] This missing access for trafficked persons is acknowledged and is one of the aims of the National Action Plan. However, so far no further progress with regard to this question is evident.[301] Linked to the residence permit is also the payment of 'basic care', which is € 180 per month.[302]

3.2.2 Right to residence

According to the Council of Europe Convention on Action against Trafficking in Human Beings, as well as DIR 2004/81/EC,[303] Austria

---

[297] M. Ammer, M. Nowak, FRA Thematic Study on Child Trafficking, Austria (2008)(82) <http://fra.europa.eu/fraWebsite/attachments/Child-trafficking-09-country-at.pdf> accessed 23 November 2010.

[298] Austrian Task Force on Combating Human Trafficking, *Report by the Working Group on Child Trafficking* (2008) p. 17.

[299] Cf. Austrian Task Force on Combating Human Trafficking, *First Austrian Report on Combating Human Trafficking* (2008) p. 14.

[300] Cf. SRA s. 69(a)(3).

[301] Cf. Austrian Task Force on Combating Human Trafficking, *First Austrian Report on Combating Human Trafficking* (2008) p. 15.

[302] Cf. LEFOE-IBF, *2009 Annual Report* (Vienna 2010) p. 17.

[303] Council Directive (EC) 2004/81 of 29 April 2004 on the residence permit issued to third-country nationals who are victims of trafficking in human beings or who have been

implemented a residence permit for trafficked person and has to implement a recovery and reflection period.

The recovery and reflection period implemented by Austria encompasses a minimum of 30 days.[304] Within these 30 days, a presumed trafficked person must not be deported. This period is implemented by an internal decree.[305] An assessment of the implementation of the DIR 2004/81/EC holds that an implementation by an internal decree does not fulfil the criteria of the directive. The directive is therefore not sufficiently transposed in Austria.[306] Additionally, according to jurisprudence of the ECJ, amendments of administrative practices are not sufficient because beneficiaries need to be able to know these rights and to claim these rights before courts.[307]

The main regulation regarding residence for trafficked persons is SRA s. 69a. This regulation was amended in 2010 and, in comparison to the previous regulation, several improvements have been made. The residence permit *for special protection* offers different groups a permit, including witnesses or victims of THB (CC s. 104a) or of the transnational prostitution trade (CC s. 217)[308] as well as unaccompanied minors or minors who are *inter alia* in the custody of the youth welfare authority.[309] The residence permit can be issued *ex officio* or upon well-founded application despite the fact that the trafficked person does not fulfil all necessary prerequisites - normally necessary for a residence permit.[310] For trafficked persons, this permit is issued in order to ensure criminal investigation or to ensure the enforcement of civil law claims linked to THB or the transnational prostitution trade. The permit is not granted when no criminal investigation is conducted or when no civil law claims are issued.[311] The residence permit has to be issued within six weeks. This means that the Ministry of Interior has to decide within six weeks whether the permit is granted or not. Additionally, the permit is granted for at least six months and

---

the subject of an action to facilitate illegal immigration, who cooperate with the competent authorities [2004] OJ L 261/19.

304 Cf. Explanatory Notes 1565 d.B. XXII. GP 14 (government bill regarding the Council of Europe Convention on Action against Trafficking in Human Beings).

305 Ministry of Interior, internal decree BMI-FW1700/0090-III/4/05.

306 Cf. Academic Network for Legal Studies on immigration and Asylum in Europe, 'Directive 2004/81 Victims of Trafficking Synthesis Report' (2010) p. 31 <http://ec.europa.eu/home-affairs/doc_centre/immigration/docs/studies/odysseus_2004_81_victims_trafficking_synthesis_en.pdf> accessed 16 December 2010.

307 T. Öhlinger and M. Potacs, *Gemeinschaftsrecht und staatliches Recht* (3rd edn, LexisNexis, 2006) p. 113.

308 SRA s. 69(a)(1)(2).

309 SRA s. 69(a)(1)(4)(a).

310 Prerequisites which have to be normally fulfilled are for example that the foreigner is holder of a valid health insurance or has access to adequate housing. Cf. SRA s. 11(2).

311 SRA s. 69(a)(3).

is renewable.[312] Consequently, Austria fulfils all requirements regarding a residence permit for the DIR 2004/81/EC and the Council of Europe Convention on Action against Trafficking in Human Beings. But, as shown above, Austria does not fulfil the requirements regarding the recovery and reflection period. Austria's regulation does not take into account granting a residence permit based on the personal situation of the trafficked person.[313] An issuance of the residence permit solely based on the personal situation would not be possible according to SRA s. 69a. Additionally, it is not clear whether the trafficked person has to cooperate with the authorities in order to receive the permit. The provision does not explicitly mention the necessity to cooperate with the authorities and at the same time does not explicitly exclude this necessity. According to the Ministry of Interior, this provision does not at all require the cooperation of the trafficked person. The decisive factor is whether the criminal investigation started in this case or not.[314]

After the residence permit, next step would be the unlimited authorisation to settlement *(Niederlassungsbewilligung-unbeschränkt)*.[315] In addition to the initial requirements of the permit *for special protection* (on-going criminal investigation and/or civil law claims), persons have to fulfil the integration agreement (*Integrationsvereinbarung*).[316]

Trafficked persons from other EU Member States do not require the residence permit *for special protection*. EU citizens need a specific confirmation of registration (*Anmeldebescheinigung*) if they stay longer than 3 months in Austria. Prerequisites for this confirmation can create obstacles for victims of THB. It requires, for example, a passport or identification card as well as enough earnings or health insurance. Some of these requirements might be difficult to fulfil for trafficked persons. The relevant municipal department of the city of Vienna agreed to amend the requirements for victims of THB.[317]

3.2.3 Victims as witnesses in proceedings

In recent years, the Code on Criminal Procedure has been amended several times. The improvement in the rights of victims was of central interest in these amendments and led to the introduction of a chapter on victims' rights in the code. In general, victims of crimes have rights with regard to participation in

---

[312] SRA s. 69(a)(3).

[313] As the Council of Europe Convention on Action against THB suggests for example in Art. 14(1)(a).

[314] Cf. Explanatory Notes XXIV. GP regarding the amendments of the Law on Asylum 2005, the APA 2005 and the SRA (government bill 88, 11).

[315] Cf. SRA s. 43(3).

[316] Cf. SRA s. 14(5). The integration-agreement requires inter alia sufficient knowledge of German.

[317] Cf. LEFOE-IBF, *2009 Annual Report* (Vienna 2010) p. 25.

criminal proceedings, and right to protection as well as compensation.[318] In order to ensure that victims can make use of their rights, the Code on Criminal Procedure states that police, public prosecution and the court are under an obligation to inform the victim.[319] Furthermore, the rights of victims encompass the right to have access to court files, the right to have interpretation free of charge as well as the right to receive psycho-social and legal assistance.[320]

Essential within these amendments is the implementation of the institution on psycho-social and legal assistance.[321] This assistance is provided to victims during criminal proceedings and is free of charge. Those who are entitled to this assistance are the victims of deliberate offences which exposed them to violence or serious threat and may have been harmful to their sexual integrity. Additionally, relatives of a victim who died because of a criminal offence as well as relatives who have been witnesses of the offence are entitled to this assistance.[322] The assistance consists of legal and psychosocial support. The legal support encompasses legal representation during the proceedings; the psychosocial support includes preparation for the proceedings and for example accompanying the victim to all questionings. LEFOE-IBF organises prior to the criminal proceedings a legal counselling meeting with the representing lawyer. In this meeting, the client gets information on the court system and the upcoming proceedings.[323]

The Ministry of Justice entrusts specific, qualified institutions or organisations with the assistance. The psycho-social and legal assistance is in general free of charge for the victim; the Ministry of Justice bears the costs. In general, the assistance is of high importance and is used often. In 2008, 2829 persons used this assistance and the Ministry of Justice had to budget almost € 4 million for it.[324]

In 2009, the right to psycho-social assistance was extended also to civil law proceedings.[325] The psycho-social assistance is applicable when the civil proceedings are linked to the foregoing criminal proceedings.

Regarding testimony, specific groups of victims have certain special rights. Victims under the age of 14, as well as victims of offences which may have

---

[318] Marianne Hilf and Philipp Anzenberger , 'Opferrechte: Die Stellung des Opfers im Strafverfahren' (2008) ÖJZ 2008/94, p. 888.

[319] Cf. inter alia CCP s. 10(2).

[320] Marianne Hilf and Philipp Anzenberger , 'Opferrechte: Die Stellung des Opfers im Strafverfahren' (2008) ÖJZ 2008/94, p. 889.

[321] Cf. CCP s. 66(2).

[322] Cf. CCP s. 66(2).

[323] Cf. LEFOE-IBF, *2009 Annual Report* (Vienna 2010) p. 24.

[324] Dina Nachbauer, 'Die "persönliche Betroffenheit" von Opfern als Erfordernis des Rechtsanspruchs auf Prozessbegleitung' (2010) JSt 2010, p. 49.

[325] Cf. Second Act on Protection against Violence (*Gewaltschutzgesetz*), Federal Law Gazette No. I 40/2009.

violated their sexual integrity, can testify early during the investigating stage with participation of the parties *(kontradiktorische Vernehmung)*. This form of testifying allows the victim to be questioned separate from the perpetrator. On the one hand, victims can testify during the trial proceedings and sit in a separated room equipped with video equipment. On the other hand, it is also possible that, based on early testifying during the investigation stage, additional questioning during the trial proceedings can be avoided.

In some cases the victims or the public prosecutors have to make a request in order to be able to testify early, while in other cases the courts are obliged to do it that way. In any case, victims of sexual offences under the age of 14 must be provided with the opportunity to testify early. Victims of offences who have been exposed to violence or serious threat can testify during the proceedings in a separate room in the absence of the perpetrator.[326] Victims who might have been violated in their sexual sphere have in addition the right to be questioned by a same sex person. Additionally, those victims can refuse to answer questions which are too personal or which require detailed descriptions of the offence which are not bearable for the victim.[327] The trial proceedings may be conducted without any public access. However, in this case the victim may be accompanied by confidants.[328]

3.2.4 Right to compensation

Victims of crime can join the criminal proceedings as a so-called 'private party' (*Privatbeteiligung*) in order to claim compensation.[329] These victims get additional rights and have *inter alia* the right to require the acceptance of further evidence.[330] Victims become a 'private party' by declaration and have to justify the claims that they lodge. In general, the judge can defer the decision in respect of damages to the civil court. In cases where the proceedings are closed or the alleged perpetrator is acquitted, the court has to refer the victim to the civil court. Consequently, the victim has to file the complaint at a civil court. The situation is different if the perpetrator is convicted. Generally, the criminal court has to decide upon the amount of compensation paid when the results of the proceedings are sufficient to assess the amount of damage. But if further information or investigation would be necessary for the assessment, the criminal court refers the victim to the civil court. In short, the benefit for a victim being a 'private party' is that the person

[326] Cf. CCP s. 250(3).
[327] Cf. CCP s. 158(1)(2).
[328] Karin Bruckmüller and Dina Nachbaur, 'Opferrechte im Strafverfahren' (2009) JAP 2009/2010/10, p. 71.
[329] Cf. CCP s. 65(2).
[330] Cf. CCP s. 67(6)(1).

would have a better chance of receiving compensation without bearing any of the costs of the proceedings compared to proceedings before the civil court.[331]

State funded compensation is offered by the Victims of Crime Act (*Verbrechensopfergesetz*).[332] In general, this act applies when a person has been injured or has suffered other damages to health caused by an offence. Persons who have been injured in Austria, but are not from Austria, have to fulfil further criteria. The deliberate offence causing the injuries must be punishable by at least six months of imprisonment.[333] Consequently, the VCA also applies to trafficking in human beings. The VCA provides for different payments and includes *inter alia* the provision in cases of loss of income, costs of medical treatment or different forms of rehabilitation.[334] In addition, a lump sum for moral damages can be paid. The lump sum is usually € 1000, but can be increased to € 5000 based on the severity of the injury.

Access to VCA payments is handled by the Federal Social Welfare Authority. Austrian citizens can request payment when the offence happened in Austria or abroad. EU citizens also qualify for the VCA when the offence took place in Austria. Third country nationals have limited access to VCA payments. The offence must have taken place in Austria, and the victim is only entitled to payments when she/he was legally residing in Austria at the time.

In order to implement DIR 2004/80/EC,[335] the Social Welfare Authority acts as the assisting or deciding authority in cases of cross-border applications. The directive, for example, foresees that a person who was injured as a result of an offence in another EU Member State can apply not only in the country in which the offence took place, but also in the country of usual residence. Austria acts in cases of THB as the deciding authority because the persons have been injured in Austria. At the same time, it is possible that trafficked persons file the application for compensation in their home country and Austria must then decide on the application. Experience with regard to cross-border cases has remained rather limited. In 2006 and 2007, Austria adjudicated on a total of 3 cross-border cases.[336]

Additionally, according to AEL s. 29, migrants who are working, but do not fulfil the requirements of the AEL or SRA, are entitled to the same claims

---

[331] Maria Eder-Rieder, 'Die Stellung des Opfers im neuen Strafverfahren' (2008) JSt 2008, pp. 118-119.

[332] Federal Law Gazette No. 288/1972 as amended by Federal Law Gazette I No. 4/2010, in the following VCA.

[333] Cf. VCA s. 1 (1)(1).

[334] Cf. VCA s. 2.

[335] Council Directive (EC) 2004/80 of 29 April 2004 relating to compensation to crime victims [2004] OJ L 261/15.

[336] Cf. Matrix insight, 'The application of Directive 2004/80/EC relating to compensation to crime victims (2008) p. 30 <http://ec.europa.eu/civiljustice/news/docs/study_application_directive_compensation_final_report_en.pdf> accessed 17 December 2010.

as a person with a regular working contract. This would include the possibility of claiming unpaid wages. LEFOE-IBF supports trafficked women when they are claiming unpaid wages before the court in respect of social and labour law. LEFOE-IBF also cooperates with the Chamber of Labour which offers legal counselling.[337]

3.3 Application of the legal framework in practice

Identification

Usually, actors who are not involved in anti-trafficking work directly have a general awareness about the existence of cases of THB in Austria. But at the same time, as shown by interviews THB does not fall within the scope of responsibility for these actors.[338] On the one hand, responsibilities are clearly defined by law and consequently limit the scope of activity. Usually these actors are fully occupied with these responsibilities. On the other hand, organs such as the Control Unit for Illegal Employment, which are sensitised, lack sufficient information on how to identify presumed victims of THB, and also lack understanding of the necessary follow-up steps.

Cases show that there are different understandings of THB among relevant actors and the judiciary, suggesting that further awareness raising measures are needed. With regard to the judiciary, the level of general awareness regarding THB seems to be rather low. Notions such as 'working in a household is not proper work', 'persons lie in order to receive benefits' or 'the person would anyway receive more than in his or her home country' or the general belittlement of the situation of exploited workers, for example, influence proceedings in THB cases.[339] Different legal assessments of THB lead to peculiar situations in specific cases. In one case regarding exploitation of a woman in domestic work, the criminal investigation was stopped before an indictment was brought, but later on the woman successfully filed a complaint before the court for social and labour law matters and received considerable compensation.[340]

The identification of victims depends on a specific notion of 'victims of THB'. It has been observed that 'victims of THB' have certain attributes within the judiciary - being self-confident does not fit into this picture. In one case, a young woman, acting very self-confidently and speaking German fluently could not be, according to the judge, a 'victim of THB'. The alleged

---

[337] Cf. LEFOE-IBF, *2009 Annual Report* (Vienna 2010) p. 33 and case study 1.

[338] Interview with Labour Inspectorate (November 2010) and interview with District Health Insurance Fund Vienna (November 2010).

[339] Cf. Interview with NGO (August 2010), interview with Ministry of Finance (August 2010) and interview with Control Unit for Illegal Employment (August 2010).

[340] Cf. Interview with NGO (August 2010).

perpetrator was thus acquitted.[341] An obstacle may also be that people often do not consider themselves as victims. It is difficult to assess whether a case is THB if the person entered Austria voluntarily and knew what they were going to do in Austria.[342]

The lack of identification is also linked to a general uncertainty about which cases could be assessed as cases of THB for labour exploitation. Closely linked to the above mentioned notion of victims of THB is the issue regarding the circumstances under which the work is done. Persons come to Austria in order to earn money and therefore shoulder burdens, such as poor living conditions or dangerous working conditions. But uncertainty exists over where THB actually starts and ends.

Generally, indicators on identifying cases of THB for labour exploitation do not exist in Austria. In trainings for the Control Unit for Illegal Employment, the police usually refers to the general indicators developed by international organisations, but cannot refer to Austria-specific indicators. The development of indicators on THB for labour exploitation would facilitate work in this area.[343] Identified key indicators would include whether the person is able to move freely, and any form of violence.[344] However, especially with forms of THB for labour exploitation, it needs to be stressed that the definition of THB does not require violence. Other means can also be used.

Assistance

As indicated above, the situation regarding National Referral Mechanisms with a focus on children and male victims is unsatisfactory. Since there are no specified institutions or organisations which would take care of male victims of THB, police refer presumed trafficked men for housing to different charitable organisations, such as Caritas Austria.[345]

The residence permit has to be issued after a time period of six weeks according to the SRA. During the first months of implementation of this time limit, experiences have been very positive and the limit was almost never exceeded by the Ministry of Interior.[346] Experience in 2010, however, shows that issuing this permit takes between five and eight months[347], which may raise several issues. On the one hand, trafficked persons are not covered by health insurance until their residence permit is issued. Consequently, LEFOE-IBF has to rely on voluntary treatments offered free of charge by medical

---

[341] Cf. Interview with NGO (August 2010).

[342] Interview with a public prosecutor (November 2010).

[343] Cf. Interview with Control Unit for Illegal Employment (August 2010).

[344] Cf. Interview with Criminal Intelligence Service (September 2010), interview with Ministry of Finance (August 2010) and interview with Control Unit for Illegal Employment (August 2010).

[345] Cf. Interview with regional Criminal Intelligence Service (November 2010).

[346] Cf. LEFOE-IBF, *2009 Annual Report* (Vienna 2010) p. 32.

[347] Statement by LEFOE-IBF (Personal email correspondence 16 December 2010).

doctors. On the other hand, trafficked persons find themselves in a kind of legal vacuum without any residence permit. Since Austria is not properly implementing a reflection period, there is also no protection against expulsion during this period.[348]

Victims as witnesses in proceedings

The existence of psycho-social and legal assistance in criminal proceedings has constituted an enormous improvement with regard the enforcement of the rights of victims. With regard to THB-cases, LEFOE-IBF provides psycho-social assistance to victims and organises legal assistance, which is mainly undertaken by two experienced lawyers in Vienna.[349]

In practice, the cooperation of the victim with law enforcement agencies is still very important. Victims who act as witnesses in court proceedings are essential. Other types of evidence are very difficult to produce, at least without entailing very high costs.[350] As described in case study 2, it is considered key that victims act as witnesses. With regard to child trafficking, it has been suggested that in practice, children are not acting as witnesses in proceedings.

Right to Compensation

The possibility to act as a so called 'private party' within the criminal proceedings supports victims in claiming damages. Judges are not obliged to decide upon these damages and can refer the victim to the civil court. In such cases, no legal assistance is offered for civil law claims and only psycho-social assistance is accessible. Comparing the situation of compensation paid in cases of THB for sexual exploitation and THB for labour exploitation, it can be seen that with regard to THB for labour exploitation more legal opportunities are provided in respect of access to compensation. Unpaid wages can be claimed by the trafficked person at the court on social and labour law. In proceedings regarding THB for sexual exploitation, compensation is rather limited to the possibilities within the criminal court proceedings. The sums of unpaid wages granted to trafficked persons are higher than the sums for moral damage assessed in criminal proceedings. The lowest sum that a trafficked woman supported by LEFOE-IBF received was € 2500 for unpaid wages. Claims of unpaid wages can even be successful after the criminal investigation regarding the same case has ended. A woman, exploited in domestic work and supported by LEFOE-IBF, received € 15.000 for unpaid wages before the

---

[348] Cf. Academic Network for Legal Studies on immigration and Asylum in Europe, *Directive 2004/81 Victims of Trafficking Synthesis Report* (2010) p. 33 < http:// ec.europa.eu/home-affairs/doc_centre/immigration/docs/studies/odysseus_2004_81_victims_trafficking_synthesis_en.pdf> accessed 16 December 2010.

[349] Cf. LEFOE-IBF, *2009 Annual Report* (Vienna 2010) p. 24.

[350] Cf. Interview with a public prosecutor (November 2010).

court on social and labour law. At the same time, State prosecutors decided not to bring an indictment and closed the investigation.[351]

Regarding the Victims of Crime Act, victims of THB face a number of obstacles when attempting to access payments. The National Action Plan foresees, therefore, that the Task Force will assess the practical applicability of this act in cases of THB.[352] Third-country nationals have to have been legally residing in Austria at the time the crime took place. This prerequisite is rather difficult to achieve for victims of THB. Most victims are forced to stay in Austria and are not aware of their current residence status. Based on this regulation, most THB victims would be excluded. In particular, a section of the act, which excludes payments in cases where the person would have access to similar payments in their home country,[353] means that the procedure can be lengthy with regard to victims of trafficking. The authority in Austria has to assess whether the victim of THB could receive payments in the home country.

3.4 Summary of findings

3.4.1 Identified obstacles

Generally, it can be observed that the identification of victims of THB for labour exploitation, and following a referral system and assistance for victims of THB for labour exploitation, is rather difficult. The existing National Referral Mechanism in Austria covers cases of THB for sexual exploitation, women exploited in domestic work, exploitation through begging and, to a certain extent, trafficking in children. Identifying presumed victims of THB for labour exploitation requires the inclusion of further actors and sometimes different ways of cooperation. As indicated above, apart from the well-functioning and practiced ways of identification and cooperation, identification faces several obstacles.

As elaborated in Section 1, regarding THB for labour exploitation, no formalised system on identification and cooperation exists. The core functions of a National Referral Mechanism are the identification of presumed trafficked persons and the regulation of cooperation between different actors in order to ensure assistance to the presumed trafficked persons.[354] Gaps in a formalised system with regard to THB for labour exploitation can be observed.

---

[351] Cf. Interview with NGO (August 2010).

[352] Cf. Austrian Task Force on Combating Human Trafficking, *First Austrian Report on Combating Human Trafficking* (2008) p. 17.

[353] Cf. VCA s. 8(3).

[354] T. Kröger, J. Malkoc, BH Uhl, *National Referral Mechanisms – A Practical Handbook* (OSZE/ODIHR 2004) p. 16.

As indicated above, with regard to the identification of cases, indicators on THB for labour exploitation in Austria are missing, and some authorities have clear responsibilities during an inspection, excluding THB for labour exploitation. It can therefore be assumed that not all presumed trafficked persons can be identified. At the same time, means of further cooperation between various actors after identifying indicators are vague. As described, third country nationals who are illegally in the country, as so identified during an inspection, are usually referred to the police and deported.

Assuming that there are also male victims of THB, and more specifically of THB for labour exploitation, assistance for these victims has to be provided. Specialised services for men, offering housing for example, do not exist so far in Austria.

Migrant workers, who do not fulfil all the requirements of the AEL or SRA, are entitled to claim wages in the same way as persons holding regular working contracts. Although it is legally possible to claim unpaid wages, for example, the implementation in practice is rather difficult since there is no formal support for access to this right in Austria.[355] Austria's situation regarding undocumented migrant workers in general is focused on sanctioning the employer, with little access to protection and rights for the workers.[356] In Austria, some initiatives exist which seek to improve the situation of documented and undocumented migrant workers, such as the project 'work@migration' of the Union of Salaried Private Sector Employees or the initiative called 'PrekaerCafé.'[357] Services for undocumented migrant workers such as the German model, organised by the trade union ver.di,[358] do not exist in Austria. In addition to a system of national referral with regard to THB for labour exploitation, which would need further development in Austria, there is also the need for systemised awareness raising and nation-wide assistance with regard to trafficked children. Gaps in awareness within the youth welfare authorities in all provinces of Austria, and insufficient specialized institutions in all provinces for trafficked children, are reported.

An obstacle to the identification of victims is also the lack of a clearly defined notion of victims. In case study 1, the interview partner stated that awareness raising among public prosecutors and judges needs to be further supported. The acquittal in the case illustrates existing attitudes. Domestic work was not considered 'work'. It was considered that the person made false allegations in order to receive a residence permit. And – as stated in the

355 Cf. Interview with Chamber of Labour (August 2010).

356 PrekärCafé, 'Mehr als ein Stück Papier' (2010) < http://www .migrazine .at /artikel/mehr-als-ein-st-ck-papier> accessed 22 December 2010.

357 Cf. <http://www.myspace.com/prekaer> and <http://www.gpa-djp.at/ servlet/ ContentServer?pagename=GPA/Page/Index&n=GPA_4.7.1> accessed 22 December 2010.

358 Cf. <http://besondere-dienste.hamburg.verdi.de/themen/migrar/themen/anlauf stel le1> accessed 22 December 2010.

acquittal - a very self-confident and fluently German speaking woman did not fit into the accepted 'victim' identity.[359]

The current regulation regarding the residence for trafficked persons who are third-country nationals is considered unsatisfactory. The obligation to implement a recovery and reflection period is not sufficiently implemented in Austria, and the protection against expulsion is consequently also not implemented properly. Trafficked persons fall within a legal vacuum until the residence permit is issued, which can take more than half a year. Additionally, the current situation of residence does not offer enough protection and security of residence in order to persuade the trafficked person to cooperate with law enforcement and testify. Improving the regulation of residence as well as measures of victim protection would support the cooperation between the trafficked person and law enforcement.[360]

With regard to compensation, experience shows that more and more decisions on compensation are taken within criminal proceedings. However, sums of granted compensation are rather low.[361] Although the victim has psycho-social and legal support throughout the criminal proceedings, legal assistance is not offered when the judge refers the case to the civil court with regard to claims of moral damage.

The VCA provides the opportunity to receive payments, but victims of crimes have to reside legally in Austria. This regulation excludes from the outset many victims of THB from all possible payments under the VCA. Payments are not made when the person has similar claims in their home country. Lengthy and bureaucratic proceedings in order to prove that the home country does not offer similar possibilities are seen as problematic with regard to victims of THB.

3.4.2 Good practices

The implementation of psycho-social and legal assistance for specific groups of victims of crimes offers great support to victims of THB. This assistance, offered free of charge, is seen as essential in order to have access to all rights during the proceedings. The victim can be prepared before the proceedings and a lawyer ensures that the victim can use all the rights granted. According to the experience of LEFOE-IBF, the implementation of psycho-social and legal assistance works very well in practice.[362] Additionally, the right to follow the criminal proceedings as a 'private party' supports the right to have access to compensation.

---

[359] Cf. Interview with NGO (August 2010).

[360] Cf. Interview with regional Criminal Intelligence Service (November 2010).

[361] Cf. LEFOE-IBF, *2009 Annual Report* (Vienna 2010) p. 24.

[362] Cf. Interview with NGO (August 2010).

The FMEIA introduces several measures in order to raise awareness regarding THB for labour exploitation in diplomatic households. In a circular letter the FMEIA has informed all embassies and international organisations based in Vienna about the Austrian Law on Domestic Workers, especially on minimum wages and working hours. Domestic workers must get their legitimisation card on their own at the FMEIA, which allows staff to talk to the worker in privacy.[363]

[363] I Brickner, 'Hilfe für ausländische 'Haussklavinnen'' (Help for foreign 'houseslaves') *Der Standard* (Vienna 2 December 2009).

Part IV
Case studies

Case 1

This exploitative situation took place between March 2002 and July 2006. The information about this case was received within an expert interview.[364]

The person concerned (Z) was referred to the NGO LEFOE-IBF by another women's shelter (usually dealing with women who face violence). The case concerns domestic work. The legal assessment of this case is threefold. Criminal proceedings took place based on complaints including 'exploitation of a foreign person' (APA s. 116)' as well as 'misuse of authority' (CC s. 212) and 'sexual coercion' (CC s. 202). In addition, the Chamber of Labour Vienna initiated requests in order to obtain unpaid wages. The third proceeding concerns the social insurance law and whether the work done by Z can be seen as an employment relation, which would entail an entitlement to social insurance.

15-year old Z from Latin America came to Austria in order to take care of the child of the family of X and Y and to do the housework. X's father talked to the parents of Z telling them that Z should live in Austria with X and Y and support them with child care in exchange. Additionally, Z expected to be able to pursue vocational training.[365] Z had for the first six months a legal residence status. An application to prolong the residence permit was unsuccessful. Consequently, Z had as of mid 2002 no regular residence status.[366] According to Z, she worked until 2004 seven days a week from 7 am till 7 pm. Afterwards she worked less, but still five days a week for around nine hours, and on the weekends 12 hours. Additionally, according to Z, she was raped by Y several times.[367] For the first period, Z received 220 $ a month, with 100 $ of that sum being paid directly to the parents of Z. From 2006 onwards, Z received around 100 $.[368] In November 2006, Z moved out of the common apartment and found another place to live.[369] X found out about her husband's intercourse and immediately arranged a return ticket for Z. Z was supposed to show up at their place in order to discuss the return ticket. Z asked friends to call the police if she were not back within an hour. Finally, the friends called the police.

[364] Cf. Interview with NGO (August 2010).

[365] Appeal against decision of municipal department 40 of Vienna, p. 4.

[366] Decision of Regional Criminal Court Vienna, 2 October 2007, p. 7.

[367] Decision of Regional Criminal Court Vienna, 2 October 2007, p. 13.

[368] Decision of Regional Criminal Court Vienna, 2 October 2007 and record of the Social Insurance Vienna, 22 January 2008.

[369] Decision of Regional Criminal Court Vienna, 2 October 2007, p. 9.

Cooperation

The police referred Z first to a women's shelter. From there she was referred to LEFOE-IBF, with the support of the police. LEFOE-IBF initiated the usual steps for supporting women.[370] The cooperation between the NGO and the police worked as usual. The police investigated the case and legal proceedings were initiated. The NGO did not monitor any difference in the cooperation with the police because this case included exploitation in domestic work and not, as in the majority of cases, sexual exploitation in prostitution.[371]

Victim Protection

When Z moved to Austria, she was 15 years old. She, as well as the family of X and Y, have a Latin American background and come from the same country. The families of X and Z know each other. It seems that Z and X have the same father - a fact which did not initially come to light and was not clarified.[372]

After talking to the police in 2006, Z was referred first to a women's shelter, then to LEFOE-IBF. Consequently LEFOE-IBF initiated the process for obtaining a residence permit *for special protection* for Z, which was granted.[373] Up until the start of the trial, Z was supported by LEFOE-IBF for six months. Z cooperated with the law enforcement agencies. Z was able to get psycho-social and legal assistance throughout the criminal procedure.

Period after proceedings

X and Y were acquitted regarding 'exploitation of a foreign person' (APA s. 116)' and 'misuse of authority' (CC s. 212) as well as 'sexual coercion' (CC s. 202).

The court described the contact between Y and Z as an 'exchange of affectionateness', initiated by Z. Y would not have made use of his authoritative position as host, and the extramarital relationship was based on mutual agreement.[374] Regarding the exploitation in the household, it was argued that the witness Z indicated exploitation. But later on she said – in conformity with X - that she was able to decide about her spare time and work in other households.[375] Furthermore, the court then elaborated the main motive for Z staying in Austria and the possibility that she made false allegations in order to receive a residence permit *for special protection*. The return ticket was booked one day after Z initiated the complaint. The court concluded that she wanted to avoid her return. The court could not preclude

[370] Cf. Interview with NGO (August 2010).
[371] Cf. Interview with NGO (August 2010).
[372] Decision of Regional Criminal Court Vienna, 2 October 2007, p. 6 and appeal against decision of municipal department 40 of Vienna, p. 3.
[373] Based on SRA s. 69 a(1).
[374] Decision of Regional Criminal Court Vienna, 2 October 2007, pp. 8-9.
[375] Decision of Regional Criminal Court Vienna, 2 October 2007, p. 10.

the possibility that Z pretended to be sexually exploited in order to receive the residence permit.[376] Additionally, the court held that Z was a very self-confident and a fluently German speaking young lady, whereas Y does not speak German very well and therefore did not understand the questions properly during his first questioning by the police, in which he stated that sexual acts happened against Z's will.[377] The court finally concluded that there was no situation of exploitation. The court referred to the condition of *ruthless exploitation of vital interests of the victim* in order to establish exploitation. Z would have lived like a family member with X and Y and would have taken care of the children and the household. For this work she received pocket money and she was able to decide about her spare time freely. Additionally, she was able to work for others and could save this earned money. Consequently, no situation of exploitation was held to have occurred.[378]

The Chamber of Labour Vienna lodged a request for the receipt of unpaid wages. For this employment, the minimum wages for domestic workers were applicable.[379] Claims are expired after three years[380]; therefore no further steps were possible.[381]

In addition, the District Health Insurance Fund came to the conclusion that Z's work entitled her to be fully protected by the social security system (including insurance of sickness, work-related accidents and pensions). However, the higher instance decided differently. Z's work was seen as support and as a share of the household work, including caring for children, within shared accommodation. She worked in exchange for boarding. Household work did not occupy Z entirely, and did not exclude Z's full self-determination.[382] LEFOE-IBF appealed against this decision.[383]

---

[376] Decision of Regional Criminal Court Vienna, 2 October 2007, pp. 11-13.

[377] Decision of Regional Criminal Court Vienna, 2 October 2007, pp. 13-14.

[378] Decision of Regional Criminal Court Vienna, 2 October 2007, pp. 15-16.

[379] Based on the Law on Domestic Workers (Federal Law Gazette No. 235/1962 as amended by Federal Law Gazette I No. 100/2002) a minimum wage applies. For Vienna this minimum wage for an unskilled worker in the first year (without preparing meals) would be € 1.000 (pre-tax). Cf. <http://www.bmask.gv.at/cms/site/attachments/ 1/7 /8/CH0787/CMS1244015004738/hausgehilfenwien_mlt.pdf> accessed 29 November 2010.

[380] Claims regarding wages prescribe after three years (Civil Code s 1502), cf. W. Brodil, M. Risak and C. Wolf, *Arbeitsrecht in Grundzügen* (6th edn LexisNexis, Vienna 2010)(512).

[381] Interview with NGO (August 2010).

[382] Decision of municipal department 40 of Vienna, p. 11.

[383] Interview with NGO (August 2010).

Case 2

This case describes an exploitative situation in the agricultural sector in Austria.

Two asparagus-producers had been charged with exploiting 84 Slovakian harvest workers in 2006. According to the indictment, the harvest helpers had to work up to 77 hours per week and received only € 3,60 per hour instead of the minimum wage of € 5,27.[384] Since the workers officially worked for 20 hours only, the case was preliminary dealt with as case of fraudulent withholding of social security duties.[385] It is reported that social security were owed about € 46.000.[386] Representatives of the Control Unit for Illegal Employment conducted an inspection of an agricultural business and found out about the working conditions when talking to the workers. First, the workers said they worked from 8 am till midday, but after further questioning they admitted that they worked from 7 am to 7 pm. A 30-minutes lunch break as well as housing costs had been deducted from the wages. The harvest helpers complained about the working conditions.[387] In the trial, the asparagus-producers were acquitted.

Cooperation

During the control, the Control Unit for Illegal Employment received information regarding working hours. After the inspection, they requested permission to enter the premises for further authorities, including police. Special organs of the customs department and the tax authority also took part and seized several objects. Afterwards, they filed a complaint regarding fraudulent withholding of social security duties.[388] It was stated that experience with cases, including consideration of possible indicators of exploitation, was rather small. The cooperation between the public prosecution and Control Unit for Illegal Employment could be improved.[389] The public prosecutor investigated further and the case led to a trial.

Victim Protection

Information about the situation of the harvest helpers is rather lacking. The 84 female and male harvest helpers came from Slovakia. Most of them had valid working permits. The Control Unit for Illegal Employment got in touch with the harvest helpers during an inspection of the premises. There is no information on any special measure for the persons involved. During the

---

[384] R. Eiben, 'Kein Lohn für Gastarbeiter während der Spargel wächst' (No wages for migrant workers during the asparagus grows) *Kurier* (13 July 2007).

[385] Based on CC s. 153(d) *Betrügerisches Vorenthalten von Sozialversicherungsbeiträgen und Zuschlägen nach dem Bauarbeiter-Urlaubs- und Abfertigungsgesetz.*

[386] R. Eiben, 'Kein Lohn für Gastarbeiter während der Spargel wächst' (No wages for migrant workers during the asparagus grows) *Kurier* (13 July 2007).

[387] Cf. Interview with Control Unit for Illegal Employment (August 2010).

[388] Cf. Interview with Control Unit for Illegal Employment (August 2010).

[389] Cf. Interview with Control Unit for Illegal Employment (August 2010).

inspection, the harvest workers cooperated with the organs. Since it was not clear at the beginning that exploitation could be occurring, the harvest workers did not receive any specific information or specific protection.

Period after proceedings

In the trial, the producers were both acquitted. The final indictment did not only mention the charge of 'fraudulent withholding of social security duties', but also 'trafficking in human beings' and 'exploitation of a foreigner'. The defendants were acquitted in respect of all three charges. It is reported that the producers denied the accusations. The explanation for the registration of only 20 working hours per week instead of – as stated by the harvest helpers – up 70 hours per week is that asparagus could only be harvested in the early morning and in the afternoon. The waiting times in between were not reported to the AES. These hours of waiting would not be considered for payroll accounting.[390] This claim is highly doubted by the control organs. The harvest helpers did not show up at the trial and sent a letter instead saying that they did not want to testify for or against the producers. However, the testimonials of the harvest helpers would have been essential.[391] Missing evidence of guilt led to the acquittal.

[390] R. Eiben, 'Kein Lohn für Gastarbeiter während der Spargel wächst' (No wages for migrant workers during the asparagus grows) *Kurier* (13 July 2007).

[391] Cf. Interview with Control Unit for Illegal Employment (August 2010).

Part V
Recommendations

General recommendations

1) In Austria, a stakeholder meeting should be organised with representatives of all relevant authorities, institutions and NGOs, which would help to improve cooperation in THB for labour exploitation. Combating THB for labour exploitation requires the involvement of different stakeholders from those relevant with regard to THB for sexual exploitation or child trafficking. Other relevant authorities, discussed in this report, are the Control Unit for Illegal Employment, the Labour Inspectorate, the District Health Insurance Fund Stakeholders and the Construction Workers' Annual Leave and Severance Pay Fund. A stakeholder meeting discussing THB for labour exploitation requires the attendance of stakeholders representing employee's interests and migrant worker's interests, such as trade unions, labour organisations and NGOs dealing with undocumented migrant workers in Austria.
2) Generally, awareness raising measures such as trainings focusing on THB for labour exploitation are needed. These measures should follow a strategic plan and cover all relevant stakeholders. Multi-stakeholder trainings could create the basis for sustainable cooperation across the authorities or organisations.
3) It is recommended that the existing efforts for a comprehensive National Referral Mechanism in Austria be further developed. It should also focus on THB for labour exploitation. Therefore, the involvement of more stakeholders nationwide is necessary.
4) The development of a list of indicators on THB for labour exploitation specifically for the Austrian situation would support the identification of presumed trafficked persons and is therefore recommended. Bearing in mind that a list of indicators is not the only tool of identification, further accompanying measures which support identification have to be taken into account.
5) The Austrian National Action Plan against Human Trafficking includes measures, which are seen as essential for combating THB for labour exploitation. Examples include the measures regarding potential contact centres for presumed male victims of THB, further discussions on a broadened NRM which focuses also on trafficked children, a review of the criminal law regarding THB, and the improvement of statistical data regarding THB. In order to ensure the implementation of these actions, adequate resources have to be allocated.
6) Inspired by the Council of Europe Convention on Action against Trafficking in Human Beings, it is recommended that all measures

follow a gender-mainstreaming and child-rights approach in their development, conception and implementation. Trafficked children are also exploited for the purpose of labour exploitation and the role of women in THB for labour exploitation needs to be taken into consideration to the same extent as the role of trafficked men.

5.1 Recommendations regarding the definition of Trafficking in Human Beings for labour exploitation

1) In order be able to better assess the situation on THB for labour exploitation in Austria, more specified statistical data as well as further research are needed. The data and information currently available do not allow for a full understanding of the dimensions of THB for labour exploitation in Austria.
2) The National Action Plan foresees a review of all applicable legal regulations regarding THB for labour exploitation. The category of 'exploitation of a foreign person' (APA s. 116) should in particular be evaluated.
3) It should be ensured that all victims of THB, irrespective of which legal regulation on THB is applied, have equal access to support and assistance. All victims of THB should have access to psycho-social and legal assistance, provided that the requirements are satisfied.
4) Since the criminal liability of legal persons may play a vital role in combating THB for labour exploitation, it is recommended that the application of the rather new CCLA is evaluated. Measures supporting the enhanced implementation of the CCLA should follow.

5.2 Recommendations regarding investigation and prosecution

1) As a sustainable follow-up to the suggested stakeholder meeting, it is recommended that a working group dedicated to THB for labour exploitation is established within the Austrian Task Force on Combating Human Trafficking. Working groups on specific topics, such as child trafficking, have proved to be valuable instruments.
2) Authorities, *inter alia* the Control Unit for Illegal Employment as well as Labour Inspectorates, possess the right to enter premises. The legal competence to conduct inspections and controls are extensive, but necessary at the same time, in order to ensure effective protection of employees, for example. All authorities in addition to the police may be permitted to enter specific business premises and under certain circumstances also private homes, but only for specific purposes. Such permissions should also be made available for combating THB.

3) Since the exchange of relevant information between these authorities[392] is legally regulated in various acts, such as the AEL, it is recommended that awareness on THB for labour exploitation is raised within these authorities. Although THB is not specifically part of the scope of responsibility for these authorities, it is recommended that these authorities be able to identify, at least, indicators of THB, and so can inform the relevant authorities. In respect of information sharing and forwarding, as well as access to databases, the rights of the data subject with regard to personal data must be safeguarded.
4) Awareness raising measures, such as information round tables or trainings, need to be conducted. Trainings should be available to all relevant actors including the Control Unit for Illegal Employment, Labour Inspectorate, District Health Insurance Fund Stakeholders and the Construction Workers' Annual Leave and Severance Pay Fund. At the same time, on-going trainings are recommended for all police units that may have contact with presumed trafficked persons, including the aliens' police unit, youth welfare authorities, State prosecution and judges. Trainings should explicitly focus on THB for labour exploitation and integrate a human rights based approach against THB. This would include *inter alia* the protection of victim's rights and interests, ensuring access to compensation for victims and access to justice for trafficked children.
5) The existing efforts for a comprehensive NRM needs to be further developed in order to tackle the needs of combating THB for labour exploitation. It should therefore define the cooperation between relevant stakeholders. The parameters of information sharing and access to assistance have to be outlined, and cooperation between various authorities and organisations on an operational level must also be determined. Examples include contacting the relevant unit of the police or ensuring residence of the presumed victim and the referral to an adequate institution.
6) Enhanced cooperation between relevant authorities and exchange of information between e.g. police, Labour Inspectorate and Control Unit for Illegal Employment may have a positive impact on gathering more evidence on THB for labour exploitation in specific cases. The gathering of more evidence would minimise the dependency on testimonials of victims.

[392] See for detailed information M. Heemskerk and C. Rijken, 'Combating Trafficking in Human Beings for Labour Exploitation in The Netherlands', Chapter 2, para 2.1 in this book.

7) The usage of JITs should be further actively promoted. Further awareness raising within public prosecutors on THB in general, and the advantages of JITs in transnational cases of THB, may facilitate access to creating JITs.
8) The translation of documents or requests plays an important role within various frameworks, such as transborder investigations or the directive on compensation of victims of crime. Translations may lead to delays. Therefore, it is recommended that adequate resources for translation costs be allocated.
9) Further efforts are needed on the part of the international community and EU Member States to set up single points of contacts within States to deal with the prosecution of THB. These specified units need to have adequate competences.

5.3 Recommendations regarding victim protection

1) The current regulations regarding residence of trafficked persons need improvement. The residence of victims of THB cannot be fully secure since there is no comprehensive protection from expulsion. It has to be ensured that presumed victims of THB, including victims of THB for labour exploitation, do not face deportation. Additionally, access to justice has to be guaranteed for all victims of THB, including trafficked children.
2) Austria needs counselling facilities for documented and undocumented migrant workers, especially legal counselling. In order to ensure access to rights, such as the right under AEL s. 29, specified services are needed.
3) The existing efforts for a comprehensive NRM needs to focus more specifically on trafficked children. Enhanced awareness and cooperation of the relevant actors should be the focus. Additionally, support for children in specialised institutions has to be ensured. The NRM should also take into account access to residence and education, and access to justice for trafficked children, including compensation, in Austria.
4) Access to compensation within criminal proceedings for trafficked persons should be further evaluated and improved.
5) It is recommended that access to payments resulting from the VCA for trafficked persons be improved. Barriers for trafficked persons, such as the prerequisite of having a legal residence status in Austria at the time of the offence, should be removed.

Chapter 2
Combating Trafficking in Human Beings for Labour Exploitation in the Netherlands

Marijn Heemskerk and Conny Rijken[1]

Part I
The legal framework on defining Trafficking in Human Beings for labour exploitation and the dimensions of this crime

1.1 The definition of Trafficking in Human Beings for labour exploitation in the Netherlands

Introduction to Article 273f of the Dutch Penal Code

The crime of human trafficking is included in Article 273f of the Dutch Penal Code (***DPC***). Article 273f DPC reads as follows:

> *'1. Guilty of trafficking in human beings and as such liable to a term of imprisonment not exceeding eight years and/or a fifth category fine*[2] *shall be any person who:*
>
> *1° by coercion, violence or any other act or by the threat of violence or any other act, by extortion, fraud, deception or the abuse of authority arising from the actual state of affairs, by the abuse of a vulnerable position or by giving or receiving payments or benefits in order to obtain the consent of a person who has control over this other person recruits, transports, moves, accommodates or shelters another person, with the intent of exploitation of this other person or removing his or her organs;*
>
> *2° recruits, transports, moves, accommodates or shelters a person with the intent of exploitation of that other person or removing his or her organs, when that person has not yet reached the age of eighteen years;*
>
> *3° recruits, takes with him or abducts a person with the intention of inducing that person to make himself/herself available for performing sexual acts with or for a third party for remuneration in another country;*

---

[1] Marijn Heemskerk is lawyer in Amsterdam. Conny Rijken is Associate Professor at Tilburg Law School, European and International Public Law Department and research fellow at INTERVICT (International Victimology Institute Tilburg).

[2] Dutch Criminal law recognises maximum fines divided into six categories, which are listed in Article 23 sub 4 DPC. The fines range from €380 (1st category) to €760,000 (6th category). For fifth category crimes like human trafficking a penalty not exceeding €76,000 may be imposed.

4° forces or induces another person by the means referred to under (1°) to make himself/herself available for performing work or services or making his/her organs available or takes any action in the circumstances referred to under (1°) which he knows or may reasonably be expected to know will result in that other person making himself/herself available for performing labour or services or making his/her organs available;

5° induces another person to make himself/herself available for performing sexual acts with or for a third party for remuneration or to make his/her organs available for remuneration or takes any action towards another person which he knows or may reasonably be expected to know that this will result in that other person making himself/herself available for performing these acts or making his/her organs available for remuneration, when that other person has not yet reached the age of eighteen years;

6° wilfully profits from the exploitation of another person;

7° wilfully profits from the removal of organs from another person, while he knows or may reasonably be expected to know that the organs of that person have been removed under the circumstances referred to under (1°);

8° wilfully profits from the sexual acts of another person with or for a third party for remuneration or the removal of that person's organs for remuneration, when this other person has not yet reached the age of eighteen years;

9° forces or induces another person by the means referred to under (1°) to provide him with the proceeds of that person's sexual acts with or for a third party or of the removal of that person's organs;

2. *Exploitation comprises at least the exploitation of another person in prostitution, other forms of sexual exploitation, forced or compulsory labour or services, slavery, slavery-like practices or servitude.*

3. *The person found guilty shall be punishable with a term of imprisonment not exceeding twelve years and/or a fifth category fine, or either of these penalties:*

   1° offences as described in the first paragraph if they are committed by two or more persons acting in concert;

   2° offences as described in the first paragraph if such offences are committed in respect of a person who is under the age of sixteen.

4. *If one of the offences described in the first paragraph results in serious physical injury or threatens the life of another person, it shall be punishable with a term of imprisonment not exceeding fifteen years and/or a fifth category fine.*

5. *If one of the offences referred to in the first paragraph results in death, it shall be punishable with a term of imprisonment not exceeding eighteen years and/or a fifth category fine.*

6. Article 251 is applicable mutatis mutandis.'[3]

Article 273f was introduced pursuant to international law instruments and entered into force on 1 January 2005 as Article 273a.[4] It was renumbered from 273a to 273f mid-2006, without changes to the contents being made. The article replaces the old Article 250a, which prohibited human trafficking for the purposes of sexual exploitation only. The current Article 273f is broader and covers all forms of human trafficking and the removal of organs, which is emphasised by the fact that it was moved from Title XIV of the DPC devoted to crimes against morality (*misdrijven tegen de zeden*)[5] to Title XVIII of the DPC dealing with crimes against personal freedom (*misdrijven tegen de persoonlijke vrijheid*). Article 273 sub 1(1), sub 1(2), sub 1(4), and sub 1(6) may apply to THB for labour exploitation, the other parts of paragraph 1 deal with THB for sexual exploitation.

Since 1 July 2009, the terms of imprisonment included in Article 273f were augmented as a consequence of the '*re-evaluation of the seriousness of THB by society*'.[6] A person found guilty of human trafficking is subject to a term of imprisonment of 8 years and/or a fine not exceeding €76,000.[7] In paragraphs (3), (4), and (5) higher punishment for qualified forms of the criminal

[3] Taken from the unofficial translation text provided by the Bureau of the Dutch National Rapporteur on Trafficking in Human Beings (BNRM) <http:// english. bnrm.nl/legislation/index.aspx> accessed 30 October 2010, with additional translation from the authors.

[4] Optional Protocol to the Convention on the Rights of the Child on the Sale of Children, Child Prostitution and Child Pornography, 25 May 2000, A/RES/54/263 (Trb. 2001, 63), United Nations Convention against Transnational Organised Crime, 15 November 2000 A/RES/55/25 (Trb. 2001, 68), Protocol to the United Nations Convention against Transnational Organised Crime to Prevent, Suppress and Punish Trafficking in Persons, Especially Women and Children, 15 November 2000 A/RES/55/25 (Trb. 2001, 69), Protocol to the United Nations Convention against Transnational Organised Crime against the Smuggling of Migrants by Land, Sea and Air, 15 November 2000, A/RES/55/25 (Trb. 2001, 70), Council Framework Decision on combating trafficking in human beings, 19 July 2002, 2002/629/JHA [2002] OJ L203/1, Council Directive defining the facilitation of unauthorised entry, transit and residence, 28 November 2002, 2002/90/EC [2002] OJ L328/17, Council Framework Decision on the strengthening of the legal framework to prevent the facilitation of unauthorised entry, transit and residence, 28 November 2002, 2002/946/JHA [2002] OJ L328/1, Council Framework Decision on combating the sexual exploitation of children and child pornography, 22 December 2003, 2004/68/JHA [2003] OJ L13/4.

[5] Literally, the Dutch word *[misdrijven tegen de zeden]* means 'crime against morality'. Title XIV of the DPC lists crimes against morality, the majority of which are related to sexual acts.

[6] BNRM, *Trafficking in Human Beings – 7th Report of the National Rapporteur* (BNRM October 2009) (BNRM7) p. 18.

[7] A combination of imprisonment and a fine is possible (Article 9 sub 3 DPC).

behaviour listed in paragraph (1) are given. Paragraph (6) provides that a person holding a specific position may be discharged of that position if found guilty of THB.[8]

The main principle for jurisdiction of the Dutch courts is the territorial principle; the Dutch Penal Code applies to anyone committing a crime in Dutch territory and the person committing such crime may be prosecuted before the Dutch courts (Article 2 DPC). Pursuant to the Council of Europe Convention on Action against Trafficking in Human Beings (the ***Warsaw Convention***)[9], the jurisdiction of Dutch courts in THB cases was extended in three ways. Firstly, in case THB is committed abroad by a Dutch national or a person having domicile in the Netherlands, the Dutch courts have jurisdiction if the victim is younger than 18 years (Article 5 sub 1(3) and Article 5a sub 1 DPC). If THB was committed abroad and the victim is older than 18 years, the Dutch courts have jurisdiction if the crime was committed outside any jurisdiction (Article 5 sub 1(5) DPC and Article 5a sub 3). Secondly, Dutch courts have jurisdiction if a Dutch national or a person having domicile in the Netherlands commits THB abroad if the victim is over 18 years of age, provided that THB is penalised in the country where it was committed (Articles 5 sub 2 and 5a sub 2 respectively). Thirdly, Dutch courts have jurisdiction if the victim of THB is of Dutch nationality or has domicile in the Netherlands (Article 5b).[10]

Labour exploitation under Article 273f.

Article 273f is a rather complex and lengthy provision and aims to cover a very broad range of activities.[11] Parts of it stem from international law instruments, most notably the United Nations' Protocol to Prevent, Suppress and Punish Trafficking in Persons, especially Women and Children (the ***Palermo Protocol***) and the EU Framework Decision on Trafficking in Human Beings (the ***Framework Decision THB***),[12] and parts of it find their origin in the old Article 250a DPC, which prohibited sexual exploitation only. Most of the terms that are derived from international legislation are not further defined in Dutch law.

---

[8] If the crime is committed by two or more persons in concert, the maximum term of imprisonment is 12 years (Article 273f sub 3(1)). The same applies if the victim has not yet reached the age of 16 years (Article 273f sub 3(2)). If one of the offences described in the first paragraph of Article 273f results in serious physical injury or threatens the life of another person, the maximum term of imprisonment is fifteen years (Article 273f sub 4), if it results in death the maximum term is eighteen years (Article 273f sub 5). A person convicted for human trafficking may also be discharged of his/her duties (Articles 273f sub 6 and 251 DPC).

[9] Council of Europe Convention on Action against Trafficking in Human Beings, 16 May 2005 (Trb. 2006, 99).

[10] Act related to partial amendment of the DPC, the Dutch Code of Criminal Procedure and certain other related acts in the context of legal developments, international obligations and legal defaults, 26 November 2009 (Stb 2009, 525).

[11] It is the longest provision in the DPC. See BNRM7 (n. 6) p. 436.

[12] See footnotes 4 and 9 respectively.

The Dutch legislator did not give much guidance in the legislative history and left it to the judiciary to further define the terms. This leads to uncertainty regarding certain elements of the crime.

Most notably, practice showed that the means of coercion '*abuse of authority arising from the actual state of affairs*' and '*abuse of a vulnerable position*'[13] as well as the element of '*(intent to) exploitation*'[14] were unclear.[15] Courts applied strict tests for the establishment of these elements.

It was established in case law quite quickly and consistently that a person is in a '*vulnerable position*' if there is a combination of illegal residence, a poor economic situation and being unable to speak the Dutch language. Establishing in which cases abuse is made of that vulnerable position proved more difficult, especially in cases where (illegal) migrants approached the employers themselves, and requested work. In such cases, the District Court and the Court of Appeals of Den Bosch held that certain '*initiative and actions*' were required from the suspect, whereby the suspect '*intentionally*' abused the weaker or vulnerable position of the victims.[16] Other courts subsequently followed this consideration.[17]

Article 273f sub 2 contains some – but not much – guidance for the meaning of 'exploitation': '*Exploitation comprises at least the exploitation of another person in prostitution, other forms of sexual exploitation, forced or compulsory labour or services, slavery, slavery-like practices or servitude.*' In the cases that were rendered before the first Supreme Court's decision in a THB for labour exploitation case on 27 October 2009, courts applied a very strict test and were reluctant to establish exploitation. Reference was made to the parliamentary history, the fact that Article 273f is based on international law instruments that refer to human rights instruments, the Dutch National Rapporteur on Trafficking in Human Beings (***BNRM***) [18] position, and the Guideline on Human Trafficking (the ***Guideline***) issued by the Board of Procurators General.[19] The BNRM held, in

---

[13] Both elements of Article 273f sub 1(1) and Article 273f sub 1(4).

[14] Element of Article 273f sub 1(1) and Article 273f sub 1(6).

[15] BNRM7 (n. 6) 509. See also the contribution of L. van Krimpen, 'The interpretation and application of labour exploitation in Dutch case law', Chapter 11 in this book.

[16] District Court Den Bosch, 8 March 2007, LJN: BA0145 and LJN: BA0141; Court of Appeals Den Bosch, 30 January 2008, LJN: BC3000 and LJN: BC2999.

[17] E.g. District Court Zwolle, 29 April 2008, LJN: BD0860.

[18] The Bureau of the National Rapporteur on Trafficking in Human Beings was established on 1 April 2000. The Rapporteur's main task is to report on the nature and extent of human trafficking in the Netherlands. The reports contain information on relevant regulations and legislation, as well as information on prevention, criminal investigations, prosecution and victim support. They also contain policy recommendations. The Dutch Rapporteur works independently and reports to the Dutch government. See <http://english.bnrm.nl/about/> accessed 8 February 2011.

[19] Guideline on Human Trafficking (Aanwijzing Mensenhandel), 31 December 2008 (Stc. 253). The Board of Procurators General, which heads the OM, may issue guidelines

2005, that not each abuse in relation to employment constitutes exploitation. When exploitation in the context of THB is at stake, according to the BNRM, fundamental rights such as human dignity, personal freedom, or personal integrity are at stake.[20] The BNRM also considered that a situation amounts to exploitation if there is some form of coercion, poor working conditions, multiple dependency and the victim does not have the freedom (or is under the impression of not having the freedom) to escape from the labour situation.[21] The Guideline states that the Public Prosecution Service (*Openbaar Ministerie or* ***OM***) in the combat of THB for labour exploitation needs to focus on excesses.

Courts often started by making reference to the abovementioned sources, then established a list of (very) poor working conditions, and subsequently held that these poor working conditions did not amount to excesses or violations of fundamental human rights andd therefore could not qualify as THB.[22]

For both the definition of 'exploitation' and 'abuse of a vulnerable position', the so-called Chinese case, rendered in October 2009, provided some clarity. In judgments issued since, courts have applied more lenient tests to establish the above two elements (see further below).

Furthermore, the elements that need to be proven under the several sub parts of Article 273f, and how they relate to one another are unclear. This is particularly the case for sub 1(4) and sub 1(1). Although the required elements in and the distinction between these two parts seem clear, this is not so much the case in reality. Some courts have held that although paragraph 1(4) does not require the element of exploitation, this element must be assumed considering the introduction of the provision.[23] This means that an element is added to the paragraph. Other courts have held that it is sufficient that the perpetrator coerced another person into making him/herself available for performing work/services.[24] The legislative history does not provide clarity whether or not exploitation should be added to the elements in 273f 1(4).[25]

---

on how the OM should perform their duties on the basis of Article 130 sub 4 Act on the Judicial Organisation.

[20] BNRM7 (n. 6) p. 535; D. Korvinus, D. Koster and H. de Jonge van Ellemeet, 'Mensenhandel: het begrip uitbuiting in art. 273a Sr' (2006) TREMA Nr. 7, p. 287.

[21] BNRM7 (n. 6), p. 536.

[22] The so-called Moonfish case is an example of such a case. In that case, Indian employees were working six days a week, with long working days and for very low wages in a tofu factory. The court held that, although this situation was 'socially undesirable', these circumstances were not sufficient to establish a violation of fundamental human rights. See District Court Zwolle, 29 April 2008, LJN: BD0860; LJN: BD0846 and LJN: BD0857.

[23] E.g. District Court Dordrecht, 20 April 2010, LJN: BM1743, District Court The Hague, 3 May 2010, LJN: BM3374.

[24] Most explicitly: District Court Haarlem, 8 December 2010, LJN: BO8985, under 4.4.2.

[25] The legislator seems to have copied the text of the old Article 250a DPC, which prohibited sexual exploitation, without considering the consequences of copying this text

The legislative history does mention that sub 1(4) '*is aimed at exploitation*', but does not specify whether that means that forcing or inducing another person to make him/herself available automatically amounts to exploitation, or that, in fact, sub 1(4) only applies in cases where the work/services would be exploitative.

Also, the legislator did not adjust the wording of 273f 1(4) to fit the rest of Article 273f; most notably those parts that are based on international law, adding to the lack of clarity on how this part relates to the other parts of Article 273f.[26] There is also confusion with regard to Article 273f 1(1), which contains the elements act-means-purpose. According to the text of the provision, the means of coercion need to be aimed at the act (housing, transferring, etc.). However, exploitation seems to imply a certain unwillingness of the victim to perform labour/services, and thus a certain amount of coercion too. The distinction between coercion aimed at the acts and the coercion aimed at the labour is artificial and causes confusion.[27]

It does not help – especially considering the fact that the legislator left it to the courts to further define the elements of Article 273f – that courts, in their considerations, often do not differentiate between the several subsections of Article 273f (even in cases where charges are brought under several subsections) and do not specify which elements need to be proven in order to establish any of the subsections of Article 273f.

Consequently, the scope of Article 273f 1(4) and the interpretation of its elements are unclear[28] and there were not many prosecutions in labour exploitation cases. In the cases that *were* pursued, the courts set a high standard to establish the means of coercion on the one hand and (intent to) exploitation on the other. Again, this resulted in a hesitance by the (special) investigation

---

into a broader provision. Article 250a DPC read: 'who forces by violence or any other act or by the threat of violence or any other act, or induces by the abuse of authority arising from the actual state of affairs or by deception another person to perform sexual acts with a third person for remuneration, or takes any action in the aforementioned circumstances which he knows or may reasonably be expected to know will result in that other person making himself/herself available for the performing of such acts'. By copying this text, the legislator does not seem to have taken into account that inducing another person into prostitution is by definition exploitation, but that performing labour is not necessarily.

[26] E.g. in the 2nd half of sub 1(4), reference is made to 'the circumstances listed in paragraph 1(1)'. It is unclear to which 'circumstances' reference is made. The parliamentary history is, again, not very helpful: 'The term 'circumstances' refers to all situations mentioned in paragraph 1(1).' Neither the word 'circumstances', nor the word 'situations' is used in the rather complex paragraph 1(1), meaning that the parliamentary history does not clarify much. Is reference made to the means of coercion, to the intention of exploitation, to the acts of recruitment, transportation, etc.?

[27] Cf. conclusion Advocate-General (Knigge) accompanying the decision of the Supreme Court of the Netherlands, 27 October 2009, LJN: BI7097, under 52.

[28] BNRM7 (n. 6) p. 509.

services, police and public prosecutors to investigate and prosecute cases involving THB for labour exploitation.[29]

This situation improved somewhat when the Supreme Court rendered its decision in the so-called Chinese case on 27 October 2009.[30] The Supreme Court's decision provides some guidance with regard to the elements '*abuse of a vulnerable position*' and '*abuse of authority arising from the actual state of affairs*', as well as '*(intent to) exploitation*'. By doing so, the Supreme Court seemed to point towards lower standards for establishing these elements.

The Supreme Court held that by imposing the condition that the suspect intentionally abused the vulnerable position of the victims, the Court of Appeals applied too strict a test. '*Most notably, it is not required that the initiative was taken by the suspect, nor that the victim was brought into an exploitative position [i.e. when there is authority arising out of the actual state of affairs] by the suspect.*' For the question whether there is abuse of authority arising out of the actual state of affairs, conditional intent (*voorwaardelijke opzet*) is required; the suspect must or could have been aware of the factual circumstances in which the victim resided and of which the authority have pursued or may be assumed to have pursued. The same applies to cases in which the vulnerable position as referred to in Article 273f sub 1(1) DPC is in question.[31]

Like the District Court, the Court of Appeals had established that the Chinese persons worked illegally in the restaurant six days a week, 11 to 13 hours a day for a remuneration of €450 to €800 per month, with no more than five free days a month. The workers slept several persons to a room. The District Court and the Court of Appeals held that although these were '*undesirable*' working conditions, this did not amount to exploitation, since the working conditions (apart from the long working hours) were not poor, the earned income could be freely spent by the employees, and it could not be reasonably established that the Chinese did not have an option other than to work and stay in the restaurant. The Supreme Court considered that '*although it is impossible to answer the question whether a certain situation amounts to exploitation in general, in this case the following elements are of relevance: the nature and duration of the employment, the restrictions to the employee resulting from such employment, and the financial gain of the employer*'. The Supreme Court also considered that Dutch standards need to be taken as frame of reference, and it is not required that the victim was actually exploited. Against that background, the Supreme Court held that the Court of Appeals' consideration that there was no (intent to) exploitation was, without further motivation, incomprehensible because the Court of Appeals had established the abovementioned conditions (i.e. the illegality of the work, working hours, limited amount of free days per month, remuneration, and sleeping several persons to a room).

---

[29] From the introduction of Article 273f DPC in 2005 to 27 October 2009 only 12 prosecutions took place in which labour exploitation was charged. Of these cases, only 4 cases led to a conviction for THB.

[30] Supreme Court of the Netherlands, 27 October 2009, LJN: BI7097.

[31] Supreme Court of the Netherlands, 27 October 2009, LJN: BI7097, under 2.5.1 and 2.5.2.

Although the Supreme Court's decision leaves certain questions unanswered regarding the exact meaning of the term 'exploitation', [32] the effect in subsequent case law has been that lower standards for establishing exploitation were applied. In other words, the question whether a certain situation exceeds 'merely' poor working conditions and is in fact exploitation is answered in the affirmative more easily. The number of prosecutions and convictions in THB for labour exploitation cases has risen since the Supreme Court's decision.[33] Most notably, exploitation has been established in business-like situations, and when no physical force was involved.[34]

However, courts are still struggling with the definition of Article 273f: courts are each applying a different test, they often do not specify which of the subparts of 273f 1 is/are under consideration, and what elements need to be proven to come to a conviction under these subparts.[35]

Also, the lack of clarity regarding the scope and elements of paragraph 1(4) and how it relates to the other paragraphs (most notably paragraph 1(1)) still exists. Three cases relating to the induced subscription to phone companies illustrate the lack of clarity relating to Article 273f sub 1(4). In these cases, the suspect induced the victims to subscribe to a phone company. The phones that accompanied the subscription were handed over to the suspect, who sold or used the phones with the subscription. The victims were faced with substantial phone bills. The suspects were charged with THB for labour exploitation on

[32] The Supreme Court does not refer to breaches of fundamental human rights when considering the meaning of exploitation. Does that mean that the Supreme Court follows the conclusion of the Advocate-General (Knigge) by determining that a breach of fundamental human rights is not a requirement for exploitation? The Supreme Court refers to 'a case like the current case'. At which specific elements of this case does the Supreme Court aim? How are factors to be weighed; does any deviation from the Dutch standards mean that exploitation is established? Do the Advocate-General's remarks that circumstances are interlinked (e.g. the more restrictions for the worker, the less poor the working conditions need to be in order to establish exploitation) apply? More generally, the Advocate-General issued a very detailed analysis of the questions at hand. It is unfortunate that the Supreme Court did not indicate to what extent their considerations were based on – or deviated from – the Advocate-General's conclusions. The case was referred back to the Court of Appeals in Den Bosch, which issued an abbreviated judgment on 17 September 2010 in which the suspect was found guilty of THB. Also in this judgment the above-mentioned questions remained unanswered.

[33] From 27 October 2009–31 December 2010, 11 judgments were published, in the first instance, or became otherwise known to the author in which charges were brought for THB for labour exploitation. At least 7 of these led to convictions for THB.

[34] Cf. L. van Krimpen, 'The interpretation and application of labour exploitation in Dutch case law', Chapter 11 in this book.

[35] E.g. District Court The Hague, 17 February 2010, LJN: BL4298; District Court The Hague, 18 March 2010, LJN: BL8022; District Court The Hague, 12 May 2010, LJN: BM4240; District Court Leeuwarden, 13 July 2010, LJN: BN 1234; District Court Utrecht, 5 October 2010, LJN: BO2835; District Court Roermond, 26 October 2010, LJN: BO3022.

the basis of Article 273 sub 1(4). In two of these cases, this led to a conviction of THB for labour exploitation on the basis of Article 273f sub 1(4). One of the courts that came to the conviction held that the mere inducing of another person to make him/herself available to perform a service constitutes THB in the sense of Article 273f sub 1(4), although it held that '*the acts do amount to trafficking in human beings, although the acts that took place resemble more a form of deceit. This term is also better suited to the use of everyday language and to society's perception regarding the facts of this case*'.[36] The two other courts held that exploitation needed to be added as an element to Article 273f sub 1(4).[37] In one of these cases, this led to a conviction, in the other it did not. In the case that did not result in a conviction, the court considered that, although the victim was deceived and induced to subscribe to the phone company, this did not amount to a violation of fundamental rights and the element of exploitation was not established.[38]

Another noteworthy feature of Dutch case law is that, although criminal exploitation is not mentioned in Article 273f DPC, the Dutch courts did not have any difficulty in including this under the scope of Article 273f DPC. The criminal acts, e.g. hemp cutting or drug trafficking, are deemed to be '*work or services*' as referred to in Article 273 sub 1 (4) DPC.[39]

1.2 Other legislation and policies relevant for Trafficking in Human Beings for labour exploitation

1.2.1 Criminal law

Slave trade

Slavery, as such, is not prohibited under Dutch criminal law, but slave trade is under Articles 274–277 DPC. Article 274 DPC is hardly ever applied in practice, and was not charged in any of the published judgments relating to labour exploitation.

Human smuggling

Human smuggling is prohibited by Article 197a DPC. Article 197a prohibits as human smuggling the providing of entrance to, transit through, or illegal stay in, the Netherlands, another EU country or a Member State of the Smuggling

---

[36] District Court Haarlem, 8 December 2010, LJN: BO8985.

[37] District Court The Hague, 18 March 2010, LJN: BL8022, under 3.4.2; District Court Dordrecht, 20 April 2010, LJN: BM1743, under 4.1.2.

[38] District Court The Hague, 18 March 2010, LJN: BL8022, under 3.4.2.

[39] BNRM, *Trafficking in Human Beings – 10 years National Rapporteur Trafficking in Human Beings in the Netherlands - 8th Report of the National Rapporteur* (BNRM8 2010) 30; L. van Krimpen, 'Mensenhandel en arbeidsuitbuiting. Recente ontwikkelingen in de jurisprudentie' *[Trafficking in Human Beings and Labour Exploitation; recent developments in case law]* (2010) 36 nr. 7 Justitiële Verkenningen (van Krimpen) p. 56.

Protocol[40], or facilitating such entrance/transit/stay, if the perpetrator knows or has '*serious reasons to suspect*' that such entrance, transit or stay is illegal. Although the crimes of human smuggling and human trafficking are related, they are distinct offences. Human smuggling is a crime against the public authorities, whereas human trafficking is a crime against personal freedom. For human smuggling to occur, the person who was smuggled, by definition, crossed the border at some point, whereas human trafficking may also occur when victims of Dutch origin are exploited within the Netherlands. Human smuggling and human trafficking are often charged cumulatively or alternatively.

Illegal labour

Articles 197b–197d DPC prohibit the employment of individuals illegally residing in the Netherlands where the employer has '*serious reasons to suspect*' that the individual is residing in the Netherlands illegally. Illegal employment is also prohibited by Article 2 sub 1 of the Aliens Employment Act (*Wet Arbeid Vreemdelingen* or ***WAV***) (see below). A person violating the Aliens Employment Act is subject to administrative fines (Article 18 sub 1 WAV), a person violating Articles 197b–197d DPC is criminally liable. Concurrence between Articles 197b–197d DPC and Article 2 of the Aliens Employment Act is possible.

Illegal deprivation of liberty

Illegal deprivation of liberty/unlawful detention is prohibited in Article 282 DPC. In THB for labour exploitation cases the means of coercion are usually more subtle than in cases of sexual exploitation: in the latter cases, there is often a form of illegal deprivation of liberty. Having said that, illegal deprivation of liberty charges can also be brought in THB for labour exploitation cases, e.g. District Court The Hague, 5 October 2007.[41]

Forgery and falsification of travel documents

Forgery is penalised in Article 225 DPC. The documents to which Section 225 DPC relates are documents that serve as evidence of any fact, e.g. forms with which social benefits may be obtained. Also the business accounts or working instructions may be forged. Falsification of travel documents is penalised in Article 231 DPC.

Means of coercion

Some of the means of coercion mentioned in Article 273f DPC are also criminalised independently in Article 326 DPC (deceit), Article 284 DPC

---

[40] Protocol to the United Nations Convention against Transnational Organised Crime against the Smuggling of Migrants by Land, Sea and Air, 15 November 2000, A/RES/55/25 (Trb. 2001, 70).

[41] District Court The Hague, 5 October 2007, LJN: BB5303.

(coercion) and Article 285 DPC (threat/intimidation).

Participation in a criminal organisation
Participation in a criminal organisation is penalised in Article 140 DCP. Charges are often brought in THB for labour exploitation cases.

Tax evasion
In cases of labour exploitation, the trafficker will not report his/her illegally obtained profits to the Tax Authorities, which may result in the fact that no taxes will be incurred over his/her profits. The employer thereby violates Articles 68 and 69 of the General Act on Royal Taxes (*Algemene Wet Rijksbelastingen* or ***AWR***). Often the trafficker will also not pay social premiums and taxes on the victims' wages. On that basis he/she will be liable for administrative fines on the basis of the Aliens Employment Act (*Wet Arbeid en Vreemdelingen* or ***WAV***) (see below).

Housing regulations
The Housing Act (*Woningwet*) provides that buildings may only be used for the purposes described in the regulations relating to that specific building (Article 7b sub 2 under the Housing Act). Anyone who intentionally violates such a rule is criminally liable on the basis of Article 1a sub 2 and Article 2 sub 1 of the Economic Crimes Act (*Wet Economische Delicten*). Municipality officers check whether housing is in compliance with the relevant legislation. This means that municipality officials may detect signs of THB (See Part II).

Non-punishment principle
In case a victim of THB is also a suspect of a crime (e.g. obtaining false travel documents or – in case of criminal exploitation – drug trafficking), the non-punishment principle becomes relevant. Dutch law does not contain a specific provision on non-punishment. However, the principle may be applied since the OM may decide not to further investigate a case in so far as such an investigation is not opportune (*seponeren*), a court may find a suspect guilty without applying any punishment or measure (Article 9a DPC), and the rules on distress (*overmacht*) may be applied. However, there are several difficulties regarding the non-punishment principle. If a court finds a victim guilty without applying punishment or sanction, this may have consequences for the victim's residence status in the Netherlands. Also, in order to apply the non-punishment principle, victims need to be recognised. This is especially important in cases of criminal exploitation, partly because even the victim him/herself may perceive him/herself as a perpetrator instead of a victim.[42]

[42] BNRM7 (n. 6) p. 274.

1.2.2 Labour law

Acts monitored by the Labour Inspectorate *(Arbeidsinspectie,* **AI**)
The Minimum Wage and Minimum Holiday Allowance Act (*Wet Minimum Loon en Minimum Vakantietoeslag* or ***WML***) provides that every employee between 23 and 65 years of age should receive at minimum the minimum wage and minimum holiday allowance. The Working Conditions Act (*Arbeidsomstandighedenwet*) provides the minimum working conditions to which employers have to adhere. The Working Hours Act (*Arbeidstijdenwet*) lists the minimum standards relating to working hours. Finally, the Decree relating to Risk of Serious Accidents (*Besluit risico's zware ongevallen*) regulates the prevention of serious accidents involving dangerous substances. The Labour Inspectorate is (jointly) responsible for monitoring and enforcing these acts. As such, the inspectors may come across THB for labour exploitation in the course of their duties (See Part II).

1.2.3 Migration law

Aliens Employment Act
On the basis of the Aliens Employment Act (*Wet Arbeid Vreemdelingenwet* or ***WAV***) an employer is subject to an administrative fine if he/she employs a person without a valid work permit (Article 2 sub 1 WAV in conjunction with Articles 18 sub 1 and 19a sub 1 WAV). In the case of repetitive violations, the employer may become criminally liable (Article 19c WAV in conjunction with Article 1 sub 4 Economic Crimes Act).

Employees from within the 'old' Member States of the EU may work in the Netherlands without a work permit. Employees from the Member States that acceded to the EU on 1 May 2004 may work in the Netherlands without work permit as of 1 May 2007 (Estonia, Hungary, Latvia, Lithuania, Poland, Slovenia, Slovakia and the Czech Republic), and as of 1 May 2004 (Malta and Cyprus).[43] Employees from Bulgaria and Romania, which acceded to the EU on 1 January 2007, need a work permit. This regime will terminate on 1 January 2012.[44]

With the flexible working relations and the free movement of workers and services within the EU (with exceptions for Bulgarians and Romanians), it can be quite complicated to determine whether a person is illegally employed in

[43] <http://ec.europa.eu/eures/main.jsp?acro=free&lang=nl&countryId=NL&fromCountryId=CY&accessing=0&content=1&restrictions=1&step=2> accessed 14 November 2010.

[44] <http://www.europadecentraal.nl/menu/645/Vrij_verkeer_van_werknemers.html> accessed 14 February 2011.

the Netherlands or not. Under the current regime, EU citizens and citizens from Lichtenstein, Norway, Iceland and Switzerland have to register with the immigration service in case they wish to work in the Netherlands for a period longer than three months. They have to inform the immigration service about their goal and the requirements are that they (i) are financially self-sufficient, (ii) have health insurance and (iii) are registered at the municipal administration (***GBA***). If their stay is shorter than three months, registration is not required.

If Romanian or Bulgarian citizens want to be employed in the Netherlands, they need a work permit and – if they wish to work in the Netherlands for a period exceeding 3 months – an EU citizen's residence permit, with notification that the work is allowed. A work permit is only required for the first year. A work permit will be refused if the labour conditions are below the normal standard (Article 9(b) WAV) or where no sufficient accommodation is available (Article 9(f) WAV). The residence permit can be obtained if the following conditions are met: they (i) are of Bulgarian or Romanian nationality, (ii) have health insurance, (iii) are registered at the GBA, (iv) have a valid travel document, (v) will not be a threat to public order, and (vi) will earn sufficient financial means (€991.20 gross per month for singles). Because Romanian and Bulgarian citizens are allowed to stay in the Netherlands without a residence permit, the question arises what happens if they are caught working without a residence permit? Are they allowed to stay in the Netherlands, or are they considered aliens and required to leave the country?

Third country nationals (people from outside the EU, the EER region and Switzerland), need a residence permit, a work permit[45] and a mandate for provisional stay (*machtiging voor voorlopig verblijf* or ***MVV***), unless excluded from this condition. Only with the MVV can one apply for a permanent residence permit. They have to register with the GBA.

Accommodation for workers from within the EU is often provided by the employers (or in the case of posted workers by the employment agency), most likely because registration at the GBA is a prerequisite for the residence permit for workers from Bulgaria and Romania and the registration at the immigration service for other EU citizen. In cases where the employer needs a work permit for the foreign employee (for instance, for Bulgarian and Romanian nationals and for persons from outside the EU), one of the conditions for the work permit is that the employee has accommodation at a reasonable distance from the work place. Although formally not required, it seems logical that the employer will help the employee find accommodation.

[45] Certain categories of workers are excluded from the working permit requirement. These categories can be found in the Act implementing WAV, and further regulations can be found in the delegation and implementation decision of the WAV, as well as the policy rules of the UWV regarding WAV.

However, dependency on the employer for accommodation, or living on the employer's premises may be indicators of THB.
Other possibilities for EU, EER and Swiss citizens to work in the Netherlands are as a self-employed person or working as a posted worker. For the former category, Dutch law cannot impose additional requirements and Romanians and Bulgarians are not excluded. What they need is a residence permit with the notification that work is allowed or that they have a permit for self-employed persons. They have to notify the Employee Insurance Agency (*Uitvoeringsinstituut Werknemersverzekeringen* or ***UWV***) in advance about their services and have to be registered at the chamber of commerce in their home country or in the Netherlands. Furthermore, they need a declaration of independent contractor status (*verklaring arbeidsrelatie* or *VAR*) which they have to obtain through the tax service. This declaration aims to guarantee the commissioner that he does not have to pay social premiums above the remuneration paid to the worker. They have to perform the work as a self-employed person, which means that this may not be a bogus self-employment construction.

Posted workers will need a work permit as well, but that is normally organised by the posting employer with whom the worker has a contract. If a Dutch employer hires workers through an employment agency or a foreign company, the Dutch employer is still under an obligation to check the work permits of the workers. Following a proliferation of employment agencies and suspicion of illegal practices in these agencies, a new law on hirer's liability came into force on 1 January 2010. This law is part of a package of measures to combat mala fide employment agencies. The act aims to give extra protection to the person who performs work via the employment agency, regardless of the law applicable to the employment agreement. Hirers that hire employees through non-certified employment agencies become jointly liable for the employees' wages, meaning that the employees can claim wages both from the hirer directly as well as from the employment agency.

There is discussion about the quality label (the certificate) granted to employment agencies, since some say that this is not a guarantee that illegal practices do not take place at these agencies. The General League for Employment Agencies (*Algemene Bond Uitzendondernemingen* or *ABU*) is one of the parties responsible for the granting of certificates (there are several leagues for employment agencies that may or may not apply a certification scheme). To make it even more complicated there is also the European Legal Labour Certificate (*Stichting Keurmerk Internationale Arbeidsbemiddeling* or *SKIA*) that issues certificates to organisations such as employers, enterprises, and locations for housing.

1.3. The dimensions of Trafficking in Human Beings for labour exploitation in the Netherlands

1.3.1 Characterisation of Trafficking in Human Beings for labour exploitation at the national level

Scope/perception

When the current Article 273f DPC (then Article 273a DPC) was introduced in 2005, it was yet unclear to what extent THB for labour exploitation occurred in the Netherlands. The BNRM performed an explorative study, the outcome of which indicated that labour exploitation did exist in the Netherlands, although it was impossible to say on which scale. Still, this is difficult to say.[46]

The awareness of labour exploitation and the prohibition thereof in Article 273f needed some time to grow after its introduction in 2005. Initially, there was not much attention to THB for labour exploitation, but in recent years the parties involved, including the government, police and the media, devoted more and more attention to the problem.[47]

Still, it seems as if there is a perception that labour exploitation is less serious than sexual exploitation. Although the number of prosecutions of THB for labour exploitation cases rose since the Supreme Court issued its judgment on 27 October 2009, still the number of prosecutions of THB for labour exploitation cases is substantially lower than the number of prosecutions of THB for sexual exploitation cases. This may be caused by the fact that the Guideline states that THB for sexual exploitation, victims who are minor, and the removal of organs have priority in the combat of THB.[48] Also, victims of THB for labour exploitation are approached differently from victims of THB for sexual exploitation. Victims of THB for labour exploitation are not always recognised as such and are not always made aware of the B-9 procedure and the reflection period (see Part III).[49]

Victims

The most important source of information regarding the number of THB victims, their gender, age, nationality, and cultural background, as well as the industries in which the victims were exploited, originate from the Coordination Centre for Human Trafficking (*Coördinatiecentrum Mensenhandel* or ***CoMensha***). CoMensha is the national reporting, registration and coordination desk for victims of human trafficking. Officially, all (possible)

[46] BNRM8 (n. 39) p. 29.

[47] BNRM7 (n. 6) p. 509. An example is the information campaign regarding THB for labour exploitation launched by the victim support organisation CoMensha (2009-2010) <http://www.mensenhandel.nl/cms/index.php?option=com_content&task=view&id=254&Itemid=72> accessed 12 December 2010.

[48] Guideline (n. 19), paras 1 and 8.

[49] BNRM7 (n. 6) p. 510.

victims of human trafficking in the Netherlands should be reported to CoMensha. However, parties like CoMensha, the BNRM and Bonded Labour in the Netherlands (***BLinN***) estimate that there are more victims of THB for labour exploitation than show up in CoMensha's figures.[50]

In the period 2007–2009, the majority of victims registered with CoMensha were victims of sexual exploitation. In this period, 1230 victims of THB were reported, of which 161 were victims of THB for labour exploitation (7%).[51] From January 2010 up to and including November 2010, 810 victims were registered, of which 110 were victims of other exploitation (13%).[52] The majority of the reported THB for labour exploitation victims were female, except for the year 2009.[53]

People that are vulnerable to exploitation are people that reside illegally in the Netherlands, especially minors, and members of closed migrant communities in the Netherlands (e.g. the Chinese and Turkish communities).[54] However, besides employees that work in the Netherlands illegally, other foreign nationals who are in fact eligible to work in the Netherlands also fall victim to THB for labour exploitation, especially those from the new EU Member States. They often think they do not have the same rights as Dutch employees with regard to the amount of remuneration, working hours, etc.[55] Also mentally disabled,[56] and mentally troubled[57] persons are prone to fall victim of labour exploitation, as are domestic nurses.[58]

---

[50] Not all victims of human trafficking are reported by CoMensha. Some victims do not want to report out of fear of the authorities; others do not know they can report (nor do their potential carers); yet others do not know which rights they can assure by registering, to mention but a few reasons. On the other hand, some persons may report themselves to CoMensha in the hope of obtaining a residence permit on the basis of the B9 procedure (see Part III). Overall, parties like CoMensha, the BNRM and victim support organisation BLinN estimate that there are more victims of THB for labour exploitation than show up in CoMensha's figures. Cf. interview with Project Leader BLinN (November 2010); BNRM8 (n. 39) p. 96.

[51] BNRM8 (n. 39) pp. 184-185.

[52] It should be noted that these figures are based on the victims reported to CoMensha. Some institutions report to CoMensha quarterly or each half year, meaning that not all reports may have been included in the report. Also, in cases where a victim is exploited in several sectors, CoMensha lists them more than once in their figures.

[53] 2007:65%, 2008:74%, 2009:42%, 1 January 2010–30 November 2010:64%. Calculated on the basis of the number of victims included in BNRM8 (n.37) p. 184-185 (2007-2009) and CoMensha's monthly report (1 Jan 2010–30 Nov 2010) to be found at <http://www.mensenhandel.nl/cms/docs/maandrapportage-november2010.pdf> accessed 12 December 2010.

[54] Guideline (n. 19), para 12; BNRM8 (n. 39) p. 71; Eline Willemsen, *Report on Exploitation in sectors other than the sex industry* (Bonded Labour in the Netherlands (BLinN) 2010) (BLinN Report) 6.

[55] BLinN report (n.54) p. 5.

[56] BNRM8 (n. 39) p. 71; District Court Utrecht, 17 June 2008, LJN: BD7426.

Perpetrators

The 8th report of the BNRM contains information regarding gender, age, and country of birth of persons suspected and convicted of THB. The information is based on data provided by the public prosecution service. Since the OM does not distinguish between THB for labour exploitation and other exploitation, it is impossible to provide information on the gender, age, and country of birth of THB for labour exploitation perpetrators/convicts. The BNRM recommended that the public prosecution service make this distinction in the future.[59]

Recruitment

The methods of recruitment differ by case and are not always traceable from judgments rendered in criminal proceedings. Some victims migrate to the Netherlands by their own means and initiative, and request work upon arrival in the Netherlands. Others come to the Netherlands through employment agencies, human smugglers or 'snake heads' (Chinese) for a specific (promised) job.[60] Sometimes the employers directly arrange for the victims to come to the Netherlands (especially in cases of domestic work), but in most instances there is a third person who mediates.[61] Especially in cases related to criminal exploitation (drug trafficking, induced subscription to phone companies) and other atypical cases such as the exploitation of a mentally handicapped person, the victims are recruited in the Netherlands by creating some sort of 'friendship' or personal relationship.[62]

Means of coercion

The most common form of coercion is creating dependency, most notably financially, and creating fear of the authorities. Consequently, the means of coercion '*abuse of authority arising from the actual state of affairs*' and '*abuse of a vulnerable position*' are most often brought as charges in THB for labour exploitation cases. The perpetrators ensure that the victim is financially dependent upon the perpetrator. Debt bondage is one of the ways in which this is done. The debt concerns the travel to the Netherlands (through smugglers, employment agencies, or otherwise), but victims also incur 'debts' upon arrival in the Netherlands, for instance for rent and personal hygiene, so

---

57 District Court Leeuwarden, 10 February 2009, LJN: BH2373.

58 Expert Meeting in the project Combating THB for Labour Exploitation in the EU (February 2011).

59 BNRM8 (n. 39) p. 122.

60 E.g. Supreme Court of the Netherlands, 27 October 2009, LJN: BI7097; District Court The Hague, 5 October 2007, LJN: BB5303.

61 Interview with Project Leader BLinN (November 2010); Interview with legal researcher BNRM (October 2010).

62 E.g. District Court Leeuwarden, 10 February 2009, LJN: BH2373; District Court Utrecht, 17 June 2008, LJN: BD7426.

that the debt remains high and the worker dependent.[63] Some perpetrators also issue 'fines' for all kinds of behaviour, such as chewing gum at work, being late, etc. Other perpetrators simply do not pay wages, or only part of them, so that victims remain working for them in the hope that they will receive their wages at a later stage.[64] Another way of creating dependency is by taking in the passport of the employee. Threatening to inform the authorities is also often used as a means of coercion. The threat of actual violence occurs less often than in cases of sexual exploitation; the same applies to actually confining the victim to the work place.[65]

Perpetrators also create or stimulate some form of loyalty, especially in cases of domestic servitude. A sort of relationship materialises because the victim is living in the perpetrator's house, often taking care of the children, and so forth. Also, for other reasons, the position of domestic workers, more specifically domestic workers of diplomats, deserves attention. Au pairs and servants of diplomats are often isolated, living in their employer's house, and have a dependent residence status.[66]

Sectors

Information about the sectors in which the reported victims were exploited is available as of 2007. The table below provides an overview up to 30 November 2010.

[63] E.g. the victims in the so-called asparagus case discussed in Part IV were reported to have had to pay €8 for a bottle of shampoo, although this could not be established in the criminal investigations.

[64] This happened in the so-called asparagus and krupuk cases, discussed in Part IV.

[65] Interview with Project Leader BLinN (November 2010).

[66] Interview with Project Leader BLinN (November 2010); BLinN Report (n. 54) p. 6.

Reported victims 1 January 2007–30 November 2010 by sector[67]

	Female	Male	Total
Sexual exploitation			
Total sexual exploitation	**1798**	**83**	**1883[68] (57%)**
Other exploitation			
Agriculture	49	52	101
Other	56	52	108
Domestic work	38	6	34
Drug trafficking	16	5	21
Au pair	9	-	9
Criminality	4	2	6
Bar/restaurant	9	16	26[69]
Abattoirs	4	-	4
Construction	1	18	19
Cleaning	5	2	7
Textile	2	-	2
Food industry	4	11	15
Total other exploitation	**197**	**164**	**362 (11%)**
Miscellaneous			
Forced organ donation	-	1	1
Unknown	704	49	753
Not yet worked	279	33	314[70]
Total miscellaneous	**983**	**83**	**1068 (32%)**
Total	**2978**	**330**	**3313[71] (100%)**

In addition to these sectors, the Guideline mentions road transport, taxi companies, clothing factories, flower auctions, and newspaper and magazine

[67] Based on figures included in BNRM8 (n.37) pp. 184-185 (2007–2009) and CoMensha's monthly report (1 Jan 2010–30 Nov 2010) to be found at <http://www.mensenhandel.nl/cms/docs/maandrapportage-november2010.pdf> accessed 12 December 2010.

[68] For 2 reported victims exploited sexually the gender was unknown, meaning that to the sum of female and male victims 2 victims with unknown gender were added.

[69] For 1 reported victim exploited in the bar/restaurant sector the gender was unknown, meaning that to the sum of female and male victims 1 victim with unknown gender was added.

[70] For 2 reported victims who had not yet worked the gender was unknown, meaning that to the sum of female and male victims 2 victims with unknown gender were added.

[71] For 5 reported victims the gender was unknown, meaning that to the sum of female and male victims 5 victims with unknown gender were added.

delivery as sectors where labour exploitation may occur.[72] THB for labour exploitation may also occur in the employment agency business and by means of forced marriages.[73] Some interviewees emphasise that THB for labour exploitation is likely to occur in sectors where peaks in employment need occur, and/or low wages are common, and/or where unskilled (or low skilled) labour is required.[74] Two other 'sectors' have risen in the recent years. Firstly, criminal exploitation whereby the trafficker lures or coerces the victim into performing a criminal act (e.g. drug trafficking, working in a hemp factory).[75] Secondly, judgments were rendered in which the coercing of a person to subscribe to a phone company was considered to be THB for labour exploitation (see above).

1.3.2 Facts and Figures on Trafficking in Human Beings for labour exploitation in the Netherlands

The police cannot easily see how many complaints of human trafficking were made, nor how many investigations have been concluded or are pending. Other investigative bodies that may investigate THB, such as the SIOD and the KMar do not publish figures on the number of investigations concluded or pending either.

The data related to prosecutions is mainly based on information from the public prosecution service. However, the OM does not distinguish between THB for labour exploitation and other exploitation. The BNRM recommended the OM make this distinction in the future.[76]

On the basis of the judgments that were published since the introduction of the prohibition of labour exploitation on 1 January 2005, the following may be concluded. In almost five years since its introduction (1 January 2005–October 2009), there were twelve cases in which charges of THB for labour exploitation were brought; four of these cases led to a conviction for THB for labour exploitation. In October 2009 the so-called Chinese case (see above) was rendered. Since October 2009 the number of prosecutions has risen substantially. In a little over a year (October 2009–31 December 2010), 11 cases were published or became otherwise known to the author. At least 7 of these led to convictions for THB.

[72] Guideline (n. 19), para 12.

[73] BNRM7 (n. 6) pp. 522-525 and 530-532.

[74] Interview with senior policy advisor SIOD (July 2010); Interview with policy advisor AMF (AI) (October 2010).

[75] Van Krimpen (n.39) pp. 62-65.

[76] BNRM8 (n. 39) p. 122.

1.4 Summary of the findings

1.4.1 Identified obstacles

Article 273f DPC is a very lengthy and complex provision. Most of its terms are derived from international law, without being further defined in Dutch law. The legislative history gives little guidance for the interpretation of the relevant terms, as the legislator left it to the courts to define the provision's terms as well as the scope of the article.

Practice shows that courts struggle with the definition of the elements contained in Article 273f, as well as the scope of the article. Before the Supreme Court rendered its decision in the Chinese case in October 2009, courts tended to apply a very strict test for establishing 'exploitation' and 'abuse of a vulnerable position', thereby creating a narrow scope for especially Article 273f sub 1(1), which contains both elements. Since the Supreme Court's decision, courts tend to be more lenient in establishing these terms.

The elements that need to be established under Article 273f sub 1(4) and the scope of this subparagraph remain unclear. Most notably, the question is whether the 'mere' inducing of a person to offer labour/services is sufficient to constitute THB, or whether the situation needs to be exploitative. Recent case law illustrates this. In three cases the question whether coercing another person to subscribe to a telephone provider constitutes THB was at stake. In two of these cases, the question was answered in the affirmative.

Furthermore, courts often do not specify which subparagraph they are considering, which elements are required to be met in these subparagraphs, and how these elements need to be interpreted. Consequently, the distinction between the several subparagraphs, the definition of the respective elements, and the scope of Article 273f remain blurred, meaning that public prosecutors cannot use these differences strategically.

It seems that sexual exploitation is still perceived as a more serious crime than labour exploitation. There are substantially fewer prosecutions in THB for labour exploitation cases, and victims are not always recognised as such.

Finally, it is not yet possible to achieve a complete picture of the scope and nature of THB for labour exploitation in the Netherlands, and the investigations/prosecutions in such cases. Most notably, the investigative departments (the police, SIOD, KMar) and the OM in their data gathering do not distinguish between THB for sexual exploitation and THB for labour exploitation, nor between the sectors in which the exploitation took place. Likewise, in data gathering by CoMensha and other parties no distinction is made between the age, nationality, and cultural background of victims and perpetrators by sector in which THB for labour exploitation occurred.

1.4.2 Good practices

Recently, more and more initiatives have been taken by the media, the government, and other parties to create more awareness about THB for labour exploitation.

The Supreme Court has given some guidance for the interpretation of the terms 'exploitation' and 'abuse of a vulnerable position' as included in Article 273f sub 1(1). Courts tend to be more lenient in establishing these terms since the Supreme Court's decision. This has had an effect on the number of prosecutions in THB for labour exploitation cases. The number of prosecutions has risen substantially since the Supreme Court's decision. In essence, this is a positive development, although the risk exists that too many situations are now considered to be THB for labour exploitation (see above).

Part II
Cooperation in the investigation and prosecution of cases of Trafficking in Human Beings for labour exploitation

In paragraph **Fout! Verwijzingsbron niet gevonden.** the most important actors that may detect (signs of) THB for labour exploitation are listed, as well as the parties responsible for criminally investigating and prosecuting such cases. The cooperation between these parties in the sense of investigating and prosecuting THB for labour exploitation will be further elaborated upon in paragraph 2.2.
International cooperation in the detection, investigation and prosecution of THB for labour exploitation is discussed in paragraph 2.3.

2.1 Actors involved in investigating and prosecuting Trafficking in Human Beings for labour exploitation

The Labour Inspectorate

The Labour Inspectorate (*Arbeidsinspectie* or ***AI***) falls under the authority of the Ministry of Social Affairs and Employment. There are three directorates within the AI, each of which focuses on the monitoring of specific legislation. Most notably, the Directorate for Labour Market Fraud (*Directie Arbeidsmarktfraude* or **AMF**) focuses on the implementation of the WAV and the WML, and the Directorate for Labour Conditions (*Directie Arbeidsomstandigheden* or ***Arbo***) focuses on the implementation of the Working Conditions Act and the Working Hours Act.[77] The AI works closely together with the Aliens Police and/or the general police. More than 50% of the inspections occur in conjunction with the Aliens Police.

Within the AI, the AMF teams come across cases of THB for labour exploitation most often. The AMF teams are in charge of inspecting the WAV and the WML and visit approximately 11,000 working places per year. In the context of monitoring the WAV and the WML, AMF inspectors ask questions regarding identity, wages and payments, work permits, etc. The information obtained on that basis may lead to signs of THB. Also, the majority of AMF visits take place in risk sectors such as the bar/restaurant sector, agriculture, employment agencies and construction sites.[78] However, the Arbo teams may also come across signs of THB for labour exploitation, such as poor working conditions.[79]

---

[77] Interview with policy advisor AMF (AI) (October 2010).
[78] Taskforce Trafficking in Human Beings, Toolkit (Select CD-Rom B.V. 2009) (Toolkit), under 'Partners'. This toolkit, in the form of a DVD, was launched by the Taskforce THB and aims to provide all relevant information to the parties involved in the combat of THB. As such it contains information on the relevant parties, legislation, policies, publications, etc. The Toolkit has been criticised for focusing on sexual exploitation.
[79] BNRM7 (n. 6) p. 519.

The AI passes on signs of THB to the SIOD and (via the SIOD) to the Expertise Centre for Human Trafficking and Human Smuggling (the *Expertise Centrum Mensenhandel Mensensmokkel* or ***EMM***).[80] Signs are detected on the basis of a brochure issued by the EMM, which lists certain core signs of THB on the basis of five topics.[81] Arbo teams run the signs through the AMF.[82] In 2009, the BNRM recommended that the instructions within the AI about when and which signs should be reported to the SIOD should be improved.[83] The BNRM also observed that the identification of THB for labour exploitation cases should be improved. According to the BNRM, a more active role may be expected of the Labour Inspectorate, including that the AI inspectors explicitly question possible victims and actively look for signs of THB.[84]

Since 2007–2008 AI inspectors have been trained and/or made aware of THB for labour exploitation.[85] In the 7th national report (2009), the BNRM observed that training within the AI should be improved, and made three recommendations in that regard. First, the BNRM emphasised that training needs to be repeated and that it should also be given to newly recruited inspectors. This training should focus on recognising signs of THB and the approach taken towards victims.[86] Secondly, the BNRM recommended that *Arbo* inspectors should receive THB training. Thirdly, the BNRM recommended that the AI (both AMF and *Arbo*) organise joint training with the Aliens Police in order to create more awareness of each other's tasks and authorities, and the division of roles if (potential) victims of THB are at stake.[87] Although working on the first and second recommendations, such training has not yet been realised.[88] The newly recruited inspectors should have received

---

[80] Interview with policy advisor AMF (AI) (October 2010).

[81] Multiple dependency (e.g. the employer arranges for housing, clothing, transportation), strong limitation of employees' basic freedoms (e.g. the employee cannot avail of his/her own wages), poor working conditions (e.g. extremely low wages), violation of physical integrity (e.g. signs of physical abuse), exploitation is not incidental (e.g. working at different locations).

[82] Interview with policy advisor AMF (AI) (October 2010).

[83] Recommendation 11, BNRM7 (n. 6) p. 602.

[84] Recommendation 12, BNRM7 (n. 6) p. 602.

[85] BNRM7 (n. 6), p. 519.

[86] Recommendation 18, BNRM7 (n.6) p. 603.

[87] Recommendation 18, BNRM7 (n.6) p. 603.

[88] Interview with policy advisor AMF (AI) (October 2010). The AI indicated that it is working on training in cooperation with the victim support organisation BLinN, that refresher training is being developed, and that the AI is considering whether or not to develop more extended training for Arbo inspectors.

training at the beginning of 2011.[89] Some persons question whether the training within the AI is sufficiently in-depth.[90]

There has been an increase in the number of signs of THB for labour exploitation that the AI reported to the SIOD. In 2008 only five signs were reported; it is unknown how many signs were reported in 2009, but in 2010 the AI reported more than 50 signs to the SIOD. Also, data originating from the AI was sent to the EMM in order to be analysed. On the basis of the outcome of this analysis, the AI intends to consider improvement of its own data processing, as well as training efforts. However, the EMM does not function optimally, and no outcome has been generated yet.

One of the reasons why the AI does not detect as many signs as one would expect, is that victims are not likely to have the courage to speak up if the AI performs an inspection. In many instances, the employer instructs the employees not to speak up. Furthermore, employers are often present when the AI speaks to employees and the AI inspectors are trained to build a working relationship with the employer. Often the AI inspectors will start an inspection by having a private meeting with the employer. The employee may experience this as the AI siding with the employer. Also, the fact that the inspectors ask for identity papers in the first conversation and that officers from the Aliens Police are present may create fear within the employee. Consequently, it is difficult for the AI to recognise a victim. If the AI does not question further, the victim's situation may remain unnoticed.[91] Also, the AI in some instances announces in which sector it will hold its inspections, the inspectors are instructed to focus on specific violations, and the inspectors are evaluated on the basis of the amount of fines applied. The AI is criticised by some that, consequently, employers may cover up exploitative situations, and that inspectors do not have the incentive to look beyond violations of these acts and apply fines.[92]

In general, the AI is giving more attention to the issue of THB for labour exploitation, and the number of signs reported to the SIOD rose in 2010. Although aware that the AI is taking steps to create more awareness amongst its officials, most interviewees were of the opinion that the detection of THB for labour exploitation by the AI is open to improvement.[93]

Social Intelligence and Investigation Department (*SIOD*)

The Social Intelligence and Investigation Department (*Sociale Inlichtingen en Opsporingsdienst* or ***SIOD***) is the Special Investigation Department of the

[89] Interview with policy advisor AMF (AI) (October 2010).

[90] Expert Meeting in the project Combating THB for Labour Exploitation in the EU (February 2011).

[91] BLinN Report (n. 54) pp. 36-37.

[92] Expert Meeting in the project Combating THB for Labour Exploitation in the EU (February 2011).

[93] Interview with public prosecutor in the National Office (July 2010); Interview with victim support lawyer (November 2010); Interview with legal researcher BNRM (October 2010); Interview with Project Leader BLinN (November 2010).

Ministry of Social Affairs and Employment. The SIOD is a so-called special investigation service (*bijzondere opsporingsdienst*) and may criminally investigate THB for labour exploitation.[94]

An important part of the SIOD's work relates to illegal employment, organised forms of social benefits fraud, and fraud with employment subsidies. Since the introduction of labour exploitation in Article 273f DPC, the criminal investigation of THB for labour exploitation was added to the SIOD's tasks.[95] The SIOD works repressively; controls in the field of work and income are performed by the AI. Signs resulting from such controls are reported to the SIOD.[96] The SIOD also receives reports from foundation 'Report Crime Anonymously' (*Stichting Meld Misdaad Anoniem*), the Aliens Police and the KMar.[97] Since 2006, the investigation of exploitation for labour and/or services is marked as a priority in the SIOD's year plans.[98]

Since 2007, SIOD detectives receive training in the recognition of THB for labour exploitation and the approach to be taken towards victims.[99] In 2009, the BNRM stressed that more awareness relating to labour exploitation should be created within the SIOD.[100] In 2010 the SIOD started a new course on THB for 18 SIOD inspectors, a specialist of the Labour Inspectorate and a CoMensha employee. Skills relating to victim identification and interaction with (possible) victims of THB are central themes in this course.[101] In 2009 the SIOD sent two cases they had investigated to the prosecution service, two in 2010, and they had 7 investigations operational by 31 December 2010. Also, the SIOD in conjunction with the National Agency against Trafficking in Persons (Ministry of Administration and Interior, Romania) organised the first international seminar focusing on the everyday practice of the efforts to combat labour exploitation. The conference, named LABOREX2010, was held from 31 January–2 February 2010. The most important findings of the conference were published.[102]

---

[94] THB for labour exploitation may also be investigated by the police and the KMar.
[95] BNRM7 (n. 6) p. 516.
[96] Toolkit (n.78) under 'Partners'.
[97] Expert Meeting in the project Combating THB for Labour Exploitation in the EU (February 2011).
[98] BNRM7 (n. 6) p. 517.
[99] Oral information SIID.
[100] Recommendation 12, BNRM7 (n. 6) p. 602.
[101] BNRM8 (n. 39) p. 72.
[102] F.H. van Dijk and R.N. Ungureanu, *Labour Exploitation in Europe, A Practical Guide with Operational Observations and Recommendations on European Inspection, Investigation and Prosecution of Labour Exploitation* (Van Dijk/Ungureanu). Copies may be requested from the SIID.

Most of the interviewed parties involved in the combat of THB for labour exploitation are positive about the progress the SIOD is making and the attention it is giving to this problem.[103]

Police

The Dutch police are divided into 26 police departments. Of these departments, 25 concern regional departments for each of the 25 police regions the Netherlands is divided into. The 26th department concerns the National Police Services Brigade (*Korps Landelijke Politiediensten* or ***KLPD***).[104] Each of the 26 police departments is autonomous and organised in its own way.[105] The Aliens Police, charged with monitoring of the legal stay of aliens within the Netherlands, is part of the regional police departments.[106] The detecting role of the police lies, for a large part, with the Aliens Police as a result of their involvement in the inspections on illegality. It should be noted that currently a draft bill is pending for the reorganisation of the police; envisaged is one national police organisation with 10 police regions, which will be managed centrally.

The police have a role identifying and investigating warning signs regarding THB for labour exploitation, but they are also required to give victim support. Certified police officers are required to assist (potential) victims in filing their complaint, and are also required to inform victims about their rights (see Part III).

According to the BNRM, many police departments are still searching for the most effective approach towards THB for labour exploitation. The '*eye and ear*' for THB for labour exploitation is open to improvement. Improvement and intensifying the detection of exploitation outside the sex industry is essential to diminish the scope of THB in the Netherlands.[107] Illegal aliens who are arrested should be asked about them being victims. This does not happen everywhere.[108] Some suggest that the Aliens Police should have standard boxes to tick with warning signs of THB.[109] In 2009, the BNRM recommended that the police intensify training efforts. Training should focus on warning signs of THB for labour exploitation and the way in which these signs should be

[103] Interview with Legal Researcher BNRM (October 2010); Interview with Project Leader BLinN (November 2010).

[104] <http://www.politie.nl/Overdepolitie/organisatie/> accessed 17 December 2010.

[105] Interview Expert THB DNR (November 2010).

[106] <http://www.dienstterugkeerenvertrek.nl/samenwerking/vp.aspx> accessed 8 January 2011.

[107] BNRM7 (n. 6) p. 329. The BNRM mentioned that illegal aliens should always be asked questions to establish whether or not they are (potential) victims of THB. Also, it is not always clear to police officers what 'the smallest indication' is that the person may be a victim, which is of relevance because if there is such an indication, the person has to be offered the reflection period under the B9 procedure (see Part III).

[108] BNRM7 (n. 6) p. 330.

[109] Interview with Legal Researcher BNRM (October 2010).

processed in order to promote investigations of THB, as well as victim support.[110]

Royal Netherlands Marechaussee (*KMar*)

The Royal Netherlands Marechaussee (*Koninklijke Marechaussee* or ***KMar***) may be best described as a police service with military status, and has a role both identifying and investigating signs of THB for labour exploitation.[111] Part of the KMar's functions relate to guarding the Schengen borders, the combating of illegal immigration over the internal borders, and determining the identity of foreign nationals.[112]

During the performance of tasks in the abovementioned fields, the KMar may detect signs of THB for labour exploitation.[113] The BNRM recommended in 2009 that the identification of THB by the KMar should be improved. The KMar should play a more pro-active role, in which officers explicitly question possible victims and in which officers actively look for signs of THB.[114] The KMar has taken several initiatives to better identify victims, including drafting victim profiles. In the context of the Task Force for combating Human Trafficking, in which the KMar participates, the KMar drafted an action plan, in which attention is given to the awareness of KMar officials regarding THB.[115] The KMar may also investigate cases of THB.

The Immigration and Naturalisation Service (*IND*)

Officials of the Immigration and Naturalisation Service (*Immigratie en Naturalisatie Dienst* or ***IND***) may also detect THB. The IND is responsible for executing the Dutch policy regarding aliens.

Signs of THB should be passed on to the EMM, the KMar, and other investigative bodies. The IND is also responsible for transferring victims to the police or the KMar (who, in turn, may refer victims to CoMensha and/or other aid organisations). Only confirmed (and not potential) victims are registered.[116] In 2009 the BNRM recommended that the IND develop an automated system in which all (potential) victims of THB who apply for residence status with the IND or are otherwise known to the IND are registered.[117] Also, the BNRM recommended that the identification of THB for labour exploitation cases by the IND should be improved. According to the BNRM, a more active role may be expected of the IND, including that IND officials explicitly question possible victims and actively look for signs of

---

[110] Recommendations 17 and 18, BNRM7 (n. 6) p. 603.
[111] Toolkit (n.78) under 'Partners'.
[112] Ibid.
[113] Ibid; BNRM7 (n. 6) p. 333.
[114] Recommendation 12, BNRM7 (n. 6) p. 602.
[115] BNRM7 (n. 6) pp. 333-334.
[116] BNRM7 (n. 6) p. 332.
[117] Recommendation 45, BNRM7 (n. 6) p. 606.

THB.[118] The IND officials should also receive training aimed at recognising signs of THB and how to support victims.[119]

Municipalities
Several departments of municipalities may come across signs of THB for labour exploitation. The municipal division that comes across THB for labour exploitation most often is the department responsible for checking housing/construction regulations, as they may come across victims of THB when performing inspections. Both in the asparagus case and the krupuk cases described in Part IV, this municipal department played a role. Apart from identifying existing THB cases, the municipalities are also crucial in preventing THB for labour exploitation with the so-called administrative approach, as will be further elaborated upon in paragraph 2.2.[120]

Labour Associations, Sector Organisations, and Employee Councils
Labour Associations, Sector Organisations, and Employee Councils may also come across signs of THB. Labour Associations represent employees in the Netherlands, including labour migrants.[121] Sector organisations often monitor the quality of the products produced in a certain sector. As such, they may also monitor the labour conditions of the employees working in a certain sector.[122] Too little attention to 'compliance' may facilitate THB.[123] Employee Councils represent the employees within a company. In June 2010, the Ministry of Employment and Social Welfare launched a campaign raising awareness of THB for labour exploitation, (partly) aimed at Sector Organisations and Employee Councils.[124]

Other parties
Other parties that may detect signs of THB for labour exploitation are the Ministry of Foreign Affairs/Dutch Embassies/Dutch consulates,[125] Foreign Consulates and Embassies,[126] the Treasury,[127] the Chamber of Commerce, the Fiscal Intelligence and Investigation Department,[128] the Employment Insurance

---

[118] Recommendation 12, BNRM7 (n. 6) p. 602.
[119] Recommendations 18 and 20, BNRM7 (n. 6) p. 603.
[120] Interview with the Chairman of the Task Force THB (October 2010).
[121] BLinN Report (n.54) p. 16.
[122] Interview with the Chairman of the Task Force THB (October 2010).
[123] Programme (n.146) p. 6.
[124] Task Force Progress Report (n.211) p. 8.
[125] BLinN Report (n.54) p. 16.
[126] Ibid.
[127] Toolkit (n.78), under 'Partners'. Labour exploitation is often accompanied by financial and tax crimes. In that case the FIID can play a role in identifying THB. Consequently, the Treasury can play a role in identifying THB.
[128] Toolkit (n.78) under 'Partners'. The FIID's main tasks are to combat fiscal and financial-economical fraud and organised crime. Labour exploitation is often

Agency, the General League for Employment Agencies, the Financial Intelligence and Investigation Service (*Fiscale Inlichtingen- en Opsporingsdienst* or ***FIOD***), victim support organisations like CoMensha and civil society.[129]

Investigation and prosecution

There are 28 investigative departments that may criminally investigate THB for labour exploitation: each of the 25 local police departments (including the Aliens Police), the National Investigation Team of the KLPD (*Dienst Nationale Recherche* or ***DNR***), the KMar and the SIOD.[130] Each of the police departments is autonomous and organised in its own way. This means that, although each region has certain officers dealing with cases of THB for labour exploitation, this falls under a different team in each of the departments.[131] According to the Guideline, it is preferable to form multi-disciplinary teams in THB cases, e.g. teams consisting of the Aliens Police, regional police, regional investigation service, SIOD, and KMar. In case this is not possible, structural information exchange should be established.[132]

Prosecution of cases regarding THB for labour exploitation may be done by three different offices within the public prosecution service (***OM***). Each office has a contact public prosecutor for THB cases. There are no specialised judges/courts yet, although at the end of 2010 the Council for the Judiciary (*Raad voor de Rechtspraak*) advised appointing four District Courts to handle exclusively THB cases in the Netherlands.[133]

National Office (*Landelijk Parket*)

The National Office aims at combating (international) organised crime and is in charge of the investigations by the DNR, which focuses specifically on crimes like international smuggling and trafficking in human beings, the production and export of synthetic drugs, laundering of criminal money, and terrorism.[134] Within the National Prosecutor's Office, there is a national

---

accompanied by financial and tax crimes. Consequently, the FIID can play a role in identifying THB.

[129] CoMensha often receives messages from foreign employees working directly with Dutch businesses, who request help because they think they are being exploited. CoMensha forwards such messages to the SIID. In 2010, CoMensha forwarded about 20 messages. Cf. CoMensha Monthly Report for October.

[130] Guideline (n. 19) para 6.

[131] Interview with Expert THB DNR (November 2010). Some police regions have specialised THB teams; others leave it to the Aliens Police to investigate THB cases (although trafficking may concern victims that reside in the Netherlands legally as well); others leave it to the vice squad (although THB does not necessarily concern a sex crime).

[132] Guideline (n. 19).

[133] Information received from the Judicial Council by email.

[134] <http://www.om.nl/organisatie/landelijke/landelijk_parket/> accessed 26 November 2010.

coordinating public prosecutor for THB. This public prosecutor leads THB investigations performed by the DNR. This public prosecutor also performs national coordinating tasks related to the investigation and prosecution of THB.[135]

Functional Office (*Functioneel Parket*)
The Functional Office combats criminality in the fields of the environment, economics and fraud.[136] The Functional Office is responsible for the investigation and prosecution of criminal cases in which a special investigation service (e.g. the SIOD) plays the lead role.[137]

Regional Office (*Arrondissements Parket*)
There are 19 regional offices in the Netherlands. Regional offices are responsible for the investigation and prosecution of THB cases for which the Functional Office and National Office are not responsible. Within 11 regional offices, one public prosecutor acts as the contact person for THB.[138]

Furthermore, the **Bureau for the Deprivation of Illegally Obtained Profits (*Bureau Ontnemingen Openbaar Ministerie*)** may start proceedings for the recovery of illegally obtained profits (*ontneming onrechtmatig verkregen voordeel*).

Usually, the National Office leads investigations performed by the DNR, the Functional Office the investigations performed by the SIOD, and the relevant Regional Office the investigations run by the other parties. To this extent multi-disciplinary teams are formed, but the different offices decide which office takes the lead.[139]

Once every three months there is a meeting between all THB public prosecutors within the regional offices. The National Office and the Functional Office are also present. Sometimes other actors like the SIOD and the AI are also present. Furthermore, there is an informal circle of THB public prosecutors, where they exchange information (e.g. case law) and expertise.[140]

Information exchange
As mentioned before and as will be elaborated upon in more detail in paragraph 2.2, information exchange is an important element in the combat of THB in the Netherlands. The most important institutions involved in information exchange are the following:

---

135 Guideline (n. 19) para 3.
136 Toolkit (n.78), under 'Partners'.
137 <http://www.om.nl/organisatie/landelijke/functioneel_parket/> accessed 26 November 2010.
138 Toolkit (n.78), under 'Partners'.
139 Interview with the Chairman of the Task Force (October 2010).
140 Interview with public prosecutor in the Regional Office Rotterdam (November 2010).

Expertise Centre for Human Trafficking and Human Smuggling (*EMM*)
In order to obtain a national view of the nature and scope of THB, the Expertise Centre for Human Trafficking and Human Smuggling *(Expertisecentrum Mensenhandel en Mensensmokkel* or ***EMM)*** was established in 2005. It is a collaboration between the information service of the National Investigations Team (*dienst Nationale Recherche Informatie*), the DNR, the KMar, the SIOD, and the IND.[141] The EMM is the national information and knowledge centre for human smuggling and human trafficking, and aims to support the investigation of THB cases by painting the broader picture.[142] The EMM partners and the police are obliged to transfer indications of THB to the EMM; all other parties that may identify warning signs of THB can only pass on such information to the EMM in so far as privacy legislation applicable to such parties allows.[143] The EMM combines the information in order to arrive at the 'full picture' of THB cases.

Regional Information and Expertise Centres (*RIECs*) and National Information and Expertise Centre (*LIEC*)
Pursuant to the programme Administrative Combat of Organised Crimes (*Bestuurlijke Aanpak Georganiseerde Misdaad*) in 2009, 11 Regional Information and Expertise Centres (*Regionale Informatie en Expertise Centrum*) (***RIEC***) were established in the Netherlands, as well as one National Information and Expertise Centre (*Landelijk Informatie en Expertise Centrum* or ***LIEC***). The primary task of the RIECs is to facilitate the local municipalities in the administrative combat of organised crime, which includes THB. RIECs are supposed to facilitate more intensive information exchange. RIECs play the role of information broker between the investigation departments on the one hand, and the municipalities on the other, so that the decision can be made to take legal or administrative steps in a particular situation.[144] Each RIEC is in a different stage of development. In some regions RIECs still have to be set up. Not every RIEC sets THB as a priority; the RIECs are free to determine which crimes are prioritised.[145]

2.2 Cooperation between actors within the country

Under this section, first the legal framework for cooperation between the abovementioned parties is discussed. Attention will be given to the policy,

---

[141] Toolkit (n.78), under 'Partners'; Guideline (n. 19) paras 2-3. NB The BNRM also mentions the Task Organisation of the Aliens Police *[Taakorganisatie Vreemdelingen or TOV]* as a partner of the EMM. See BNRM7 (n. 6) p. 341.
[142] Toolkit (n.78), under 'Partners'.
[143] Interview with Expert THB DNR (November 2010).
[144] Interview with Expert on THB DNR (November 2010).
[145] Ibid.

legislation and rules regarding such cooperation. Furthermore, the legal framework for special investigative methods will be described. Subsequently, the application of the legal framework in practice will be evaluated.

2.2.1 Legal framework for cooperation

2.2.1.1 Policy

In recent years the Dutch government issued many policy documents in the area of combating organised crime, which includes THB. In this report, the most fundamental elements introduced in these policy documents are discussed. Key in the policies issued in recent years is that information is exchanged between investigative actors (e.g. the police, SIOD), administrative actors (e.g. the mayor, municipal departments that monitor housing regulations), prosecution departments (public prosecutor's offices), and private parties (NGOs). Below a few key terms introduced in the policy documents are briefly explained.

Programmatic approach

In 2007 the Dutch Government issued the Programme for the Reinforcement of the Combat of Organised Crime (*Programma Versterking Aanpak Georganiseerde* Misdaad)[146] (the ***Programme***). Although it is recognised in the Programme that the combat of organised crime has an important repressive component, the Programme follows the principle that the effective combat of organised crime requires more than just criminal investigation and prosecution. According to the Programme, a combined effort of preventive, administrative and penal measures on the local, regional, national and international level is needed to combat organised crime. In order to achieve this, the Programme includes goals and activities in the three pillars of combating organised crime, i.e. (i) the preventive and administrative approach,[147] (ii) the criminal approach, and (iii) international cooperation.[148]

---

[146] Programma Versterking Georganiseerde Misdaad (Annex to Kamerstukken II 2007/2008, 29 911 nr. 10) (Programme).

[147] The following is meant by 'preventive and administrative approach': administrative bodies and/or private parties may unknowingly facilitate THB. Establishing certain administrative rules or legislation, the failure of enforcing certain legislation, and the toleration of certain (criminal) behaviour during a long period of time are examples of administrative behaviour that may facilitate THB. The fact that no attention is given to 'compliance' in certain business sectors is an example of behaviour by private parties (e.g. sector organisations) that may facilitate THB. Hence, administrative bodies may prevent THB by amending the rules/legislation, enforce legislation, not tolerate criminal behaviour, etc. This can be very specific (e.g. denying a person convicted of THB a license to run a brothel), but also high level (e.g. amending rules so that a person trying to obtain a license to run a brothel needs to show whether or not he/she has ever been convicted of THB). Private organisations such as sector organisations may prevent THB by drafting rules for compliance. Also information campaigns in countries of origin are part of preventive measures that may be taken. See Programme (n.146) pp. 5-6.

[148] Programme (n.146).

The Programme aims to seek a method to develop and implement measures within the three pillars that fit in with the daily practice of preventing and combating organised crime. To facilitate this, a so-called '***programmatic approach***' in four themes was introduced. One of these four themes concerns THB. A programmatic approach means that the phenomenon is approached at local, regional and national level, as well as at the international level, and that all involved parties develop an approach in which preventive, administrative, criminal and international aspects are sufficiently included.[149] In this approach, effective information exchange between the OM and the police on the one hand, and administrative bodies on the other is key. Administrative information and instruments are used in concrete criminal investigations. On the other hand, information from criminal investigations is used to adjust policy and (administrative) instruments.[150] The programmatic approach may be used in concrete criminal investigations, but also in initiatives in which information exchange is institutionalised by means of setting up structures in which parties structurally exchange information regarding THB. Information exchange with the EMM and RIECs may be part of that information exchange.

In order to make the programmatic approach operational, a Task Force for each of the themes was set up. The Task Force THB (the ***Task Force***) is a collaboration between different parties involved in combating THB, who from their own responsibilities come up with measures to prevent THB, combat THB, and support victims of THB.[151] Also, the Task Force takes the initiative for policy measures and monitors concrete THB investigations in pilot criminal investigations in which the programmatic approach is followed (*proeftuinen*).[152]

Barrier model

Part of the programmatic approach is the use of the so-called barrier model. In the barrier model, five barriers are defined that must be overcome in order to commit THB when foreign victims are concerned. These barriers are (i) entrance into the Netherlands, (ii) housing, (iii) identity, (iv) labour, and (v) financial flows. Besides the core perpetrators and their direct facilitators (i.e.

---

[149] Programme (n.146) p. 4.

[150] OM National Office, *Handbook to combat Trafficking in Human Beings* (OM National Office June 2009) (Handbook) p. 111.

[151] The Task Force includes the Head Public Prosecutor of the OM Regional Office in Amsterdam, the BNRM, representatives of the National Police Services Brigade, the Procurator General, R.M, the judiciary, the Ministry of Employment and Social Affairs, the Ministry of Health, the Ministry of Justice, the Ministry of Foreign Affairs, municipalities, and CoMensha.

[152] <http://www.om.nl/onderwerpen/mensenhandel_en/@151310/plan_van_ aanpak/ >accessed 4 December 2010.

pimps, forgers, bodyguards), for each of the barriers the following parties are identified: the parties that knowingly facilitate the overcoming of a barrier (e.g. human smugglers and drivers for the barrier 'entrance'), the parties that unknowingly facilitate the overcoming of the barriers (e.g. customs officers for the barrier 'entrance'), and the parties that may prevent the overcoming of the barriers (e.g. the municipalities, KMar, police, IND, and Aliens Police for the barrier 'entrance').[153]

The barrier model may be used to identify the (administrative) actors that are to be involved in concrete criminal investigations, as well as (further) barriers to prevent THB that transpired in concrete criminal investigations.[154] The barrier model may also be used to identify the parties that should be included in an institutionalised information exchange as foreseen in the policy documents. It may be adjusted to better suit THB for labour exploitation and domestic cases.[155]

Intelligence-led investigations and financial investigations

Signs of THB need to be detected, relevant starting points for criminal investigations are to be investigated and should – as far as possible – lead to investigations.[156] THB investigations are to be intelligence-led.[157] This means that strategic and tactical decisions in criminal investigations should be based upon the analysis of information, meaning that the investigations are not (or are less) dependent upon victims' statements. Also in this regard, it is important that information is exchanged between the investigative departments, and parties like the administrative authorities and the AI, so that information may be compiled ('*gestapeld*').[158] The EMM and RIECs may play a role in the intelligence-led investigations. Furthermore, financial investigations are to be part of THB investigations.[159]

2.2.1.2. Legislation and rules

Below will follow a description of the most important legislation related to the exchange of information between the police, special investigation departments (e.g. the SIOD and FIID), the prosecution services, and third parties. The legislation is extensive and detailed, and several different acts may apply to one party. This means that information exchange is very complex. The complexity of information exchange was recognised by several ministries, who jointly issued – in the light of the policy of stimulating information exchange between a wide range of parties as described above – certain guidelines for cooperation in practice.

---

153 Ibid.

154 Ibid.

155 E.g. by adding the barrier 'cultural-religious background'.

156 Guideline (n. 19), para 1.

157 Ibid, paras 1-2.

158 Ibid, paras 6-7.

159 Ibid, paras 1-2.

Act for the Protection of Personal Data (Wet bescherming persoonsgegevens)

The Personal Data Protection Act of 6 July 2000 (*Wet bescherming persoonsgegevens*) applies to all persons processing information, to the extent that other legislation does not provide otherwise. Most notably, the Personal Data Protection Act is applicable to the processing of information by the municipalities (to the extent that it is not related to the municipal personal records database, see further below), the special investigations services (except for information processing on the basis of Articles 10 sub 1(a) and 12 in the Police Data Act, see further below), and other parties, to the extent that special legislation does not provide otherwise.[160] The Supervisory Board Personal Data Protection Act (the ***Supervisory Board***) is responsible for monitoring the correct application of the act.[161]

Under the Personal Data Protection Act, personal data may only be collected for well- and explicitly defined purposes, and only to the extent that it is relevant in the light of the purposes for which it was collected.[162] Personal data may only be processed in six listed types of situations, most notably when the processing is necessary to duly execute the public tasks of an administrative body (being either the administrative body that is processing the information, or the administrative body that is receiving the information) (Article 8e), or when the information processing is '*required for the representation of justified interests of the person responsible for processing the information or of a third party to which the data is provided, unless (...) the right to privacy prevails*' (Article 8f). Data may not be processed in a manner that is not reconcilable with the purpose for which it was obtained, except for when this is necessary for the prevention, investigation and prosecution of criminal offences (Articles 9 sub 1 and 43 b).[163]

The processing of personal data is to be reported to the Supervisory Board preceding the actual processing.[164] The act also contains a duty to inform the person involved that the information is being processed.[165] However, this duty

[160] The Personal Data Protection Act does not apply to the processing of information for the purposes of the execution of a police task, which is regulated by the Police Data Act *[Wet Politiegegevens]*, nor to the processing of information related to criminal proceedings, which is regulated by the Judicial Data and Data Related to Criminal Proceedings Act *[Wet justitiële en strafvorderlijke gegevens]*, nor to the processing of information that is regulated in the Municipal Personal Records Database Act *[Wet gemeentelijke basisadministratie persoonsgegevens]*. Consequently, the Personal Data Protection Act is not applicable to information processed by the police and the public prosecutor's office. It is not applicable to information processed by the municipalities only to the extent that data included in the municipal personal records database is being processed.

[161] Personal Data Protection Act, Chapter 9.

[162] Personal Data Protection Act, Articles 7 and 11.

[163] Personal Data Protection Act, Articles 9 sub 1 and 43 b.

[164] Personal Data Protection Act, Chapter 4.

[165] Personal Data Protection Act, Articles 33-35.

does not apply in cases where the prevention, investigation and prosecution of criminal offences are concerned.[166]

Police Data Act (Wet Politiegegevens)

The Police Data Act of 21 July 2007 entered into force on 1 January 2008. Compared to the legislation it replaced, the Police Data Act offers more possibilities to share information within the police, with third parties, and internationally.[167] Simultaneously with the Police Data Act, the Decree on Police Data – specifying certain elements of the act – entered into force.[168] The Supervisory Board is responsible for monitoring the correct application of the Police Data Act.[169] The Police Data Act also applies to the processing of information by the special investigation services (e.g. the SIOD and FIID).[170]

Police data may only be processed to the extent that the processing is necessary to achieve the purposes defined in the act, that the data was lawfully obtained, and that the exchange is proportional and relevant to the purpose for which it was collected. Police data may only be processed for a purpose other than for which it was collected in so far as the Police Data Act provides explicit grounds for such a purpose.[171] Sensitive information, for instance regarding religion or health, but also membership of a branch organisation, may only be processed in addition to other police data, and only to the extent that this is inevitable for the purpose of processing.[172] Police data must be corrected or destroyed if incorrect.[173] The access to the information that is being processed needs to be secured and the access has to be limited by means of requiring authorisation. The persons processing the information are subject to confidentiality obligations.[174]

Article 10 in the Police Data Act (processing of information for the establishment of involvement in serious crimes) is of particular relevance to THB for labour exploitation. Under the conditions mentioned in Article 10, police data may be processed to achieve insight into the involvement of individuals in committing or plotting THB (whether or not in organised form) (Article 10 sub 1a), or the involvement in activities that may indicate the

---

[166] Personal Data Protection Act, Article 43.

[167] BNRM7 (n. 6) p. 23.

[168] Besluit van 14 december 2007, houdende bepalingen ter uitvoering van de Wet Politiegegevens (Besluit Politiegegevens).

[169] Police Data Act, Article 35.

[170] Besluit van 3 juli 2009, houdende bepalingen inzake de overeenkomstige toepassing van de Wet politiegegevens op de verwerking van persoonsgegevens door een dienst van een publiekrechtelijk lichaam die is belast met de opsporing van strafbare feiten (Besluit politiegegevens bijzondere opsporingsdiensten) (Stb. 2009, 305), amending the Police Data Act, Article 46.

[171] Police Data Act, Article 3.

[172] Police Data Act, Article 5.

[173] Police Data Act, Article 4.

[174] Police Data Act, Articles 6 and 7.

plotting or committing of THB (Article 10 sub 1 b).[175] In the Decree on Police Data, this is referred to as '*theme processing of serious crimes*' (Chapter 3).[176] On the basis of Article 10, police data may be transferred to the EMM in order to investigate the involvement in (or activities that may indicate) the plotting or committing of THB by certain individuals. The information that is received by the EMM is processed in a 'theme register' as referred to in Article 3:2 Decree on Police Data. The EMM may retain the information on THB longer than for what is standard for a regular police task (Article 8 Police Data Act) and criminal investigations (Article 9 Police Data Act) because it is maintaining a theme register.[177]

The Police Data Act also provides the possibility to establish connections between police data processed in different investigations. Article 11 regulates the automatic comparing and searching in combination of police data. Most notably and relevant to the combating of THB, the EMM and other parties subject to the Police Data Act may automatically compare data processed on the basis of Article 10 sub 1 with other police data that is processed for other purposes, in order to establish whether connections exist between the relevant data.[178] Under certain circumstances, police data may also be automatically compared to data other than police data by the EMM or by other parties to which the Police Data Act applies.[179]

Chapter 3 of the Police Data Act regulates the provision of information to third parties (i.e. all parties other than the police departments and the KMar). Most notably, information may be provided to the extent necessary: to SIOD and FIID officers to perform the criminal investigation tasks assigned to them; to members of the public prosecutor's office for their authority over persons charged with investigations of criminal offences; and to mayors in connection with their authority over the police or in the context of their maintaining public order.[180]

Furthermore, Article 18 provides for the provision of police data to specific third parties (listed in the Decree on Police Data) on a structural basis for the performance of these third parties' tasks. Article 19 provides for the provision of police data to unspecified third parties on an *ad hoc* basis. Article 20 provides for the provision of police data to unspecified third parties in structural collaborations. Information under Articles 19 and 20 may be provided to third

---

175 Police Data Act, Article 10 sub 1a1 (involvement in plotting or committing THB in organised form and which may cause serious violations of the public order), sub 1a3 and 3:1 Decree on Police Data (involvement in plotting or committing THB which may cause serious violations of the public order), and sub 1b and 3:2 Decree on Police Data (activities which may indicate the involvement in committing or plotting of THB).

176 Decree on Police Data, Chapter 3.

177 Police Data Act, Article 10 sub 6.

178 Police Data Act, Article 11 sub 2.

179 Police Data Act, Article 11 sub 5.

180 Police Data Act, Articles 16a, 16c, and 16d.

parties in special circumstances with an eye to a serious public interest, and only for the following purposes:

a. the prevention and investigation of criminal acts;
b. the enforcement of public order;
c. the providing of assistance to victims and others who are involved with a criminal offence;
d. the supervision of compliance with legislation.

Act on Judicial Data and Data related to Criminal Proceedings (Wet justitiële en strafvorderlijke gegevens)

The Act on Judicial Data and Data related to Criminal Proceedings of 7 November 2002 (***Judicial Data Act***) regulates the processing of judicial data and data related to criminal proceedings by the OM. Certain elements of the act are further specified in the Decree on Judicial Data.[181] As long as certain data is not yet included in a criminal file or in automatic form, the data may not be regarded as data related to criminal proceedings, and – to the extent that it is included in a police register – the Police Data Act applies.[182]

In cases of grave public interest, the public prosecution service may provide judicial data and data related to criminal proceedings to the police and the special investigation services like the SIOD and the FIID. The Public Prosecutor's Department may, under these circumstances, also provide judicial data and data related to criminal proceedings to third parties, when this serves one of the following purposes:

a. the prevention and investigation of criminal acts,
b. the enforcement of public order and safety,
c. the supervision of compliance with legislation,
d. the taking of an administrative decision,
e. the assessment of the need to apply a measure regarding the legal position (*rechtspositionele maatregel*) or a disciplinary measure, or
f. the providing of assistance to victims and others who are involved with a criminal offence.

Information on this basis may only be provided (a) to the extent that this is necessary in consideration of a serious public interest or in the establishment, invocation or defence of a right, and (b) in such form that the tracing of persons other than the person involved is prevented in all reasonableness.[183]

---

[181] Besluit van 25 maart 2004 tot vaststelling van de justitiële gegevens en tot regeling van de verstrekking van deze gegevens alsmede tot uitvoering van enkele bepalingen van de Wet justitiële gegevens.

[182] Guideline Judicial Data Act *[Aanwijzing vertsterkking strafvorderlijke gegevens voor buiten de strafrechtspleging gelegen doeleinden] [Aanwijzing wet justitiële en strafvorderlijke gegevens]* (Scr. 2010, 11804), para 1.

[183] Judicial Data Act, Articles 8a and 39f.

Other
Besides the abovementioned legislation specifically applicable to the processing of information, certain legislation that primarily regulates other subjects contains provisions on the exchange of information. The following provisions in the following acts are most notable:

The parties responsible for monitoring labour legislation, including the AI and SIOD, may exchange information between each other on the so-called SUWI Act (*SUWI wet*). Furthermore, the AI may exchange information with other administrative bodies on the basis of the WAV (Article 16) and the WML (Article 18p).

Articles 96, 98 and 100 of the Act on the Municipal Personal Records Database (*Wet gemeentelijke basisadministratie persoonsgegevens*) list the requirements the municipality has to fulfil in the context of providing information from the municipal personal records database. Most notably, information may be provided to the regional police departments on the same conditions as provision of information within the municipality internally.[184]

Article 67 of the General Act on Royal Taxes provides that all information received in the enforcement of the tax legislation is to be kept confidential. Article 67 sub 2 of the General Act on Royal Taxes provides that exceptions to this rule may be provided by Ministerial Decree. Article 43c sub 1 of the Implementing Regulations to the General Act on Royal Taxes provides such exceptions. On the basis of Article 43c sub 1 under l of the implementing regulations, the Treasury may provide certain specified types of information to the Public Prosecutor's Department, including information regarding criminal offences.[185] The Treasury may also provide information to municipalities, the police, and the Public Prosecutor's Department as long as there is an integral execution and enforcement of government regulations and that there is a covenant on the basis of which the cooperation takes place.[186] Although the KMar, the SIOD and the FIOD are not explicitly mentioned, it is to be assumed that the same applies to the exchange of information with these parties.[187]

The Administrative Agreement (Bestuurlijk Akkoord)[188]
In order to facilitate structural information exchange between investigative and administrative bodies, the Ministries of Internal Affairs, Justice, Finance,

[184] Article 96 sub 2 Act on the Municipal Personal Records Database of 9 June 1994.
[185] Implementing Regulations of the General Act on Royal Taxes *[Uitvoeringsregeling Algemene Wet inzake Rijksbelastingen 1994]*, Article 43l.
[186] Ibid., Article 43m.
[187] Administrative Agreement (n.188) p. 5. NB the text in this document refers to Article 43m, but considering the content, it is to be assumed that 43l has to be read where 43m is mentioned.
[188] Bestuurlijk Akkoord Geintegreerde Decentrale Aanpak Georganiseerde Misdaad (September 2008) (Administrative Agreement).

Employment and Social Affairs, the Chairman of the Society of Dutch Municipalities, and the Chairman of the Board of Procurators General concluded the 'Administrative Agreement regarding Information Exchange'.[189] The Administrative Agreement sets out the legal framework in which the exchange of information may occur in regional partnerships.[190] Each of the participating bodies is responsible for providing information to the extent that the legislation applicable to that body allows such provision of information.[191] The processing of information by the partnership is a distinct processing of information that should comply with the Personal Data Protection Act. A model-covenant for cooperation on the regional level, as well as a checklist for compliance with relevant legislation, is attached to the Administrative Agreement.[192] From the covenant and the checklist it shows that information exchange remains difficult.

2.2.1.3. Special investigation techniques

Special investigation techniques may be used in preliminary investigations[193], 'classical investigations'[194], and 'modern investigations'.[195]

---

[189] Task Force Plan of Action (1 January 2009) p. 3.

[190] Attention is given to the Personal Data Protection Act, the Police Data Act, the Judicial Data Act, and the General Act on Royal Taxes.

[191] In summary (additional provisions of the relevant acts may have to be complied with in certain situations), information may be provided by the following parties on the following basis. Municipalities: Article 8 sub e Personal Data Protection Act (to the extent that it is not related to information from the municipal personal records database). Police/RM: Article 20 Police Data Act. Public Prosecution Department: Article 8a and 39f Judicial Data Act. Treasury: Article 67 sub 2 General Act on Royal Taxes and Article 43m of its Implementing Regulations. Special investigation services like the SIID: Article 8 sub e Personal Data Protection Act and Article 20 Police Data Act (to the extent that the information is processed on the basis of Articles 10 sub 1 and/or 11 Police Data Act). All parties may receive data on the basis of Article 8f of the Personal Data Protection Act and the police/RM/Public Prosecutors' Department and Treasury on the basis of Article 22 sub 1 Personal Data Protection Act.

[192] It is unclear currently how many regional covenants have been concluded in the Netherlands.

[193] Preliminary investigations may be started '[if] from facts or circumstances clues arise that within groups of persons crimes are plotted or committed as described in Article 67 sub 1 DPC that constitute a serious violation to the public order taking into account their nature or the connection with other crimes that are plotted or committed within those groups of persons, the Public Prosecutor may order that investigative officers start investigations with the goal of preparing criminal investigations.' (Article 126gg DPC).

[194] Classical criminal investigations are investigations on the basis of a reasonable suspicion that THB was committed. Classical criminal investigations may be started if there is a suspect as defined in Article 27 DCPP. Article 27 DCPP reads as follows: 'Before prosecution is started, an individual is regarded as a suspect if a reasonable suspicion of guilt of any criminal offence results from facts or circumstances.'

[195] Criminal investigations on the basis of a reasonable suspicion that an organised form THB was plotted or committed (modern criminal investigations) may be started if 'facts or circumstances result in a reasonable suspicion that crimes as described in Article 67 sub

Title Ve of Book 1 of the Dutch Code of Criminal Procedure (***DCPP***) regulates the special investigation techniques that may be used in preliminary investigations, which are two in number. As one of those applies only to investigations into terrorist crimes, in THB cases only one special investigation technique exists (i.e. the ordering of data from a person that in the performing of his/her tasks processes information of relevance for the investigations).

The use of special investigative techniques in the context of so-called 'classical investigations' is regulated in Book I, Title IVa of the DCPP. Title IVa is divided into eight parts, each concerning a distinct special investigative technique. Many of the techniques may only be applied if the investigations concern a crime subject to a term of imprisonment of a minimum of four years; in addition, sometimes it is required that the crime would mean a serious violation of public order, taking into account the nature of the crime or its connection with other crimes committed by the suspect. For each of the techniques, conditions for the application are included (e.g. the formalities for the order issued by the Public Prosecutor for the use of the investigative method), as well as certain limitations (e.g. the duration of the use of the method). Most of the special investigative techniques may be ordered by the Public Prosecutor. Only three special investigative methods require authorisation by the investigating judge, i.e. recording confidential communication (Article 126l DCPP), recording telecommunications (Article 126m DCCP), and the continuous or regular provision of information by a person processing information regarding the suspect (Article 126ne sub 3 ff DCCP).

Title V of Book 1 regulates the special investigative techniques that may be used in 'modern' criminal investigations. The techniques are the same as the techniques included in Article IVa DCPP (i.e. the techniques allowed in classical criminal investigations), although different conditions and limitations to the application of the techniques apply. Again, the Public Prosecutor may order most of the techniques, except for the recording of confidential communication (Article 126s DCPP), recording telecommunications (Article 126t DCCP), and the continuous or regular provision of information by a person processing information regarding the suspect (Articles 126ue sub 3 ff DCCP).

Title Va provides for three types of civilian assistance in criminal investigations: (i) civil collection of information, (ii) civilian infiltration, and (iii) civilian pseudo-purchase and pseudo-services. Finally, Title Vd DCCP provides general rules that apply to the use of special investigative techniques in all different types of investigations.

---

1 DPC are plotted or committed in an organised structure that, taking into consideration their nature or the connection with other crimes that are committed or plotted in an organised structure result in a serious breach of the public order.'

Schematically, the possibilities for using special investigative techniques in criminal investigations are as follows:[196]

	Preliminary investigations (Title IVc)	Classical investigations (Title IVa unless otherwise indicated)	Modern investigations (Title V unless otherwise indicated)
(Systematic) Observation	-	126g	126o
Entering locked premises	-	126k	126r
Requesting information concerning telecommunications	-	126n–126ni	126u–126ui
Recording telecommunications (phone and e-mail)	-	126m	126t
Recording confidential communications	-	126l	126s
Systematic information-gathering by an investigative officer	-	126j	126qa
(Systematic) Information-gathering by a civilian	-	126v (Title Va)	126v (Title Va)
Pseudo-purchase and pseudo-services by an investigative officer	-	126i	126q
Pseudo-purchase and pseudo-services by a civilian	-	126ij (Title Va)	126z (Title Va)
Infiltration by police officers	-	126h	126p
Civilian infiltration	-	126w (Title Va)	126x (Title Va)
Other	-		
Ordering data	126hh	126n–126ni	126u–126ui

2.2.1.4. Financial criminal investigations

Apart from criminal investigations described above, financial criminal investigations may be started if a suspect is suspected of a crime for which a

[196] The numbers in the columns refer to the relevant provisions in the DPPC.

fine of the fifth category may be imposed. THB is one of these crimes. In so far as the suspect may have obtained financial profits of any substance, financial investigations may be started in accordance with Book I, Title IV DPPC.[197] The investigations may be started on the authorisation of the investigating judge, and are aimed at determining the amount of illegally obtained profits for the deprivation thereof on the basis of Article 36e DPPC.[198] The financial investigations are distinct from the criminal investigations, and have their own time frame. This means that the financial investigations may continue even though the criminal proceedings against the suspect have already started and possibly even when the suspect has already been convicted.[199] Investigation techniques include the ordering and confiscation of information (Article 126a DPPC), the confiscation of goods (Article 126b sub 1 DPPC), the searching of premises by the investigating judge (Article 126b sub 2 DPPC), and urgent financial searching of premises (Article 126c DPPC).

Even though the aim of the financial investigations is distinct from the aim of the criminal investigations against the suspect, information obtained in the financial investigations may be used as evidence in the criminal proceedings against the suspect, to the extent that the financial investigations are not primarily aimed at obtaining evidence for the criminal proceedings (as opposed to obtaining evidence regarding illegally obtained profits for the purpose of confiscating such illegally obtained profits).[200] The information may also be used as evidence for the damages claimed by a victim of THB who joined the criminal proceedings against his/her trafficker.[201]

The Guideline states that financial investigations need to be part of the investigations in cases of THB, in order for the illegally obtained profits to be confiscated. Since THB is such a profitable 'business', the perpetrators should be deprived of their profits.[202]

2.2.2 Application of the legal framework in practice

Detecting (signs of) THB

Besides parties who may traditionally have come across THB for sexual exploitation (e.g. the Aliens Police), the detection of THB for labour exploitation signs mainly concern parties for whom THB is a 'new' phenomenon (e.g. the Labour Inspectorate, SIOD, Sector Organisations). Although virtually all parties that may come across THB for labour exploitation have taken initiatives to increase awareness regarding THB for

---

[197] Article 126 sub 1 DPPC.

[198] Articles 126 sub 3 and 126 sub 2 DPPC.

[199] Commentary to DPC *[Tekst en Commentaar Strafrecht]* Book I, Title IV, Article 9, introductory remarks, point 1.

[200] Ibid. point 2.

[201] Handbook (n.150) p. 57.

[202] Guideline (n. 19) p. 2.

labour, signs of THB are not always picked up by them.[203] This was discussed above where the different parties that may detect signs were described. The following elements may amount to not all warning signs being picked up. Article 273f is a very lengthy and complex provision, meaning that, for a lot of individuals who may detect signs of THB, it is still unclear what THB actually is. Officials that may come across signs of THB for labour exploitation (e.g. AI inspectors, KMar officials at the borders, and police officers) are not always aware that certain signs, added to other signs, may amount to THB. They do not recognise such signals and do not actively look for them. Training efforts have been taken, but need to be intensified and repeated in order to raise awareness about this phenomenon. Finally, it seems that certain parties that may come across victims of THB for labour exploitation are insufficiently equipped to take into consideration the victims' position; for all kinds of reasons victims often choose not to talk about their situation, meaning that the THB can only be detected if the party in question actively engages with the victim to find out about his/her position. Inspectors should be aware of the impression they leave with potential victims, who often come from countries where authorities cannot be trusted. Finally, parties such as sector organisations, may not (yet) have realised that they may come across THB for labour exploitation.

Not only do signs need to be detected, they should also be shared with the relevant parties in order to obtain 'the full picture'. Without effective cooperation and sharing of information between the parties that may detect signs of THB, a particular situation can be perceived as a combination of different violations of administrative, labour and maybe even criminal law, but not as THB. This is illustrated by the so-called asparagus case discussed in Part IV. In that case, the municipality, police and AI were each aware of certain poor conditions under which workers worked and lived, but the information was not 'added up'.

Practice shows that this information exchange is subject to all kinds of hurdles and therefore often does not happen. The so-called asparagus case described in Part IV is an example of inadequate information exchange. These hurdles are partly technical, most notably automated systems from different parties cannot be synchronised, and partly a result of attitude.[204] The fact that often the provider of information does not receive feedback about what happened with the information may play a role here. The complexity of the legal framework applicable to information exchange does not stimulate information exchange either. With respect to the Police Data Act specifically, it is felt that the enhanced opportunities for information exchange introduced by the act are not yet visible in practice. For instance, the Police Data Act provides for horizontal information exchange between the special investigation

[203] Interview with public prosecutor from the National Office (July 2010); Interview with victim support lawyer (November 2010); Interview with legal researcher BNRM (October 2010).

[204] BNRM7 (n. 6) p. 358.

services and the police.[205] However, the systems have not yet been adapted to each other and the attitude from the police is that they dislike the special investigation services accessing their data, and *vice versa*. Furthermore, the Police Data Act provides for certain safeguards regarding the information to be exchanged; only certain persons may access certain data for certain goals. An authorisation matrix needs to be established, with one person responsible for determining whether someone may access the data or not. As a consequence, it takes more formalities and time to obtain information. Also, responsible persons may be reluctant to exchange information because they do not have much experience of the act and wish to be on the safe side by rejecting a request for information. A factor that plays a role here may be that the parties subject to the Police Data Act are monitored biannually about the application of the act. Finally, the finesse of the Police Data Act, which is relatively new, has not yet reached all layers of persons working under that act. On the basis of the required safeguards under the act, certain persons are under the impression that the act does not facilitate, but rather limits the possibilities of information exchange.[206]

Furthermore, the two institutions designed to facilitate information exchange do not function optimally. As for the EMM, not all police departments and other parties pass on signs to the centre.[207] The data exchange between the EMM partners and the EMM is not automatic, since the different parties work with different information systems that cannot be linked to each other. Consequently, signs of THB need to be reported to the EMM manually.[208] Of the information that *is* received by the EMM, too little analysis is made. Not only does this mean that THB cases are not detected, it also means that as a result of disappointing output the partners and chain partners have become sceptical and may be (come) reluctant to transfer information. Another reason for reluctance to pass on signs to the EMM is that there is insufficient feedback on what happens with the signals transferred.[209] In a study regarding the information exchange between the police departments and the EMM that was performed in 2009, recommendations were given in six categories.[210] The implementation of these recommendations is not running smoothly.[211]

---

205 Police Data Act, Article 15.

206 Telephone interview with information expert SIOD (28 February 2011).

207 BNRM7 (n. 6) p. 340.

208 Interview with Expert THB DNR (November 2010).

209 BNRM7 (n. 6) p. 340.

210 Ibid. It concerns recommendations for improved ICT, better division of tasks and roles, concrete agreements about the quality of information supplied and feedback to (chain) partners, quality of the analytical process within the EMM, and reinforcement of cooperation with the management.

211 Task Force, Progress Report (September 2010) (Task Force Progress Report) p. 3.

Information exchange through the RIECs and the LIEC does not function optimally (yet) either. Many of the RIECs have not yet been established, or do not focus on THB. Some feel that adding another party to the already dysfunctional system of information exchange (the EMM) unnecessarily complicates matters.[212]

Structural information exchange

More and more initiatives are taken for structural information exchange between all parties that may detect THB, prevent THB, act administratively against THB, criminally investigate and prosecute THB, and provide victim care. In such initiatives, covenants for information exchange are usually completed, mostly based on the Administrative Agreement. In some initiatives, the parties to be involved are identified on the basis of the barrier model.

The most important aims of such structural information exchange are to detect THB cases at an early stage, and to jointly decide on the most appropriate intervention (criminal, administrative, or otherwise).[213] In most initiatives some form of administrative reports are also incorporated, through which the police provide feedback to administrative bodies on the basis of information they obtained in their criminal investigations, in order for the administrative bodies to adjust policies that may facilitate THB. This is all at an early stage and is work in progress. It is unknown in how many regions initiatives have been taken, which parties are involved, how exactly they work together, and how they perform.[214] What is known is that structural information exchange does not run optimally.[215]

Criminal investigations and prosecutions

Information exchange in concrete criminal investigations and prosecutions seems to work well. In more and more investigations multidisciplinary teams are formed, conforming to the Guideline. An example is the team in the so-called asparagus case (see Part IV), involving the regional police Brabant South East (which include the Aliens Police and the investigation service), and the SIOD. If it happens that two or more public prosecutors' offices are involved in a case, the different public prosecutors' offices and investigation departments work together. They discuss and mutually decide who has the main responsibility for a particular case.[216]

Also, public prosecutors cooperate with (administrative) bodies, such as the AI and the municipal service responsible for monitoring housing legislation. In the asparagus case (see Part IV) the public prosecutor cooperated with the AI. In that case, the AI had established violations of labour law by the suspect and

[212] Expert Meeting in the project Combating THB for Labour Exploitation in the EU (February 2011).

[213] In some initiatives the provision of victim care is also sought by including victim support organisations in the information exchange.

[214] BNRM7 (n. 6) pp. 318-319.

[215] Ibid.

[216] Interview with the Chairman of the Task Force (October 2010).

imposed fines on the suspect on numerous occasions. The extensive documentation relating to the suspect was shared completely with the public prosecutor, on the basis of which a good view of the extent of exploitation (duration, economic gain) could be obtained. The AI also assisted in the prosecution by knowledge transfer (what minimum wages are, what net minimum wages are, what the meaning is of the relevant provisions in the WAV, how work permits are requested, etc.).[217] In the krupuk case, the Criminal Intelligence Unit (*Criminele Inlichtingen Eenheid* or ***CIE***), the municipal department responsible for monitoring the implementation of the housing regulations (*Dienst Stedelijke Ontwikkeling* or ***DSO***), the Aliens Police and the SIOD cooperated with each other. The public prosecutor in that case noted that due to the input of the DSO and the Aliens Police all aspects of the case were covered. She states that it was an asset to have other agencies watch 'from a different perspective'.[218] It is unknown whether information from other parties, such as sector organisations, has been used in THB for labour exploitation cases.

As far as is visible in the THB for labour exploitation judgments that were published, evidence is most often based on witness statements and police reports. This shows that the intelligence-led investigations have not yet become standard in THB for labour exploitation cases.

In the cases studied in Part IV, the phone of the suspect was tapped, information concerning telecommunications was submitted, and premises were observed and entered. Use of other special investigation techniques cannot be seen in the files, nor were they mentioned in interviews. Interviewees did indicate that special investigative techniques such as pseudo-purchase cost a lot of time, which is usually not available in THB investigations.[219] There is no clear insight into the effectiveness of special investigative techniques.[220] According to one interviewee, it may be useful to investigate the effectiveness of (civilian) infiltration and the tapping of the victim's phone, which is done in Portugal.[221]

As mentioned before, the Guideline determines that financial investigations should be started in cases of THB. The two public prosecutors who led the investigations described in Part IV indicated that in *hindsight* financial investigations could have been developed further and/or financial inspectors could have been involved in the investigations at an earlier stage. They both emphasised the importance of the timely involvement of financial inspectors in the investigations. This is of relevance not only for the confiscation of illegally

[217] Interview with the public prosecutor from the Regional Office Rotterdam (November 2010)

[218] Interview with public prosecutor from Functional Office (July 2010).

[219] Interview with public prosecutor from Functional Office (July 2010); Interview with senior policy advisor SIOD (October 2010).

[220] Van Dijk/Ungureanu (n.102) p. 50.

[221] Interview with senior policy advisor SIOD (July 2010).

obtained profits, but also to establish the economic gain incurred by the employer, which is – since the Supreme Court decision in the Chinese case – of relevance to establish the element of exploitation.[222] The information may also be used to determine the damages incurred by the victim.

Pilot criminal investigations
In the context of the Task Force, there are two pilot criminal investigations related to THB for labour exploitation in which the programmatic approach is followed.[223] As yet, no results from these pilot projects (*proeftuinen*) are (publicly) known.

2.3 Cooperation between States

2.3.1 Legal framework for cooperation in trans-national Trafficking in Human Beings-cases

Dutch law, with respect to information exchange in criminal investigations, is to a large extent based on international instruments.[224] Therefore, a short description of the international instruments most relevant for criminal investigations into THB for labour exploitation will be given, before going into the Dutch law provisions with respect to information exchange.

International instruments
International instruments of relevance for information exchange within Europe are the Schengen Implementation Convention,[225] the Treaty of Prüm,[226] the Framework Decision on simplifying information exchange,[227] the

---

[222] Interview with public prosecutor from Regional Office Rotterdam (November 2010); Interview with public prosecutor from Functional Office (July 2010).
[223] One (Den Bosch) sees to agriculture, one (Drechtsteden) to the employment agency sector.
[224] Commentary on international penal law (*Tekst en Commentaar Internationaal Strafrecht*), B. I General Introductory Remarks, point 4. See for an elaborate discussion on the relevant instruments A. Middelburg and C. Rijken, 'The European Legal Framework to Combat THB for Labour Exploitation', Chapter 6 in this book.
[225] The Schengen acquis – Convention implementing the Schengen Agreement between the Governments of the States of the Benelux Economic Union, the Federal Republic of Germany and the French Republic on the gradual abolition of checks at their common borders, 14 June 1985.
[226] Convention between the Kingdom of Belgium, the Federal Republic of Germany, the Kingdom of Spain, the French Republic, the Grand Duchy of Luxembourg, the Kingdom of the Netherlands and the Republic of Austria on the stepping up of cross-border cooperation, particularly in combating terrorism, cross-border crime and illegal migration, 27 May 2005 (Trb. 2005, 197).
[227] Council Framework Decision on simplifying the exchange of information and intelligence between law enforcement authorities of the Member States of the European Union, 18 December 2006, 2006/960/JHA [2006] OJ L386/89, also called the Swedish Framework Decision.

Treaty of Enschede,[228] the Treaty of Senningen, [229] and the EU Convention on Mutual Legal Assistance.[230] Treaties of relevance for information exchange outside Europe are bilateral treaties such as with the United States [231]and Canada[232], as well as the UN Convention against Transnational Organised Crimes,[233] which contains a provision on mutual legal assistance with no less than 30 paragraphs (Article 18).[234]

National law

Book IV, Title X DCCP (International Legal Assistance)

International Legal Assistance is regulated in Book IV, Title X DCCP. This Title contains three parts, of which the first part is of most relevance. This part regulates the execution of international requests for legal assistance, as well as joint investigation teams (see further below).[235] It concerns Articles 552h–552q DCCP.

In so far as a request for legal assistance is based on an international instrument in which the provision of legal assistance is obligatory, the request will be executed 'to the extent possible' (Article 552k sub 1). In the absence of an international instrument, or an instrument in which information exchange is discretionary, the request will be executed provided that the request is 'reasonable' and does not violate the law or a direction issued by the Minister of Justice (Article 552k sub 2). Basically, in such cases, information may only be exchanged when no compulsion measures are to be applied to obtain the information, and the investigating judge does not need to be consulted.[236]

[228] Treaty between the Kingdom of the Netherlands and the Federal Republic of Germany concerning cross-border cooperation by police and in criminal law matters, 2 March 2005 (Trb. 2005, 86 and 241).

[229]Treaty between the Kingdom of the Netherlands, the Kingdom of Belgium and the Grand Duchy of Luxembourg concerning cross-border police intervention, 8 June 2004 (Trb. 2005, 35).

[230] Convention of 29 May 2000 on Mutual Assistance in Criminal Matters between the Member States of the European Union, 29 May 2000 (Trb. 2000, 96).

[231] Kingdom of the Netherlands – US Treaty on Mutual Assistance in Criminal Matters, 12 June 1981 (Trb. 1981, 188).

[232] Treaty between the Kingdom of the Netherlands and Canada on Mutual Assistance in Criminal Matters, 1 May 1991 (Trb. 1991, 85).

[233] See n. 3.

[234] Further details in A. Middelburg and C. Rijken, 'The European Legal Framework to Combat THB for Labour Exploitation', Chapter 6 in this book.

[235] Part 2 regulates legal assistance regarding criminal offences committed on board aeroplanes landed on Dutch territory, and part 3 regulates the transfer and acceptance of criminal prosecution.

[236] Commentary to the DPPC (*T&C Strafvordering 2009*), Book IV, Title X, Part. 1, Introductory remarks, note 2c.

Articles 552l and 552m provide for imperative and discretionary grounds for refusal to execute a request for legal assistance.[237]

On the basis of Article 552i DPPC, in principle, requests for legal assistance need to be transferred to the Public Prosecutors' Service. Also Article 552j emphasises the central role of the Public Prosecutors' Service.[238] In certain circumstances the investigating judge needs to be involved (Articles 552n–552o).

However, the police may provide data to foreign authorities without involvement of the public prosecutor under certain circumstances. Most notably, this is the case if: [239]

a. police data is requested; on the basis of Article 17 of the Police Data Act the police may provide police data to foreign authorities as long as the relevant conditions are met (see further below);
b. no special investigative techniques as referred to in the Articles 126g–126z, 126zd–126zu, 126gg, and 126ff are required to obtain the requested information;
c. no compulsion measures are required to obtain the requested information;
d. the requested information is not used as evidence in criminal proceedings;
e. the requested information does not concern CIE information;
f. none of the grounds for refusal listed in Articles 552k, 552l, and 552m is applicable;
g. the requested information does not concern judicial information that may be provided on the basis of the Judicial Data Protection Act (see further below).

Use of special investigative techniques pursuant to foreign requests for legal assistance

On the basis of Article 552oa sub 1 DCCP, in so far as a valid request for legal assistance based on a treaty so requires, the following special investigative techniques may be used in classical and modern criminal investigations: recording confidential communications (Articles 126l and 126s DCCP), recording telecommunications (phone and e-mail) (Articles 126m and 126t

---

[237] To the extent that the applicable international instruments leave room for the application of the grounds for refusal.

[238] It provides that the public prosecutor who receives the request decides on the (manner of) execution. To the extent that the execution takes place in several regions, each regional public prosecutor is competent to be responsible for the execution of the request. To the extent necessary, this public prosecutor will involve the public prosecutors of the other relevant regions.

[239] Guideline regarding information exchange in the context of mutual legal assistance in criminal matters *[Aanwijzing inzake de informatie-uitwisseling in het kader van de wederzijdse rechtshulp in strafzaken (552iSv)]* (Guideline 552i DPPC) (Stcr. 2008, 232) paras 4.1 and 4.2.

DCCP), and certain of the investigative techniques relating to requesting information concerning telecommunications (Articles 126nd sub 6, 126ne sub 3, 126nf, 126ng, 126ue sub 3, 126uf, 126ug DCCP). Police reports and other objects obtained through the application of these techniques may only be transferred to foreign authorities to the extent that the court allows this (Article 552oa sub 4). Other investigative techniques listed in Book I, Titles IVa–Vc and Ve DCCP[240] may be applied where a valid request for legal assistance so requires, regardless of whether or not this request was based on a treaty (Article 552oa sub 2).

Direct provision of police data on the basis of the Act and Decree on Police Data

Police data may be provided to authorities in another country that are charged with the execution of the police task, or part of the police task, in so far as this is necessary for the due execution of the police task in the Netherlands or the police task in the requesting State (Article 17 sub 2 Police Data Act). The Police Data Act, which entered into force on 1 January 2008, gives the statutory framework for the already existing practice with regard to the exchange of personal and other data between police departments of different countries. Because police data may be provided to authorities that are charged with part of the police task, police data may also be provided to special investigation departments.[241]

The provision of data to foreign authorities is further regulated in the Decree on Police Data in paragraph 5. Paragraph 5 specifies that data may only be exchanged for the purposes of certain listed elements of the police task, and that the data may not be used for other purposes (e.g. as evidence in criminal proceedings) without prior consent from the Dutch Public Prosecutor.[242]

A much more lenient set of rules applies to the exchange of information within the EU pursuant to the Treaty of Prüm and the Swedish Framework Decision. Information must be exchanged under the same requirements as information exchanged with Dutch investigative officers, and may only be denied on the basis of the grounds listed in Article 5:2 of the Decree on Police Data. Information may be exchanged for all elements of the execution of the police task instead of certain specified elements thereof. Also, the Decree on

[240] It concerns Title IVa (classical investigations), V (modern investigations), Va (civilian assistance in classical and modern investigations), Vb (terrorist crimes), Vc (civilian assistance in investigations regarding terrorism), Ve (preliminary investigations).

[241] Commentary on international penal law *[Tekst en commentaar Internationaal Strafrecht]* note 3 with Article 17 Police Data Act.

[242] Decree on Police Data, Article 5:1 sub 2. See also Commentary on international penal law *[Tekst en commentaar Internationaal Strafrecht]*, para 5 Decree on Police Data, introductory remarks, no. 3.

Police Data offers the possibility of direct automated provision of police data within the EU.[243]

Police data may also be provided to Interpol and Europol pursuant to international treaties or statutory provisions.[244] According to the Decree on Police Data, such provision of information to Europol is even obligatory.[245] The provision of information to Interpol is not regulated in the Decree on Police Data. Provision of data to Eurojust is not regulated in the Police Data Act, because it is assumed that the provision of information to Eurojust, in most cases, happens on the basis of Articles 39e and 39f of the Judicial Data Act.[246]

Direct provision of judicial data on the basis of the Judicial Data Protection Act

On the basis of Article 39e sub j of the Judicial Data Protection Act, judicial data may be provided by the Board of Procurators General to foreign legal officers and institutions that, on the basis of international law, have a task in the context of criminal law. On the basis of Article 39f, judicial data may be provided to institutions to the extent necessary on six listed grounds, which include the prevention and investigation of criminal offences.

Outgoing requests for legal assistance

The outgoing requests for legal assistance abroad is not regulated. Determining factors are the treaty, legislation of the State receiving the request, as well as Dutch legislation. If Dutch investigation departments wish to avail themselves of information from a State with whom a treaty has been concluded, the principle of good faith applies.

The Netherlands may trust that the information was legally obtained in the requested country. The information may, even if it was obtained in a manner that does not conform to Dutch policy or legislation (e.g. a certain investigative technique was used that is unknown under Dutch policy/legislation), be used in national criminal investigations, unless it is clear that there is a flagrant violation of the essential principles of law, e.g. the fair trial principle or the 'classic' human rights (e.g. the use of torture and inhuman or degrading treatment).[247]

Dutch police officers may exercise certain criminal investigation powers abroad on the basis of Article 549a DCPP.

Parallel investigations

In parallel investigations, criminal investigations into the same phenomenon are pursued in different countries. In such investigations, police information is

---

[243] Decree on Police Data, Article 5:3.

[244] Police Data Act, Article 17 sub 4.

[245] Decree on Police Data, Article 5:5.

[246] Commentary on international penal law *[Tekst en commentaar Internationaal Strafrecht]* note 4 with Article 17 Police Data Act.

[247] Guideline 552i DPPC (n.239) under 6.

exchanged more directly and intensively, and assistance is requested and provided more directly and intensively.[248]

Joint Investigation Teams

Pursuant to Article 13 of the European Convention on Mutual Assistance in Criminal Matters, Book IV, Title X, Part 1A (sections 552qa–552qu) DPPC regulates the Dutch participation in Joint Investigation Teams (***JITs***). The Guideline Joint Investigation Teams sets rules regarding the establishment, scope, composition and authorities of JITs.[249] Furthermore, Article 5:4 of the Decree on Police Data regulates the provision of police data in the context of JITs. A JIT must be based on a treaty or the EU Framework Decision on JITs and a request for legal assistance. Treaties that provide regulations for JITs are the European Convention on Mutual Assistance in Criminal Matters, the Convention on Mutual Assistance and Cooperation between Customs Administrations, the UNCTOC and the Second Additional Protocol to the European Convention on Mutual Assistance in Criminal Matters.[250]

European Arrest Warrants

The EU Framework Decision regarding the European Arrest Warrant[251] was implemented in Dutch law by means of the act of 29 April 2004.[252] The act applies to the extradition from and to the Netherlands within the European Union. The Public Prosecutor, the investigating judge and the Court of Amsterdam are authorised to deal with incoming European arrest warrants. Every public prosecutor is authorised to issue European arrest warrants.

European Evidence Warrants

The term for implementation terminated on 19 January 2011. The Dutch government has not yet implemented the EU Framework Decision concerning the European Evidence Warrant, but agreement within the

---

[248] Guideline (n. 19) para 15.

[249] Guideline Joint Investigation Teams *[Aanwijzing Joint Investigation Teams]* (Scr. 2008, 45) (Guideline JIT).

[250] Guideline JIT (n.249) under 2.

[251] Council Framework Decision on the European arrest warrant and the surrender procedures between Member States – Statements made by certain Member States on the adoption of the Framework Decision, 13 June 2002, 002/584/JHA (PbEG Official Journal L 190).

[252] Wet van 29 april 2004, Stb. 195, tot implementatie van het kaderbesluit van de Raad van de Europese Unie betreffende het Europees aanhoudingsbevel en de procedures van overlevering tussen de lidstaten van de Europese Unie, zoals deze wet laatstelijk is gewijzigd bij de Wet van 22 December 2005 (Stb. 2006, 24).

Ministerial Council on implementing the law was reached in February 2011. The proposal has now been sent for advice to the Council of State.[253]

Guideline

The Guideline states that, since THB is often transnational and a form of organised crime, international cooperation with foreign and transnational authorities should be actively sought. When, in Dutch criminal investigations, the full THB chain can be revealed by international cooperation, the investigations should include such cooperation. Opportunities for international cooperation, such as requests for legal assistance, parallel investigations and JITs are to be used. [254] Since profits are often transferred abroad, international information exchange is specifically necessary in financial investigations.[255]

2.3.2 Application of legal framework in practice

There is not much information available regarding the international cooperation of Dutch investigative bodies with foreign bodies. Little academic research has been performed in this regard.[256] The BNRM does mention that there are several bottlenecks in international cooperation, such as differences in legal systems and interests.[257] Also one of the interviewees marked the international exchange of information as 'difficult.'[258] In any event, it seems that international cooperation in criminal investigations is more developed in investigations regarding THB for sexual exploitation than in investigations regarding THB for labour exploitation.[259]

Interviewees indicated that most of the information exchange in criminal investigations regarding THB for labour exploitation runs through personal contacts with foreign investigative officers, or through liaison officers. International cooperation depends to a large extent on personal relationships.[260] Use is hardly made of opportunities such as exchanging information with Europol and Interpol. Also little to no use is made of Eurojust's services. To a certain extent, this has to do with attitude; despite the fact that international cooperation is prescribed in the Guideline, it is often felt within investigative departments that they 'can do it themselves' and that there is no need for

---

[253] <http://www.rijksoverheid.nl/documenten-en-publicaties/wetsvoorstellen/2011/02/07/wetsvoorstel-implementatie-kaderbesluit-europees-bewijsverkrijgingsbevel-v-j>.

[254] Guideline (n. 19) para 1.

[255] Ibid, para 7.

[256] Exceptions in relation to THB are: C. Rijken, *Trafficking in Persons. Prosecution from a European Perspective* (Asser Press 2003), and more generally on cooperation and in Dutch J. Koers, *Nederland als verzoekende staat bij de wederzijdse rechtshulp in strafzaken*, (Wolf Legal Publishers 2001)

[257] BNRM7 (n. 6) p. 353.

[258] Interview with senior policy advisor SIOD (July 2010).

[259] Interview with public prosecutor from the National Office (July 2010).

[260] Van Dijk/Ungureanu (n.102) p. 31.

assistance from other (foreign) parties.[261] In the policies of the SIOD, for instance, there is little or no attention paid to international cooperation. It also has to do with the fact that a phone call to a known foreign police officer results in information much quicker than when the formal procedures are followed. In so far as information is found that may be of use for criminal prosecution, this information may be formally requested afterwards in order for the information to be admissible in criminal proceedings. Finally, the little use of Europol can be explained by the fact that certain countries do not make use of it at all. Consequently, there is no information to share or compare, which is Europol's task. Also, no JITs have been established (yet) in THB for labour exploitation cases.[262]

Another factor that hinders information exchange is that the organisation of inspection, investigation and prosecution of labour exploitation differs a lot between European Member States. Also, it is felt that too many national agencies are involved in the combat of THB for labour exploitation (e.g. in the Netherlands: 28 investigative departments, 4 public prosecution departments, the EMM, the RIECs, and the LIEC).[263]

When evidence for the criminal proceedings is collected, it is common to request legal assistance from foreign authorities on the basis of a formal request. Both in the krupuk and the asparagus case (see Part IV), witness testimonies from abroad were obtained through a formal request for legal assistance. It seems as if witness testimonies are the most common, if not the only, way in which evidence is requested from abroad in THB for labour exploitation cases.

The asparagus case shows that the amount of time involved in obtaining the evidence very much depends upon the efficiency of the foreign party dealing with the request.[264] The krupuk case shows that the Dutch authorities involved in the evidence gathering abroad have to deal with cultural differences.

2.4 Summary of findings

2.4.1 Identified obstacles

Not all parties that may detect signs of THB for labour exploitation are always successful at doing so. First of all, this may be caused by too little awareness about the crime, or about the fact that a certain sign may add up to exploitation. It may also be the result of inspectors taking too little initiative to actively ask the victim about his or her position; victims often initially deny or

[261] Interview with senior policy advisor SIOD (July 2010)

[262] Interview with public prosecutor from the National Office (July 2010).

[263] Van Dijk/Ungureanu (n.102) p. 32.

[264] Interview with public prosecutor in the Regional Office Rotterdam (November 2010).

do not recognise their situation for various reasons. It may also be caused by the fact that the (scope of the) crime is still unclear (see Part I).

Furthermore, practice shows that, although the awareness about the need to exchange information has risen within the parties that may detect signs of THB for labour exploitation, this information exchange does not yet function optimally. Such information exchange is essential because a certain situation will often not be recognised as THB as long as different elements of the situation are not brought together and made sense of. As long as the different parties do not exchange information, a certain situation will be perceived as a violation of administrative law, labour law, and maybe even criminal law, but not as THB. First of all, it seems that there is no incentive to pass on warning signs in certain instances. The lack of feedback about what happened to previous information may add to this lack of incentive. In other words, a change of attitude is required. Furthermore, two important instruments designed to facilitate information exchange, the EMM and the RIECs, do not function well. Other factors that temper effective information exchange are that such exchange is subject to complex legal instruments, and that technical hurdles exist, such as the use of different automated systems by the different parties that cannot be synchronised.

As will be described under 'good practices' below, information exchange in concrete criminal investigations – once a suspicion of THB for labour exploitation has arisen – seems to work well. However, structural information exchange, as foreseen by the several policy documents regarding the programmatic approach, does not seem to function well. Cooperation between partner organisations is not always established, most notably since not all parties that should be included are identified. Furthermore, the administrative reports do not (yet) have the desired effect. Moreover, the RIECs and the EMM do not function effectively. Finally, there is no overview of the (outcomes of the) different initiatives that have been taken with regard to the programmatic approach.

Although the Guideline specifies that financial investigations are supposed to be part of all THB investigations, not all the attention given to this part of the investigations is timely and effective. Financial inspectors are not involved, or involved at a late stage of the investigations.

There is not much information on the effectiveness of the different special investigation techniques in THB for labour exploitation cases.

There are many parties that may investigate and prosecute THB. It may be investigated by (different departments of) the regional police departments, the DNR, the KMar, and the SIOD. The investigation and prosecution may be led by the Functional Office, the National Office or one of the Regional Offices of the OM. This means that many different parties need to manage knowledge about THB for labour exploitation, which is, as described in Part I, a very complex crime that is subject to difficulties in interpretation. This does raise the question whether it would not be more efficient to centralise knowledge about and experience of this crime in one investigative department, supervised by one OM department.

There is not much information on international cooperation in THB for labour exploitation cases. In any event, it is clear that too little use is made of instruments like Europol and Interpol. Also the potential of bodies like JITs is not explored sufficiently. In so far as evidence is collected abroad, this mainly seems to comprise witness testimonies.

2.4.2 Good practices

Most of the parties that may detect signs of THB devote attention to this topic by means of training. Also, public campaigns about the awareness of THB for labour exploitation were launched to sensitise 'new' actors such as Sector Organisations about THB.

The awareness of the need to exchange information at an early stage seems to have been raised (e.g. krupuk case).

Multidisciplinary teams are formed in concrete criminal investigations. Furthermore, information exchange between the OM and bodies like the AI and the municipal service responsible for monitoring housing regulations seems to work well. In that way, a good overview of the exploitation (number of hours worked, amount of remuneration, Dutch standards on working hours and remuneration, and housing conditions) can be obtained.

The international cooperation to obtain evidence from abroad seems to be working well, especially if relationships exist as in cases where the person seeking cooperation already knows a colleague in the other country. The fact that the evidence gathering takes place within Europe does not necessarily seem to be an advantage, as seen in the asparagus case described in Part IV.

Part III
Victim protection and assistance

3.1 Identification of victims

The list of parties that play a role in detecting THB, and thus its victims, is long. Besides the parties mentioned in Part 2.2 of this report, lawyers, victim support networks,[265] shelters, youth welfare organisations,[266] and other welfare organisations (e.g. the International Organisation for Migration) may identify victims.

3.2 Legal framework for the protection of the rights of victims of Trafficking in Human Beings for labour exploitation

3.2.1 Assistance to victims

Victims may be referred to CoMensha, which is the national reporting, registration and coordination desk for victims of human trafficking. The police and KMar are obliged to refer victims to CoMensha.[267] The most important tasks of CoMensha are the registration of victims and the coordination of victim support.

CoMensha established local networks throughout the Netherlands with the aim of providing integrated assistance to victims of THB. There are 11 networks. In these networks, all parties that play a role in the shelter and support of victims (e.g. shelter organisations, the police, aid organisations, and lawyers) work together. If a victim is registered with CoMensha, CoMensha helps the victim in receiving shelter. Subsequently, the network (in so far as it is available) arranges for other victim care.[268] The networks are supervised by a care coordinator, or, in the absence of such a care coordinator, by CoMensha. Not every municipality is linked to such a network including a care coordinator.[269] In addition, only eight care coordinators are appointed at the moment.

Chapter B9 of the Aliens Act Implementation Guidelines (*Vreemdelingen-circulaire*) advises law enforcement to inform CoMensha of police actions,

---

[265] CoMensha established local networks throughout the Netherlands with the aim of providing integrated assistance to victims of THB. The networks reported the second most victims to CoMensha in the period 2001–2009.

[266] Child Welfare Council *[Raad voor de Kinderbescherming]*, Youth Care Desks *[Bureaus Jeugdzorg]* and custody social work of the foundation Nidos *[Voogdijmaatschappelijk werk van Stichting Nidos]*.

[267] Paras B9/3.2.6 and 3.2.7.

[268] <http://www.mensenhandel.nl/cms/index.php?option=com_content&task= view&id =7&Itemid=11>.

[269] <http://www.mensenhandel.nl/cms/index.php?option=com_content&task= view&id=39&Itemid=59>. accessed 26 November 2010; BNRM8 (n. 39) p. 187.

possibly involving trafficking victims, before these actions actually take place, so that CoMensha can prepare assistance.[270] The Guideline does not contain a similar provision.

The assistance available for non-Dutch victims of THB is closely connected to the possibility of residence. As such, this assistance will be discussed under the heading 'right to residence' below.

3.2.2 Right to residence

Residence connected to criminal proceedings

Aliens who become victims of THB or who witness THB may be granted a temporary residence permit in accordance with the procedure described in Chapter B9 of the Aliens Act Implementation Guidelines part B (*Vreemdelingencirculaire (B) 2000*). This procedure is typically referred to as the ***B9 procedure***.[271] In theory the B9 procedure has two aims, namely, to serve the prosecution of traffickers, and to serve the interest and wellbeing of the victims and testifying witnesses.[272] However, in practice it turns out that the B9 procedure is primarily used to serve criminal investigation and prosecution, although recent developments give reason to be more optimistic, as will be illustrated below. By granting a temporary residence permit the person remains available for law enforcement. Although grounded in regulations regarding aliens, the B9 procedure also applies to EU citizens and residents from the EER region and Switzerland.[273]

The B9 procedure foresees a reflection period and a temporary residence permit. A victim of THB has the right to a reflection period of a maximum of three months, during which the victim may decide whether or not to report the crime to the police or otherwise cooperate with law enforcement (for conditions to obtain the temporary residence permit, see further below). The expulsion of the alien from Dutch territory is postponed for the duration of this reflection period.[274] The reason for the reflection period is that victims are

---

[270] Para B9/3.2.6.

[271] Article 14 sub 2 Aliens' Act *[Vreemdelingenwet]* provides the basis for the issuance of temporary residence permits for certain goals described in Article 3.4 of the Decree on Aliens *[Vreemdelingenbesluit 2000]*. According to Article 3.4 of the Decree on Aliens, temporary residence permits in connection with the prosecution of THB may be provided under certain limiting conditions. These limiting conditions are described in Article 3.48 of the Aliens' Decree and relate to criminal investigations/prosecution being pursued, and the cooperation of the applicant in such proceedings. The procedure for application and issuance of such residence permits is further described in Chapter B9 of the Aliens Act Implementation Guidelines *[Vreemdelingencirculaire 2000]*

[272] Advice ACVC, De mens beschermd en de handel bestreden, Advisory Commission on immigration, Protect victims and fight human trafficking.

[273] Thus including Iceland, Lichtenstein and Norway.

[274] B9 para 3.2.1.

often too traumatised to immediately take a well-considered decision on whether and to what extent they wish to cooperate with law enforcement.[275] The reflection period is offered by the superintendent of the police. During the reflection period, the alien will stay legally in the Netherlands and can apply for shelter, legal aid, medical and psychological care, and remittance based on the Regulation on Remittance for Aliens of Certain Categories (*RvB*), and medical insurance. The victim is not allowed to work. The reflection period terminates when the victim decides to cooperate or to testify in the criminal proceedings against the trafficker, or decides not to cooperate or testify, when the person leaves the accommodation, applies for a residence permit, or after a period of three months. The reflection period is not open for testifying witnesses.

When a victim files a complaint against the trafficker or otherwise decides to cooperate with law enforcement, this is considered as an application for a temporary residence permit based on B9. In theory, the victim will first have an informative talk with an investigative officer before the actual testimony is recorded, however, in practice, these two can and do collide. The hearing of a victim is in principle conducted by a certificated police officer. The police or KMar file the application for the residence permit with the IND and must inform CoMensha on the application. The IND will take a decision within 24 hours in the case of victims; no time limit applies for testifying witnesses.

A victim of THB may receive a temporary residence permit on the basis of the B9 procedure as long as criminal investigations and/or criminal proceedings are pending against the suspect and the victim reports the crime to the police and/or cooperates with law enforcement. A testifying witness of THB may only receive such a temporary residence permit as long as criminal investigations and/or criminal proceedings are pending against the suspect, the witness reported the crime to the police, and the Minister of Justice deems the presence of the witness in the Netherlands necessary for the criminal investigation and/or prosecution of the suspect.[276] The duration of the temporary residence permit is dependent on the duration of the criminal proceedings. It is granted for a year and may be renewed until 'a decision is taken on the facts' in the criminal proceedings.[277] Upon termination of the criminal procedure, either by conviction, acquittal or dismissal, the legal residence based on B9 terminates as well.[278] During the period of the temporary residence permit on the basis of B9, the victim/witness has the same rights as during the reflection period. In addition, the victim/witness is

[275] B9 para 3.2.

[276] Aliens Decree *[Vreemdelingenbesluit 2000]* Article 3.48.

[277] This may include a decision of the Supreme Court, because it can refer the case back to the Appeal Court which then again has to deal with the facts of the case.

[278] The OM has a monopoly in deciding whether or not to criminally investigate and prosecute a case. However, both victims and testifying witnesses can complain about a decision to dismiss the case at the Court of Appeals in The Hague on the basis of Article 12 DPC. They are allowed to stay in the Netherlands until the Court of Appeals has decided on the complaint.

allowed to work and the remittance is based on the Work and Welfare Act (*Wet Werk en Bijstand*) instead of the *Rvb*.

In case there is the slightest indication that a case of THB exists, the police and/or KMar have to inform the alien of the possibility to report the crime and/or cooperate with law enforcement. In so far as the alien is eligible for the reflection period, the police/KMar also have to inform the alien of this right. These obligations also explicitly exist in cases where the alien is residing in aliens' detention.[279] The Guideline includes indicators for the existence of THB in its annex 3. These indicators are divided in five categories:

a. multiple dependency: i.e. the exploiter also organises accommodation, clothes, transport or that the victim has a debt
b. limitation of basic rights; i.e. isolation and the victim does not have possession of his/her own travel documents
c. working in very bad conditions; i.e. low wages, dangerous work, long working hours, intimidation
d. violation of physical integrity; i.e. (threatened with) violence
e. exploitation takes place on regular basis

The obligations to inform the alien of the possibility of cooperating with law enforcement and to register the victim with CoMensha do not exist for other parties who may come across victims of THB.[280] Furthermore, the Guideline provides that only skilled officers who receive training to interact with (possible) THB victims should interact with such victims, and that it is '*desirable*' that they should be certified.[281] To date, only certain police officers are certified. There are no officers from, e.g. the SIOD, who are certified.[282]

On 22 December 2010 an amendment to the B9 procedure entered into force, adding a paragraph 13 to Chapter B9 of the Aliens Act Implementation Guidelines Part B.[283] According to this amendment, victims of THB who do not cooperate with the investigation and prosecution of THB may also apply for temporary residence status on the basis of Article 3.4 sub 3 of the Decree on Aliens.[284] Such a temporary residence permit is granted if the victim cannot

[279] B9 paras 3.1 and 3.2.

[280] BNRM7 (n. 6) p. 171. The BNRM stresses that parties like the SIID and the AI should also be able and be obliged to point out the B9 possibilities to possible victims.

[281] Guideline (n. 19) p. 6 under 3.

[282] Pursuant to a recommendation from the BNRM, several SIID inspectors received training in order to become certified to hear possible THB victims. However, up to now (February 2011) no certificates have been issued on the basis of this training.

[283] Besluit van de Minister voor Immigratie en Asiel van 14 december 2010, nr. WBV 2010/20, houdende wijziging van de Vreemdelingencirculaire 2000 (22 December 2010 Stc 20701), Article I under F.

[284] Decree on Aliens, Article 3.4 sub 1 lists the goals for which temporary residence permits may be granted. As noted before, prosecution of THB is one of these goals. In addition, Article 3.4 sub 3 Decree on Aliens states that the Minister may issue a temporary residence permit for goals other than those defined in Article 3.4 sub 1.

report the crime or otherwise assist in the investigation and prosecution because of (i) serious threats and/or (ii) medical or psychiatric restraints. The victim must establish these circumstance(s) by means of (a) a declaration from the police which shows that the alien is a victim of THB, and (b) a declaration from the police which shows that the victim cannot be expected to cooperate in the penal proceedings following serious threats from the trafficker in the Netherlands, and/or medical information showing that physical or psychological disorders prevent cooperation in the penal proceedings. As a prerequisite for the temporary residence permit, the victim needs to be sufficiently insured against medical costs. The temporary residence permit has a duration of one year, and cannot be extended. If a victim obtains a temporary residence permit on this basis, he/she is free to work. After a year, the victim may apply for a continued stay permit (see below). The victim may also opt to cooperate in the penal proceedings and obtain a (temporary) residence permit based on B9.

Continued stay after criminal proceedings
After the termination of the residence permit based on B9, there are two possibilities for a victim to apply for a further residence permit. First, a victim may apply for an asylum residence permit or a regular residence permit. Second, there is the possibility of continued stay, in accordance with Article 3.52 of the Aliens Decree (*Vreemdelingenbesluit 2000*), which is further elaborated in Chapter B16/17 of the Aliens Act Implementation Guidelines (*Vreemdelingencirculaire*).

A permit for continued stay may be granted if the victim has been availed of a B9 temporary residence permit for more than three years, regardless of whether the criminal proceedings are still pending or not at the time of application. Apart from that, the victim may apply for a residence permit for continued stay on the basis of urgent reasons of a humanitarian nature, or in cases of poignant individual circumstances. Factors that play a role in granting a residence permit for continued stay are:

- the risks a victim faces upon return to the country of origin, taking into account possible reprisals, and the amount of support that may be received from aid organisations;
- the risk of prosecution in the country of origin (most notably when having worked in prostitution);
- the opportunities for reintegration in the country of origin.

The burden of proof rests with the victim.

Residence regardless of criminal proceedings
Victims of THB who do not wish/dare to report the crime to the police or otherwise cooperate with law enforcement and cannot obtain a temporary residence permit under B9 as extended on 22 December 2010 (see above), may also apply for a residence permit under poignant individual circumstances.

The test is identical to the test for continued stay, i.e. there have to be urgent reasons of a humanitarian nature.

Unaccompanied minors
The stay and care of unaccompanied minors is organised until they are 18 years old. When they turn 18 they have to leave the Netherlands, unless they have a specific ground to stay.

3.2.3 Victims as witnesses in proceedings

In principle, a suspect in criminal proceedings has the right to hear witnesses, including the victim. The interests of protecting the privacy, security and health of the victim on the one hand, should be weighed against the right of the suspect to cross-examine the victim on the other.[285] The OM can propose to hear the victim without the presence of the suspect. Also, the OM may be opposed to a victim, who has not yet reached 18 years of age, being examined at the hearing. The lack of direct examination by the suspect may be remedied by having an examination by the investigating judge, to play a recording of the testimony given by the victim during the hearing, or to hear from the police officers who conducted the examinations. In very limited circumstances, the victim may be labelled as a threatened witness and be examined anonymously. In very limited cases, a witness protection programme exists for such witnesses.[286]

3.2.4 Right to compensation

There are three ways in which a victim may obtain compensation; (i) in criminal proceedings, (ii) in civil proceedings, and (iii) through the Violent Offences Compensation Fund (*Schadefonds Geweldsmisdrijven*). Because civil proceedings are lengthy and costly, the most common route for compensation is to obtain it in criminal proceedings and/or request payment from the Violent Offences Compensation Fund.

Compensation in criminal proceedings
There are three ways in which a victim of a crime committed in the Netherlands may obtain compensation in criminal proceedings; (a) the victim may participate in the criminal proceedings and submit a civil claim, (b) the court may apply a compensation measure (*schadevergoedingsmaatregel*), or (c) the court may apply a special condition of sentence (*bijzondere voorwaarde bij strafoplegging*). Since the introduction of the compensation measure under Dutch law, the special condition of sentence is hardly ever applied. It is more

---

[285] Guideline (n. 19) para 8; Supreme Court, 20 May 2003, LJN: AF5704.
[286] Ibid.

common that a victim submits a claim, and/or the court applies the compensation measure.

In order to file a claim in criminal proceedings, the victim has to fill out a form indicating the type and amount of damages incurred. Contrary to when a civil action is commenced, the victim does not have to pay any court fees to submit the claim. The victim's claim is based on civil law and is of an accessory nature to the criminal proceedings. Most notably, this means that the claim is admissible only to the extent that it does not '*burden the procedure disproportionately*'[287] and the victim has limited opportunities to elaborate on the claim.[288] This disproportionate burden test was introduced on 1 January 2011 by means of the Victim's Position Act.[289] The test for admissibility of the victim's claim used to be that the claim could be '*established easily*'. Under the old legislation, claims for compensation were often (partly) dismissed on the basis that they could not easily be established. Rationale for the amendment is that this should happen less frequently. It remains to be seen what the effect of the new test is.

In principle, the court decides on the claim in its final judgment.[290] In cases where the claim is declared inadmissible, the victim still has the possibility of submitting a civil claim. In cases where the claim is dismissed, this possibility does not exist. If the claim is awarded, the victim has an enforceable title against the convicted person; the victim him/herself is responsible for enforcing the judgment in accordance with the relevant provisions of the Dutch Code of Civil Procedure. In practice, such enforcement is almost always problematic.

Like the victim's claim, the compensation measure is also based on (the scope of) the civil law liability of the perpetrator for damages incurred by the victim as a consequence of the committed crime.[291] The victim may request

[287] Article 361 para 3 DCCP.

[288] The victim may orally substantiate his/her claim each time the public prosecutor pleads, and may submit evidence supporting the claim to the extent this evidence is easily established. The victim cannot bring forward witnesses or experts, but may ask questions regarding his/her damages claim to experts and witnesses called by the public prosecutor and/or the defendant. The victim may also request the public prosecutor to call experts or witnesses for the purposes of testifying on the amount of damages incurred. See AC Bijlsma, Handbook Injured Party *[Handboek benadeelde partij]* (2005) (Bijlsma) p. 80.

[289] Act of 17 December 2009 Strengthening Position of the Victim in Criminal Proceedings *[Wet van 17 december 2009 tot wijziging van het Wetboek van Strafvordering, het Wetboek van Strafrecht en de Wet schadefonds geweldsmisdrijven ter versterking van de positie van het slachtoffer in het strafproces]*.

[290] Articles 335 and 333 DCCP.

[291] F.F. Langemeijer, *The Victim and the Criminal Proceedings [Het slachtoffer en het strafproces]* (Kluwer Deventer 2004) (Langemeijer), p. 87. In this regard, Article 23 WAV may be of relevance. An employment agreement is null and void in the absence of a valid work permit. If an employer employs a person without a valid work permit, the presumption is made that the worker was employed by the employer for a period of a minimum of six months for the customary remuneration in the relevant sector for the customary working

the compensation measure to be applied, or the judge can impose it *ex officio*. If the compensation measure is applied, the suspect becomes liable for payment to the State. As such, the Central Fines Collection Agency (*Centraal Justitieel Incasso Bureau* or ***CJIB***) is responsible for collecting the compensation on behalf of the victim. Often the court decides that the suspect will be imprisoned if he does not fulfil the compensation measure. This term of imprisonment does not relieve the suspect of his obligation to pay the compensation measure. However, the system used to be that the CJIB was relieved of the duty to collect the compensation measure after the suspect was imprisoned, and that the title was transferred to the victim in order for the victim to enforce it. As collection by the CJIB was often unsuccessful, victims became responsible for the enforcement themselves, and, considering the difficulties in enforcing titles against human traffickers, were practically left empty-handed. An important change regarding the collection of the compensation measure was introduced by the Victim's Position Act. If the CJIB is not successful in collecting the claim within eight months of the judgment becoming irrevocable, the victim will receive the money from the State as a kind of advance payment.[292] This regime applies unlimitedly for victims of THB.

Usually, the court applies the compensation measure in so far as the victim's claim is awarded. This means that the victim is not him/herself responsible for enforcing the judgment.

Compensation through the Criminal Injuries Compensation Fund

Victims can also receive an allowance from the Criminal Injuries Compensation Fund (*Schadefonds Geweldsmisdrijven*). According to Article 3 of the Compensation For Victims Of Violent Crimes Act (*Wet Schadefonds Geweldsmisdrijven*), anyone who, due to a violent crime committed in the Netherlands, incurs serious physical or psychological damage can ask for compensation. To that end, the victim has to submit an application. A commission decides on the request and may hear witnesses and experts to receive further information. If a request is dismissed, the victim can appeal at the Appeal Court in The Hague.

Other rights of victims in criminal proceedings

On 1 January 2011 the Victim's Position Act entered into force. The following aspects of this act are most notable:

- The right to be informed about the criminal procedure, and the right to correct treatment and information on the possibilities for compensation for damages.[293]

---

hours (Article 23 WAV). An employee filing a wages claim may base this claim on this presumption.

[292] Art. 36f DCCP.

[293] Art. 51a DCCP. This is actually a codification of well-established practices and they are further elaborated upon in paragraphs 2, 3, and 4 of Article 51.

- The right of access to the file and to add documents to the file.[294] Under certain conditions the prosecutor can refuse access and/or the adding of documents. He needs to inform the victim of this decision and the victim can appeal against this decision.
- Right to judicial aid and an interpreter.[295]
- Right to speak in court.[296] This right equally applies to the bereaved.
- As discussed above, one important aspect is the change in the criteria for the admissibility of damages claims, and the introduction of advance payment by the government.

3.3 Application of the legal framework in practice

Identification and referral

As described (partly) in Part II, many of the organisations that may identify victims of THB are not aware of their role or have become aware only recently. This means that not all (possible) victims are referred to CoMensha for registration and assistance, and to the police, who can – if necessary – explain and offer opportunities under the B9 procedure.

Apart from the difficulties in the identification of victims described in Part II, there have been signs that victims in detention are often not identified by detention personnel and not referred to the police or to CoMensha. BLinN conducted an investigation on this issue in January 2009.[297] In the same research, BLinN concluded that there are '*structural problems*' regarding the role of the police/KMar in the detention context. One of these problems was that victims were not recognised as such when they were arrested.[298] The other problems identified by BLinN concerned the refusal to register the victim's complaint, delay in registering the complaint, and simply quitting without officially dismissing (*seponeren*) the case for lack of evidence.[299] Likewise, BLinN described several difficulties in the work performed by the Repatriation and Departure Service (*Dienst Terugkeer en Vertrek*) of the IND.

---

[294] Art. 51b DCCP. This was previously limited to those who participated in the criminal proceedings but is now extended to all victims. Furthermore, since 1 May 2004 victims could add a written declaration to the file to inform the judge and prosecutor of the consequences of the crime.

[295] Art. 51c DCCP. This right was previously contained in Article 337 DCCP.

[296] Article 51e DCCP. This was introduced on 1 January 2005 in Article 336 and is now included in Article 51e.

[297] Bernice Boermans, 'Uitgebuit en in de bak' *[Exploited and imprisoned!]* (Bonded Labour in the Netherlands (BLinN) 2009, p. 25. BLinN Report (n. 54) p.15.

[298] For instance, if many young migrants arrive at Schiphol International Airport and tell identical (asylum) stories. This fits into the THB victim profiles as established by the police and the RM. Still, BLinN encountered 20 such young migrants in detention after they were denied asylum.

[299] Bernice Boermans, 'Uitgebuit en in de bak' *[Exploited and imprisoned!]* (Bonded Labour in the Netherlands) (BLinN 2009) pp. 29-38.

The most important factors that contribute to the lack of identification are insufficient awareness of THB, perception that labour exploitation is less serious than sexual exploitation, and insufficient awareness of the position that victims take. As mentioned before, often victims do not dare to speak up out of fear of the authorities or the traffickers. But also victims often do not recognise themselves as victims. Especially foreign victims are often not aware of their rights, and are not aware that they may be a victim of THB.[300] In addition, victims often prefer to find other work in the Netherlands, and are afraid that their illegal status will become known to the authorities if they speak up, which would hinder finding other work.[301]

As described above, only the police/KMar are obliged to refer victims to CoMensha. Although other institutions are not under such an obligation, they are free to do so. As shown in the table below, other parties indeed often refer victims of THB (for sexual exploitation and other exploitation) to CoMensha. In 2009, BNRM recommended that all administrative bodies that may come across victims of THB be under the obligation to report them to CoMensha.[302]

Parties reporting victims to CoMensha 1 January 2010–30 November 2010

	Female	**Male**	**Total**[303]	
Lawyers	9	–	9	7
Police	515	65	580	1
KMar	36	2	38	4/5
SIOD	21	17	38	4/5
Networks	73	11	84	2
MO/VO	25	–	25	6
Victim him/herself	5	2	7	8
Other	74	4	78	3
Total	**758**	**101**	**859**	

Assistance

The lack of safe and suitable shelter is a substantial problem, especially for male victims. In June 2010 a pilot was started with shelter specifically for THB victims. The rationale is that the needs of victims will be better addressed if they are sheltered in a place that specialises in THB victims. In this pilot, 50 places were made available at three different locations, where victims may

---

[300] BNRM7 (n. 6) p. 514; BNRM8 (n. 39) p. 50.

[301] Interview with Project Leader BLinN (November 2010).

[302] BNRM7 (n. 6) p. 224; Recommendation 42, p. 606.

[303] The total number of reporting parties is higher than the total number of reported victims; some victims are reported by more than one party.

reside for a period of three months.[304] Forty of these places are reserved for women, 10 for men.[305] However, since subsequent shelter is not well-arranged, the expectation is that these places will be filled quickly, and that the problems will not be resolved. The responsibility for subsequent shelter lies with the municipalities.[306] In addition, a pilot was started in The Hague, Amsterdam, Rotterdam and Utrecht in 2008 whereby 10 places for male victims of domestic violence and THB were established. The duration of this pilot was extended to the end of 2011.[307] Two out of the 10 places are reserved for victims of THB.[308]

The lack of shelter is illustrated by the krupuk case (discussed in Part IV). In that case, the SIOD themselves arranged shelter for the victims in a hotel. Later, the victims were placed in a shelter that lay around the corner from the place where they had been exploited.[309]

CoMensha does not seem to be informed about actions taken by the investigative departments before these actions take place, as the B9 procedure suggests. Considering the limited shelter availability, it is difficult for CoMensha to find appropriate shelter pursuant to police operations.

The police play a central role in the B9 procedure. This means that, for instance, if the SIOD investigates a case (for instance, when the AI found indications of THB and referred the matter to the SIOD), the SIOD is dependent on the police for the application of a reflection period or residence permit. It is not definite that the police will act immediately the SIOD requests them to, and the division of tasks between the SIOD and the police in such situations is not clear.[310] Some might feel the need to first see or even hear the victims. The same situation exists in cases where institutions and authorities other than the police find indications of THB, such as civil servants or the municipalities, the fire brigade, etc. The problems in relation to the central role of the police and the connection between criminal law and migration law are discussed in the summary of findings below.

Compensation

In general, figures from the BNRM show that a relatively small number of THB victims file a claim for damages.[311] The amount of damages awarded is

---

[304] BNRM8 (n. 39) pp. 45-47.

[305] Task Force Progress Report (n. 211) p. 5.

[306] BNRM8 (n. 39) pp. 45-47.

[307] <http://www.trouw.nl/nieuws/nederland/article3280715.ece/Opvang_voor_ bedreigde mannen_is_ populair.html> accessed 3 November 2010.

[308] BNRM8 (n. 39) p. 50.

[309] BNRM7 (n. 6) p. 136. Also F. van Dijk and P. Vonk, 'The European efforts in combating human trafficking for the purpose of labour exploitation; on milestones, migration, Member States and mutual assistance?', Chapter 9 in this book.

[310] Interview with Project Leader BLinN (November 2010).

[311] In 2007 108 criminal cases for human trafficking were recorded, meaning that there were at least 108 victims who could submit a damages claim. Only 37 (alleged) trafficking

typically low, most notably since claims are often declared inadmissible in part or in full because they would not be 'easily established.' No cases under the new standard, i.e. that claims may not 'burden the procedure disproportionately' have become known to the authors yet. Usually, in cases where a victim's claim is awarded, a compensation measure to the same amount is applied. Under the old system (up to 1 January 2011), the collection of such compensation measures was problematic, and victims often became responsible for enforcing the title themselves, meaning that, in effect, they remained empty-handed. There are no cases known to the authors yet under the new system, under which the State would have to pay the amount due to the victim under the compensation measure, in case the perpetrator does not comply with the measure.

With regard to THB for labour exploitation specifically, the following may be noted. Out of the judgments known to the authors, 10 convictions for THB for labour exploitation were rendered. In only four of these cases, a claim for damages was awarded to the victim.[312] In all of these four cases, a compensation measure was also applied.

The SIOD and the AI can be very helpful in determining the amount of money to be claimed. Aside from sexual services, for other forms of labour, minimum wages have been established as well as working hours and holiday allowances. In this way it becomes clearer what the profit of the exploiter has been in a particular case. Since it falls to the expertise of the SIOD and the labour inspectorate to trace cases in which these rules have been violated and to calculate the profit made, their reports and investigations can be very helpful in determining the amount of a claim in any particular case. This, for instance, was the case in the asparagus case (see Part IV), where the labour inspectorate had fined the suspect year after year and had a complete file on the violations of social laws. The prosecutor made use of these reports to make a calculation for the claim, but also in an attempt to prove the illegal practices. This information should also be made available to the victims for their compensation claim.

3.4 Summary of findings

3.4.1 Identified obstacles

Not all victims are identified as such. Reasons for this are: that parties that may identify victims are insufficiently aware of THB, the perception exists that

---

victims did so in 2007, which means that approximately 30% or less of victims submitted a damages claim.

[312] It concerns District Court Utrecht, 17 June 2008, LJN: BD7426, District Court Haarlem, 24 April 2009, LJN: BI3519, District Court The Hague, 18 March 2010, LJN: BL8022; District Court Haarlem, 8 December 2010, LJN: BO8985.

labour exploitation is less serious than sexual exploitation, and that the victims remain silent about or deny their victimhood. Furthermore, there is no obligation to refer victims to the police, whereas the police are the only party that may ensure that a victim can avail him/herself of the possibilities outlined in the B9 procedure (see below). Also, only the police and the KMar have the obligation to report and refer victims to CoMensha.

Victim care is not centralised and differs by municipality. Not every municipality has a care network and care coordinator. Furthermore, there is insufficient shelter for victims of THB.

One of the major problems in relation to the B9 procedure is the link between criminal law and migration law, and the fact that the police have a decisive role in the application of B9.

The link with criminal law is threefold:

- In general, cooperation with law enforcement or reporting the crime is a prerequisite for a victim being granted a reflection period or temporary residence permit based on B9, unless a victim falls within the new category under paragraph 13.
- The legal status of the victim is dependent upon the duration of the criminal investigations. When the authorities decide to dismiss the case, or decide not to investigate the case, the victim loses his/her legal status based on B9.
- The legal status of the victim is dependent upon the duration and outcome of the criminal proceedings. If there is a conviction for THB, the person can be granted an extended residence permit. If the suspect is acquitted from THB, the victim will lose his/her legal status regardless of the reasons for the acquittal. An exception is made in cases where the victim has been residing in the Netherlands for more than three years on a temporary residence permit.

The central role of the police/KMar is based on the following:

- The police/KMar are the only parties that are obliged to report victims to CoMensha.
- The police/KMar are the only parties that are obliged to inform a (possible) victim about the possibility of cooperating with law enforcement or reporting the crime.
- Since only certain police officers are certified to interact with victims of THB, only these police officers can do the admission and examination of THB victims.
- Applications for and the granting of the reflection period and temporary residence permits are run through the police/KMar.

First of all, this means that if a victim is not referred to the police, or does not dare to cooperate with the police, he/she cannot avail him/herself of the possibilities outlined in the B9 procedure.

Secondly, it means that other parties that may identify victims of THB are dependent on the police for ensuring the victim's rights under the B9 procedure. Since, in the case of labour exploitation, many more authorities and organisations other than the police are likely to find indications of THB (e.g. the AI, SIOD), there is a risk that victims and witnesses will not be granted the reflection period or the temporary residence permit, simply because the police are not (always) directly involved in the case, or only at a later stage. Furthermore, the fact that only police officers may interact with (possible) victims means that, for instance, when the SIOD is involved, the division of tasks becomes unclear and the SIOD is dependent on the police to inform the victim about his/her rights under the B9 procedure.

Thirdly, the tasks related to migration status are not primarily tasks for law enforcement officers and it seems that the police are taking over some of the tasks of the IND. Most notably, it was reported and expressed during the interviews that law enforcement officers often make a judgement on whether, and to what extent, the information given will lead to a successful investigation and prosecution. If they think the chances are low, they will not offer the reflection period. Also, the evaluation of whether a successful investigation and prosecution will be conducted seems to indicate to the IND whether or not to grant an application for temporary stay. Furthermore, this places the police in a difficult position as, on the one hand, they have a responsibility for the wellbeing of victims and, on the other, they have an interest in getting the victim to testify. To make it even more complicated, the information given by the victim is decisive in the granting of a residence permit. Although formally, the fact that there are indications of a successful investigation is irrelevant, it becomes decisive in the way the (application of the) B9 regulation is structured at the moment. To make the procedure more transparent the IND must act more independently and victims must be given the opportunity to apply for the reflection period and residence permit themselves at the immigration service.

Fourthly, the police are occupied by the admission of victims and witnesses because the admissions process can only be done by certified officers. This means that it may take a while before a victim can get an appointment with the police. In the meantime, the victim does not have legal status, shelter or financial support and is dependent on other institutions and persons.[313] In general, the relief for victims before they may avail themselves of B9 are inadequate.

Fifthly, an important consequence of the link between criminal law and immigration law and the fact that the police are instrumental in safeguarding rights under the B9 procedure is that if a case is not dealt with under criminal law, there are no grounds for the B9 procedure. In some cases, it seems more efficient to impose administrative fines upon employers that do not respect

---

[313] Yearly report CoMensha 2009, p. 8.

labour legislation, than to act under criminal law. In fact, this is an important part of the policy to combat organised crime in the Netherlands. In such cases, victims cannot apply for a residence permit based on B9 or apply for the reflection period.

Another problem in relation to the B9 procedure is that it is not always applied to EU citizens.

The burden of proof to establish urgent reasons of a humanitarian nature (a condition of obtaining a residence permit for continued stay after expiration of a B9 permit) rests with the applicant. It is very difficult to show that it is too dangerous to return to the home country, that shelter/support in the home country is insufficient, or that there is no possibility of reintegration into society.[314]

There is insufficient shelter for victims of THB, in particular male victims.

Victim care is not organised centrally and differs by region. There are insufficient networks and care coordinators.

The system of compensation in criminal proceedings is not adequate. First of all, claims are often declared (for a large part) inadmissible because they would not be 'easily established'. This test for admissibility has been replaced since 1 January 2011 by a new test that the claim may not 'burden the criminal procedure disproportionately'. It remains to be seen what the consequence of this newly introduced test is. Secondly, only a small number of victims of THB submit a claim for damages. Thirdly, it is difficult to prove a claim for damages, not in the least because if the evidence is extensive this would mean that the claim cannot be 'easily established.' Again, it remains to be seen whether more extensive evidence will be considered now that the test for admissibility has been amended. Also, information established in the proceedings for the deprivation of illegally obtained profits, that may well substantiate the victim's damages claim, is not automatically taken into account in the establishment of the victim's claim. This is partly due to the fact that deprivation proceedings run independently of the criminal proceedings against the suspect, and may even continue after the suspect has been convicted. In the light of the fact that financial investigations are to be part of the criminal investigations into THB from an early stage,[315] the information collected in the context of the deprivation proceedings should be taken into account in the decision on the victim's claim.

3.4.2 Good practices

The residence permit and the assistance and protection of victims is not fully dependent on the intention of the victim to testify in a case, as used to be the case under Dutch law, but cooperation with law enforcement otherwise suffices. Furthermore, a new provision has been included making it possible in certain

---

[314] Interview with victim support lawyer (November 2010).

[315] Cf. Guideline (n. 19).

cases to apply B9 without cooperating with law enforcement, bringing Dutch law further into compliance with Article 12(6) of the Warsaw Convention.

There are some positive developments with regard to compensation. First, the test for the admissibility of compensation claims in criminal proceedings has been amended since 1 January 2011. It is hoped that this will mean that compensation claims are declared inadmissible less frequently. Also, courts tend to apply a compensation measure in so far as a victim's claim is awarded. It is recommended that this practice is continued in the light of the introduction of the advance payment; in so far as the perpetrator does not comply with the compensation measure, the State will pay the amount to the victim. Finally, there is a lot of emphasis on financial investigations in THB cases. It would be very helpful if the information obtained in financial investigations is made available in the context of the victim's damages claims.

Part IV
Case studies

Two cases regarding THB for labour exploitation that were recently investigated and prosecuted in the Netherlands will be discussed in this Part IV.

The asparagus case

Each asparagus season, foreign workers worked on the asparagus farm of suspect J. In 2009, the AI, the municipality, and the police had been aware that for years J. had not adhered to the rules regarding the employment of foreign persons.[316] After discussions between the mayor, the chief of police and the public prosecutor's department (the so-called 'triangle-discussions' or *driehoeksoverleg*), in 2008 the municipality decided to outlaw the situation administratively on the basis of the Housing Act. J. tried to oppose this by submitting a request for an injunction, but the injunction was denied. Although during the injunction hearing it transpired that the employees were locked in overnight, and that one foreign worker had informed the police of maltreatment, the decision was taken to act administratively and not criminally. The premises were cleared on 15 May 2009. During the clearance operation, 55 workers of Romanian, Polish, and Portuguese origin were found at the premises. The mayor declared to the press that the circumstances in which the workers were found were '*reminiscent more of a form of slavery than a modern business*.'

Despite the fact that the circumstances were described by the mayor as '*a form of slavery*', and the AI had information indicating THB, initially no penal action was taken against J. The case drew much attention in the local and national media, as well as politically. After some time, the OM decided to start preliminary investigations and later criminal investigations into THB for labour exploitation. The investigations were conducted by the DNR, the regional police Brabant South East, the Aliens Police, the SIOD and the AI, and supervised by the regional office of the OM. The division of tasks was decided upon by the Regional Office and the Functional Office. The cooperation between the Regional Office and the AI in the THB investigations was very good. Because the AI had been monitoring J. since 2005, they had extensive documentation on the situation. Their extensive documentation was shared with the public prosecutor. On the basis of that documentation, the public prosecutor could get a clear picture of the extent of exploitation (duration and economic gain).

[316] In four years as of 2005, the AI applied fines to the amount of €566,250 for illegal employment, not paying minimum wages and not reporting an accident. The police had received complaints of maltreatment, intimidation, underpayment and the withholding of identity papers. The municipality was aware that foreign workers were living at J's premises in violation of the housing regulations.

It transpired that J. operated alone, with some assistance from her mother and brother. Toni, a Romanian employee, functioned as intermediary between employees and J. Also a certain Mr. Stijnen was involved, who is married to a Romanian woman and who lives in Romania. He owns a camp site there. He recruited for J. by placing an advertisement in a local newspaper and by giving J´s contact details to interested persons.

It was decided to focus on the period March–June 2009. In this period, about 70 victims were identified, ¾ of whom were male and ¼ female. Of the victims identified, 15 were interviewed.[317] Most of them had returned to their home country. All were interviewed after their repatriation by the Dutch police in cooperation with the foreign authorities.[318] The timing of their interviews depended on the pace with which the requests for international legal assistance were processed in the respective countries, and how active the liaison was. The requests for international legal assistance were sent simultaneously. In Portugal, additional testimonies were conducted by the Portuguese police (without judge commissioner, counsel, or public prosecutor being present). The defence wanted to question these persons further. This request was submitted in April 2010 to the judge commissioner, who transferred the request to Portugal for videoconferencing. However, videoconferencing is impossible in Portugal. Therefore, the rogatory letter still has to be performed, and the judge commissioner, defence counsel and public prosecutor will travel to Portugal to hear the victims a third time. This has led to a lot of delay in the proceedings. Consequently, the first hearing on the merits of the case has been postponed several times and is still pending.

Although in total at least six signs of THB were known at the time of clearing the premises, the workers were not informed about the B9 procedure, nor was the reflection period offered to them. The employees were not registered with CoMensha. Although they had a claim for unpaid wages against J., a group of 36 Romanian victims preferred to return home without money. The municipality arranged for a bus. Before they entered the bus, the municipality had them sign an agreement in which it was stated that the victims would repay the cost of the travel back home. That same day the victims returned back home. They did not receive after- care in their country of origin. The remaining workers, about 20, chose to remain working for J. After all, they would be paid at the end of the season and were hoping to actually receive the money if they remained working for J. Several weeks after the clearance, the municipality gave permission for the workers to be housed in tents at J's premises. Also, at the end of May the UWV granted 35 work permit applications that J. had applied for, despite the fact that employees were found under bad conditions and criminal investigations against J. were pending. The workers who did remain at J's farm were informed about their

[317] 2 Polish, 9 Romanian, and 4 Portuguese persons.

[318] The Romanians were interviewed in October 2009, the Polish in November 2009, and the Portuguese in January 2010.

rights at a later stage by the police, on the basis of the B9 procedure. They did not avail themselves of these rights.

All the victims who testified received a letter in their own language with information about the possibility of joining the criminal proceedings and submitting a claim. Five victims are taking this opportunity.

The krupuk case

On 8 July 2009 and 23 July 2009, the CIE received reports regarding illegal Asian people being housed at Herman Costerstraat 264 under poor conditions who were working in the owner's satay factory. After the first report, an observation camera was placed to observe Herman Costerstraat 264, but no unusual movements were noticed. Discussions between the SIOD and the public prosecutor's office resulted in the conclusion that there was no reason for criminal investigations, since there was no reasonable suspicion of guilt. Since mention had been made about very poor conditions and the substantial number of persons that were residing at the same address, it was decided to inform the DSO of the municipality in The Hague, which is responsible for monitoring housing regulations. The DSO decided with the Aliens Police to inspect Herman Costerstraat 264 on 28 July 2009 at 12:00 hrs. If it turned out that there were large numbers of illegal persons residing and working in the house, the SIOD and the public prosecutor's office could decide whether or not to start criminal investigations. On 28 July 2009 at 10:00 hrs the SIOD received a report that one day earlier a report had been made to the Aliens Police in The Hague that there were illegal people residing at Herman Costerstraat 246 and that sounds coming from the house suggested that people were working there. On the basis of that information, the suspicion arose that the first reports to the CIE had erroneously referred to Herman Costerstraat 264 instead of 246. When the registers were checked, it turned out that the inhabitants of Herman Costerstraat 246 owned an Indonesian shop. It was also known to the DSO that deep frying pans had been emptied in the municipal back garden of Herman Costerstraat 246. This did match the information received by the CIE. On this basis, it was decided to start criminal investigations after all.

It turned out that indeed there was a large number of persons present in the building. The living and working conditions at this address, as well as at the address where the shop was located, were very poor. The 11 persons found at Herman Costerstraat 246 who were illegally residing in the Netherlands were taken by the Aliens Police. The owner of the house and his wife were arrested by the SIOD. A third person, an illegal Indonesian male who had his own room with air-conditioning and who was involved in dividing the tasks, was also made a suspect. Later on in the investigations, a contact person for the agents in Indonesia (responsible for recruiting, smuggling, making travel arrangements) was also considered a suspect and arrested.

On 31 July 2009 the main suspects were brought before the investigating judge. The two male suspects (the house owner and the Indonesian intermediary) were detained; the woman (the partner of the house owner) was released under the condition that she remained a suspect and as such should remain available for investigations (*geschorst*). The public prosecutor subsequently had her phone tapped, which revealed the abovementioned contact person in Indonesia.

Testimonies were taken from all illegal persons encountered. From their statements and the conditions established during the search of the premises, the suspicion arose that the workers had been exploited. They had to work long days for a small salary, and had to pay a high price for a mattress on the floor. They did not speak Dutch, did not know the Netherlands, did not have a residence status there, had no money, and no family or friends around as back-up. Criminal investigations into THB were started under supervision of the Functional Office. The public prosecutor decided to bring charges of THB primarily, and human smuggling additionally. According to the public prosecutor, the leading factor in the charge of THB was that the employer had control over both the working and living conditions of the victims, which could be connected to the limitation of a person's freedom. The directorate responsible for labour conditions within the AI was requested to draft a report on the labour conditions. All (potential) victims were interviewed in that context. The examinations were filmed.

On 3 May 2010 the District Court in The Hague rendered its judgment (the judgment) in the case against the owner of the house. The judgments in the cases of the other three suspects have not been published. The house owner was found guilty of (jointly committing) THB under Section 273 sub 1 under 1, 4 and 6. He was sentenced to 4 years' imprisonment. Due to the seriousness of the violations committed by the suspect, the court applied a higher sentence than requested by the public prosecutor.

The Aliens Police offered the reflection period outlined in the B9 procedure to the workers that were found during the search. Four of the (potential) victims availed themselves of the reflection period; the others chose to return to Indonesia. All (potential) victims were reported to CoMensha. Because CoMensha could not find shelter for the four (potential) victims, the SIOD arranged shelter in hotels and in a holiday house. More than a week later, places became available in a shelter arranged by CoMensha, which was located two streets away from the house where they had been exploited.

Lessons learnt from the asparagus and krupuk cases

Both cases illustrate clearly that without effective cooperation and sharing of information between the parties that may detect signs of THB, a particular situation can be perceived as a combination of different violations of administrative, labour and maybe even criminal law, but not as THB. The asparagus case is an example of the different authorities (i.e. the AI, municipality, police) not communicating with each other, resulting in a very late realisation that this situation possibly amounted to THB. One of the consequences was that many victims returned to their home countries without receiving assistance. Also, the UWV granted work permits to J. despite the fact that employees were found under bad conditions and criminal investigations against J. were pending. The krupuk case is an example of effective cooperation and sharing of information between the relevant authorities at an early stage (i.e. the DSO, Aliens Police, SIOD, and public prosecutor), leading to an early detection of THB. The authorities involved were well aware that THB could be at stake. In the search that was performed, there was a clear understanding about the role of the different actors involved. The SIOD and the Aliens Police, for instance, agreed that if only illegal employment was concerned, the Aliens Police would take the lead and the workers would be brought to aliens' detention. However, if there was also poor labour conditions, the SIOD would take the lead and investigate whether this was a case of THB.

In both criminal investigations specific information from certain (administrative) authorities (the AI, DSO, and Aliens Police) on living and working conditions was used to establish the element of exploitation.

The asparagus case shows that the perception seems to be that labour exploitation is less serious than sexual exploitation. It is hard to imagine that, should the workers have been sex workers, they would have been put on a bus to be returned home at their own cost.

The public prosecutor, in both the asparagus and the krupuk case, indicated that financial specialists should be involved from the start of the investigations. This is of relevance for painting a picture about the financial profit the suspect made. According to the Supreme Court decision in the Chinese restaurant case, that is of relevance to determine whether the workers were being exploited.

Finally, the krupuk case underlined that there is insufficient shelter for male victims. The SIOD first arranged shelter for them. After spaces had become available, the victims were then taken to a location close to where they had been exploited. This does not seem to be an ideal situation.

Part V
Recommendations

5.1 Recommendations regarding the definition of Trafficking in Human Beings for labour exploitation

1) A framework for the interpretation of 'exploitation' in the sense of Section 273f sub 2 DPC should be designed. We propose a framework along the following lines:
The following elements may add to exploitation:
   (i) unwillingness of the victim to perform the labour/services,[319]
   (ii) poor labour conditions,[320]
   (iii) profit obtained by the suspect on the basis of labour/services performed by the victim.

   In case any – or a combination – of these elements is present, exploitation may be established if the situation is excessive, taking into account Dutch/European standards. The elements are 'communication vessels'; a mere deviation from Dutch/European labour standards is insufficient if the victim was not in any way coerced to perform the

---

[319] Indicators of unwillingness (not limitative):
a. means of coercion (listed in Section 273f sub 1(1) or other) are used to have the victim perform labour/services (e.g. the suspect imposes debts upon the victim);
b. victim is not free to leave the situation (e.g. the victim is socially isolated by the suspect, and/or the suspect keeps the identity papers of the victim, and/or the suspect does not pay out sufficient wages for the victim to leave);
c. victim is under the perception that he/she is not to free to leave the situation (e.g. suspect creates or stimulates fear of Dutch authorities).
It should be noted that consent of the victim is irrelevant if any means of coercion is used by the suspect aimed at making the victim perform work/services. Conditional intent *[voorwaardelijke opzet]* is sufficient to establish that means of coercion were used in order to persuade the victim to perform the work/services.
Other elements supporting the conclusion that there is a certain extent of unwillingness may be found in Annex 3 to the Guideline.

[320] Relevant labour conditions (not limitative):
a. working hours;
b. amount of remuneration;
c. other labour conditions (e.g. having to work under hazardous circumstances, standing, working under high temperatures, and/or under (other) conditions mentioned in Annex 3 to the Guideline);
d. to the extent the suspect provided housing for the victim: conditions under which the victims are living, and for what price (e.g. having to pay 40% of remuneration for renting a mattress that is placed shoulder-to-shoulder to other mattresses).

work/services and the suspect had no or limited gain from the work performed by the victim. If, on the other hand, the victim was in any way coerced to perform the work/services and/or the suspect made substantial profits from the work/services performed by the victim, exploitation may be established in so far as the situation may be labelled as excessive in the context of Dutch standards. In order to establish whether a situation is excessive, due notice should be taken of the fact that the seriousness of the situation may be taken into account in determining the punishment.[321] In other words, the situation needs to be serious, but there is no need to interpret the meaning of 'excessiveness' very restrictively.

2) The scope of Section 273f sub 1(4) should be clarified. We propose to limit the scope, in the sense that Section 273f sub 1(4) only applies in cases of excessive situations. Again, Dutch/European standards need to be taken into consideration, and due notice should be taken of the fact that the seriousness of the situation may be taken into account in determining the punishment. Cases such as District Court Haarlem, 8 December 2010, LJN: BO8985, that are typical cases of deceit under Section 326 DPC, *and nothing more*, should be tried on the basis of deceit, not on the basis of THB.
3) It should be clarified which standards apply to the question whether a situation is exploitative or not, taking into consideration (i) that European legislation refers to standards of the host country (workers), standards determined by the self-employed (self-employed persons) or a combination of those (posted workers), and (ii) that these standards differ considerably across the EU.
4) Part of the complexity of Section 273f DPC originates from the fact that the provision attempts to cover many different acts that constitute THB. It may add to the clarity of the concept of THB to make distinct provisions regarding (i) sexual exploitation, (ii) labour exploitation, and (iii) forced organ donation. Also, it may provide clarity if the trafficking act and exploitation are penalised in separate (sub-) provisions. The provision on labour exploitation could be formulated as follows:

   1 Guilty of trafficking in human beings for labour exploitation and as such liable to a term of imprisonment not exceeding eight years and/or a fifth category fine shall be any person who:
      1° takes any action with the intent to exploit another person or have that person exploited;
      2° takes any action he knows or may reasonably be expected to know will result in another person being exploited;
      3° exploits another person;
      4° wilfully profits from the exploitation of another person.

[321] Cf. conclusion Advocate-General (Knigge) accompanying the decision of the Supreme Court of the Netherlands, 27 October 2009, LJN: BI7097.

2 Means of coercion include coercion, violence or any other act or the threat of violence or any other act, extortion, fraud, deception, abuse of authority arising from the actual state of affairs, abuse of a vulnerable position, and giving or receiving payments or benefits in order to obtain the consent of a person who has control over another person.

3 Exploitation comprises at least forced or compulsory labour or services, slavery, slavery-like practices or servitude.

4 Section 273f paragraphs 3 up to and including 6 DPC apply simultaneously.

5) The distinction between trafficking and labour exploitation may also be made by including a separate provision on labour exploitation as such, in the DPC. If this is done, it should be guaranteed that victims receive all assistance that is accorded to THB victims in international instruments.
6) Courts need to specify which paragraph of Section 273f paragraph 1 DPC they are considering, which elements need to be established pursuant to the relevant paragraph(s), and to what extent such elements are established in the case at hand.
7) THB for labour exploitation is still perceived to be less serious than THB for sexual exploitation. Initiatives such as public information campaigns raising awareness about this phenomenon should be continued.
8) In order to effectively combat THB, more insight should be created with respect to the nature and scope of victims and perpetrators in the Netherlands. Therefore, we recommend that
   a. the OM and investigative services register THB for labour exploitation cases; i.e. the number of reports made, the number of investigations started, the outcome of the investigations, etc.;
   b. the OM, the investigative services and CoMensha register information regarding the age, gender, and cultural background of victims and perpetrators by the sector in which the (alleged) exploitation took place.

5.2 Recommendations regarding investigation and prosecution

1) Parties that may detect signs of THB for labour exploitation should be aware of this crime and of the elements that may add up to THB.[322] Therefore:

[322] Examples of such parties are the Aliens Police, the police, the AI, the RM, the IND, municipal bodies monitoring housing regulations, Chamber of Commerce, Labour Associations, Sector Organisations, Employee Councils, embassies and consulates, the Employee Insurance Agency, and the employment agency sector.

a. training efforts should be pursued, intensified and repeated;
b. the instructions to officials working for the abovementioned parties should as standard include that the officials should actively look for and report signs of THB.
c. officials should be aware of the perception of victims, since for many reasons they often do not dare to speak up about their situation.

2) Parties involved in the combat of THB for labour exploitation in the EU should receive joint training and/or exchange know-how.
3) 'New' actors – i.e. those not typically involved in the combat of THB for sexual exploitation – should be identified and made aware of THB for labour exploitation. There may be a role here for the Task Force.
4) Signs of THB need to be exchanged. Apart from the solution of technical problems regarding information exchange within the EMM and RIECs, attitude with regard to information exchange needs to be improved. Individuals who possess information that may indicate THB should be aware of the importance of exchanging such information. Individuals receiving information should provide feedback to the provider about what actions were taken on the basis of the information received, in order to create the incentive to continue information exchange.
5) Research should be conducted with respect to the outcome of the initiatives taken to exchange information on a structural basis between actors in the combat against THB for labour exploitation. Most notably, this research should include whether the complexity of privacy legislation and data protection poses hurdles to such information exchange.
6) Information from the AI and municipal services responsible for monitoring housing regulations should be made available in the context of criminal proceedings in order to establish the element of exploitation.
7) Research should be conducted to determine whether it is feasible to centralise all THB for labour exploitation investigations with the SIOD, considering their expertise with labour conditions.
8) Financial investigations should be started at an early stage in the criminal proceedings. The information obtained in such investigations should be used not only for establishing the illegally obtained profits, but also to establish the victim's losses.
9) Research should be conducted regarding the effective use of special investigation techniques in THB cases.
10) Research should be conducted regarding the effectiveness of international information exchange between investigative departments.
11) The possibilities for information exchange in international situations, such as the establishment of JITs, information exchange through EUROPOL and Interpol, should be taken advantage of more frequently by the Dutch investigative bodies.

5.3 Recommendations regarding victim protection

1) All parties that may come across victims of THB for labour exploitation[323] should:
   a. create awareness amongst their officials about THB by means of (continuous) training. In this training, attention should be given to the position of the victim, and the perception that labour exploitation is less serious than sexual exploitation.
   b. (be obliged to) refer victims – as long as the victims consent – to the police or make clear agreements with another party regarding victim referral (e.g. the AI could agree with the SIOD that the SIOD refers victims to the police).
   c. (be obliged to) report victims to CoMensha or make clear agreements with another party regarding victim reporting (e.g. the AI could agree with the SIOD that the SIOD reports victims to CoMensha).
2) The identification of THB victims in aliens' detention should be improved.
3) Possibilities to further de-link criminal law and migration law should be investigated.
4) Research – taking into account the practice of States like Belgium and Italy – should be done as to whether victims should be enabled to apply for the reflection period and temporary residence permit at the IND themselves or have CoMensha do it on their behalf.
5) Further research should be conducted into the needs of victims of THB in general, and the needs of victims of THB for labour exploitation in particular, in order to find out to what extent the support provided does meet the needs of THB victims.
6) The government should assign funds so that more victim support networks may be created.
7) The government should assign funds in order that more shelter accommodation may be created, especially for men.
8) SIOD officers should be certified in order to enable them to offer the reflection period under B9 and to interact with victims.
9) The burden of proof for continued stay should be reversed.
10) Information from parties like the AI and the municipal division for checking housing regulations should be made available to victims in order to support their damages claim, or should otherwise be taken into account in the decision on the victim's claim.
11) Deprivation proceedings should be run simultaneously with the main criminal proceedings. Information from the deprivation proceedings

[323] Examples are the parties mentioned in the preceding footnote, as well as lawyers, victim support networks, shelters, youth welfare organisations, and other welfare organisations.

should be made available to the victim to support his/her claim, or otherwise be taken into account to decide on the victim's claim.

12) The common practice that a court applies a compensation measure as long as a victim's claim is awarded should be continued.

13) The requirement for admissibility of a victim's claim, i.e. that such a claim '*may not unreasonably burden the proceedings*', should not be applied restrictively.

14) It should be investigated whether the courts can be obliged to apply a compensation measure. In cases where the victim does not wish to receive the compensation, the amount can be paid to the Violent Crimes Compensation Fund.

Chapter 3
Combating Trafficking in Human Beings for Labour Exploitation in Romania

G. Cristinel Zaharia[1]

Part I
The legal framework on defining Trafficking in Human Beings for labour exploitation and the dimensions of this crime

1.1 The definition of Trafficking in Human Beings for labour exploitation in Romania

In Romania, the central legal instrument addressing trafficking in persons in general, not just for labour exploitation, is Law no. 678/2001.

This law, on preventing and combating trafficking in persons, was aimed at harmonising the Romanian legislation with the *acquis communautaire* and adjusting it to European and international standards. It also represents an adaptation and a complement to the internal legislation, as compared to the Protocol regarding Prevention, Suppression and Punishment of Trafficking in Persons, especially women and children, supplementing the UN Convention on Transnational Organised Crime. The Protocol and the Convention were signed by Romania in Palermo, in December 2001.

During its drafting, other international documents were taken into account, such as the Joint Action of 24 February 1997 on combating human trafficking and sexual exploitation of children, adopted by the Council of the European Union on the basis of Art. K3 of the Treaty of the European Union and the Recommendations of the Council of Europe: No. R (2000) 11 focussed on action against trafficking in human beings for sexual exploitation, No. R (91) 11, concerning sexual exploitation, pornography, prostitution and trafficking of children and young people, No. 1325 (1997) regarding trafficking of women and forced prostitution in the Member States of the Council of Europe, No. 1099 (1996) on the sexual exploitation of children, and No. 1065 (1987) concerning child trafficking and other forms of child exploitation. Other documents of the ILO have also been considered, such as Convention No. 182 on the Prohibition and Immediate Action for the Elimination of the Worst Forms of Child Labour (1999).[2]

---

[1] George - Cristinel Zaharia; PhD candidate on Human Trafficking, Bucharest University, Romania; Assistant Professor, Craiova University, Romania; Judge at District Court in Drobeta, Turnu Severin, Romania.

[2] According to the preamble of Law No. 678/2001.

The above mentioned law contains provisions regarding the prevention and punishment of trafficking, the protection and assistance given to victims of such trafficking, the judicial proceedings conducted, as well as the promotion of cooperation between States in this field.

It should be pointed out from the very beginning that Law No. 678/2001 does not deal specifically with combating human trafficking for labour exploitation, but it aims to combat human trafficking in general and other forms of exploitation, such as sexual exploitation and the removal and transplant of organs, etc.

The Law includes five crimes:

1. Adult trafficking (Art. 12),
2. Child trafficking (Art. 13),
3. The offence under Art. 17, to which the legislature does not give a specific name, but is intended to allow punishment of exploitation of a human trafficking victim in Romania, who is not Romanian citizen,
4. The offence of child pornography, which is not of interest in this study, and
5. Organising the trafficking of persons and minors (Art. 15, Para 2).

The crime of trafficking in persons (Art. 12) and the offence of trafficking in minors (Art. 13) include certain activities designed to exploit the victim, including the execution of work or performance of services either by force or in circumstances that violate the legislation on working conditions, wages, health and safety.

Whenever the trafficker seeks a victim's submission to execute work or to perform services forcibly or violates the legal norms on working conditions, wages, health and safety at work, the condition of purpose is fulfilled. If the other conditions of the offence are met, in addition to the purpose, the crime of trafficking in adults or child trafficking will be applied.

It is not necessary for the victim of crime to have actually been subjected to the execution of labour exploitation or to the violation of the legal norms on working conditions, wages, health and safety at work for the crime of trafficking to be applied.[3] The intent of the trafficker to do so is sufficient. Consequently, it is not necessary to prove that the violation of these legal provisions has taken place. If the goal is achieved, for example if the victim is actually subjected to forced labour, both the offence of trafficking and the crime of submission to forced or compulsory labour will be applied. In certain circumstances, the achievement of purpose can also fall under the administrative law. For example, non-compliance with the stipulation of ensuring payment of the gross minimum wage in the country (which is a violation of the provisions on wages); a stipulation in an employment contract that breaches the legislation (including aspects which may affect the health and safety of workers) and hiring people without giving each one an employment

[3] M. Hotca, M. Dobrinoiu, *Offences stipulated in Special Laws* (C. H. Beck Publishing House, Bucharest 2008) p. 51.

contract, are all considered to be administrative offences. In such situations, regional labour inspectorates may apply sanctions for the administrative offences committed. Also, the courts can convict the employers of the crime of THB for labour exploitation if the act was preceded by the recruitment; transportation; transfer; accommodation or receipt of persons by threat, force or other forms of coercion; by abduction, fraud or deception; by abuse of authority or taking advantage of that person's inability to defend himself/herself or to express their will; or by offering, giving or receiving payments or benefits to achieve the consent of the person who has authority over another person, in the case of adults. In the case of minors, it is enough that the recruitment, transportation, transfer, accommodation or receipt of these persons took place for the purposes mentioned above.

In case law, we frequently see cases where victims are compelled to engage in various activities by force or by violating the legal provisions on working conditions, wages, and health, and we only see very few cases that include the violation of the provisions on safety in the workplace. In the cases that we have investigated, actual exploitation did take place. We have not encountered situations where traffickers have been convicted both for the crime of human trafficking and the crime of submitting victims to forced labour. By contrast, in other situations, as in the H.A. case commented on in this study, the Bucharest Territorial Labour Inspectorate sanctioned the company that exploited victims for labour, who belonged to the principal trafficker, H.A., for not signing employment contracts with the victims in accordance with Romanian Labour Law.

1.1.1 Definition of Adult Trafficking

According to Art. 12 of the Law,

(1) The recruitment, transportation, transfer, accommodation or receipt of persons by threat, force or other forms of coercion; by abduction, fraud or deception; by abuse of authority or taking advantage of that person's inability to defend himself/herself or to express their will; or by offering, giving or receiving of payments or benefits to obtain the consent of the person who has authority over another person for the purposes of exploitation, constitutes a crime of trafficking and is punishable by 3 to 12 years imprisonment and to the interdiction/withdrawal of certain rights.

(2) Trafficking in persons committed in one of the following circumstances:
- a) By two or more persons together;
- b) When it causes serious harm to the victim's bodily integrity or health;
- c) By a public servant performing official duties,

shall be punished by 5 to 15 years imprisonment, including the interdiction of certain rights.

(3) If the offence results in the death or suicide of the victim, the punishment is 15 to 25 years imprisonment, including the interdiction of certain rights.

Attempted human trafficking is also punishable according to Art. 15, Para 1 of Law No. 678/2001.

In order to understand what 'attempt' means, from the point of view of the Romanian legislation, we must look at Art. 20 of the Romanian Penal Code:

> *'An attempt is to enforce the decision to commit the crime, but enforcement has been discontinued or its effect has not appeared. There is attempt, even when committing the offence was not possible, due to failure or insufficiency of the means used or due to the fact that during the period when they committed the acts of execution, the object was missing from the place where the offender believed it to be. There is no attempt when the crime is impossible as a result of how the execution was conceived.'*

Romanian penal law establishes two different offences, according to type of victims, minors or adults. The exploitation of victims is not explained in Art. 12, which criminalises trafficking in adults, but in Art. 2, Paragraph 2 of the law.

In accordance with Art. 2, Paragraph 2:

1. *'In this Law, terms and expressions below have the following meanings:*

   (...)

2. *By exploitation of a person we understand:*

   a) execution of a work or performance of services forcibly or by violation of the legal norms on working conditions, wages, health and safety;

   b) keeping a person in a state of slavery or other similar means of depriving them of their freedom and maintaining them in servitude;

   c) imposing the practice of prostitution and pornographic performances with the express purpose of producing and disseminating pornographic materials or other forms of sexual exploitation;

   d) organ harvesting;

   e) carrying out other activities that violate human rights and fundamental freedoms.'

1.1.2 Definition of child trafficking

According to Article 13 of the Law,

(1) The recruitment, transportation, transfer, hosting or receiving of a minor/child in order to exploit him/her, represents the crime of trafficking in minors or child trafficking and is punishable by 5 years to 15 years imprisonment, including the interdiction of certain rights.

(2) If the fact referred to in Para (1) is committed by threat, violence or other forms of coercion; by abduction, fraud or deception; by abuse of authority or profiting from a child's inability to defend himself/herself or to express his/her will or by offering, giving, accepting or receiving

payments or benefits to obtain the consent of the person who has authority over the minor, the penalty is 7 years to 18 years imprisonment, including the interdiction of certain rights.

(3) If the facts referred to in Para (1) and (2) are committed in accordance with Art. 12, Para (2); the penalty is 7 years to 18 years imprisonment, including the interdiction of certain rights in the case of Para (1) and 10 years to 20 years imprisonment, including the interdiction of certain rights, in the case of Para (2).

(4) If the facts contained in this article result in the death or suicide of the victim, the punishment is 15 years to 25 years imprisonment, including the interdiction of certain rights.'

The crime of 'Attempted trafficking' is also punishable according to Art. 15, Para 1 of Law No. 678/2001. 'Attempt' is punished in the same way as indicated above.

At the same time, we shall no longer insist on the notion of exploitation, which we have also presented, in defining the crime of trafficking in adults. In terms of labour, child exploitation methods are identical to those used to exploit adults: performing work or performing services forcibly or by violating the legal norms on working conditions, wages, health and safety at work.

1.1.3. Description of the crime stipulated in Art. 17 of Law No. 678/2001

The Romanian legislature has not established a name for this criminal offence, but the crime includes punishment for the exploitation of non-Romanian citizens who are victims of THB.

According to Art. 17:

(1) 'The act of knowingly inducing or permitting (either directly or through an intermediary) the entry into or detention in the country of a person who is not a Romanian citizen and is subject to trafficking in persons:

a) by using fraudulent means, violence or threats or other forms of coercion; or

b) by abusing that person's position, because of his illegal or precarious situation of entry or residence in the country, or due to pregnancy, illness or a physical or mental infirmity,

is an offence and is punishable with the penalties stipulated for the crime of trafficking in persons.

(2) If the act referred to in Para (1) is committed repeatedly; the maximum penalty shall be increased by two years.'

This is not considered to be a crime of human trafficking, but a crime associated with human trafficking and is included in Section 2 of the Law, entitled 'Offences relating to trafficking in persons'.

1.1.4. Content of the crime stipulated in Art. 15, Paragraph 2 of Law no. 678/2001

According to this article, the organisation of the offences/crimes mentioned in this chapter (adult trafficking and child trafficking) is a crime and is punishable as 'organised crime', according to Art. 15, Para 2 of the law.

1.1.5. Considerations strictly related to the trafficking in persons for labour exploitation

The type of trafficking in persons this study is interested in differs from other types of human trafficking in terms of purpose. 'Human trafficking for labour exploitation' is defined as trafficking in persons that are intended to be subjected to the execution of work or the performance of a service, either by force or in working conditions that are in violation of legal rules, wages or health and safety.

Considering the legal provisions, it can be observed that the purpose of exploitation appears as a constituent element in the structure of the crime. If the facts provided by Art. 12 of Law No. 678/2001 were not committed in order to exploit the victim, this will not constitute a crime of trafficking. It should be emphasised that the mere existence of purpose is sufficient for the existence of the crime, and it is not necessary for the crime to occur in order to prove that the victim has actually been exploited.[4] For example, according to Romanian law, if a person is recruited and transported against her will through the use of violence with the express purpose of being exploited by forced labour, this constitutes the crime of 'trafficking in persons', even if that person has not actually been exploited (for example, the police identified the victim during transportation and rescued her/him before they have been exploited).

The Romanian legislator distinguishes between the execution of work and performance of services. Work is a conscious activity, specific to human beings, targeted towards a specific goal, satisfying a necessity. In turn, a service, performed for the benefit or interest of someone, is a task that someone has as an employee. The service sector and the work sector are interconnected. It was therefore not necessary for the legislator to distinguish between the execution of work and the performance of services.

If the work or service is conducted either forcibly or in violation of the legal rules on working conditions, wages, health and safety, this constitutes a crime of trafficking, the conditions are applied alternatively and not cumulatively. The victim's consent is not required when force is used, and consent is usually not given when the legal rules are being violated. It can also occur that both can be identified: the victim is forced to perform a specific job

---

[4] G. Cristinel Zaharia, 'Harmonisation of the crimes stipulated in Law no. 678/2001 on preventing and combating trafficking in persons with other crimes' (2008) Criminal Law Notebooks Review, CH Beck Publishing House, No. 4, p. 19.

that does not comply with the laws on working conditions, wages, health and safety. The forcible submission to the execution of work or services is the act by which a person obliges another person to supply an activity against his/her will, in cases other than those allowed by law. [5]

It can be noted that unlike the express provisions in the Palermo Protocol, Romanian law penalises as 'trafficking in persons' acts that target subjecting victims to work in violation of the legal rules on working conditions, wages, health and security.

Also, as another specific feature, one notes that there is a difference between Art. 3 of the Palermo Protocol and Art. 12 of Law No. 678/2001. Thus, while the Protocol uses the term 'harbouring', the Romanian law on preventing and combating trafficking in persons uses the notion of 'accommodation' with trafficking in adults and 'hosting' for trafficking in minors. The term 'accommodation' is also used in Law No. 300/2006, which implements the Convention of the Council of Europe on the Action against Trafficking in Human Beings, adopted on 16 May 2005. With regard to the relationship with Law No. 678/2001, we note that Law No. 300/2006 has just adopted the Convention and represents the normative act under which Romania engaged to respect it. Law No. 300/2006 does not criminalise offences, as is the case with Law No. 678/2001.

The official version of the above mentioned Protocol uses the term 'harbouring' to describe the situation which the Romanian legislator, in translation, as stipulated in Art. 12 of Law No. 678/2001, refers to as 'accommodation.'

The word 'harbouring', derived from the verb 'to harbour' has a much broader sense than the equivalents the Romanian legislator has selected, giving a proper sense of the circumstances in which the crime of human trafficking is usually committed. [6] 'To accommodate' someone means, according to the Romanian Explanatory Dictionary, 'to install someone temporarily in a house', while 'to host' is 'to put someone up in your house for some time, giving them shelter and food'. 'Accommodation' is the temporary installation of a person in a household or in another location for this purpose. Usually, it is an activity of an organised nature and involves a cooperative relationship between the parties.[7]

Romanian law makes a clear distinction between the submission of the victim to execute the work or perform services forcibly or in violation of the laws on working conditions, wages, health and safety on the one hand and, on the other, keeping the victim in a State of slavery or other similar method of deprivation of freedom or servitude. In both cases, the limits of punishment

---

[5] V. Dongoroz, *Theoretical Explanations of the Romanian Criminal Code, 3rd Volume* (All Beck Publishing House Bucharest 2003) p. 286.

[6] G. Cristinel Zaharia, 'Harmonisation of the crimes stipulated in Law no. 678/2001 on preventing and combating trafficking in persons with other crimes' (2008) Criminal Law Notebooks Review, CH Beck Publishing House, No. 4, p. 23.

[7] *Ibid.*

are identical. As we mentioned before, it is not necessary to achieve the goal. If the person is actually exploited, certain aspects of exploitation will fall under the influence of criminal law, others will fall under the influence of administrative law.

At the same time, trafficking in persons for labour exploitation must not be confused with the submission of victims to 'carry out other activities that violate human rights and fundamental freedoms.' For example, there are frequent situations in which victims are forced to steal property or beg (in this case, minors are used). From a strictly legal perspective, such situations cannot be classified as a means of labour exploitation according to Romanian law.

To conclude, the Romanian legislator has determined that keeping people in slavery, or using other similar methods to deprive people of freedom, keep them in servitude or perform other such activities that violate human rights and fundamental freedoms, such as obliging a person to beg or steal, does not fall within the definition of human trafficking for labour exploitation. In this case, the purpose is represented by exploiting the victim through carrying out activities that violate their human rights and fundamental freedoms, in accordance with Art. 2 Para 2 Letter e) of Law No. 678/2001.

1.2 Other legislation and policies relevant for Trafficking in Human Beings for labour exploitation

1.2.1 Criminal law

There are other legal provisions which are also relevant to THB for labour exploitation in Romanian criminal law.

Such provisions are found in the Romanian penal code. According to Art. 191 of the Criminal Code, 'the act of subjecting a person, in other circumstances than those provided by law, to work against his/her will or to forced labour is punishable by 6 months to 3 years imprisonment.'

Also, according to Art. 190. of the Criminal Code, 'keeping a person in a state of slavery or making him/her a slave, and trafficking in slaves as well, shall be punished with 3 to 10 years imprisonment, including the interdiction of certain rights.'

At first glance, one could argue that there is an overlap between the texts on human trafficking crimes and crimes of slavery (pertaining to the subjection of victims to forced or compulsory labour), but in reality these texts complement one another, meaning that they should be applied bearing in mind the trafficker's aim. This is because, as we have already said, to apply the crime of trafficking in persons is not necessary to effectively result in the exploitation of the victim. It is sufficient that the acts are committed to pursue this goal. If the victim is exploited, being subjected to forced labour, both the offence of trafficking and the crime of submission to forced or compulsory labour will be applied.

From a practical perspective, until now we have not yet encountered a situation in which only trafficking in human beings is applied. The same problem arises in the case of slavery, because, until now, there has been no data showing that any offender has been convicted for the crime of slavery.

1.2.2 Labour Law

In terms of labour law, there are legislative measures and policies involving the Ministry of Labour and Social Solidarity with regards to trafficking for labour exploitation. According to Art. 4 of Law No. 678/2001, the Ministry of Labour and Social Solidarity will take the necessary measures in its field of activity for the elaboration and implementation of the National Action Plan for countering trafficking in persons.

At the same time, according to Art. 6 of the Law:

(1) 'The Ministry of Labour and Social Solidarity, through its specialised structures at central and regional levels, develops and implements special measures to integrate individuals at high risk of being trafficked, especially women in disadvantaged areas and socially marginalised people in the labour market .

(2) For people at a high risk of being trafficked, the National Agency for Employment develops information programmes regarding the labour market and employees' rights, professional training programmes, and information for economic agents, in order to give priority in employment to the above mentioned individuals.

(3) The Ministry of Labour and Social Solidarity, together with the Ministry of Finance, studies the opportunity to elaborate some incentives for economic operators who employ both people at a high risk of being trafficked and victims of trafficking, who have completed professional training courses, making proposals in this regard'.

The failure to ensure the minimum wage is paid, stipulations in the individual employment contract of clauses that contravene the legislation, hiring people without an individual employment contract, violating the provisions regarding overtime and the statutory provisions on weekly rest all constitute administrative offences, according to the Labour Code.[8]

Hazardous child labour is prohibited in Romania under Government Decision No. 867/2009. All activities carried out by a child or achieved through a child's direct involvement are considered hazardous work in formal and informal sectors, if, by their nature or the circumstances in which they are exercised, they are injurious to the children's health, safety, morals and development. These include the following: those conducted in hazardous economic sectors or in dangerous occupations in which child labour is prohibited by law; those with a frequency, duration and/or intensity that prevents attendance at compulsory education, participation in orientation programmes or training approved by the competent authority, or the ability of

[8] Article 256 of the Labour Code describes these administrative offences.

children to receive instruction. Violations of the provisions of this decision represent legal offences.

According to the Labour Law, the normal amount of working time is 40 hours per week. The period worked after the 40 hours are completed is considered to be overtime, and this cannot be enforced without the employee's consent. The employee is entitled to compensation for overtime hours with time off. In Romania, the gross guaranteed minimum wage is 600 lei (about 145 euros), according to Government Decision (G.D.) 1051/2008.

1.2.3. Migration Law

Government Emergency Ordinance (G.E.O.) No. 105/2001 regarding the Romanian State border criminalises trafficking in migrants.
According to Art. 71 of this legal norm:

(1) The recruitment, mentoring and guidance of one or more individuals to cross the State border illegally and the organisation of these activities constitutes a crime of 'trafficking in migrants' and is punishable with 2 to 7 years imprisonment.
(2) If the act referred to in Para (1) is likely to endanger the life or safety of migrants or subject them to inhuman or degrading treatment, the punishment is 5 to 10 years imprisonment.
(3) If the act referred to in Para (2) results in the death or suicide of the victim, the punishment is 10 to 20 years imprisonment.
(4) Attempted acts stipulated in paragraphs (1) and (2) will be punished.

The crime of trafficking in migrants, as provided by Art. 71 of G.E.O. 105/2001, differs from a human trafficking crime in that it sanctions the illegal crossing of the border. In a human trafficking case, where the intention is to exploit the victim, border crossings often occur legally. Furthermore, in the former case, migrants cannot be considered to be victims as violence is not used against them.

If people that are victims of trafficking for labour exploitation are illegally brought across the border, the trafficker can be sentenced both for the crime of human trafficking and the crime of trafficking in migrants.

1.3. The dimensions of Trafficking in Human Beings for labour exploitation in Romania

1.3.1 Characterisation of Trafficking in Human Beings for labour exploitation at the national level

First, we must point out that Romania is a country of origin and transit in terms of trafficking for labour exploitation. In almost all cases, Romanian citizens are trafficked abroad.[9]

The method of operation is almost identical. Victims are chosen from among those with modest levels of education and poor living conditions seeking a better life. Victims from rural areas are preferred, but people are recruited from urban areas as well. Their ages range, usually, between 20 and 45 years. In principle, the victims are Romanian citizens who are trafficked abroad. Foreign citizens from Honduras, Nicaragua, Mexico and the Philippines have been trafficked in Romania. Both men and women are trafficked and their numbers vary depending on nature of the work. For example, men are trafficked more in the construction business. In agriculture, the percentage is balanced and women are mostly trafficked for domestic work. Victims can also be trafficked in different sectors such as the hotel and restaurant industries, or media distribution services. Victims are transported either by car or coach, or by plane.

The recruiter is a very clever person, who manages to capture the attention of victims with stories of success, convincing them that he will enrich them overnight. Deception is therefore used to convince the victims. Recruiters are usually people the victims know and who are travelling abroad or have settled in the country where the victims will be exploited. For example, in a case that was brought to my attention by an NGO representative, a twenty-four year old youngster from Bucharest, who had only completed four years of primary school, was persuaded by a neighbour who had settled in England that he would find a better paid job there. The trafficker's offer was accepted and he set off. The youth had not realised that he needed a visa to travel through the territory of certain countries. He was therefore tied under an international road transport vehicle (a truck) to avoid being detected at the border.[10]

After recruitment, the border crossing is next, which can be done either legally (with the victims not knowing at this point that they are being trafficked), or illegally, as in the case described above. Transportation is done in the traffickers' own cars or in coaches. Although we have not found an explanation for this, in many cases, victims are transported by traffickers to a point near the border crossing by minibus. They then get out and climb into another car or another minibus that takes them over the border. After crossing

---

[9] D. Baloş, *Trafficking in human beings. Prevention and Elimination of the Worst Forms of Child Labour* (Eurodidact Publishing House , Cluj-Napoca 2005) p. 3.

[10] Interview with the President of the Association for the Development of Alternative Practices of Reintegration and Education (ADAPRE) (06.10.2010).

the border, they are loaded back into the minibus that originally brought them to the border and they continue their journey to their destination. These facts were established by a Romanian court and applied during sentencing.[11]

The victims are most often trafficked to countries such as Spain, Italy, France, Czech Republic, Cyprus and Greece. After reaching their destination, the victims begin to realise that they have been deceived and that they are being trafficked. The victims are either exploited by their recruiters, or by intermediaries who hand them over to others to exploit them. Further on into the process, the violence starts to occur; victims are required to perform work against their will. Usually ID documents are retained. The intimidation can take a milder form, such as threats, but also more serious forms, such as physical violence, beatings, etc.

In some cases, the violence can be unimaginable. For example, there were some Romanians trafficked to Cyprus, who were forced to pick oranges. They were kept on a plantation and were guarded by armed Albanians. Albanians are known for their brutality. They did not hesitate to shoot the victims if they did not obey. The conditions under which the victims were living were miserable. The places where they were living were not designed to house people. Housing for the victims often included a tent; victims often had to sleep outdoors or in a warehouse.

In another case, a Romanian group was brought to Spain by Romanian traffickers, who took the victims to work on a plantation belonging to a Spanish owner. The victims were sleeping outside in the open air, meals were prepared using pet food, to wash they were given water taken from sewers and irrigation pumps, and their passports were withheld. Moreover, they worked 12 to 14 hours a day. The number of boxes of products filled by each injured party was calculated and held in evidence against the defendants. As they were being coerced, the victims continued working in the difficult conditions. After about three weeks, the Romanian traffickers received wages for 19 Romanians from the Spanish owner. The victims were refused payment of the money they were entitled to for their work under the pretext that they had to pay the traffickers 200 Euros each, as compensation for the cost of their transport from Romania to Spain.[12]

As indicated in the above case, the victims' working schedule included very long days, almost from dawn to dusk, apart from rest and meal breaks.

Victims are exploited mainly in agriculture, harvesting fruit, but also in the construction and clothing industries. The representative of ADAPRE also claims that there are cases of mixed exploitation, both sexual and labour. For example, a girl who was being sexually exploited performed several tasks including: having sex with the clients, dancing in the club, cleaning and

---

[11] Timisoara Court of Appeal – Criminal Decision No. 147/A/27.10.2008, Mehedinti Court House – Criminal Decision No. 32/29.01.2007.

[12] Ploiesti Court of Appeal, Criminal Division for cases involving minors and family - Decision No. 113/12.09.2008, published by Jurindex service <www.jurisprudenta.org>.

arranging the tables after closing time. She also had to take care of the trafficker's child, performing the duties of a nanny, during her free time.

Traffickers refuse to pay the promised wages to the victims under the pretext of fictitious debts, implying that the victims must work to pay back the money spent by the traffickers on their transportation.

Finally, the victims escaped, either reaching the police in their country of destination or the Romanian diplomatic missions. In a particular case to which an NGO representative made reference, some Romanian citizens trafficked to Spain also complained about the treatment that they had been subjected to by the Spanish police, who had in turn reported them to the diplomatic mission of the Romanian State. It is obvious that there are situations in which police officers do not manage the victims' complaints as they should.[13]

Where victims are trafficked within the country, transportation is unnecessary. Cases of trafficking in persons for labour exploitation within the country are rare.

1.3.2 Facts and Figures on Trafficking in Human Beings for labour exploitation in Romania

Currently, there are no statistics produced in Romania about investigations, prosecutions and convictions for cases of human trafficking for labour exploitation. The National Agency against Trafficking in Persons only holds a record of victims of trafficking, but no record is made for the persons prosecuted and convicted for committing this crime. There are, however, statistics regarding the victims exploited through labour and those exploited in other ways.

For example, in 2009, there were a total of 314 victims trafficked for labour exploitation as follows: 20 in the hotel industry, 81 in construction and 213 in agriculture. Out of the 314 victims, 304 were trafficked abroad and 10 in Romania. According to the statistics of NATP, 91 were exploited in Spain, 65 in Italy, 52 in Czech Republic, 23 in Greece, 21 in Finland, 7 in Germany, 10 in Britain, 16 in Cyprus, 2 in Austria, 7 in U.S.A., and 6 in Slovakia and several were exploited in other States.[14]

In 2010, according to a statistical evaluation report on human trafficking in the first half of 2010, for the first time in NATP records, human trafficking of victims for labour exploitation is no longer the number one offence, as there are presently higher instances of human trafficking for sexual exploitation. In the first six months of the year, a total of 144 victims exploited for labour were identified, of which 31 were women exploited in agriculture, construction and other sectors. The 113 men were exploited mainly in agriculture and construction. For the 1st half of 2010, statistics do not show if the exploitation

[13] Interview with the President of the Development of Alternative Practices of Reintegration and Education (ADAPRE) (06.10.2010).

[14] National Agency Against Trafficking in Persons - Summary of human trafficking in 2009, pp. 3-4.

of victims for labour occurred in Romania or abroad.[15]

With regard to the penalties imposed on traffickers, they can vary from case to case, depending on many factors, such as the punishment limits attached to the particular crimes, the severity of the crime committed, the character of the offender and the circumstances that mitigate or worsen criminal liability. For example, in two cases, a sentence of three years imprisonment was imposed.[16] In another case, traffickers were sentenced to a four year suspended sentence (which means that they were free[17]).

The above cases have transnational implications and involve Romanians who are trafficked abroad. Almost all cases of human trafficking in Romania investigated so far concern Romanian citizens trafficked abroad. We have not encountered cases in which Romanians were trafficked within Romania. We encountered several cases in which foreigners were trafficked to Romania.

If the victims are minors, the penalty is higher, i.e. between 5 and 15 years at least. When victims are adults, the punishment is between 3 and 12 years. In principle, the traffickers are sentenced only for the crime of trafficking. However, it is possible for them to be convicted for other offences as well. The crime of trafficking in migrants can be added to the convictions when illegal border crossing is organised, alongside the offence of forging the victims' official identity documents; tax evasion, when traffickers evade the amounts obtained from paying taxes or murder, when victims are killed, etc.

1.4 Summary of the findings

1.4.1 Identified obstacles

1. In terms of defining trafficking in human beings, the inadequate translation of the terms 'harbouring' and 'accommodation' with regards to the trafficking in adults and the term 'hosting' with reference to trafficking in minors is an obstacle in Romanian legislation. According to the Romanian Explanatory Dictionary, "to accommodate" someone, means 'to install a person temporarily in housing', while 'to host', signifies having someone in your house for some time, giving them shelter (and food). "Accommodation' is interpreted as the installation of a person temporarily in a household or in another location built for this purpose. Usually, it is an activity of an organised nature and involves cooperation between the parties.[18]

---

[15] National Agency Against Trafficking in Persons - Statistical evaluation of human trafficking in the first half of 2010, p. 8.

[16] See Timisoara Court of Appeal – Criminal Decision No. 147/A/27.10.2008, and Craiova Court of Appeal – Criminal Decision No. 115/24.09.2008.

[17] See High Court of Cassation and Justice - Criminal Decision No. 2680/22.04.2005.

[18] G. Cristinel Zaharia, 'Harmonisation of the crimes stipulated in Law no. 678/2001 on preventing and combating trafficking in persons with other crimes' (2008) Criminal Law Notebooks Review, CH Beck Publishing House, No. 4, p. 19.

The word 'hosting' derived from the verb 'to host', has a much broader sense than the current Romanian legislation accepts, implying a proper sense of the circumstances in which the crime of trafficking is usually committed.

Therefore, a first recommendation would be that the measures adopted internationally should be correctly translated by the States that target their implementation into national legislation. An inaccurate translation of international normative acts at national level can partially affect the goal of an international law.

2. The second difficulty is the fact that Romanian law does not punish the actual exploitation of victims in the provision of THB, but only if preceded by preparatory acts (recruitment, transportation, transfer, accommodation or receipt of persons by threat, force or other forms of coercion; by abduction, fraud or deception; by abuse of authority or taking advantage of that person's inability to defend himself/herself or to express their will; or by offering, giving or receiving of payments or benefits to obtain the consent of the person who has authority over another person for the purposes of exploitation – in the case of adult trafficking and the recruitment, transportation, transfer, hosting or receiving in case of a child). For example, if a person is recruited by deception in order to be exploited for labour, we are in the presence of human trafficking. If the person is actually exploited, for examples is forced to work against his/her will, we are in the presence of another crime, represented by submission to forced or compulsory labour. The crime of trafficking will be applied, even if the operation did not take place, but the goal was pursued by performing the acts described as crimes in the legal text.

3. Another inconsistency is the fact that the actual exploitation of the victim is punished more leniently than the planning of the operation. For example, the crime of 'trafficking in persons' is punishable by 3-12 years imprisonment, if the crime is committed for the purpose of coercing the victim to forced labour. By contrast, the offence of 'submitting people to forced labour' is itself only punishable with imprisonment for six months to three years.

   The differences between the two punishments are huge, and this fact cannot be justified in terms of criminal law. The intention to commit the crime of THB for labour exploitation is punished more harshly than the actual exploitation itself, although the latter has a higher degree of risk. In our opinion, it is much worse actually to force a person to work rather than just create this danger.[19]

[19] G. Cristinel Zaharia, 'Harmonisation of the crimes stipulated in Law no. 678/2001 on preventing and combating trafficking in persons with other crimes' (2008) Criminal Law Notebooks Review, CH Beck Publishing House, No. 4, p. 19.

4. Another obstacle is the fact that failure by the employer to provide the proper conditions of employment for the employees can easily be classified as a misdemeanour. For example, misdemeanours include the offences of non-compliance with the stipulation of ensuring payment of the minimum wage in the country; a stipulation in the individual employment contract that breaches the legislation; hiring people without giving each one an individual employment contract, and violation of the provisions on overtime and the statutory provisions on weekly rest.

   According to Law No. 678/2001, exploiting the victim means a failure to comply with the laws regarding wages and working conditions. A labour inspector can easily demonstrate negligence, without searching for evidence of human trafficking. Of course, it does not follow that if an employer fails to comply with the legal norms on wages or causes the employee to perform an activity that violates the safety rules, that we are witnessing the crime of human trafficking. However, the exploitation of an employee in these forms may be an indication of trafficking. As we have mentioned above, human trafficking does not include exploitation of the victim in the Romanian legislation. For example, in the case of adult victims, the act of recruitment, transportation, transfer, harbouring or receiving the victim by using threats, violence or other forms of coercion, deception, etc., is required for proving the purpose of exploitation. Thus, it is possible for an employee to perform an activity in violation of the provisions on safety at work, although he might not have been compelled to do so by the employer. In such cases, a labour inspector should talk to the employee to find out whether he is a victim of human trafficking, and to notify the competent criminal authorities if it is the case.

5. The legislation does not provide special training for labour inspectors in identifying trafficking cases. To identify cases of trafficking, the labour inspectors must also have knowledge of criminal law, so that they can conclude whether or not there is trafficking in persons, by reference to the provisions in the penal law.

6. Another obstacle is the trafficked persons' lack of information about the criminal nature of the acts committed against them. Consequently, the prosecution structures may not be made aware of it by the victims. The labour inspectors are also not informed in good time. For example, one labour inspector said that employees only reported that their wages were not being paid or that no employment contract had been drafted, once they were no longer working. Such reports are too late, as the victims' assertions are impossible to verify.

7. Lack of an effective social security system that protects the unemployed is also a drawback in the labour market. For example, unemployment benefit is granted for different periods, depending on the length of employment: six months for people who have paid contributions for at least one year; 9 months for people who have paid contributions for at least 5 years and 12 months for people with a contribution period of more than 10 years. For a person who has not had a period of social contributions exceeding one year, the unemployment benefit is 75% of the guaranteed gross minimum wage, which in Romania is about 145 Euros. In these circumstances, victims are inclined to accept poor employment conditions, even in violation of the laws, just to earn more money.

1.4.2 Good practices

In the category of good practices, we find the following:

1. Law No. 678/2001 is an adaptation and a complement to national laws in line with the stipulations of the Protocol on the Prevention, Suppression and Punishment of Trafficking in Persons, especially Women and Children, supplementing the UN Convention against Transnational Organised Crime. Both the Protocol and the Convention were signed by Romania in Palermo in December 2001.
   During its drafting, other international documents were taken into account, such as the Joint Action of 24 February 1997 on combating human trafficking and sexual exploitation of children, adopted by the Council of the European Union on the basis of Art. K3 of the Treaty of the European Union and the Recommendations of the Council of Europe; No. R (2000) 11, focused on action against trafficking in human beings for sexual exploitation; No. R (91) 11, concerning sexual exploitation, pornography, prostitution and trafficking of children and young people; No. 1325 (1997) regarding trafficking in women and forced prostitution in the Member States of the Council of Europe; No. 1099 (1996) on the sexual exploitation of children; No. 1065 (1987) concerning child trafficking and other forms of child exploitation. Other documents from the International Labour Organisation have also been considered, such as Convention No. 182 on the Prohibition and Immediate Action for the Elimination of the Worst Forms of Child Labour (1999).

2. Law No. 678/2001 contains some provisions in addition to the Palermo Protocol, this means that the Romanian law penalises actions that seek to subject victims working in violation of the legal rules on working conditions, wages, health and safety as trafficking in human beings. The conclusion is that Romanian law is more comprehensive in this regard.

3. Trafficking in minors is punished more harshly, given the greater implications of such acts, resulting from the physical and psychological frailties of minors.

4. Law No. 678/2001 regulates the framework on preventing and combating trafficking in persons, the assistance granted to victims, the international cooperation, and the methods to provide compensation to victims.

5. The Romanian legislation has established specialised structures for the investigation and prosecution of trafficking crimes in the form of specialised prosecutors and police officers.[20]

[20] The prosecution is conducted by the Department for the Investigation of Organised Crime and Terrorism (DIOCT). Also the Romanian Police General Inspectorate is organised into Divisions for countering Organised Crime, Brigades for countering Organised Crime or Services for countering Organised Crime.

Part II
Cooperation in the investigation and prosecution of cases of Trafficking in Human Beings for labour exploitation

2.1 Actors involved in investigating and prosecuting Trafficking in Human Beings for labour exploitation

The following actors are involved in investigating and prosecuting trafficking offences:

- The Romanian Police General Inspectorate, through the Divisions for countering Organised Crime, the Brigades for countering Organised Crime or Services for countering Organised Crime;
- The Border Police General Inspectorate;
- The Prosecutor's Office of the High Court of Cassation and Justice – Directorate/Department for the Investigation of Organised Crime and Terrorism;
- The Territorial Labour Inspectorates, but only in terms of making controls and provision of information in terms of employment;
- The non-governmental organisations, where victims can be accommodated and they can be interviewed. Non-Governmental Organisations play a very important role because they are used to stabilise the victims in the area, allowing investigators to make contact with them whenever they need to while carrying out the investigation;
- The National Agency Against Trafficking in Persons, through its regional centres, coordinated by the Ministry of Internal Affairs. One of its tasks is the coordination of victims in criminal proceedings;
- The Courts.

The main actor in the investigation and prosecution of trafficking in persons is the Prosecutor's Office of the High Court of Cassation and Justice – Directorate/Department for the Investigation of Organised Crime and Terrorism, within which prosecutors specialised in countering trafficking in persons operate. Prosecution for this type of crime is carried out by these prosecutors.[21]

The role of this actor and of the prosecutors is to gather the necessary evidence on the crime, to identify offenders and establish their liability, in order to decide whether or not it is appropriate to have them prosecuted.This actor is acting in accordance with the Code of Criminal Proceedings and other laws applicable to human trafficking. Victims are interviewed, evidence is gathered, financial investigations are made and phone calls are intercepted, etc.

Prosecutors from the Prosecutor's Office of the High Court of Cassation and Justice – Directorate for the Investigation of Organised Crime and Terrorism are specialised prosecutors and THB falls within their mandate.

[21] DIOCT was founded by Law No. 508/2004.

They are given specialist training in this field. In principle, the training is general and not aimed in particular at trafficking in persons for labour exploitation. Meetings and exchanges with other European magistrates are held periodically, at least once on a year, within programmes at European level. Also, over time, as a result of the investigation of several crimes of human trafficking for labour exploitation, prosecutors gain more experience, which helps them perform their work. Basically, this is a self-specialisation.

Another actor is the Romanian Police General Inspectorate, through the Divisions for countering Organised Crime, Brigades for countering Organised Crime or Services for countering Organised Crime. Officers specialising in combating trafficking are active in these institutions. Their role is to help the public prosecutor to collect information, data and evidence.

Police officers work under the supervision of the prosecutor and are required to complete the tasks assigned in this respect by the prosecutor. Police officers are involved in gathering evidence and can listen to victims and offenders, etc. Also, police officers can organise a *flagrante delicto*, which means they catch the trafficker exactly at the moment when the crime is committed and record him using the equipment supplied. Police specialisation is achieved through training that is focused not only on labour exploitation of trafficking victims, but also on more general issues.

The role of the Border Police General Inspectorate is to oversee the Romanian State border.

This actor operates by means of border guards, carrying out inspections at the border of Romania with other States. Instances of trafficking for labour exploitation can be identified when these checks are made. When such cases are detected, the competent prosecutors are informed as well as the Regional Centres of the National Agency against Trafficking in Persons, to assess victims' situations and report them to institutions that can secure the assistance they need. The specialisation of these police officers in human trafficking is still minimal, and is accomplished first through training, and secondly by gaining experience when new trafficking crimes are investigated.

Territorial Labour Inspectorates carry out inspections on the employers' compliance with the general and specific rules pertaining to labour relations, safety and health at work. Labour inspectors go to the employers' premises and check the conditions under which the employees have to operate, they talk to them and examine the employees' labour contracts and other documents, etc.

Labour inspectors are specialised in the research of labour law compliance on employment and pass some exams in order to occupy these posts. They regularly take part in training courses. We did not met inspectors who had taken part in seminars on criminal issues about trafficking in persons for labour exploitation.

Non Governmental Organisations are designed to accommodate victims of trafficking in their own shelters. It must be pointed out, based on the data collected, that the shelters are provided mainly by Non Governmental Organisations, although it should be the Romanian State that provides such shelters, according to Law No. 678/2001. The cause of this failure is a lack of financial means.

Non Governmental Organisations operate under the rules of the Government Emergency Ordinance No. 26/2000. They cooperate with State institutions and provide information and assistance to victims, etc. By accommodating the victim, their place of residence is known, and the prosecution can contact him/her if they deem it necessary to hear from him/her.[22] The representatives of Non Governmental Organisations usually specialise by attending training in these matters and by gaining experience over time, by providing assistance to victims.

The National Agency against Trafficking in Persons was created in 2005 and its aims are to coordinate and evaluate the activities to prevent trafficking in persons and the assistance provided to victims. The Agency cooperates both with Romanian and foreign Non-Governmental Organisations and Inter-Governmental Organisations in order to raise public awareness of the problem and its consequences.

The NATP has initially worked under the provisions of Government Decision No. 1584/2005, and then in line with Government Ordinance No. 20/2009. The NATP registers all the victims of trafficking, makes statistics, assesses the needs of the victims, guides them towards the specialised services providing assistance, etc.This institution organises training on human trafficking for specialists in combating human trafficking, such as police officers, representatives of NGOs and judges.

The courts are responsible for organising the trafficker's preventive arrest, for authorising the completion of searches or phone tapping, etc. Judges manage these activities under the applicable legal provisions.

A national network of judges, specialists in prosecuting human trafficking cases, was established in Romania.[23] Unfortunately, the number of judges in this network is quite low. Theoretically, the judges in this network are better trained than their colleagues.

Judges participate in training on trafficking in persons as well.

The actors involved in investigating and prosecuting crimes of trafficking in persons for labour exploitation are identical to those involved in investigating and prosecuting crimes of trafficking for the sexual exploitation of victims, with the exception of the Territorial Labour Inspectorates. In the case of the victims' labour exploitation, cases of human trafficking can also be identified by labour inspectors, who then refer these to the prosecution authorities. The

---

[22] Interview with the President of the Young Generation Romania Association (03.11.2010).

[23] By Order of the Minister of Justice No. 1806 from the 2nd of July 2004, whose provisions are supplemented by SCM Decision No. 269 of the 6th of July 2005, the Network of judges specialised in solving cases of trafficking in persons was established; it is composed of 56 judges, one judge from each court and Court of Appeal. The network has been made known internationally to the European Commission, Eurojust, the Council of Europe, the United Nations Organisations and other international structures with responsibilities in this area.

labour inspectors only have the powers to check and register the legal infringements, but have no powers to conduct criminal investigations, only prosecutors and the police having the jurisdiction to do so.

The victims are identified by the police either through routine checks that they carry out, through victims' complaints or a result of denunciations from citizens who have information about cases of human trafficking for labour exploitation of victims.

The prosecutors identify the victims either from direct reports and reports received from citizens, or by examining the work done by the police.

Labour inspectors can identify victims as a result of the checks performed in connection with the activity of the employer, who is actually the trafficker. These checks can be made ex officio or following complaints received.

Non-Governmental Organisations can identify the victims as a result of information gathered from other victims whom they are already assisting, or as a result of complaints received from victims or citizens.

The National Agency against Trafficking in Persons may identify victims as a result of complaints received through the free telephone service TelVerde, which allows any person who has knowledge of any case of trafficking in persons to report it. Also, citizens or victims can flag this type of case.

Romanian embassies and consular offices identify victims amongst Romanian citizens abroad.

2.2 Cooperation between actors within the country

2.2.1 Legal framework for cooperation

The exchange of information takes place between the institutions involved in combating human trafficking in the country, according to the provisions of the law.

The law does not establish explicit conditions for the exchange of information between institutions, however certain conditions are inferred. A first condition is that the institution that has requested that information actually needs it as part of its activity. A second condition is that the information requested is the type of information that is allowed to be transmitted.

According to Art. 97 of the Romanian Criminal Procedure Code, 'any physical or legal person, in possession of an object or a document that can serve as evidence, is obliged to present it and deliver it to the criminal prosecution body or court, at their request.' Also, in Romania, the Law No. 544/2001 on free access to public information was adopted. Any person, including public institutions, has the right to request and obtain public information from the authorities and public institutions under the present law's provisions.

According to Art. 7 of this law, 'authorities and public institutions are obliged to reply in writing to the request for public information within 10 days or, where appropriate, within 30 days from the submission of the request, depending on the difficulty, complexity, volume of documentary work and the urgency of the request. If the time required to identify and disseminate the information requested exceeds 10 days, the response will be communicated to the applicant within 30 days, provided he receives a written notice regarding this delay within 10 days. A refusal to communicate the requested information shall be justified and communicated within 5 days from the receipt of the petitions.'

According to Art. 12 of this legislation, the following may not be accessed by citizens:

a) Information concerning national defence, public security and public order if, according to the law, it belongs to the categories of classified information;
b) Information on the deliberations of authorities, and those relating to the economic and political interests of Romania if, according to the law, it is classified information;
c) Information on commercial or financial information if, according to the law, its disclosure infringes intellectual or industrial property rights, as well as the principle of fair competition;
d) Information on personal data, according to the law;
e) Information on proceedings during criminal or disciplinary investigation, if it jeopardises the outcome of the investigation, discloses confidential sources or endangers the life, physical integrity or health of a person consequent to an investigation carried out or under way;
f) Information on court proceedings, if their disclosure is undermining a fair trial or the legitimate interest of any party involved in the process;
g) Information whose publication is prejudicial to the measures meant to protect young people.

The judges and the prosecution structures may request any information from the other actors, who have the obligation to disclose such information.

Protocols may be completed between the other institutions with regards to the sharing of information. For example, there are protocols between the Romanian Immigration Office and the Labour Inspectorate, in terms of identifying foreigners who are not entitled to work in Romania and are identified on the labour market. There are also such protocols between NGOs and police inspectors regarding the housing of victims of trafficking and to communicate information from NGOs to police inspectors. Sometimes, information exchange operates in one direction only, from NGOs to the police, prosecutors and courts.

There are institutions that are obliged to provide information without the right to receive certain information themselves. For example, NGOs are required to provide any information they hold to the prosecution, but the prosecution is not obliged to provide information to NGOs about the evidence, the status of the research, the intention to carry out searches, the plans to arrest a trafficker, etc. The prosecution's information is secret in

Romanian criminal law, i.e. the defendant does not know all the evidence.[24] Due to its secret nature, the prosecutors and police are not obliged to disclose such information. It should be pointed out that, in Romania, during the investigation, even the defendant is not aware of all the evidence in the file, since the prosecution is not obliged to disclose it. Of course, the defendant will be aware if an on-site investigation, a search at the trafficker's home or a reconstruction of the crime is being carried out. But under no circumstances during the prosecution will the criminal authorities present the accused with the witnesses' statements, any telephone or video recordings, or documents obtained by the prosecution which incriminate him. Only after all the evidence has been collected and the prosecution has been completed, according to Art. 250 of the Criminal Procedure Code, does the prosecutor call the defendant and go through all the evidence collected against him. He is then sent to trial before a judge.

The representatives of NGOs have expressed their dissatisfaction with this situation because sometimes, for instance, they cannot answer questions from victims housed in shelters or whom they assist regarding the status of their cases.

In turn, the police are obliged to inform the prosecutor about information they hold, but the prosecutor is not obliged to inform the police about information they consider the police has no need of.

The court also has the right to request information from any institution, if that information would be useful during trial. Failure to provide the information requested can result in a fine from the judge. But the court cannot be required to provide information that would jeopardise the prosecution's right to secrecy.

The Territorial Labour Inspectorates are obliged to inform the prosecuting authorities whenever they consider that the crime of trafficking of victims for labour exploitation has been committed. However, the information exchange between these parties is not reciprocal. There are also situations when the Territorial Labour Inspectorates are informed of possible cases of trafficking for labour exploitation precisely to carry out inspections, and their results are then be made available to the prosecution.

As a rule, the police, prosecutors and courts have the right to request all the information they need from other institutions. However, the exchange of information is not always compulsory.

Information obtained by the prosecution (i.e. the police, prosecutors from other institutions and the courts) concerning when they should decide to approve an application for a search, or a demand for preventive arrests, can be used during criminal investigations and proceedings and during the trial.

The National Action Plan is meant to implement a national strategy against trafficking in persons for the period 2006-2010, adopted by Government

[24] I. Neagu, *Criminal Procedure Law. Special Part. Treaty* (Global Lex Publishing House, Bucharest 2008) pp. 39 – 43.

Decision No. 1.720/2006 and to provide the following measures relating to the exchange of information:

- Establishing a centralised database on trafficking in persons, including active non-governmental organisations and anti-trafficking projects/measures. These databases must contain all information necessary for the fight against human trafficking, such as characterisation of the victims, age groups, level of education, origin, sectors in which victims are trafficked, mode of operation, trafficking routes, NGOs that can provide assistance, etc.
- Determination of the communication channels and contact points for the exchange of data between institutions with responsibilities in the investigation and prosecution of trafficking cases;
- Conclusion of cooperation agreements on data exchange with all relevant institutions and organisations, governmental and non-governmental, national and international, and with hotel networks, international transport companies, taxi companies, construction companies, impresarios, labour recruitment companies, etc. to inform, identify and report issues relating to trafficking;
- Connecting the central database with the institutions involved in preventing and combating trafficking in persons and providing the necessary assistance to victims of trafficking;
- Dissemination of information to the institutions with relevant expertise in the field, within the country and abroad.

Investigative methods

The following investigation methods can be used:

a) (Systematic) Observation;
b) Entering locked premises;
   In this situation, the approval of the court is necessary. Searches can be made only pursuant to a search warrant given by the judge.
c) Requesting information concerning telecommunications;
   This category includes, for example, the prosecution's requests regarding the list of calls made by the trafficker or the owner of a number, etc., without revealing the contents of the communication. Telecommunication companies are legally required to provide this type of information to the prosecution.
d) Recording telecommunications (phone and e-mail)/Recording confidential communications;
   Romanian law protects the secrecy of correspondence. The law provides that if there is a report regarding an offence that is being prepared or being committed, and interception and tapping are required to establish the facts, or if the identification or location of the participants cannot be obtained by any other means and the research would delay matters, then permission to intercept and tap conversations or communications by telephone or by any electronic means of

communication may be granted by the judge, at the request of the prosecutor who performs or supervises the prosecution.
Also, the court, at the prosecutor's request, during the prosecution, or by default, during the trial, may order that any postal or transport company must retain and not deliver letters, telegrams and any other correspondence or articles sent by the dealer, or addressed to him, either directly or indirectly.

e) Information systematically gathered by an investigative officer;
This is the method used in all cases of human trafficking. The prosecution has an obligation to collect all information necessary to solve a criminal case. In this respect, institutions have the right to seek all the information they need from the other institutions.
f) (Systematic) Information gathered by a civilian officer;
This method is rarely used. For example, a labour inspector may collect information which he then submits to the prosecution. Collecting this information can only be done within the jurisdiction conferred by law.
g) Staged purchases and services by a police officer/Staged purchases and services by a civilian;
These methods are used if you want to achieve a *flagrante delicto*.
h) Infiltration by police officers;
If there is good and concrete evidence that a crime of human trafficking has been committed or is going to be committed and that this crime cannot be discovered or the crime's perpetrators can not be identified by other means, investigators can assume a false identity and use this method to collect data pertaining to the crime and identify the individuals suspected of committing a crime. Undercover investigators are operatives from the judicial police and they can only be used for a specified period. Undercover investigators have a permit issued by the prosecutor to collect data and information.
i) Financial investigation;
As part of a financial investigation, information may be requested by the prosecution from banks, who are required to submit data from their records.

2.2.2 Application of the legal framework in practice

The prosecutor conducts the criminal investigation. The prosecution is focused on gathering the necessary evidence on the existence of the crime, identifying offenders and determining their criminal liability so as to establish whether or not it is appropriate to have them taken to court.[25] During the trial, the prosecutor is involved in the hearing and has the right to require the use of evidence and take appropriate measures that will help decide the best outcome for the case.

---

[25] This aim of prosecution is established by Art. 200 of the Romanian Criminal Procedure Code.

Police officers are involved in conducting a criminal prosecution by the following prosecutor's directions. They effectively interview witnesses, collect evidence, and are involved in conducting searches and assessing the goods.

Judges have the power during the trial to rule on measures of particular importance, such as approvals to carry out house searches, the preventive arrest of traffickers, authorising the interception of telephone conversations, so as to ensure compliance with Art. 6 of the European Convention on Human Rights. During the trial, judges use the evidence gathered during the criminal investigation and consider any other evidence deemed necessary. Finally a court ruling is given.

Employees of the intelligence services participate by making telephone interceptions or recordings.

The Territorial Labour Inspectorates help by providing the information obtained during the investigations to the prosecution and the courts.

Non-Governmental organisations help to stabilise the victims by granting them accommodation or assistance, allowing the investigation teams to contact them.

As for the cooperation between the police, prosecutors and judges, we have illustrated that police officers comply with the requests of the prosecutor and the court. The prosecutor is subject to the court's jurisdiction and can request that certain measures be taken, such as the arrest of the trafficker, the authorisation for wire tapping and house searches. The court may require the police to carry out certain measures, such as collecting objects and documents, etc.

After obtaining an authorisation for phone tapping, Romanian Intelligence Service employees (the Secret Service) are called in to conduct the technical aspects since they have the required technology. All the other institutions are obliged to provide the information they hold to the prosecution and the courts.

The Department of Investigation of Organised Crime and Terrorism (DIOCT) within the Prosecutor's Office of the High Court of Cassation and Justice, operates as follows:

The DIOCT is managed at both central and territorial levels. Services, offices and departments directed by chief prosecutors are organised within the central structure by order of the Chief Prosecutor of the DIOCT. Territorial services led by chief prosecutors are established by order of the Chief Prosecutor of the DIOCT in the territorial jurisdiction of the prosecutor's offices attached to courts of appeal. By order of the Chief Prosecutor of the DIOCT, territorial offices under the jurisdiction of the territorial prosecutor's offices attached to tribunals may be established or abolished. Offices are directed by chief prosecutors.

All the DIOCT prosecutors, both at central and regional levels, have the same mandate/competences pertaining to the categories of crimes they can investigate. In terms of territory, each jurisdiction is different and every prosecutor investigates crimes within his criminal jurisdiction.

According to Art. 20 of Law No. 508/2004 governing the creation, organisation and operation of the DIOCT, within the Public Ministry, prosecutors within the central structure or in the territorial services of the DIOCT can take over cases for prosecution that are under the jurisdiction of the territorial structures subordinated to the DIOCT, subject to the approval of the Chief Prosecutor of DIOCT. In cases that are taken over, prosecutors within the central structure and territorial services have the right to invalidate acts and measures made by the prosecutors within the subordinated territorial structures, if they are contrary to law, and these more senior prosecutors may then carry out any of the relevant tasks.[26]

The indictments prepared by the prosecutors from the territorial services and offices of the DIOCT are in turn checked by the chief-prosecutors from these services or offices. Indictments made by chief-prosecutors of the territorial offices are verified by the chief prosecutors of territorial services. Indictments made by the chief prosecutors of the territorial services, as well as by prosecutors from within the central structure of the DIOCT are verified by the DIOCT services' chief prosecutors, according to their particular area of expertise. When the indictments are prepared by prosecutors that are Heads of Departments within the central structure, this is verified by the DIOCT's Chief Prosecutor.

The police report to the Prosecutor during the criminal investigation. As such, the allocation of tasks is irrelevant at central or regional level, because the prosecutor's provisions must be complied with rather those of superiors within the police force itself. According to Art. 219 of the Criminal Procedure Code, 'a higher-level police chief cannot give instructions to a judicial police investigation officer in a criminal investigation; the prosecutor is the only competent authority in this regard.' This is a rule. To explain this better: each judicial officer who conducts prosecution activities has a superior, an officer in the police force. However, their activities must follow instructions given by the prosecutor. Only he is able to guide the police in carrying out the prosecution activities. The police officer's superior is not allowed to tell the police officer how to conduct the criminal investigation.

The Labour Inspectorate is a specialised body of the central public administration that functions under the authority of the Ministry of Labour

---

[26] For example, let us assume that the prosecution of a crime of human trafficking of victims for labour exploitation is initiated by the Territorial Office X. The DIOCT's central structure considers, for example, that in order to prosecute the case more effectively, it is necessary to take over this case at a central level. The central structure takes over the case from the territorial office and the prosecutor working on the case can then take any action that the initial prosecutor had had authority to do. Furthermore, he can invalidate the actions and measures taken by the prosecutors within the subordinate territorial structures, if they are contrary to law. The measures prosecutors can take may refer to: the management of evidence, seizure of trafficker's assets, retaining the accused in order to make preventative arrest after the detention permit has been issued by the judge, etc.

and Social Solidarity. The Labour Inspectorate has subordinate Territorial Labour Inspectorates, legal entities that are organised in each country and in Bucharest.

Inspectors from the central Labour Inspectorate have the power to carry out inspections within the jurisdictions of the regional Territorial Labour Inspectorates.

The National Agency against Trafficking in Persons includes a central structure and several regional centres. The regional centres are responsible for referring victims to institutions that can provide assistance to them and for performing statistics and analysis at regional level. The central structure of the NATP coordinates the Regional Centres and generates statistics at central level, after collecting data from regional level.

There are situations in which a case surpasses the regional level. If a particular case, due to the geographical locations in which offences are committed, falls into the jurisdiction of several structures of criminal prosecution (prosecutors and judicial police) in different districts, jurisdiction over the case reverts to the organisation that was first informed. Any conflict of jurisdiction between two or more prosecutors is resolved by their common superior prosecutor. When a conflict arises between two or more criminal courts, the jurisdiction shall be exercised by the prosecutor supervising the criminal investigation of these courts.

Regarding the courts, the rules of Art. 35 of the Code of Criminal Proceedings apply. In cases that are indivisible or connected, if the jurisdiction under the law in relation to various perpetrators and different facts belongs to several courts of equal rank, the jurisdiction to hear all the facts and judge all the perpetrators belongs to the court before which the case was first brought. If jurisdiction over the facts or perpetrators belongs to different courts of unequal rank, the jurisdiction in all such combined cases lies with the higher court.[27]

It should be noted that Romania has four categories of courts: law courts, tribunals, courts of appeal and the High Court of Cassation and Justice.[28] Each of these courts has jurisdiction in the first instance in certain cases. Trials on human trafficking are judged in the first instance by the law courts, the decisions of the courts can be appealed to the courts of appeal and courts of

[27] There is indivisibility: when several persons were involved in committing an offence; when two or more crimes were committed by the same act; in the case of an ongoing offence or in any other cases where two or more material acts constitute a single crime. There is connection: a) when two or more crimes are committed by different perpetrators, by one or more persons together, at the same time and same place; when two or more crimes are committed in different time periods or in different places, as a result of an understanding between criminals; when a crime is committed to prepare, facilitate or conceal another offence, or is committed to facilitate or ensure the avoidance of criminal liability by the perpetrator of another crime; when there is connection between two or more crimes and bringing the crimes together is necessary to administer justice.

[28] This hierarchy of courts is established by Law No. 304/2004, concerning the judicial organisation.

appeal decisions can be appealed to the High Court of Cassation and Justice. Sometimes, the jurisdiction over a process of human trafficking may belong to a court other than the law court, because of the traffickers' particular circumstances. For example, jurisdiction belongs to the High Court of Cassation and Justice if the trafficker is a member of the government, a senator or a deputy. If a senator committed the crime of human trafficking in conjunction with an ordinary citizen, both would be judged by the High Court of Cassation and Justice, whereas the case would have been judged by a law court if neither of them was a senator.

When two or more courts are competent to judge the same case or decline jurisdiction, the positive or negative conflict of jurisdiction is settled by the common higher court. With regards to labour inspections, each inspector has to carry out inspections in its territorial jurisdiction.

Representatives of the regional centres of the National Agency against Trafficking in Persons only conduct the assessment and referral of those victims who have presented themselves at the Regional Centres. Cooperation between institutions is provided under the law and takes place as described above.

With regards to the procedure used to report victims of trafficking, there is a National Mechanism to identify and report victims of trafficking in persons, which provides a formalised form of cooperation between institutions. The Law No. 678/2001 on preventing and combating trafficking in persons also stipulates cooperation between State institutions.

When an illegal immigrant is found to be working, the statutory provisions that apply are those governing the status of foreigners in Romania. A number of situations must be considered.

If the person who is found working has illegally entered Romanian territory, he/she is investigated for the crime of illegally crossing the border and can be sentenced to prison. After serving his/her punishment, he/she may be forced to leave the Romanian territory.

If the person has entered the Romanian territory legally, but without having the right to work, and he/she is found to be working, a repatriation order against him/her will be issued by the Romanian Immigration Office. This measure is taken because the immigrant has not respected the regulations under which he/she was permitted to enter the country. For example, if a foreigner was allowed to enter the country for tourism, he/she is not entitled to work.

At the same time, if a person enters Romania legally with the right to stay for a limited period and he/she does not leave the country at the end of this period and is found to be working, a repatriation procedure will be initiated for that foreigner.

2.3 Cooperation between States

2.3.1 Legal framework for cooperation in trans-national Trafficking in Human Beings-cases

In general, international cooperation on trafficking in persons is complex and very difficult considering the variety of judicial systems, non-standardised legislation, and the very different criminal and social policies of European States. In most cases, human trafficking takes place with the participation of a number of individuals, each under the jurisdiction of a different State.

Being a form of organised crime, human trafficking can be prevented and controlled through effective international cooperation between all institutions responsible for law enforcement, with the help of non-governmental organisations and through the adoption of some appropriate international and national laws. Articles 45-47 of Law No. 678/2001, amended, relate to international cooperation on trafficking in persons. Under these provisions, the Ministry of Public Administration and the Interior and the Public Ministry (in Romania, all prosecutors are from the Public Ministry) are required to appoint liaison officers and prosecutors to cooperate with police officers and judges from other States in order to coordinate actions during a prosecution.[29] To this end, there are points of contact with similar institutions in other States within the Ministry of Foreign Affairs and Prosecutor's Office of the High Court of Cassation and Justice.

According to Article 22 of Law No. 508/2004, 'regarding mutual consultation with similar structures in other countries, concerning offences under the jurisdiction of the Department for the Investigation of Organised Crime and Terrorism and the exchange of data and information on the research of these crimes, an international legal aid office is constituted that functions within the Department for the Investigation of Organised Crime and Terrorism, reporting directly to the Chief Prosecutor.'

According to Art. 47 of Law No. 678/2001, international transport companies are required to verify if passengers are in possession of the identity documents required for entry into the country of transit or destination when tickets are issued. Drivers and ticket inspectors working for international road transport companies, are also obliged to check this when passengers board. This measure is useful because, in most cases, the traffickers confiscate victims' travel documents.

International cooperation in preventing and combating trafficking in human beings is not confined to these provisions. International conventions on this matter, to which Romania adhered by signature or ratification, represent legal instruments which allow both informal and judicial cooperation.

[29] In accordance with the provisions of Law No. 304/2004, the Public Ministry exercises its powers through public prosecutors organised under the law in prosecutor offices. The Public Ministry represents the general interests of society and defends legal order and the rights and freedoms of citizens through its judicial activity;

Cooperation between EU Member States takes place by using measures adopted within the EU, such as the European arrest warrant.[30]

Romania cooperates on trafficking in persons for labour exploitation with Eurojust. Law No. 58/2006 was adopted on 22 March 2006 to ratify the agreement on cooperation between Romania and Eurojust, signed in Brussels on 2 December 2005, and to regulate certain measures relating to the representation of Romania to Eurojust, in the period preceding and following Romania's accession to the European Union.

On 1st August 2007, Romania signed up to the Convention and the Additional Protocols to the Convention, which established the creation of European Police Office.

The European arrest warrant is a judicial decision by which a competent judicial authority of a Member State of the European Union calls for the arrest and surrender by another Member State of a person for the purpose of prosecution, or to serve a sentence or as a safeguard measure with freedom being withdrawn. The European arrest warrant is executed on the basis of mutual recognition and confidence, in accordance with the provisions of the Council Framework Decision No. 2002/584/JHA of 13 June 2002.

In Romania, the courts are designated as the judicial authorities responsible for issuing warrants. The Romanian judicial authorities responsible for executing these are the courts of appeal. The Romanian authorities accredited to receive European arrest warrants are the Ministry of Justice and the offices attached to the appeal courts designated under Para (2), in whose district the person being sought is located. If the location of the person is not known, the European arrest warrant is transmitted to the Prosecutor's Office of the Bucharest Court of Appeal.

The Romanian Central Authority is the Ministry of Justice. As such, the Ministry of Justice:

a) receives European arrest warrants issued by a judicial authority in another EU Member State and forwards these to the prosecutor's office attached to the court of appeal in whose district the person was located or to the Prosecutor's Office of the Bucharest Court of Appeal, if the person sought has not been located, whenever the issuing judicial authority fails to transmit the European arrest warrant directly to the Romanian judicial authority;
b) forwards the European arrest warrant issued by a Romanian judicial authority, if it cannot be transmitted directly to the foreign judicial authority receiving it or if the executing Member State has designated the Ministry of Justice as the recipient;
c) keeps track of European arrest warrants issued or received by the Romanian judicial authorities, for statistical purposes;

[30] For an elaborate overview of these instruments see A. Middelburg and C. Rijken, 'The EU Legal Framework to Combat THB for Labour Exploitation', Chapter 6 in this book.

d) performs any other tasks prescribed by law, designed to assist and support the Romanian judicial authorities in issuing and enforcing the European arrest warrants.

In Romania, the framework law governing judicial cooperation in criminal matters is law No. 302/2004. In transnational cases, the following special investigative techniques can be used, whether European Union Member States or other countries are involved. In some cases, the law contains special provisions for cooperation with the EU Member States, and we shall refer to those in this study.

a) (Systematic) Observation;
   This method can be used at the request of another State, and the observation's results can be shared with the other State, following a request for judicial assistance in this regard.
b) Entering locked premises;
   To use this method of investigation it is necessary to respect the laws of the State in whose territory they are applied. For example, in Romania, a court approval is needed to conduct a search.
   According to Art. 163, Para 1: 'the letters rogatory concerning searches, seizure of property and documents are subject to the following conditions:
   - the offence motivating the letters rogatory shall be liable to give rise to extradition in Romania, as the requested State;
   - the execution of the letters rogatory is consistent with Romanian law.
     For example, a house search in the case of a magistrate's home can be done only with the agreement of the Superior Council of Magistracy. A house search of a Member of Parliament can only be done with the agreement of the Romanian Parliament. Without these agreements, the Romanian State cannot act on the requests made by the letters rogatory.
     According to Art. 187, the provisions of Art. 163, Para (1) shall not apply in relation to the States that are parties to the Convention implementing the Schengen agreements. In order to execute the requests set out in the letters rogatory concerning searches and seizure, the following conditions may, however, be imposed:
   - the Romanian legislation and the laws of the State requesting it must provide a punishment with deprivation of liberty or some measure characterised by restriction of freedom, lasting a maximum of 6 months, for the offence that triggered the request of the letters rogatory, or the law of at least one of the parties should provide an equivalent penalty and, according to the law of the other party involved, the offence should be punishable as a violation of legal rules, established by the administrative authorities, whose decision may be appealed before a criminal court;
   - the execution of letters rogatory is consistent with Romanian law.

c) Requesting information concerning telecommunications;
Each country involved obtains such information on telecommunications carried out in its own territory. For example, if a telephone conversation takes place between two people from two different countries, each country may request information from the telephone company operating within its territory. We should mention that a Romanian phone company has no obligation to provide such information to anyone other than the Romanian State authorities, and has no obligation to another country making such a request.
To achieve international judicial cooperation, the Romanian State may request the necessary information from the national telephone company, who is then obliged to provide this information to the Romanian authorities. This information will be made available by the petitioned State (Romania) to the petitioning State, based on a request for international judicial assistance.
d) Recording telecommunications (phone and e-mail)/Recording confidential communications;
Telecommunications may only be recorded by each country only within its own territory. Thus, the Romanian State will tap conversations using its own Telephone Company, and the other country involved will record the phone conversations made through the telephone company within its territory. If a State is interested in a conversation that has taken place on the territory of another State, it should request assistance in this regard.
For example, according to Art. 171 (interception and recording of conversations and communications) of Law No. 302/2004 on international judicial cooperation in criminal matters:
'(1) In order to solve a criminal case, the judicial authorities of the petitioning State or the competent authorities so designated by the petitioning State may submit an application to the Romanian authorities seeking legal assistance for the interception of telecommunications and their immediate transmission to the petitioned State or interception of the registration and subsequent transmission of telecommunications to the petitioning State, if the person investigated:
   a. is located on the territory of the petitioning State and it requires technical assistance in order to intercept communications from the target;
   b. is located on Romanian territory, when communications can be intercepted from the target in the Romanian State;
   c. is located in a third country, which has been informed, and if the petitioning State requires technical assistance to intercept communications from the target.
(2) The applications submitted under this article must meet the following conditions:

d. to indicate and confirm the issuing of an order or a warrant for interception and recording, during criminal proceedings;
e. to contain information that will allow the identification of the interception's target;
f. to indicate the criminal acts that are the object of criminal investigation;
g. to mention the duration of interception;
h. to contain sufficient technical data, if it is possible, especially the number of the network connection so as to allow processing of the application.

(3) If the request is made in accordance with Paragraph (1), Letter b), it must also contain a description of the facts. The Romanian judicial authorities may request any additional information needed to enable them to assess whether the measure should be taken and applied in a similar national case.'

e) Systematic information gathering by an investigative officer;
Investigating police officers may be used in each State involved in a case. Sharing information obtained by them can be done following a request for international judicial assistance.

f) Infiltration by police officers;
Romanian law provides in Art. 168 the possibility of conducting undercover investigations, as follows:
'(1) The Romanian State may agree with a foreign State to assist one another in conducting investigations made by undercover agents.
(2) The Romanian authorities will decide on a case-by-case basis, according to Romanian law.
(3) Under the conditions of Romanian law, Romanian and foreign judicial authorities will establish the concrete methods of investigation and legal status of undercover agents.'

g) Financial investigation;
Law No. 302/2004 contains provisions relating to financial investigations only in relation to European Union Member States.
Art. 187 of Law No. 302/2004 provides for information on banking operations between countries to be supplied. Upon request, the Romanian authorities will provide details of bank accounts specified by the petitioning foreign authorities, and on banking transactions which took place in a clearly defined period through one or more bank accounts specified in the application, including details on any sender or beneficiary.
Data will be provided only to the extent that information is available to the bank holding those bank accounts. When the information is requested, the applicant authority will explain in the application why

the requested information is considered to be of substantial value to the investigation of the respective crime.

The request is subject to the following conditions:

a) the execution of the request is compatible with the Romanian law;

b) the criminal act under investigation is a criminal offence under Romanian law.

Art. 187 regulates banking supervision. The Romanian authorities will, for a specified period, at the request of a Member State of the European Union, provide supervision of banking operations which are carried out on one or more bank accounts specified by the petitioning authorities. The applicant will show in the application why the information requested is considered to have substantial value for the research of the respective offence. The Romanian judicial authorities shall, as provided by Romanian law, authorise banking supervision. Under the jurisdiction of Romanian law, Romanian and foreign judicial authorities will determine the practical aspects of supervision.

The banks will ensure both the confidentiality of the information transmitted to the applicant and of the criminal investigation being conducted, without disclosing this data to the client or any other person.

Another method of cooperation in investigating crimes of human trafficking is the formation of joint investigation teams.

According to Art. 169 of Law No. 302/2004, 'in order to facilitate the resolution of a request for rogatory commission, joint investigation teams may be established, with a specific purpose and limited duration that may be extended by agreement of the States involved. The composition of the team shall be agreed by all parts involved'.

A joint investigation team may be created especially when:

a) during proceedings pending in the petitioning State, difficult investigations are required to be carried out, involving significant human and other resources in both States;

b) several States conduct investigations that require a coordinated and concerted action in the countries concerned.

The application to mount a joint investigation team may be made by any of the States involved. The team is formed in one of the countries where the investigation is to be conducted.

2.3.2 Application of legal framework in practice

The actors referred to in Para 2.1 are competent to cooperate with authorities abroad. Law No. 678/2001 provides for cooperation between the Romanian police and prosecutors and the police and prosecutors from other States involved. According to Art. 45, 'liaison officers within the Ministry of Interior and magistrate's office, are based in the prosecutors' offices, which are attached to tribunals, who must ensure mutual consultation with liaison officers, or liaison magistrates from other States, in order to coordinate their actions during the prosecution'.

A contact point with similar institutions in other States was established within the Ministry of Interior and Prosecutor's office of the Supreme Court of Justice to exchange data and information on the investigation and prosecution of crimes under this law.

According to Article 22 of Law No. 508/2004 on the establishment, organisation and operation of the Public Ministry's Department for the Investigation of Organised Crime and Terrorism, for the mutual consultation with similar structures in other countries, regarding offences under the jurisdiction of the Department for the Investigation of Organised Crime and Terrorism and the exchange of data and information on investigation of these crimes, an international legal aid office was set up and works within the Department for the Investigation of Organised Crime and Terrorism, reporting directly to the Chief Prosecutor.'

The courts also have the right to cooperate, requesting assistance from other similar courts in other States or by issuing European arrest warrants, etc.

The NGOs also cooperate with other foreign NGOs. According to the 'National Mechanism for the Identification and Referral of Trafficked Persons', if the victim is identified by an NGO from another country, the representative of a Romanian NGO will meet the victim at the border crossing point or at the place agreed with the partner in question. If the victim agrees to participate in an assistance programme organised by that NGO or other organisations or institutions, depending on the particularities of the case, the victim will be included in a special assistance programme.

The National Agency against Trafficking in Persons is an organisation that specialises in the protection of victims. It is organised under the Romanian Police General Inspectorate, and consequently cooperates with similar structures in other States.

The Territorial Labour Inspectorates can collaborate with their counterpart institutions abroad, and foreign labour inspectors may, for example, be invited to assist in conducting an investigation of the Romanian labour inspectors.

The actors mentioned above are familiar with the laws and procedures on international judicial cooperation. Some of them have direct contact with their counterparts from other States (e.g. NGOs or the representatives of National Agency against Trafficking in Persons). Moreover, in principle, mediation is required to achieve direct contact between actors in different countries. For example, according to Art. 46 of Law No. 678/2001, 'to exchange data and information on the investigation and prosecution of crimes under this law, a contact point with similar institutions in other States will be established within the Ministry of Interior and Prosecutor's Office of the Supreme Court of Justice.' A European arrest warrant is transmitted via the Ministry of Justice.

Cooperation between the Romanian and foreign labour inspectors can be achieved in cases concerning transnational labour services. If collaboration is requested in terms of labour relations, the Single Liaison Offices Network is used. There is a single liaison office in each State. If the aim is to obtain information on safety and occupational health, the KSS network is used.[31]

The Romanian prosecution organisations cooperate with Europol and Eurojust. In Romania, one of the last operations in which Europol was involved was the dissolution of a network that was trafficking minors, located in Tandarei (Romania). The network was recruiting gipsy children and taking them illegally over the border to Great Britain, where they were then exploited by being forced to beg or commit crimes on the streets.
In this instance, cooperation was very good, although from interviews we conducted, it was revealed that sometimes, in the case of Europol, the information is not obtained quickly enough.

Decision No. 664/2010, issued on 07.14.2010, regarding the approval of the 2010 Action Plan for implementing the National Strategy on Migration for the period 2007-2010, approved by Government Decision No. 1.122/2007, allows border police officers to participate in joint operations between Member States and in training activities through the FRONTEX Agency, as well as exchanging operational information of interest through authorised agencies /institutions: SECI (Agreement on Cooperation for the prevention and control of transnational crime in South-East Europe), EUROPOL, FRONTEX.

Good practice is represented by the sharing of information between institutions in different countries, the creation of joint teams of cooperation, by the possibility of catching traffickers who are not in one of the States involved, etc.

Bad practice is exemplified by the length of time it takes to organise the letters rogatory, the lack of financial resources to pay translators, the lack of authorised translators for certain languages.

In our opinion, coercive investigation measures include: detention, arrest, being ordered not to leave the city, and ordered not to leave the country.

Such preventive measures can be taken in cases of trafficking in human beings for labour exploitation. Moreover, in a case analysed by us, there are details on taking such action against traffickers.

2.4 Summary of findings

2.4.1 Identified obstacles

1. The main obstacle is the length of time taken in obtaining letters rogatory. Often, information must be obtained quickly, but this is only managed following a lengthy period;
2. The creation of joint investigative teams requires a certain period of time, during which time the traffickers may disappear;[32]

[31] KSS is a European network composed of inspectors specialised in safety and occupational health.

3. Another obstacle is the lack of translators. For example, if cooperation with non-European countries, such as India, (where there are many dialects) is required, there are no accredited translators;[33]
4. Lack of financial resources needed to pay translators.

2.4.2 Good practices

1. Exchange of information and transfer of experiences, know-how and best practices, at bilateral and multilateral level;
2. Participation in specific programmes and activities undertaken b the EU institutions to prevent and combat trafficking in persons;
3. Flexibility of contact and exchange of intelligence procedures with foreign liaison officers or corresponding structures from abroad, Europol, Romanian and foreign liaison officers on mission in Romania, through the network of contact points;
4. Conducting joint investigations on specific cases, by direct contacts with the competent authorities from the countries of destination. We have met professionals who have spoken of their participation in such joint teams.[34]

---

[32] Interview with the National Agency against Trafficking in Persons – Oradea Regional Centre (03.11.2010).

[33] Interview with the Prosecutor's Office of the High Court of Cassation and Justice - Department for the Investigation of Organised Crime and Terrorism – Iaşi Territorial Office (05.11.2010).

[34] Interview with the National Agency against Trafficking in Persons – Oradea Regional Centre (03.11.2010). For example, in one case, Romanian officers went to Spain, collaborated with Spanish officers and presented the prosecution material to the traffickers arrested in Spain.

Part III
Victim protection and assistance

3.1 Identification of victims

3.1.1 Methods of identification and actors involved

Victims may be identified in several ways: by the judicial organisation; with the help of the diplomatic missions and consular offices abroad; by using the free telephone service TelVerde, requests for assistance from the victims of trafficking can be retrieved and referred or concerns about the possible instances of the crime of trafficking in persons; by other people, for instance former clients (of victims, both sexual and labour exploitation); by the inspectors of regional labour services, the medical personnel of hospitals or other health care facilities, or by employees of schools or other community institutions. Most victims are identified as a result of their complaints, because they know the exact situation and are directly involved and affected.
Victims can be identified by:

- policemen specialised in combating human trafficking, namely the Romanian Police General Inspectorate, and the Divisions for countering Organised Crime, the Brigades for countering Organised Crime or Organised Crime Control Services, or the Border Police General Inspectorate;
- Other structures of the system of national defence and public order, which do not have the fight against trafficking as their main objective – the criminal investigation police, transport police, the public order police, the gendarmerie;
- Prosecutor's Office of the High Court of Cassation and Justice – Department for the Investigation of Organised Crime and Terrorism, the central structure and regional offices and services;
- National Agency against Trafficking in Persons, the central structure and the regional centres;
- Territorial Labour Inspectorates, during inspections;
- Romanian Immigration Office, when foreign citizens are involved;
- International Organisation for Migration;
- Non-Governmental Organisations;
- Romanian embassies and consular offices abroad and those of other States in Romania;
- Ordinary citizens, representatives of hospitals and the Church, etc.

In Romania, inspections aimed at identifying possible cases of victims of trafficking for labour exploitation are carried out by the Ministry of Labour in cases where firms are mediating the conclusion of contracts for work abroad. Otherwise, from the information we have, the institutions do not seek to identify victims of trafficking for labour exploitation, but act only after obtaining this information, either from referrals or through regular checks.

Romanian law does not specify a particular authority to determine the age of the victim who may be a child. The age may be determined by any State institution, based on documents, such as a birth certificate, or identity documents, such as an identity card or passport. Unless false information is revealed, the age mentioned in these documents is considered to be the real one.

A problem arises when the child has no documents to prove his/her age. In such a situation, the institutions involved need to collect information on the individual's name and place of origin and details of their family and relatives, so that they can identify the individual and determine their age based on civil status documents kept at the person's place of birth.

Finally, if the age cannot be determined in this manner, either because the birth of this child was never declared or they cannot trace the civil status documents or individuals who can provide them, the victim's age is determined by anthropological surveys conducted by the Institute of Forensic Medicine.[35]

3.1.2. Victim status

From our point of view, it can only be established with certainty whether or not a person has been victim of 'trafficking in persons' after the trial has ended.

However, prior to that, so that people who appear to be victims of trafficking can receive assistance, they are granted this status based on a minimum amount of information and proof. The analysis is carried out by institutions with expertise in the field. It is a prerequisite for granting the status of 'victim', that there be a minimum amount of information to justify the presumption that the person was a victim of human trafficking. The status of 'victim of trafficking' is established by the police, prosecutors and judges. This qualification is based on the victim's statements, other people's statements and is based on the material evidence collected and documents obtained, using audio or video recordings, etc.

There is no procedure in Romania by which a person, on their own, is allowed to claim and be able to obtain the status of a victim of human trafficking. The status of the victim is determined by the authorised institutions, following the complaints received, and the victim is free to choose whether they wish to benefit or not from the legal provisions adopted in his/her favour.

In Romania there is no conflict between the tasks/responsibilities specified in the work of the authorities in relation to combating trafficking in persons. Legislation has been designed so that the authorities support each other in the fight against human trafficking.

[35] Interview with Prosecutor's Office of the High Court of Cassation and Justice - Department for the Investigation of Organised Crime and Terrorism – Central structure.

3.1.3 The needs of victims

The needs of victims are initially evaluated by representatives of the Regional Centres of the National Agency against Trafficking in Persons. They carry out the initial assessment of a victim in order to identify her/his needs for professional advice. It may be observed that the victim needs medical assistance and psychological counselling. It is possible that the trafficked person also needs shelter.

The needs of the victim can be identified by those providing assistance effectively. For example, a psychologist, a doctor or representatives of NGOs can fulfil this task. Needs are analysed based on discussions with the victims and based on their requirements. They are given psychological, legal and medical assistance, as well as shelter, etc.

Sometimes, failures can occur because of the organisations providing assistance. For example, although the law provides for the provision of accommodation for victims who need it, the authorities, who should provide shelter, may not be able to accommodate the victims due to lack of funds. In Romania, accommodation is provided mainly by NGOs, but there are relatively few of them and they are not financed by the Romanian State.

If a case only falls under labour law and the victim is not harmed, he/she will not benefit from the provisions relating to assistance, protection and compensation. Damages can only be sought in a civil lawsuit, initiated by the victim.

If the victim is a foreigner in Romania and the situation is not considered to be a criminal case, but is considered to fall under immigration law, the victim may even suffer sanctions. In such a situation, he/she is not considered a 'victim of human trafficking'. Violation of the provisions concerning the status of foreigners in Romania may result, as appropriate, in the criminal, civil and administrative liability of the person responsible for the act.

3.2 Legal framework for the protection of the rights of victims of Trafficking in Human Beings for labour exploitation

3.2.1 Assistance to victims

Romanian law does not establish special conditions for victims of human trafficking for labour exploitation to receive assistance. Any victim of trafficking in persons is entitled to such assistance. It is understood that this assistance is granted only if the victim needs it and wants to receive assistance.

The assistance given to victims may be psychological; to help them overcome the trauma they have suffered. Also, medical care is given as required. If they do not have a place to stay, they are housed in the NGOs' shelters or in assistance and protection centres for trafficking victims belonging to the State. One problem is that there are a very small number of such shelters and a lack of financial resources.

The victims' social reintegration will be pursued. A job will be sought for victims of trafficking who have Romanian citizenship, so they can earn a living. Victims who are foreign citizens may remain in Romania for a period, but they do not automatically acquire the right to work. Trafficked persons may be granted some compensation for the damage suffered. During the legal process, they will receive legal support and counselling. According to Art. 44 of Law No. 678/2001, victims of trafficking are entitled to compulsory legal assistance in order to exercise their rights at all stages of the criminal proceedings, prescribed by law, and to support their requests and civil claims against the persons who committed offences against them under this law. Legal aid lawyers are provided by default. Unfortunately, the legal assistance offered is not very good, these lawyers are not interested in the case, in the same way that a paid lawyer representing the party would be. There have been cases in which the legal aid lawyers conclude a legal contract with the trafficker after dumping the victim and go on to represent the accused in the legal process. As the lawyer understands the victim's position and how they intend to plea, they are able to help the accused.[36] If there is a risk of the victims being targets for retaliation, their physical integrity will be protected.

According to Art. 26, Paragraph 4, of Law No. 678/2001, 'because of their age, if minors are victims of crimes under this law, they receive special protection and assistance.'

According to Article 24, Paragraph 3, of Law No. 678/2001, 'in cases involving offences under this law, the hearing of a child who has not attained the age of 14 years should be held in the presence of one parent or guardian or of the person to whom the care and education of the minor is entrusted'. According to G.E.O. 194/2002, 'juveniles placed in accommodation centres should have free access to compulsory education.'

The situation for unaccompanied foreign minors who enter or remain unaccompanied after entering Romanian territory is as follows: their identity and means of entry into the country is established; according to the law, their representation is assured by a competent institution, which will ensure the necessary protection and care for them, including accommodation in special child care centres under the same conditions as for Romanian children; steps are taken to identify the parents, regardless of their place of residence for the purpose of family reunification; until the parents are identified, school-aged children must have access to the compulsory education system; if a child's parents are not residing in Romania, the child is returned to the parents' country of residence or the country where other family members have been identified, with their consent; if parents or other family members are not identified or if the minor is not accepted in his home country, temporary residence in Romania shall be allowed. In order to find the appropriate

[36] Interview with the President of Young Generation Romania Association (03.11.2011);

solutions, the Romanian Immigration Office will cooperate with other institutions, as well as with national and international organisations specialising in protecting minors.

Male victims are more difficult to assist. They have more pride and often refuse to believe that they have been trafficked. They do not consider themselves to be victims of trafficking for labour exploitation, but think that they have been deceived by the employer or trafficker who has not respected the contract that had been agreed. For this reason, those attempting to assist them must be better trained, as it is more difficult to work with male victims than female victims. An NGO female representative claimed that because they need to earn their own living, male victims accept the situation more readily after they have found a new job. Once they find a job, it can be easier to work with them.[37]

Although the law makes no distinction with regards to shelters, almost all shelters are meant for women. Moreover, the number of shelters in Romania is very low. We encountered just one case where an NGO had given shelter to Hondurans.[38]

The victim is informed of his rights by the police. Also, according to legal procedure, after the identification process, the victims are referred to the regional centres of the National Agency against Trafficking in Persons. Here the victims are informed about their rights. They are assessed to determine whether they need psychological and medical counselling, housing, etc.

Victims may be placed in the care of NGOs, which, in turn, can inform victims of their rights such as, for example, the right to obtain compensation.

3.2.2 Right to residence

A. Residence granted

The Right of Residence granted to foreigners in general

In Romania, the granting of a residence permit to a foreigner is done under the conditions of the G.E.O. 194/2002, concerning the status of foreigners in Romania. The right of residence means the right granted to a foreigner to remain in Romania by the Romanian competent authorities, in accordance with the legal stipulations.

Foreigners who are temporarily in Romania can legally remain on Romanian territory until the right of residence is terminated by the visa granted or, where appropriate, by a residence permit. Where the period for which visas are abolished is not clearly mentioned (in the case of international conventions or regulations which unilaterally abolish the visa regime),

---

[37] Interview with the President of the Association for the Development of Alternative Practices of Reintegration and Education (ADAPRE) (06.10.2010).

[38] Assistance was provided by the Romania Young Generation Association.

foreigners who do not require visas in order to enter Romania are allowed access to Romanian territory and may remain for up to 90 days, within a 6 month period, from the date of their first entry into the country.

The right of residence granted may be temporary or permanent.
According to Art. 107 of the G.E.O. No. 194/2002, for foreigners to whom the right of residence in Romania is granted or extended, a residence permit is issued by the Romanian Immigration Office, through its territorial units, as follows:

a) Temporary residence permit, for a foreigner to whom the right of temporary residence is granted or, where appropriate, extended;
b) Residence permit for work, for a foreigner to whom the right of temporary residence and the right to work is granted or, where appropriate, extended;
c) Permanent residence permit, for a foreigner to whom permanent residence is granted.

The conclusion is that a foreigner must have a residence permit for work or permanent residence granted in order to be able to work in Romania. Foreigners with temporary residence permits shall not be allowed to work.

Allowing victims that are foreign citizens to remain in Romania
Victims of the crime of trafficking for labour exploitation may remain on Romanian territory according to several legal statutory provisions.
First of all, Law No. 678/2001, regarding the prevention and fight against the trafficking in persons, stipulates in Art. 39[1]:

> *'(1) For those foreigners for whom there are serious grounds for believing they are victims of human trafficking, a period of 'recovery and reflection' is granted of up to 90 days, to allow them to escape the influence of the perpetrators and to make a conscious decision to cooperate with the competent authorities. During this period, they are allowed by the Authority for Foreigners, at the request of the prosecutor or the court, to remain on Romanian territory.*
>
> *(2) During or at the end of the period of reflection, foreign victims of trafficking may, upon request, be granted a temporary residence permit, as stipulated by Government Emergency Ordinance No. 194/2002 republished, with subsequent amendments.'*

Secondly, G.E.O. 194/2002 sets out two ways of permitting foreigners to remain in the country.

First, Articles 102-104 of this legal document establish a first form of permission, entitled 'tolerance to remain in Romania', by which permission is granted by the Romanian Immigration Office allowing foreigners to remain in the country if they do not have the right of residence and do not leave Romania, for reasons beyond their control. Foreigners are tolerated in certain circumstances, including when there is reasonable cause to believe that they are victims of human trafficking. In this case, tolerance is granted at the request of the prosecutor or the court. As a result of these provisions, if the prosecutor or the court finds that there is reasonable cause to believe that a person has been trafficked, they must ask the Romanian Immigration Office to grant the status of 'tolerated person' to the potential victim. This period of tolerance cannot be longer than 90 days, and this is the time during which the potential victim must decide if he wants to cooperate with the authorities.

Secondly, Art. 130 regulates 'the granting of temporary residence for foreign victims of trafficking.' Under this article:

> *'(1) a temporary residence permit can be granted at the request of the prosecutor or court to foreigners who are victims of trafficking, (...) (even if they have entered Romania illegally), provided that:*
>
> *a) They manifest a clear intention to cooperate with the Romanian authorities in order to facilitate the identification and prosecution of the perpetrators of criminal offences committed against them;*
>
> *b) They have ceased relations with individuals suspected of committing crimes against them;*
>
> *c) Granting residence is appropriate to carry out judicial investigations;*
>
> *d) Their staying in Romania is not a danger to public order and national security.*
>
> *(2)' The right of residence can be granted for a period of six months, and can be extended for further periods under the same conditions.'*

Consequent to the aforementioned stipulations, the granting of temporary residence can only be done at the request of the prosecutor or the court and only after the victims have expressed their willingness to cooperate with the authorities. This right of residence cannot exceed 6 months, but may be extended for new periods of six months.

B. Access to the labour market

During the period in which the victim is tolerated, as well as when temporary permission to stay is granted, he/she does not have the right to work. However, the victim may apply for a residence permit to work, just like any other foreigner, as long as he/she qualifies under the Romanian legal provisions for foreigners. However, if the right of residence is granted based on the status of a 'victim of human trafficking', this does not automatically confer entitlement to work in Romania.

3.2.3 Victims as witnesses in proceedings

A victim of trafficking may participate in a trial as follows:

a. Injured party;
According to Art. 24, paragraph 1 of the Criminal Procedure Code, 'a person participating in criminal proceedings who has suffered physical, moral or material injury by a criminal act, is referred to as an 'injured party'.' Thus, the right to participate in the process and contribute to gathering evidence against the defendant is given to the victim of the offence.

b. Civil Party;
According to Art. 24, Para 2 of the Criminal Procedure Code 'the aggrieved person engaged in a civil action during a criminal trial is called a 'civil party'.' The 'injured party' is entitled to damages in criminal proceedings, without the need to resort to civil court later. In this situation, the 'injured party' seeks only to obtain compensation and cannot contribute to the criminal prosecution of the defendant.

c. Injured party and civil party;
The 'aggrieved person' may participate at the same time as an 'injured party' and a 'civil party', should he/she wish to do so.
d. Witness.[39]
According to Art. 82 of the Criminal Procedure Code: 'the 'aggrieved person' may be heard as a witness if he is not already constituted as a 'civil party' or participating in the process as a victim.'

When the victim gets involved in a trial as a civil party, his intention is to be compensated for damage suffered. The court will consider this issue and will force the trafficker to cover (part of) the unpaid wages, the cost of medicines, moral injury, etc.

If the victim is a witness, the first requirement is to protect his/her identity, so that the employer/trafficker does not know who has testified against him.

If the victim is heard as a witness whose identity is protected, his/her hearing will be completed under a false identity. The victim's actual data is placed in a sealed envelope which is deposited at the prosecutor's office, in a special place, in conditions of maximum security. Documents on the true identity of the witness will be presented to the panel of judges in strict confidence. Also, the witness will be heard through closed-circuit television, with his/her image and voice distorted so that he/she cannot be recognised. Art. 86 of the Criminal Procedure Code regulates this proceeding.

However, a witness may be placed in a protection programme throughout the investigation and the prosecution, and, in this case, the prosecutors, work with the National Office for Witness Protection, with whom the witness signs a Protocol setting out his/her duties and rights. The protection granted to witnesses is governed by Law No. 682/2002.

---

[39] I. Neagu, *Criminal Procedure Law. General Part* (Global Lex Publishing House, Bucharest 2007) pp. 172 – 175 and 402.

After completion of the trial, the presence of the victims is no longer necessary. As such, the right of residence granted in order to assure the participation of the victims in the judicial proceedings cannot be extended. Once the permit has expired, the victim must leave Romanian territory, as long as he has not regained the status of tolerated person and cannot leave the country, or if he has not been given back a right of temporary residence or for work purposes, as provided by Romanian law for any foreign citizens.

Sometimes, the right of residence can be revoked before the end of judicial proceedings.

Art. 130, Paragraph 3 of G.E.O. 194/2002 stipulates that the right of residence granted to victims for their cooperation with the authorities may be revoked in the following situations:

1. The conditions set out in Para (1) are no longer met;
2. The residence grantee has intentionally renewed contacts with persons suspected of committing offences under Para (1);
3. If it is discovered that the foreigner has misled the authorities about the status of a victim or the data and information he/she has offered them was false;
4. If the victim ceases to cooperate;
5. If the competent authorities determine the existence of any of the cases provided for in Art. 10 of the Criminal Procedure Code. (In cases specified in Art. 10 of the Criminal Procedure Code, the perpetrator cannot be condemned).

3.2.4 Right to compensation

The victims of trafficking for labour exploitation are entitled to pecuniary compensation. There are three ways a victim can obtain compensation for the crime committed against him.[40]

A. Being a civil party in criminal trial.

Victims of human trafficking may participate as a civil party and may request to be compensated for the damage that has been inflicted on him/her by the offence.

According to Art. 14 of the Civil Procedure Code, 'a civil action has to prove the liability of the defendant and identify the civil party responsible'.

The judge must rule on the civil action, where a civil party is constituted. In accordance with Art. 348 of the Criminal Procedure Code, even if a civil party is not constituted, the court shall decide on the compensation for material and moral damages. If the victim is a minor/child, and/or in other cases, the court shall rule only on their return to work, full or partial withdrawal of a document, and reinstating the status quo prior to the crime.

---

[40] G. Mateuţ, *Trafficking in human beings. Offender. Victim. Crime* (Social Alternatives Association, Iasi 2005) p. 63.

Damages are paid according to the provisions of civil law:

a) By payments in kind, by the return of an object, by restoring the situation that existed prior to the crime, through the total or partial revision of a written document or by any other appropriate means;
2) Through cash compensation payments, when compensation in kind is not possible.

Also, financial compensation is given for any benefits the civil party has lost. A civil action may also pursue the liability of the defendant under civil law and request compensation for moral damages.

The conclusion is that the victims of trafficking for labour exploitation have the right to compensation for both material damages (including the return of ID documents seized by the trafficker from the victim, the abolition of illegal contracts, payment of monies that were not received from the employer, costs of medical expenses incurred, etc.) and non-pecuniary or moral damages (represented by the mental suffering the victim has been subjected to).
The amount is calculated based on the actual loss suffered by the victim. The advantage of this procedure is that it offers full compensation to the victim. The amount that can be granted is not dependent on any limit. It is equivalent to the damage caused to the victim. According to Art. 14 of the Civil Procedure Code, damages will be paid according to the provisions of civil law. In accordance with Art. 998 and 999 of the Civil Code, compensation must be paid in full.

B. Formulation of a civil action

Secondly, the victim of human trafficking, if he/she considers it unadvisable to seek redress for damages suffered through a criminal trial, may formulate a civil action, by which he/she sues the trafficker/dealer. This procedure also offers the possibility of full compensation of damages for the victim.

C. Compensation under Law No. 211/2004

According to Art. 21 of Law No. 211/2004, 'financial compensation is granted, upon request, under the law, to individuals who are victims of the crime of trafficking'. It should be noted that this legal bill establishes a procedure for granting financial compensation to the victim from the Romanian State, distinct from the legal process between the victim and the trafficker, during which the victim may request compensation directly from the trafficker.

In conclusion, whereas in the trial held between the victim and the trafficker, the compensation of damages is made by the trafficker, in the proceedings reviewed by the Law No. 2004 compensation is granted by the Romanian State.'

Compensation shall be granted if the criminal offence was committed in Romania and the victim is a:

a) Romanian citizen;
b) Foreign citizen or stateless person who resides legally in Romania;
c) Citizen of a European Union Member State, who is legally in Romania at the time of the offence; or
d) Foreign citizen or stateless person resident in an EU Member State, who is legally in Romania at the time of the offence.

If victims do not fall into the categories of persons referred to above, financial compensation is granted under international conventions, to which Romania is party.

According to Art. 23 of Law No. 211/2004, financial compensation is granted only if the victim has notified the prosecution or the court within 60 days of the date of the offence. If the victim was unable, physically or mentally, to notify the prosecution or the court, the 60 days are calculated from the date on which the state of incapacity ended. Victims who have not attained the age of 18 years or are banned are not required to notify the prosecution or the court about the offence. The legal representative of the minor or the person under interdiction may report the crime to the prosecution bodies.

According to Art. 27 of Law No. 211/2004, the victim's financial compensation is granted for the following categories of damages suffered by the victim, depending on the crime committed:

- Hospitalisation costs and other medical expenses incurred by a victim,
- Material damage resulting from destruction, degradation, disabling or divestment of a victim's assets due to the crime,
- A victim's loss of earnings due to the crime.

Financial compensation for material damage resulting from destruction, degradation, disabling or divestment of the victim's assets by the crime is calculated based on an amount equivalent to 10 minimum national gross salaries established for the year in which the victim has formulated the request for financial compensation.

Based on the above mentioned stipulations, the procedure mentioned in Law No. 211/2004 does not always provide satisfactory recompense for the damage caused to the victim.

On the one hand, the financial compensation for material damages resulting from destruction, degradation, disabling or divestment of the victim's assets by the crime is compensated by an amount equivalent to 10 minimum national gross salaries established for the year in which the victim has submitted the request for financial compensation. Where the actual loss is greater than the equivalent of 10 minimum national gross salaries, the difference cannot be covered by this procedure, but can only be covered by a civil process between the victim and the trafficker. On 01/12/2010, the minimum national gross wage was 600 lei (about 145 Euros).

On the other hand, non-pecuniary damages are not covered by this procedure. A victim's mental suffering can only be compensated by means of a legal trial between the victim and the trafficker. Payment of compensation for moral damages caused can only be made by the trafficker. A victim may participate in criminal proceedings as a civil party, according to Art. 15 of the Criminal Procedure Code.

It should also be pointed out that, according to Art. 27, Para 3 of Law No. 211/2004, the amounts paid by the defendant by way of civil damages and the compensation awarded to the victim from an insurance company for damages caused by the offence shall be deducted from the amount of financial compensation given by the State to the trafficking victim.

Also, for financial compensation grants to be approved based on the Law No. 211/2010, certain conditions, specified in Art. 24, have to be met:

1. the victim's request for compensation has to have been within the statutory period;
2. the victim must have been constituted as a civil party in the criminal trial, unless if it was ordered for the criminal prosecution not to begin for legal reasons;
3. the offender must be insolvent or has disappeared;
4. the victim has not received full compensation from an insurance company for damages incurred

It should also be mentioned that the procedure established by Law No. 211/2004 can be implemented only after a decision by the court or the prosecutor on the crime of human trafficking.

Also, financial compensation is granted by the Romanian State only as a last solution, should compensation not have been paid by the trafficker or by an insurance company, or because the trafficker is insolvent or has disappeared.

Victims seek to obtain compensation from the defendant in a criminal trial when constituted as a civil party, because the alternative procedure established by Law No. 211/2004 is more difficult and several conditions have to be fulfilled.

I was not informed of any case in which victims received compensation under the provisions of Law No. 211/2004. There have been initiatives in this respect from some NGOs, but because of the amount of documentation required, the victims have given up.

3.3 Application of the legal framework in practice

In our opinion, Romanian legislation on trafficking in persons is very advanced as it is based on laws that have been adopted and ratified at international level.

At central level, meetings of the Inter-ministerial Working Group are regularly organised to coordinate and evaluate activities aimed at preventing and combating trafficking in persons and developing the National Strategy against Trafficking in Persons (NSTIP).[41]

The application of legal frameworks may prove to be difficult for a number of reasons. In terms of granting assistance, one obstacle is the lack of financial resources. There are not enough shelters for victims. NGOs are not funded by the State. Male victims are more difficult to help because they are reluctant to accept that they have been trafficked for labour exploitation, instead they argue that they were simply deceived. Only after they have been given a job do male victims agree to be given psychological counselling. For women, the situation is the opposite and they receive psychological counselling first.[42]

With regards to the right to stay in Romania, victims are disadvantaged by the fact that they do not automatically receive the right to work as well. Therefore, unable to earn a living, the victim is put in great difficulty and has no means of subsistence. Consequently, although the law provides that the victim who wants to cooperate with the authorities can obtain the right to remain, in reality the victim's right to remain on Romanian territory is limited by a lack of material resources. In such a case, the victim will want to leave Romanian territory quickly, in order to work in another country.[43]

With regards to the participation of victims as witnesses in judicial proceedings, a drawback is the fact that trials take too long. If the victims are foreigners, they can testify before the prosecutor, but victims are not able to talk to the judge because they are obliged to return to their country of origin before the trial has ended.

Then, with each hearing, the victim relives the trauma that he/she went through. We have met police officers and prosecutors who have expressed the opinion that victims should be allowed to make just one statement during the trial. It should be emphasised that according to the Romanian system, the victim is heard first by a police officer and a prosecutor and then by a judge. The victim is called several times to testify during a criminal trial.[44]

Another aspect is the fact that victims are often threatened by traffickers. The statements given before the prosecutor are usually changed before they are heard by a judge. Victims withdraw their testimonies when faced with pressure from traffickers. Often, following the withdrawal of a witness statement, traffickers cannot be convicted due to a lack of evidence. They therefore receive lower penalties or are convicted for other (less serious) crimes.

---

[41] M. Adrian Hotca, *Protection of victims. Elements of victimology* (CH Beck Publishing House, Bucharest 2006) p. 203.

[42] Interview with the President of Association for the Development of Alternative Practices of Reintegration and Education (ADAPRE) (06.10.2010).

[43] Interview with the President of the Young Generation Romania Association (03.11.2010).

[44] Interview with the Prosecutor's Office of the High Court of Cassation and Justice - Department for the Investigation of Organised Crime and Terrorism – Iaşi Territorial Office (05.11.2011).

In many cases, the victim has to travel hundreds of miles from his home to the prosecutor's office where the case is being researched or to the court where the proceedings are taking place in order to testify. Since victims are usually poor, they rarely have the money needed to pay for transportation.

Since trials are very lengthy (often spanning several years) and because the victims are usually not able to find work in Romania, they are most likely to choose to go abroad, thus losing contact with the investigators.

With regards to compensation, it is not something that the victims can easily access. On the one hand, if the victim tries to seek compensation from the traffickers, the traffickers manage to dispose of their assets using various tricks, so that they cannot pay up due to a lack of funds, although they are ultimately legally obliged to pay. On the other hand, if the victims find out that the employer/trafficker is insolvent, they can employ the procedure set out in Law No. 211/2004, which states that after the criminal proceedings have been completed, the victims are allowed to request compensation from the Romanian State. However, this procedure is more cumbersome and requires the fulfilment of a very large number of conditions and the gathering of a number of documents. So far no one that we have interviewed was aware of any case in which a victim of trafficking in persons had received financial compensation from the State. In almost all cases, the victims have no legal knowledge and are therefore unable to manage on their own after the trial is completed. At this stage, practical assistance is no longer offered to the victim, because a lawsuit takes several years, and assistance is not granted for long once the victim has been identified.

There are no statistics kept about this in Romania. As such, there is no record of the number of victims that have actually testified.

We can only appreciate, by taking into account the cases and interviews studied, that most victims trafficked for labour do cooperate with the authorities. Clearly, the number of victims exploited for labour that cooperate with the authorities is much greater than the number of victims of sexual exploitation that cooperate. This is because the traumas caused by the exploitation of victims for labour is less than the traumas caused by the sexual exploitation of victims. Consequently, victims exploited for labour may be able to cope more easily during the trial.

3.4 Summary of findings

3.4.1 Identified obstacles

With regards to the identification of victims, obstacles could include:

- A lack of cooperation from victims, so that it can not be determined whether or not they have been trafficked. There are people who do not want to cooperate for various reasons such as fear of the traffickers or the desire not to be involved in lengthy legal proceedings;
- Non-involvement of the authorities. For example, if the Romanian victims are trafficked abroad and their identity documents are withheld,

they cannot return to Romania unless they are issued ID/Travel documents by the Romanian embassies and consulates from the country where they were trafficked to in order to facilitate their repatriation. In one interview, the interviewee said that such documents are very hard to obtain from the Romanian embassies;
- Poor management of human resources. One of the interviewees stated that there are situations where very good officers (who had managed to obtain good results in the fight against trafficking in persons) are engaged in other tasks, police officers with less experience and worse results are brought in to replace them.

In terms of granting assistance to victims, difficulties could include:
- A lack of financial resources needed to ensure effective assistance. From a legal point of view, assistance is provided to the victims, but in practical terms it is necessary to have the necessary financial resources;
- A shortage of shelters needed to accommodate the victims;
- The Victims' lack of cooperation. For example, it was discovered that men trafficked for labour decline psychological counselling, insisting that they were deceived;
- NGOs are not funded by the Romanian State, despite the fact that victims who are under the protection of the Romanian State benefit from their services.

As far as the right of residence is concerned, the main obstacle is the fact that victims who are given the right to remain in Romania do not have the right to work.

The following issues also prevent victims from participating as witnesses in judicial proceedings:
- The victims refuse to cooperate because they are threatened by traffickers or do not want to relive the trauma which they have experienced by recalling events while providing their statements;
- The victims cannot take part in court proceedings because they are being conducted a long distance away from where they live and they can not afford the transport expenses or they have left the country.[45]

The issues surrounding compensation may include:
- The insolvency of traffickers that are required to pay compensation;
- A large number of conditions which must be met in order to obtain compensation under Act No. 211/2004, making this procedure very difficult.

---

[45] Interview with the National Agency against Trafficking in Persons – Oradea Regional Centre (03.11.2010).

- The capping of the amount awarded as compensation in respect of pecuniary loss, resulting from the destruction, degradation or disabling of victims' assets or the dispossession of the victim during the criminal act. According to Art. 27 of Law No. 211/2004, 'the limit of compensation awards for such damage is, equivalent to 10 times the gross national minimum salary established for the year in which the victim submitted the request for financial compensation.'

3.4.2 Good practices

- The development of standards for identifying and reporting victims;
- The development and dissemination of methodologies for the immediate reporting of victims of human trafficking to the relevant services that grant assistance and protection;
- The training of local police officers and those from rural communities in identifying the phenomenon in their area of jurisdiction;
- The development of guidelines for identifying and reporting issues related to trafficking and their distribution in the local communities;
- The organisation of meetings and the preparation of information materials on how to identify trafficking victims;
- The development of specific national standards for granting assistance and protection to victims of human trafficking;
- The employment and training of NATP personnel to operate the TelVerde telephone service, intended for complaints relating to trafficking cases;
- The education of staff from the Romanian diplomatic missions about the rights of victims of trafficking and the procedures for the repatriation of Romanian citizens that are victims of human trafficking;
- Improving the victim's chances of obtaining financial compensation for the harm suffered;
- The provision of psychological, physical, and legal assistance to victims of human trafficking.

Part IV
Case studies

Case one[46]

The situation is as follows:

In June 2008, a company from Honduras initiated a campaign to recruit labour in Central America. The Honduran company had, as its partner, a trust in Romania, with headquarters in Bucharest, that was seeking to attract a cheap workforce. The victims, mostly men, aged between 25-37 years, arrived in Romania in two groups from the following countries: Honduras, Nicaragua, Indonesia and Mexico. Although they were informed that they would be signing employment contracts in Romania to work here, they came to Romania with a tourist visa for 5 days. They were instructed by the recruiting company to declare that the purpose of their visit was tourism and that they were not seeking employment.

Upon arrival, they were all called to the IBS trust's headquarters. Here they were told that IBS would provide for a Romanian language course and that they would work for a probationary period of three months and that training would be provided. They were also informed that they had been lied to in Honduras and that they would not be receiving 700-800 Euros as had been promised, but would only receive 300 Euros. Their passports were taken and locked in a safe. They were asked to sign some contracts in Romanian and English, languages that they did not know. One of the clauses specified that they agreed that their passports should be kept by the company. Also, the 300 Euros promised for the period worked was not paid, all they received for about two months of work was around 125 Euros. When they were paid, they were also asked to sign another contract. They were not aware of its content, nor did they receive a copy of it. The actual trafficking was done by several people, traffickers from Lebanon and Romania. The main dealer H.A. was a Lebanese-American citizen. The others involved, including his subordinates, were Romanian.

The living conditions for all the victims were unsanitary. Most lived in Bucharest, housed in the basement of the firm's building, in a makeshift bedroom, with no kitchen and a shared bathroom which had no hot water and no heating. About nine people lived in that room in bunk beds. They had no natural light. Though they were initially promised that they would have three free meals a day, they received nothing from the company.

The victims were exploited in the construction industry and in media services. For example some victims had to carry buckets of mortar and were required to lift heavy objects. Others woke up at 3:00 am to load, transport and deliver bales of newspapers to newsagents. Some victims were forced to sell newspapers, although they did not speak Romanian. With no food, they

[46] This case of THB for labour exploitation is reviewed by the Prosecutor's Office of the High Court of Cassation and Justice of Romania, in the file No. 304/D/P/2008.

were living at the mercy of their Romanian colleagues who, from time to time, offered sandwiches to them.

After a while, they requested to change jobs. The main shareholder of the trust, called H.A., told them that their jobs would not be changed; spoke to them rudely and threatened to throw them out into the street without returning their passports, where they would die of hunger. Since H.A. had brought the victims to Romania, found them accommodation and offered them training, they were warned that they owed him money,

One Honduran called the police and, unable to write in Romanian, verbally reported what had happened. The police asked for the cooperation of the Labour Inspectorate of Bucharest for a joint inspection. The other victims were then discovered. The Prosecutor was then informed about this case and the legal prosecution began. H.A. left Romania around this time.

In Romania, the following institutions were involved in the investigation: the General Inspectorate of Police; the Prosecutor's Office of the High Court of Cassation and Justice who conducted the investigations and the prosecution; the Labour Inspectorate of Bucharest, who examined the press, and the Romanian Immigration Office, which granted the right of residence to two of the victims during the criminal hearing. There has been no cooperation with Honduras until now. The Honduran authorities are going to be involved in the near future with the investigation of the Honduran firm's activity.

The institutions within our country involved in the case worked together. The General Police asked the Labour Inspectorate of Bucharest to investigate and find out if one of the victim's stories is true. The conclusions were brought to the attention of the prosecutor, who began a criminal investigation. During the prosecution, the prosecutor asked the Romanian Immigration Office to grant residence to two victims who would be cooperating with the authorities.

The methods of investigation used were: searches, witness' statements, police verifications, verification of banking transactions, and use of undercover investigators. The victims were informed of their rights by the police, protocols were signed accordingly. Among the victims of trafficking, only two wanted to stay on in Romania to cooperate with the authorities and they received assistance from the Young Generation Romania Association. They received psychological support and material aid was granted in the form of accommodation, food and some modest amounts of money for expenses. The other victims were not assisted.

The investigation is ongoing. A decision has not yet been reached. From a legal point of view, the case has been analysed both in terms of the provisions of the labour laws and the criminal law's stipulations. Some of the crimes committed were misdemeanours (e.g. the victims had no contract of employment for the work they rendered), and others constituted the offence of trafficking persons, legally classified as criminal.

Case two[47]

The situation is as follows:

The main trafficker, P.I, a Cypriot citizen, managed a limited liability company in Cyprus, whose object was not labour recruitment and placement. In the spring of 2006, the company began collaborating with several Romanian recruitment companies, run by Romanian traffickers. More than 130 victims were trafficked from Romania in about two years through five Romanian companies that sent labour to Cyprus, to be distributed by the Cypriot trafficker P.I. The victims were mainly young people aged between 17-35 years.

'The Romanian traffickers' directors or recruitment associates and job placement firms, posted various job advertisements offering appealing jobs abroad, for various levels of qualifications in the newspaper 'Evenimentul de Iasi'. There was a very short period of time between the time of recruitment and departure to Cyprus, typically a few days. The Romanian dealt with the transportation of the victims, via Henri Coanda International Airport, located near Bucharest, to Larnaca, Cyprus.

Once in Cyprus, the traffickers seized the victims ID documents and P.I. informed the aggrieved parties that he was not their employer, that they would not be doing what they had come to do, and that the contract that they had signed in their country was no longer valid. Some of the victims were immediately sent by P.I. to the new employer, but others were accommodated at the firm's office in miserable conditions until he found them a job. Also, P.I. told them that they owed him a fee for the job he was guaranteeing them, a fee of 500 Euros each to have their passports returned, as well as air travel costs, which were actually twice as much as the price of the plane tickets.

The victims became totally dependent on the defendants because they did not speak the language and had no ID documents or income. After they succeeded in stopping the victims' freedom of movement, the traffickers organised the so-called 'placement of labour' from the Cypriot firm's headquarters. This in fact resembled a slave market, since the victims were sold to the employers. Very rarely were victims employed in disciplines that they were familiar with and had agreed to when in Romania, nor did they work according to the conditions stipulated in the contracts they had signed.

At the firm's headquarters, P.I. organised an area to house the victims that was totally unsuitable and dirty. This is where they lived until they were distributed to employers. The complex was surrounded by a 2 m high fence and protected by guards.

---

[47] The human trafficking case that we present below has been reviewed by the Prosecutor's Office of the Romanian High Court of Cassation and Justice - Department for the Investigation of Organised Crime and Terrorism - Iasi Territorial Office, file No. 3/D/P/2008. Currently, the case is pending before the Iasi Court of Appeal and is registered under No. 915/45/2009. A final decision has not been made in this case.

The victims worked as waiters in hotels and restaurants, and also in construction and agriculture. Some provided gardening services. In each case, the conditions of the accommodation were unsuitable. They worked up to 19 hours a day, the salary promised was never paid in full, and the victims were terrorised when they expressed dissatisfaction.

Some victims lodged complaints at the Romanian Embassy in Cyprus; others returned home and reported their experiences to the Romanian authorities. Others made reports to the Cypriot authorities, who carried out checks, confirming the complaints received. In Romania, the Romanian traffickers were indicted and arrested. After being freed, some resumed their criminal activities and were arrested again. Evidence was collected about the Cypriot trafficker P.I. and a warrant was even issued for his arrest, but this could not be enforced because he has not returned to Romanian territory. The authorities tried to issue a European arrest warrant, but the procedure took more than 8 months before the Iasi Court of Appeal, without any positive result being obtained.

The following institutions were involved in the investigation in Romania: the General Inspectorate of Police; the Prosecutor's Office of the High Court of Cassation and Justice that conducted the investigations and prosecution; the Ministry of Justice that prepared the letters rogatory, and the Iasi Court of Appeal, before which the case is now being tried. The Cypriot institutions that were involved in the case in Cyprus were the Cypriot Police; Prosecutor's Office; the Cypriot Ministry of Justice, in preparing the letters rogatory; and the Romanian Embassy in Cyprus where the victims went in the first place.

With regards to cooperation with other States, the Romanian police and prosecutors met with their Cypriot counterparts in Bucharest, at the Romanian General Police Inspectorate headquarters, where evidence was presented by both parties and a transfer of jurisdiction from the Romanian to the Cypriot authorities was made in the case of the Cyprus trafficker P.I. The meeting was mediated by Europol. Letters rogatory were prepared in which the Cypriot authorities collected evidence in Cyprus for their Romanian counterparts. The Romanian State has sent some victims to be tried in Cyprus by the Cypriot authorities.

The methods of investigation used were: the taking of statements from victims and witnesses, phone tapping and financial investigations.

The cooperation between institutions in our country was very good. Cooperation with the institutions in Cyprus has been very good as well, yielding the information required by the Romanian authorities required to be able to complete their investigation.

Concerning international cooperation, the following issues have been noted: a lack of translators to translate the documents that had to be sent to the Cypriot authorities, a lack of financial support for the translation, the length of time required to complete the letters rogatory, which took up to 6 months.

The victims were informed about their rights by the police. They cooperated with the law enforcement authorities. No specific protection measures were taken during the legal proceedings.

The process is ongoing. The prosecutor said that the crime of human trafficking was committed, and the case has come to court. No decision has yet been given by the court.

Part V
Recommendations

5.1 Recommendations regarding the definition of Trafficking in Human Beings for labour exploitation

1) The definition of trafficking in persons for labour exploitation of victims does not punish the act of exploiting the victims' services by third parties.
   For example, in the case of the Cypriot Ioannis Piripitzis, Piripitzis recruited the labour, but other employers, who did not use restrictive methods on the victims, were benefiting of the victims' services.
   Therefore, our proposal would be also to criminalise the use of services performed by the victims by those people who are aware of the fact these individuals have been trafficked, when the customer benefiting from the victims' services is someone other than the trafficker.
2) When laws are adopted nationally to implement rules and regulations that have already been adopted internationally, an accurate reflection of the provisions of the international law should appear in the national law. For example, in Romanian law, the term 'harbouring', as stipulated in the Palermo Protocol, has been translated as 'accommodation' for the crime of human trafficking and 'hosting' for the crime of trafficking in minors.
   Our proposal is that Law No. 678/2001 should be amended to correct the translation of the term of the Palermo Protocol, the purpose being to punish the acts of 'harbouring' and not of 'accommodation', respectively 'hosting'.
3) Romanian law does not punish the victim's effective exploitation under the THB provision, but the acts prior to the exploitation. Therefore, the crime of trafficking in persons will be sanctioned even if the victims' labour exploitation did not take place.

A victims' effective exploitation by labour may be another crime, namely the crime of forced or compulsory submission to labour, if the victim is required to perform a specific job. But in situations where the exploitation of the victim implies subjecting her/him to carry out work that is in violation of the legal rules on working conditions, wages, health and safety, we cannot always find another offence to cover these situations. Consequently, exploitation of the victim remains unpunished.

Therefore, we propose changing the definition of the crime of human trafficking for labour exploitation, so as also to punish the effective exploitation of the victims, and not just the instruments and activities that are used for the exploitation. Sometimes, laws that may have some bearing on the matter are somewhat contradictory. For example, exploiting the labour of the victim also means subjecting the victim to conduct work in violation of the legal rules on working conditions, wages, health and security.

But according to the Romanian Labour Code, the following crimes are misdemeanours, so they are punished by fines and not imprisonment:

1. The failure to satisfy the requirements of ensuring payment of the minimum wage in the country,
2. The stipulation of clauses that are contrary to the law in the individual employment contract clauses,
3. Employing people without a contract of employment,
4. The failure to respect the provisions for overtime work,
5. Violation of the legal provisions on weekly rest.

We propose that the exploitation of a victim's labour should no longer be penalised as a misdemeanour, because it creates difficulties in the prosecution of the crime of trafficking in persons, because of the temptation to see the facts as minor offences.

5.2 Recommendations regarding investigation and prosecution

1) Cooperation can be achieved both with European countries and with countries on other continents. There are situations in which the Romanian authorities do not know the language used by the authorities with which they are cooperating, and accredited translators cannot found. For example, India has many languages.
   The proposal would be to conduct a study so to ascertain the geographical areas in which victims are recruited, and run parallel operations to identify or train specialised translators for that language.
2) Translation is done by certified translators for a fee. During interviews, we have become aware of the lack of financial resources for carrying out translations.
   Our proposal would be to guarantee financial resources for this purpose.
3) Over the duration of process, the victim, in principle, testifies several times, including in front of the judge. At each hearing, the victim relives the trauma.
   From this point of view, we think that a system should be designed to investigate and prosecute crimes of trafficking for labour exploitation of victims whereby victims should only need to testify once.
4) One problem faced by the Romanian legal system is that victims make a statement immediately after the crime has been committed against them, and afterwards change their statements at new hearings. This situation arises due to threats from traffickers, who manage to scare the victims.
   We propose a system where victims can be protected from these threats. We consider that interviewing the victim once, immediately after the crime is discovered, would solve this problem.
5) Identifying and investigating crimes of human trafficking requires

workers involved in such cases to be specialised. In the interviews we carried out, it became evident to us that there are situations in which highly trained officers, who have been fighting against human trafficking for a long time, have been replaced even during major investigations and by other police officers that did not have the same training.

As such, we suggest that investigators should not be replaced while the investigations are being conducted if they have not violated any laws.

6) As the victims of human trafficking are often in a poor state of mental health, the investigators should be delicate in the way they handle the victims.

   We propose the development of standards aimed at setting rules on how to develop relationships with victims.

7) Assistance to victims also requires a legal element. Almost always, the victims do not have legal training and do not defend themselves, so a lawyer is provided to defend their interests.

   However, the lawyer's fee is not very high. There were situations where the lawyer stopped defending a victim and subsequently started to work for the trafficker. Such a situation is not beneficial to investigating a case because the information obtained from the victim can be used by the traffickers or to assist their defence in a criminal trial.

   We therefore propose that the legislation be amended in order to forbid lawyers who have defended victims of trafficking to defend traffickers later.

8) Regarding international cooperation, it was evident in our interviews that the process can take a very long time, with foreign authorities only responding after long delays.

   In criminal legal aid, international letters rogatory is a form of legal assistance that consists in power being granted by the judicial authority of one State to the legal authority of another to exercise judicial activities relating to a certain criminal lawsuit, in their name.

   We propose that maximum time limits be established within which responses should be given to letters rogatory.

9) Romanian law does not allow trafficking victims to work in Romania. We suggest it is very important to make a change in this respect, allowing victims to have access to employment, so they are no longer forced to leave the country and thereby lose the opportunity to take part in the criminal proceedings.

10) With regards to the conditions determining the granting of the right of temporary residence in return for the cooperation of the victims, we do not believe that this measure helps to achieve a better investigation of the crime of trafficking in persons.

    It is possible for the victims to change their minds later, but it would then be too late for them to be able to participate in the criminal proceedings. We propose that the granting of the temporary residence should no longer be subject to the victims' cooperation with the legal authorities.

5.3 Recommendations regarding victim protection

1) During this study, we have found that the NGOs complain that there are not given the information they require to be able to talk to the victims. The NGOs are interested in the ongoing investigations and subsequent events , but the prosecuting authorities do not provide them with the information. There are cases when other NGOs do not provide the necessary information. For example, in one case, the Romanian NGO did not know that the victim had tuberculosis, and the foreign NGO has not reported this to them. One of the employees of the Romanian NGO was forced to have an abortion after having had a lung X-ray.
   Therefore, our proposal would be to regulate the way in which the NGOs can formally request certain information that they need to deal with victims from the authorities, so that this information does not affect the investigation.
2) Regarding victims of trafficking remaining in Romania, the problem is that, either during their tolerated period of stay or while they are being granted a right of temporary residence, they do not have the right to work. Furthermore, the temporary residence can only be granted after they have expressed their intention to collaborate with the authorities.
   In terms of the failure to grant the right to work, we see that this practice actually hasten the departure of victims who are foreign nationals from Romania. We should not lose sight of the fact that it is mainly men who refuse psychological counselling, saying that they were not victims of trafficking but were simply deceived. In these cases, the best means to protect and assist them is to get them back into work, so that they have the satisfaction of earning an income by themselves. Only then do they agree to receive material support and psychological counselling. However, since the victims are not allowed access to the labour market, we cannot use this as a way of assisting the victims.
   We propose to amend the Romanian legislation, by granting foreign victims of trafficking in persons, the right to work during the period in which they are on Romanian territory.
3) With regards to the compensation awarded, the procedure established by Law No. 211/2004 is, in our view, very hard to achieve. However, the time period between when the victim is identified and when compensation is awarded is very long, because the procedure established by Law No. 211/2004 may only be used after the criminal proceedings have ended, which can often take several years.
   We propose to amend this legislation in order to establish a more streamlined and faster procedure for obtaining compensation from the State.

Chapter 4
Combating Trafficking in Human Beings for Labour Exploitation in Serbia

Prof. Dr. Vesna Nikolić-Ristanović
Dr. Sanja Ćopić[1]

Introduction

Serbia is primarily a transit country for human trafficking, but also a country of origin and country of destination (permanent or temporary) for trafficking victims.[2] Victims of trafficking include both men and women, adults and children, who are trafficked *in*, *through* and *from* Serbia, or inside the country, for the purpose of sexual exploitation, labour exploitation, begging, committing crimes, adoption, etc.

Anti-trafficking initiatives in Serbia started at the end of the 1990s, primarily launched by NGOs, which were providing victim support and advocating for victims' rights.[3] Nevertheless, only after the ratification of the *UN Convention against Transnational Organised Crime and the supplementary Protocol to Prevent, Suppress and Punish Trafficking in Persons, especially Women and*

---

[1] Prof.dr Vesna Nikolić-Ristanović is the director of the Victimology Society of Serbia and Professor at the Faculty of Special Education and Rehabilitation, University of Belgrade.
Dr. Sanja Ćopić is a researcher and President of the Executive board of the Victimology Society of Serbia and research assistant at the Institute for Criminological and Sociological Research in Belgrade.
Prof. Vesna Nikolić-Ristanović wrote the section on victim protection, while Dr Sanja Ćopić wrote the sections on the legal framework for defining THB for labour exploitation and the dimensions of this crime, and on cooperation in the investigation and prosecution of cases of THB for labour exploitation.

[2] V. Nikolić-Ristanović, S. Ćopić, S. Milivojević, B. Simeunović-Patić, B. Mihić (2004) *Trafficking in People in Serbia*. Belgrade: Victimology Society of Serbia and OSCE; Bjerkan (ed.) *A life of one's own: the rehabilitation of victims of trafficking for sexual exploitation*. Oslo: Fafo-report 477; Nikolić-Ristanović (ed.) (2009) *Male Trafficking in Serbia*. Belgrade: Victimology Society of Serbia; US Department of State (USDS) (2009) *Trafficking in Persons Report*. U.S. Department of State Publication 11407, Office of the Under Secretary for Democracy and Global Affairs and Bureau of Public Affairs, Washington, D.C.; US Department of State (USDS) (2010) *Trafficking in Persons Report* <http://www.state.gov/g/tip/rls/tiprpt/2010> accessed 13 July 2010.

[3] B. Simeunović-Patić, S. Ćopić, 'Protection and Assistance to Victims of Human Trafficking in Serbia: Recent Developments' (2010) European Journal of Criminology, 7(1) pp. 45-60; V. Nikolić-Ristanović, S. Ćopić (2010a) 'Izazovi pružanja pomoći žrtvama trgovine ljudima u Srbiji' ['Challenges in supporting victims of human trafficking in Serbia'] in J. Kovačević i V. Vučinić (eds), *Smetnje i poremećaji: fenomenologija, prevencija i tretman (II deo)*, Beograd: Fakultet za specijalnu edukaciju i rehabilitaciju Univerziteta u Beogradu, pp. 559-573.

Children (more commonly referred to as the 'Palermo Protocol') in 2001[4] and the *Council of Europe Convention on Action against Trafficking in Human Beings* (hereinafter referred to as Council of Europe Convention) in 2009[5], did Serbia intensify its efforts towards establishing the legal and institutional frameworks for combating trafficking in persons.

The aim of this chapter is to provide further information about the legal and institutional framework for combating 'trafficking in persons for labour exploitation' in Serbia, taking due account of the prosecution of offenders and protection of victims. The data for this research was collected through interviews and desk research. Interviews were conducted with two police officers in Belgrade[6], while written materials about one case of trafficking for labour exploitation were collected from a local NGO involved in anti-trafficking activities - NGO ASTRA[7]. Most of the cases described by the respondents were actually cases we had already come across in previous research. These interviews enabled us to obtain some additional information about cases that were already known, but also to collect data on three other cases of trafficking for labour exploitation. As part of our research, we have analysed relevant legal documents, reports from the Serbian Statistics Bureau, court judgments and other available materials.

In addition, we have made use of two recent research projects conducted by the Victimology Society of Serbia-VDS[8] - the *research on male victims of trafficking in Serbia*[9] and the *research on the system of assistance and support to female victims of trafficking in persons in Serbia.*[10]

The *Research on male victims of trafficking* was conducted during the course of 2008 and 2009 with the aim of obtaining an insight into the scope, structure

---

[4] The Law on the Confirmation of the UN Convention against Transnational Organised Crime and Supplementing Protocols was passed on 22nd June 2001, Official Gazette FRY – International contracts No. 6/2001.

[5] The Law on the Confirmation of the Council of Europe Convention on Action against Trafficking in Human Beings was passed on 18th March 2009, Official Gazette RS No. 19/2009.

[6] One respondent was from the Ministry of the Interior, Border Police Directorate, Department for Suppressing Cross-border Crime and Criminal Intelligence Matters, Section for Suppressing Illegal Migration and Trafficking in Persons, while the second respondent was from the Belgrade Police Administration, Department for Suppressing Illegal Migration and Trafficking in Persons.

[7] 'The Case of Labour Exploitation of the Citizens of the Republic of Serbia, the Republic of Bosnia and Herzegovina and the Republic of Macedonia in the Republic of Azerbaijan, Country of Origin Report', ASTRA, La Strada Bosnia and Herzegovina and NGO Partnership for Social Development, 2009.

[8] Both authors of the Country Report for Serbia were directly involved in both research projects.

[9] V. Nikolić-Ristanović (ed), *Male Trafficking in Serbia* (2009).

[10] V. Nikolić-Ristanović, S. Ćopić, *Pomoć i podrška ženama žrtvama trgovine ljudima u Srbiji* [*Assistance and support to women victims of trafficking in persons in Serbia*] (2010).

and characteristics of trafficking in male persons in Serbia, as well as into the social response to this phenomenon. The data was collected using the ethnographic multi-method.[11] The largest portion of data was collected through interviews with 82 professionals from different backgrounds (State officials and representatives of NGOs and international organisations); followed by interviews with 13 victims / potential victims of trafficking and 12 individuals convicted for trafficking in persons, who were serving their prison sentences at the time the data was collected. Data was collected on 55 cases of trafficking in male persons that occurred in the period from 2003 to 2007, and 407 male victims of trafficking were identified: 342 adult and 65 child victims (those below the age of 18).[12]

The second research project, conducted in 2009, focused on the practical side of the system to provide assistance and support to female victims of trafficking. Data was collected on 11 cases of trafficking in women and girls that occurred in 2009 and 12 female victims were identified, which made 18.7% of the total number of female persons identified that year by the Agency for the Coordination of Protection of Victims of Trafficking in Human Beings.[13] The data was collected through interviews and mailed questionnaires, with the representatives of both State and non-State actors directly involved in providing assistance and support to victims, as well as through the content analysis and monitoring of court trials for trafficking in persons. For each case, we obtained insights from various actors involved in providing support and assistance, which enabled us to obtain a more comprehensive and realistic picture of the mechanism of reaction in each individual case of trafficking, but also a clearer insight into the functioning of the system of support in general and the status and role of different stakeholders within it.

[11] V. Nikolić-Ristanović, J. Dimitrijević, 'About the research on male trafficking in Serbia: the subject, goal, sample and method' (2009) in V. Nikolić-Ristanović (ed), *Male Trafficking in Serbia*, pp. 51-61 Belgrade: Victimology Society of Serbia.

[12] S. Ćopić, J. Dimitrijević, 'The scope and structure of male trafficking in Serbia' (2009) in V. Nikolić-Ristanović (ed), *Male Trafficking in Serbia*, pp. 63-80 Belgrade: Victimology Society of Serbia.

[13] The Agency for the Coordination of the Protection of Victims of Trafficking in Human Beings is an organisational unit of the social welfare system, which is seen as the central part of the referral mechanism, being 'the first point of contact for victims after they have encountered the police or other actors' (B. Simeunović-Patić, S. Ćopić, 'Protection and Assistance to Victims of Human Trafficking in Serbia: Recent Developments' (2010) pp. 50. However, clear mandates of the Agency and cooperation with other actors 'have not yet been formalised' (UNODC, 2009: 276; V. Nikolić-Ristanović, S. Ćopić, *Pomoć i podrška ženama žrtvama trgovine ljudima u Srbiji* [*Assistance and support to women victims of trafficking in persons in Serbia*] (2010).

Part I
The legal framework on defining Trafficking in Human Beings for labour exploitation and the dimensions of this crime

1.1 The definition of Trafficking in Human Beings for labour exploitation in Serbia

Article 26 of the Constitution of the Republic of Serbia[14] explicitly states that no one can be held in slavery or slave-like conditions, and it bans any form of trafficking in persons and forced labour, including the sexual and economic abuse of a person in an unfavourable position.

The Republic of Serbia does not have a special law on combating trafficking in persons; rather the legal framework encompasses a series of legal acts: Criminal Code, Code of Criminal Procedure, Law on Organisation and Jurisdiction of Government Authorities in the Suppression of Organised Crime, Corruption and other Particularly Serious Crimes, Law on the Protection Programme for Participants in Criminal Proceedings, Law on Juvenile Perpetrators of Criminal Offences and the Criminal Legal Protection of Minors, Law on Foreigners, Law on State Border Protection etc.

1.2 Other legislation and policies relevant for Trafficking in Human Beings for labour exploitation

1.2.1 Criminal law

The first step in developing a legal framework for combating trafficking in persons was taken in 2003 when trafficking in persons entered the Criminal Code of Serbia as a separate criminal offence. Nowadays, the Criminal Code of the Republic of Serbia[15] contains two separate incriminations relevant to the suppression of human trafficking: one refers to trafficking in persons in general (Article 388) and the other one to trafficking in children for the purpose of adoption (Article 389). Both criminal offences are considered crimes against humanity and other entities protected by the international law.

Trafficking for labour exploitation is not defined separately but rather within the general crime of trafficking in persons. According to Article 388 of the Criminal Code, this criminal offence may encompass one or more of the following acts: recruitment, transport, transfer, selling, buying, acting as intermediary in a sale, hiding or holding another person. The act has to be undertaken by the use of one or more of the following means: force or threat,

---

[14] Official Gazette RS, No. 98/06.

[15] Official Gazette RS, No. 85/2005, 88/2005, 107/2005, 72/2009, 111/09.

deception or maintaining deception, abuse of authority, trust, a dependency relationship, making the circumstances of the other party difficult, retaining identity papers or giving or accepting money or another benefit. The aim of trafficking is the exploitation of another person. Consequently, the offender has to act with the intent of exploiting this person's labour, forced labour, committing offences, prostitution, mendacity, pornography, removing organs or body parts or forced service in armed conflict. Imprisonment of three to twelve years is envisaged for this form of crime. If the crime is committed against a juvenile (a person from 0 to 18 years)[16], the offender shall be punished even if there was no use of force, threat or any other means.

The crime gets its qualified form if a victim of the basic form of crime is a juvenile, if it results in serious bodily injuries or in the death of one or more persons; if this criminal offence is committed habitually or if it is committed by an organised group. The latest changes in the criminal legislation dated from 2009 have contributed to better harmonisation of the national legislation with international standards, being an example of direct and efficient implementation of the Council of Europe Convention that was confirmed by the Serbian Parliament earlier that year. These amendments set the basis for the prosecution and punishment of 'service users', i.e. persons who knew or should have known that a person is a victim of trafficking and abuse his / her position or enable another person to abuse the victim's position for the purpose of exploitation, including labour exploitation. In addition, they introduced a provision that provides that the victim's consent to the intended exploitation or being held in slave-like conditions is irrelevant for the criminal liability of an offender if some of the proscribed means have been used.

In terms of the legal definition of trafficking in persons, we may conclude that it complies with the definition in the Palermo Protocol and particularly with the one contained in the Council of Europe Convention. We do not envisage any particularities in the legal definition of trafficking in persons in comparison to the definitions set forth in the relevant international documents, ratified by Serbia. Yet, when we come to the point regarding labour exploitation we notice that the terms 'exploitation of person's labour' and 'forced labour' are not defined in the Criminal Code. As stated by Stojanović[17] with regard to these terms, either other provisions of the Code or other relevant international documents will be used. This seems quite clear with regard to the term 'forced labour', which is defined in various international

[16] According to the Criminal Code, a person from 0 to 18 years is considered a juvenile, a person from 0 to 14 is considered a child who does not have criminal responsibility, while minors are those between 14 and 18 who are responsible and could be sanctioned for committing crimes.

[17] Z. Stojanović, *Komentar Krivičnog zakonika [Commentary of the Criminal Code]* (2006). Beograd: JP 'Službeni glasnik'.

documents.[18] However, we argue that 'exploitation of person's labour' should be defined more precisely in order to provide for better identification of victims of such practice, but also to eliminate any form of legal uncertainty. This seems particularly important if we bear in mind the fact that labour exploitation is not a crime as such in the Criminal Code of Serbia. In this respect, only provisions relating to the violation of labour rights may be used. Notwithstanding this, we argue that it is still necessary to make a clearer distinction between exploitation on the one hand, and the violation or restriction of labour rights or social justice on the other, because it is quite obvious that not every case of violation or restriction of labour rights can be considered to be exploitation.

The territorial principle is the main principle for claiming jurisdiction in Serbia. According to Article 6 of the Criminal Code of the Republic of Serbia, the criminal legislation shall apply to anyone who commits a criminal offence, including trafficking for labour exploitation on its territory. If the perpetrator is a foreigner, the case can be transferred to a foreign State on the basis of reciprocity. As to the extraterritorial jurisdiction of Serbia, it is envisaged that Serbia can have jurisdiction over the following cases: a citizen of Serbia who commits a criminal offence abroad, but is found on Serbian territory or is extradited to it; a foreigner who commits a criminal offence against Serbia or its citizen outside Serbian territory and is found on Serbian territory or is extradited to it, and a foreigner who commits a criminal offence abroad against a foreign State or foreign citizen, when such an offence is punishable by five years' imprisonment or a heavier penalty, pursuant to the laws of the country of jurisdiction, if such person is found on Serbian territory and is not extradited to the foreign State. These general rules can be applied in the case of trafficking in persons for labour exploitation.

Nevertheless, the prosecution cannot be undertaken in Serbia if the offender has served the full sentence for the same criminal offence for which he was convicted abroad; if the offender was acquitted abroad by a final judgment or the statute of limitation has set a limit in respect of the punishment, or the offender was pardoned; or if the offender is of unsound mind and was subject to a relevant security measure abroad. In addition, in the above mentioned cases, the criminal prosecution shall be undertaken only when the criminal offences are also punishable by the law of the country where they were committed. If the law of the country where the offence was committed does not provide for criminal prosecution for such an offence, the prosecution may only be undertaken with the permission of the Republic's Public Prosecutor. Yet, if the act was considered a criminal offence at the time

---

[18] C.R.J.J. Rijken and E.J.A. de Volder 'The European Union's struggle to realise a human rights-based approach to trafficking in human beings: A call on the EU to take THB-sensitive action in relevant areas of law' (2010) Connecticut Journal of International Law 25(49) pp. 49-80.

it was committed under general legal principles of international law (which refer to the cases of trafficking in persons), the prosecution may be undertaken in Serbia subject to permission from the Republic's Public Prosecutor, regardless of the law of the country where the offence was committed. However, insofar as we still lack a case-law with regard to trafficking for labour exploitation, it is hard to discuss this issue in greater depth with respect to this particular field.

1.2.1.1 Other provisions of the Criminal Code

In addition to the aforementioned provisions, there are some other provisions that could be relevant to suppressing trafficking in persons, such as provisions on smuggling migrants and slavery.

1.2.1.2 Smuggling of people

The exploitation of immigrants does not co-exist to the aforementioned definition of trafficking in persons, which means that criminal legislation provides for equal legal protection for both Serbian citizens and foreigners. On the other hand, a certain number of trafficking victims could be hidden behind illegal migrants. Consequently, provisions relating to illegal migration and the smuggling of persons could be relevant in suppressing trafficking in persons. This applies in particular to countries such as Serbia, which, as we will point out later, is mostly positioned as a transit country for trafficking adult men, most frequently for the purpose of labour exploitation.

Illegal crossing of the State border and smuggling of persons is a criminal offence against public peace and order (Art. 350 of the Criminal Code). It is envisaged that anyone who crosses or attempts to cross the border of Serbia without the required permit, armed or by the use of force, shall be punished by up to one year's imprisonment. The smuggling of persons consists in enabling another person to cross the Serbian border illegally or to remain or transit through Serbia illegally with the intent of acquiring a benefit for themselves or for another person. Six months to five years' imprisonment is envisaged for this form of crime. Qualified (serious) forms of crime include the following: a crime being committed by an organised group, by the abuse of authority or in a manner that endangers the lives and health of individuals whose illegal crossing of the Serbian border, stay or transit through the country is being facilitated or if a larger number of persons is being smuggled.

According to the research data, two crucial problems may occur with regard to the criminal prosecution of trafficking in persons: difficulties in distinguishing between trafficking and smuggling cases, and proving the liability of those suspected of trafficking. Both problems are particularly linked to cases of trafficking in adult male foreigners, discovered on Serbian territory en route to EU countries, where exploitation did not occur.[19] The analysis of the irrevocable verdicts, brought by the Serbian courts in the period from 2003 to 2007, for both trafficking in and smuggling of persons, suggest that cases that are almost identical are frequently classified in different ways.[20] Thus, legal practice is still wondering when to classify certain behaviour as trafficking or smuggling. This is illustrated by the words of the Nis deputy public prosecutor:

> *Sometimes, depending on the evidence available, the legal classification of the act being committed may be a problem. Due to certain similarities between the acts in a criminal offence of trafficking in persons and the illegal crossing of the State border and smuggling of persons, it is often not possible to determine for sure if the passive subject of the crime is a victim of trafficking in persons or not. It is necessary to determine the reasons why a person crossed the border illegally, i.e. how did the offender take advantage of the victims' circumstances and for what purpose.* (Excerpt from the interview with the deputy public prosecutor from Nis)[21]

Thus, the purpose of undertaking certain criminal acts should be crucial in distinguishing these crimes in practice: the purpose of trafficking in persons is the exploitation of the victim, while the aim of smuggling is to achieve material gain. Nevertheless, in practice, it is not so easy to prove the purpose, particularly in cases of trafficking in which the exploitation did not occur yet. In this respect, the intention of the perpetrator is debatable: whether the perpetrator's intent, directed at achieving certain goals (various forms of exploitation) is demanded as a special subjective element.[22] Stojanović correctly noted that for trafficking in persons, it is sufficient for the perpetrator to know that the victim will be used by any person for some of the purposes stated in the definition of the criminal offence. However, the dilemma is how to prove that the perpetrator knew that the victim would be exploited. In one case, this intent was proven in the following way:

> *As individuals who illegally enter the countries of Western Europe, they would have to work illegally; hide from the authorities of the final destination countries; accept and work the hardest and the most low-paid*

---

[19] S. Ćopić, 'Criminal prosecution of perpetrators of male trafficking' (2009) in V. Nikolić-Ristanović (ed), *Male Trafficking in Serbia* Belgrade: Victimology Society of Serbia, p. 260.

[20] Ibid., p. 260.

[21] Ibid., p. 260.

[22] Z. Stojanović, *Komentar Krivičnog zakonika [Commentary of the Criminal Code]* (2006) p. 811.

> *jobs - jobs as agricultural labourers, without social insurance or protection. Thus, compared to the employed individuals in the countries of their final destination, they would not have equal rights to work and pay; every employer or intermediary would be able to blackmail them and pay them below the market rate. In the position such as the one described, they would be prone to exploitation, which means taking advantage of another person's work.* (Except from the Court judgment of the District Court in Nis, K 205/05)

This actually confirms the theory by some authors that victims of smuggling, if they reach the country of destination, almost inevitably turn to other illegal markets and the informal economy,[23] being forced to accept 'dirty, dangerous and difficult jobs'.[24] In such conditions, smuggling can very easily turn into trafficking in persons.[25] Besides, in the course of smuggling, the abuse of the human rights of migrants can also occur.[26] Consequently, we may argue that trafficking in persons and the smuggling of migrants are criminal offences that are not mutually exclusive. Yet, although it is not easy to distinguish between them in practice in each individual case, it is important for the authorised agencies to put more effort into doing so. One of the reasons is the fact that trafficking in persons is a more serious crime than smuggling, which is reflected in higher penalties proscribed by the law. Another reason relates to the victims: if a case is considered to be trafficking, different forms of assistance and support will be available to the victims identified, while, unfortunately, these will usually not be available to the smuggled persons. Nevertheless, as the research results suggest, in the transit countries, the criminal offence of smuggling still remains important as a sort of supplement to the provision on trafficking: if there are no elements of trafficking or there is a lack of evidence, there are grounds to declare the case as smuggling (in cross-border cases); otherwise, the perpetrators may remain unpunished, which raises the question

---

[23] N. Ely-Raphel, Trafficking in human beings (2002) in D. Vlassis (ed), *Trafficking networks and logistics of transnational crime and international terrorism*, International Scientific and Professional Advisory Council of the United Nations Crime Prevention and Criminal Justice Programme, p. 173; V. Nikolić-Ristanović, *Ilegalna tržišta, trgovina ljudima i transnacionalni organizovani kriminalitet [Illegal markets, trafficking in human beings and transnational organised crime]* (2003). Temida, 4, p. 10.

[24] L. Kelly, *Fertile fields: trafficking in persons in Central Asia* (2005) Vienna: IOM, Technical Cooperation Centre for Europe and Central Asia, p. 54 <http://www.iom.int/jahia/Jahia/cache/offonce/pid/1674;jsessionid=1662869D20A3ECBD2F7CB0D85C1E8CB2.worker02?entryId=8002> accessed 13 April 2008.

[25] L. Kelly, 'A conductive context: Trafficking of persons in Central Asia' (2007) in M. Lee (ed) *Human trafficking*, pp. 73-91 Devon: Willan Publishing, p. 87.

[26] J. Salt, 'Trafficking and Human Smuggling: A European Perspective' (2000), International Migration Vol. 38(3), Special Issue 2000/1, p. 34.

of the penal policy governing the special and general prevention of this and similar criminal offences.[27]

1.2.1.3 Holding in slavery and transportation of enslaved persons

Article 390 of the Criminal Code envisages a punishment for holding in slavery and transportation of enslaved persons. It stipulates that 'whoever in violation of international law enslaves another person or places a person in a similar position, or holds a person in slavery or similar position, or buys, sells, hands over to another or mediates in the buying, selling and handing over of such a person or induces another to sell his freedom or the freedom of persons under his support or care, shall be punished by imprisonment of one to ten years'. In addition, it is foreseen that 'whoever transports persons in slavery or other similar position from one country to another, shall be punished by imprisonment of six months to five years'. If committed against a minor - imprisonment of five to fifteen years is stipulated.

As pointed out in the Commentary of the Criminal Code,[28] in practice there could be problems in distinguishing this crime from the criminal offence of trafficking in persons, because trafficking in persons may encompass acts that are directed towards the establishment of slavery or slavery-like conditions. However, as already pointed out with regard to distinguishing trafficking from smuggling cases, we may argue that the demarcation line between trafficking and slavery is also in the intent of the perpetrator. Namely, in the definition of slavery, the intent to exploit an enslaved person is not a constitutive element of the criminal offence.

1.2.1.4 Other relevant legislation and policies

Provisions related to labour issues could also be relevant in detecting and preventing trafficking in persons, as well as some policy documents, which will be discussed in this part. In addition, we will also point out the importance of the Law on the Confiscation of Property Acquired through Criminal Acts.

1.2.2 Labour law

Provisions related to the field of labour and employment are contained in several laws, primarily in the Law on Labour, Law on Employment and Unemployment Insurance and the Law on the Conditions for the Employment of Foreign Citizens.

The Law on Labour[29] provides for the conditions for the employment, as well as the rights and obligations of both employer and employee. The provisions of this Law are applied in cases of the employment of both nationals

---

[27] S. Ćopić, 'Criminal prosecution of perpetrators of male trafficking' (2009) p. 260.

[28] Z. Stojanović, *Komentar Krivičnog zakonika* (2006) Commentary of the Criminal Code.

[29] Official Gazette No. 24/2005, 61/2005, 54/2009

and foreigners. However, as to the Law on the Conditions for the Employment of Foreign Citizens[30], a foreign citizen can only be employed in Serbia if he/she has a permanent or temporary residence permit, and a working permit. Yet, the former law does not comply with the EU and other relevant provisions in this field and it needs to be changed.

Granting temporary or permanent residence permits to foreigners comes under the jurisdiction of the Ministry of the Interior. This issue is regulated by the Law on Foreigners.[31] According to Article 26 of this Law, a foreigner can be granted a temporary residence permit of more than 90 days for the purpose of work, education, a family reunion or other justifiable reasons. Some general conditions for granting a temporary residence permit include: a foreigner has enough financial resources to live on; he/she has health insurance, and the reason for the foreigner's stay in Serbia is justifiable. If a residence permit is given for work reasons, it may last as long as the permit for the working arrangement. Permanent residence permits can be granted on the basis of a continuous stay for a period of at least five years on the territory of Serbia on the basis of a temporary residence permit; marriage to a Serbian citizen or a person that was already granted permanent residence permit; heritage and in the case of a juvenile when one parent is Serbian citizen.

Work permits for foreigners are granted by the National Agency for Employment. Yet, the number of foreigners in the labour market in Serbia is limited by the annual rates of work permits that could be issued, which is decided upon by the Serbian Government. In addition, it is stipulated that the National Agency for Employment could reject the requirement for issuing a work permit to a foreigner if its data includes evidence about unemployed Serbian citizens who fulfil the same conditions for employment as a particular foreigner and those set forth by the employer. These solutions aim at protecting Serbian citizens on the labour market. However, if a foreigner gets a job in Serbia, the provisions in the Law on Labour will apply.

According to the Law on Labour, a person over the age of 15 can be employed. When hiring people aged between 15 and 18 years, the consent of the parent or the guardian given in the written form is required. The employment is established on the basis of a written agreement between the employer and employee. Every employee has the right to a wage, health and safety in the workplace, health care, integrity and other rights in the case of illness, a decrease or loss of working capacity and ageing, material support in the case of unemployment, and other forms of protection. Particular emphasis is placed on the protection of women during pregnancy and maternity leave, children (15 to 18 years) and the disabled. Youngsters (15-18 years) are

[30] Official Gazette of SFRY No. 11/78 and 64/89, Official Gazette of the FRY No, 42/92, 24/94 and 28/96 and Official Gazette of Serbia No. 101/2005.

[31] Official Gazette of Serbia No. 97/2008.

protected from particularly heavy physical work; work underground, or under the water, on high sites or in conditions that could negatively impact on their health. This Law also provides for the conditions for the employment of domestic labour, stating that an employee must receive at least 50% of the agreed wage in money, while the rest may be in the form of food and accommodation, which can be observed as a form of preventing exploitation. However, additional research into this field is needed. The Law also stipulates that full-time employment is 40 working hours per week.

According to the provisions of the Law on Labour, the Social Economic Council shall set the minimum wage in the country. However, if the Council fails to bring the decision within a timeframe stipulated by this Law (i.e. within 10 days from the day when the negotiation started), the Government of the Republic of Serbia will decide upon it. That is exactly what happened in the second half of 2010. The Government reached a decision in November that year regarding the minimum wage for the period July-December 2010. The average minimum net amount for this six month period was 16,140 RSD, which is 150 EUR.[32]

The Law on Employment and Unemployment Insurance[33] seems to be important in terms of preventing trafficking for labour exploitation in Serbian citizens who are getting jobs abroad. It contains provisions on employment abroad, stating that the Ministry of Economy and Regional Development, the National Agency for Employment or the agencies for mediation in employment are crucial stakeholders in the process of employment aboard. In this respect, the Ministry can sign the contract on employment with the relevant agency, organisation or employer in a foreign country. The National Agency for Employment and the registered agencies for mediation in employment are obliged to protect a person employed abroad. This protection should at least encompass the equal treatment of a Serbian citizen compared to the citizens of the country of employment during his/her stay and work in a foreign country. Protection also encompasses providing a work permit in the country of employment, expenses for different health examinations, transport expenses, information on living and working conditions, as well as on the rights and obligations pertaining to their employment status abroad, concluding the contract before the person departing to the country where they will work.[34] The National Agency for Employment and mediation agencies

[32] On 3 December 2010 the currency rate was 1 EUR=106.9252 RSD. The data on average wages is obtained from <http://www.praksa.rs/aktuelni_podaci.php?open=28> accessed 3 December 2010.

[33] Official Gazette No. 36/2009.

[34] In this respect, the National Agency for Employment has established the Migration service centre. The aim of this service is to provide assistance and counselling to citizens wishing to migrate. The Centre offers information about the risks of illegal migration and possibilities of getting a job in the scope of legal migration. In addition, it refers potential migrants, Serbian citizens, to relevant national institutions in order to develop their

are offering information about possibilities and conditions of employment abroad, living and working conditions, labour rights and obligations and forms of protection of labour rights abroad, as well as about rights upon return to Serbia. Finally, it is envisaged that the National Agency for Employment and the mediation agencies are obliged to provide the Ministry of Economy and Regional Development with information on persons employed abroad, their number and structure and other relevant data in advance, i.e. before they leave Serbia. Thus, by providing for the control of job offers abroad and the process of employment abroad, these provisions provide a better legal basis for preventing trafficking for labour exploitation.

Nevertheless, as stated by one of our respondents, it is rather hard to distinguish between trafficking for labour exploitation and illegal employment in practice, because the demarcation line is very tiny. He pointed out that illegal employment or working in the grey economy could be considered to be indicators of trafficking, but they do not necessarily involve elements of trafficking. Respondents from the Labour inspectorate of the Ministry of Labour and Social Policy interviewed during research on male victims of trafficking stated that illegal work, i.e. working without a contract ('black labour') is mostly prevalent in the construction industry, trade and catering. Young and non-qualified people with low levels of education, without regular wages, as well as unemployed people over 40 years of age and recipients of welfare are most frequently recruited for this kind of illegal work (so-called 'black labour').[35] In 2008, 9054 individuals were discovered to be working without contracts, and this number was a little bit lower in 2009 – 5734.[36] However, in most of these cases (approximately 70%) after the inspection, the employers signed contracts with the employees, which meant that the inspectors did not then report these cases as an instance of trafficking for labour exploitation.

---

knowledge and increase the possibilities of employment abroad. A guideline is available on the web site of the National Agency for Employment, providing information about different countries, their legal systems, possibilities for education and employment, visa regimes, procedures of getting residence and work permits, conditions for studying, family reunions, rights and support to migrants in the destination country, as well as other relevant information for migrants and programmes of reintegration upon return to Serbia. This information is available on <http://www.nsz.gov.rs/page/ services/ sr/migr_centar.html> accessed 2 March 2011.

[35] 'Rad na crno cveta zbog niskih novčanih kazni', Blic online, 10th April 2010, <http://www.blic.rs/Vesti/Drustvo/184451/Rad-na-crno-cveta--zbog-niskih-novcanih-kazni> accessed 3 December 2010.

[36] *Izvestaj o radu Inspektorata za rad za 2009. godinu [Report on the work of the Labour Inspectorate for 2009]*, available on <http://www.vip-bzr.com/uploads/IZVESTAJ%20O%20RADU%20INSPEKTORATA%20ZA%20RAD%20ZA%202009.GODINU.pdf> accessed 2 March 2011.

1.2.2.1 Law on confiscation of property

In 2008, the *Law on Confiscation of Property Acquired through Criminal Offences*[37] was passed. It contains provisions on the conditions, procedure and the authorities qualified to disclose, confiscate and manage property acquired by criminal means (Article 1). The term 'property acquired by criminal means' refers to the 'property of the accused, cooperating witness or the witness which is obviously disproportionate to his legal income' (Article 3, paragraph 1, point 2). The Law enables the investigation of the origin of the whole property of the accused and not only of the property which is suspected to be acquired by a crime. The burden of proof lies with the accused, who would have to prove that he had acquired the property legally. The Law is applied in cases of enlisted criminal offences, including trafficking in persons, which may have certain effects on the suppression of this form of crime.

1.2.2.2 Policy documents

In 2006, the Government of the Republic of Serbia adopted the *Strategy for Combating Trafficking in Persons*.[38] It presents the first and, up to now, the only, but important policy document that defines the institutional framework for combating trafficking in persons and providing support to victims of this form of crime. It defines the strategic goals, measures and activities of the stakeholders in combating human trafficking. There are eleven strategic goals divided into five areas: institutional framework; prevention; assistance, protection and reintegration of victims; international cooperation, and monitoring and evaluation. It foresees *inter alia* the necessity of permanent improvement of the legal framework, in accordance with the international obligations undertaken, continuous international and regional cooperation with relevant services, institutions and organisations with the goal of achieving more efficient suppression of trafficking in persons, i.e. more efficient prosecution of traffickers and perpetrators of other criminal offences containing elements of exploitation. In addition, one of the strategic goals set forth in this document refers to the development of the mechanism of monitoring and evaluation of the results achieved in this field. However, the State failed to undertake the necessary measures so far in order to define the way and the stakeholder of the monitoring process that would guarantee the objectivity and impartiality of the results obtained.[39] In other words, Serbia has not yet established a national rapporteur or a similar independent agency that would be in charge of the continuous monitoring and evaluation of anti-trafficking activities.

---

[37] Official Gazette RS, No. 97/2008.

[38] *Strategy for combating trafficking in persons*, Official Gazette RS, No. 111/06.

[39] V. Nikolić-Ristanović, S. Ćopić, *Pomoć i podrška ženama žrtvama trgovine ljudima u Srbiji* [*Assistance and support to women victims of trafficking in persons in Serbia*] (2010).

The problem of trafficking in persons is also addressed by the *Strategy for Combating Illegal Migrations in the Republic of Serbia in the period from 2009 to 2014*,[40] which stipulates different proactive and reactive measures for suppressing illegal migration.[41] It focuses on the development of human and other resources, cooperation and legal procedures in the field of control of illegal migration. It envisages a series of proactive measures in the field of identifying persons at risk, implementing media campaigns, cooperation with citizens and the local community and combating illegal migration. It emphasises the need for signing agreements on employment in other countries and a series of other measures directed towards 'frequent causes' and various types and forms of manifestation of illegal migration. If adequately implemented, it could also result in preventing the victimisation through trafficking in persons.

1.3 The dimensions of Trafficking in Human Beings for labour exploitation in Serbia

Keeping records about cases of trafficking in persons in Serbia is not sufficiently legally regulated and there are no appropriate systems solutions. Although the records of victims or perpetrators are maintained by different institutions and organisations, it is noted that there is no consistency in the manner in which they are kept. They are kept in different ways, and different methodological approaches are used in the data collection. Therefore, existing records are different, uneven and very difficult to compare. In addition, there is a lack of a single database in Serbia, which would contain data on the recognised victims of trafficking, perpetrators, the method of trafficking, and the manner in which organisations and institutions act in each individual case.[42] This significantly obstructs the monitoring of the phenomenon, as well as finding out its dimensions, structure and characteristics, and the procedures undertaken in individual cases. As a result, it is hard to estimate the dimension of trafficking in general, and trafficking for labour exploitation in particular on the basis of the data of different institutions and organisations.[43]

---

[40] *Strategy for Combating Illegal Migrations in the Republic of Serbia from 2009 to 2014*, the Government of the Republic of Serbia passed on 26 March 2009. Official Gazette No. 55/05, 71/05,101/07, 65/08.

[41] B. Simeunović-Patić, 'The legal and institutional framework of the social reaction to the problem of trafficking in persons in Serbia' (2009) in V. Nikolić-Ristanović (ed) *Male Trafficking in Serbia*, pp. 219-234 Belgrade: Victimology Society of Serbia.

[42] V. Nikolić-Ristanović, S. Ćopić, *Pomoć i podrška ženama žrtvama trgovine ljudima u Srbiji* [*Assistance and support to women victims of trafficking in persons in Serbia*] (2010).

[43] However, we should point to the steps that have been taken during the past few years related to the establishment of such a database. Namely, models of databases on the victims and traffickers were set up in a project carried out by ICMPD in 2008. It was envisaged that in Serbia a database of trafficking victims should be managed by the

According to the data of the police, and the Agency for the Coordination of the Protection of Victims of Trafficking in Human Beings, presenting the key institutions that have evidence on trafficking cases, trafficking for labour exploitation still accounts for a smaller proportion of the trafficking cases identified in Serbia. The police data[44] shows that in 2009, out of 85 victims identified, 12 (14.1%) were trafficked for labour exploitation[45] - 7 male (4 adults and 3 minors) and 5 female. In the same year, based on the evidence of the Agency for the Coordination of Protection of Victims of Trafficking in Human Beings, out of 127 identified victims of trafficking, 18 (14.2%) were trafficked for labour exploitation.[46]

According to data from the Serbian Statistics Bureau, the overall number of adults reported for trafficking in persons in Serbia in the period 2004-2009 was 342, of which 339 were adults and 3 were minors. However, in the same period, there was a much lower number of those accused and convicted for this criminal offence: 85 people were accused (84 adults and one minor), while 72 were convicted (71 adults and one minor). This data suggests a huge decrease in the number of accused and convicted for trafficking in persons in comparison to the number of those reported. However, without an in-depth analysis of the reasons for dismissing the cases it is hard to explain this decrease. Yet, as illustrated, we can only assume that one of the most important reasons for this decrease lies in the problem of proving the guilt of those suspected of trafficking in persons and the fact that the crime occurred due to a lack of

---

Agency for the Coordination of the Protection of Victims of Trafficking in Human Beings, while the database on traffickers should be managed by the Ministry of the Interior. In an interview conducted with the representative of the Agency into the research on the system of protection for female victims of trafficking, she pointed out that the Agency received the software; they started to enter the data but stopped rather quickly, because of the complexity of the programme. The same was found to be the case in the interview with the police officer carried out in the research into trafficking for labour exploitation. So, it remains to be seen whether and how this way of keeping records about trafficking issues will work in practice and if it will serve as a basis for monitoring the phenomenon. For more on these databases see R. Surtees, *Handbook on Anti-Trafficking Data Collection in South-Eastern Europe: Developing Regional Criteria* (2007) Vienna: International Organisation for Migration Policy Development (ICMPD).

[44] The data obtained in the interview with the police officer from the Ministry of the Interior, Border Police Directorate, Department for suppressing cross-border crime and criminal intelligence matters, Section for suppressing illegal migration and trafficking in persons, conducted on 21st September 2010. Also available on <http://www.mup.gov.rs/cms_cir/sadrzaj.nsf/trgovina-ljudima.h>.

[45] According to the same source of data, 53 victims were trafficked for the purpose of sexual exploitation, 14 for begging, 6 for forced marriage and 3 for committing crimes.

[46] The data obtained from the statistical data available on the web site of the Ministry of Interior of the Republic of Serbia <http://www.mup.gov.rs/cms_cir/ sadrzaj.nsf/trgovina-ljudima.h> accessed 3 December 2010.

evidence. The distribution of reported, accused and convicted adult persons by years is presented in Table 1.

Table 1: Adult persons reported, accused and convicted in Serbia in the period 2004-2009

	2004	2005	2006	2007	2008	2009	Total
Reported	69	68	50	51	51	50	339
Accused	4	11	18	16	14	21	84
Convicted	2	10	13	14	12	20	71

Most of the individuals reported, prosecuted and convicted for trafficking were male adults, although females and minors were also present. Most of the convicted adult traffickers were sentenced to imprisonment – 60 or 84.5%, while 11 (15.5%) were convicted to a conditional sentence. Most of the prison sentences were of short duration, i.e. less than 3 years. The maximum sentence in this period, according to the statistical data, was between 3 and 5 years.

However, the data of the Serbian Statistics Bureau refers to all cases of trafficking regardless of the form of trafficking, i.e. the form of exploitation. In other words, the data available at this State institution is not separated according to the form of exploitation. As a result, we cannot provide the exact number of individuals accused and convicted of trafficking for labour exploitation.

Finally, the research on male victims of trafficking has shown that in 36 out of 55 cases of trafficking in male persons analysed that occurred in the period 2003-2007, the victims were adults, while in 16 out of these 36 cases, which makes 44.4%, adult male victims were trafficked for labour exploitation.[47]

1.3.1 Characterisation of Trafficking in Human Beings for labour exploitation at the national level

According to the research data,[48] trafficking in persons for labour exploitation is the dominant form of trafficking in men, while women, both adult and underage, only occasionally appear to be trafficked for this purpose. As to the age, we note that a 'broader age range appears to be more common among

---

[47] S. Ćopić, J. Dimitrijević 'The scope and structure of male trafficking in Serbia' (2009) in V. Nikolić-Ristanović (ed), *Male Trafficking in Serbia*, pp. 63-80 Belgrade: Victimology Society of Serbia, p. 80.

[48] S. Ćopić, 'The characteristics of male trafficking in Serbia' (2009) in V. Nikolić-Ristanović (ed), *Male Trafficking in Serbia*, pp. 81-133 Belgrade: Victimology Society of Serbia; S. Ćopić, J. Dimitrijević 'The scope and structure of male trafficking in Serbia' (2009) in V. Nikolić-Ristanović (ed), *Male Trafficking in Serbia*, pp. 63-80 Belgrade: Victimology Society of Serbia.

victims trafficked for labour and begging'.[49] The majority of trafficked men are therefore between 18 and 50 years of age, and within this category, most are between 30 and 40; so, these are individuals who are able to work. Trafficking for labour exploitation is predominantly transnational trafficking, with Serbia primarily positioned as the country of transit, although it appears as the country of origin and sporadically as the country of destination.

The main nationalities in the structure of foreign male victims found on the territory of Serbia (who were either exploited in Serbia or were intended to be exploited in the EU countries and were in transit through Serbia) were Chinese and Turkish, followed by citizens of Afghanistan, Albania, India, Pakistan, Bangladesh, Kazakhstan, Macedonia, Moldova and Romania. The main country of final destination of these victims is Italy, followed by other EU countries, mostly Germany, France, Greece, Spain, as well as Scandinavian countries. On the other hand, adult Serbian men were primarily trafficked to Russia, Saudi Arabia, the United Arab Emirates, and Azerbaijan. Just occasionally, Serbia was the country of final destination, primarily for victims from Romania.

The most frequent form of recruitment is by job offer. Men are mostly offered traditional male jobs, such as jobs on construction sites, while women are offered work as babysitters, waitresses, domestic workers (servants) or in agriculture. The job is usually offered in two ways: by individuals and by employment agencies. Recruitment is usually through employment agencies in the cases of trafficking in Serbian citizens. In the cases identified, the agencies that were offering supposedly legal jobs were actually doing so illegally: without the necessary employment agency business licence that is issued by the Sector for Employment at the Ministry of Labour and Social Policy. Jobs were advertised through newspapers and the Internet.

The victims are transported both legally and illegally, but also a combination of these two methods was identified.[50] The method of transporting the victims depended on their citizenship. Serbian citizens were legally transported to destination countries, mostly by aeroplane or, perhaps, by some other means, using valid travel documents, visas and other necessary documentation, but most of them remained illegally in the countries of destination, because their residence permits were not renewed. Illegal and combined methods of transportation of victims were more common in the cases of foreign citizens. In a number of cases, the victims were travelling illegally from their country of origin towards a destination country and had

---

[49] R. Surtees, *Second Annual Report on Victims of Trafficking in South-Eastern Europe 2005*, Regional Clearing Point, IOM 2005, p. 499.

[50] Combined methods of transport means that some victims are travelling legally from their home countries towards Serbia, but entering Serbia illegally and continuing their journey illegally, while in some cases victims come to Serbia legally, and then continue their journey from Serbia illegally.

illegally entered Serbia when their trafficking route was cut off (e.g. Albanian citizens). In the majority of cases, foreign victims, although they entered Serbia illegally, used combined forms of transport, which at one point in the journey also involved legal methods of transportation. This was particularly characteristic for Turkish, Chinese and citizens of other Asian countries, who are usually legally transported to Kosovo (by aeroplane, ship or by land), often from Turkey (especially the airport in Istanbul), then illegally cross the administrative border towards Serbia and illegally continue the journey towards Hungary or Croatia and the Republic of Srpska (Bosnia and Herzegovina) and then on to the countries of Western Europe. In some cases, foreign victims came to Serbia legally, with the necessary travel documents and visas, only to continue the journey illegally upon entering Serbia. Finally, in a certain number of cases, victims came legally to Serbia, but remained on its territory after their visas expired, which means they were illegally staying in the country. Victims are transported by different means, while the illegal transport of the victims across the territory of Serbia is often conducted in highly inhumane conditions.

Labour exploitation is the most common form of exploitation of adult men as victims of trafficking in persons, primarily in the construction industry, and then in agriculture or some other branches of the economy (for example, work in a slaughter house). In these cases, the exploitation consisted in longer working hours (10 to 12 hours per day, sometimes even longer), without suitable breaks and protection; followed by lower payments than agreed or even not getting payments at all. In some cases, adult male victims were exposed to different forms of control and victimisation. The main method of keeping them under control was by withholding their passports and depriving or limiting the victims' freedom of movement. In a number of cases, victims of trafficking were also exposed to other forms of victimisation, mostly poor living conditions,[51] inappropriate, insufficient and poor food, as well as relocation to other sites, threats and even physical violence.

In practice, it is hard to estimate to what degree these elements are decisive in the classification of trafficking for labour exploitation, but they are important. One respondent justified it as follows:

> *A person signs an agreement with an employer that stipulates particular conditions (with regard to accommodation, food, payments, etc.), giving the employee a certain degree of security. However, the employer does not respect the provisions of the agreement. In this situation, the employee can file a charge with the commercial court for violation of his/her labour rights. Yet, nobody can say for sure at which stage this case could become*

[51] In terms of living in collective accommodation, with 12-24 or even more persons in a room, an insufficient number of toilets, strict house rules, no running water for several days a week, no heating, etc.

> *a trafficking case; but, this can be an indicator of trafficking, which may be a starting point for the law enforcement agencies to start proactive work. On the other hand, if a foreigner comes to Serbia and his passport has been taken away, he has been accommodated in a collective centre, and he works and lives in inadequate conditions; we can then assume that there are elements of trafficking. Namely, this person, who is capable of work, has been subjected to deception; he has a fictional agreement; he is placed under the control of an employer and his freedom of movement is restricted, so, in this instance there is no doubt that we are talking about labour exploitation.*

With this observation in mind, we can argue that it is important for the law enforcement agencies to find out as much as possible about the above mentioned elements in order to classify a case as trafficking for labour exploitation. Nevertheless, for as long as there is still an absence of case-law, it is hard to elaborate on this issue in greater depth.

Part II
Cooperation in the investigation and prosecution of cases of Trafficking in Human Beings for labour exploitation

In this section, we will primarily focus on the actors involved in investigating and prosecuting trafficking for labour exploitation, the existing cooperation of these actors, both in the country, and between countries, as well as on the possibilities of the use of special investigative techniques in cases of trafficking in persons.

2.1 Actors involved in investigating and prosecuting Trafficking in Human Beings for labour exploitation

The *Strategy for Combating Trafficking in Persons* defines the institutional framework for combating this form of crime. It defines the National Mechanism for the Coordination and Creation of the Policy of Combating Trafficking in Persons, which consists of two parts: strategic and operational. The strategic level includes the Council of the Government for Combating against Trafficking in Persons,[52] the National Coordinator for Combating Trafficking in Persons and the Republic Team for Combating Trafficking in Persons.[53] The operational level encompasses the police, judiciary and the Agency for the Coordination of the Protection of Victims of Trafficking in Human Beings. As pointed out in this policy document, specialised non-governmental and international organisations are providing important support at operational level, although this document does not define what is meant by specialised non-governmental organisations.

Taking the provisions of the Strategy as a departure point, we may argue that the main actors involved in the investigation and prosecution of trafficking for labour exploitation are the police, prosecutors' offices and courts, i.e. the same actors as those involved in detecting, investigating and prosecuting cases of trafficking for sexual exploitation. Besides, in the cases of trafficking for labour exploitation, an important role is or should be played by some other State institutions, primarily by the market inspection of the Ministry of Trade and Services and the Labour Inspectorate of the Ministry of Labour and Social Policy.

---

[52] The Council was established by the Decision of the Serbian Government in October 2004 (Official Gazette No. 113/04), as an expert body authorised to advise the Government. It is composed of ministers of the interior, education, sports, finance, health, labour and social policy and justice.

[53] The Republic Team for Combating Trafficking in Persons is composed of state agencies, national NGOs and representatives of relevant international organisations, such as the IOM, OSCE, UNHCR, and UNICEF.

2.1.1 Police and judiciary

The Ministry of the Interior (MoI) has an important role in the institutional framework for combating trafficking in persons in the Republic of Serbia. In order to enable more efficient suppression of trafficking in persons and the identification of victims, special police teams or units for suppressing illegal migration and trafficking in persons were established within two police directorates: the Directorate of the criminal police (within its Service for combating organised crime), and the Border police directorate (within its regional police administrations or police stations).[54] In addition to investigating activities, the MoI is the main institution dealing with the issues of the entrance and stay of migrants in Serbia, undertaking measures related to regular and irregular migration, control of borders, visas, asylum, residency of foreigners in the country and the issuing of citizenships. The MoI is authorised to refuse to allow those illegally in the country from remaining in Serbia, as well as to organise their return in accordance with the agreements on readmission.[55]

When speaking about the judiciary, we may say that both basic (municipal) and higher (district) prosecutors and judges are involved in investigating and prosecuting trafficking cases, depending on the severity of a particular case. Judges and prosecutors in the Republic of Serbia have instituted various forms of education organised by various international and local organisations, with the aim of raising their level of efficacy, but also with a view to adopting a human-rights based approach to the problem of trafficking and introducing European and international standards in this field.[56] However, as one of the respondents emphasised, there is still a need for specialisation by prosecutors and judges when dealing with trafficking issues in general, and trafficking for labour exploitation in particular. In his opinion, specialisation by prosecutors and judges can contribute to the efficiency and quality of their work and, consequently, suppress trafficking, which is important if we consider how quickly traffickers act.

---

[54] There are 27 police administrations in Serbia.

[55] B. Simeunović-Patić, 'The legal and institutional framework of the social reaction to the problem of trafficking in persons in Serbia' in Vesna Nikolić-Ristanović (ed), *Male Trafficking in Serbia* Belgrade: Victimology Society of Serbia 2009.

[56] International Centre for Migration Policy Development - ICMPD (2006) *Trgovina ljudima – Regionalni standardi. Priručnik za sudije i tužioce. Program obuke u Jugoistočnoj Evropi* (*Trafficking in human beings – regional standards. Manual for judges and prosecutors. Program of education in the South East Europe*) Belgrade: OSCE Mission in Serbia and Montenegro.

If a particular case fits into the definition of organised crime[57] special police and prosecuting authorities, special investigation techniques and probative rules as well as provisions on victims' protection will be applied. The Law on the Organisation and Jurisdiction of Government Authorities in the Suppression of Organised Crime, Corruption and other Particularly Serious Crimes contains provisions on the establishment, organisation, jurisdiction and authorities of the special State agencies (police, public prosecution and judiciary) involved in discovering, investigating and prosecuting the offenders of the criminal offences that include elements of organised crime. Within the Service for combating organised crime in the Directorate of the Criminal Police, there is a special department that deals with cases of smuggling and trafficking in persons.[58] The Law on Public Prosecutors[59] envisages the establishment of the Prosecutor's office for organised crime as the prosecutor of special competence for the territory of the Republic of Serbia. Finally, within the Higher (District) Court in Belgrade, there is a Special department for organised crime, which runs trials in cases of organised crime at the first instance court on the territory of Serbia. With this in mind, we can see that in the case of organised crime, jurisdiction is established by the crime, rather than territorially, providing for a basis for more efficient suppression of this form of crime and protection of its victims. Nevertheless, as suggested by the research, in the legal practice, trafficking in persons is only occasionally treated as a form of organised crime.[60] Consequently, the above mentioned provisions are just occasionally applied to suppressing trafficking in persons.

---

[57] The current definition of organised crime is given in Art. 2 of the *Law on Organisation and Jurisdiction of Government Authorities in the Suppression of Organised Crime, Corruption and Another Particularly Serious Crimes* (Official Gazette RS, No. 42/02, 27/03, 39/03, 67/03, 29/04, 45/05, 61/05, 72/09). Organised crime is defined as 'committing criminal offences by organised criminal groups, i.e. another organised group or its members for which an imprisonment of four years or a more severe sentence is prescribed'. The term 'organised criminal group' in Art. 2 of this law, implies 'a group of three or more persons, which exists for a certain period of time and acts in agreement with the aim of committing one or more criminal offences for which an imprisonment of four years or a more severe sentence is prescribed, for the purpose of, directly or indirectly attaining financial or other material gains' (Art. 3, para. 1). The term 'organised group' implies a group which has not been formed with the aim of committing criminal offence, nor does it have such a developed organised structure, defined roles and the continuity of members, but its function is organised crime (Art. 3, para. 2).

[58] This department is authorised to discover cases of trafficking in and smuggling of persons and the use of special investigative measures and techniques, i.e. the use of the proactive investigations.

[59] Official Gazette RS, No. 116/08.

[60] S. Ćopić, 'Criminal prosecution of perpetrators of male trafficking' (2009) p. 264.

2.1.1.1 Market and labour inspectors

Market inspection of the Ministry of Trade and Services is authorised to conduct inspections of the implementation of laws and other provisions regulating conditions for providing services by legal and physical entities and entrepreneurs, the protection of customers and advertising. This department plays a key role in prohibiting the work of agencies which deal with illegal mediation in employment, as well as in preventing their advertising (most frequently the offer for employment abroad) and with that the recruitment of potential victims of trafficking in persons for labour exploitation.[61]

The Labour Inspectorate is part of the Ministry of Labour and Social Policy of the Republic of Serbia.[62] The central office is located in Belgrade, while there are 25 regional offices, i.e. departments in administrative districts in Serbia. In 2009, this institution had 324 employees, of which 301 were labour inspectors.

The Labour Inspectorate conducts inspections in the field of employment and health and safety at work. In other words, it carries out inspections on the implementation of the Law on Labour, Law on Occupational Health and Safety and other relevant laws, as well as on the implementation of the general collective agreement, individual and special collective agreements, general acts and agreements on employment, which regulate the rights, obligations and responsibilities of employees in different organisations and institutions. However, the labour inspectors can only undertake control measures towards company owners – labour inspectors are not competent in cases where people are employed by those that do not have a registered company.[63] This problem is stressed in the *Strategy for Combating Illegal Migration in the Republic of Serbia.* In this policy document, it is emphasised that there is a need to changing the existing regulations 'in order to enable the labour inspectors to have legal authorisation to undertake measures against all legal and physical entities that illegally employ foreigners' (*Strategy for combating illegal migration,* Paragraph 2.1.1.). This seems particularly important if we bear in mind the fact that when

---

[61] The Law on Advertising was implemented on 1st January 2006 (Official Gazette RS, No. 79/05). It provided more opportunities for building mechanisms for the prevention of illegal mediation in employment considering that for the first time it introduced the responsibility of the person advertising, the party transmitting the advertisements and all those in the advertising chain. In the first half of 2008, five agencies were discovered and advertising of mediation in employment was prohibited. One of them illegally mediated in the process of 80 Serbian citizens going abroad for the purpose of obtaining illegal employment. B. Simeunović-Patić, (2009) 'The legal and institutional framework of the social reaction to the problem of trafficking in persons in Serbia'.

[62] Information about the Labour Inspectorate can be found in *Izvestaj o radu Inspektorata za rad za 2009. godinu* [*Report on the work of the Labour Inspectorate for 2009*] available on <http://www.vip-bzr.com/uploads/IZVESTAJ%20O%20RADU%20IN SPEKT ORATA%20ZA%20RAD%20ZA%202009.GODINU.pdf> accessed 2 March 2011.

[63] B. Simeunović-Patić, *The legal and institutional framework of the social reaction to the problem of trafficking in persons in Serbia* (2009).

conducting inspections, labour inspectors discover so-called 'phantom companies', i.e. companies that are not registered, where employers hire workers without contracts ('black labour'), but labour inspectors are not authorised to react, because that is the jurisdiction of the market or tourist inspections.[64]

Apart from 'black labour', some of the most frequent forms of violation of labour rights revealed in 2009 by labour inspectors refer to payments, i.e. delays in payments or absence of payment for a certain period of time; overtime work, which is rather frequent, but also hard to detect by labour inspectors due to the employees' unwillingness to report this and the lack of legislation on keeping records in the workplace.[65] Labour exploitation and even trafficking for the purpose of labour exploitation could be hiding behind these problems. It is obvious how important the Labour Inspectorate is in suppressing and preventing both labour exploitation and trafficking for the purpose of labour exploitation. In this respect, it is necessary to organise training for labour inspectors so they can obtain the skills needed to recognise cases of trafficking for labour exploitation. In other words, they need some tools to detect and react properly in such cases, because up to now they have not been included in seminars and training dedicated to this topic.

2.1.1.2 Education of anti-trafficking actors

To recognise the trafficking in persons in general, and trafficking for labour exploitation in particular there is a need for continuous and systematic education of all those that are likely to come into contact with victims or potential victims of trafficking. Training and seminars have been organised in Serbia so far, primarily by NGOs, the Ministry of Labour and Social Policy, the Ministry of the Interior, the Association of Judges of Serbia, the Association of Public Prosecutors, etc., with the support and assistance of international or inter-governmental organisations (OSCE, IOM, UNDP, ICMPD, etc.). Seminars and training were organised for social workers, police officers, judges, prosecutors, NGO activities. Yet, there is still a lack of perception by professionals in Serbia in the field of trafficking, particularly in trafficking for labour exploitation. As Simeunović-Patić pointed out, 'there are still a significant number of professionals who have never attended one single seminar or some other form of training on trafficking in persons (33%)'.[66] In other words, there are still professionals from different backgrounds, including those involved in investigation and prosecution (police, prosecutors and

---

[64] *Izvestaj o radu Inspektorata za rad za 2009. Godinu [Report on the work of the Labour Inspectorate for 2009]* p. 45.

[65] Ibid., pp. 7-8.

[66] B. Simeunović-Patić, 'Sensibility of professionals and the recognition of male victims of trafficking' (2009) in V. Nikolić-Ristanović (ed), *Male Trafficking in Serbia*, pp. 205-217 Belgrade: Victimology Society of Serbia, p. 211.

judges), market inspectorates, labour inspectorates, social workers and others who are not specifically trained to recognise and act if there is an indication of trafficking for labour exploitation.

On the other hand, we note that the training and seminars organised so far in Serbia were rather *ad hoc*, lasting one or two days, addressing mainly the issue of trafficking in persons in general and sex trafficking in particular.[67] We can therefore argue that, based on the research results, there is still a need to develop and organise the systematic and ongoing education of professionals from different backgrounds, with an emphasis on labour exploitation issues.

2.2 Cooperation between actors within the country

In practice, the cooperation of the above mentioned institutions, but also NGOs, centres for social work, the Agency for the Coordination of the Protection of Victims of Trafficking in Human Beings, etc. is relatively good. As suggested by the research on male victims of trafficking, 44% of professionals interviewed and the majority of those who had been cooperating with different actors in specific cases of trafficking thought the inter-agency cooperation to be 'especially good', 'good' and 'mostly good', while only 5.5% thought it to be 'bad'.[68] Cooperation with NGOs[69] and the police ranked highly, while cooperation with the centres for social work was felt to be relatively poor.[70] However, quite a few respondents revealed that the key problem in cooperation between the relevant actors is seen in the informal nature of the cooperation and the fact that it is often based on personal contacts.[71] One respondent interviewed during the research on male victims of trafficking stressed:

[67] Ibid.

[68] Ibid., pp. 201-202.

[69] Above all, the ASTRA and Atina NGOs.

[70] With regard to the mentioned issues, some NGOs are directly involved in providing assistance and support to victims of trafficking, including shelters, as well as reintegration programmes, but primarily for adult female victims of trafficking. On the other hand, Centres of social work are organisational units within the state system of social protection, who have jurisdiction in the field of social and family protection. In the case of trafficking in children, with the exception of other institutions in the social welfare system, the centres for social work are the only institutions authorised to act. Also see V. Nikolić-Ristanović, S. Ćopić, *Pomoć i podrška ženama žrtvama trgovine ljudima u Srbiji [Assistance and support to women victims of trafficking in persons in Serbia]* (2010).

[71] B. Simeunović-Patić, 'Sensibility of professionals and the recognition of male victims of trafficking' (2009) p. 202.

> *What is missing is that formal cooperation has still not been established with the key people, most of it is happening at a personal level.... Cooperation is good but is completely informal. There are no binding laws. A problem may occur when people in certain positions change.* (Representative of the IOM Office in Belgrade - excerpt from the interview carried out on research into male victims of trafficking in Serbia)

Consequently, during the process of further institutionalisation of the anti-trafficking mechanism and the improvement of mutual cooperation between the relevant actors, an important step was taken at the end of 2009 when the Agreement on Cooperation was signed between the Ministry of the Interior, Ministry of Finance, Ministry of Justice, Ministry of Health, Ministry of Education and Ministry of Labour and Social Policy. As pointed out in this Agreement, this cooperation should include the following:

- Harmonisation of work and coordination of activities in the field of the protection of victims of trafficking in order to enable the sustainability of the programmes of protection and reintegration of victims;
- Exchange of information in all fields;
- Mutual professional and technical assistance in order to improve the identification of victims of all forms of exploitation;
- Joint risk assessments aimed at decreasing the risk factors;
- Organising joint actions and other activities in order to raise the level of public awareness on trafficking in persons;
- Organising joint expert groups to solve particular cases;
- Improving the statistical monitoring of the phenomenon in order to improve the national response to trafficking in persons;
- Education of all actors involved in the procedure of identification and assistance to victims, in order to improve the identification, assistance and protection;
- Acting in the case of unexpected circumstances;
- Improvement of the legal framework for combating trafficking in persons;
- Preventing secondary victimisation of victims / witnesses and providing for the timely recognition of the problem;
- Other forms of cooperation agreed upon by the parties.

This Agreement is accompanied by an additional document – the Guidelines for the standard operational procedures in dealing with victims of trafficking.[72]

[72] The Guidelines were developed within the Programme of support for the establishment of transnational referral mechanisms (TRM) for victims of trafficking in south-eastern Europe, which was implemented by the ICMPD.

These documents may contribute to further formalisation of the mechanism for combating trafficking in persons. However, we do not have any data on the implementation of these documents so far, particularly not in the field of trafficking for labour exploitation. Consequently, it is necessary to monitor the implementation of the agreement, to estimate the level of cooperation achieved and to assess its effectiveness in order to conclude if it really contributes to suppressing this form of crime in general, and certain forms of trafficking, including trafficking specifically for labour exploitation.

As to the information exchange between anti-trafficking actors, the Strategy for Combating Trafficking in Persons provides that the Republic Team for Combating Trafficking in Persons will form a strategic part of the National Mechanism for Coordination of the Activities and Creation of an Anti-Trafficking Policy. It is defined as a 'multidisciplinary body, composed of representatives of State institutions, NGOs and international organisations, and presents a forum for discussing and developing a long-lasting, multi-sector and coordinated policy for combating trafficking in persons'. This forum should provide for the possibility for a faster information exchange with regard to the activities undertaken in this field and feedback on the results achieved. However, as we will point out later, the role, duties and responsibilities of the members of the Republic Team are not defined by the Strategy or any other legally binding instrument. Consequently, there is no legal basis for regular information exchange, which is still somewhat based on personal contacts. The above mentioned agreement is therefore important, because it contains provisions on the need to develop the exchange of information in all fields.

2.3 Cooperation between States

In cases of trafficking in persons, cooperation between States is rather narrow and mainly regional.[73] This can, at least partly, be explained by the fact that Serbia is not yet an EU Member State and many forms of cooperation established at EU level are not applied in the country.

The Ministry of the Interior of the Republic of Serbia cooperates with other countries in the region. This cooperation is primarily based on a safe partnership, which has been formed by the signing of the *Police Cooperation Convention for Southeast Europe*[74], with Albania, Bosnia and Herzegovina, Macedonia, Moldova, Romania and Montenegro, as well as through participation in the *Regional Centre for Combating Transborder Crime* in Bucharest

[73] B. Simeunović-Patić, 'The legal and institutional framework of the social reaction to the problem of trafficking in persons in Serbia' in V. Nikolić-Ristanović (ed), *Male Trafficking in Serbia* Belgrade: Victimology Society of Serbia 2009.

[74] The Law on Affirmation of the Police Cooperation Convention for Southeast Europe, Official Gazette RS – International contracts, 70/07.

(SECI centre)[75] and the *Migration, Asylum, Refugees Regional Initiative* (MARRI) are of significant importance.

Notwithstanding the importance of regional cooperation and good examples of joint investigations in cases of smuggling in persons,[76] the lack of broader international cooperation still presents an obstacle to solving other cases of trafficking, primarily those that involve Serbian citizens who have been trafficked aboard. As suggested by the research results, in cases of cross-border trafficking of Serbian citizens for the purpose of labour exploitation, international police cooperation primarily worked through Interpol. For example, in the case of trafficking in Serbian citizens to the United Arab Emirates, Serbian police asked for information from the UAE through Interpol, but the information never reached the Serbian police. As pointed out by one respondent, the police of one country are not obliged to act upon the request of any other country, which can be considered an obstacle to effective investigation in certain cases. Consequently, as the same respondent said, bilateral cooperation must be established with certain countries (countries of destination for Serbian citizens), because without such formal cooperation, State agencies, primarily the police of other countries, are not willing and also not obliged to act and provide the information requested. At the moment, in such cases (meaning those that include countries outside the region of Southeast Europe) the only possible form of cooperation is international mutual legal assistance, which is primarily based on the Law on International Legal Aid in Criminal Matters.[77] Yet, this form of cooperation, as stressed by one of the respondents, is rather slow and is applied randomly, primarily in cases of organised crime. However, as already emphasised, trafficking in persons is rarely treated as a form of organised crime in legal practice in Serbia, so one can hardly count on the use of the international mutual legal assistance in these cases.

An important step was taken in October 2009 in the process of developing police cooperation further, when the Working Arrangement between Frontex and the Ministry of the Interior of the Republic of Serbia was signed in Belgrade.[78] On this occasion, it was pointed out that 'cooperation between Frontex and the Border Police of Serbia will be developed gradually, with the aim of reaching a sustainable partnership', as well as one that will 'focus on joint operational activities in the field of Border Control, training and technical cooperation in the field of research and development'. In addition, in

[75] The SECI centre was established on the basis of the Agreement on cooperation in preventing and combating transnational crime signed in May 1999 in Bucharest. Serbia has appointed representatives of police and customs officers and actively participates in operations at the Centre.

[76] S. Ćopić, 'The characteristics of male trafficking in Serbia' in V. Nikolić-Ristanović (ed), *Male Trafficking in Serbia* Belgrade: Victimology Society of Serbia 2009, pp. 121-122.

[77] Official Gazette No. 20/2009.

[78] Information available on <http://www.frontex.europa.eu/newsroom/ news_releases/ art54.html> accessed 3 December 2010.

September 2008, Europol and Serbia concluded a strategic cooperation agreement, while in 2010, Serbia signed three cooperation measures with Europol: a roadmap for cooperation between Serbia and Europol, a memorandum of understanding on the establishment of a secure communication line between Serbia and the Europol headquarters, as well as a bilateral agreement for the interconnection of computer networks.[79] Although these forms of cooperation have not so far been applied in identified cases of trafficking in persons in general and trafficking for labour exploitation in particular, they certainly present important developments. The implementation of these agreements and measures in the near future must be monitored in order to see how effective they are in suppressing cross-border cases of trafficking in persons.

The international and regional cooperation of the judicial bodies is also important for the efficient suppression of cross-border trafficking in persons. Serbia is a member of the *Southeast European Prosecutors Advisory Group* (SEEPAG) which was founded with the aim of promoting more direct cooperation of the prosecutors from eleven countries who are members of South East Europe (Albania, Bosnia and Herzegovina, Bulgaria, Croatia, Greece, Macedonia, Moldova, Romania, Serbia and Montenegro, Slovenia and Turkey), and to strengthen the capacities of the police, the customs and the prosecutors in the region in order to resolve cases of transnational crime.[80] In addition, in 2003, a contact person was appointed to facilitate cooperation with Eurojust. However, in the trafficking cases we have come across up to now, there were no data about this form of cooperation in investigating and prosecuting these cases.

2.3.1 Special investigative techniques

The Code of Criminal Procedure of the Republic of Serbia provides the possibility for the use of special investigative techniques in cases of trafficking in persons, which is of special importance in detecting and proving trafficking in persons.

Special investigative techniques, set forth in the Code of Criminal Procedure, are primarily oriented towards the investigation of organised crime cases. However, the Code envisages the possibility of the use of some of the techniques in cases of very serious crimes, even if they are not committed by an organised criminal group, i.e. even if they cannot be subsumed under the

---

[79] EUcrim - The European Criminal Law Association Forum, 2010/2, p. 41, available on <http://ec.europa.eu/anti_fraud/publications/agon/eucrim_10-02.pdf> accessed 4 December 2010.

[80] The initiative for the founding of this group was given by Serbia in 2003 and in Belgrade in 2005. The Secretariat of SEEPAG was established with the financial support of the government of the USA.

definition of organised crime in a particular situation. The list of these criminal offences is defined by the Code, and it includes the criminal offences of trafficking in persons. This means that some special investigative techniques could be applied in every case of trafficking, while some of them can be used only in cases in which trafficking in persons has elements of organised crime.

The Code envisages the following special investigative techniques that could be applied in any trafficking case: surveillance and recording of telephone and other conversations or communications, rendering of simulated business services and concluding simulated legal affairs, controlled delivery, and automatic computer search of personal and other data. The use of the special investigative techniques is limited in terms that they can be applied only if the evidence for the prosecution cannot be collected in another way or if it would be extremely difficult to collect them.

On the other hand, in cases in which trafficking in persons takes the form of an organised crime, the criminal justice agencies can also apply some additional investigative techniques, including undercover investigators and the examination of the witness collaborator. Both techniques can be applied under the same conditions as the aforementioned measures, i.e. only if the evidence for the prosecution cannot be collected in another way or if collecting them would be extremely difficult.

The data on the research conducted so far suggests that special investigative techniques are applied only occasionally and primarily in cases in which there were elements of organised crime. In such cases, the most frequently applied technique was surveillance and the recording of telephone and other conversations or communications. Nevertheless, in none of the cases of trafficking for labour exploitation described were special investigative techniques used.

According to the Law on International Legal Aid in Criminal Matters, it is possible formally to request the relevant agencies in the foreign country to provide some forms of legal aid. Apart from extradition, undertaking or transferring criminal prosecution and the execution of a criminal judgment, international legal aid also covers the undertaking of other procedural acts and measures, including special investigative techniques. Yet, the Code of Criminal Procedure does not contain explicit provisions on the use of evidence collected abroad, particularly evidence collected through the use of special investigative techniques. However, insofar as the Law on International Legal Aid in Criminal Matters provides a legal basis for collecting evidence in other countries, we can only assume that evidence collected in this way can be used in the criminal procedure in the same way as evidence collected in the country. This also leads us to the conclusion that the Code of Criminal Procedure needs to be amended in accordance with the recent Law on International Legal Aid in Criminal Matters.

Part III
Victim protection and assistance

In Serbia, there is no special system of victim protection designed specifically for victims of labour exploitation. The legal framework and institutional framework for THB victim protection in theory serves all victims, although in practice, the entire system is mostly created to serve the needs of female victims of trafficking for sexual exploitation. In the text below, we will describe the institutional and legal framework for the protection of victims of trafficking and present research findings about the operation of this system in practice in relation to victims of THB for labour exploitation.

3.1 Identification of victims

3.1.1 Institutional framework for supporting and protecting victims of trafficking

In accordance with the international liabilities undertaken by the ratification of the UN Convention against Transnational Organised Crime and the Protocol to Prevent, Suppress and Punish Trafficking in Persons, Especially Women and Children; apart from prosecuting offenders, a system for the protection of victims within the framework of a broader national mechanism for combating trafficking in persons has started to develop in Serbia. Within this system, the central role in victim protection is given to the Agency for the Coordination of Protection of Victims of Trafficking in Human Beings (henceforth, the 'Agency'), although up to now, significant support in this domain at operational level has been provided by international and local NGOs.[81]

The Agency is a 24 hours / 7 days a week State service, which is part of the Ministry of Labour and Social Policy. Its main aim is to certify victims, i.e. to determine who is to be recognised as a victim, and refer him / her to safe housing and / or other support and assistance services. The Agency is charged with being the first point of contact for victims after they have been encountered and pre-identified as victims by the police or other actors. It is intended to identify them as victims, carry out an assessment of their needs, refer them to services, and provide assistance and monitor the protection of the trafficked person's human rights. The identification process is primarily based on the following indicators:

---

[81] B. Simeunović-Patić, 'The legal and institutional framework of the social reaction to the problem of trafficking in persons in Serbia' in V. Nikolić-Ristanović (ed), *Male Trafficking in Serbia* Belgrade: Victimology Society of Serbia 2009, p. 186.

- Documents and transportation: missing personal documents, possessing false documents and visas, illegal entry to Serbia, etc.
- Exploitation: false promises with regard to working and living conditions, forced labour, exposure to different forms of violence, threats, punishment, etc., non-payment or payment below what was agreed upon, isolation, debt bondage, etc.
- The person's appearance and behaviour: lack of trust, fear, anxiety, emotional disturbance, precariousness, physical injuries or scars, etc.
- Credibility: giving contradictory information, not remembering details, not being ready to cooperate, etc.
- Fear: of punishment, traffickers' reprisal, police, etc.

The Agency is thus expected to have a central role in identifying victims, but also in providing direct support to victims.

Apart from the Agency, direct assistance to victims of trafficking in persons is provided through the activities of NGOs and the International Organisation for Migration. Female victims are housed in one of two shelters in Belgrade. One of them is managed by the NGO – *Counselling against family violence* and the other one by the NGO *Atina*. Victims housed in the shelter are provided with medical[82] and psychological assistance as well as legal counselling and assistance. The NGO Atina also provides assistance in reintegrating victims and assistance in professional training. The NGO *ASTRA* has a helpline for victims of trafficking in persons, for members of their families and other people who need information related to trafficking. It provides medical, legal, psychological and technical assistance. In 2007, it started running a reintegration programme, within the framework of which a daily centre 'Skill house',[83] was opened for victims of trafficking in persons of both sexes. Also, the NGO *Victimology Society of Serbia* – VDS, through its *VDS info and victim support* service, offers victims of both genders and of all crimes, including trafficking in persons, information on their rights and services available, as well as emotional support and support in court. VDS also monitors the status of victims of trafficking in persons in criminal proceedings. The NGO *Centre of integration of youth* runs a drop-in centre for street children, a lot of whom are victims of trafficking.

NGOs which support victims, including those that run shelters, rely predominantly on erratic funding from international donors. The State funding is only symbolic and provided on an *ad hoc* basis. Also, there is no law so far which regulates their work and victim support services in general, although the

---

[82] As far as medical assistance to foreign citizens who are victims of trafficking in persons in Serbia is concerned, legal rights of access to free health service covered by the compulsory health insurance in the Republic should be mentioned; see Art. 241. Law on Health Protection, Official Gazette RS, No. 107/05.

[83] More about the programme on <http://www.astra.org.rs>.

draft of the new Law on Social Protection is expected to contribute to that. *The International Organisation for Migration* (IOM) in Belgrade was involved in providing some financial assistance to victims of trafficking (150 US dollars), interpreting services and financial assistance to the NGO Atina, which offers direct assistance to victims.[84] The IOM has, for quite a long time, also been involved in a programme of assistance in returning the victims of trafficking in persons to their countries of origin.

Protection, assistance, and support are provided to all trafficked persons, both foreign and national, regardless of their actual recognition as 'victims of crime' by law enforcement agencies, or the willingness of the trafficked person to be repatriated or to cooperate with the authorities in crime control. Moreover, as already mentioned, there is free medical aid available to foreign victims of trafficking covered by public health insurance. The only two conditions for receiving help relate to the trafficked person's consent to be assisted and supported and to positive identification by the Agency.

However, this solution had many shortcomings in its practical implementation.[85] Victim certification is centralised in the hands of only one actor - the Agency, which is supposed to cover the entire country. This precludes good use of overall victim support resources, and direct victims to the Agency whose own material and personal resources and capacities are more than modest, so that in practice it is not able to accomplish its mission effectively.[86] The practical operation of the Agency depends on information received from other actors, such as the police, IOM, NGOs, magistrate courts and social welfare institutions, which, as the Agency itself recognises, are often not even informed about its existence and role. In practice, the Agency barely plays the role of a coordinating body, and offers mostly the same direct assistance services as specialised NGOs. Even when the Agency does refer victims to other services, the referrals are mostly limited to organisations and institutions in Belgrade and general victim services and women's organisations

---

[84] S. Jovanović, *Victim Protection in the SEE in a Mirror of the Council of Europe Convention on Action against Trafficking in Human Beings: Serbia, Montenegro, Croatia, Bosnia and Herzegovina, Macedonia and Romania* (IOM Belgrade, Technical report November 2007) p. 9.

[85] V. Nikolić-Ristanović, 'Supporting victims of trafficking: toward reconciling the victims' and state's security', Security and Human Rights, forthcoming.

[86] S. Jovanović, M. Savić, *National Referral Mechanism for Victims of Human Trafficking in the Republic of Serbia* (2008) Belgrade: NGO Atina.; V. Nikolić-Ristanović, 'Support, assistance and the protection of male victims of trafficking: results of the research' (2009) in V. Nikolić-Ristanović (ed), *Male Trafficking in Serbia,* pp. 219-234 Belgrade: Victimology Society of Serbia; V. Nikolić-Ristanović, S. Ćopić, *Pomoć i podrška ženama žrtvama trgovine ljudima u Srbiji [Assistance and support to women victims of trafficking in persons in Serbia]* (2010).

are always excluded.[87] The lack of proper education and special referral systems for children, male victims and victims of trafficking for labour exploitation is also a serious obstacle to more effective victim identification and protection.

Recent research findings[88] show that the process of recognising and assisting both female and male victims of trafficking in Serbia involves a relatively small number of actors. A limited number of actors leads to a small number of identified victims, and as a consequence, a small number of those receiving assistance. The non-governmental organisations created to provide victim support for women-victims of trafficking are mainly concentrated in Belgrade. Thus, it is clear that only a small portion of total resources available to assist victims in Serbia is used to provide victim support. This leads to inappropriate use of existing, already limited, resources and also to the problematic quality of the services provided. This is certainly a consequence of the non-systematic development of the whole national referral mechanism for victims of trafficking, which still does not have a shaped and coherent legal framework. In particular, the place and the role of the Republic's team in Combating Trafficking in Human Beings seem unclear. This team is, together with the Agency for the Coordination of Protection of Victims of Trafficking in Human Beings, a part of the national referral mechanism. The role of institutions and organisations that are the part of the Republic team, as well as their relationship with the Agency is not fully or sufficiently legally regulated. In addition, the place and the role of other organisations and institutions (which are not part of a national referral mechanism) that come into contact with victims and / or provide assistance and support is also not clear, nor is their relationship to the overall National Mechanism for Coordination of the Activities and Creation of an Anti-Trafficking Policy. Finally, since there is no victim support NGO that is known to be specialised in assisting male victims, it is unclear whom male victims are to be referred to, i.e. what kind of assistance they can obtain. Since victims of trafficking for labour exploitation in Serbia are mainly men, it is important to consider what serious obstacles exist for their proper protection and support.

Thus, in the absence of clearly-defined procedures and standards for the treatment of different subjects, the referral mechanism and the victim support system are still working on an *ad hoc* basis. The lack of protocols on cooperation that would clearly define the roles, the order of inclusion and the manner of treatment is also connected with this. There are also no protocols

[87] V. Nikolić-Ristanović, 'Support, assistance and the protection of male victims of trafficking: results of the research' (2009); V. Nikolić-Ristanović, S. Ćopić, *Pomoć i podrška ženama žrtvama trgovine ljudima u Srbiji [Assistance and support to women victims of trafficking in persons in Serbia]* (2010).

[88] V. Nikolić-Ristanović (ed), *Male Trafficking in Serbia* (2009); V. Nikolić-Ristanović, S. Ćopić, *Pomoć i podrška ženama žrtvama trgovine ljudima u Srbiji [Assistance and support to women victims of trafficking in persons in Serbia]* (2010).

that would define the multi-sector cooperation of different actors at a local, horizontal level (for example, the coordinated action of the police, social work centres and NGOs in local communities throughout the country), as well as connecting different actors vertically (for example, the Agency, centres for social work and non-governmental organisations). The fact that the support system for victims of trafficking has been developing independently from the support system for victims of other forms of gender-based violence, prevents the proper use of the experiences, resources, and approved standards developed within the women's groups and other organisations that are supporting victims of crime. Given that there is no clear and coherent legal framework and that the existing agreements on the cooperation of some actors are considered to be internal documents that are not disclosed even to the scientific public, it is clear that the victim support system for victims of trafficking has a high level of arbitrariness and lack of transparency. This all contributes to a lack of flexibility and the inefficiency of the entire victim support system, with many victims, particularly male victims of trafficking for labour exploitation, being left out of it.

3.2 Legal framework for the protection of the rights of victims of Trafficking in Human Beings for labour exploitation

An *Instruction on the conditions for obtaining temporary residence permit for foreign citizens, victims of trafficking in persons* was issued by the Minister of the Interior in 2004. It prescribes that a recovery and reflection period of three months is available to those persons who are identified as victims by the Agency for the Coordination of Protection of Victims of Trafficking in Human Beings, and for whom the Agency requests a residence permit – for purely humanitarian reasons, i.e. not requesting that the victim cooperates with the authorities at all. The residence permit may be extended for another six months if a victim is willing to cooperate with the law enforcement agencies in discovering the crime and the offender, as well as to one year if a victim is actively involved in the court proceedings as a witness or an injured party or if her personal safety is endangered. Insofar as the Ministry of the Interior and its Department for Foreigners is responsible for deciding upon residence permits, this agency will also be responsible for deciding upon the existence of the aforementioned reasons for the renewal of the temporary permits. A decision should be made on the basis of information that needs to be provided by different actors. Namely, when applying for the renewal of the temporary residence permit, the documentation must contain a letter of the Agency for the Coordination of the Protection of Victims of Trafficking in Human Beings, a letter from the organisation providing assistance stating that the victim is involved in the programme of support, assistance and reintegration, as well as an official letter from the relevant State institution (police, prosecutor's office or court), depending on the stage in the procedure, in which it is stated that a victim is cooperating in discovering the crime and the trafficker or that a victim is actively involved in the related criminal proceedings, or that there is a threat to the victim's safety. Finally, the Instruction requests that efforts are made so that the victims of trafficking are either not punished at all for illegal border crossing, or that their penalty is lenient one.

The Law on Foreigners from 2008 regulates the issue of temporary residence permits to foreign citizens – victims of trafficking in persons in paragraph 5 of Article 29. It prescribes that temporary residence in the Republic of Serbia will be granted 'if it is in the interest of conducting criminal proceedings for the criminal offence of trafficking in persons, to the foreigner who is the victim of this criminal offence' under the condition that there are no obstacles in terms of threat to the public order or safety of the Republic of Serbia and its citizens. Also, the same article prescribes that during the course of temporary residence in the Republic of Serbia, such a foreigner, if he / she does not possess the required means of support, will be provided with adequate accommodation, food, and basic living conditions. Article 47 of the law is also relevant to the protection of the victims of trafficking in persons. It refers to the ban on forced removal of a foreigner to a territory where he / she will be faced with persecution on account of his / her race, sex, religion, nationality, citizenship, membership of a particular social group or his / her political opinion, and where there is a risk of him/her being subjected to torture, inhumane or humiliating conduct or punishment.[89]

Apart from the above-mentioned, the most recent legal changes relate to protection from repeated and secondary victimisation. The New Code of Criminal Procedure[90] introduced a new regulation which, if continuously applied in practice, is supposed to protect victims and witnesses from offensive behaviour and intimidation. Thus, it was intended that the court would protect a witness or an injured party from an offence, threat or any other type of attack, and reprimand or set a fine for the offenders. In the event of violence or a serious threat, the court had to notify the State prosecutor in order to initiate criminal prosecution. Also, at the suggestion of the judge or council president, the president of the court or the State prosecutor were able to demand that the police take the necessary precautions to protect a witness or

---

[89] According to the information received from the National coordinator for combating trafficking in persons in an informal interview conducted on 6th May 2009, the *Instruction on conditions of obtaining temporary residence to foreign citizen victims of trafficking in persons* remained in effect after the *Law on foreigners* (2008) came into effect. Currently new regulations are being prepared and the plan is that the solutions regarding the period for reflection and temporary residence for victims of trafficking in persons, who are foreign citizens, be the same as the solutions contained in the Instruction (Simeunović-Patić, 2009).

[90] V. Nikolić-Ristanović, S. Ćopić, 'Položaj žrtve u Srbiji: klasični krivični postupak i mogućnosti restorativne pravde' [*The state of victim in Serbia: traditional criminal procedure and possibilities for restorative justice*] (2006), Temida, pp. 67-77.

an injured party. The Code of Criminal Procedure, as well as the *Law on the Programme of Protection of Participants in the Criminal Proceedings*[91]and the *Law on Juvenile Perpetrators of Crimes and the Criminal Legal Protection of Minors*[92] also provides measures for protection from secondary victimisation.

The protection of victims as witnesses has been especially improved with the 2006 *Code of Criminal Procedure*. The most significant improvements were the provisions on interrogation of 'especially vulnerable' witnesses, which prescribed measures of protection for the purpose of preventing secondary victimisation of the victim and the witnesses for whom the authority conducting the procedure establishes that they are, considering their age, life experience, lifestyle, sex, health, nature or the consequences of the criminal offence, that is, other circumstances of the case, especially vulnerable.[93] This *Code of Criminal Procedure*, however, was later replaced by another one, which did not contain the provisions about protection of vulnerable victims and witnesses and prohibition of certain questions. At the moment of writing of this report, the draft of the new *Code of Criminal Procedure* had been prepared, which again incorporated the provisions about the protection of vulnerable victims and witnesses, but no mention of the prohibition of some questions.

According to the Code of Criminal Procedure, the status of 'protected witness' can also be applied to victims of trafficking in persons considering

---

[91] Official Gazette RS, No. /85/05.

[92] Official Gazette RS, No. 85/05.

[93] Those measures include: interrogation outside the premises of the authority conducting the proceedings, if the interrogation at those premises might have damaging consequences on the physical and psychological state of the witness; interrogation with the assistance of a psychologist, social worker or other expert when this is needed in order to prevent the criminal proceedings from having damaging consequences on the individual, his physical and psychological state (the authority conducting the proceedings may decide to conduct the interrogation using audiovisual technology), as well as without the presence of parties and other participants in the room in which the victim or the witness is present, so that the parties, defence lawyer and the person authorised to question him / her through an authority conducting the proceedings, may make use of a psychologist, pedagogue, social worker or other expert; appointing a representative during the interrogation when the authority conducting the proceedings believes that this is needed for the purpose of helping such a victim or witness; the possibility of questioning the victim or the witness only through the authority conducting the proceedings who will treat the victim or the witness with special attention trying to prevent the criminal proceedings from having damaging consequences on their personality, physical and psychological state; a ban on confronting the victim or the witness with the accused, while they can be confronted with the other witnesses only at their request. The witness and the victim may not be asked questions related to their sexual life and sexual orientation; political and ideological beliefs; racial, national and ethnic origin, moral criteria and other personal or family circumstances, except if this is needed for the sake of clarification of significant characteristics of the crime which is the subject of the proceedings (Art. 107 of the Code of Criminal Procedure, 2006).

both the formal conditions (that the act in question is an act for which ten years' imprisonment or a more severe penalty is prescribed) and the material condition for its implementation (that there exist circumstances which obviously show that interrogation of a certain witness would endanger the life, health, physical integrity, liberty or property of the witness or people close to him/her). In these cases, the court may pass a decree by which the person is allocated the status of protected witness and a special method of interrogation in the criminal proceedings may be prescribed, so that his/her identity is not revealed during the proceedings. Non-disclosure of the identity of the witness is primarily secured by the implementation of measures of protection during interrogation prescribed by the Code, as well as by assigning responsibilities to participants in the proceedings to protect the data on the protected witness as an official secret.[94] However, the research so far suggests that these provisions have not been applied in practice in cases of trafficking in persons, not even in cases before the Special department for organised crime.

The Law on the Programme for the Protection of Participants in Criminal Proceedings prescribes special measures of extra judicial protection for the participants in criminal proceedings and those closely related to them whose lives, health, physical integrity, freedom or property are in danger due to statements or information given, which form significant evidence. This law prescribes the possibility of special protection for the victims of criminal offences against humanity and other values protected by international law, as well as for the victims of organised crime. Protection of the victims (and individuals closely related to them) may be granted before, during and after the completion of the criminal proceedings. Protection measures are broad in character and in accordance with the provisions of *the Council of Europe Convention on Action against Trafficking in Human Beings*, which are the measures that it prescribes as 'effective and appropriate protection' and which include: physical protection of the person and property, change of residence, hiding the identity and data on possessions and change of identity.[95]

The *Law on Juvenile Perpetrators of Crimes and the Criminal Legal Protection of Minors* which has been in force since 1st January 2006, has provisions which represent a significant improvement in the protection of victims in the criminal procedure, including minor victims of trafficking in persons. A minor must have a representative (who has acquired special knowledge in the area of children's rights and the criminal legal protection of minors) while all officials (police officers, judges and prosecutors) involved in the proceedings must have

---

[94] The court will of course, choose one or more special measures of protection in interrogation in order not to disclose the identity of the witness. These include: excluding the public from the main hearing; concealing the witness; testifying from a special room with equipment being used to change the witness's voice.

[95] B. Simeunović-Patić, 'The legal and institutional framework of the social reaction to the problem of trafficking in persons in Serbia' (2009).

a suitable certificate. Techniques of interrogation are also prescribed (with the compulsory presence of a psychologist, pedagogue or other expert) the aim of which is to prevent secondary victimisation. The number of interrogations of a minor is limited to two. Only in special cases can an interrogation be conducted more than once and in those cases the judge is obliged to take special care to protect the personality and the development of a minor.
Finally, conditions under which the victims of trafficking in persons in Serbia can receive compensation for damage are the same as for other victims of criminal offences – they must have the status of the injured party in the criminal proceedings and they must submit a claim for redress in the criminal proceedings or in a civil suit. The criminal court is not obliged to discuss a claim for redress if the discussion would significantly prolong the criminal proceedings. However, the court is obliged to gather evidence and inspect what is needed to decide on the claim if this does not prolong the court proceedings significantly. Otherwise, the court will limit itself to information that cannot be established at a later date or which would be significantly more difficult. The court is obliged to pronounce the confiscation of property gain acquired through crime (this might be a source of compensation for the victim). In practice, however, the victims are most frequently referred to civil suits. Civil suits, however, last a long time, they are exhausting and complicated for the victim, especially for foreign citizens.[96]

The 2008 *Law on the Confiscation of Property Acquired through Criminal Acts* prescribes that through a decree on the permanent confiscation of property, the court may decide on the legal property request of the victim whose existence is established by a valid verdict. However, since the criminal proceedings for trafficking in persons are predominantly conducted against low level perpetrators, rarely against the organisers and those who obtain the greatest material gain from it, it is difficult to imagine that this will contribute toward a significant improvement in victim compensation.[97]

3.2.1 Protection of victims of trafficking for labour exploitation in Serbia: research findings

All available research findings suggest that the victims of trafficking for labour exploitation in Serbia are predominantly men. The results of research on male victims of trafficking for labour exploitation show that the police and the Agency for the Coordination of the Protection of Victims of Trafficking in

[96] It should also be stated that in Serbia there is no obligation to provide free legal assistance to the victims of trafficking in persons – only minors must have a representative and if the parents / guardians do not engage one, he/she will be appointed ex officio. Some NGOs still provide this sort of assistance, primarily to women.
[97] Ibid.

Human Beings are the State agencies that male victims mostly come into contact with. In certain cases, victims were also helped by their embassies and consulates. However, the victims also come into contact with the State authorities when they have committed the offence of illegally crossing the State border and illegally residing on the territory of Serbia. In these cases, they come into contact with the magistrate courts and prison. In this regard, the experience of female victims of trafficking for labour exploitation is very similar to that of the male victims.[98]

In the majority of cases of male trafficking for labour exploitation identified, the police performed the primary identification of victims and after that informed the Agency for the Coordination of the Protection of Victims of Trafficking in Human Beings, or non-governmental organisations specialised in assisting victims of trafficking in persons. The police also provided sheltered accommodation for foreigners, which operates under the auspices of the Ministry of the Interior in Serbia. Sometimes, the police informed the victims of the existence of the Agency. Respondents from the organisations to which the victims were referred mostly showed that they were satisfied with their cooperation with the police on cases being referred to them. Although rarely, magistrate judges also sometimes carry out primary identification of the victim when they interrogate them as illegal migrants. One of our respondents described a case where the magistrate judge recognised a minor victim of trafficking for labour exploitation from Romania, who was trafficked together with his minor brother and mother. The judge informed the Agency, who offered accommodation and informed the police.

3.2.2 Police and victim identification and protection

Police identification of the victims is most frequently performed during the process of disclosing criminal offences and gathering evidence to lodge criminal charges and encompasses cases of transnational trafficking. The disclosure of male victims of trafficking is primarily the result of a proactive approach by the police (the operation of cutting off the chain of trafficking and smuggling, patrols, etc.) but frequently victims, migrants above all, are disclosed by accident (that is by the police coming across foreign migrants by chance).

As is expected, data from research shows that the role of the police in identifying and assisting male victims is determined by the framework set by the national referral mechanism and their own institutional framework, which is mandatory. Nevertheless, descriptions of cases given by our respondents show that there is a practice of police behaviour deviating from the national mechanism of referral, which results from the victims' refusal to contact the

---

[98] V. Nikolić-Ristanović (ed), *Male Trafficking in Serbia* (2009).

Agency for the Coordination of the Protection of Victims of Trafficking in Human Beings and a conflict between the need for a quick and efficient reaction to the needs of the victim and the inefficiency and non–operational nature of the Agency.[99] So far, research has shown that victims of trafficking, as with other crime victims, need information, emotional support, outreach, referrals, legal, medical, financial and other assistance. They need to feel out of reach of the abusers and must have a safe place to stay, compensation and witness support. They also have specific needs connected with their (illegal) migrant status, as well as with the complexity of the consequences of lasting and multiple victimisations. These specific needs include in particular: information in their own language, including information about assistance, especially when moving from one secure place to another or when they are imprisoned; culturally sensitive support and assistance to leave their abusive situation; feeling in control of their decision to return home and testify against the traffickers; witness support adapted to their increased concerns, and residence permits in the country of destination.[100] In this sense, it seems that this type of police behaviour can be used as a way of overcoming the limitations of the national referral mechanism and that it is in the interest of the victims, depending on the circumstances.

In accordance with the national referral mechanism, referral is primarily to the Agency for the Coordination of the Protection of Victims of Trafficking in Human Beings. If however, the representatives of the Agency are not available or in emergency cases, NGOs for victims of trafficking are informed or welfare centres if the victims are children. The activity of the police related to the victims of trafficking in persons is mostly limited to referral and emergency accommodation for the victims. The police itself does not offer the victims, that is, potential victims, any other form of direct assistance (for example, giving information or distributing informative leaflets on the rights and possible forms of assistance) nor do they refer the victims to a broader range of institutions and services which could be of assistance in case they should need it – such as general services for victims of crime, Roma organisations or

---

[99] For similar regarding female victims, see S. Jovanović, M. Savić, *National Referral Mechanism for Victims of Human Trafficking in the Republic of Serbia* (2008) p. 35.

[100] U. Hedin, S. Manssen, 'The Importance of Supportive Relationships Among Women leaving Prostitution' (2003) in M. Farley (ed), *Prostitution, Trafficking and Traumatic Stress* Binghamton: The Haworth Maltreatment & Trauma Press, p.234.; H. Clawson, K. Small, E. Go and B. Myles, *Needs Assessment for Service Providers and Trafficking Victims* (2003), National Institute of Justice, p.8; V. Nikolić-Ristanović, *Support, assistance and protection of victims of male trafficking: research findings* (2009) pp.199-220; V. Nikolić-Ristanović, S. Ćopić, *Pomoć i podrška ženama žrtvama trgovine ljudima u Srbiji* [*Assistance and support of victims of trafficking in persons in Serbia*] (2010).

services intended for the disabled or people with special needs.[101] Actually, only in cases when the victim, whom they have recognised as such, refuses contact with the Agency or the NGO, are the victims pointed towards existing assistance programmes and given information on whom they can turn to for assistance in case they need it later.[102]

It is obvious that the limitation of such a practice has especially negative consequences on the support and assistance provided to male victims of trafficking for labour exploitation, considering that by referring them to organisations of a more general type, it would be possible to avoid their otherwise complete refusal to identify themselves as victims in general, especially as victims of trafficking in persons. Namely, men identify victims, and particularly victims of trafficking, primarily to be women, and, thus, refuse to accept what they consider to be a part of the female identity.

Still, police identification of someone as a victim of trafficking is no guarantee that you will not be brought in and interrogated and then punished by the judge of the magistrates' court for illegally crossing the border (or the administrative border with Kosovo) or illegal residence on the territory of Serbia. The practice of filing reports for misdemeanours against male victims, which has long since been abandoned where female victims are concerned[103], is sometimes justified by providing witnesses in the criminal proceedings against the perpetrators, thus providing a minor benefit to the victims. Men do not consider themselves victims of trafficking because they associate this with women.

The research results also pointed out the omissions of the police related to the identification and the treatment of male victims of trafficking for labour exploitation. Namely, not all victims are identified by the police. Data received through the Victimology Society's research on male trafficking shows that some of the male victims were not identified by the police as victims of trafficking in persons. In a system in which providing assistance to victims depends to a large extent on their being identified by the police, this has significant consequences on a great number of males being 'left out' of the assistance programme. Jovana Mihajlović from IOM described such a case from 2007 in which there were a number of victims (two aeroplanes full of Serbian citizens):

---

[101] V. Nikolić-Ristanović, 'Support, assistance and protection of victims of male trafficking: research findings' in V. Nikolić-Ristanović (ed), *Male Trafficking in Serbia* Belgrade: Victimology Society of Serbia 2009.

[102] S. Jovanović, M. Savić, *National Referral Mechanism for Victims of Human Trafficking in the Republic of Serbia* (2008).

[103] It is important to note that the Instruction of the MOI of Serbia on the conditions for granting a temporary residence permit to foreign citizens also prescribes that victims of trafficking not be penalised for illegal entry and staying in the country.

> *They were travelling by plane to Moscow and Abu Dhabi, but the police 'took them off' the plane. The police felt that they should not be disturbed by anybody, especially not the NGO, so nobody got involved in these cases. The police say that they told them of the Agency's existence. They did not call the Agency.*

Jovana Mihajlović also pointed to the difference between women and men who are victims of the same criminal offence. Describing a case of trafficking in women and a man from Moldova, she says:

> *I think that the man was punished for a misdemeanour, while the women in the same group were not. For this exact reason we insisted on him obtaining a temporary residence permit as well, so that he be treated as a victim and not be punished, but we did not succeed. The police that had found them had not done anything special for him, that is, they had not treated him as a victim of trafficking. The women were accommodated in the Shelter, they received temporary residence permits and he was accommodated in the Shelter for foreigners and was later voluntarily returned to Moldova.*[104]

Aleksandra Galonja, who was also from IOM at the time of collecting data on the research into male victims of trafficking, said that non-identification of adult males is not the exception, but rather the rule. This is why all men are automatically placed in the Shelter for foreigners and are generally not identified as victims of trafficking, but rather as illegal migrants. The experiences of Serbian citizens trafficked for labour exploitation to Azerbaijan was even worse, since the police did not do anything in spite of the reports from victims themselves that they were being threatened and were in need of protection.

3.2.3 The Agency for the Coordination of the Protection of Victims of Trafficking in Human Beings

Research findings suggest that the Agency for the Coordination of the Protection of Victims of Trafficking in Human Beings undertake the following activities with the aim of assisting male victims of trafficking for labour exploitation: assistance in obtaining a temporary residence permit, establishing contact with the embassy of the country the victim comes from, contact with the NGOs and institutions who run safe accommodation, as well as other

---

[104] V. Nikolić-Ristanović, 'Support, assistance and protection of victims of male trafficking: research findings' in V. Nikolić-Ristanović (ed), *Male Trafficking in Serbia* Belgrade: Victimology Society of Serbia 2009.

forms of direct assistance to victims of trafficking in persons. However, as far as the male victims are concerned, the Agency's assistance is provided primarily to male children - cases of providing specific assistance to adult males are rare. Of a total of 407 male victims identified in the Victimology Society's research on male trafficking, the Agency was in contact with only four children and four adult men.[105]

One of the rare male adults whom the Agency assisted was an eighteen-year old Roma person. The Agency conducted an interview with him and provided him with financial assistance from the Red Cross. The Agency also offered assistance in cases of Serbian citizens trafficked to the United Arab Emirates, Russia and Azerbaijan. However, the victims did not want assistance, and in some cases they even refused to talk to the Agency. According to many respondents 'the victims were only interested in redress – and that is the reason why some of them had reported this case, as well as so that the perpetrators could be punished'.[106] However, according to NGO Astra, the Agency failed to identify victims that were trafficked to Azerbaijan and to offer appropriate assistance for their needs, such as transportation to the place of residence, psychological and legal assistance, etc.

Within the framework of the cases identified both by this research and previous research by the Victimology Society of Serbia, the Agency for the Coordination of Protection of Victims of Trafficking in Human Beings asked for a residence permit for only one adult male victim and this application was granted.[107] Namely, a Romanian citizen, a victim of trafficking for the purpose of labour exploitation, was provided with a residence permit on humanitarian grounds for three months. He then received a temporary residence permit for a period of another six months (as he took part in the criminal proceedings).

A significant problem as far as male victims are concerned, is the absence of a proactive approach from the Agency for the Coordination of the Protection of Victims of Trafficking in Human Beings. Namely, as we were informed by a representative of the International Organisation for Migration, the Agency has a contract with the Shelter for foreigners, but persons from the Agency do not go there, although they should, as that is the way they could identify

---

[105] Ibid.

[106] It is interesting that the number of victims trafficked to the UAE was over a 100, and so rightfully the manner in which the assistance would be provided in this case, if the victims wanted it, can be questioned considering the more than modest capacities of the Agency.

[107] It is interesting that in the recently published report on the results of the research into the functioning of the national referral mechanism of the victims of trafficking in persons in Serbia, it is stated that all victims who were identified by the Agency received residence permits, and that residence permits were issued even in those cases in which the police officers did not share the opinion of the Agency on the need for the same. S. Jovanović, M. Savić, *National Referral Mechanism for Victims of Human Trafficking in the Republic of Serbia* (2008) pp. 20-21.

victims of trafficking for labour exploitation. The same applies to prisons in which the men are imprisoned as illegal migrants, as well as to the institutions where male children are accommodated, such as the Shelter for children and young persons, the Drop-in centre for street children, etc.

The problems noted with the Agency for the Coordination of Protection of Victims of Trafficking in Human Beings are to a large extent of a general nature and, as such, have been observed in the recent research on the operation of the national referral mechanism in Serbia.[108] However, problems are especially acute where men and children are involved as victims of trafficking in persons for the purpose of labour exploitation; this is because the national mechanism as a whole, and especially the work of the Agency, has been designed around the needs of female victims of trafficking for sexual exploitation.

3.2.4 The punishment of male victims of trafficking for labour exploitation

The results of the Victimology Society's research[109] showed that a significant number of the adult male victims of trafficking in persons were sentenced for a misdemeanour – 57 or 16.6 %. This number is probably significantly higher as for 82 (24%) of them there was no data on the verdict. This is totally discrepant with the above mentioned Instruction and the established practice of not punishing female victims and represents a drastic form of secondary victimisation of victims.

Victims that were punished for an offence were Chinese citizens, citizens of Bangladesh, Afghanistan, Albania, Macedonia and Albanians from Kosovo. There is no particular time period when the offences were committed, so it is obvious that it is a broadly established practice. Namely, the cases of identified male victims of trafficking in persons who were punished for an offence date to the period from 2003 to 2008 with the exception of 2005, a year in which not one case of punishment of a male victim was recorded. Also, male victims from Serbia trafficked to the United Emirates were also punished there, put in prison with serious criminals where they stayed for 15 days, and were then deported. The same happened to Roma woman from Serbia, trafficked to the Netherlands for exploitation in domestic work.

Considering the obvious omissions in the process of identifying male victims of trafficking in persons in Serbia, it is important to add to the above mentioned also the data on the convicted victims of smuggling, amongst which are undoubtedly some male victims of trafficking. Namely, out of a total of 403 adult male victims of smuggling, identified by the Victimology Society of Serbia's survey, 170 (42.2%) were convicted of misdemeanours for

---

[108] Ibid.

[109] V. Nikolić-Ristanović, *Support, assistance and protection of victims of male trafficking: research findings* (2009).

illegally crossing the State border, while for 224 there is no data. Out of 253 minors, 31 (12.2%) were convicted of misdemeanours. Nine minors were sentenced to educational measures, nine were given a fine and there are no data on the type of penalty for the others. In nine cases, it is only stated that the minors were arrested. From the data, it is obvious that the percentage of convicted victims of smuggling is greater compared to the number of victims of trafficking. Also, it is obvious that the minors were also given a fine and not only an educational measure as in the case of trafficking.

During the interviews with the convicted migrants in prison, researchers tried to find out how the men (victims or potential victims of trafficking) convicted for illegally crossing the State border, that is illegal residence, were treated in the proceedings and prison, whether any form of support was available to them or assistance or anything similar.[110] The men that were interviewed did not have any special complaints with regard to the manner in which they were treated by the judges of the magistrate court and the prison staff. However, from their statements, an inadequate practice is noted, which can have especially serious consequences for the victims of trafficking. Namely, the majority of interviewees were originally sentenced with a fine, but as they did not have enough money to pay it, the penalty was substituted with a prison sentence. Also, Albanians (from Kosovo) who were interviewed did not always have an interpreter, despite the fact that their Serbian was very poor. The language barrier prevents normal communication, which can lead to major misunderstanding and can endanger the rights of the victims. The best illustration of this is the responses of the respondents which show their (mis)understanding of the fine being replaced with imprisonment. At the same time, this illustrates that it is meaningless to punish individuals who are victims of trafficking in persons, that is, the people whom the traffickers robbed of money.

The words of the judge of the Magistrate Court in Belgrade also refer to the delicate nature of the position of the victims of trafficking in the magistrate proceedings:

> *It is hard to obtain information from the victims. Half of them want a defence lawyer and representative and half do not for they are afraid of repressive measures in their countries. Sometimes, some embassies see in the media that the people in question are their citizens so they approach the court.*[111]

People convicted were predominantly satisfied with the conditions and the conduct of the prison staff towards them. In most cases, they implied that their

---

[110] Ibid.

[111] Ibid.

basic needs were met and they did not suffer mistreatment. On the other hand, some of them complained that they did not have enough food, that they did not receive the medical treatment that they needed, that the conduct of the guards was inadequate and that they did not receive information that was important to them (i.e. the access number for calling outside Serbia so that they could contact their family) and such like. Also they do not receive basic information on their status and on how to leave the country. It is clear that neither the Agency for the Coordination of the Protection of Victims of Trafficking in Human Beings nor an NGO visited them.

The Albanians from Kosovo whose status (whether citizens of Serbia or not) is unclear are particularly confused, as there is a discrepancy regarding them leaving the country after the sentence has been served. The researchers have noted the following cases:

> *After spending 30 days in prison he will be allowed to return to Kosovo. He therefore asked if we knew the costs of the ticket to Kosovo for he had very little money with him. He also asked whether there was a Western Union in the vicinity for his wife to send him money. He did not know what would happen once he came out, whether he was going alone or how.*

> *They asked us about a bus to Vranje and Prizren*[112] *and explained that they were anxious because nothing worked on Sundays in Kosovo. They also asked if we knew where they could get money, from which bank, that is, whether there was a bank open on Sundays, so they could call their relatives to send them money in order to buy a ticket to get home. They seemed anxious. Obviously nobody had advised them how they could return to Kosovo.*

Researchers asked the prison warden and he told them that the prison informs the police and the police decide whether they will escort them to the UNMIK police at the administrative border or not. This means that, if they are not escorted, they are released to fend for themselves, without money, in a city where they do not know anybody, except maybe the traffickers, which automatically places them in a position of higher exposure to re-victimisation. The risk is particularly high as the prison is located near the Hungarian border, where a large number of people participate in trafficking in human beings.

Individuals treated as foreign citizens are escorted to the Shelter for foreigners and from there to their own countries. As far as the citizens of

[112] Towns in Southern Serbia and Kosovo, respectively.

Kosovo are concerned, the police decide whether they will be escorted or allowed to go alone. It is very important to note the practice that even foreigners who are punished for misdemeanours, after having serving their sentence, if they have a valid passport, are released with residency denied, so that they have a limited time to leave the territory of country. In this case they are not escorted either so they are exposed to similar risks.[113]

3.2.5 Non-governmental organisations and support to victims of trafficking for labour exploitation

Non-governmental organisations offering some sort of assistance to male victims of trafficking were described by interviewees as: organisations which are specialised in providing assistance to the victims of trafficking, including organisations who run shelters for victims of trafficking in persons; organisations specialised in providing assistance to the disabled; humanitarian organisations (for example the Red Cross) and non-governmental organisations who work with street children (Centre of Youth Integration).

Forms of assistance which minors and younger adult victims received from the local non-governmental organisations were: information, emotional support, referral to specialised organisations for working with people with disabilities, other NGOs and health institutions, specialised assistance (legal, including representation in court, and psychological), practical assistance (for example, financial, purchase of mobile phone and computer), assistance in the process of being accommodated in the Shelter or foster family and the monitoring of his situation, assistance with regard to education (i.e. continuing schooling, taking a language course – young Roma man) and becoming involved in the programmes of social inclusion (NGO Atina) and (re) integration (NGO Astra). As can be noted, NGOs have offered various forms of direct assistance to victims, so they represent the most significant players in providing support and assistance, not only to female, but also to male victims of trafficking and primarily to male children. However, some organisations, such as NGO Astra, have played a significant role on several occasions in assisting adult male victims of trafficking for labour exploitation.

In the case of the citizens of Serbia who were trafficked to Malta, NGO Astra gave the information needed to the victims that approached it. They did not want any other assistance. Apart from that, NGO Astra also contacted all other NGOs and international organisations dealing with issues related to trafficking in order to provide assistance. However, according to the

[113] Important here is the protective and not the repressive aspect of escorting, that is the police escort of victims. See more in V. Nikolić-Ristanović, 'Support, assistance and protection of victims of male trafficking: research findings' in V. Nikolić-Ristanović (ed), *Male Trafficking in Serbia* Belgrade: Victimology Society of Serbia 2009.

information received from Astra, assistance was not offered, since no organisations in Malta were found who were able to assist, and the State institutions contacted did not want to become involved. It should also be said that INTERPOL stated that in this case there are no trafficking elements. Also, NGO Astra, along with national and international organisations and State institutions, offered assistance to Serbian citizens trafficked to Azerbaijan, such as meeting them at the airport. Money for transport to the bus station was provided for a smaller number of workers whom family or friends did not pick up at the airport; emergency accommodation was found for a worker who did not want to return to his place of residence out of fear for his safety, as well as for six exploited workers in Belgrade.[114]

Moreover, they 'requested the competent authorities in the Republic of Azerbaijan to provide urgent protection and assistance to workers who were still in the territory of this country, to make the risk assessment together with the competent authorities of the Republic of Serbia, Macedonia and Bosnia and Herzegovina and ensure the safe return of the workers to their countries of origin, as well as include the workers in their National Referral Mechanism'.[115] 'They requested all actors involved in the provision of assistance to the workers, both in the country of destination and the countries of origin, to coordinate their activities in future. They also asked for adequate assistance to be provided to the workers whose safety was most compromised before they left Azerbaijan. Finally, they requested support for the establishment of the Association of Workers from Azerbaijan in Bosnia and Herzegovina and financial support for their work. In the event of legal action being started, the request was for comprehensive and appropriate legal assistance to be provided to them.'[116]

As far as the attitude of the NGOs towards male victims is concerned, respondents from certain NGOs have noticed that some organisations refuse to provide assistance to the victims, either because they do not provide assistance to male victims or because of inadequate expertise in working with certain groups of people (for example persons with disabilities). The same objection applies to NGOs who are specialised in providing assistance to the victims of trafficking as to the Agency – the absence of a proactive approach in providing support and assistance to victims in general, especially male victims, both adults and children. Generally speaking, outreach work, i.e. visits to institutions which are supposed to have victims, is still rare in Serbia, even where NGOs

---

[114] The Case of Labour Exploitation of the Citizens of the Republic of Serbia, the Republic of Bosnia and Herzegovina and the Republic of Macedonia in the Republic of Azerbaijan, Country of Origin Report, ASTRA, La Strada Bosnia and Herzegovina and NGO Partnership for Social Development, 2009.
[115] Ibid.
[116] Ibid.

are concerned. The Roma and organisations providing support to street children are somewhat of an exception.[117]

Apart from the Serbian NGOs, victims and foreign citizens were offered assistance by the International Organisation for Migration and, in Azerbaijan, by the Azerbaijani Migration Centre - AMC. This organisation mostly conducted interviews with the victims and offered assistance with regard to mediation in the process of obtaining documents (e.g. travel document and visas).

3.2.6 Provision of safe accommodation and leaving the country

As already mentioned, there are two types of safe accommodation in Serbia specifically intended for victims of trafficking. One serves foreigners, and the other accommodates national victims. However, they are both created to serve the needs of female, primarily adult, victims.

Safe accommodation intended specifically for children and male victims of trafficking does not exist, so if needed, various *ad hoc* solutions are found. These are often not adequate for victims at all and especially not for victims of trafficking. Also, as was well observed by Marija Andjelković from NGO ASTRA, men are rarely recognised as victims by the support system and the existing programmes are created to suit the needs of women.[118] There is a difference in the accommodation of male minors and adults, as well as Serbian and foreign victims.

Adult foreigners are accommodated in the Shelter for foreigners, while foreign minors are also accommodated in the Shelter for foreigners, but also in the Shelter of the Correctional Institution for Children and Young Persons. Underage male foreigners, in other words, children from 10 to 14 years of age are accommodated in the Shelter of the Correctional Institution for Children and Young Persons and older ones in the Shelter for foreigners.

Serbian underage victims are accommodated in the Shelter for women victims of trafficking, in the Shelter of the Correctional Institution for Children and Young Persons and in the safe house for women and children victims of violence in the welfare centre in Novi Sad. Serbian male children are accommodated in foster families.

While the victims are accommodated directly by the police in the shelter for foreigners, in the shelters managed by the NGOs and the welfare centre and the shelter of the Correctional Institution for Children and Young Persons, the victims are accommodated based on a referral by the Agency for

---

[117] V. Nikolić-Ristanović, 'Support, assistance and protection of victims of male trafficking: research findings' in V. Nikolić-Ristanović (ed), *Male Trafficking in Serbia* Belgrade: Victimology Society of Serbia 2009.
[118] Ibid.

the Coordination of Protection of Victims of Trafficking in Human Beings and directly by the police or NGOs.[119]

At the time of this research, not one single Serbian adult male victim was in safe accommodation. As far as Serbian citizens from Kosovo are concerned, insofar as the available findings suggest, thus far there has not been a need for this, since they have had somewhere to stay, i.e. they had their houses or flats, and support from their families. However, if it were needed, it is difficult to imagine what solution could be found and to what extent it would be adequate.

Also, although accommodation was provided for underage male victims and adult male foreigners, it cannot be considered remotely adequate, let alone stressed as an example of good practice. The accommodation used is intended for other purposes and is not created to serve the needs of victims of trafficking. A big problem is both the absence of shelters for men and the absence of shelters for children. Also, the issue of the provision of safe accommodation for Albanians from Kosovo is raised. They are treated as national victims and as such are deprived of this form of assistance.[120]

An example of bad practice is stressed by Aleksandra Galonja from IOM who noticed that all adult male victims, who were foreign citizens, were automatically accommodated in the Shelter for foreigners and not identified as victims of trafficking, but rather as illegal migrants. Accommodation in the Shelter for foreigners is actually intended for the purpose of isolating illegal migrants and not for the purpose of protecting them and providing them with support. This also means that, if victims have legal travel documents, they are not accommodated in the Shelter for foreigners, but are expected to leave the country immediately.[121]

Absence of support for victims accommodated in the Shelter for foreigners is a big omission in the system of providing assistance to male victims in Serbia, especially considering the fact that victims are often scared, in a poor physical and psychological state and have no information. As the judge in the Magistrate Court in Belgrade said, in the case of trafficking in Turkish citizens, the victims were: 'scared, neglected, hungry, there was no evidence of violence nor did they complain, they only asked what would happen to them'.[122]

Foreign citizens, who are victims of trafficking, mostly leave Serbia in one of the following ways:

[119] Ibid.
[120] Ibid.
[121] Ibid.
[122] Ibid., p. 237.

- Some of the victims are included in the IOM programme of voluntary return, for example victims who did not obtain the temporary residence permit.
- Some of the victims are deported, that is, they are denied residence in Serbia for a certain period.

Victims who were denied residence in Serbia were, as a rule, escorted by the police to the border of the country from which they entered Serbia. Thus the victims who were trafficked through Kosovo were escorted to the 'Merdare' check point, in other words, to the administrative border with Kosovo – including Albanians from Albania and citizens of other countries who were trafficked through Kosovo and occasionally Albanians from Kosovo. Albanians from Kosovo and foreign citizens who have valid documents were previously allowed to leave the territory of Serbia alone, that is, without a police escort.

A certain number of victims remained in Serbia in order to testify in the criminal proceedings, mostly thanks to the involvement of the Embassy of their country (for example a citizen of Turkey). Citizens of Serbia who were trafficked to other countries were mostly deported to Serbia.

3.2.7 Refusal of assistance by the victim

Research findings showed that refusal of assistance by the victims is more common with male victims of trafficking for labour exploitation than with female victims.[123] Refusal is expressed as a complete refusal to accept assistance and then leaving the shelter or other safe accommodation.

> *The victims were somehow discovered by the police in Bosnia and Herzegovina. They were brought to Serbia in order to enable their return to Georgia, for it was easier to obtain the necessary documents in Serbia and to organise their return. They stayed in the shelter for two or three days and then they fled when a woman from the shelter took them to get photographed for their documents. (Vesna Stanojević – Counselling against family violence)*

One of the explanations for the refusal of assistance by the male victims given by individual interviewees is the limited assistance in securing safe accommodation and services within it, as well as the lack of a broader range of measures of support and assistance. It has been noted that this is not acceptable to men. In the case of adult males, their refusal is connected with the broader

[123] On the refusal of assistance by female victims please see A. Brunovskis, R. Surtees, *Leaving the past behind? When victims of trafficking decline assistance* (2007) Oslo: Fafo-report 40.

aspect of gender, that is, the general refusal of men to identify themselves as victims at all, and especially as victims of trafficking in persons. Namely, the role of the victim is mostly associated with passive behaviour and helplessness, which are seen to be innate characteristics of the female gender identity.[124] The gender aspect of the social construction of the term 'victim' is more emphasised when it is a case of a victim of trafficking in persons: the term which primarily implies a female victim of trafficking for sexual exploitation. The interviewees have noticed that refusal to identify oneself as a victim is connected to their fear of repression by the trafficker, but also with their denial of their own victimisation which is connected to the fact that they do not wish to believe that they have been tricked by the traffickers. Also, some victims of trafficking for labour exploitation consider themselves to be victims of fraud rather than victims of trafficking, so that a refusal of assistance is connected to the avoidance of being treated as a victim of trafficking.[125]

From the above, it can be concluded that the data received through research obviously suggests that there is a need to creating a more comprehensive, more diverse and better adapted programmes of support, assistance and protection for victims of trafficking in general, and especially male victims and street children.

3.2.8 Victims in criminal proceedings

The research so far also gives a certain insight into the status of victims in criminal proceedings. What we have learned mostly points to the general problem of inadequate conditions for trials and the testifying of victims. This problem was especially emphasised recently. In the majority of cases of trials for trafficking and smuggling of persons, the trials are conducted in the ordinary courts and not in the Special Department of the Higher Court in Belgrade for organised crime. So, most of the court rooms in these courts are small and there is no possibility of employing modern technical equipment, such as video links, voice and image-changing equipment and so on, which is important when protecting the victims from secondary victimisation. A problem is noticed with the so-called leaking of information, especially information related to the identity of the victim, which furthermore endangers the victim and negatively influences their readiness to testify. While observing a trial before the Higher Court in Belgrade, VDS volunteers noticed the discomfort of the victims and their families due to the fact that contact with

---

[124] For a similar explanation, see R. Surtees, *Listening to Victims: Experiences of Identification, Return and Assistance in South-Eastern Europe* (2007) Vienna: International Centre for Migration Policy Development, p. 196.

[125] V. Nikolić-Ristanović, 'Support, assistance and protection of victims of male trafficking: research findings' in V. Nikolić-Ristanović (ed), *Male Trafficking in Serbia* Belgrade: Victimology Society of Serbia 2009.

the family of the accused and the witnesses was unavoidable in the hall before and during the break in the trial.

The results of research do not show that measures of protection are being implemented in cases of adult male victims of trafficking for labour exploitation. Still, the results do show that the professionals feel for the difficult life circumstances of the male victims. In some cases, the victims were interrogated at the main hearing, while in others only their testimonies were read. In the latter case, the victims were mainly interrogated before the investigative judge and then they left the country so they were unable to attend the main hearing. It has also been noticed that in cases where minors and younger male adults appear as victims in the criminal proceedings, measures to protect children from secondary victimisation are applied and the victims are listened to very attentively. For example in one case, the judge first found out from the legal advisor of the young man – the victim - whether the young man would be capable of testifying, considering that he would have to be taking insulin at a set time. When it was established that the young man was ready to testify, the judge told him that he could stop the testimony at any time if he felt weak.

In one criminal proceeding the audio recording of the victim's testimony was used, while in the other, the testimony was recorded with a video camera, so on the basis of that testimony, secondary victimisation was avoided and it was used in further court proceedings. In some cases, from the very beginning of the proceedings, victims had a representative provided by the NGO ASTRA. The presence of the NGOs' representative is very important in providing support and legal assistance to the victim, but also as a way of mitigating the problems related to the lack of space. For example, victims and their families would usually sit together with the representatives of the NGOs on one side, while the families of the accused would sit on the other side. In addition, the presence of the legal advisors from the NGOs was important in safeguarding the rights of the victim in the criminal proceedings, especially the right to restitution.

Part IV
Case studies

Case one: Trafficking of an adult Romanian male person in Serbia

Source of information: the interview with the police officer in the Ministry of the Interior, Border Police Directorate, Department for suppressing cross-border crime and criminal intelligence matters, Section for suppressing illegal migration and trafficking in persons, which was conducted on 21st September 2010, and the interview with the representative of the Agency for the Coordination of the Protection of Victims of Trafficking in Human Beings conducted on 22nd January 2008, as part of the research on male victims of human trafficking.

The case was discovered in 2007 in Veliko Gradiste, a town in the North-Western part of the country, close to the border with Romania. The case was discovered by accident. One police officer was under investigation for corruption. The corruption case was being investigated internally at the Ministry of the Interior. During this investigation, it was discovered that a friend of the police officer being investigated was holding an adult male Romanian citizen in his slaughter house, in rather poor conditions, for the purpose of labour exploitation. The police officer being investigated was not involved in the exploitation, but he was familiar with the whole story and he even assisted in obtaining the forged residence permit for the Romanian citizen.

The victim was an adult Romanian citizen, who was born in 1977. He had a low level of education: he had only completed primary school and had lived in an orphanage in Romania. Since 2000, he had regularly been coming to Serbia, in search of a job. He was entering Serbia legally, staying for 30 days (as permitted), then leaving the country and returning. He had regular entry and exit stamps in his passport. He was coming to Serbia (and Veliko Gradiste in particular) on his own, just as many other Romanian citizens did at that time. He was doing various different jobs involving manual labour.

On one occasion when he came to Serbia in 2002, he got a job in a slaughterhouse and agreed his wage with the owner. This should have been 150 EUR per month. The owner of the slaughterhouse agreed to provide him with accommodation and food. His exploitation started in 2002 and lasted for the next five years – from 2002 to 2007, when he was recognised as a victim of trafficking. During his stay in this slaughterhouse, he was living in sub-human conditions and was only paid occasionally. He lived in a windowless basement. He slept on the floor, and the premises did not have any heating or electricity. In 2004, the passport of the Romanian citizen expired. The owner took the victim's passport with the excuse of legalising his stay in Serbia. His freedom of movement was restricted; he was not allowed to talk to anyone. He was living in complete isolation.

As pointed out by the police officer being interviewed, the key characteristics of this case that made it a case of trafficking for labour exploitation were: false promises (on the sum to be paid, working and living conditions, the issuing of a resident permit, etc.), the withholding of a passport, bad living and working conditions, restricted freedom of movement, longer working hours than had been agreed, and fear of custody and deportation.

Once rescued, he was referred to the Agency for the Coordination of the Protection of Victims of Trafficking in Human Beings. The Agency identified him as a trafficking victim. After being identified as a victim of trafficking, he was issued a temporary residence permit on humanitarian grounds (three months), which was renewed for another six months on the basis of his cooperation with law enforcement and the judiciary in the procedure against the offender. He was not placed in the shelter or other accommodation; all he wanted was a residence permit, no other assistance. During his stay on the basis of the temporary residence permit he had been granted, he got another job in a restaurant.

According to the police data, a criminal charge of trafficking in persons (Art. 388 of the Criminal Code) was filed against the offender – the owner of the slaughterhouse. The case went before the District court in Pozarevac. It is still going on. Five months after being rescued, the Romanian citizen returned to Romania.

Case two: Trafficking of Serbian citizens to Azerbaijan

Source of information: The Case of Labour Exploitation of the Citizens of the Republic of Serbia, the Republic of Bosnia and Herzegovina and the Republic of Macedonia in the Republic of Azerbaijan, Country of Origin Report, ASTRA, La Strada Bosnia and Herzegovina and NGO Partnership for Social Development, 2009,[126] and the interview with the police officer from the Belgrade Police Administration Department for suppressing illegal migration and trafficking in persons, which was conducted on 26th August 2010.

This is the case of trafficking for labour exploitation of the citizens of Serbia, Bosnia and Herzegovina, and Macedonia in Azerbaijan, dated 2009. It probably represents one of the largest registered cases of trafficking for labour exploitation in this region. Apart from the citizens of the above mentioned countries, the citizens of Moldova and Pakistan, as well as of Azerbaijan were also exploited.

In Serbia, the first news about the case was received by the NGO ASTRA, which forwarded the information to the police. The case was discovered by a certain number of international organisations and foreign embassies in

[126] This report was made available by the NGO ASTRA.

Azerbaijan, as well as by the local NGO Azerbaijan Migration Centre, when some workers started to complain, alarming some of these organisations with details of their case. The exact number of exploited workers could not be established, because the workers were going to Azerbaijan in groups, while several groups had already returned from Azerbaijan when the case was discovered. In the report of the Azerbaijan Migration Centre, it was stated that during 2009 there were around 500 workers in Baku and Mingachevir. According to the workers' estimates, in October 2009, there were between 920 and 1040 workers at construction sites run by the SerbAz Company in Azerbaijan. Serbian police have identified about one hundred workers who were exploited in Azerbaijan.

Most of the exploited workers were young males, mostly between 18 and 22 years of age. There were several women among them, mostly working in the kitchen or doing administrative jobs. They were recruited in their countries of origin and offered jobs. The construction company SerbAz Project and Construction LLC (hereinafter referred to as SerbAz) had been managing construction works at several sites in Azerbaijan and it was looking for workers. The investor of this construction work was the Government of Azerbaijan. SerbAz had offices in the Netherlands, in Russia and Azerbaijan, but it was not registered in Serbia. Information on the employment opportunity for construction workers in Azerbaijan was spread by word of mouth, but also through advertisements.

In order to sign a contract, workers had to pay a fee of up to 200-250 EUR. If they did not have the money, they were allowed to pay it out of their first pay packet. Instead of normal contracts, they were asked to fill in questionnaires, detailing their qualifications and skills. The workers were told that they needed to pay 10 EUR for their visa and the company would arrange the travel. They were promised accommodation in flats with five persons at most, as well as not more than ten hours per day of work for a salary of between 700 and 800 USD a month, depending on skills and qualifications.

The workers went to Azerbaijan legally by aeroplane. However, once they reached Azerbaijan, their passports and travel documents were taken away, with the explanation that this was needed in order to legalise their residence status. Nevertheless, the majority of workers stayed in Azerbaijan illegally: they entered the country on tourist visas which they paid for themselves (the visa is obtained at the border checkpoint, i.e. at the airport). Only a certain number of workers had residence permits, which they were issued after the entry visa, but these permits also expired during their stay and were not renewed.

Most workers lived in collective accommodation – dormitories accommodating between 40 and 110 people. Living conditions were bad. Every dormitory had bedrooms for 12-24 people and a small living room which could fit 10-12 people. The number of toilets and bathrooms was insufficient and the workers had no running water for at least four days a week. It was rather cold in the dormitories and the electricity was often cut off. Strict house rules were applied. Workers had to work when they were ill;

they could not be hospitalised and examinations were carried out by a nurse instead of a doctor. The food was rather poor and insufficient.

As to the working hours, shifts were supposed to last for 12 hours (day shift and night shift), but the employer could extend the working hours at any time, without notice. The workers did not have the right to complain or refuse to work. There were no toilets in the workshops. They were completely separate, dirty, without running water, soap or toilet paper. Workers were not protected in the workplace: they were working without standard protection gear.

According to the 'contracts' that were signed, the workers should have been paid in cash, on a regular basis, at a rate of USD 5-7 per hour. However, the workers received only a portion of the expected payment, i.e. they were paid at an hourly rate of USD 3-4. The total amount they received was therefore reduced by USD 1000-3700. From May until August 2009, the workers were not paid at all.

Workers were punished for a series of different punishable acts. For each of these acts, a fine was imposed. They were also exposed to physical punishments, threats, relocation to other construction sites and dormitories, etc. Their freedom of movement was restricted.

A criminal report against 14 individuals was filed in Bosnia and Herzegovina, although when they were asked by Interpol and the police in Azerbaijan to provide some information on the case, the Azerbaijan authorities said that there had not been labour exploitation in this case. As far as Serbia is concerned, one must find out which Serbian citizens were involved in this chain and then open the case before the court.

Part V
Recommendations

Based on the research, we have drafted recommendations for the development of a social response to trafficking in persons in general and for the purpose of labour exploitation in particular in Serbia. The proposals have been split into five main groups: enhancement and legal regulation of the anti-trafficking mechanism, enhancement of the system of referral and support and assistance to victims of trafficking in human beings, prosecution, prevention, and monitoring and evaluation.

Enhancement and legal regulation of the anti-trafficking mechanism

1. Explicitly define the status, role and concrete activities of the Republic's Team for Combating Trafficking in Human Beings as a part of the National Mechanism for the Coordination of Activities and Creation of an Anti-Trafficking Policy.
2. Explicitly define and legally regulate the status, role and relationships between all actors involved in the National Mechanism for the Coordination of Activities and Creation of an Anti-Trafficking Policy, so as to guarantee maximum use of the existing resources.
3. Regulate procedures for the inclusion of new members into the Republic Team for Combating Trafficking in Human Beings in order to enable all actors, who are important to victim identification and support, to be included.

Enhancement of the system of referral and support and assistance to victims of trafficking in human beings

1) Create the conditions for including more actors in the process of identification and provide support and assistance to victims of trafficking in persons in general and trafficking for labour exploitation in particular by:
   a. Educating all those that are coming or might come into contact with victims of trafficking in human beings, including trafficking for labour exploitation (particular emphasis should be placed on the employees in the social welfare system, market inspectors and labour inspectors, judges in magistrate courts, persons employed in the diplomatic consular offices, etc.).
   b. Raising the awareness of the citizens on whom to address if someone needs assistance;
   c. Raising the awareness of potential and actual victims so that they know whom to address if they are in need of assistance.
2) Establish a National information centre that would:
   a. Keep and regularly update the database on the existing services / organisations that could be useful for victims of trafficking.
   b. Provide for and distribute information about existing services to:

    i. Actors that are coming or might come into contact with victims of trafficking in human beings;
    ii. Potential and actual victims;
    iii. All those that need this information.

  c. Set up and regularly update the library with domestic and foreign literature on trafficking in persons in general and trafficking for labour exploitation in particular.

3) Legally regulate the role of different actors in providing assistance to underage victims of trafficking in persons in a way that enables a clear distinction of their competencies.
4) Develop and formalise mechanisms for the cross-sector connection and cooperation between different actors at local level (horizontal connecting).
5) Connect mechanisms for cross-sector cooperation at local level with the National Mechanism for the Coordination of Activities and Creation of Anti-Trafficking Policy (vertical connecting).
6) Develop outreach programmes and other proactive approaches to recognition, support and assistance of victims and potential victims, including illegal migrants, street children, persons employed on the black market and other persons at risk.
7) Strengthen the capacities and resources (material and human) for market and labour inspection, with the aim of improving their work on disclosing cases of trafficking in persons for labour exploitation.
8) Create programmes of support and assistance to victims and potential victims (safe accommodation, information, emotional support, expert assistance, referrals, etc.), which would be adapted to the specific needs of various categories of victims, including victims of trafficking for labour exploitation.
9) Establish a State fund to compensate victims of crime (including victims of trafficking in persons).
10) Legal regulation (through the law on foreigners) of the reflection period, i.e. issuing temporary residence permits to victims of trafficking for humanitarian reasons and protecting their safety.
11) Create adequate programmes for the (re)integration of victims of trafficking for labour exploitation.
12) Develop regional and international cooperation to provide assistance and support to victims of trafficking in persons.

Prosecution

1) The term 'exploitation of a person's labour' should be defined more precisely in the Criminal Code in order to provide for better identification of victims of such a practice, but also to eliminate any form of legal uncertainty.
2) Develop mechanisms of cooperation between actors involved in prosecution both at national, European and international level.

3) Improve bilateral cooperation, particularly with the countries identified as countries of destination for Serbian citizen who are trafficked for labour exploitation.

Prevention

1) Connect the measures for suppression of trafficking in persons with the broader social policy especially;
   a. Measures for poverty reduction
   b. Measures for suppressing the grey economy
   c. Measures for creating legal employment (for both employees and the employers)
   d. Employment / self-employment programmes
2) Raise the awareness of the public to the problem of trafficking for labour exploitation (through information campaigns, media content, etc).
3) More energetic suppression of corruption and strengthening of institutions and the trust of citizens in them.
4) Raise the awareness of the citizens with regard to the risks connected with the acceptance of illegal offers of jobs, migration, etc.
5) Develop preventive measures directed towards individual groups of potential victims (e.g. adult males and male children, the Roma, people with disabilities, people with special needs, illegal migrants, etc.)
6) Develop a system to support and inform illegal migrants.
7) Improve the systems at State level for informing citizens of job offers abroad.

Monitoring and evaluation

1) Establish a National rapporteur that would conduct continuous monitoring and evaluation of anti-trafficking activities in general, with a particular emphasis on assistance and support to victims, in accordance with the ODIHR model, based on which this role should be given to a non-governmental organisation.
2) Explicitly define the role of the National rapporteur and its relationship with the National Mechanism for the Coordination of Activities and the Creation of an Anti-Trafficking Policy and everything associated with it.
3) Continuous monitoring should be carried out with the use of quantitative and qualitative methods, combined with different techniques for collecting data from different actors (including data on victims, traffickers, ways of committing trafficking, and victim support).
4) Legally regulate the conditions for allowing the professional and scientific public to be present during the actions of State agencies in the pre-trial criminal procedure.

Chapter 5
Combating Trafficking in Human Beings for Labour Exploitation in Spain

F. Manrique López,
F.J. Arrieta Idiakez,
F. Manrique Rojo[1]

Part I
The legal framework on defining Trafficking in Human Beings for labour exploitation and the dimensions of this crime

1.1 The definition of Trafficking in Human Beings for labour exploitation in Spain

Recently, Spain has proceeded to amend its Criminal Code, Organic Law 10/1995 of 23rd November[2], through Organic Law 5/2010 of 22nd June.[3] Among the new aspects introduced by this new piece of legislation, is the creation of an *ex novo* Title, within Book II of the Code, on trafficking in human beings ('Title VII Bis. On trafficking in human beings'), which now contemplates, through its Art. 177 bis, the criminalisation of human trafficking.

With this new piece of legislation an end has been put to a major loophole, which was criticised institutionally by the European Commission in its report of 6th December 2006[4], expressing that Spain did not establish a clear distinction between human trafficking and smuggling illegal immigrants.

Furthermore, the now resolved matter, involved the breach of the commitments acquired by Spain at international level, as well as those regarding the existing European Community legislation.

As a matter of fact, real change in Spanish legislation on trafficking in human beings is a result of the ratification by Instrument of 23 February 2009, of Convention No. 197 of the Council of Europe, on Action against Trafficking in Human Beings, done at Warsaw on 16 May 2005.[5] This assertion becomes proven when observing the language and interpretation given to the new Art. 177 bis of the Criminal Code, and becomes even clearer

[1] Fernando Manrique López is Professor in Labour Law and Social Security at University of Deusto, Law Faculty; Francisco Javier Arrieta Idiakez is lecturer in Labour Law and Social Security at University of Deusto, Law Faculty. Fernando Manrique Rojo is a lawyer specialized in labour law in Bilbao.
[2] Official State Gazette of 24 November 1995, No. 281.
[3] Official State Gazette of 23 June 2010, No. 152.
[4] COM (2006) 770 final.
[5] Official State Gazette of 10 September 2009, No. 219.

upon close examination of the Spanish Statutory instrument on Foreigners, as amended by the provisions for the protection of the dignity of the victim, since references to this Convention, lie therein.[6]

Accordingly, under Spanish legislation, the concept of Trafficking in Human Beings for labour exploitation necessarily needs to be drawn from the sum of the elements constituting the criminal offense contained under Art. 177 bis, of the Spanish Criminal Code:

a) The Spatial or Geographical Consideration (Where): The crime must have been committed while maintaining some form of link with Spain. The need for a connecting link is further clarified by expressly covering the different possibilities:[7]
   - *ON Spanish territory:* this means that all aspects characteristic and necessary to carry out an action of Trafficking in Human Beings, would have been brought into effect within the scope of Spanish territorial sovereignty.
   - *FROM Spain:* draws our attention to the individual that is carrying out the crime, as well as the individual that is being subject to the actions of the criminal. Here it could be possible to have the victim be picked up in Spain, for the purpose of being exploited abroad. Or alternatively, to have the offender be located in Spain, and then contact, through a different number of means, a potential victim living abroad, in order to achieve their subsequent exploitation in Spain or another State.
   - *IN TRANSIT THROUGH Spain:* implies that at least one of the parties needs to have the offence be committed, takes place in Spain. For example, the victim may be transported through the Spanish territory, or carried on board a Spanish vessel or aircraft, or handed over to an intermediary who is in Spain.
   - *With DESTINATION Spain:* in this case, Spain is the state where the victim will be arriving. His or her final destination, where they will be subject to a form of labour exploitation.

b) Instrumental Consideration (How): in order to adequately incorporate instrumental considerations into the Spanish national legislation, as

---

[6] An identical conclusion is reached in the Report by the State Prosecutor□s Council on the Organic Draft Bill for the amendment of Organic Law 10/1995 of 23 November on the Criminal Code in respect of Title VII bis on trafficking in human beings at <www.fiscal.es>, where it provides that it may be said that Art. 177 bis performs an almost verbatim transposition of the commands contained in the Council of Europe Convention to combat trafficking in human beings, although completed with some amendments originating in the Directive of the European Parliament and of the Council on preventing and combating trafficking in human beings, and protecting victims.

[7] I. Rodríguez Fernández, 'Trata de personas' in I. Ortiz de Urbina Gimeno (ed), *Memento Experto Reforma Penal 2010. Ley Orgánica 5/2010* (Madrid: Francis Lefebvre 2010) p. 74.

contemplated by international Law, the Spanish legislator has preferred to avoid the route of literal translation, and has instead chosen to refer to legal concepts that already exist in our national Laws, which provide a perfect equivalent:[8]

- *Violencia e intimidación (Violence and Intimidation):* includes all coercive forms covered under international law ('threat', 'use of force or other forms of coercion', 'abduction', 'kidnapping').
- *Engaño (Deception):* includes all forms of fraud or fraudulent action.
- *Abuso de una situación de superioridad, o de necesidad o vulnerabilidad (Abuse of a position of power or vulnerability, or of necessity):* with this expression, all three forms of abuse that exist under Spanish law, are incorporated into the statutory provision. All other hypothesis are covered under the umbrella provided by this broader legal concept. This includes payments or benefits provided to those who hold some form of power over the victim, which can be exercised with a view to taking advantage of the vulnerability of the latter (because of their dependence or reliance on a third party). Alternatively to reinstate the prevalence and superiority of the former (who would collaborate in exercising that power over the victim, and would accordingly be considered, at least, necessary cooperator in the crime of Trafficking in Human Beings). Notwithstanding the aforementioned, and as established under the Directive of the European Parliament and Council, on the prevention and combating of trafficking in human beings and protection of victims, a situation of 'vulnerability' must be understood to have occurred when the person has no real or acceptable alternative but to yield.

c) Personal Consideration (upon whom): the crime can be committed regardless of whether the victim is a 'national' or a 'foreign' citizen. The adoption of the term 'foreign' citizen, without taking into consideration whether the victim holds a legal or illegal status of residence, has important positive consequences for the prosecution of this crime. This new language caters for the legal prosecution of cases where Trafficking in Human Beings for labour exploitation may be carried out under circumstances where a non-national victim falls subject to Trafficking in a country of origin different to Spain, and is then taken to Spain, in order to endure labour exploitation under legal conditions that could not only mask the crime, but even serve to obtain the necessary administrative authorisations. The language of the new provision, would equally contemplate the possibility of the 'foreign' victim having acquired a valid resident permit before falling subject to trafficking, or even a situation where the victim was a 'national', even if the latter is believed to be able to more easily avoid the sphere of influence of the

[8] I. Rodríguez Fernández, 'Trata de personas' in I. Ortiz de Urbina Gimeno (ed), *Memento Experto Reforma Penal 2010. Ley Orgánica 5/2010* (Madrid: Francis Lefebvre 2010) p. 83.

criminals.

d) Commisive Consideration (carrying out what kind of action): sets out the actions already described at international level, namely:[9]
   - *Recruitment:* is the act of overcoming and breaking the will of the victim, through any of the instrumental considerations described herein above. Sometimes, to favour the recruitment, the criminal will resort to the instrumental element of deception or fraud. Once the victim arrives at the destination, a number of additional measures will normally be adopted in order to have the victims give in to the labour exploitation they are intended to be subject to. Such would be actions of violence, intimidation or abuse, exercised in any of the three situations of superiority, need or vulnerability.
   - *Transport and Passage:* these are clearly intermediate comportments, and are to be construed in a broad manner. All actions carried out in aid of moving the victims to the place where they will be subject to actions of labour exploitation, should accordingly be encompassed herein.
   - *Housing and accommodation:* these are also intermediate behaviours, foreordained to the subsequent exploitation of the victims. Such behaviour should therefore not be mistaken with the housing and accommodation occurring after the arrival of the victim at the destination, since such action and their subsequent acts would overreach the specifics of trafficking, and should accordingly be confined within the scope of the crime that constitutes each specific form of labour exploitation. Moreover, in order to open up criminal liability of actions related to trafficking and include the handover of the victim from one criminal to another[10], these concepts should be interpreted in accordance with their grammatical meaning, in order to include the concept of 'transfer', as used by the Council of Europe's Convention on human trafficking.
   - *Delivery and Reception:* assumes that the subject that will be carrying out the crime of labour exploitation, contacts the victims, either directly (for example, waiting for them at an airport, bus station or any point of arrival in Spain), albeit indirectly, (the victim is handed over to him by the trafficker). In both cases the operator becomes the perpetrator of a crime of trafficking prior to the crime of Labour Exploitation.

e) *Purposive Consideration* (what for): as part of the present subject of analysis, and report, actions carried out must obey the unlawful purpose

---

[9] I. Rodríguez Fernández, 'Trata de personas' in I. Ortiz de Urbina Gimeno (ed), *Memento Experto Reforma Penal 2010. Ley Orgánica 5/2010* (Madrid: Francis Lefebvre 2010) pp. 76-80.

[10] J.M. Terradillos Basoco, 'Trata de seres humanos' in F.J. Álvarez García and J.L. González Cussac (eds), *Comentarios a la Reforma Penal de 2010* (Valencia: Tirant lo Blanch 2010) p. 210.

of the crime, including labour exploitation. Once again, national legislation has willingly adopted the criteria used at international level, whereby, labour exploitation has been defined in accordance with the following standards: the imposition of forced labour or services, slavery or practices similar to slavery, servitude or begging. Of all these actions, the incorporation of forced begging is most relevant, since it anticipates a most likely future matter to be incorporated into Member States□ national legislation, as advocated by the European Directive of the European Parliament and Council on the prevention and combating of trafficking in human beings and protection of victims. However, no action has yet been taken to include the use of the victim to commit criminal acts within the unlawful purpose of the crime, even though this is a matter that is also foreseen and already contemplated in the Directive.

After examining the different elements that make up the crime of trafficking, it must be concluded that the crime of trafficking is consummated upon completion of the specific action of trafficking, regardless of whether or not the effective exploitation of labour occurred. Moving on from this conclusion, we find that where an alleged case of labour exploitation has effectively occurred, the crime of trafficking will concur with crimes committed in violation of workers rights, which is a specific field of the Law also known as Criminal Labour Law.[11] Given the importance of this field of Law for our study, we will look into this matter with great detail in the following subsection, which will deal with statutory instruments, Regulations and relevant policies for the prosecution of the crime of trafficking for labour exploitation. This broad picture associated with the concept of trafficking, necessarily draws our attention to the penalties to which criminals may be convicted. Accordingly, it must be noted that having the crime of trafficking be covered, through the inclusion of specific language to this end, needs to be the first step in guaranteeing that the Spanish law incorporates the different measures that are advocated at international level, and in particular, those related to the protection and recovery of victims.[12]

Thus, Art. 177 bis of the Criminal Code contemplates convictions of imprisonment from 5 to 8 years. Furthermore, that particular article establishes that where the subject being at risk is a child (underage person), a special degree of protection needs to be afforded to the victim, and accordingly establishes that under such circumstances, the crime associated to the action carried out for the purpose of Labour Exploitation, will automatically be considered to be Trafficking in Human Beings, regardless of whether the

---

[11] Report by the State Prosecutor's Council on the Organic Draft Bill for the amendment of Organic Law 10/1995 of 23 November on the Criminal Code in respect of Title VII bis on trafficking in human beings at <www.fiscal.es>.

[12] Ibid.

different instrumental considerations associated to this crime, are met or not. Finally, Art. 177 bis, affords an additional degree of protection where the instrumental means are employed in the course of the action of trafficking. Under such circumstances, the victims' degree of consent, and whether it was obtained, will be irrelevant.

The language used in the new provisions has also established more severe penalties associated to the gravity of the crime definition. These must be read in accordance with the provisions of the Convention of the Council of Europe on combating trafficking in human beings, as complemented by the provisions of the Directive on the prevention and combating of trafficking in human beings and protection of victims:

a) When as a result of trafficking, the victim is put at risk; a higher-grade penalty to the one that would have been attributable to the actions effectively carried out by each individual, will be established. This same principle will apply where the victim is underage; or where the victim is particularly vulnerable owing to an illness, a disability, or its situation. Moreover, where more than one of these facts associated to the crime, is present in the crime definition, then, the conviction to be imposed, must be for the upper half of the penalty under consideration.
b) Where actions are carried out by individuals that hold a public authority position, act as agents of such, or belong to the Civil Service, a higher-grade penalty to the one attributable to their actions, will serve as a basis for the conviction.
c) Where convicted individuals belong to a chartered profession, a registered trade, association of more than two people, industry or business, even if in a temporary or transitory manner, a higher-grade penalty to the one that would have been attributable to the actions effectively carried out by each individual, will be established.
d) When the criminal actions described are headed by a legal entity, a fine, equivalent to three to five times the profit made will be imposed.
e) Finally, enticement, provocation, and conspiracy to commit the crime of trafficking is punishable with a lower-grade penalty in one or two degrees, to the one that would have been attributable to the effective criminal actions of Trafficking.

1.2 Other legislation and policies relevant for Trafficking in Human Beings for labour exploitation

In order to get a grasp of the broader picture associated with the criminal activity of Trafficking, we must examine a number of additional (criminal) actions, which may also be present when examining an action of trafficking for labour exploitation. This needs to be done without leaving aside the field of Criminal Law, and always bearing in mind the protection afforded by the Spanish Criminal Code. In order to do so, we must take into account the legal dimension of trafficking, and the actions associated therewith, bearing in mind that these crimes will be related to the field of Labour Law and Immigration Law.

1.2.1 Criminal labour law

As has already been noted, where the action of trafficking leads to labour exploitation, the crime of trafficking will concur with other crimes, amongst which, there will necessarily be crimes against the rights of workers. This particular field of action has been called Criminal Labour Law.[13] The Spanish Criminal Code has a special section covering 'crimes against the rights of workers', under Title XV of its Book II. This section is specifically aimed at targeting such criminal actions, and as has been noted, actions known as exploitation or exploitation of mankind by other human beings, are contained therein, together with the penalties associated to these criminal, unlawful labour activities.[14] Without doubt, this translates into there being the need to have an unlawful action that outreaches the punitive scope of sanctions, attributable to administrative law and immigration law. The former being a field of the law covered by Royal Legislative Decree 5/2000, of 4th August, which approves the 'Consolidated Law on Offenses and Penalties in the Social Order' (TRLISOS)[15], while matters related to the latter are regulated under Organic Law 4/2000, of 11th January, on the 'Rights and freedoms of foreigners in Spain and their social integration' (LOEx).[16] In this way, we must now contemplate the specific crimes that may concur with the crime of Trafficking for Labour Exploitation.

It should be noted, that in order to facilitate the analysis carried out as part of this work, the penalties discussed herein below, share a protected interest. This interest has been traditionally characterised by its nature, which shares in

---

[13] As Baylos Grau and Terradillos Basoco noted at the time, 'the term "Criminal Labour Law" does not have a univocal meaning, other than by way of the generic reference to the criminal classification of some aspects of the individual or collective employment relationship, and of the (concomitant therewith) relationship with the Social Security' A. Baylos Grau and J. Terradillos Basoco, *Derecho penal del trabajo* (Madrid: Editorial Trotta, 1990) 15. For the purpose of greater precision, it has been interpreted that Criminal Labour Law is composed of those offences that affect the interests held by employees, not because they are persons, but rather because they belong to a social class, and this is where Criminal Labour Law appears as a reinforced system of sanctions to overcome the ineffectiveness of the employment regulations laying down the minimum conditions for the employment relationship, i.e. the rights of the employees, J. Muñoz Sánchez, *El Delito de Imposición de Condiciones Ilegales de Trabajo del Art. 311 del Código Penal en el Marco del Derecho penal del trabajo* (Cizur Menor: Aranzadi 2008) p. 24.

[14] This has been upheld, *inter alia*, by the Judgements of the Supreme Court of 30 June 2000 (rec. 995/2000), 29 March 2004 (rec. 438/2004), 24 February 2005 (rec. 221/2005), and 17 March 2005 (rec. 372/2005).

[15] Official State Gazette of 8 August 2000, No. 189.

[16] Official State Gazette of 12 January 2000, No. 10.

the collective interest of workers. An interest which, however may be of a collective nature, stems from each individual's rights, affording them protection through their employment contract. It is because of this nature of the 'interest' that we can argue that it is a protected interest of a collective nature, with an individual basis. More specifically, the collective projection of this legally protected interest is directly associated with a correct and proper functioning of the labour market, as established through the State's interest in defending a minimum level of rights for workers, arising from their employment contract. Hence, that in the specific crimes that are being discussed, the threshold to be observed is the minimum guarantees, established as an indispensable condition of hiring.[17]

a. *Forcing workers into harmful working conditions, or detrimental Social Security terms (Art. 311 Criminal Code).* This crime is considered the 'central figure' or 'general crime' of all those contained under the heading 'Of the crimes against the rights of workers.' According to the definition of this crime, actions attributable to the crime are punished with imprisonment, which may range from 6 months to 3 years, and a fine. These penalties will be imposed on those individuals whom by means of deception, or through the abuse of a situation of need, impose on workers in their service, working conditions or Social Security terms that lessen, suppress or diminish their Statutory rights. This is also applicable to rights to which they may be entitled, in accordance with an applicable Collective Agreement or their individual contract of employment (as per section 1). Where these actions are carried out thereof by individuals using force or intimidation, a higher-grade penalty to the one that would have been attributable to the actions effectively carried out by each individual, will be established (as per section 2).

   As regards the actions associated with committing the crime of Labour Exploitation a difference must be drawn between the different events that fit into the criminal iter. Thus, it is possible that for a number of reasons (reaction of the victim, intervention of third parties etc.) the crime never materialises, with the actions carried out being no more than an attempt to commit a crime of this nature. However, when the crime has effectively been carried out, in addition to the criminal penalties, a number of additional consequences must be taken into account. One such is the case where there is a party that profits from the criminal action: such party must bear the consequences of the application of Art. 1305 of the Spanish Civil Code (treatment of unfair enrichment). In addition, the workers will be

[17] With regard to this characterisation, see J.M. Lorenzo Salgado, 'La protección de las condiciones laborales o de Seguridad Social en los arts. 311 y 312.2, inciso 2.º, CP' in L. Varela Castro and M. Marchena Gómez (eds), *La protección penal de los trabajadores: tipos, instrucción y enjuiciamiento* (Madrid: Consejo General del Poder Judicial. Centro de Documentación Judicial. Cuadernos de Derecho Judicial 2008, V) pp. 252-253.

afforded the protection provided by the Labour Law, by means of the application of Art. 9.2 of the TRLET. This establishes the duty to preserve the underlying engagement, as a means of guaranteeing the rights and entitlements that stem from the employment relationship.

Indeed, the Spanish legislator has established that where the underlying engagement needs to be called void, this should be done from a prospective approach, since this allows the worker holding a judicial declaration of nullity, to remain entitled to receive the remuneration owed to him for the work carried out, and to bring a claim for any other rights or entitlements he may have accrued in law, as a consequence of the performance of his work.

Moving forward with the present study, we must look, albeit briefly, at the additional aspects required to carry out the main action associated with committing the crime of Labour Exploitation, which essentially is to 'impose' one of the following terms:

- Working conditions: Broadly speaking, these should include among them all those that affect the content of the employment relationship. Here we must include all matters that have an effect on the conclusion, execution and fulfilment of the contract: wages, working hours, vacation etc.
- Social Security Conditions: they all find their origin in the basic legal relationship of protection afforded by the public System of Social Security. Inherent to this System, we find: (1) Legal relations pertaining to the System (membership, registration, cancellation, or modification of data in a manner that is detrimental to workers' rights); (2) Contributions (their absence or failure to perform them); (3) Protection (e.g. absence of direct payment of temporary disability benefits). However broad the public System may be in its protection, the terms and conditions resulting from the action of Private or Supplemental Social Security Benefits, established through collective bargaining, must also be taken into account. The bulk of the latter consisting basically of voluntary contributions, pension schemes and funds.

b. The recruitment in adverse conditions of foreign nationals, who do not hold valid work permits (Art. 312.2, under section two, of the Criminal Code). According to the definition of this crime, actions pursuant to the recruitment of foreign nationals, with a view to having them perform services in accordance with conditions that lessen, suppress or diminish their Statutory rights, or rights to which they may be entitled to, in accordance with an applicable Collective Agreement, or their contract of employment, are punished with imprisonment from 2 to 5 years, and a fine of 6 to 12 months.

As may be observed, this is a specific definition, for it is only applicable to cases where the person that is being subject to the action of Labour Exploitation is a foreign national, who does not hold a valid work permit. The present article aims to cater for the particularly defenceless situation with which foreign nationals who do not hold a valid work permit, are faced. Hence, the requirement contained under Art. 311 of the Criminal Code, that the action is carried out through deceit, or abuse of a position of need, is done away with, in order to provide protection to the precarious situation associated with not holding a residence permit.[18]

There is an important aspect to be distinguished between Art. 312.2 and Art. 311. This is because Art. 312.2 talks about foreign nationals' 'conditions' in general, and not about 'working conditions and Social Security terms'.

So, when faced with determining what those 'conditions' may be, the most signified jurists have agreed upon their being considered to be Labour ones, bearing an identity of terms to those established under Art. 311.1 of the Criminal Code.[19] Accordingly, when contemplating the crime definition established thereto, a crime would be committed where such an employee was to be provided with a remuneration below the national minimum wage, he was forced to endure extended shifts, poor housing conditions, working conditions of extreme hardship, or any such conditions considered to be of a detrimental nature to human dignity, as well as working in conditions that are contrary to health and safety regulations, etc.

The ordinary course of action of this analysis, will now have us focus on the Social Security conditions of foreign nationals who do not hold valid

---

[18] J.M. Lorenzo Salgado, 'La protección de las condiciones laborales o de Seguridad Social en los arts. 311 y 312.2, inciso 2.°, CP' in L. Varela Castro and M. Marchena Gómez (eds), *La protección penal de los trabajadores: tipos, instrucción y enjuiciamiento* (Madrid: Consejo General del Poder Judicial. Centro de Documentación Judicial. Cuadernos de Derecho Judicial 2008, V) pp. 288-289. Also J. Figuera Albert and J. Tomàs Salàs Darrocha, 'Los delitos de tráfico ilegal de mano de obra (Art. 312.1 y 2 CP)' (2009) Revista Técnico Laboral, 14, p. 119. Even the case law has referred to this point, the most notable example of which, *inter alia*, would be the Judgement of the Provincial Court of Cadiz of 13 January 2000, which held that sub-section 2 of Art. 312.2 of the Criminal Code 'does not require, in contrast to Art. 311.1, that the unlawful conditions should be imposed by way of dishonesty or an abuse of a situation of necessity. This is without doubt due to the fact that the legislator considered that the recruitment of a foreign worker without a work permit inherently entails dishonest behaviour and that the employer is taking advantage of a situation of illegality in order to be able to impose such unlawful working conditions. Specifically, the social reality of our country reveals to us the increasing prevalence of these kinds of illegal workers who are obliged to survive by taking any kind of work and under any unlawful conditions, and this situation of necessity is doubtless exploited by certain unscrupulous employers, who can thus obtain substantial profits …'.

[19] J. Figuera Albert and J. Tomàs Salàs Darrocha, 'Los delitos de tráfico ilegal de mano de obra (Art. 312.1 y 2 CP)' (2009) Revista Técnico Laboral, 14, p. 119.

residence or work permits, and are affected by the crime definition established under the second schedule of Art. 312.2 of the Criminal Code. The questions that naturally arises when contemplating what occurs under such circumstances, shifts our attention once again to the employer, and to whether from the particular perspective of this crime definition, he may employ such foreign nationals subject to Social Security terms and conditions that lessen, suppress or diminish their Statutory rights, or rights to which they may be entitled to, in accordance with an applicable Collective Agreement, or contract of employment. And where such may be the case, what may those terms and conditions be.

The response to this question must be consistent with what we have already established as regards actions being void, where a contract of service is entered into by this kind of foreign nationals. Accordingly, this general principle must be further reinforced by the principles of equity and protection against unfair enrichment. Finally, regarding industrial accidents, it must be taken into account the Convention 19 of the ILO, 5th June 1925, on Equality of Treatment (Accident Compensation).

1.2.1.1 Criminal Law on Foreigners

Although, as noted above, in its Criminal Code Spain has clearly differentiated between the legal concepts of trafficking and smuggling human beings, either through the regulation of trafficking in Art. 177 bis, or through the modification of the sections of 318 bis giving deficient coverage to international orders on the persecution of trafficking of people (e.g. through applying said precept exclusively to foreign citizens, and, with respect to what might be understood as trafficking, only in cases for purposes of sexual exploitation) the truth is that a number of aspects of Art. 318 bis are still difficult to interpret, as a result of the extreme abstraction, not to say the occasionally outright obscurantism, of the legal concepts used, and the confusion into which the legal operator is plunged when trying to establish and apply the simultaneous relations between the type of offence defined in Art. 318 bis, and other definitions of offences found in the Criminal Code, including trafficking of human beings in 177 bis.

a. *Problems arising from the legal concepts used.* Starting from the definition made, as a way of understanding what has been said previously, in its first section 318 bis establishes that 'anyone who, directly or indirectly, promotes, favours or facilitates illegal smuggling or clandestine immigration of people from, in transit or with destination in Spain, or with destination in any other country of the European Union, shall be punished with a sentence of 4 to 8 years of prison.' Subsequent sections are then devoted to the regulation of more serious types.

   There is an undoubted conceptual problems deriving from the terms 'illegal smuggling' (*tráfico ilegal*) and 'clandestine immigration' (*inmigración clandestina*). We consider that, as a starting point, a clear distinction between the two terms is needed. Specifically, to this end, the arguments contained in the 1st Point of Law of the Sentence of the Spanish Supreme Court, Courtroom Two, for Criminal Offences, dated 3 April 2007 (rec. 1393/2006) should be followed. According to this argument, the difference in the legal meaning consists in the fact that *tráfico* should be understood not just as the transit of people but, at the same time, as trading or exploitation of any kind, ordinarily with the object of obtaining personal or economic profit, and that this should be 'illegal', i.e. that it contravenes the administrative regulation of frontiers, which brings us to a regulatory element of the definition. Contrariwise, *inmigración clandestina* (clandestine immigration) should be understood as a more or less surreptitious move to avoid the legal controls on immigration, also without administrative authorisation. However, while sharing the idea that *inmigración clandestina* encompasses that which is not visible because it is carried out in places not established for such activity, beyond the reach of the authorities (e.g. boats of the kind known as *pateras* and *cayucos*, other vessels or 'human engines', hidden in motor vehicles), and that which is performed by means of mechanisms designed to distort or hide the illegal aspects of such activity (e.g. falsified documentation) we consider the nuance introduced by the magistrate MARTÍN PALLÍN in his dissenting vote in the Sentence of the Supreme Court, dated 30 May 2005 (rec. 884/2005), must be taken into account. Thereto in contrast to the criterion adopted in that Sentence, and in many other sentences, by which the act of accessing Spanish territory or a Schengen zone with absolutely legal documentation (e.g. as a tourist for a legal period) while not revealing the real motive for the journey (to exercise a particular profession beyond the legal period of the stay) is also *inmigración clandestina*, the judge's dissenting decision declares that there has been no 'illegal' entry. In such cases, two clearly different situations become mixed up, since there is a world of difference in the creation, after a legal entry into Spain, of a situation of irregular residence, whether on the immigrant's own initiative or on the initiative of some third party that forces such a situation (as happens in cases of labour exploitation).

b. Problems arising from simultaneous relations. In cases of trafficking in illegal aliens for the purpose of labour exploitation, it is possible that smuggling offences occur simultaneously as envisaged under 318 bis. However, in practice, it is unlikely that these two offences will ever arise simultaneously. We refer to those situations where trafficking coincides with smuggling and yet the trafficking does not arise for the purpose of labour exploitation. Imagine the typical situation where vessels, dinghies or fishing boats are intercepted out to sea with illegal immigrants bound for the Spanish coast. Unless there is an adequate police investigation, which in the majority of cases requires certain cooperation with the law enforcement authorities of other States, or unless the victims cooperate – which is very hard to persuade them to do – in order to reveal that beyond the smuggling there is also a situation of trafficking going on, the simultaneous occurrence will be impossible. To make things worse, the 'avalanches' of immigrants arriving or attempting to arrive at the Spanish coast in the said situation make us ask ourselves if the procedural rules for the acknowledgement of international protection are being followed to the letter in all cases. These rules entail the right to asylum and subsidiary protection, governed by Act 12/2009 of 30 October, on the right to asylum and subsidiary protection[20], which in the event of being respected would facilitate the simultaneous occurrence of smuggling and trafficking.[21] The Community rules contained at Directive 2008/115/EC, of the European Parliament and of the Council, of 16 December, on common standards and procedures in Member States for returning illegally staying third-country nationals[22], do not help in identifying the true reasons for illegal immigration either. Whilst it is true that those who have sought asylum are exempt from the application of this Directive, the fact is that in addition to the question that ought to be asked about the proper expression, already referred to, of the Right to international protection, it should not be forgotten that this Directive conceals, behind the term 'return'[23], an actual expulsion which frequently means that immigrants are 'abandoned to their fate' in completely unknown, not to mention hostile, States, as a result of the lack of investigation of this fact, with regard to their person, and even in the middle of the desert![24] And this is because according to such Directive,

[20] Official State Gazette of 31 October 2009, No. 263.

[21] However, the truth of the matter shows us that on occasions the actions taken are incorrect, as occurred on 2 February 2007 when the Spanish tug *Luz del Mar* made contact in international waters with the *Marine I*, a vessel with 372 immigrants on board which suffered a breakdown when it was on its way to the Canary Islands and was consequently adrift. The tug towed the vessel to the closest port, the Mauritanian port of Nouadhibou, but the Mauritanian authorities refused permission to dock, arguing that Spain ought to take charge of the passengers, given that Spain had found them. Ten days went by before the passengers, most of whom were from Bangladesh, could disembark at Nouadhibou. Spain negotiated the disembarkation of these people with Mauritania and their subsequent detention in a hangar, in very poor living conditions and without Spanish law being applied in any way, despite the fact that these persons were under the effective control of the Spanish armed forces case extracted from M. Aldalur Balbás, *Clandestinos. Qué hay detrás de la inmigración ilegal?* (Barcelona: Ediciones B 2010) pp. 46-47.

[22] OJEU of 24 December 2008, L 348.

[23] This follows the comments made in J. Cruz Villalón, 'La política comunitaria de inmigración' in R. Escudero Rodríguez (ed), *Inmigración y movilidad de los trabajadores* (Madrid: La Ley 2010) pp. 100-104.

[24] M. Aldalur Balbás, *Clandestinos. ¿Qué hay detrás de la inmigración ilegal?* (Barcelona: Ediciones B 2010) pp. 108, 120, although the events took place within a clear example of 'externalisation', in other words, economic aid is given to those countries bordering the Mediterranean (Morocco, Algeria, Libya...) so that they may act as a border or a stopper. Therefore it is very difficult for someone to ask for international asylum at the border.

'return' is not just sending or transporting illegal non-EU nationals to their country of origin, but also includes the possibility that they will be sent to another non-EU state, using coercion and force, with which Community or bilateral agreements are in place for this purpose between any particular Member State and such third countries.[25] Ultimately, all of these consequences go towards creating the right conditions for ending up once again in the hands of organised networks dedicated to people trafficking, given their vulnerability and desperate need.

1.3. The dimensions of Trafficking in Human Beings for labour exploitation in Spain

1.3.1 Characterisation of Trafficking in Human Beings for labour exploitation at the national level

From the point of view of this report, the characterisation of trafficking for the purpose of labour exploitation should be examined taking into account the fact that the reports drafted by the United Nations and, in particular, the report issued by the Office on Drugs and Crime (UNODC) entitled 'Trafficking in persons: global patterns', published in May 2006, as well as the different authorities consulted (Law Enforcement Authorities, Public Prosecutor, Labour Inspectorate and NGOs), consider Spain to be a country that is both a destination and one of transit on the way to the rest of Europe, given its special geographical situation (the main entry point for migrants from the African continent).

As with all forms of trafficking in human beings, the *modus operandi* of the offence of trafficking for the purpose of labour exploitation is characterised by two distinct stages: the recruitment of the victims and their exploitation.

Variations in the commission of the offence are abundant. Despite the fact that the definition of the offence contained in Art. 177 bis of the Criminal Code provides for the possibility that the victims may be both nationals and foreigners, the truth is that the authorities or organisations consulted, and references to be found in the case law or in learned opinion under examination, concentrate exclusively on cases where the victims are always foreign.

Although not the most common scenario, there could exist a criminal racket composed of members of different nationalities, controlling the entire trafficking process, and which might even carry out the exploitation (e.g. the 'escort and prostitution' sectors and manual workers in the agricultural sector; children dedicated to begging), but in the majority of cases a distinction should be made between the recruitment and labour-exploitation stages. Thus,

[25] This is, for example, the policy that Spain has maintained since 1992 with Morocco, although the enforcement of the agreement has not always been peaceful, see I. González García, 'El acuerdo España-Marruecos de readmisión de inmigrantes y su problemática aplicación: las avalanchas de Ceuta y Melilla' (2006) Anuario Español de Derecho Internacional, 22, pp. 225-284.

recruitment may take different forms, out of which the following should be highlighted:

a) With the cooperation of persons or organisations in the countries of origin, who are responsible for deceiving the victims through false offers of work in Spain (e.g. through press advertisements, e-mails, contacts with family members or relatives). Normally, in these cases, it is the same people who are responsible for organizing the trip to Spain using legal methods (e.g. documents in order, although obviously, as a result of the deception, not those that are required to work, using, for example, stay or transit visas) or illegal methods (e.g. travel in dinghies, fishing boats or other kinds of vessels).
b) The racketeers installed in Spain resort to lawful forms of recruitment in the country of origin, as governed by the Organic Foreign-Nationals Act and its implementing provisions, although with the aim of deceiving the future workers, given that once they are in Spain, in practice, the aim is to exploit their labour. Even though the initial residence and work permits involved in recruitment in the country of origin are limited in terms of time, territory and sector, given that they are in force for one year and apply to a particular territory and sector of activity, the employer may subsequently abuse this situation. Furthermore, a double situation may arise: that the immigrants should return (giving rise to the paradox that they may be recruited in their country of origin once again by the same employer, without the one-year period already spent in Spain lawfully counting for any purpose) or that once this one year term has elapsed they should find themselves in an irregular situation and, as such, endure or continue to endure labour exploitation. Similar consequences may arise for foreign non-EU workers lawfully recruited to occupy fixed-term positions of employment in Spain. What the foreign nationals want is to be able to obtain a 'long-stay residence permit' authorizing them to reside and work in Spain indefinitely. For this purpose, the requirements are 5 years of lawful and unbroken residence in Spain (although certain absences of up to 6 months are allowed, provided that they do not total over one year out of the 5 required), resulting from the sum of the durations of the initial authorisation (1 year) and of the subsequent renewals to be applied for by the foreign national directly (first renewal for 2 years, and second renewal for a further 2 years). In this sense, for 5 long years, Spanish legislation on foreign nationals itself generates a precarious situation, caused by the worries of the foreigner, who rather than report the continual deceptions, is prepared to accept real situations of labour exploitation (e.g. handing over money that has been previously earned, directly or in payment for other items similar to the former truck-system remuneration systems), despite the appearance of legality created by the employer.

c) With regard to Portuguese citizens, in the agricultural, forestry and construction sectors, it is common for racketeers to rely on the Hispano-Portuguese agreement on cross-border recruitment in order to subsequently commit offences and abuses in its enforcement which ultimately end up in the form of labour exploitation. Frequently, the Portuguese companies which recruit their fellow nationals are no more than a legal fiction, and limit themselves to trafficking for the purpose of labour exploitation, given that their aim is that their victims, who will be providing services in Spain, will not be subject to the Spanish collective bargaining agreement, but rather they will be very poorly paid and have to work very long hours.

We also find a large number of Rumanians providing their services in the construction industry for these kinds of recruitment companies, with the exact same infringement consisting in not applying the Spanish sectoral collective bargaining agreements. In all of these cases, Act 45/1999 of 29 November, on the posting of workers within the framework of the trans-national provision of services[26], which amounts to the transposition into Spanish law of Directive 96/71/EC of the European Parliament and of the Council of 16 December 1996 concerning the posting of workers in the framework of the provision of services.[27]

In those cases where victims are transported to Spain from abroad, there are many routes to be taken into account, although their precise definition is a very complex question, as they are constantly changing in order to avoid police investigations. Broadly speaking there are four main routes:

a) *African routes.* A distinction should be made between Moroccan routes and sub-Saharan routes.
   On the Moroccan routes, and taking into account the reinforcement of the terrestrial borders, the alternative formula of access by sea has arisen. Maritime routes have become complicated following the start-up in 2002 and subsequent expansion of the Integrated Border Patrol System (SIVE)[28]

[26] Official State Gazette of 30 November 1999, No. 286.

[27] OJEC of 21 January 1997 [1997] OJ L018.

[28] This is defined as an integrated system of radars, infra-red cameras, and visible-light cameras capable of detecting and identifying very small vessels, and then transmitting the information to the command centre, which subsequently issues the pertinent orders to the interception units. It was first installed at Algeciras (2002), and has then been extended to Cadiz, Malaga, Granada, Almeria, Huelva, Ceuta, Fuerteventura, Lanzarote and Gran Canaria. It is currently being installed in Murcia, Alicante, Valencia, Ibiza Tenerife, La Gomera and El Hierro. Surveys and procurement are underway in Castellon, Majorca, Minorca and Pontevedra. It is at the survey and project stage in the Bay of Biscay and Catalonia (with regard to this organisation, see R. Cortés Márquez, 'La vigilancia de las fronteras marítimas en la Unión Europea' in S. Zaragoza Soto (ed), *Impacto de los riesgos emergentes en la Seguridad Marítima* (Madrid: Ministerio de Defensa. Cuadernos de Estrategia 140 2009) pp. 70-72.

and the greater control by the Moroccan authorities (Royal Navy) over the Mediterranean coast, which provides significant maritime control. For this reason, traffickers use more subtle channels, such as embarking immigrants on fishing vessels with a Moroccan crew, mixing them in with the other crew members, and then disembarking them as soon as they are in Spanish waters a few yards from the beach or in Spanish ports. In many cases Spanish fishermen are also involved.

Organisations or networks dedicated to trafficking in this field have existed, and every so often they continue to operate. Tangiers is the waiting room for this kind of illegal immigration, although a movement towards Algeria has been detected. Specifically, the organisations transfer illegal Moroccans, Mauritanians, Senegalese, Algerians and even Orientals during the hours of darkness to the Spanish coast of Almeria, Barbate, Tarifa, Motril and Malaga. Once in Spain, the immigrants are collected by individuals who make up the lower levels of the networks. This infrastructure is normally made up of a series of compatriots who have their own vehicles, who transfer them the last stage of the way to agricultural enterprises in Almeria, Valencia or Catalonia, or to cities such as Madrid or Barcelona.[29]

Air travel is also used. From Casablanca Airport Moroccans attempt to get through the border controls at Spanish Airports (mainly through Madrid) using false documents.

---

[29] This type of approach has been in evidence recently in the so-called 'Operación Patera 7', in which the Spanish Civil Guard dismantled an organisation dedicated to people-smuggling between Morocco and Spain. The operation allowed 6 people to be arrested, and a further 3 were charged as the alleged perpetrators of the offences of 10 homicides, trafficking in human beings, conspiracy, and offences against the rights of foreign nationals and against public health. The investigations commenced on 29 June 2009, when a dinghy carrying some 40 people sank off the coast of Barbate. It would appear that the captain performed an inappropriate manoeuvre, which caused the vessel to destabilise and capsize, with the result that 10 people died, including the captain. During the investigation, which lasted for approximately one year, the Civil Guard, in coordination with the Moroccan authorities, took numerous steps to clarify the sequence of events. As a result of this investigation, Morocco has been able to dismantle the apparatus for attracting people to undertake the voyage and for charging them for it (€1,500). In Spain, the group that was in charge of collecting the travellers and subsequently transporting them to various locations around Spain, especially to the Murcia region, where they were put up in very precarious conditions in flats until illegal and likewise precarious and badly-paid work was found for them, taking advantage of their irregular situation, was also dismantled. Thus, in Cadiz, 3 members of the group have been identified and arrested: the head of the expedition and 2 voyage controllers. Two more people have been arrested in Murcia, and when searches were carried out at two flats, it was found that three Moroccans were staying there under very precarious conditions, whose presence in Spain was irregular. In Seville, a sixth person who formed a part of this criminal gang has been arrested.

Immigrants from countries located to the south of the Sahara Desert and from the rest of the African continent travel on the sub-Saharan routes. The gradual tightening of French regulations has caused them to select Spain as their destination, despite the fact that the visa requirement has led them to choose illegal methods. The main route used is by sea, although access to Spain is also attempted by air, as has been described in the foregoing section. Senegal, Mauritania and Mali are the main exporters of sub-Saharan emigrants to Spain. The reason for this was the sealing of the Ceuta and Melilla borders at the end of 2006, with the dismantling by force of illegal camps and the monitoring of the Gibraltar straits. All sorts of vessels depart from the coasts of the States referred to, and in particular small fishing boats, with the aim of transporting immigrants to Spain. As a result, also within this area of activity, the number of organisations dedicated to trafficking has grown, although they limit themselves to smuggling, given that once in Spain the victims are received by unscrupulous employers who have the intention of obtaining cheap labour. The fishing boats racket consists in the costs of the trip (between €3,000 and €5,000) and the issuing of a fictitious contract (€5,000) or false visa (€2,000).

b) *The American routes*. South Americans enter Spain for the most part through Barajas Airport (Madrid). They enter as tourists with valid passports and return tickets, but their real intention is to settle in Spain, and so the majority do not return to their countries once their period of stay has expired. Bearing in mind the fact that there is a significant group of South-American nationals residing in Spain, it is also commonplace for the foreigner to say that the reason for the visit is to see relative or friend, who will be more than happy to send a letter of invitation. For this reason, some even use fraudulent letters of invitation. There are also those who attempt to use false travel documents and papers (e.g. false passports). Lastly, some foreigners go on a tour of various European countries, where controls are not so rigorous, and then board a flight to Spain. As it is an internal flight they do not have to pass through Spanish border controls, and provided they are not detained at the transfer halls of the airport, they will have obtained their objective.

   Given the high cost of the trip for the majority of these foreigners, criminal organisations operate in their countries of origin for the most part dedicated to smuggling, although some are involved in trafficking as well, especially in the escort and prostitution sectors. These organisations tend to perform the function of sponsors, i.e. they take care of financing the trip, and then charge their victims a high percentage for this.

c) *The Eastern-European routes*. The recent accession of a number of Eastern-European States to the European Union has helped in the free movement of citizens[30], but it should not be forgotten that for as long as situations of poverty persist with societies and governments lacking the necessary cohesion, their citizens will continue to be the victims of trafficking. For this reason, there are also illegal-immigration networks in these countries, which in the majority of cases choose road transport in order to transfer their victims. Guided by assistants belonging to the organisation, they use vans or minibuses to cross the Western-European countries (Germany, Austria and France), entering Spain mainly through the Pyrenees. On some occasions, vessels originating from European ports have transported illegal immigrants from the said countries hidden in containers. In non-EU States (e.g. Moldova, Ukraine, Russia) the situation is made worse by the use of techniques already referred to with regard to the extortionate charges for travel expenses and necessary documents.

d) *The Asiatic routes*. Illegal immigration originating from Asia is concentrated mainly on the Chinese population coming from the poorest regions of the country such as Zhejiang, Fujian and Guangdong. They tend to go first to Hong Kong, Bangkok and Singapore, where they are supplied with stolen and subsequently doctored documents or completely false documents, with which they subsequently travel to various European airports. Indians, Nepalis and Bengalis also use the same tactics, operating for the most part from Thailand, and the cities of Bangkok, Pattaya and Hat Yai constitute strategic points.

Another modus operandi is that the Chinese will travel by land in order to enter the Schengen area. In this regard, Moscow has been for many years the most important hub for illegal immigration from China, using the same routes used for immigration from Eastern Europe.

But it is noteworthy that in recent years Asians have increased their use of maritime routes in order to enter Spain, following stricter police controls at European airports. In this regard, one of the routes runs as follows: Hong Kong – Cambodia – Kuala Lumpur – Abu Dhabi – Casablanca – Algeciras.

---

[30] With regard to the possibility of imposing restrictions in the European Union on workers from the East, envisaged in the accession documents signed by the 8 States joining the European Union in 2004 (Poland, Lithuania, Czech Republic, Estonia, Latvia, Hungary, Slovenia, and Slovakia), by way of a deferment of the free movement of labour for a minimum of 2 and a maximum of 7 years, Spain opted for the minimum of 2 years. Thus, once the said deferment expired, in May 2006, the régime envisaged in Spain for the citizens of Member States of the European Union has been applied automatically and in full to workers of the nationality of the said States. As in the case of the 8 States referred to, upon the accession of Rumania and Bulgaria to the European Union in 2007, this has put an end to the time when citizens from the said countries would seek to enter Spain as false tourists, with counterfeit documents or in an irregular situation.

> Following the detection and police monitoring of this route, more recently the organisations dedicated to smuggling have opted for more reliable routes. For this purpose they buy up large disused vessels at knock-down prices ('scrap vessels'), and depart from their respective countries towards some region of the Persian Gulf, mainly Dubai, which normally issues visas (basically to Indians and Pakistanis). From here they transfer to the African continent, which they cross by truck or minibus through Kenya, Nigeria and Tanzania until they reach Ivory Coast, Cape Verde and principally, Guinea-Conakry, where they transfer to the scrap vessels once again to travel to the Canary Islands.

After having examined the four main routes, we should now concentrate on the specific forms in which labour exploitation takes place, once the immigrants have arrived in Spain, mentioning the main sectors in which this arises.

The abuses or control mechanisms used in order to keep the victims at their place of work normally consist in widespread deceit or coercion on the basis of the debt owed for the trip and for being found work; confiscation of documents on the pretext that they need to be updated or just simply by force; threats against the victim's person or his/her family members; explicit use of physical violence; abuse of situations of superiority and vulnerability; imposition of sanctions for any reason that give rise to new situations of debt servitude; control of movements.

For their part, the exploitative conditions, in addition to what might have been stated already when discussing the different forms of recruiting victims, tend to consist in the non-application of Spanish employment law in general, but in particular, in the reduction of the wages that they ought to receive; in long grinding working hours exceeding 10 hours a day, including weekends; in having no holidays; in the performance of unhealthy, insanitary and hazardous tasks, in breach of health and safety in the workplace regulations; in discrimination; in physical and psychological abuse.

Finally, the most vulnerable sectors detected are those of escorts and prostitution (clubs, apartments, massage parlours, the street), catering/service industries/commerce, construction, agriculture (mainly picking olives, oranges and grapes), domestic service, sewing shops, road transport and the maritime-fishing sector (mainly the Merchant Navy).

Following the information supplied by the Section on offences relating to trafficking in human beings within the Judicial Police Technical Unit of the Civil Guard, the commonest nationalities of the victims of labour exploitation are Rumanian and Moroccan. Bulgarians, Brazilians, Paraguayans, Bolivians and Portuguese are also exploited.

The Labour Inspectorate Directorate-General points out that in accordance with its activities, immigrants who are victims of trafficking for the purpose of labour exploitation originate from sub-Saharan Africa, Maghreb, Latin-America and Eastern Europe. With regard to sectors, it points out that the overall majority (over 56%) are concentrated in nocturnal clubs and brothels (in accordance with sexual exploitation) and the rest in activities connected with the service industry/catering sector (21%), commerce (10.58 %) and agricultural and livestock farms (7.77%). In the same manner, the Delegated Foreign-National Affairs Public Prosecutor of the Pontevedra (Galicia) Public Prosecutor's Office apportions nationalities within the sectors as follows: Paraguayans, Brazilians and Nigerians work in the escort and prostitution sector; Rumanians and Bulgarians work in construction; and the Chinese work in the sewing shops.

The Delegated Foreign-National Affairs Public Prosecutor of the Malaga Public Prosecutor's Office, who also has powers in the Autonomous City of Melilla, has communicated to us his experience in matters of labour exploitation carried out at clandestine sewing shops, involving being held at the place of work and having documents confiscated. He has dealt with the cases of Chinese citizens aged between 25 and 40. But he acknowledges that the most common cases are those of trafficking for the purpose of sexual exploitation which normally also entail labour exploitation.

The NGO 'Save The Children' states that within the field of prostitution, NGOs detect the presence of children mainly from Rumania, Bulgaria, sub-Saharan African countries (Nigeria, Sierra Leone and Ghana) and South-American countries (Paraguay, Brazil). This fact is confirmed in the 2009 Review of the Integrated Plan to Combat Trafficking in Human Beings for the purposes of Sexual Exploitation, approved in December 2008 by the Spanish Government, when 13 minors were detected as victims of sexual/labour exploitation. Likewise, it refers to the presence on the streets of Spanish cities of children being exploited in the commission of thefts and begging (of Roma origin) coming, for the most part, from camps located in Rumania. Lastly, it warns of some methods used by traffickers in order to persuade and undermine the wishes of their victims. There is evidence that children exploited for sexual/labour purposes are recruited by people known to them, 'boyfriends' and even family members who offer false promises of work (in the domestic sector, catering or as models or actresses).

The territorial delegation of SOS Racismo in Gipuzkoa states that it is aware of situations where, whilst the women are not deceived as to the work to be performed as prostitutes, once they are in Spain, they find that the working conditions are nothing like what was agreed in their countries of origin. The same situation has been reported by the Delegated Foreign-National Affairs Public Prosecutor of the Pontevedra (Galicia) Public Prosecutor's Office.

With regard to domestic service, the work carried out by researchers working for the ACCEM NGO warns us that this economic sector constitutes one of the darkest, both with regard to the supervision of working conditions, and to compliance by employers with employment duties. This is so because the family home as a place of work represents an important barrier to the performance of any inspection and monitoring of the business activity. The peculiarities of the sector, which in Spain has a special employment relationship and a special Social Security classification that is completely outdated, do nothing to improve the problems that exist.

The Spanish trades unions UGT (Basque-Country office), CCOO-CITE (Salamanca, Leon, Navarre and Basque-Country offices) and ELA (more representative in the Basque Country) coincide, in general terms, with what has been stated above. Nevertheless, they draw attention to the use of Portuguese, South-American and Rumanian nationals in the construction industry, with the corresponding collective bargaining agreements not being applied. For its part, the ELA trade union has also denounced the situation of Rumanian and Portuguese haulers, who are obliged to work without hours in order to pay off certain debts acquired in their countries of origin (e.g. joining false cooperatives).

Finally, in the Merchant Navy sector we have it on record that in the Canary Islands Special Register of Ships and Shipowners (known as REBECA, the second Spanish Register located in the Canary Islands, covering vessels and shipping companies, which operates, as all registers do, as a flag of convenience) resort is often made to the legislation applicable in the country of origin of the crew members, in order to reduce labour costs, alleging that they have consented. These crew members are of a multitude of different nationalities, but with the common denominator that they are all under-developed countries and that they find themselves in a clearly subservient situation. This is an infringement of the principle of Spanish law that the law of the country whose flag is carried shall apply, as well as of the international treaties ratified by Spain and European law and the regulations of the Council of Europe.[31]

1.3.2 Facts and Figures on Trafficking in Human Beings for labour exploitation in Spain

Whilst it is difficult enough to obtain facts and figures on trafficking for the purpose of labour exploitation given the lack of reporting of this offence, the mixing-up of the offences and the blurred line that separates sexual exploitation from labour exploitation, the situation in Spain has become much more complicated over the years. This is due to the absence of any codified offence of trafficking, in all its different forms, until the reform of the Criminal Code in 2010, which has proceeded to enact Art. 177 bis of the Criminal Code, in force since 23 December 2010.

Despite the fact that, obviously, following the said reform, it will be possible to collect more accurate facts and figures as from next year, we can refer here to the data for 2008 and 2009, extracted from the reports supplied

[31] Extensively on these matters, see F.J. Arrieta Idiakez, *La Seguridad Social de los trabajadores del mar en el Derecho español* (Vitoria-Gasteiz: Servicio de Publicaciones del Gobierno Vasco 2007) pp. 289-358.

by the Section on offences relating to trafficking in human beings within the Judicial Police Technical Unit of the Civil Guard.

Thus, during 2008 and 2009, a total of 1760 victims were identified (offences against the rights of employees, illegal labour smuggling, clandestine labour immigration). Of these, 74% were men (1302) and the remaining 26% were women (457). As for their ages, the following table shows the distribution of victims by ages, where it may be seen that the highest percentage is to be found in the 26 to 33 age range, which is logical bearing in mind that the victims must have a high production capacity:

Age range	Number of victims (percentage)
Under 18	24 (1.3%)
18 - 25	454 (26%)
26 - 33	539 (31%)
34 - 41	360 (20%)
42 - 49	223 (13%)
50 - 57	97 (5.6%)
58 - 65	21 (1.1%)
Age undetermined as yet	42 (2.4%)

During 2008 a total of 462 offences relating to trafficking in human beings for the purpose of labour exploitation were detected, pursuant to which a total of 433 persons were arrested, 378 men and 55 women. In 2009, a total of 286 offences of this kind were detected, pursuant to which a total of 228 persons were arrested, 200 men and 28 women.

Finally, in addition to the figures offered, and with regard to the offence of trafficking for the purpose of labour exploitation, we should refer at this point to the information collected from the Labour Inspectorate Directorate-General. However, before offering the exact data, it would be convenient to take into account an important qualification that may be extracted from the said data. Thus, it should be stated that aside from the number of offences of trafficking for the purpose of labour exploitation, there are many cases in which, even though they are not ultimately considered to be offences, they nonetheless constitute 'new forms of labour exploitation', which whilst of low intensity, continue to be harmful to people's freedoms and dignity. The problem is that these new forms of labour exploitation go unnoticed when it comes to assessing the extent or seriousness of cases of trafficking, as a phenomenon that needs to be fought.

Moving on to the data collected between 2007 and 2009, it should be borne in mind that inspection activities come close to the phenomenon of trafficking when situations of unregulated economic activities or those involving the 'black economy' are tackled. Therefore, given the difficulty in carrying out such inspection activities, there is a need for cooperation with the law enforcement authorities. These kinds of joint actions follow mutual cooperation protocols, and are the result of prior planning with regard to campaign targets or control of the information received on the illegal smuggling of immigrants, black-economy activities or sexual and/or labour exploitation of persons.

Now then, the data on the results received by way of the Labour Inspectorate information system only reveal infringements of employment, immigration or Social Security law. And this is because criminal activities are controlled and processed by the law enforcement authorities, and are forwarded directly to the Public Prosecutor's Office. Furthermore, it should be borne in mind that under Spanish law, due to the caselaw of the Constitutional Court in application of the principle of *non bis in idem* (the same facts should not be punished twice), where the same set of facts and conduct gives rise to a legal infringement (employment, immigration or Social Security in this case) that could give rise to administrative penalties (fines), whilst at the same time possibly constituting criminal offences (trafficking) codified under criminal law and giving rise to criminal liability, priority is given to hearing the alleged criminal liability, whilst the administrative penalty proceedings are suspended and are then either re-started in the event that the criminal proceedings are dropped or dismissed, or dropped in the event that the criminal proceedings end in a conviction.

Thus, out of the 50 Provincial Inspectorates, 14 have reported that they have detected situations that could be defined as labour exploitation. The 26 remaining Provincial Inspectorates have responded that within their jurisdiction no situations of labour exploitation have been detected, or that it is not possible to provide that information, because when the law enforcement authorities detected any such situations, proceedings were commenced by the law enforcement authorities through the criminal courts, and the Labour Inspectorates were unaware of the data, scope and results of the said situations.

With regard to the most significant conclusions, the Labour Inspectorate Directorate-General has stated as follows:

The results of actions taken can only show the actions under administrative infringements within the jurisdiction of the Labour Inspectorate.

Within the situations verified during the 2007-2009 period, out of the 17,245 inspections carried out, situations of labour exploitation contrary to personal freedoms and dignity were detected at 220 companies, although according to the Inspectorate only in 51 cases was this caused by the existence of trafficking or an organised network of sexual or labour exploitation (31 cases of sexual exploitation and 20 situations of labour exploitation).

Out of the 605 companies where situations of employment infringements were detected, 56.53% correspond to escort bars or clubs; this was followed by 21.33% at other places of employment for other activities in the services sector; 10.58% at places of employment for wholesale or retail trade activities, and 7.77% at agricultural or livestock farms.

With regard to one part of the Provincial Inspectorates in which it has not been possible to detect situations of labour exploitation, it should be pointed out that despite the fact that in some cases clear evidence for criminal activity was detected, these cases were transferred directly to be handled and pursued by the law enforcement authorities, and the Labour Inspectorate is unaware of the final result and assessment of these matters.

The prevalence of situations involving the sexual exploitation of women explains that out of a total of 1823 employees affected, 1457 (79.92%) were women.

Out of the 605 companies at which situations of employment infringements were detected, at 7.10% of them, in 43 cases the existence of labour (non-sexual) exploitation was detected, 20 of them involving trafficking.

The vast majority of the cases of sexual and labour exploitation affect the immigrant foreign (non-EU) population: 87.54% of the affected employees (1596 employees out of a total of 1823 affected by the employment inspections carried out in order to monitor the black economy). Furthermore, 79.92% are women (1457 women in total out of 1823 employees affected).

With regard to infringements of employment rights detected, and which have given rise to infringement proceedings with proposed economic penalties (fines), the overall figures show that 41.20% of the affected employees were not in possession of the required work permit (751 employees, which make up 47.06% of 1596 foreign employees affected by the inspections), and 37.36% of employees (681 employees) were working without being registered for Social Security.

1.4 Summary of the findings

We would highlight the aspects set forth below as being the main conclusions of this first section.

1.4.1 Identified obstacles

One. Despite the fact that Spanish legislation (Art. 177 bis of the Criminal Code) is in line with international and European regulations with regard to trafficking in human beings for the purpose of labour exploitation, it may be seen that the terminology used, as occurs with the reference regulations cited, makes no express reference to 'labour exploitation', but rather prefers a series of concepts ('forced work or services, slavery or practices similar to slavery or servitude or begging) which seem to be rather too detached from the day-to-day reality of the European Union of the 21st century, although it may serve, at an international level, as a minimum standard of protection.[32] As such, in

[32] This is derived from the main international regulations, which are also applicable in Spain, such as ILO Convention number 29 on forced labour, approved on 28 June 1930, and in force since 1 May 1932; the Slavery Convention, signed at Geneva on 25 September 1926, and which came into force on 9 March 1927; and the United Nations Supplementary Convention on the Abolition of Slavery, the Slave Trade, and

order to identify labour exploitation arising as a result of trafficking under the Spanish Criminal Code, it is necessary to resort to the definition of 'offences against the rights of employees' (Arts. 311 and 312). These statements are more than justified bearing in mind the fact that slavery is envisaged in the Spanish Criminal Code only amongst the offences of crimes against humanity (Art. 607 bis 2.10) and is defined as 'the situation of a person over whom another exercises, including *de facto*, all or some of the attributes of the right of ownership, such as buying, selling, lending or exchange.'

Two. Even when arguing in favour of 'labour exploitation' being identified with 'offences against the rights of employees', the regulation of the existing precepts ought to be improved. The improvements need to go in two directions. On the one hand, the precepts that address these offences must overcome their internal logic, in the sense that they should concentrate solely and exclusively on the Employment Law perspective, with regard to the definition of the subjects involved (employer/employee) and the working conditions, in order to also cover the relationship between self-employed persons and clients. And in the Spanish case not just because of the existence of many bogus self-employed persons, as occurs in the rest of Europe (e.g. in the road transport sector), but also because of the recent regulation in the 20/2007 Self-Employment Act of the concept of the economically-dependent self-employed person, which is envisaged as a *tertium genus* that may be added to traditional self-employed persons and salary-earning employees; in other words, with their own regulatory Act consisting in having more rights than the former, but fewer rights than the latter, with regard to their clients. On the other hand, with regard to offences of labour exploitation committed against illegal aliens (Art. 312.2, second sub-paragraph of the Criminal Code) it is regrettable that the offences that may be committed against such persons in matters of Social Security are not more clearly defined.

Three: Often the legislation governing foreign nationals itself generates situations that encourage trafficking for the purpose of labour exploitation, for example by way of the excessively-long time periods required in order to acquire residence and an indefinite permit. The latest interpretations by the Court of Justice of the European Union with regard to the posting of workers within the transnational provision of services, limiting the possibility to apply the regulations applicable in the host country, have likewise done nothing to assist the prevention of trafficking, given that by protecting free competition between undertakings, it increases the risk of social dumping amongst workers of different nationalities. Furthermore, free competition would only be protected in order to allow undertakings belonging to States with lower employment conditions to provide their services in Member States that have higher social costs, and never the other way around.

Institutions and Practices similar to Slavery, signed in Geneva on 7 September 1956, and which came into force on 30 April 1957.

1.4.2 Good practices

One. In 2010 Spain has amended its regulations with regard to trafficking in human beings for the purpose of labour exploitation in order to comply with international and Union requirements. In this manner, it has proceeded to distinguish the concepts of trafficking and smuggling, although in practice, the real distinction ought to arise following proper investigation of the facts and the safeguarding of the right to adequate protection for victims, especially in the case of illegal immigrants found at sea.

Two: The so-called 'Criminal Labour Law', which deals with defining offences against the rights of employees, is an essential complement for the prosecution of labour exploitation where the trafficking takes place for this purpose. In this regard, Spanish legislation is more than compliant with Directive 2009/52/EC, of the European Parliament and of the Council of 18 June 2009 providing for minimum standards on sanctions and measures against employers of illegally staying third-country nationals.[33]

Three: With the aim of preventing trafficking for the purpose of labour exploitation from arising when workers are posted within the framework of transnational provision of services, it is fundamental, despite the latest interpretations by the Court of Justice of the European Communities, to uphold the principle of *lex loci* as envisaged under Act 45/1999 of 29 November. Faced with the breach of this principle, mostly within the construction industry, in the relationship between contractors and sub-contractors, good practice has been detected, *lege ferenda*, at the proposal of the ELA trades union in the Basque Country, consisting in introducing penalty clauses both in the tenders for public works, and principally, into collective bargaining agreements. The said penalty clause would consist in paying compensation by way of an indemnity equivalent to two times the annual salary laid down in the collective bargaining agreement, whenever it is shown by way of an infringement report by the Labour Inspectorate or a court judgement that the collective bargaining agreement has not been applied with regard to wages or working hours.

---

[33] OJEU of 30 June 2009 [2009] OJ L168.

Part II
Cooperation in the investigation and prosecution of cases of Trafficking in Human Beings for labour exploitation

2.1 Actors involved in investigating and prosecuting Trafficking in Human Beings for labour exploitation

The parties involved in the investigation and prosecution of trafficking in human beings all have different profiles, given their different functions, but ought to be coordinated by way of cooperation in the manner set forth in the following sub-section. We will now specify who the said parties are, and provide a brief description of the role they perform in the fight against trafficking for the purpose of labour exploitation.

(a) The Spanish Government and the Regional Governments. The Spanish Government is responsible for institutional coordination with regard to trafficking in human beings, for which purpose an inter-ministerial group has been set up composed of the following Departments: Ministry of Foreign Affairs and Cooperation; Ministry of Justice; Ministry of the Interior; Ministry of Education, Social Policy and Sport; Ministry of Health and Consumer Affairs; Ministry of Work and Immigration and the Ministry of Equality. Likewise, it is responsible for setting up the necessary public services in order to ensure the effectiveness of the investigations and prosecutions. Furthermore, given that Spain is a devolved State, composed of 17 Autonomous Regions, the Governments of these Regions, within the powers devolved to them, may also pursue their own policies with regard to trafficking in human beings for the purpose of labour exploitation. Ultimately, coordination between the various central and regional Authorities is essential, all the more so when one recalls that matters concerning immigration, foreign nationals and the right to asylum fall within the exclusive purview of the State. Furthermore, it should be recalled that following the amendments made to the Organic Foreign-Nationals Act pursuant to Organic Law 2/2009 of 11 December[34], all Public Authorities must base the exercise of their powers in relation to immigration on respect for, amongst other principles, the prosecution of trafficking in human beings (Art. 2 bis h).

(b) *The law enforcement authorities.* [35] At a policing level, in Spain, the criminal investigation and prosecution of offences concerning trafficking in human beings is carried out by the law enforcement authorities of the State [Civil Guard and National Police Force (Foreign-National Brigade)], as well as by

---

[34] Official State Gazette of 12 December 2009, No. 299.

[35] The information supplied by the Section on offences against trafficking in human beings of the Judicial Police Technical Unit of the Civil Guard has been taken into account.

the regional police forces within their jurisdiction. With regard to the Integrated Border Patrol System (SIVE), it should be pointed out that the relevant powers are held by the Civil Guard.

From the point of view of training in matters concerning trafficking in human beings, the Civil Guard, through its Section on offences relating to trafficking in human beings within the Judicial Police Technical Unit, has confirmed to us that work is being done on this subject. In this regard, it is stated that the training carried out by the Civil Guard in its courses for specialists in the investigation of offences against the person (which also includes specialists in the women and children sector), as well as in the various specialist courses and specific workshops, tends to cover all aspects of the investigation of trafficking in human beings in general, irrespective of the purpose of the exploitation. In fact, the commitment of the Civil Guard to the fight against trafficking in human beings is clear when one sees that it forms a part of their strategic objectives.

(c) The Public Prosecutor.[36] The task of the Public Prosecutor is to draw up criminal charges to be filed against activities involving trafficking in human beings through the courts. For this purpose, the Public Prosecutor is able to rely on a special Public Prosecutor dedicated exclusively to matters involving foreign nationals. Its basic structure consists in a Coordinating Trial Public Prosecutor specializing in Foreign-National affairs, two Public Prosecutors under the direction of the Trial Public Prosecutor, and as many Delegated Public Prosecutors specializing in Foreign-National affairs as there are provinces in Spain (50).

The Reform of the Organic Public Prosecutors's Office Act undertaken by way of Law 24/2007 of 9 October[37] was of particular relevance to the prosecution of the offence of trafficking, given that it entailed not only the necessary assignment of the Delegated Public Prosecutors specializing in Foreign-National affairs to the new territorial bodies that had been created (50 Provincial Public Prosecutors), but also the appointment of those vacancies that had arisen. Thus, during 2007 and pursuant to Instruction 5/2007 of the Attorney-General of 18 July, on coordinating trial public prosecutors specializing in health and safety in the workplace, road safety and foreign-national affairs, and on the corresponding sections of the territorial Public Prosecutors' Office, foreign-national services started to be set up with all the Provincial Public Prosecutors' Offices across Spain. As a result, in February 2008, the start-up stage of the net Criminal Codework of territorial foreign-national Sections or Units of the Spanish Public Prosecutors Office was finally concluded, with the specific objectives as dictated in Instruction 5/2007,

[36] The Reports of the State Prosecutor's Office corresponding to years 2008, 2009, and 2010 have been consulted.

[37] Official State Gazette of 10 October 2007, No. 243.

which included 'regarding offences committed against foreign nationals under Art. 318 bis of the Criminal Code', which as has been stated in the first part of the report, did not adequately distinguish the concepts of smuggling and trafficking. However, following the reforms implemented in 2009 and 2010 respectively, with regard to the Organic Foreign-Nationals Act and the Criminal Code, aimed at providing adequate regulation of trafficking in human beings, in accordance with international regulations and in particular, the Warsaw Convention of the Council of Europe on Action against Trafficking in Human Beings, those aspects relating to trafficking have also become a part of the remit of Public Prosecutors specializing in foreign-national affairs.

Likewise, the Provincial Public Prosecutors were strengthened during 2009, with the assignment of a further 51 public prosecutors as assistants, associates, back-ups, or auxiliaries to the Delegated Public Prosecutor specializing in Foreign-National affairs.

The only negative point recorded in the Attorney-General's Office Report for the years 2008, 2009 and 2010 that needs to be mentioned is the serious inadequacy of the various computer systems in operation in the Provincial Public Prosecutors' Offices. In this regard, all of the said Reports comment on the need to roll out a complete unified computer system for all of the Provincial Public Prosecutors' Offices, irrespective of the Autonomous Region in which they are located, that is up to the task of storing and processing the specific data of the Foreign-National Section.

But it is recorded that the Foreign-National Public Prosecutors' Office database is not just composed of information generated by the computer systems, but also of the records of the Trial Public Prosecutor specializing in foreign-national affairs who, with the help of his/her assistants, receives, examines, analyses and files the documents that the Deputy Public Prosecutors of each Provincial Public Prosecutors' Office supply throughout the year in the matters under examination. Furthermore, the essential statistical data diligently supplied by the General Foreign-Nationals and Borders Commissariat and by the Organized Crime Intelligence Centre is taken into consideration.

(d) Labour Inspectorate. Pursuant to Law 42/1997 of 14 November, whereby the Labour Inspectorate is governed[38], the 'Labour Inspectorate is a public service which is responsible for monitoring compliance with rules of a social nature and for ensuring that they are enforced, as well as for advising and, where appropriate, providing arbitration, mediation and conciliation in the said matters. It shall exercise the said responsibilities in accordance with the principles of the social and democratic Rule of Law enshrined in the Spanish Constitution and Conventions numbers 81 and 129 of the ILO' (Art. 1.2).

The investigation and prosecution of offences against the rights of employees, which offences, as it has been argued in this report, are the

[38] Official State Gazette of 15 November 1997, No. 274.

ultimate manifestation of the labour exploitation that flows from trafficking in human beings, falls under Art. 3 of Law 42/1997, where it is provided that 'the inspection powers cover the tasks of monitoring and ensuring compliance with the statutory, regulatory and normative provisions of the collective bargaining agreements in the following areas; the regulation of employment and trades-union relations; health and safety at work, as well as the technical-legal rules affecting working conditions in the said area; the Social Security System; employment and migrations.'

With regard to the powers held by Labour Inspectors, these are defined at Art. 5 of Law 42/1997, where it is provided that they have public-authority status and they are authorised as follows:

- To freely enter any centre, establishment or place of employment, at any time and without prior notice and to remain there.
- To be accompanied during their visit by such employees or the representatives thereof and by such experts and technicians (whether of the company or officially qualified for this purpose) as they may think fit for the proper performance of the inspection activity.
- To carry out any investigation, examination or test procedure that they may think fit in order to verify that the statutory provisions are being correctly observed, such as: to request information from the employer or from the company staff, or to require the identification of the persons present at the place of employment that is being inspected.
- To inspect the documents and books of the company, its records, computer software and files held in electronic format, at the place of employment or at the premises being inspected.
- To obtain or procure samples of the substances and materials in use or being handled at the establishment, to take measurements, obtain photographs, videos and recorded images, to draw diagrams and plans.

Lastly, with regard to training, the Labour Inspectorate Directorate-General states that there are training and methodology activities regarding trafficking within the Labour Inspectorate System, which have the aim of improving efficiency.

(e) NGOs.[39] Despite the fact that there are many NGOs working in the area of foreign nationals and therefore aware, indirectly, of situations of trafficking for the purpose of labour exploitation, *Red Española Contra la Trata de Personas* ought to be highlighted, as it is made up of 23 NGOs that work in the said area from a global perspective in accordance with the national and international legal instruments applicable in Spain, considering all persons who are trafficked for the purpose of sexual or labour exploitation, forced marriages,

[39] Information received from a number of NGOs has been taken into account, such as APRAMP, Sos Racismo (Gipuzkoa office), Save The Children, and Compañía de Jesús Foundations in Bilbao and Madrid, which have Social Centres for immigrants.

begging, slave labour, etc. to be the victims of trafficking. As will be seen in the following sub-section, *Red Española Contra la Trata* acts in conjunction with various public institutions. Further to what is to be set forth in the said sub-section, NGOs, in addition to providing the necessary help and protection to victims (accommodation, psychological assistance...), also file complaints and report to the Labour Inspectorate. Likewise, it may be seen that NGOs that do not belong to the *Red* refer cases where they suspect that some form of trafficking may be involved to NGOs that are members.

(f) Trade Unions.[40] In so far as trade unions have the aim of defending and promoting workers' economic and social interests, their relationship with situations of trafficking in human beings for the purpose of labour exploitation arises from time to time. Therefore, their role normally consists in, basically, reporting cases they become aware of and seeking to legalise the situation of the illegal immigrants. Through campaigns against labour exploitation, questions of human trafficking are dealt with indirectly, thereby increasing social awareness of this problem. However, when it comes to providing help and protection to the victims, they normally refer any cases to the corresponding NGOs.

2.2 Cooperation between actors within the country

2.2.1 Legal framework for cooperation

The legal framework for cooperation within the State between the various organisations referred to above is made up of instruments of many different kinds. In some cases, there are regulations in place, as in the case of the Labour Inspectorate. But in the majority of cases, cooperation takes place through a series of accords, instructions and similar instruments.

In addition to these instruments, we should make special mention of two newly-created instruments which amount to a significant step forward in the fight against trafficking in Spain and which are essential when tackling cooperation between different organisations or actors. We refer to the Integrated Plan to Combat Trafficking in Human Beings for the purposes of Sexual Exploitation, approved on 12 December 2008 by the Spanish Cabinet and which has been in force since January 2009, with a three-year term, and which amounts to the first integrated instrument in Spain with regard to trafficking. A second and more important framework is the Galicia Protocol on institutional action to approve measures to prevent, investigate and treat women who are the victims of trafficking for the purpose of sexual exploitation, approved on 18 January 2010 by the Senior Public Prosecutor of

---

[40] Information supplied by the following trades unions has been taken into account: UGT (Basque Country office), CCOO-CITE (Salamanca, Leon, Navarre, and Basque Country office), and ELA (more representative in the Basque Country).

the Autonomous Region of Galicia and the Galicia Regional Government, which according to the Report of the Attorney-General's Office for 2010, 'has been able to correctly implement' the Integrated Plan referred to within the Autonomous Region of Galicia. Furthermore, the said Report goes on to express the Public Prosecutor's desire that the Galicia Protocol should become a 'model agreement that should become standard in the rest of Spain.'

Evidently, both the Integrated Plan and the Galicia Protocol are focussed on sexual exploitation, but for as long as no similar instruments are developed in order to specifically tackle trafficking for the purpose of labour exploitation, it is our understanding that many of its aspects ought to be taken very much into account and applied on an analogous basis, without overlooking the fact that, normally, sexual exploitation goes hand in hand with labour exploitation, as may be deduced, furthermore, from the Galicia Protocol itself. In this manner, recent regulation in Spain of the offence of trafficking and the various measures implemented in order to protect the victims of such trafficking would be complemented, principally through the Organic Foreign-Nationals Act and Law 12/2009 of 30 October, governing the right to asylum and subsidiary protection.

Thus, focussing on the Integrated Plan, with regard to coordination and cooperation measures, 5 objectives are implemented, which we now examine:

(a) *Objective 1: To strengthen police operational cooperation.* The aim is for the different national, regional and local police forces to work together: harmonizing procedures, sharing methodologies, experiences and good practice, and establishing fluid communication mechanisms when undertaking police investigations and operations. This is to be achieved by way of the following steps: the implementation of a code of procedure and police coordination between different police authorities; and the performance of police operations through the Organized Crime Intelligence Centre, with the involvement of the national, regional and local law enforcement authorities in the dismantling of organised gangs that traffic in human beings, including mechanisms to provide immediate assistance to the victims through the NGOs.

(b) *Objective 2: To have a specific statistical tool with regard to trafficking in human beings, harmonised at a European level.*

(c) *Objective 3: To strengthen cooperation at an international level.* The intention is to increase the mechanisms that allow the best possible information to be obtained and the most complete collaboration between the countries of origin, transit and destination. Emphasis is placed on the fact that the availability of information in the countries of origin to potential victims and their peers regarding the basic legal aspects affecting emigration and employment in Spain, as well as making them aware of the dangers and the commonest reasons with regard to this phenomenon, can make an effective contribution to the tasks of prevention and discouragement of trafficking in those areas. Furthermore, the importance of the NGOs operating in Spain providing assistance to the victims should be borne in mind, given that on many occasions they are also present in the places of origin, or they have accords with other NGOs that are participating in the provision of international cooperation in those areas. In order to be able to comply with the said objective, the following actions are proposed: the performance of information and awareness campaigns in the countries of origin in order to avoid the recruitment of victims; and the identification and inclusion of the priority countries from which the victims of trafficking originate in the corresponding Country Strategy Papers (CSP), in order to encourage the creation of agreements and projects by the parties to Spanish cooperation.

(d) *Objective 4: To enable more effective cooperation with regard to investigations and in bringing cases of trafficking to court.* The following actions are proposed for this purpose: the exchange of police information with the countries of origin, transit and destination; coordination of police units with INTERPOL and EUROPOL; increasing the coordination of the Organized Crime Intelligence Centre with similar centres and services in other countries; encouragement of judicial coordination at a European level, through EUROJUST and at a Latin-American level, through Iber-Red.

(e) *Objective 5: To draw up and strengthen coordination mechanisms and effective links with NGOs and institutions committed to the fight against trafficking and to providing assistance to victims.* The following actions are proposed for this purpose: the creation of a Forum to combat Trafficking, composed of the relevant Public Authorities, NGOs and other institutions involved.

For its part, 3 lines of activity concerning institutional cooperation may be extracted from the Galicia Protocol which are relevant to the investigation and prosecution of trafficking for the purpose of labour exploitation, to wit: the filing of regular reports, at least once a year, by the law enforcement authorities to the Foreign-National Section of the Provincial Public Prosecutor's Office; the filing of a report once a year by the Labour Inspectorate to the Foreign-National Section of the Provincial Public Prosecutor's Office regarding the inspection minutes drafted at the corresponding places of employment; the filing of as many reports as may be considered pertinent by NGOs to the Foreign-National Section of the Provincial Public Prosecutor's Office, regarding persons at risk of trafficking.

2.2.2 Application of the legal framework in practice

By taking into consideration the instruments mentioned above as a whole, we can describe the manner in which cooperation between the various parties involved in the investigation and prosecution of trafficking in human beings for the purpose of labour exploitation is being undertaken in Spain.

As a direct result of the Integrated Plan, as may be seen from the Review for the first year offered by the Spanish Government[41], with regard to institutional coordination, we may highlight the start-up of two of the activities envisaged. On the one hand, the Inter-ministerial Coordination Group for Combating Trafficking in Human Beings has been set up, composed of members from the Ministries of Foreign Affairs and Cooperation, Justice, Interior, Health and Social Policy, Work and Immigration, Presidency, Education, Industry, Tourism and Trade, Defence, and the Ministry of Equality, which is coordinating the plan. On the other hand, the Social Forum on Trafficking has been set up, on which the main organisations within the sector are represented, Central Government, the Autonomous Regions and Local Authorities, through the Spanish Federation of Borough Councils, with the aim of ensuring coordination with the tasks carried out by the NGOs. Amongst the technical-operational measures implemented, we may highlight the start-up of the Data-Management System regarding Trafficking in Human Beings (BDTRATA), created by the Organized Crime Intelligence Centre, in order to provide more accurate information on this kind of criminal activity. Lastly, and with regard to training, the Ministry of Equality has given a course for all Intervention Areas on trafficking and its consequences. The Ministry of the Interior has provided training for the Specialist and Operational Units of the Civil Guard and the Police. The Ministry of Foreign Affairs and Cooperation has organised training courses for consular staff. The Ministry of Defence has done the same for its staff posted in areas of conflict. And the Ministry of Justice has organised courses for professionals in the Judiciary.

We now focus more specifically on each one of the parties involved and the examination that has been carried out allows us to provide the description set forth below.

a) The Section on offences relating to trafficking in human beings of the Judicial Police Technical Unit of the Civil Guard is in charge of the coordination of the operations of all units that the Civil Guard has based in Spain (Organic Judicial-Police Units, of which there is normally one per province), of national police coordination and coordination with international bodies (INTERPOL, EUROPOL, SIRENE, etc.) and of training and updating the skills of members of the Organic Judicial-Police Units. Furthermore, a new Service Directive has recently been approved, number 40/2009, which regulates and coordinates the tasks of the various Civil Guard Units in the prevention, investigation and prosecution of this kind of criminal activity.

[41] <http://www.la-moncloa.es>.

Activities consisting in carrying out the initial investigation and verifying the alleged criminal offences are performed by the various police forces, collecting evidence that is later compiled in the Committal Report. The Judicial bodies (judges and State prosecutors) which are leading the investigation are responsible for committing the case for trial and for classifying the criminal offences.
In respect of the Civil Guard, the investigation of offences regarding trafficking is de-centralised at the level of the different Command Centres (at a provincial level) and all actions are coordinated through a Central Unit, the Judicial Police Technical Unit. There is also a Central Operational Unit for complex investigations which require the latest technology. There may, according to the province, be specific resources to attend to the victims of trafficking, most of which are exclusively for women.

The investigation methods may be very varied. Systematic observation and the search for evidence is normally carried out through administrative inspections at places of employment. Telecommunications tapping and in particular telephone tapping, may also be used. However, it should be borne in mind that this measure may only be authorised with regard to a specific and serious offence. Therefore, the Investigating Judge may only authorise this method where, in accordance with Art. 579.3 of the Criminal Procedure Act, there is evidence of such specific criminal liability and that the suspect uses the communications being tapped for criminal purposes. Therefore, when this method of investigation is employed as a judicial response to a police request, as occurs in the majority of cases, the judge before whom the request is made must verify, *inter alia*, that the request contains evidence from which it may be inferred: a) that the serious offence in question is real (in this case, trafficking for the purpose of labour exploitation); b) that the person being investigated – the telephone subscriber whose line is going to be tapped – is a party to the said offence. These points, with the necessary details, must be stated in the judicial ruling. However, both the Supreme Court and the Constitutional Court have allowed the requirement that the said evidence be contained in the judicial ruling to be met by way of referring back to the reasons given in the originating police communication.[42] Likewise, information from witnesses or evidence provided by associations providing victim support, such as NGOs, is also important. From the victims□ point of view, the main problem is that, quite often, they are not considered to be victims and

[42] Judgement of the Supreme Court, Second Criminal Chamber, of 13 May 2008 (rec. 11134/2006). With regard to these points, see also the judgements of the same chamber of 12 November 2007 (rec. 934/2007), 22 May 2001 (rec. 816/2001), and judgement 167/2002 of 18 September, of the Constitutional Court. In the same regard, see the case law of the European Court of Human Rights, compiled in its ruling of 25 September 2006.

as such, they do not report the offences. Even where they are considered to be victims, they often fail to report through fear, mistrust or because, despite everything, they think they have 'a lot to lose' given their opinion that they are worse off in their countries of origin. In those cases where the victims do take the step of reporting an offence, it was commonly the case that they returned to their countries of origin without ratifying their evidence on the day of the hearing. However, this problem is now being tackled by using the form of evidence given in advance. There is no doubt that evidence given by victims is very important, even though the investigation has commenced following a complaint filed by a third party or as a result of a different kind of investigation. But at the same time, it is essential to keep a documentary record of all evidence in proof that an offence of trafficking has really taken place, for example by collecting air tickets, documents in the possession of the organisation, false contracts, etc.

With regard to exchange of information, the National Police Force and the Civil Guard have at their disposal a system of mutual access to the information contained in the databases of previous convictions. The regional police forces have recently joined the said system. In those specific aspects in which organised gangs are involved, coordination is carried out by the Organized Crime Intelligence Centre.

Lastly, consideration should be given to the proposal made by the Deputy Foreign-National Affairs Public Prosecutor of Pontevedra (Galicia), to the effect that the various law enforcement authorities, in their preventive inspections, ought to conduct a series of tests aimed at identifying the existence of evidence of victims of trafficking in human beings, as well as a questionnaire relating to their employment conditions and their journey to Spain, in addition to informing them of their rights (period of reflection, asylum, residence and work permits etc.). In this manner, copies of the minutes setting out the data obtained would be forwarded to the pertinent Foreign-National Public Prosecutors' Office, which could then instigate a criminal investigation if evidence of trafficking were found.

b) Cooperation with various authorities and organisations is essential for the Public Prosecutor, as may be seen from the Report of the Attorney-General's Office for 2008. Specifically, cooperation, as described below, represents the solution to a series of different shortcomings, such as the problem of international judicial coordination, which is essential in situations where there is organised cross-border crime and, above all, the difficulty in proving the existence of trafficking offences.

   In the 2008 Report, the Public Prosecutor linked this aforementioned idea to the more widespread reporting with regard to the complex way in which evidence is obtained from victims, due to a variety of factors, which as shall be seen in part four, regarding the protection of victims, have been taken into account to a certain extent in the reforms implemented in 2009. Thus, with regard to the said factors, reference was made to the fact that, in the majority of cases, the said evidence must necessarily be given in advance, which means that it is impossible to do this using the normal services when these are provided by a Court that is on call 24 hours a day and the number of depositions to be recorded is very large; on account of the rapid deportation by the government of the foreign witness, and the restrictions on the application of the provisions of the Organic Foreign-Nationals Act aimed at avoiding the said deportation; on account of the unwillingness of many victims to provide evidence, who fear their traffickers more than any other option; on account of the shortcomings and flaws of a system for the protection of witnesses that is manifestly inadequate, governed by Organic Law 19/1994, of 23 December, on the protection of witnesses and expert witnesses in criminal cases[43]; on account of the reluctance, and in some cases, refusal, of some Courts with regard to evidence being taken by way of rogatory letters from the Court hearing the case where the victims of gangs are residing in a different judicial district, and on account of there being no essential qualified personnel available to take evidence (interpreters).

As has been stated, in order to remedy these problems, in 2008 the Foreign-National Public Prosecutors' Office based its approach on cooperation.

Thus, first of all, a permanent and periodical communication system was set up (meeting at least once a month in ordinary session and as often as required in exceptional situations) with the General Foreign-National Commissariat (Criminal-Gang and Counterfeit Documents Commissaries), through which all significant investigations into trafficking in human beings for the purposes of sexual and labour exploitation are examined, with the aim of establishing the corresponding cooperation measures between the police force and the Public Prosecutor within their respective powers. It as well included provisions on items being forwarded to the various Provincial Public Prosecutors, where a start was also made on encouraging the involvement of the Delegate Public Prosecutors with their respective Units to combat Immigration Gangs and Counterfeit Documents.

Secondly, a similar channel of communication, in terms of nature and frequency, was established with *Red Española de Lucha contra la Trata de Seres Humanos*, which brings together 23 NGOs, both national and international. Meetings with the *Red* are carried out with two precisely-defined objectives: communication by the said organisation of facts of which it is aware that could constitute a trafficking offence, and cooperation with the said organisation where necessary in order to implement measures to

[43] Official State Gazette of 24 December 1994, No. 307.

protect the victims and witnesses of such offences, as well as to facilitate the collection of evidence and the presence of the witnesses at the trial.

c) Cooperation between the Labour Inspectorate and other parties or organisations is envisaged under Law 42/1997 in two respects, although the said cooperation always revolves around the exchange of information.

In this manner, on the one hand, there is the requirement on certain parties to provide their assistance and cooperation to the Labour Inspectorate (Art. 9). In this regard, the Public Authorities and all persons exercising public authority are under a duty to provide assistance to the Inspectorate upon request as necessary for the exercise of the inspection activity, and to provide the said body with any information they may have. Specifically, the Tax Authorities shall assign their data and background information to the Inspectorate, and those bodies managing and cooperating with the national services of the Social Security are also required to provide their assistance and to supply, upon request, such information, background facts and data as they may have that are relevant to the performance of the inspection, even where these are of a personal nature subject to automated handling without the affected party being required to give his/her consent. For this reason, Tax and Work and Social Security Inspections must establish mutual correspondence and coordination programmes for the performance of their aims. Likewise, the pertinent law enforcement authorities are under a duty to provide their assistance and cooperation to the Inspectorate in the performance of its functions, through the officers designated for this purpose by the corresponding authority. Finally, the Courts shall provide the Inspectorate, either of their own motion or upon request, with the essential information required for the inspection task and which they collect from the cases they hear, with the exception of those cases where the proceedings are being conducted in secret.

Furthermore, and contrary to what occurs in the above situations, the Labour Inspectorate is also required to cooperate with all other parties (Art. 10).

In effect, the Inspectorate is required to provide cooperation and support to the Public Authorities and, in particular, to the employment authorities, management bodies and national services of the Social Security, to which it supplies the information they request as necessary for their functions, provided that any confidentiality requirements are met, where appropriate. Likewise, the Inspectorate must always seek to ensure the cooperation of business organisations and trade unions; in this regard, the Inspectorate supplies information on points of general interest arising in its inspection tasks, reports on its activities, and any other background facts, to business organisations and trade unions. Lastly, where the Inspectorate should detect that a possible public offence has been committed, it sends the Public Prosecutor a detailed report on the events that it has become aware of and the persons who may be involved.

But as might have been concluded in part one, by referring to the facts and figures for trafficking for the purpose of labour exploitation, the main cooperation provided by the Labour Inspectorate occurs with the law enforcement authorities, and only obliquely with the Public Prosecutor.

And the fact is that, as has been stated by the Work and Social Security Inspectorate Directorate-General, in order to prosecute the new forms of labour exploitation, which impose conditions that infringe people's liberty and dignity, it is necessary to coordinate the activities of the different systems of control with powers in the relevant areas: labour (the Labour Inspectorate), public safety (law enforcement authorities) and the prosecution of the offences and imposition of the corresponding criminal liability (Public Prosecutor).

Precisely as a result of the need to coordinate these different powers, a Cooperation Protocol was signed in April 2008 between the Ministries of the Interior, Justice, and Work and Immigration, the latter being represented by the Labour Inspectorate. Amongst the aims of the said Protocol is the control and monitoring of the organised criminal gangs participating in labour exploitation. For this purpose and as part of the General Council on Citizen Security, which is a participation and consultation body, the Control and Monitoring of Criminal Labour-Exploitation situations Working Group has been set up. The said Working Group is composed of the three Ministerial Departments referred to, along with those Social Agents with majority representation in the State, as well as other public or private bodies or organisations within civil society. The aims of this group are fundamentally those of prevention and observation with regard to awareness of these situations, coordination of the different areas of competence for the control and prosecution of these offences. Without doubt, what is most relevant for our purposes is the objective this group has of drawing up a proposal for a draft National Plan to combat trafficking in human beings for the purpose of labour exploitation, which is to be submitted before the office of the Deputy Prime Minister. However, for as long as no such steps are taken, the current form of procedure shall remain in operation, based on cooperation instructions, for the most part between the Labour Inspectorate and the law enforcement authorities. Thus, in accordance with the current procedure, different stages may be distinguished:

- Where in the course of activities being carried out exclusively by the Labour Inspectorate, the possible existence of a possible offence with regard to labour exploitation is discovered, the case is referred to the Public Prosecutor for it to be pursued. However, this situation arises only infrequently.

- In the majority of cases where the possible existence of an offence involving trafficking for the purpose of labour exploitation arises, this occurs during joint operations between the Labour Inspectorate and the law enforcement authorities (in this regard, see the comments made in part one, on the facts and figures on trafficking for the purpose of labour exploitation). The following procedure is then followed:
  i. Either of the two parties may ask the other for joint action to be taken, which is decided upon by mutual agreement.
  ii. A preliminary investigation stage and exchange of information stage is carried out. The information may originate from the activities of either party and also from complaints filed by third parties.
  iii. The inspection and police activities are carried out jointly, in accordance with the procedures agreed following the prior exchange of information.
  iv. Where the same facts and persons amounting to alleged offences also give rise to administrative infringements within the jurisdiction of the Labour Inspectorate, pursuant to the principle of *non bis in idem*, the law enforcement authorities shall refer the case to the Public Prosecutor and the processing of the penalty proceedings by the Labour Inspectorate shall be suspended until the Public Prosecutor has given notice that the criminal proceedings have either been dropped, or that a verdict has been reached in such proceedings. Should the criminal proceedings end in a conviction, any employment-related penalty proceedings are dropped.

Amongst the negative aspects of the coordination between the Labour Inspectorate and the law enforcement authorities, the Labour Inspectorate is constantly stating that it is only in possession of up to date specific information relating to investigations, prosecutions and verdicts in offences relating to trafficking for the purpose of labour exploitation in those cases where administrative penalty proceedings have been simultaneously commenced and suspended within the competence of the Labour Inspectorate, and subsequently, once the case has reached court, the criminal proceedings have been dropped and dismissed, given that in these cases the penalty proceedings are re-opened by the Labour Inspectorate. For this reason, there is a criticism that the Labour Inspectorate System does not have complete information on the results of the procedure when the administrative proceedings are definitively dropped following a conviction in the criminal courts.

Likewise, and central to the criticisms of the Labour Inspectorate Directorate-General, is the long time it takes the criminal courts to reach a decision (criminal proceedings can take between 5 and 10 years to be resolved, and sometimes longer), given that where the administrative penalty proceedings must be re-opened following the said belated decision, this delay neutralises the effect of the penalty proceedings of the Inspectorate, given that it is understood that in order for punitive and penalty proceedings to be effective, they must be swift and exemplary. The solution proposed by the Directorate-General consists in changing the procedure for safeguarding the principle of *non bis in idem*, such that administrative penalties in employment matters imposed by the Inspectorate are not suspended where criminal liability is subsequently found to exist, in which case the guilty verdict would have to take into account and discount from the sentence those administrative penalties that have already been imposed.

At another level entirely, it is considered that in order to achieve greater effectiveness in the fight against situations of trafficking for the purpose of labour exploitation, systematic and planned activities aimed at controlling the black or unregulated economy ought to be increased.

2.3 Cooperation between States

2.3.1 Legal framework for cooperation in transnational Trafficking in Human Beings-cases

As is the case at an internal level, the legal framework concerning trans-national cooperation is articulated through various instruments, in this case, at a European, Latin-American, or simply internal level.

(a) Instruments at a European level.

Firstly, at a European level, we must consider the presence of Spain within the European Judicial Network (EJN), which is a tool aimed at facilitating judicial protection within the framework of the fight against trans-national crime. In Spain, the contact points in charge of providing the necessary legal and practical information in order to assist the authorities interested in filing applications for judicial cooperation in an effective manner are to be found at the Ministry of Justice, the General Council of the Judiciary and the Public Prosecutor□s Office. It should be pointed out that in respect of the Public Prosecutor, the contact points are to be found, specifically, at the Technical Secretariat, the Special Public Prosecutors, the National Court and the Provincial Public Prosecutor for Malaga.

A further point should be made about EUROJUST, a body of the European Union that has its own legal personality and which has powers covering investigations and activities relating to serious criminal conduct affecting at least two Member States, with the aims of promoting coordination between the competent authorities of the different Member States and facilitating judicial cooperation between them, for which purpose it maintains privileged relations with the European Police Office (Europol) and the European Agency for the Management of Operational Cooperation at the External Borders (Frontex). Furthermore, it is noteworthy that its territorial scope may go beyond the territories of the Member States, where appropriate, given that pursuant to Art. 27.3 of Council Decision 2002/1987/JHA of 28

February 2002, setting up EUROJUST with a view to reinforcing the fight against serious crime[44], applications for judicial cooperation addressed to and received from third-party States are acceptable. Specifically in Spain, Law 16/2006 of 26 May governs the EUROJUST National Member Act and relations with this EU body.[45] This Law, in addition to amending the Spanish legal system in order to comply with the needs arising from compliance with the duties imposed by Decision 2002/1987/JHA, also sought to introduce minimum regulation into Spanish law relating to other bodies or structures which, in matters of judicial cooperation, had arisen in recent years and which were not codified under Spanish law, as in the case of European judicial networks, to which reference has already been made, and the concept of liaison magistrates.[46]

Therefore, the presence of Spain in both the European Judicial Network and in EUROJUST entails strong links to both Europol and Frontex. But given that we shall refer to the former in the following sub-section, in relation to the application in practice of the legal framework described here, we shall now refer briefly to Spain's role in Frontex.

It should be recalled that prior to the creation of Frontex by way of Council Regulation (EC) No. 2007/2004 of 26 October 2004[47], the maritime centres were created at the proposal of Greece and Spain at the SCIFA meeting of 29 October 2003, and were located at Piraeus (Greece), for the Eastern Mediterranean (ESBC), and Madrid for the Western Mediterranean (WSBC). During their brief lifetime they coordinated maritime operations and performed some research into the technology to be applied in maritime patrols.[48] Subsequently, when Frontex was set up as the Agency in charge of coordinating operational cooperation between Member States in matters of the management of the external borders, operations have been carried out every year in those zones with the highest migratory pressure, i.e. Italy, Greece and Spain.[49] Each operation is led by the country in which the resources are

---

[44] OJEU of 6 March 2002 [2002] OJ L63.

[45] Official State Gazette of 27 May 2006, No. 126.

[46] The go-between judges shall promote, and facilitate legal cooperation in civil and criminal matters between Spain and the State before which they have been accredited, and shall encourage direct contact between the competent judicial and administrative authorities. Likewise they shall exercise all those powers conferred on them by the European Union law, international treaties, or the agreements reached with regard to reciprocity (First Additional Provision of Law 16/2006).

[47] OJEU of 25 November 2004 [2004] OJ L349.

[48] R. Cortés Márquez, 'La vigilancia de las fronteras marítimas en la Unión Europea' in S. Zaragoza Soto (ed), *Impacto de los riesgos emergentes en la Seguridad Marítima* (Madrid: Ministerio de Defensa. Cuadernos de Estrategia 140 2009) p. 51.

[49] It should be borne in mind that Frontex does not replace the national border-control services, nor does it have border agents, or its own boats or aircraft. Its mission is to draw up risks analyses, to coordinate and finance the resources of the Member States in joint operations, to support the States in the training of their border police and in joint

deployed and the participation of other countries is very irregular. The most important of all such operations, known as HERA, is performed and led in the Atlantic under Spanish initiative. The initiative has also been and continues to be with the Police Directorate-General and the Civil Guard Directorate-General, with their participation in the various European and international forums and especially at Frontex[50], and all the more so since the installation in Spain of the Integrated Border Patrol System, given that the success of this system has been acknowledged even by EUROSUR, and has been exported to various countries. The importance of the HERA joint operation, which incidentally is the successor to the ATLANTIS project which was initiated by Spain in 2005, resides in its innovative features in a number of aspects. Firstly, never before had there been such advanced patrolling in the fight against illegal immigration. This need arises from the enormous SAR zone that Spain has in the Atlantic (over one million square kilometres) which means that any dinghies sighted in the said zone are the responsibility of Spain should they founder. Secondly, the Regulations governing Frontex did not envisage operations beyond the European borders. Finally, never before had the Spanish Civil Guard deployed so many maritime resources in foreign countries. In this operation activities are based on the Canary-Islands Regional Coordination Centre, which centre has become, furthermore, the best European platform for the performance of tests with new technical devices in the fight against illegal immigration, from satellites to unmanned aerial vehicles, which makes it an unbeatable starting point for the developments that are currently being examined in Europe.[51] In addition to the HERA operation, a three-year project was commenced in 2006 known as SEAHORSE, with the aim of initiating more intensive cooperation with African countries, through the exchange of liaison officers, courses of various kinds, and an annual conference on immigration with the attendance of European and African nations, which has led to the SEHAORSE-Network projects (with the aim of setting up a communications network, via satellite, for the exchange of information between contact points in Spain, Portugal, Mauritania, Senegal and Cape Verde) and the SEAHORSE-Cooperation Centres (with the aim of expanding the communications network to Morocco, Gambia and Guinea Bissau).[52]

---

repatriation flights, to assist them in crisis situations, and to provide technical assistance to the European Commission and to the Member States.

[50] R. Cortés Márquez, 'La vigilancia de las fronteras marítimas en la Unión Europea' in S. Zaragoza Soto (ed), *Impacto de los riesgos emergentes en la Seguridad Marítima* (Madrid: Ministerio de Defensa. Cuadernos de Estrategia 140 2009) p. 70.

[51] R. Cortés Márquez, 'La vigilancia de las fronteras marítimas en la Unión Europea' in S. Zaragoza Soto (ed), *Impacto de los riesgos emergentes en la Seguridad Marítima* (Madrid: Ministerio de Defensa. Cuadernos de Estrategia 140 2009) p. 73.

[52] R. Cortés Márquez, 'La vigilancia de las fronteras marítimas en la Unión Europea' in S. Zaragoza Soto (ed), *Impacto de los riesgos emergentes en la Seguridad Marítima* (Madrid: Ministerio de Defensa. Cuadernos de Estrategia 140 2009) p. 74.

Even so, those intercepted in African waters are handed over to the authorities of the country with sovereignty over the said waters, whilst those intercepted in the Canary Islands are subject to legal process, i.e. an attempt is made to return them within the statutory time limits, which is not at all easy.[53] There is no doubt that this fact ought to serve as a warning to prevent the infringement of international protection, constituted by the right to asylum and subsidiary protection, and eventually, to the creation of favourable circumstances for the trafficking in human beings, as has been stated in part one (1.2.2. b above).

(b) Instruments at a Latin-American level

As a counterpart to the European Judicial Network (EJN), the Latin-American Network of International Judicial Cooperation arose at a Latin-American level following the Inaugural Meeting held on 27 to 29 October 2004, commonly referred to as IberRed.[54] In this manner, this network is a structure formed of Central Authorities and contact points from the Ministries of Justice, Public Prosecutors' Office and Public Ministries, and the Judiciaries of the 22 States that make up the Latin-American community of nations[55], as well as the Supreme Court of Puerto Rico. Its aim is to optimise the instruments of civil and criminal judicial assistance and to reinforce the ties of cooperation between Member States. Ultimately, it constitutes a fundamental step in the creation of a Latin-American Judicial Area, which is understood to mean a specific area within which the activity of judicial cooperation can benefit from reinforced and dynamic mechanisms and instruments that allow effective judicial protection to be simplified and expedited. Specifically in Spain, throughout 2010 the plan for the dissemination of IberRed has been put into practice. As such, the task of disseminating this tool has been carried out in Barcelona, Seville, Malaga and Valencia, with both judges and public prosecutors in attendance, by way of a participatory and theoretical-practical methodology, showing the advantages, effectiveness and potential of the said tool.

(c) Instruments of an internal nature.

In 2002 the International Cooperation Network of Public Prosecutors was set up with the aim of providing a specialised service in matters of international judicial cooperation at each one of the Provincial Public Prosecutors' Offices.[56]

---

[53] R. Cortés Márquez, 'La vigilancia de las fronteras marítimas en la Unión Europea' in S. Zaragoza Soto (ed), *Impacto de los riesgos emergentes en la Seguridad Marítima* (Madrid: Ministerio de Defensa. Cuadernos de Estrategia 140 2009) pp. 73-74

[54] <http://www.iberred.org>.

[55] Andorra, Argentina, Bolivia, Brazil, Chile, Columbia, Costa Rica, Cuba, Ecuador, El Salvador, Spain, Guatemala, Honduras, Mexico, Nicaragua, Panama, Paraguay, Peru, Portugal, Dominican Republic, Uruguay, and Venezuela.

[56] <http://www.fiscal.es>.

Specifically at the Provincial Public Prosecutors' Offices and, on the basis of the need for specialisation in this matter, the Attorney-General's Instruction 2/2003, based on a structure set up previously on an informal basis, established a Special International Cooperation Service at the Public Prosecutor's Office of each Provincial Court. In accordance with the provisions of the Instruction, 'the said service shall be composed of the Public Prosecutor(s) at each Office belonging to the Network of international judicial cooperation of the Public Prosecutors' Office, who given their specialist training, shall be fully qualified to perform the functions which this Instruction confers on them.'. At the specialist Public Prosecutors' Offices, such as the one dedicated to foreign-national affairs, the Instruction provides that 'the said task shall be provided in the first instance and, in so far as the caseload permits, by the Public Prosecutor(s) acting as contact points for the European Judicial Network.'.
This special service and, in particular with regard to the international judicial protection afforded to those Public Prosecutors who make up the Network, is responsible, *inter alia*, for the functions set forth in Instruction 2/2003, which are transcribed below by way of example of an organisation that is useful:

The enforcement, or at least the coordination and monitoring of the enforcement, of all letters rogatory received that are to be enforced by the Public Prosecutor's Office at which they provide their services, including postings.

Assistance, where necessary, to all other Public Prosecutors on the staff in the drafting of letters rogatory to be issued, for which purpose they shall have at their disposal, where appropriate, the model letter rogatory drawn up by the European Judicial Network.

Cooperation with all other Public Prosecutors in the drafting of the reports requested by the judicial bodies of the respective Public Prosecutor's Office in matters of international judicial cooperation.

The supply of the direct contacts of the Public Prosecutor with the international judicial authorities where the said contacts are necessary for the enforcement or drafting of a request for international judicial protection.

The regulation of this Network of Public Prosecutors is carried out through Instructions 2/2003 and 2/2007 of the Attorney-General.

Finally, objectives 3 and 4 of the 2008 Integrated Plan to Combat Trafficking in Human Beings for the purposes of Sexual Exploitation should be mentioned, which are likewise applicable when the aim of the trafficking is labour exploitation, and these have already been discussed when we referred to the legal framework for cooperation within the State (2.2.1 above).

2.3.2 Application of legal framework in practice

The application of the instruments described in the previous sub-section is carried out in Spain, with regard to situations of trafficking for the purpose of labour exploitation, mainly through European arrest warrants, with the intervention of EUROJUST and EUROPOL, at a European level.

Although on the negative side, as is stated by the Deputy Public Prosecutor specializing in Foreign-National affairs for Malaga, in the interview given, it should be pointed out that, in principle, the Spanish jurisdictional bodies have been traditionally unwilling to use means of international judicial cooperation, on the grounds that these slow down procedures, but the reality of the facts has shown us that the instruments referred to function well.

Thus, in addition to the so-called 'Operación Libertad' which shall be referred to as case number one in part four, the proper functioning and the method for proceeding with the said instruments may be extracted from the examination of the so-called 'Operación Trufas', with which the participation of the Deputy Public Prosecutor specializing in Foreign-National affairs of Malaga, has been classified by the Deputy Foreign-National Affairs Public Prosecutor of Pontevedra, in the interview given, as 'an example and a success in the committal stage'. Specifically, 'Operación Trufas' focuses on the smuggling of Ukrainian citizens into the European Union by an organised gang. This gang was likewise responsible for supplying false documents from various countries within the European Union in order to facilitate their access to the labour market, although the gang was not concerned about the specific activity that each one of the immigrants was later going to engage in. Well then, following an arrest in Malaga (Spain), in application of the regulations governing foreign-national affairs, and a statement made by the person arrested as a protected witness, with regard to which it was likewise agreed that enforcement of the deportation decision would be suspended, as it was considered that his presence at the committal stage of the proceedings and in the eventual hearing, irrespective of the place where it was carried out, was fundamental, a series of telephone taps were carried out which allowed the identification of the drivers who carried out the transport through the different countries, and even the registration numbers of the vehicles used for this purpose. As a result, the Spanish police applied, through the SIRENE International Police Cooperation unit, for the cross-border surveillance of the trafficking that the gang was undertaking with these immigrants on one of its trips through France and Italy; all of which with the aim of ascertaining the location of the flats or houses where they were accommodated by way of the surveillance carried out on the drivers of the vehicles used. The said cross-border surveillance was authorised verbally and later in writing by the Judge of the Mission of Justice of the Central Headquarters of the French Judicial Police, as well as by the Procurator-General of Genoa. Subsequently, the renewal of the said surveillance was applied for again after being authorised, in this last instance also by the Portuguese authorities. The investigations allowed the police to obtain information on the vehicle used, the identity of two of the recent victims and the person to whom they were handed over, and even the identity of a number of the drivers who had performed journeys entering into Schengen territory through Slovakia with the ultimate destination of Portugal. With all of these background facts, the Spanish Public Prosecutor forwarded all of this information to the Spanish national member at EUROJUST, in order to assess whether it was appropriate to call a coordination meeting at the said institution, given the probability that other States would have commenced investigations into the same gang, and maybe even begun proceedings, all of which with the aim of avoiding duplication. Finally, the said meeting was held at the Headquarters of EUROJUST, with the attendance of representatives of the Spanish Public Prosecutor and delegations from the Public Prosecutors of various States, mainly those States with the biggest involvement such as Italy, Portugal, Austria, Germany or Hungary. The said meeting served to coordinate actions and to set the day on which the police were to carry out the arrests in coordinated manner. As a result of all this, numerous arrests were made and some of the gang members are now in jail.

Outside of Europe the importance of IberRed is growing, as has been noted by the Deputy Foreign-National Affairs Public Prosecutor of Pontevedra. In effect, in the interview given, she defends the very valuable contribution made by this tool, indicating that she recalls cases in which IberRed was essential to the trial being able to go ahead and, specifically, for the witnesses being able to give evidence by video link.

Lastly, from the 2009 Review of the Integrated Plan to Combat Trafficking in Human Beings for the purposes of Sexual Exploitation, we may extract the level of achievement of the objectives proposed in matters of cooperation with other States. Without doubt, the most significant aspect in this regard has been the joint effort and the collaboration with the originating countries. For this purpose, the main tool has been the Spanish International Cooperation for Development Agency (AECID). Thus, its Master plan for Spanish Cooperation 2009-2012, approved by the Spanish Cabinet on 13 February 2009[57], contains strategic lines and priority actions amongst which is included the following: 'to establish or strengthen the regulatory frameworks governing social protection for migrants at a bilateral or regional level, combating trafficking and the exploitation of migrants…'.[58] And during 2009 funding was commenced for cooperation projects to combat trafficking in Central America and South East Asia. These projects include the following: Central America Project (with the UNODC and COMMCA); the creation of a Regional Centre for Victim Support and Empowerment for Mexico and Central America; Convention for the Strengthening of Powers for the Protection of Childhood and Adolescence with regard to trafficking in Ecuador, El Salvador, Guatemala, Honduras and Nicaragua 2007-2010; Multidisciplinary Project for the fight against trafficking for the purpose of sexual exploitation, and support and integration of victims in the Mekong sub-region. Finally, Order TIN/3498/2009 of 23 December, which regulates collective management of recruitment at source for 2010[59], provides that 'the

---

[57] <http://www.aecid.es>.

[58] Spanish Cooperation Master Plan 2009-2012, approved by Cabinet on 13 February 2009, p. 168.

[59] Official State Gazette of 29 December 2009, No. 313.

Immigration Directorate-General shall maintain information and collaboration relations with the pertinent authorities of those countries with which there is an Agreement on the regulation and coordination of migratory flows, with the aim of facilitating the availability of workers who meet the professional profile of the occupations required by the labour market, and it shall, within the collaboration framework established in these agreements, promote the creation of databases of persons seeking work in their countries of origin in order to simplify the process and improve the quality of the selection procedures. For these purposes the use of the CV Europass curriculum vitae format approved by Decision number 2241/2004/EC of the European Parliament and of the Council of the European Union of 15 December 2004'[60] (Art. 1.3) shall be promoted.

2.4 Summary of findings

The following aspects may be highlighted as the main conclusions of part two.

2.4.1 Identified obstacles

One. At an internal level, it may be seen that there is an excessive diversity of initiatives with regard to trafficking. Likewise, the main instruments of cooperation created (Integrated Plan at a national level and Galicia Protocol at the level of the said Autonomous Region) concentrate exclusively on trafficking with the purpose of sexual exploitation, although there is a tendency to apply them also to situations of labour exploitation. Furthermore, with the exception of Galicia, at the level of the Autonomous Regions the Integrated Plan has not been substantiated by way of the corresponding protocols.

Two. The cohesion between the various parties involved at an internal level in the fight against trafficking is not wholly adequate. The main flaws are to be found in the lack of support from the Judiciary; the lack of communication between NGOs and the law enforcement authorities; the scant preparation of the majority of trade unions in order to tackle matters of trafficking directly, as well as their lack of information; the limited participation of the Labour Inspectorate in the information on trafficking, in so far as their awareness of the said information is limited to situations in which the facts under investigation do not go beyond the mere administrative infringement, over which they have jurisdiction.

Three. Spain's participation in Frontex and Spanish leadership in the HERA operation and in the SEAHORSE projects saga in order to prevent illegal immigration is at risk of becoming a massive and uncontrolled enforcement of

---

[60] OJEU of 31 December 2004, No. 390.

the EU deportation policy. Unless sufficient human and material resources are established in order to safeguard international protection, constituted by the right to asylum and subsidiary protection, the balance that must exist between border protection and the protection of human rights will break down. Trafficking is precisely one of the things that the thousands of people who are intercepted in the waters being patrolled will have to face once again after being deported through the return Directive.

Four. To date, international cooperation in the prosecution of offences involving trafficking in human beings has been established for the most part at a police and judicial level, which means that there is an absence of contacts for the purpose of collaboration and exchange of information between the different Labour Inspectorates at a European level. These bodies only have collaboration protocols for the exchange of information in cases of trans-national companies within the framework of the European Union, and never in respect of criminal offences.

Five. Outside of the European area and, in particular, with regard to Africa, international judicial cooperation is typically slow and is characterised by letters rogatory not being processed.

2.4.2 Good practices

One. The generalisation of Provincial Public Prosecutors specializing in foreign-national affairs with powers in matters of trafficking for the purpose of labour exploitation amounts to the most significant advance that has occurred in Spain in the fight against trafficking. Furthermore, the efforts that are being made in cooperation must be positively acclaimed, as there now exists permanent communication with the law enforcement authorities, as well as with *Red Española de Lucha contra la Trata de Seres Humanos*, which brings together the NGOs that are most closely involved in matters of trafficking.

Two. With regard to cooperation between States, the experiences at EUROJUST, Europol and Iber-Red are positive, although these instruments need to be promoted much more up and down the whole of Spain.

Three. The joint works and collaboration with the countries of origin commenced by Spain are a good initiative. Specifically, the fact that it should be envisaged that the said countries should set up databases of persons looking for work that simplify the performance and improve the quality of the selection processes for so-called recruitment at source would amount to a big step forward in the avoidance of fraud that normally provides cover for true situations of trafficking for the purpose of labour exploitation, but this is not enough. It is also necessary to ensure the interaction of the Spanish Labour Inspectorate, such that it has available to it all the information in this regard and can carry out direct control over the provision of services by the said immigrants at the corresponding companies offering employment, certifying that the employment conditions and Social Security arrangements are lawful.

Part III
Victim protection and assistance

With regard to the treatment of the victims of trafficking in recent times, Spain has made huge steps forward, once again as a result of the ratification of the Warsaw Convention of the Council of Europe on Action against Trafficking in Human Beings.

Thus, the amendment made to the Organic Foreign-Nationals Act by way of Organic Law 2/2009 has amounted to the regulation *ex novo* of Art. 59 bis, under the heading 'Victims of trafficking in human beings'. Furthermore, this regulation has transposed Directive 2004/81/EC into Spanish law, for which breach Spain was found guilty in Case C-266/08, Commission of the European Communities vs. Kingdom of Spain, by the Court of Justice of the European Union in its Judgement of 14 May 2009. For its part, Law 12/2009 of 30 October, governing the right to asylum and subsidiary protection has also considered the victims of trafficking in human beings to be vulnerable persons who deserve special protection. Lastly, the recent Instruction 1/2010 of the Secretary of State for Security lays down a procedure to be followed for the enforcement of Art. 59 bis of the Organic Foreign-Nationals Act. It is precisely in the light of this regulatory framework that the matters that are going to be examined in this part of the report will be analysed.

3.1 Identification of victims

With regard to the identification of victims, Art. 59 bis of the Organic Foreign-Nationals Act refers directly to the provisions of Art. 10 of the Warsaw Convention of the Council of Europe on Action against Trafficking in Human Beings, where it provides that the pertinent authorities shall implement such measures as are necessary for the identification of the victims of trafficking in accordance with the provisions of the said rule.

Well then, given the lack of regulations developing Art. 59 bis of the Organic Foreign-Nationals Act, in accordance with what has been stated by the Coordinating Trial Public Prosecutor specializing in Foreign-National affairs[61], only police officers who have had specific training and preparation with regard to dealing with and identifying victims should have contact with actual or potential victims, with all due assistance and coordination from civil support organisations (NGOs). For this purpose, it has been considered appropriate to set up 'rescue units' along the lines of those existing in Latin-American countries composed of a variety of multi-disciplinary experts (police detectives and psychologists and social workers, both from the Authorities and the NGOs), which can carry out the initial interviews of the victims affected

---

[61] State Prosecutor of the Foreign-National Coordination Chamber, 'Ficha Extranjería. Síntesis de la lucha contra la trata de seres humanos', p. 24 <www.fiscal.es>.

jointly, and inform them of their rights and plan welfare and protection strategies.

For this purpose, the map of resources that Spain has available at the moment in order to be able to implement a similar rescue institution are as follows: On the one hand the members of the law enforcement authorities themselves, composed of the members of the foreign-national brigade and the documents and investigation brigade, as well as the body of expert witnesses, psychologists and the professionals available to both the National Police Force and the Civil Guard. On the other hand, the human and material resources of the NGOs dedicated to the rescue and recovery of these victims. Now then, taking into account the need that the law enforcement authorities should be able to perform their functions under optimal conditions of safety and efficiency, the approach is that this institution of experts making up the rescue office should come from the law enforcement authorities themselves, without prejudice to the subsequent assistance of the NGOs.[62]

In this regard, it is understood that all other parties, such as Labour Inspectors or members of NGOs or trade unions should report their suspicions of trafficking to the law enforcement authorities.

The following signs should be taken as evidence that someone is a victim of trafficking:

General signs: lack of identity documents (especially passport) and immigration documents (visas, residence permits, etc.) or false documents; no or little money or lack of control over money; isolation and inability to communicate freely with family members, or members of his/her ethnic group or religious community; excessive price paid for the journey and/or money owed for the journey (debt); social isolation: limited contact with persons other than the traffickers; subject to control/supervision measures in order to ensure that this is only superficial; inability to or difficulty in communicating in Spanish, especially if he/she has already been in Spain for a long time; endurance of verbal, psychological and/or physical abuse with the aim of intimidating, humiliating, or scaring the victim.

Signs relating to his/her surroundings: victims are held under supervision and/or control; victims have a dependent relationship with regard to other persons in their day-to-day life.

Non-verbal signs in their conduct: victims seem reticent or unwilling to talk, and it is observed that they lie or act in accordance with instructions. Their appearance is scruffy, untidy and show signs of ill-treatment (bruises or other signs of being beaten, evidence of rape or sexual abuse, cuts, contusions,

[62] S. García Baquero (State Prosecutor for foreign-national affairs in Pontevedra), 'Respuestas eficaces en la identificación de la víctima de trata de seres humanos con fines de explotación sexual' <www.fiscal.es>.

burns). They appear anxious, fearful and/or especially tense or impressionable. They are very nervous; especially if a companion who normally acts as a translator and who forms a part of the trafficking gang is present during the interview or interaction.

Verbal signs: they may express fear or concern for their situation or that of their family, either in their country of origin or somewhere else; they give evasive answers or appear frightened, especially in front of persons who could be their traffickers or part of the criminal gang; in the case of children the information might be unclear with regard to the family relationship of their carers, they say they are accompanied by extended family but this is unclear.

Signs relating to servitude in order to pay off debts: a situation of servitude in order to pay off debts, victims are under pressure to pay or state they are honour-bound to pay the debt.

Signs relating to children who are victims of trafficking: the existence of emotional problems; the existence of indicators of sexual conduct; the existence of physical indicators of sexual abuse.

In those cases where there is doubt as to whether or not the victim of trafficking is a minor (which circumstance tends to arise with regard to immigrants who are not accompanied), pursuant to Art. 35 of the Organic Foreign-Nationals Act, the Public Prosecutor has powers to determine his/her age, with the assistance of the appropriate health organisations. The determination of age should be resolved as quickly as possible. In this regard, Instruction 2/2001 of the Attorney-General's Office classified the transfer of the suspected minor to a health centre and his/her stay there whilst tests are carried out as a situation of deprivation of liberty which should last for as short a time as possible, and in which the interested party ought to be informed immediately and in a comprehensible way of the reasons for his/her situation and of his/her rights, even where the presence of a Lawyer is not required in order to adequately safeguard the said rights. Amongst those items that the Public Prosecutor must provide information on are the medical tests that are going to be performed (physical examination: anthropometric tests; radiological exploration: bone maturity, dental maturity).[63] Thus, the suspected minor should be informed that the tests are suitable in order to determine his/her age; that the tests will provide a range within which what is most favourable to his/her interests will be chosen; that it is in principle necessary, given that with the current state of medical science reliable results can be obtained; and that there is no other less invasive option that allows the same

[63] See in this regard M.S. Gisbert Grifo, 'Determinación de la edad en menores. Aspectos médico-legales' (2003) Estudios Jurídicos. Ministerio Fiscal, 2, pp. 678-685; J.L. Prieto, 'Determinación de la edad de jóvenes indocumentados (Protocolo de actuación médico-forense) in <http://www.justizia.net/docuteca> .

objective to be achieved with the same efficiency. Where the suspected minors seek international protection, refusal by the said persons to submit to medical tests shall not prevent a decision being taken as to their application for international protection. Having determined their age, in the case of minors, the Public Prosecutor shall hand them over to the pertinent services for the protection of minors.[64]

3.2 Legal framework for the protection of the rights of victims of Trafficking in Human Beings for labour exploitation

3.2.1 Assistance to victims

Until such time as Art. 59 bis of the Organic Foreign-Nationals Act is developed into regulations, the procedure for assisting the victims is currently governed on a temporary basis by Instruction 1/2010 of the Secretary of State for Security. In this manner, when it comes to assistance, different stages need to be identified.

(a) Identification of the victim by the Foreign-National Brigade or other police units: Firstly, once the existence of a foreign national in an irregular situation who could be a victim of trafficking in human beings is known about, and without prejudice to providing the victim with such assistance and protection as may be required immediately, and to commencing the appropriate investigation procedures and performing any other activities envisaged in the corresponding police protocols, the procedure shall be as follows:

The said person shall be interviewed in order to find out about his/her situation, detect the existence of evidence that would support his/her status as a victim of trafficking, and advise him/her of his/her rights and the possibility of reporting an offence, as well as putting him/her in touch with specialist bodies or services that could provide assistance.

Elements that could have a negative effect at the interview shall be taken into account: the interviewer and the victim not being of the same sex, an administrative situation, fear of reprisals, command of the language, cultural differences, circumstances that he/she has been through, etc. For this reason, measures that serve to generate a comfortable and secure context for the victim shall be implemented. In this regard, through the interviews carried out, the Section on offences relating to trafficking in human beings within the Judicial Police Technical Unit of the Civil Guard has confirmed to us that the Civil Guard has set up Immigrant Assistance Teams (EDATIS) in order to assist immigrants in administrative matters and to help them trust the law enforcement authorities. Furthermore, as is recalled by Instruction 1/2010, the assistance of NGOs that have the aim of providing refuge and protection to

[64] Articles 47 and 48 of Law 12/1992 of 30 October, which governs the right to asylum and subsidiary protection, refer to the international protection of minors.

the victims of trafficking in human beings may be sought in the detection, treatment, and provision of assistance to victims.

In those cases where required, interpreters shall be on hand to provide support, avoiding the use of the traffickers or any other persons related to the place of the exploitation in the performance of this task.

Before starting the interview, the interviewee shall be informed of the confidentiality of the entire process.

The interviewer shall ensure that he/she fully understands the content and the purpose of the interview, and his/her right not to answer questions or to end the interview at any time.

The victim shall be informed, in writing and in a language that he/she can understand, of the provisions of Art. 59 bis of the Organic Foreign-Nationals Act (grant of a recovery and reflection period in order to decide whether or not he/she cooperates with the authorities in the investigation of the offence, and if so, in the criminal proceedings; right to necessary safety and protection; possibility of waiver of administrative liability; grant, at his/her choice, of the possibility of undergoing assisted return to his/her country of origin, or authorisation to reside and work on the grounds of exceptional circumstances), and all other rights that he/she may be entitled to. Likewise, pursuant to Art. 46 of Law 12/2009 of 30 October, governing the right to asylum and subsidiary protection, the specific situation of persons applying for or benefiting from international protection in a vulnerable situation shall be taken into account, which is deemed to cover those persons who are the victims of trafficking in human beings. In particular, given their situation of particular vulnerability, such measures as may be necessary shall be implemented in order to provide distinct treatment, where necessary, to applications for international protection that may be made by such victims. The document providing information on rights shall be signed by the victim and by the official in attendance.

The pertinent proposal with regard to the grant of a recovery and reflection period shall be filed (always by the Foreign-National Brigade)[65] as soon as possible with the Government Delegate or Sub-delegate, for a decision. Should the proposal be favourable, the term thereof shall be specified, which should be at least 30 days, and under all circumstances, sufficient for the victim to be able to decide if he/she wishes to cooperate with the authorities in the investigation of the offence and, where appropriate, in the criminal proceedings that have been instigated. The proposal shall be accompanied by a

---

[65] In the event that other police units have intervened, these shall compile a report stating their reasons for contending that there is reasonable evidence that the interested person could be a victim of trafficking in human beings. Said report shall be sent as soon as possible to the pertinent Foreign-National Brigade. The application for a cooling-off period, should there be one, shall under all circumstances be attached to the said report, as well as any documents that may be of interest in deciding on the grant (copies of the documents supplied by the victim, reports supplied by other entities or institutions, etc.).

copy of the file and a complete report on the administrative situation of the victim, as well as the reports supplied by other bodies or institutions.

(b) Resolution on the recovery and reflection period: In view of the documents and proposal received, the Government Delegate or Sub-delegate shall decide, as soon as possible and by way of a reasoned decision, whether or not the grant of a period of reflection is appropriate, and how long it should last.

As part of the same decision resolving on the period of reflection, the Government Delegate or Sub-delegate shall also decide as follows:

- The temporary suspension of any penalty proceedings that may have been commenced against the interested party pursuant to the Organic Foreign-Nationals Act and over which it has powers to decide. Should there exist penalty proceedings over which the decision rests with a different Government Delegation or Sub-delegation, this shall be reported immediately to the said body, together with the resolution granting the period of reflection, so that the pertinent Delegation or Sub-delegation may also agree to the immediate temporary suspension thereof.
- The temporary suspension of the enforcement of deportation or expulsion orders that the same Government Delegation or Sub-delegation may have ordered against the interested party. Should there exist a deportation order imposed by a different Government Delegation or Sub-delegation, this shall be immediately notified thereto, together with the resolution granting the period of reflection, so that the pertinent Delegation or Sub-delegation may also agree to the immediate temporary suspension of the enforcement thereof.
- The immediate release of the victim, should he/she be held at a Foreign-National Internment Centre.

The Government Delegate or Sub-delegate may refuse or revoke the recovery and reflection period for reasons of public order or where the person has been incorrectly classified as a victim.

3.2.2 Right to residence

The provisions of Instruction 1/2010 of the Secretary of State for Security shall also apply to the right to reside and work for as long as Art. 59 bis of the Organic Foreign-Nationals Act is not developed into a set of regulations. In this regard, the Instruction distinguishes the following stages:

(a) Care for the victim: The police unit that has commenced the investigation shall put the victim into contact with the pertinent assistance services (services, municipal, provincial and regional bodies and offices). Likewise, the police unit shall adopt, where necessary, such measures as may be necessary in order to ensure the victim's safety and protection. During this stage, the fundamental

role of NGOs is acknowledged when it comes to providing refuge and protection for the victims.

(b) Proposal for the waiver of administrative liability, residence and work permit for exceptional reasons and assisted return: The prosecutor pursuing the penalty proceedings may propose a waiver of liability to the Government Delegate or Sub-delegate, prior to making a definitive proposal, where he/she should consider that the conditions set forth at Art. 59 bis of the Organic Foreign-Nationals Act have been met (cooperation of the victim for the purpose of the investigation or the criminal proceedings, or in accordance with the personal situation of the victim).

Should a waiver of liability be agreed, the victim may apply, at his/her choice, for a residence and work permit for exceptional circumstances, or assisted return to his/her country of origin.

In the case of residence and work permit on the grounds of cooperation, the General Foreign-Nationals and Borders Commissariat shall forward the proposal to the corresponding Secretary of State for Security, which shall decide on residence and, should it be granted, shall forward the case file to the Secretary of State for Immigration and Emigration for the grant of the work permit.

In the case of residence and work permit on the grounds of the personal situation of the victim, the application shall be sent to the Secretary of State for Immigration and Emigration for a decision, following a prior report by the Secretary of State for Security.[66] It should be pointed out that there is a special provision regarding the contractual forms through which it is possible to recruit victims of trafficking pursuant to which the use employment contracts in order to encourage indefinite contracts is only allowable in the case of women.[67]

---

[66] In this regard, Article 31.3 of the Organic Foreign-Nationals Act refers to the possibility that the Authorities could grant a temporary residence permit, *inter alia*, for humanitarian reasons. These humanitarian reasons are linked to the foreign-national having been, for example, a victim of certain crimes. Curiously, the Foreign-Nationals Regulations, which are still in force, approved by Royal Decree 2393/2004 of 30 December (Official State Gazette of 7 January, No. 6), provide that permits may be granted for humanitarian reasons to foreign-nationals who have been the victims of the offences defined at Articles 311 *et seq.* of the Criminal Code, i.e. victims of offences against the rights of employees, which offences, in our understanding, exemplify the labour exploitation suffered by the victims of human trafficking, as has been set forth in the first part of the report.

[67] By way of this contractual format, the Spanish Government seeks to encourage employers to offer indefinite contracts, concentrating on a series of social groups which have grown in size over the years up to the point that it can now be said that currently this contractual format has become the standard form for recruitment by way of indefinite contracts. And this is because of the resulting advantages for employers in the

In the processing of these permits, the victim may be released from the duty to supply documents where obtaining the said documents might put the victim at risk.

As soon as the permit procedure has been decided upon, a provisional permit may be granted.

Where the victim should opt for assisted return, the case file shall be forwarded to the Secretary of State for Immigration and Emigration.

3.2.3 Victims as witnesses in proceedings

In principle, the participation of the victims in the criminal investigation and proceedings is considered to be essential, but as is stated by the Coordinating Trial Public Prosecutor specializing in Foreign-National affairs, evidence must be found that does not necessarily depend on the complaint and testimony of the victims, and that is compatible with the accused's right to a defence. In his opinion, steps should be taken for the proceedings to follow their course even if the victim retracts or withdraws the complaint. Telephone tapping, surveillance with electronic means and financial investigations are useful and suitable methods for the investigation of the offence of trafficking, but it is also necessary to be able to rely on specialist operational detective groups.[68]

In those cases where the victims decide to cooperate in the criminal proceedings, the Coordinating Trial Public Prosecutor specializing in Foreign-National affairs emphasises the importance of there being no possibility of visual contact between the accused and the victim; the confidentiality of the victim's particulars must be ensured; the victim must make his/her statements behind closed doors, and the victim should not be required to repeat his/her testimony during the proceedings.[69]

Art. 771.1 of the Criminal Procedure Act places a requirement on the Judicial Police to inform victims or injured parties, in writing, of the rights to which they are entitled, such as: to be a party to the proceedings, without any need to file an action; the right to appoint a lawyer or to be assisted by a duty solicitor; and in general to allege whatever is in their interests in law.

For its part, in Spain, the protection and safety of victims is carried out by way of Organic Law 19/1994 of 23 December, on the protection of witnesses and expert witnesses in criminal cases. Thus, in principle, where the Investigating Judge should reasonably detect that there is a serious danger for the victim, the Judge may order, stating the grounds, either *ex officio* or *ex parte*, such measures as may be necessary in order to preserve the identity of the witnesses.

---

form of cheaper objective unfair dismissal, and government subsidies at a fixed rate for each contract executed.

[68] State Prosecutor of the Foreign-National Coordination Chamber, 'Ficha Extranjería. Síntesis de la lucha contra la trata de seres humanos', p. 10 <www.fiscal.es>.

[69] State Prosecutor of the Foreign-National Coordination Chamber, 'Ficha Extranjería. Síntesis de la lucha contra la trata de seres humanos', p. 11 <www.fiscal.es>.

Likewise, once the judicial body with powers to try the facts has been served with the case file, it must issue a ruling as to whether or not some or all of the measures for the protection of witnesses and expert witness imposed by the Investigating Judge ought to be maintained, amended, or lifted, stating its grounds for its decision and also stating whether or not any new measures ought to be imposed.

However, this same rule governs certain aspects which leave victims unprotected. Firstly, should any party apply in its provisional assessment, accusation, or defence pleading, stating its grounds, to be informed of the identity of the witnesses or expert witnesses put forward, whose statement or report is considered to be pertinent, the Judge or the Court that is to try the case must, in the same ruling in which it is held that the evidence adduced is pertinent, disclose the forenames and surnames of the witnesses and expert witnesses. Secondly, any statements or reports by the witnesses and expert witnesses that have been subject to protection during committal stage shall only be deemed to be admissible evidence for the purpose of reaching a verdict if they are ratified during the trial hearing by the person who gave the said evidence. If the evidence is found to be impossible to reproduce, it must be ratified by way of being read out verbatim so that it may be subjected to adversarial debate between the parties.

In summary, in addition to the difficulty victims face in keeping their identity secret where it may be deduced from the content and context of their stories, they may end up being named and, as such, put at risk.

With regard to the activity of collecting evidence, so-called 'evidence given in advance' is essential. This not only means that victims are unable to change statements they have made previously once they reach court, but also, likewise, it avoids the risk that the victims will fail to appear for whatever reason, which would make it impossible for oral trials to go ahead.

Thus, pursuant to Art. 777.2 of the Criminal Procedure Act, where there are any reasonable grounds for suspecting that it will not be possible to hear some particular evidence during the oral trial, or that the said trial may be suspended, the Investigating Judge shall hear the said evidence immediately, ensuring under all circumstances that the parties are given an opportunity to debate the evidence adversary. In other words, in order to be able to assess the statement made by the victim at the committal stage subsequently at the oral trial, it is essential that counsel for the defendant is in attendance during the said statement. This stage shall be documented in a format that is suitable for audio-visual recording and reproduction, or by way of minutes authorised by the Judicial Secretary, listing those in attendance. Furthermore, in order to be assessed as evidence when reaching a verdict, the interested party must apply at the oral trial for the reproduction of the recording or for the deposition to be read out in full.

3.2.4 Right to compensation

The chances of the victims being able to obtain some kind of compensation are mixed.

On the one hand, from the point of view of their social rights, it should be recalled (see above 1.2.1) that the victims may pursue an action against the person who has exploited them in order to obtain such remuneration and any other rights they may be entitled to by law as would apply to a lawful business for the work they have performed until such time as the employment relationship with the employer was held to be void. Likewise, where appropriate, they may apply to the Social Security for any contingencies arising from professional risks; and in the case of contingencies arising from common risks, they may pursue the exploitative employer through civil contractual liability.

Furthermore, pursuant to Law 35/1995 of 11 December, on help and assistance for the victims of violent offences and offences contrary to sexual freedom[70], victims may obtain certain public aid. Despite the fact that amongst the requirements in order to be able to benefit from this aid is the requirement to be habitually resident in Spain, it is our understanding that the grant of a residence permit to the victims of trafficking covers this aspect. The value of such aid may not exceed under any circumstances the indemnity set in the conviction. This sum shall be determined by way of the application of the following rules, in so far as it does not exceed the amount stated:

- Should a situation of temporary incapacity arise, the amount due shall be equivalent to double the minimum inter-professional daily wage in force, during the time that the victim was in the said situation after the first six months have elapsed.
- Should disabling injuries be suffered, the maximum amount due shall be pegged to the minimum inter-professional monthly wage in force on the date on which the harm or damage to health is consolidated, and shall depend on the degree of disability in accordance with the following scale: Permanent partial disability: forty months; Complete permanent disability: sixty months; Absolute permanent disability: ninety months; serious disability: one hundred and thirty months.

The value of the aid shall be established by way of the application of adjustment coefficients on the maximum sums stated and, in accordance with: the economic circumstances of the victim; the number of persons who depend economically on the victim; the degree of harm or impairment suffered by the victim.

---

[70] Official State Gazette of 12 December 1995, No. 296.

3.3 Application of the legal framework in practice

Although it is still early to assess the reform brought about by the Organic Foreign-Nationals Act with the introduction of Art. 59 bis, it is possible to say, reiterating the criticisms of the Attorney-General's Office[71], that the current regulations are inadequate in that they do not amount to a complete legal text for the victims of trafficking in human beings in the same way as the text covering the victims of domestic violence. In the reform of the Organic Foreign-Nationals Act, what continues to prevail is the idea of ensuring the normal application of administrative penalty provisions. This is so because the subjective scope of the application of Art. 59 bis is limited to foreign victims in an irregular situation, and because the administrative bodies with jurisdiction to pursue the penalty proceedings are acknowledged as having exclusive powers to identify the victims and to grant the associated rights, which powers they may exercise with a wide margin of discretion.

For this reason, the success of the measures implemented depends on the development of proper regulations, which we should point out has not happened yet, despite the fact that their approval was envisaged for 12 June 2010.

3.4 Summary of findings

The following aspects may be highlighted as the main conclusions of this part:

3.4.1 Identified obstacles

One. Spanish legislation has yet to provide for an effective method of identifying victims, that allows for the collaboration of various organisations or parties. The lack of specific rescue units is a notable flaw, as is the lack of protocols enabling the law enforcement authorities and NGOs specializing in matters of assisting and protecting the victims of trafficking to operate in coordinated manner.

Two. The current rules on the protection of witnesses and expert witnesses in criminal cases has some significant flaws, which have the effect of harming victims and leaving them unprotected.

Three. The lack of regulations to develop the measures implemented by Art. 59 bis of the Organic Foreign-Nationals Act means that victims cannot be protected in an integrated way, with a complete legal text. In effect, with regard to the prosecution of the offence of trafficking, and mainly with regard to the rules on foreign-national affairs, human dignity ought to prevail, with the aim of the complete physical and psychological recovery of the victims,

---

[71] Report by the State Prosecutor's Office for 2010, pp. 855-856 <www.fiscal.es>.

and ultimately, their integration into society.

3.4.2 Good practices

One. By way of Art. 59 bis of the Organic Foreign-Nationals Act, the system for the identification of victims contained at Art. 10 of the Warsaw Convention of the Council of Europe on Action against Trafficking in Human Beings is declared to be applicable directly.

Two. By way of Art. 59 bis of the Organic Foreign-Nationals Act, the so-called recovery and reflection period of at least 30 days envisaged in the Warsaw Convention of the Council of Europe on Action against Trafficking in Human Beings, as well as in Directive 2004/81/EC, is introduced into Spanish law.

Three. Art. 59 bis of the Organic Foreign-Nationals Act allows for the possibility of victims of trafficking being granted residence and work permits on humanitarian grounds, without any requirement to cooperate with the authorities in the investigation of the offence, and where appropriate, in the criminal proceedings.

Four. The victims of trafficking in human beings are considered to be persons who are in an especially-vulnerable situation, for the purpose of the grant of international protection, constituted by the right to asylum and subsidiary protection, and as such they are entitled to differentiated treatment.

Part IV
Case studies

Case 1: 'Operation Freedom'

(a) General features

'Operation Freedom' is a case of trafficking in human beings for labour exploitation launched in several Spanish regions, including La Rioja, the Basque Country, Navarra and Aragon. The victims of the abuse, most of which occurred in grape harvesting and related activities, were Portuguese citizens.[72] The case is particular interest for a number of reasons: it gave rise to a joint investigation between Spain and Portugal, coordination was performed via EUROJUST, all the accused belonged to a criminal organisation and, finally, the length of the initiative, launched in 2005.

(b) Specific issues regarding cooperation

Cooperation between the Spanish and Portuguese authorities was coordinated by EUROJUST. Meetings attended by public prosecutors, police from La Rioja and Oporto and judges from both countries were held in Logroño (La Rioja, Spain) and Oporto (Portugal). Everyone attending the meetings made the greatest efforts to coordinate the fight against the same enemy.

Members of the Public Prosecutor's Office in Oporto, backed and coordinated by EUROJUST (223/PT/05 Operation Freedom), went to Logroño (Spain) and invited the Spanish authorities (prosecutors, police and magistrates) to meetings held in Portugal.

After conversations with the Spanish and Portuguese police, a list of all the persons accused was drawn up. As the crime was being committed in two different countries, territorial competence could have caused a serious problem endangering the success of the operation. Happily, after four meetings between procurators from Oporto and La Rioja sponsored by EUROJUST, both sides agreed to accept EUROJUST□s informal recommendation that Spain should transfer jurisdiction to Portugal, once warrants for arrest had been issued and executed, so that the persons involved could be prosecuted there.

---

[72] Sources used in this case include: (a) Questionnaires returned by the Delegate Public Prosecutor for Foreigners in Logroño and the Criminal Section against Trafficking in Human Beings of the Judicial Police Technical Unit of the Civil Guard; (b) The 2009 Report of the Spanish Fiscal General del Estado (hereafter Public Prosecutor's Office - PPO) <www.fiscal.es>; (c) Writs issued by Section 1, the Criminal Court of the National Criminal Court dated on the 27th May 2008, ordering the persons arrested to be sent to Portugal. Writs: 98/2008; 100/2008; 101/2008; In <www.wetlaw.es> JUR\2009\83752; JUR\2009\83786; JUR\2009\83765; (d) Information from the media including Europa Press (20 Minutos newspaper dated 11 March 2010; <www.lukor.com/not-neg/laboral/0504/27114831.htm> and Noticias de Alava newspaper dated 29 April 2008.

As a result, the Portuguese judicial authorities issued 29 European warrants of arrest for a range of offences, including belonging to a criminal organisation, trafficking in human beings, laundering the proceeds of criminal activities and kidnapping. Once the Spanish judicial authorities received the warrants, 21 people were arrested in April. At the same time, a further 7 people were arrested in Portugal, and twelve search and entry operations took place in Spain and five in Portugal. Finally, after Section 1, the Criminal Court of the Spanish National Criminal Court had issued writs on the 27th May 2008, the persons under arrest were handed over to the Portuguese authorities. Copies of all the writs were sent to INTERPOL SIRENE and to the prisons housing the arrested, informing them that prisoners had to be handed over within ten days, responsibility for the prisoners being taken by INTERPOL SIRENE.

On the 3rd March 2010, chief government delegate for foreign affairs Gustavo Gauthier declared in the media that the accused had not yet been tried in Portugal.

(c) Specific matters concerning the victims

All victims were Portuguese, most of them men. All freely consented to being recruited in Portugal to work on farms and vineyards in Spain. They were promised advantageous labour conditions (work and remuneration) and appropriate accommodation. However, once in Spain, mainly in the La Rioja region, but also in Navarra, the Basque Country and Aragon, they were subjected to labour and in some cases sexual exploitation, and treated as 'slave labour' (living in 'captivity', deprived of freedom of movement, under constant physical threats and even aggression).

(d) Specific issues concerning the accused

The accused were part of 'a criminal organisation' with a flexible, variable internal structure, whose activities were carried out in Spanish and Portuguese jurisdictions. Its main criminal activity was the illegal recruitment of labour by Portuguese nationals.

(e) Procedural issues

Accused were handed over by the Spanish authorities to the Portuguese in the frame of Law 3/2003, dated 14th March, on European orders of arrest.

Case 2: 'Sentence of the Criminal Court of the Spanish Supreme Court, 5th June 2006, no. 651/2006'

(a) General features
This case looks at certain events at a night club/prostitution establishment in Roquetas de Mar (Almeria, Spain) from late March 2004 that provide a clear example of trafficking in human beings for labour exploitation.[73]

(b) Specific issues concerning cooperation
Despite the fact that, in the account of the precedents in the sentence, the connection between the man convicted and several persons of Russian nationality is clearly appreciable, as the former regularly asked the latter to send him Russian women, the Spanish authorities merely exercised their jurisdiction, without attempting to open a joint investigation with the Russian authorities, a move that might have put an end to Russian citizens acting in this way with such impunity.

(c) Specific issues concerning the victims
The victims, of Russian nationality, were recruited in their own country with promises of work as waitresses in Spain. Job offers were published in the press. Once the offer had been accepted, all the victims arrived in Spain at some time in late April or early May 2004, being flown into Madrid's Barajas airport. At the airport, they were sometimes welcomed by someone working with the person convicted, who gave them a ticket to Almeria. Occasionally, the person convicted took them himself by car from Madrid to Almeria. In both cases, the victims arrived in Spain from Russia with entry visas provided by the Russian collaborators, who informed the accused that the victims had arrived in Spain.

However, once in Spain the man convicted took their passports away, and took the women to a club he owned in Roquetas de Mar, where he revealed their real job was to work as prostitutes. These events continued until the police operation took place and the accused were arrested.

(d) Specific issues concerning the persons convicted
Apart form the man referred to in the previous section, who had contacts in Russia, the role played two other women, also convicted, needs to be described. Their job was to ensure the victims were really having sexual relations with the clients.

The Russian recruiters and the convicted owner of the club in Spain where the victims were forced to act as prostitutes clearly worked in coordination. This coordination was extended even further by the victims' receiving threats in Spain, not only from the man convicted, but also from the Russian citizens.

---

[73] The source consulted for our analysis of the case was the Sentence of the Criminal Court of the Spanish Supreme Court on 5 June 2006, number 651/2006, RJ\2006\6296 <www.westlaw.es>.

Finally, the direct, rigorous control exercised by the convicted women was a key factor in the coercion and intimidation being so effective, forcing them into a situation of complete vulnerability.

(e) Procedural issues

The Provincial Criminal Court of Almeria condemned the club owner: to a prison sentence of 8 years for an offence against the rights of foreign citizens, to 2 years' prison for the offence of labour exploitation and a fine, lasting 12 months, of 12 euros a day, 2 years of prison for each of the 5 offences of inducement to prostitution and the same fine. He was also made to pay 11/21st of the legal costs. Both women were also condemned to 2 years' imprisonment for each of the five crimes of inducement to prostitution with additional penalty and fine. They were made to pay 5/21st of the legal costs. Finally the three persons involved were ordered to pay compensation amounting to 24,000 euros to each victim. The club was closed down, all cash confiscated and put to a legal purpose. And the examining magistrate was requested to decree closed civil liability in due form of law.

The Supreme Court imposed legal costs on the appellants and ratified all the sentences.

Part V
Recommendations

5.1 Recommendations regarding the definition of Trafficking in Human Beings for labour exploitation

One. Any definition of trafficking should refer expressly to 'labour exploitation', and not to an accumulation of concepts ('forced labour or services, slavery or practices similar to slavery, servitude or begging'), to provide a better match with the actual facts of the situation. Furthermore, allusions to 'labour exploitation' should be directly linked to offences against the rights of workers defined in Arts. 311 and 312 of the Criminal Code. This means that labour exploitation must be identified with the imposition on victims of labour and Social Security conditions that lessen, suppress or diminish rights recognised under labour regulations. Additionally, where national or foreign EU workers are involved, such imposition should necessarily occur by deception or the abuse of a situation of need.

Two. To complement the definition in question, improvements are needed in the regulation of precepts concerning the definition of offences against the rights of workers. These improvements are required in two directions. First, the precepts designed to cover such offences need to overcome their internal logic, in the sense of concentrating exclusively on the perspective of Labour Law, as regards the conception of the persons involved (employer/worker) and work conditions, in order to cover the relationship between self-employed persons and clients as well. Second, regarding labour exploitation offences committed against irregular foreign subjects (Art. 312.2, subsection two of the Criminal Code), infringements against them on Social Security-related issues should be clearly regulated.

Three. In line with the first two recommendations, guarantees should be given that, in all cases, the labour and Social Security conditions taken as the basis for analysis of situations lessening, suppressing or diminishing the rights of workers are Spanish, i.e. the conditions pertaining in the place where the services are rendered, with no exceptions being allowed in the framework of the transnational rendering of services.

Four. The existence of 'new low-intensity forms of labour exploitation' that are not finally deemed offences (being subject to sanctions under administrative Law as a faculty of the Labour Inspectorate) but which also harm the freedom and dignity of persons, should not go unnoticed in the evaluation of the extent or seriousness of cases of trafficking. Control of companies committing this kind of labour-related administrative infringements needs to be extended.

5.2 Recommendations regarding investigation and prosecution

One. While the present dispersal of initiatives concerning trafficking has to be overcome, there is also a pressing need to assimilate the fact that, beyond trafficking for sexual exploitation, trafficking for purposes of labour exploitation also exists, although in most cases the former usually coincides with the latter. As far as overcoming the present dispersal is concerned, the existing Integral Plan needs to be improved at State level, and also needs to be embodied in the Protocols for the country's autonomous communities or regions, to ensure absolute coordination exists between central government and the 17 region governments. This improvement will be achieved through greater cohesion between the players involved in Spain in the fight against the trafficking of human beings. And for that to happen, the present Social Forum on Trafficking needs to be restructured and given greater backing to enable the inclusion in it of the Judiciary and the Labour Inspectorate. Likewise, reinforcement is required for a range of information and communication channels: between the law enforcement authorities and NGOs and between the law enforcement authorities, the Public Prosecutor's Office and the Labour Inspectorate.

Two. Intimately connected with the first recommendation, although in the specific area of the Labour Inspectorate, some specialisation in foreigners is required, in line with the rewarding experience of the Public Prosecutor's Office. This should result in the Inspectorate becoming much more involved and being part of the leading institutional bodies against trafficking and increasing its control over the companies that employ foreign citizens, principally by increasing the regularity of visits and regulating specific action protocols. Further, in sectors detected as being prone to trafficking (e.g. the construction industry, agriculture, hostelry), the Inspectorate should issue quality certificates to any companies demonstrating best practices.

Three. Frontex-related operations (e.g. HERA, SEAHORSE) designed to protect frontiers should be subordinated to the protection of human rights. Assistance and legal services should therefore be reinforced, with personnel training given in trafficking-related issues and asylum policy and with suitable facilities also being made available to ensure such services are provided with full guarantees.

Four. At European level, relations between Labour Inspectorates need to be reinforced, beyond the mere control of multinational companies.

5.3 Recommendations regarding victim protection

One. Specific rescue units need to be set up to identify victims of trafficking of human beings. Such units will need to act in coordination, by means of the corresponding action protocols, with NGOs specializing in the aid and protection of victims.

Two. Organic Law 19/1994 of 23 December, on the protection of witnesses and expert witnesses in criminal cases, needs to be rewritten. The new text should define an integral protection system properly suited to the defence of victims of powerful criminal organisations.

Three. Regulations to develop the measures implemented by Art. 59 bis of the LOEx must lead to the creation of a genuine Statute of integral protection of victims of trafficking, oriented towards the complete physical and psychological recovery of the victims and their social integration.

Chapter 6
The EU Legal Framework on Combating Trafficking in Human Beings for Labour Exploitation

Annemarie Middelburg and Conny Rijken[1]

Introduction

This chapter aims to give an overview of the relevant EU legislation in relation to trafficking in human beings (THB) for labour exploitation.

It is generally acknowledged that THB is both a cause and a consequence of the violation of human rights and, therefore, that THB should be explicitly characterised as a human rights violation.[2] Approaches to combating THB must be inspired by human rights law. This view has been advocated both at the national level by States, as well as at the regional level by the European Union (EU). At the EU level, the European Commission (Commission) and the Council of the European Union (Council) have stated that an integrated approach based on respect for human rights is needed in order to effectively address THB.[3] Equal attention needs to be paid to both. This chapter will focus on how the EU is implementing such an integrated approach.

In general, a human rights-based approach is said to be founded upon a number of core principles: universality and inalienability; indivisibility; interdependence and inter-relatedness; non-discrimination and equality; participation and inclusion; and accountability and the rule of law.[4] In line with the human rights framework, four obligations can be identified to establish a human rights-based framework of action: (i) the criminalisation of THB, (ii) the prosecution of THB, (iii) the assistance and protection of THB

---

[1] At the time of writing, Annemarie Middelburg was a research assistant at Tilburg Law School. Conny Rijken is Associate Professor at Tilburg Law School, European and International Public Law Department and research fellow at INTERVICT (International Victimology Institute Tilburg).

[2] C. Rijken and E. de Volder, 'The European Union's Struggle to Realize a Human Rights-Based Approach to Trafficking in Human Beings: A Call on the EU to Take THB-Sensitive Action in Relevant Areas of Law' (2009) Connecticut Journal of International Law, Volume 25, No. 1, p. 52.

[3] *Communication from the Commission to the European Parliament and the Council, Fighting Trafficking in Human Beings – An Integrated Approach and Proposals for an Action Plan*, at 3, COM (2005) 514 final (Oct. 18, 2005); *The Stockholm Programme–An Open and Secure Europe Serving and Protecting the Citizens*, Council of the EU, Doc. 16484/1/09, 25 November 2009, section 4.4.2.

[4] United Nations Second Interagency Workshop on Implementing a Human Rights-Based Approach in the Context of UN Reform, 5–7 May 2003, *The Human Rights-Based Approach to Development Cooperation Towards a Common Understanding Among UN Agencies*, attachment 1, at 17, 18; United Nations Development Programme, Poverty Reduction and Human Rights: A Practice, Note 5 (June 2003).

victims, and (iv) attention to the root causes of THB.[5] These obligations correspond with the means to combat THB: prosecution (obligations i and ii), protection (obligation iii), and prevention (obligation iv), better known as the three Ps.[6]

Increased knowledge in the EU of the complexity of the crime of THB has led to the realisation that measures and strategies should no longer be limited to the fields of criminal and migration law. What is required is integrated and coordinated action in various fields. Counter-trafficking strategies must be developed in, for instance, labour law, external relations, migration, development policies, economics, gender issues and equality.[7] This report is divided into four main parts, underlining how the specific legal fields are affected by THB countermeasures at the EU level.[8] Part I will focus on criminal law and Part II will deal with labour law. Part III then addresses migration law and part IV will look at external relations. Finally, the conclusion will present suggestions with respect to the EU legislation in relation to THB for labour exploitation.

---

[5] T. Obokata, 'A Human Rights Framework to Address Trafficking of Human Beings' (2006) Netherlands Quarterly Human Rights, Volume 24, p. 387.

[6] C. Rijken and E. de Volder, 'The European Union's Struggle to Realize a Human Rights-Based Approach to Trafficking in Human Beings: A Call on the EU to Take THB-Sensitive Action in Relevant Areas of Law' (2009) Connecticut Journal of International Law, Volume 25, No. 1, p. 53.

[7] Ibid, p. 54.

[8] For the purpose of this report, the fields will be considered separately, but in many cases this fields cannot be easily viewed in separation, as legal measures impact more than one field at the same time.

Part I
Criminal Law

Until recently, THB generally was thought of as only referring to sexual exploitation. This has changed with the adoption of an international definition of THB in the United Nations Protocol to Prevent, Suppress and Punish Trafficking in Persons, Especially Women and Children[9] ('Palermo Protocol'), which extends the scope of THB to include labour exploitation.

1.1 Council Framework Decision on Combating THB[10]

The Council Framework Decision on Combating THB was adopted on 19 July 2002. The Framework Decision seeks to contribute to the fight against THB through the promotion of a common approach to trafficking. The Framework Decision obliged all EU Member States to harmonise their domestic criminal legislation on trafficking by 2004.[11]
Although Member States have generally complied with the obligation set out in the Framework Decisions, the implementation of an effective and comprehensive policy for combating THB required additional efforts. Evaluations of the Commission confirmed that the Framework Decision on Combating THB had significant shortcomings, including: (i) the low number of criminal proceedings (enabling offenders to escape justice) (ii) the lack of assistance, protection or compensation for victims and (iii) insufficient monitoring of the situation.[12]

1.2 Amending the Framework Decision on Combating THB

In March 2009, increased awareness of the limited focus of the Framework Decision on THB led the Commission to issue a proposal to repeal it in order to strengthen the framework of criminal provisions and to ensure better protection for victims. The proposal is based on the Council of Europe Convention on Action against THB, [13] but additionally provides for the

---

[9] Protocol to Prevent, Suppress and Punish Trafficking in Persons, Especially Women and Children, Supplementing the UN Convention Against Transnational Organised Crime, G.A. Res. 55/25, Annex II, U.N. Doc. A/RES/55/25 (8 January 2001).

[10] Council Framework Decision on Combating Trafficking in Human Beings, 2002/629/JHA (19 July 2002), [2002] OJ L203.

[11] C. Rijken and E. de Volder, 'The European Union's Struggle to Realize a Human Rights-Based Approach to Trafficking in Human Beings: A Call on the EU to Take THB-Sensitive Action in Relevant Areas of Law' (2009) Connecticut Journal of International Law, Volume 25, No. 1, p. 55.

[12] Procedure File CNS/2009/0050 (Summary) and MEMO/10/108 (Brussels, 29 March 2010).

[13] Council of Europe Convention on Action against Trafficking in Human Beings, CM (2005) 32 Addendum 1 final, 3 May 2005.

prevention of secondary victimisation and higher standards for assistance to victims.[14] Negotiation did lead to a political adoption on 30 November 2009, but did not lead to the formal adoption of the Framework Decision, because the Lisbon Treaty entered into force on 1 December 2009.

After the Lisbon Treaty entered into force, Framework Decisions could no longer be adopted.[15] Therefore, the proposal to amend the Framework Decision was changed into a Directive.[16] Based on the Council of Europe Convention on Action against Trafficking in Human Beings of May 2005, the European Commission in March 2010 has tabled a new proposal for a Directive on Preventing and Combating THB, and Protecting Victims, repealing Framework Decision 2002/629/JHA, that was formally adopted on 21 March 2011. It is the first agreement between the Council and the European Parliament in the area of substantive criminal law after the Lisbon Treaty came into force.[17] The new Directive applies to all Member States, except Denmark and the United Kingdom.[18] Denmark and the United Kingdom are not be bound by or subject to the application of the Directive.[19] This raises an interesting legal question, namely, to what extent Denmark and the UK remain bound by the Framework Decision when they do not become party to the directive. If they remain bound then this will at least terminate after the transition period of five years as adopted in Article 10 of Protocol 36 to the Lisbon Treaty.[20] In addition, the UK, in accordance with paragraph 4 of this article, can notify the Council that it does not accept the new competences of the institutions in the field of police and judicial cooperation in criminal matters as adopted in the Lisbon Treaty. It is explicitly mentioned in this paragraph that if the UK does make such a notification all acts in the field of police and judicial cooperation in criminal matters shall cease to apply after the period of transition.[21]

---

[14] C. Rijken and E. de Volder, 'The European Union's Struggle to Realize a Human Rights-Based Approach to Trafficking in Human Beings: A Call on the EU to Take THB-Sensitive Action in Relevant Areas of Law' (2009) Connecticut Journal of International Law, Volume 25, No. 1, p. 57.

[15] See further below, section 1.3.1.

[16] Proposal for a Directive on Preventing and Combating THB, and Protecting Victims, repealing Framework Decision 2002/629/JHA COM (2010) 95 final – 2010/0065 (COD).

[17] Before the Lisbon Treaty, EU legislation on criminal law was not decided by both institutions on an equal footing, but by a unanimous decision in the Council after mere consultation of the European Parliament.

[18] Report on the proposal for a Directive of the European Parliament and of the Council on Preventing and Combating Trafficking in Human Beings, and Protecting Victims, Repealing Framework Decision 2002/629/JHA (COM(2010)0095 – C7-0087/2010 – 2010/0065(COD)), A7-0348/2010, Recital 21–23.

[19] Ibid, Recital 22.

[20] Protocol 36 to the Lisbon Treaty, on Transitional Provisions, Article 10 paras 1–4.

[21] See also S. Peers, *'Statewatch Analysis – The New Directive on Trafficking in Persons'*, 26 November 2010 <http://www.statewatch.org/analyses/no-113-trafficking.pdf> accessed 15 March 2011.

The aim of the directive is to 'establish minimum rules concerning the definition of criminal offences and sanctions in the area of trafficking in human beings.' It also aims to 'introduce common provisions, taking into account the gender perspective, to strengthen the prevention of the crime and the protection of its victims.'[22]

Article 2(1) of the directive defines THB as: 'The recruitment, transportation, transfer, harbouring or reception of persons, including exchange or transfer of control over that person, by means of the threat or use of force or other forms of coercion, of abduction, of fraud, of deception, of the abuse of power or of a position of vulnerability or of the giving or receiving of payments or benefits to achieve the consent of a person having control over another person, for the purpose of exploitation.'[23]

The main difference with the former definition is that exploitation now also includes begging and the removal of organs, and that an open formulation of forms of force is used.[24]

The directive includes three new legal elements of added value:

(i) *Victim assistance and support*: the directive includes provisions for the establishment of mechanisms for early identification and assistance of victims (Article 10(4)). The assistance and support measures comprise a higher standard, especially regarding medical treatment (including psychological assistance, counselling and information), but also regarding accommodation, assistance, translation and interpretation where appropriate (Article 10(5)). An important provision is Article 10(3), because this article states that the victim's willingness to cooperate in the criminal investigation, prosecution and trial is not a condition for assistance and support of a victim.[25] On top of that, special measures for child victims of THB are present in the Directive. Article 12 states that the child's best interest shall be a primary consideration. There are specific provisions in Article 13 and 14, (such as physical and psycho-social assistance and the possibility of appointing a guardian or a representative for the child victim where necessary) to assist, support and protect child victims of THB.

(ii) *Protection of victims in criminal proceedings*: Article 11 of the directive includes provisions on special treatment aimed at preventing secondary victimisation, protection on the basis of a risk assessment, and legal counselling and representation (including for the purpose of claiming compensation). Legal counselling and legal representation should be free of charge when the victim does not have sufficient financial resources. More specifically, Article 11(4) includes provisions for specific

[22] Report on the proposal for the new Directive, Article 1.

[23] *Report on the proposal for the new Directive*, Article 2(1).

[24] *Report on the proposal for the new Directive*, Article 2(3).

[25] The cooperation of victims in the criminal investigation, prosecution and trial, is a condition in Directive 2004/81/EC (and similar national rules), but not in the new directive.

treatment. Member States shall avoid (a) unnecessary repetition of interviews during investigation, prosecution and trial, (b) visual contact between victims and offenders including during the giving of evidence such as interviews and cross-examination, by appropriate means including the use of appropriate communication technologies, (c) the giving of evidence in open court and (d) unnecessary questioning concerning the victim's private life.

(iii) *Prevention*: the directive includes provisions on action aimed at discouraging and reducing the demand side of THB. Member States shall take appropriate actions aimed at raising awareness and reducing the risk of people becoming victims of THB. Additionally, Member States shall consider taking measures to establish as a criminal offence the use of services which are the objects of exploitation, with the knowledge that the person has been trafficked (Article 15).

In addition, Article 7 ensures a broader scope of the provision on non-application (non-punishment clause). Member States shall, in accordance with the basic principles of their legal systems, take the necessary measures to ensure that competent national authorities are entitled not to prosecute or impose penalties on victims of THB for their involvement in criminal activities that they have been compelled to commit as a direct consequence of being subjected to THB.

In Article 9, the grounds for jurisdiction have been extended, in line with the Council of Europe Convention. Furthermore, a new provision on the seizure and confiscation of instrumentalities and proceeds of THB was adopted in the final text on the proposal of the European Parliament. A new provision on compensation was adopted as well.

Finally, Article 16 of the directive states that 'in order to contribute to a coordinated and consolidated strategy of the European Union against trafficking in human beings, Member States shall facilitate the tasks of an Anti-Trafficking Coordinator (ATC).' The ATC will improve coordination and coherence between EU institutions, EU agencies, Member States, third countries and international actors. The ATC will help elaborate existing and new EU policies relevant to the fight against THB and provide overall strategic policy orientation for the EU's external policy in this field. [26] The ATC will also contribute to the Commission reports on the progress made in the fight against THB. These reports should be presented to the Council and the European Parliament every two years.[27]

[26] Europa.eu, *'The Commission appoints an EU Anti-Trafficking Coordinator'*, IP/10/1715, Brussels, 14 December 2010, Press Release <http://europa.eu /rapid /press Releases Action.do? reference =IP/10/ 1715&format= HTML&aged =0&language=EN&guiLanguage=en> accessed 15 March 2011.

[27] Press Release, 3051st Council meeting, Justice and Home Affairs, Brussels, 2–3 December 2010, 16918/10, PRESSE 322, PR CO 41, 20–25 <http://www .consilium .europa.eu/uedocs/cms_data/docs/pressdata/en/jha/118183.pdf> accessed 15 March 2011.

The European Commission decided on 14 December 2010 to appoint Ms Myria Vassiliadou to the position of European ATC and she started on 1 March 2011. At the same time, in December 2010, the European Parliament voted in favour of the Directive on Preventing and Combating THB, and Protecting Victims which was then formally adopted on 21 March 2011.

1.3 Cooperation in Criminal Matters within the EU

In this section, the possibilities for cooperation in THB cases within the EU are explored. We will see that, within the EU, a sophisticated and widespread system exists for this cooperation which for a large part is not explicitly designed to combat THB, but which can be used when dealing with transnational THB cases. In the field of cooperation in criminal matters one can distinguish between police cooperation and judicial cooperation, both of which are, together with migration policy and police and judicial cooperation in civil matters, part of the Area of Freedom, Security and Justice. Developments in the field of police and judicial cooperation in criminal matters took place at an ever-accelerating pace, especially after the Treaty of Amsterdam and now again after the Lisbon Treaty came into force. In this section, the measures most relevant for the combating of THB for labour exploitation will be discussed after a more general explanation of the current legal framework in this field. It would go beyond the scope of this chapter to include as well the implementation, application and effectiveness of these measures and therefore these aspects are absent here.[28]

1.3.1 EU legal framework in the Area of Freedom, Security and Justice

With the coming into force of the Lisbon Treaty on 1 December 2009 the pillar structure of the EU has been abolished and the former third pillar has been communautarised. This means that, in the area of police and judicial cooperation, the ordinary legislative procedure will be applied (meaning decision-taking jointly by the Council of Ministers and the European Parliament by qualified majority voting) and that measures that can be adopted are decisions, directives and regulations. Furthermore, the European Court of Justice (ECJ) now renamed the Court of Justice of the EU (CoJ) will become fully competent in this area as well, (with some exceptions).[29] However, due to the transitional period adopted in Article 10 of the 36th Protocol to the Lisbon Treaty, the instruments that were in force on 1 December 2009

---

[28] For more general information and elaboration on the European Criminal Law see: A. Klip, *European Criminal Law*, Intersentia, 2009; S. Peers, *EU Justice and Home Affairs Law*, Oxford EU Law Library, 2011; V. Mitsilegas, *European Criminal Law*, Hart Publishing, 2009; M. Fletcher (et al), *EU Criminal Law and Justice*, Elgar European Law, 2008.

[29] K. Leanaerts, 'The Contribution of the European Court of Justice to the Area of Freedom, Security and Justice' (2010) International and Comparative Law Quarterly, Volume 59, 255–301.

(primarily Framework Decisions) remain in force until they are amended in accordance with the Lisbon Framework. That means that the competence of the CoJ only becomes fully applicable after the amendment of the pre-Lisbon instruments.

1.3.2 Law Enforcement Information Exchange

The jumble of systems available for law enforcement information exchange within the EU is the main characteristic of this field of police cooperation. Within the various systems of law enforcement information exchange, two main types can be distinguished: indirect and direct information exchange. The latter can be further subdivided into conditional and unconditional direct exchange. Indirect exchange of law enforcement information means following a formal request transmitted through the (central) authorities of a State[30] or through centralised national units.[31] This form of information exchange can be considered the traditional one, but it is still applied, especially, but not exclusively, with countries outside the EU. This type of information exchange has been formalised within Europol, for instance, where information is exchanged from, via, and to the Europol Liaison Officers (LIO), who represent the Europol National Units of the Member States.[32] Because of enhanced police cooperation within the EU and especially since the coming into force of the Convention Implementing the Schengen Agreement (CISA), this type of information exchange has been supplemented with other forms of information exchange.[33] An important document relating to indirect information exchange is the Framework Decision (Framework Decision) on simplifying the exchange of information and intelligence, which aims to streamline the procedure for information exchange on request.[34] This

[30] The exchange of information with private actors falls within this category, such as the exchange of passenger data based on the Council Directive of 29 April 2004 on the Obligation of Carriers to Communicate Passenger Data [2004] OJ L261/24; data retention based on the Directive of 15 March 2006 on the Retention of Data Generated or Processed in Connection with the Provisions of Publicly Available Electronic Communications Services or Public Communications Networks and amending Directive 2002/58/EC [2006] OJ L106/54, and the agreements between the EU and Canada and between the EU and the US on PNR (Passenger Name Record) [2006] OJ L82/14 and [2007] L 204/16 respectively.

[31] Examples of these are the Schengen Information System (SIS), the Europol Information System (EIS), the Customs Information System (CIS), the Visa Information System (VIS), and Eurodac on the storage of fingerprints and control images.

[32] Council Decision 2009/371/JHA of 6 April 2009 establishing the European Police Office (Europol) [2009] OJ L121/37, Article 9(3).

[33] Article 39 of the CISA provided for the direct information exchange between law enforcement authorities.

[34] Council Framework Decision 2006/960/JHA of 18 December 2006 on Simplifying the Exchange of Information and Intelligence between Law Enforcement Authorities of the Member States of the EU [2006] OJ L386/89. Although it was suggested that a Framework Decision should be adopted to further enhance the principle of availability,

document is new in the sense that it is not limited to law enforcement information, but also includes intelligence as well as information and intelligence, that is kept by other than competent law enforcement authorities.[35] Time limits for providing information are imposed and a request must be made using a special application form.

In case of unconditional direct exchange, law enforcement information is directly accessible to law enforcement authorities from other Member States without any further restrictions, for instance, through direct access to databases or through a direct request to law enforcement officers in another Member State. Conditional direct information exchange, in contrast to unconditional direct information exchange, is often based on a 'hit/no hit' system. In such a case, authorities from another country may search a national or EU database by inserting details on a person, an object, or a case. If there is a hit or a match, it means that further information on the person or object whose details were inserted, becomes available. The further information on the person or object will not be made directly available to the foreign authority; this authority will first have to make a request to that end.

On 27 April 2009, the Framework Decision on the Organisation and Content of the Exchange of Information Extracted from the Criminal Records between Member States came into force; it provides for the conditional direct exchange of information on sentenced persons. Convictions contained in criminal records will be exchanged EU-wide according to a common procedure based on the use of a standardised electronic form. According to Point 6, the aim of the Framework Decision is 'to improve the exchange of information on convictions and, where imposed and entered in the criminal records of the convicting Member State, on disqualifications arising from criminal convictions of citizens of the Union.' The Framework Decision is a further means to enable the execution of the Framework Decision on Taking Account of Convictions in the Member States of the EU in the course of new criminal proceedings.[36] For the smooth operation of this Framework Decision and especially with the aim of implementing Article 11, the European Criminal Records Information System (ECRIS) was established, which is

---

the Commission did not consider this document suitable for that aim. Commission Staff Working Document – Annex to the Proposal for a Council Framework Decision on the Exchange of Information under the Principle of Availability, SEC (2005)1207 of 12 October 2005.

[35] Whether information must be labelled as law enforcement information mainly depends on the aim for which information was collected and on the authority that has collected the information. Law enforcement information can be defined as 'any type or information, which is held by law enforcement authorities' and information held 'by public authorities or private entities which is available to law enforcement authorities without the taking of coercive measures'.

[36] [2008] OJ L220/32. According to Article 1: 'the purpose of this Framework Decision is to determine the conditions under which, in the course of criminal proceedings in a Member State against a person, previous convictions handed down against the same person for different facts in other Member States are taken into account.'

aimed at improving the quality of information exchange on convictions.[37]

The Prüm Decision can be considered to encompass both conditional and unconditional direct information exchange.[38] The purpose of the Prüm Decision was to create a network of national databases to facilitate information exchange between law enforcement officers by allowing access to the national databases on DNA profiles, fingerprints, and vehicle registration data. Another example of the conditional direct information exchange can be found in the Schengen Information System.[39] The information that is stored in the SIS concerns persons wanted for arrest or extradition purposes, third-country nationals who must be refused entry into the Schengen territory, missing persons, witnesses, and persons to be put under discrete surveillance. Apart from indirect information exchange through the Europol Liaison Officers, both the conditional and unconditional direct information exchange takes place at Europol.[40] In relation to direct information exchange, there are basically two options within Europol: through the Europol Information

[37] Council Decision 2009/316/JHA of 6 April 2009 on the establishment of the European Criminal Records Information System (ECRIS) in application of Article 11 of the Framework Decision 2009/315/JHA [2009] OJ L93/23.

[38] The Prüm Convention is named after the town in Germany where it was signed on 27 May 2005 by Austria, Belgium, Germany, France, Luxembourg, the Netherlands, and Spain. Although established outside the EU legal framework, the Prüm Convention was later incorporated into the EU legal framework on the basis of two Decisions; Council Decision 2008/615/JHA of 23 June 2008 on the Stepping up of Cross-border Cooperation, Particularly in Combating Terrorism and Cross-border Crime [2008] OJ L210/1, and Council Decision 2008/616/JHA of 23 June 2008 on the Implementation of Decision 2008/615/JHA on the Stepping Up of Cross-border Cooperation, Particularly in Combating Terrorism and Cross-border Crime [2008] OJ L210/12.

[39] Although the Schengen acquis was integrated in the EU system and allocated under either the former first or the third pillar, the Schengen origin of the documents is still relevant because Norway and Iceland were full partners in the Schengen acquis, and the UK and Ireland were initially not partners but joined through the adoption of the Schengen acquis with the Treaty of Amsterdam, although they have claimed a *status aparte* in the application of the whole acquis. See Protocol to the TEU on the position of the UK and Ireland. See also M. Fletcher, 'Schengen, the European Court of Justice and Flexibility under the Lisbon Treaty: Balancing the United Kingdom's 'Ins' and 'Outs'' (2009) European Constitutional Law Review, Volume 5, pp. 71–98; E. Fahey, 'Swimming in a Sea of Law: Reflections on Water Borders, Irish (-British)- Euro Relations and Opting-out and Opting-in after the Treaty of Lisbon' (2010) Common Market Law Review, Volume 47, No. 3, pp. 673–707. The Swiss joined the Schengen area later.

[40] The Europol Convention has now been replaced by the Europol Decision, which entered into force on 1 January 2010, Council Decision of 6 April 2009 establishing the European Police Office (Europol), 2009/371/JHA [2009] OJ L121/37. Europol's mandate has been extended to all serious forms of crime irrespective of their relation to organised crime. Europol staff will not be vested with operational powers, but they may request the Member States to initiate, conduct, or coordinate investigations. Member States have to inform Europol if (and why) they do not react positively to such a request.

System (EIS) or through an Analysis Work File (AWF).[41]

All these channels for law enforcement information exchange raise questions as to the reliability of the data, the purpose for which the data is collected and used, and the possibility of having your data deleted, for instance. These questions on Data Protection led to the adoption of the Framework Decision on Data Protection, with which an all-inclusive instrument, generally applicable to police and judicial cooperation in criminal matters, became available. The Framework Decision serves as the counterpart of the Data Protection Directive that was established under the EC.[42] The especially well-established principles on data protection that were developed based on the Council of Europe Convention on Data Protection were a source of inspiration for the Framework Decision.[43] However, the scope of the Framework Decision is considered to be limited and not to provide sufficient protection. Therefore, a new instrument meeting these aims is now being considered.

1.3.3 Joint Investigation Teams

As the name suggests, a Joint Investigation Team is a team in which police and judicial authorities from more than one State work together on the investigation of a case with a considerable transnational component. The JIT framework was introduced in the EU Convention on Mutual Assistance, and almost literally copied into the Framework Decision on JITs to accelerate the

[41] A. De Moor and G. Vermeulen, 'The Europol Council Decision: Transforming Europol into an Agency of the European Union' (2010) Common Market Law Review, Volume 47, pp. 1089–1121.

[42] This Directive concerns the processing of commercial data generally performed by private parties in the course of their business. Directive 95/46/EC of the European Parliament and of the Council of 24 October 1995 on the Protection of Individuals with Regard to the Processing of Personal Data and on the Free Movement of Such Data [1995] OJ L281/31.

[43] These principles can be found in Chapter II of the CoE Data Protection Convention and include the quality of data (including the purpose limitation, meaning that the data cannot be used for purposes other than that for which it was collected, that data is kept up to date and will be stored no longer than is necessary), special categories of data (meaning that data revealing racial origin, political opinions, or religious or other beliefs, data concerning health or sexual life, and personal data relating to criminal convictions is not automatically processed), data security (without any concretisation of how data must be protected), and the rights of data subjects (including the right to be informed, to have data corrected and deleted if necessary, and the right to legal remedies if the former rights cannot be exercised). The data protection principles are considered to be one of the components of data protection. The other components are the establishment of independent supervisory authorities and the notification/registration system. The rights of data subjects are sometimes considered a separate component and are not included in the data protection principles.

coming into force of this provision.[44] One of the most profitable elements of a JIT is the potential to conduct investigative activities in the Member States that are members of the JIT without the formalities of a request for mutual assistance. The seconded members of the State where the activities need to take place can conduct them as if they were requested in national proceedings.[45] The information resulting from these activities will be directly available for further investigations in the JIT, as well as for investigations in the State where the activities were carried out. In accordance with their national laws, JIT members may share information available in their home country within the JIT. Conversely, in accordance with paragraph 10 of Article 13, information obtained by a JIT may be used for the purpose: a) for which the team has been set up, b) of detecting, investigating, and prosecuting other criminal offences with prior consent of the providing MS, c) of preventing an immediate and serious threat to public security, and d) of other purposes to the extent that this is agreed between the Member States of the JIT.[46] A further additional value of a JIT is that representatives of third states, as well as agencies such as Europol and Eurojust, can also participate in a JIT.

1.3.4 Judicial Cooperation in Criminal Matters

The acts adopted in this area aim to facilitate judicial cooperation (such as mutual legal assistance, extradition, execution of sentences, etc.) and are, explicitly or implicitly, based on the principle of mutual recognition. In general, the characteristics of the legal acts adopted in the field of judicial cooperation are more or less comparable and can be summarised as follows. Requests relating to a freezing order, an evidence warrant, or an arrest warrant are communicated directly between the competent authorities and are executed as if they were requested in a national procedure. The grounds to refuse the request are generally limited and the starting point for execution is 'yes, unless'. Formally, infringements of human and fundamental rights are not considered to be grounds for refusal. In general, the double criminality requirement will not be imposed for the 32 crimes that were first listed in the European arrest warrant and later copied into a number of other documents. A requesting or issuing state may indicate the requirements that have to be taken into account when executing the request, which the executing state has to comply with, unless they are contrary to its fundamental principles of law (the principle of *forum regit actum* instead of *locus regit actum*).[47] To further facilitate judicial cooperation, often a standardised form must be used. As the procedures for traditional mutual legal assistance requests were often time-

[44] C. Rijken and G. Vermeulen (eds), *Joint Investigation Teams in the EU, From Theory to Practice,* (TMC Asser Press, 2006) pp. 10–13. On this duel legal basis see also C. Rijken, 'Joint Investigation Teams: Principles, Practice, and Problems. Lessons Learnt From the First Efforts to Establish a JIT' (2006) Utrecht Law Review, Volume 2, pp. 99–118.

[45] EU Convention on Mutual Assistance 2005, Art. 13(7).

[46] EU Convention on Mutual Assistance 2005, Art. 13(10).

[47] See, for instance, European Evidence Warrant (EEW), Art. 12.

consuming, it must be considered a considerable advantage that time limits have been included in many of the new instruments, which will speed up the procedures.

The Framework Decision on the European Arrest Warrant (EAW) is probably the most debated and, at the same time, the most used instrument in European criminal law, providing for a simplified and fast procedure for the surrender of suspects and convicted persons between Member States.[48] In the EAW, serious limitations to the 'traditional' grounds to refuse extradition of suspects or sentenced persons were also made, including the possible violation of a person's fundamental rights.[49] Based on the 'success' of the EAW and faced with the difficulties of the transmission of evidence within the EU, the Framework Decision on the European Evidence Warrant (EEW) was adopted. The EEW is also based on the principle of mutual recognition and supplements the Framework Decision on the execution in the EU of orders to freeze property and evidence.[50] The EEW has a limited scope: excluded from

---

[48] N. Keijzer and E. Van Sliedregt (eds), *The European Arrest Warrant in Practice* (T.M.C. Asser Press 2009); E. Guild and L. Marin, *Still not Resolved: Constitutional Issues of the European Arrest Warrant* (Wolf Legal Publishers 2009); E. Guild (ed), *Constitutional Challenges to the European Arrest Warrant: A Challenge for European Law: The Merging of Internal and External Security* (Wolf Legal Publishers 2006); R. Blekxtoon and W. Van Ballegooi, *Handbook on the European Arrest Warrant* (T.M.C. Asser Press 2005); E. Fahey, 'How to Be a Third Pillar Guardian of Fundamental Rights? The Irish Supreme Court and the European Arrest Warrant' (2008) European Law Review, Volume 33, pp. 563–576; O. Pollicino, 'European Arrest Warrant and Constitutional Principles of the Member States: A Case Law-Based Outline in the Attempt to Strike the Right Balance Between Interacting Legal Systems' (2008) German Law Journal, Volume 9, pp. 1313–1355; R. Davidson, 'A Sledgehammer to Crack a Nut? Should There be a Bar of Triviality in European Arrest Warrant Cases?' (2009) The Criminal Law Review, pp. 31–36; Cumberland and Carson, 'Fair Trials International Case Notes: the European Arrest Warrant and Unreasonable Delay' (2008) Journal of European Criminal Law, Volume 3, p. 59; M. Mackerel, 'The European Arrest Warrant – The Early Years: Implementing and Using the Warrant' (2007) European Journal of Crime, Volume 15, pp. 37–66; F; Impala, 'The European Arrest Warrant in the Italian Legal System, Between Mutual Recognition and Mutual Fear Within the European Area of Freedom, Security and Justice' (2005) Utrecht Law Review, Volume 1, pp. 56–78; M. Plachta, 'European Arrest Warrant: Revolution in Extradition?' (2003) European Journal of Crime, Volume 11, Criminal Law and Criminal Justice, pp. 178–194.

[49] M. Mackarel, 'Human Rights as a Barrier to Surrender' in: Keijzer and van Sliedregt (eds) pp. 139–156.

[50] Concerning the facilitation of the collection and transfer of evidence in the (pre-)trial phase, quite a number of legal acts and systems exist in parallel, which make the legal framework not only complicated and opaque for judicial authorities, but for suspects and individuals affected by these acts and systems as well. That was the reason for the Commission to produce a Green Paper to consult with the stakeholders in this field on one single system for obtaining evidence in criminal matters. Green Paper on obtaining evidence in criminal matters from one Member State to another and securing its admissibility, COM (2009)624 final, 11 November 2009. The Commission states that the existence of multiple systems for obtaining evidence is based on different principles,

the EEW are the *taking* of evidence from interviews, statements, or hearings, the *taking* of evidence from a person's body, real-time evidence, such as interceptions of communications or the monitoring of bank accounts, evidence requiring analysis of existing objects, documents, or data, and evidence related to data retention.[51] Other relevant instruments are the Framework Decision on Alternative Sanctions and Suspended Sentences which was adopted together with the Framework Decision on Transfer of Custodial Sentences (short names).[52] These two Framework Decisions supplement one another. The Framework Decisions apply to offenders not living in the State of conviction and are aimed at facilitating the social rehabilitation of the sentenced persons. They are, of course, also aimed at ensuring the EU-wide execution of measures connected to probation and alternative sanctions. Because of the large differences between the Member States, the application of the principle of mutual recognition in this regard is far-reaching since Member States receiving a request for execution are in general obliged to recognise the decision ('yes, unless'). The Framework Decision on the transfer of custodial sentences enables sentenced persons to be transferred to another MS for enforcement of their sentences, better facilitating social rehabilitation. The Framework Decision on taking account of convictions[53] concerns the multiple convictions of the same person for different acts and will encourage Member States to take into account previous convictions in other Member States.

Despite all these developments, an overall measure on procedural rights in this field has not been adopted. This issue has been under discussion since 2004 when the Commission launched its proposal for a Framework Decision on procedural rights, but Member States have not managed to give this priority

---

namely, mutual assistance and mutual recognition. This makes the application of the rules burdensome and may cause confusion among practitioners, which might hinder effective cross-border cooperation. On 29 April 2010 an initiative for a Directive regarding the European Investigation Order in criminal matters was launched, providing one overall legal mechanism for cross-border evidence gathering. Council of the EU, Brussels, 29 April 2010, 9145/10.

[51] Framework Decision on the European Evidence Warrant, Article 4(2).

[52] Council Framework Decision 2008/947/JHA of 27 November 2008 on the Application of the Principle of Mutual Recognition to Judgments and Probation Decisions with a View to the Supervision of Probation Measures and Alternative Sanctions [2008] OJ L337/112, and Council Framework Decision 2008/909/JHA of 27 November 2008 on the Application of the Principle of Mutual Recognition to Judgments in Criminal Matters Imposing Custodial Sentences or Measures Involving Deprivation of Liberty for the Purpose of Their Enforcement in the European Union [2008] OJ L327/27.

[53] Council Framework Decision 2008/675/JHA of 24 July 2008 on taking account of convictions in the Member States of the European Union in the course of new criminal proceedings [2008] OJ L220/32.

and come to an overall decision on procedural rights.[54] Only recently some progress has been made in the further development of these rights.[55] The Council has agreed on a Roadmap to identify areas for legislative initiatives and a step-by-step approach, bearing in mind the complexity of the issues.[56] The areas that are identified in the Roadmap are: translation and interpretation; information on rights and information about the charges; legal advice and legal aid; communication with relatives, employers, and consular authorities; special safeguards for suspected or accused persons who are vulnerable; and a Green Paper on pre-trial detention. The first step has now been taken with the adoption of a Directive on the right to interpretation and translation in criminal proceedings.[57] A proposal for a second directive has now been tabled.[58] Although action at EU level in this area is highly welcomed, the content and limited scope of the Roadmap is disappointing.

1.3.5 Europol and Eurojust

The Europol Drugs Unit (EDU), which became operational on 3 January 1994, preceded the establishment of Europol which took up its full activities on 1 July 1999. Its primary function is to gather and analyse information held by the different national police forces. With the adoption of the Council

[54] The first proposal for a Council Framework Decision was launched on 28 April 2004, COM (2004) 328 final. Since then, negotiations on this proposal have taken place and several counterproposals have been made, every time diminishing the guaranteed procedural rights. Also Jimeno-Bulnes, 'The Proposal for a Council Framework Decision on Certain Procedural Rights in Criminal Proceedings Throughout the European Union' in Guild et al. (eds), *Security versus Justice?* (Ashgate 2008) pp. 171–202.

[55] On 23 October 2009, the JHA Council agreed on the general approach to a package of documents aimed at strengthening procedural rights of suspected or accused persons in criminal proceedings. See Resolution of the Council on a Roadmap for strengthening procedural rights of suspected or accused persons in criminal proceedings, Brussels, 24 November 2009, Doc. 15434/09. Two proposals were launched on the first step of the Roadmap, namely, on the right to interpretation and translation; one by a group of 13 Member States on 22 January 2010 (who had already proposed a Framework Decision under the pre-Lisbon legal framework) and another by the Commission on 9 March 2010, Brussels COM(2010)82. These two proposals were merged into one document. On 16 June 2010 the European Parliament adopted the proposal. Proposal for a Directive of the European Parliament and of the Council on the Right to Interpretation and Translation in Criminal Proceedings, COM (2010)82 final.

[56] Resolution of the Council on a Roadmap for strengthening procedural rights of suspected or accused persons in criminal proceedings, Brussels 24 November 2009, 15434/09.

[57] Directive 2010/64/EU on the Right to Interpretation and Translation in Criminal Procedures [2010] OJ L280.

[58] Proposal for a Directive from the European Parliament and the Council on the Right to Information in Criminal Procedures, COM (2010) 392/3.

Decision Establishing the European Police Office[59] the Europol Convention was replaced, enabling a more rapid and flexible adaptation of Europol's legal framework and to new trends in crime if needed. The Decision entered into force on 1 January 2010. Europol's mandate has been extended to all serious forms of crime, independent of their relation to organised crime. This includes THB.

Eurojust is the counterpart of Europol for judicial cooperation in criminal matters. Although it was established much later, namely in 2002, it seems that it has consolidated its position very rapidly and Member States easily found their way in Eurojust. Eurojust is competent on all Europol crimes and may assist, at the request of Member States, in the context of any other crime, including THB.[60] Eurojust personnel can act as national members or members of the Eurojust College. If they act as national members, they keep and execute their competences in the way these competences have been granted under national law. However, since the decision to strengthen Eurojust, it has become necessary to streamline the competences of the national members. Summarising the objectives of Eurojust, Eurojust must stimulate and improve the coordination of investigations and prosecutions, improve the cooperation between the competent authorities of Member States, facilitate mutual legal assistance and the implementation of extradition, and otherwise support judicial cooperation.[61] The competences of the national members and the College, (Articles 6 and 7 of the Eurojust Decision, respectively) overlap to a large extent. They can ask Member States to undertake or refrain from undertaking an investigation or prosecution, to coordinate and assist in investigations or prosecutions, to provide information, to set up JITs, to facilitate communications, and to take special investigative measures or any other measures. The College has an extra task in such logistical support as translations, interpretation, and the organisation of coordination meetings. Furthermore, it is competent to give non-binding written opinions on conflicts of jurisdiction and on recurrent refusals or difficulties in Mutual Legal Assistance. If Member States do not follow such opinions, they have to inform Eurojust and give their reasons why.

In conclusion, it can be stated that over recent years the field of European Criminal Law has developed considerably and has now become a mature part within European Law. Although the system must be further streamlined and refined, the measures adopted so far do facilitate criminal cooperation to a large extent; however further improvements will be constantly needed in such a dynamic field.

---

[59] Council Decision of 6 April 2009 Establishing the European Police Office (Europol), 2009/371/JHA [2009] OJ L121/37, entered into force on 1 January 2010.

[60] Council Decision 2009/426/JHA of 16 December 2008 on the strengthening of Eurojust and amending Decision 2002/187/JHA setting up Eurojust with a view to reinforcing the fight against serious crime [2009] OJ L138/14, Article 4.

[61] Decision setting up Eurojust with a view to reinforcing the fight against serious crime [2002] OJ L63/1, Article 3(1).

Part II
Labour Law

2.1 Introduction

The Palermo Protocol definition of THB includes labour exploitation. Consequently, in some cases, migrants working under harsh labour conditions can be considered victims of THB. Therefore, a minimum standard of protection for social security rights has to be guaranteed within the EU. In this section it will be explored to what extent the EU does provide such a standard. But first the question of how forced labour is defined in relation to THB at the international level will be looked at.[62] Article 2(1) of the ILO Forced and Compulsory Labour Convention[63] defines forced labour as 'all work or service which is exacted from any person under the menace of any penalty and for which the said person has not offered himself voluntarily.'[64] This definition contains two essential elements: a penalty (not only including penal sanctions, but also the loss of rights and privileges) and involuntarily offered labour. In *Siliadin v. France*[65] the European Court of Human Rights (ECtHR) added that a penalty does not necessarily have to be imposed on an individual for them to be considered a victim.[66] According to the ECtHR, it is adequate that the victim feels that he/she has been penalised by the perceived seriousness of the threat he/she was under.[67] The unwillingness of the victim to provide services or labour should be seen as a subjective element. According to the European Commission on Human Rights, services cannot be treated as voluntarily accepted beforehand. [68] Even in the situation where people voluntarily accept work, they may eventually revoke their consent because of dreadful working conditions.[69] Strictly speaking, this situation is not included in the definition of the ILO Convention. However, we generally regard this

[62] For more elaboration on this aspect see J. Beirnaert, 'A Labour Perspective on Combating Trafficking in and the Role of Trade Unions', Chapter 10 in this book.
[63] ILO, Forced and Compulsory Labour Convention, ILO Doc. C29 (10 June 1930).
[64] Ibid, Art. 2.
[65] *Siliadin v. France*, 43 ECtHR 16, 36 (2006).
[66] C. Rijken and E. de Volder, 'The European Union's Struggle to Realize a Human Rights-Based Approach to Trafficking in Human Beings: A call on the EU to Take THB-Sensitive Action in Relevant Areas of Law' (2009) Connecticut Journal of International Law, Volume 25, No. 1, p. 61.
[67] *Siliadin v. France*, 43 ECtHR. 16, 36 (2006).
[68] *Van der Müssele v. Belgium*, 6 ECtHR 163, 175 (1984).
[69] C. Rijken and E. de Volder, 'The European Union's Struggle to Realize a Human Rights-Based Approach to Trafficking in Human Beings: A call on the EU to Take THB-Sensitive Action in Relevant Areas of Law' (2009) Connecticut Journal of International Law, Volume 25, No. 1, p. 61.

also as a form of forced labour.[70] Furthermore, a wider interpretation of the definition of forced labour can be seen in case law at national level.[71]

2.2 The Posting Directive[72]

The Posting Directive of the European Parliament and of the Council was adopted in connection with Article 52 of the EC Treaty on 16 December 1996 and came into force in December 1999. The Directive constituted an integral part of the EC Action programme, linked to the Community Charter of Fundamental Rights of Workers.[73] The Posting Directive applies to non-self-employed service providers. The Posting Directive introduced 'posting', which is the situation whereby an employer sends an employee to work temporarily in another country, within the juridical sphere of labour law.[74] The Directive aims to strike a balance between the economic freedoms enshrined in the TFEU, namely, the freedom to provide services, with the rights of employees during their period of posting. It is debatable whether the Directive meets this aim. The Directive seeks to ensure that workers who are temporarily posted to another Member State are subjected to and protected by the laws of that State, in relation to the so-called core conditions of employment.[75] Article 3(1) of the Directive includes the mandatory rules that make up the core conditions of employment: maximum work periods and minimum rest periods; minimum paid annual holidays; minimum rates of pay, health, safety and hygiene at work; equal treatment of men and women; and other non-discrimination provisions.[76] For all the other issues related to the posting of workers the host country may not impose any obligations apart from those allowed under Article 3.

In practice, host countries adjust the core conditions applicable to posted workers to their own labour standards. In this way, the Directive protects

---

[70] The ILO Forced and Compulsory Labour Convention dates back to 1930. Over time, the impact and forms of forced labour have developed and changed. Therefore, the definition is not quite up to date and a wider interpretation is applied in case law.

[71] See for example a case in the Netherlands about Chinese workers in a restaurant, LJN BI7097, 27 October 2009, 08/03894.

[72] Council Directive 96/71 concerning the posting of workers in the framework of the provision of services [1997] OJ L018/1.

[73] J. Cremers, J.E. Dolvik and G. Bosch, 'Posting of Workers in the Single Market: Attempts to Prevent Social Dumping and Regime Competition in the EU' (2007) Industrial Relations Journal, Volume 38, p. 527.

[74] J. Cremers, J.E. Dolvik and G. Bosch, 'Posting of Workers in the Single Market: Attempts to Prevent Social Dumping and Regime Competition in the EU' (2007) Industrial Relations Journal, Volume 38, p. 527.

[75] C. Rijken and E. de Volder, 'The European Union's Struggle to Realize a Human Rights-Based Approach to Trafficking in Human Beings: A call on the EU to Take THB-Sensitive Action in Relevant Areas of Law' (2009) Connecticut Journal of International Law, Volume 25, No. 1, p. 64.

[76] Council Directive 96/71 [1997] OJ L018/1, Article 3(1).

posted workers, but also serves as a protective measure against the social dumping of wages and bad working circumstances in countries with proper working conditions. By aiming to establish a protection threshold of core employment conditions, the Directive facilitates, among other things, the fight against labour exploitation in the Member States.[77] However, the social aspect of the Posting Directive seems to be diminishing following the court cases which will shortly be considered below. It is particularly evident when one considers judgments of the former ECJ. In the *Laval* case,[78] Laval (a Riga-based Latvian company) signed a contract concerning the construction of a school building in the city of Vaxholm in Sweden. Trade unions blocked the building, because Laval was refusing to observe the collective bargaining agreement applicable to the building sector.[79] The court decided that the freedom to provide services prevailed over collective bargaining rights.[80] The ECJ judgment in the *Rüffert* case[81] can also be included in the case law that considers social rights an obstacle to the free movement of services.[82] The ECJ found the German State Land of Lower Saxony guilty of imposing a minimum salary requirement on a construction company working under a procurement contract. Although the Polish subcontractor of a German construction company paid its workers less than half the prescribed minimum wage, the court decided that setting a minimum wage for the subcontractor was not in compliance with the Posting Directive.[83] In the *Commission v. Luxembourg* case,[84] Luxembourg wanted to apply the public order clause of Article 3(10) and impose additional requirements on posted workers. The ECJ found the requirements in violation of Article 3(10).

Concerns over poor labour standards in the above cases were mainly driven by a fear of social dumping, i.e. unfair competition on wages and working conditions of workers by foreign service providers in a host country labour

---

[77] C. Rijken and E. de Volder, 'The European Union's Struggle to Realize a Human Rights-Based Approach to Trafficking in Human Beings: A call on the EU to Take THB-Sensitive Action in Relevant Areas of Law' (2009) Connecticut Journal of International Law, Volume 25, No. 1, p. 64.

[78] *Laval v. Svenska Byggnadsarbetareförbundet*, Case C-341/05, E.C.R. I-11767 (2007).

[79] R. Eklund, 'European Developments: The Laval Case' (2006) Industrial Law Journal, Volume 35, No 2, p. 202.

[80] C. Rijken and E. de Volder, 'The European Union's Struggle to Realize a Human Rights-Based Approach to Trafficking in Human Beings: A call on the EU to Take THB-Sensitive Action in Relevant Areas of Law' (2009) Connecticut Journal of International Law, Volume 25, No. 1, p. 64.

[81] *Rüffert v. Land Niedersachsen*, Case C-346/06, E.C.R. I-01989 (2008).

[82] S. Borelli, 'Social clauses in public contracts, the Posted Workers Directive and Article 49 EC: the Rüffert Case' (2008) European Review of Labour and Research, Volume 14, p. 358.

[83] C. Rijken and E. de Volder, 'The European Union's Struggle to Realize a Human Rights-Based Approach to Trafficking in Human Beings: A call on the EU to Take THB-Sensitive Action in Relevant Areas of Law' (2009) Connecticut Journal of International Law, Volume 25, No. 1, p. 64.

[84] *Commission v. Luxembourg*, Case C-319/06, E.C.R. I-04323 (2008).

market. But the ECJ positioning also cast a different light on protection against labour exploitation. Higher labour standards were upheld with regard to the host countries where the workers were to be posted. The workers were allowed to provide their services under worse labour conditions than their domestic counterparts, which could have resulted in an exploitative situation.[85]

Therefore, the cases have highlighted some important structural weaknesses in the Posting Directive. It seems that in the ECJ the Directive is primarily interpreted as an internal market instrument, rather than as a social protection tool.[86] The Directive is therefore considered as fixing maximum social standards rather than minimum ones.[87] This development might have a negative impact on the prevention of THB. It has become increasingly questionable whether the Posting Directive still performs the important function of preventing social dumping. The Directive seems to have rather a negative effect on labour conditions in the long term. It is questionable whether the ECJ is able to find the right balance between freedom on one side and protection on the other. These doubts have become serious concerns and the European Trade Union Confederation (ETUC) finalised a report in May 2010 in which they expressed the need for revision of the Posting Directive. ETUC claims that the ECJ has interpreted the Posting Directive, and the EU legal framework in which it is functioning, too narrowly in an internal market perspective. Eight proposals were developed by ETUC and intended to ensure that the Posting Directive can 'achieve its initial social policy objectives of guaranteeing the protection of workers and a climate of fair competition.'[88] The European Commission has now adopted a communication for a highly competitive social market economy[89] including the intention to adopt a new legislative proposal aimed at improving the implementation of the Posting Directive, especially focussing on fundamental social rights.

[85] C. Rijken and E. de Volder, 'The European Union's Struggle to Realize a Human Rights-Based Approach to Trafficking in Human Beings: A call on the EU to Take THB-Sensitive Action in Relevant Areas of Law' (2009) Connecticut Journal of International Law, Volume 25, No. 1, p. 65.

[86] ETUC, *A Revision of the Posting of Workers Directive: Eight Proposals for Improvement* (Final Report from the ETUC Expert Group on Posting, Brussels 31 May 2010).

[87] S. Borelli, 'Social clauses in public contracts, the Posted Workers Directive and Article 49 EC: the Rüffert Case' (2008) European Review of Labour and Research, Volume 14, p. 359.

[88] ETUC, *A Revision of the Posting of Workers Directive: Eight Proposals for Improvement* (Final Report from the ETUC Expert Group on Posting, Brussels 31 May 2010), p. 18.

[89] COM (2010)608 fin. 11.11.2010, Communication from the Commission to the European Parliament, the Council, the Economic and Social Committee and the Committee of the Regions, *Towards a Single Market Act. For a highly competitive social market economy, 50 proposals for improving our work, business and exchanges with one another.*

2.3 The Service Directive

The European Parliament approved the Service Directive on 15 October 2006 after two years of difficult negotiations and debate on a number of issues that significantly impact on workers' rights. [90] The most contentious issues surrounded the country of origin principle and the role of labour law. According to the country of origin principle, the labour standards of the country where a self-employed service provider is registered apply. [91] In February 2005, the European Economic and Social Committee (EESC) adopted an opinion on the Commission's proposal and warned, in particular, that application of the country of origin principle would lead to a watering down of standards.[92] The Service Directive entered into force, after many amendments, on 28 December 2006. It adopted the freedom to provide services instead of the country of origin principle. It had to be implemented by Member States before 28 December 2009.[93]

However, in June 2010, the European Commission sent a reasoned opinion to 12 Member States (i.e. Austria, Belgium, Cyprus, France, Germany, Greece, Ireland, Luxembourg, Portugal, Romania, Slovenia and the United Kingdom) who had not finalised the implementation of the Service Directive. [94] Some of the 12 Member States concerned have recently communicated a number of measures to implement the Service Directive, but they still need to adapt at least some aspects of their legislation. [95] Proper implementation of the Directive will help make the freedom of establishment and the freedom to provide services, enshrined respectively in Articles 49 and 56 of the Treaty on the Functioning of the European Union, a reality for European businesses and consumers. [96] However, this also has a downside because it will negatively influence the labour standards.

---

[90] Council Directive 2006/123 on services in the internal market, Council Directive 2006/123/EC [2006] OJ L376/36, Recital 1.

[91] C. Rijken and E. de Volder, 'The European Union's Struggle to Realize a Human Rights-Based Approach to Trafficking in Human Beings: A call on the EU to Take THB-Sensitive Action in Relevant Areas of Law' (2009) Connecticut Journal of International Law, Volume 25, No. 1, p. 65.

[92] *Opinion of the European Economic and Social Committee on the Proposal for a Directive of the European Parliament and of the Council on Services in the Internal Market*, at 5, COM (2004) 2 final (10 February 2005).

[93] Council Directive 2006/123/EC [2006] OJ L 376/36, Article 44.

[94] Europa Press Release, *Services Directive: Good Progress on Implementation, But More Needs to be Done*, IP/10/821 (Brussels 24 June 2010) <http://europa.eu/rapid/pressReleasesAction.do?reference=IP/10/821&format=HTML&aged=0&language=EN&guiLanguage=en> accessed 15 March 2011.

[95] Europa Press Release, *Services Directive: Good Progress on Implementation, But More Needs to be Done*, IP/10/821 (Brussels 24 June 2010) <http://europa.eu/rapid/pressReleasesAction.do?reference=IP/10/821&format=HTML&aged=0&language=EN&guiLanguage=en> accessed 15 March 2011.

[96] Ibid.

The Service Directive applies to self-employed service providers – workers who determine their own working hours and working conditions. The Directive establishes general provisions facilitating the exercise of the freedom of establishment for service providers and the free movement of services, while maintaining a high quality of services.[97] The Directive requires EU countries to remove unjustified or disproportionate legal and administrative barriers to the setting-up of a business or the provision of cross-border services in the EU.[98] Member States must enable European citizens to offer services on a temporary basis in another Member State without any further requirements.[99] Restrictions can only be justified by overriding concerns of general interest, such as public policy, national security, or public health. Furthermore, such restrictions can only be imposed when they are proportionate. Provisions on labour law and consumer law have been excluded from the Directive.[100]

The *Viking* case[101] is of fundamental importance to trade unions and their members across the European Union. In this case, legal proceedings started when a trade union took action against a Finnish shipping company (Viking Line) to prevent it from registering a ferry as an Estonian ship, crewed by Estonian seafarers on lower wages. Following this case, workers were deprived of their basic right to collective action because the court formally allowed Viking to relocate its assets in a country where salaries and benefits were lower.[102] Apart from that, they were not protected against being fired and against possible social dumping. The trade union's action was perceived by the ECJ to be an intolerable restriction on the freedom of establishment, a fundamental freedom guaranteed under Article 43 of the EC Treaty.[103] Also in this area, the ECJ seems to give preference to economic over social interests. This case raised similar issues as the *Laval* case and this judgment may not sufficiently protect the rights of organised labour in a modern transnational and increasingly global economy.[104]

---

[97] Council Directive 2006/123/EC, [2006] OJ L 376/36, Article 1.

[98] Ibid, Recital 1.

[99] C. Rijken and E. de Volder, 'The European Union's Struggle to Realize a Human Rights-Based Approach to Trafficking in Human Beings: A call on the EU to Take THB-Sensitive Action in Relevant Areas of Law' (2009) Connecticut Journal of International Law, Volume 25, No. 1, p. 66.

[100] Ibid.

[101] *Int'l Transp. Workers' Fed'n. v. Viking Line ABP*, Case C-438/05 2007 E.C.R. 1372, 1 C.M.I.R. 51 (2008).

[102] C. Rijken and R. Römkens, 'Trafficking for Sexual Purposes as a Globalized Shadow Economy: Human Security as the Tool to Facilitate a Human Rights Based Approach' in R. Letschert and J. van Dijk, *The New Faces of Victimhood. Globalization, Transnational Crimes and Victim Rights* (Springer 2011) pp. 73–98.

[103] *Int'l Transp. Workers' Fed'n. v. Viking Line ABP*, Case C-438/05 2007 E.C.R. 1372, 1 C.M.I.R. 51 (2008), 1414-15.

[104] ETUC, *Viking Case* <http://www.etuc.org/r/848> accessed 15 March 2011.

Part III
Migration Law

3.1 Introduction

People's motives in migrating generally relate to their desire to find a better life. Migrants are very limited in their ability to migrate legally and find jobs in the regular labour market. Consequently, most low-skilled migrant workers are pushed into low-end jobs, or into the (quasi) illegal markets, thereby amplifying their vulnerability to exploitation by traffickers.[105]

THB has been, and often still is considered an issue of irregular migration. This confusion is understandable to some extent, as many victims of THB enter the EU illegally, whether wilfully or not. Irregular migration indeed often precedes THB. This must be taken into account when considering combating THB. One must be aware of the vulnerable situation of some of the migrants and their vulnerability to fall victim to THB. In the migration debate, the risks of THB have often been used as a reason for restrictive migration laws in order to keep the traffickers out. However, in doing so, people in a vulnerable position are kept out as well, and are even more likely to be driven back into the hands of the smugglers or traffickers, with detrimental effects. One must be aware of these effects, and the vulnerability of migrants to become victim of exploitative practices is reason to plea for more open borders instead of a restrictive migration policy.

EU migration law plays a role in two phases of the trafficking chain. It plays a role when Third Country Nationals (TCNs) want to enter the EU. Then migration law effectively helps determine which TCNs will enter the EU and under what conditions. It plays a role in the second place in assisting and protecting TCNs who become victims of THB. It does so through an obligation on the Member States to provide residence permits, and the imposition of the principle of non-refoulement. In this section, only the relevant migration law in force and only proposals that are relevant for combating THB for labour exploitation will be discussed.

3.2 EU Blue Card[106]

This Directive was the first instrument of the sectorial approach. The fact that this first measure regulates the entry of high qualified persons might indicate that the financial interests of the EU are the primary concern motivating EU

[105] C. Rijken and E. de Volder, 'The European Union's Struggle to Realize a Human Rights-Based Approach to Trafficking in Human Beings: A call on the EU to Take THB-Sensitive Action in Relevant Areas of Law' (2009) Connecticut Journal of International Law, Volume 25, No. 1, p. 68.

[106] Council Directive 2009/50 on the conditions of entry and residence of third-country nationals for the purposes of highly qualified employment, Council Directive 2009/50 [2009] OJ L155.

migration policy.[107] However, the measure's explanatory memorandum sets forth that: 'The proposal also complies with the EU's development policy with its central focus on eradication of poverty and the achievement of MDGs [Millennium Development Goals] . . . . [It] seeks to minimise negative and maximise positive impacts of highly skilled migration on developing countries that already face lack of human resources in certain sectors.'[108] Additionally, Article 3(3) of the Directive explains that 'This Directive shall be without prejudice to any agreement between the Community and/or its Member States and one or more third countries, that lists the professions which should not fall under this Directive in order to assure ethical recruitment, in sectors suffering from a lack of personnel, by protecting human resources in the developing countries which are signatories to these agreements.'[109]

3.3 Council Directive on the residence permit for victims of trafficking in human beings[110]

Council Directive 2004/81 is an important EU measure that was drafted specifically for victims of THB, and for those who received assistance for illegal migration who are cooperating with the authorities. The purpose of this Directive is to 'define the conditions for granting residence permits of limited duration, linked to the length of the relevant national proceedings, to third-country nationals who cooperate in the fight against trafficking in human beings or against action to facilitate illegal immigration.'[111] The aim of the Directive is two-fold: to obtain the cooperation of victims of trafficking and illegal immigration for criminal procedures on the one hand, and to provide assistance to these victims by granting a residence permit, on the other.[112] Although this Directive was enacted as part of the EU's migration policy, it is relevant to EU criminal policy as well.[113] It is to be welcomed that in the

[107] C. Rijken and E. de Volder, 'The European Union's Struggle to Realize a Human Rights-Based Approach to Trafficking in Human Beings: A call on the EU to Take THB-Sensitive Action in Relevant Areas of Law' (2009) Connecticut Journal of International Law, Volume 25, No. 1, p. 70.

[108] *Commission Proposal for a Council Directive on the Conditions of Entry and Residence of Third-Country Nationals for the Purposes of Highly Qualified Employment*, COM 637 final at 4 (23 October 2007).

[109] Council Directive 2009/50 [2009] OJ L155, Article 3(3).

[110] Council Directive 2004/81 of 29 April 2004 on the residence permit issued to third-country nationals who are victims of trafficking in human beings or who have been the subject of an action to facilitate illegal immigration, and who cooperate with the competent authorities [2004] OJ L261/19.

[111] Council Directive 2004/81 [2004] OJ L261/19, Article 1.

[112] C. Rijken, *The European Legal Framework to Fight Trafficking in Human Beings* (IOM Den Haag 2005) p. 4.

[113] C. Rijken and E. de Volder, 'The European Union's Struggle to Realize a Human Rights-Based Approach to Trafficking in Human Beings: A call on the EU to Take

Directive, THB is seen as a separate crime and not necessarily as part of illegal immigration. In many earlier documents of the EU, THB was considered as being part of illegal immigration, impeding the adoption of effective measures for trafficking.[114]

The main comment on this Directive is that a residence permit is only granted when victims are cooperating with competent authorities in the fight against THB. Article 14(d) states that if the victim ceases to cooperate, the residence permit may be withdrawn.[115] Another important comment on this Directive is that it is aimed at TNCs, with the result that nationals of other EU Member States cannot invoke this Directive. After the accession of 1 May 2004, many countries that are source countries of trafficking became part of the EU. Consequently, the victims who are nationals of these States are left empty-handed, as they no longer belong to a third country. Furthermore, it seems that nationals who are staying in one of the EU States on a valid permit fall outside the scope of this Directive as well.[116] The last point is that only residence permits of limited duration are granted linked to the length of the relevant national proceedings. Although the Directive includes provisions specifically drafted for the protection of victims, the EU's interest in combating organised crime seems to prevail over the protection of victims' rights.[117]

In October 2010, the Commission reported to the European Parliament and the Council on the application of this Directive in the Member States, according to Article 16 of the Directive.[118] The Commission concluded that the impact of the Directive 'does appear to be insufficient in the light of the overall data on victims of trafficking in the EU.' [119] Furthermore, the Commission stated that 'the potential of the Directive in dismantling networks of traffickers while protecting the rights of victims is not being put to full use.' [120] The Commission considered the need for amendments to the Directive, including the important possibility of issuing a temporary residence permit based on the vulnerable situation of the victim and not necessarily in

---

THB-Sensitive Action in Relevant Areas of Law' (2009) Connecticut Journal of International Law, Volume 25, No. 1, p. 56.

[114] C. Rijken, *The European Legal Framework to Fight Trafficking in Human Beings* (IOM Den Haag 2005) p. 5.

[115] Council Directive 2004/81 of 29 April 2004 on the residence permit issued to third-country nationals who are victims of trafficking in human beings or who have been the subject of an action to facilitate illegal immigration, who cooperate with the competent authorities [2004] OJ L261, Article 14.

[116] C. Rijken, *The European Legal Framework to Fight Trafficking in Human Beings* (IOM Den Haag 2005) p. 5.

[117] C. Rijken and E. de Volder, 'The European Union's Struggle to Realize a Human Rights-Based Approach to Trafficking in Human Beings: A call on the EU to Take THB-Sensitive Action in Relevant Areas of Law' (2009) Connecticut Journal of International Law, Volume 25, No. 1, pp. 56-57.

[118] Report from the Commission to the European Parliament and the Council (COM 2010) 493.

[119] Ibid, p. 10.

[120] Ibid.

exchange for cooperation with competent authorities. Other amendments might include 'having a specified length of reflection periods for victims; strengthening the framework of treatment, in particular for minors: reinforcement of the obligation to inform victims of their rights.'[121]

3.4 Sanction Directive[122]

This Directive further illustrates the mixed and sometimes opposing policies of restrictive migration laws and efforts to combat THB. This Directive relates to THB, because the more potential there is for illegal work, the higher the risk of exploitative and slavery-like practices.[123] The Directive provides minimum common standards on sanctions and measures against employers of illegal immigrants in order to counter, in general, illegal immigration within the Member States. The Directive is not concerned with labour, social or criminal policy, [124] but it would perhaps be better situated within the field of employment and social affairs. The Directive explicates the relationship between irregular migration and THB. It states that if certain requirements are fulfilled, irregular migration can constitute the more serious criminal offence of THB.

Despite the Directive stating that the employer concerned will be punished instead of the illegal TCN performing the work, in some cases a Member State might be obliged to issue a return decision in accordance with its national laws or the Return Directive.[125] In such cases, the Member State would have to expel the TCN from its territory.[126] When the TCN has become a victim of particularly exploitative working conditions, criminal sanctions may be imposed and the victim may be granted protective measures (for example, a temporary residence permit).

The Directive came into force on 20 July 2009 and Member States will bring into force the laws, regulations and administrative provisions necessary to comply with this Directive by 20 July 2011.

---

[121] Report from the Commission to the European Parliament and the Council (COM 2010) 493, p. 11.

[122] Council Directive 2009/52 on providing minimum standards on sanctions and measures against employers of illegally staying third-country nationals [2009] OJ L168/24.

[123] C. Rijken and E. de Volder, 'The European Union's Struggle to Realize a Human Rights-Based Approach to Trafficking in Human Beings: A call on the EU to Take THB-Sensitive Action in Relevant Areas of Law' (2009) Connecticut Journal of International Law, Volume 25, No. 1, p. 70.

[124] Council Directive 2009/52 [2009] OJ L168, Article 1.

[125] Council Directive 2008/115 on Common Standards and Procedures in Member States for Returning Illegally Staying Third-Country Nationals [2008] OJ L348/102.

[126] Ibid, Article 6.

3.5 The Return Directive[127]

The aim of this directive is to establish a horizontal set of rules for the expulsion of TCNs who stay illegally on the territory of one of the Member States. To that end standardised forms were developed related to return, entry ban and removal. A person who applied for asylum cannot be considered illegal until a negative decision on his application has been taken. If possible, voluntary return should be preferred. The EU recognises the need to conclude readmission agreements with third States in order to facilitate the return of illegally staying TCNs. According to the directive, the principle of non-refoulement should be fully adhered to. In principle a return decision taken in one Member State applies in the other Member States as well, although more favourable provisions adopted at national level may be applied. The personal situation of the individual will be taken into account when deciding on the return decision. Victims of THB who have been granted a residence permit based on Directive 2004/81 will not be subject to an entry ban or a return decision. However, it is broadly recognised that victims of THB do not easily refer themselves to the authorities and especially not when they stay illegally in a country. Often they are threatened by their traffickers that they will be expelled from the State if they go to the police, and this is unfortunately confirmed by practice. The Directive furthermore gives grounds for detention for the purpose of removal, although this can take up to six months, which period might be extended as well.

3.6 Newly proposed instruments in the field of migration law

On 13 July 2010, a proposal for a Directive on the conditions of entry and residence of TCNs for the purposes of seasonal employment was introduced by the European Parliament and the Council.[128] On the same date, a proposal for a Directive on conditions of entry and residence of TCNs in the framework of an intra-corporate transfer was introduced.[129] A proposal for a Directive on the conditions of entry and residence of remunerated trainees can be expected.[130] Below, only the first of the three will be discussed, together with the proposal on the single residence permit as these are considered to be of most relevance for our subject.

[127] Directive 2008/115/EC on Common Standards and Procedures in Member States for Returning Illegally Staying Third-Country Nationals [2008] OJ L348.

[128] *Proposal for a Directive of the European Parliament and of the Council on the conditions of entry and residence of third-country nationals for the purposes of seasonal employment*, COM 379 final (13 July 2010).

[129] Ibid.

[130] *Policy Plan on Legal Migration*, COM 669 final (21 December 2005).

3.6.1 Proposal for a Directive on Seasonal Employment[131]

The proposal on seasonal employment is of particular interest in relation to THB for labour exploitation. In contrast to the directive on highly qualified TCNs this proposal is aimed at low-skilled and low-qualified workers. The Commission recognises that the EU will remain in need of such workers, and that this gap cannot be filled with EU national workers. More importantly, it recognises that third-country seasonal workers currently face exploitative situations and sub-standard working conditions which may threaten their health and safety. Especially agriculture, tourism and horticulture are in need of seasonal workers and they turn out to be sectors where work is undertaken by illegally staying TCNs. It furthermore states that 'swift and flexible admission procedures and securing a legal status for seasonal workers can act as a safeguard against exploitation, and also protects EU citizens who are seasonal workers from unfair competition.'[132] It particularly aims to contribute to achieving the millennium development goals as well as to eradicate poverty. Since it will be a *temporary* residence permit, it is believed that it will not constitute a brain drain. According to the proposal the TCN seasonal worker is allowed to work for a maximum of six months per calendar year as a seasonal worker. States can identify sectors where seasonal workers may be employed. A worker can apply for a permit if he/she has arranged a contract or if there is a binding job offer that specifies a rate of pay. In the explanatory memorandum it states that it specifies a pay equal to or above a minimum level. However, this is not included in the text of Article 5. It is however, not clear whether this is the minimum level that applies in the host State. The contract furthermore needs to include the working hours per week or month. Once the TCN has received the permit he/she may accept other (seasonal) work. This provision was included to make the employee less dependent on one single employer, which might enhance his/her vulnerability. But if he/she accepts other work the guarantee on the salary does not apply. Legal provisions applying to working conditions are defined in Article 16 in order to prevent exploitation and the employer must prove that the worker is accommodated properly. The payment for accommodation may not be excessive in relation to the remuneration (Article 14). Further requirements are health insurance and sufficient resources during the stay. The work and residence permit must be submitted in a single application procedure and a decision must be taken within 30 days. An important reason behind the temporary seasonal work permit is to promote circular migration which will benefit the country of origin because when they return to their home country the earnings will be invested there. To further facilitate circular migration multi-seasonal permits can be granted for a maximum of three subsequent years or States can provide

[131] *Proposal for a directive of the European Parliament and of the Council on the conditions of entry and residence of third-country nationals for the purposes of seasonal employment*, COM 379 final (2010).
[132] Ibid, at 3.

a facilitated procedure for seasonal workers who apply for a second time and were permitted the first time. Re-entry in the subsequent years is then easier. Some national parliaments of Member States have argued that the proposal is not in line with the principle of subsidiarity. Although the minimum number of protests was not achieved, the European Commission did react to the complaints by stating that it did meet the conditions for subsidiarity.[133] The proposal is now awaiting its first reading in the European Parliament.

3.6.2 Proposal for a Single Residence Permit[134]

The Commission Proposal for a Council Directive on a single application procedure for a single permit for TCNs to reside and work in the territory of a Member State and on a common set of rights for third-country nationals legally residing in a Member State (COM (2007) 638) takes steps in the direction of harmonising the procedure for labour market access, if not the admission conditions which remain in the hands of the Member States. Such a Directive, once adopted, may trigger further steps towards legislative and jurisprudential harmonisation of the regulation needed for markets to function well, and integration to be viable. The proposal was rejected by the European Parliament in December 2010 especially because of the scope of the legislation, equal treatment of TCNs and EU citizens and whether Member States should be enabled to issue or require other documents, in addition to the permit. Because the Commission does not want to withdraw the proposal, further amendments should be made.

3.7 Frontex[135]

The Council Regulation 2007/2004 established Frontex, a European Agency, on 1 May 2005. Although controlling external borders has largely remained a duty of Member States, coordination of external border controls has now been mandated to Frontex. The aim of Frontex is to improve the integrated management of the external EU borders, thereby ensuring a uniform and high level of control and surveillance, which is fundamental to the maintenance of Freedom, Security and Justice within the European Union.

Frontex's main tasks are the coordination of relevant activities of Member States, assistance to Member States in the training of national border guards, the carrying out of risk analysis and assistance to Member States in circumstances requiring technical and operational assistance at external borders.

In accordance with Article 3, joint operations (the so-called 'Hera Operations') coordinated by Frontex, were conducted. The main concern of the Hera Operations was the prevention of irregular migration and the return

---

[133] Second protocol to the Lisbon Treaty.

[134] *Proposal for a Single Residence Permit*, COM 638 final (2007).

[135] Council Regulation 2007/2004, establishing a European Agency for the Management of Operational Cooperation at the External Borders of the Member States of the European Union [2004] OJ L349/3.

of illegal migrants.[136] These practices have an impact on the prevalence of THB. As stated above, migration can turn into THB and among the migrants (potential) victims of THB might be present. If these persons are denied entry into the EU they will be returned to the hands of the smugglers or traffickers. For this, and other, reasons we are in favour of a more social migration policy within the EU. However, in the development of the Hera Operations, a human rights-based perspective appears to have been absent. The activities seem to be motivated by a protectionist perspective, more specifically, the desire to protect the EU from criminal networks and irregular migration. Such operations can have a detrimental effect as these migrants are in a vulnerable position and can easily fall into the hands of smugglers and traffickers.

Article 8 of the Regulation establishing Frontex provides for the assistance of the agency to Member States in circumstances requiring increased technical and operational assistance at external borders. Such a situation might exist when 'one or more Member States [are] being confronted by an emergency situation characterised by a sudden inflow of nationals of third countries' as described in Article 78 TFEU. To that end, Frontex can establish Rabits (rapid border intervention teams).[137] Regulation 2007/2004 is amended by Regulation 863/2007[138] and has established a mechanism for the creation of Rabit teams. The purpose of the regulation is to provide rapid operational assistance for a limited period to a requesting Member State facing a situation of 'urgent and exceptional pressure, especially the arrival at points of the external borders of large numbers of third-country nationals trying to enter the territory of the Member State illegally.'[139]

The establishment of a Rabit can be requested by one or more States. According to consideration 3 of Regulation 863/2007, 'Effective management of the external borders through checks and surveillance helps to combat illegal immigration and trafficking in human beings and to prevent any threat to the internal security, public policy, public health and international relations of the Member States.' Within the teams, national authorities act within the framework of the agency although they remain employed by their national organisations. The competences they have are governed by the regulation in the Schengen Border Code[140] and not by the separate national laws.[141] According to the Schengen Border Code they can control persons and secure the borders. To that end they may check whether travel documents have been falsified, question a person that wants to pass the border, check whether a

---

[136] C. Rijken and E. de Volder, 'The European Union's Struggle to Realize a Human Rights-Based Approach to Trafficking in Human Beings: A call on the EU to Take THB-Sensitive Action in Relevant Areas of Law' (2009) Connecticut Journal of International Law, Volume 25, No. 1, p. 73.

[137] Regulation 2007/2005 as amended by regulation 863/2007 [2007] OJ L199, Article 8(a).

[138] Council Regulation 863/2007 [2007] OJ L199.

[139] Ibid, Article 1.

[140] Regulation 562/2006 [2006] OJ L105.

[141] Council Regulation 863/2007 [2007] OJ L199 Art. 6(1).

person has triggered an alert in the Schengen Information System and stamp travel documents (Article 7 Schengen Border Code). Furthermore, they are allowed to prevent the crossing of the border into the host State (Article 12 Schengen Border Code). In principle, members of the Rabits are allowed to carry service weapons, ammunition and equipment as authorised according to the home Member State's national law. According to Article 6(3) 'members of the teams may only perform tasks and exercise powers under instructions from and, as a general rule, in the presence of border guards of the host Member State.' In addition: 'Decisions to refuse entry in accordance with Article 13 of Regulation (EC) No 562/2006 shall be taken only by border guards of the host Member State.'[142] Article 9 then includes a provision on applicable law; for the performance of their tasks in accordance with Article 6(1) the law of the host State applies, in relation to disciplinary measures for these tasks the law of the home State applies, for the carrying and use of service weapons, etc. the law of the home State applies unless the host State has indicated otherwise, and finally for civil and criminal liability Articles 10 and 11 of the regulation apply. This illustrates the complexity of the structures in which the officers have to operate, as well as the risks of exceeding powers in these operations.

In recent months, Frontex became more active in the field of THB. The Belgian Presidency organised a conference called *'Towards a multidisciplinary approach to prevention of trafficking in human beings, prosecution of traffickers and protection of victims'* as part of the 4th EU Anti-Trafficking Day on 18 October 2010. During this conference, Ilkka Laitinen, Executive Director of Frontex, called for more powers in order to be more effective in detecting and preventing THB.[143] He underscored the need for Frontex to have the authority to process personal data: 'Border guards are the potential first and last officials that are in contact with a victim of trafficking when entering or leaving the European Union.'[144] The judicial authorities and the police depend on the first-hand information collected at the border. This is one of the reasons why the Commission proposed a new Frontex Regulation, which is currently being negotiated in the Council Working Groups and in the European Parliament. In this proposal provisions for a more human-rights friendly approach are proposed. Also when looking at the first established Rabit in Greece in October 2010, the right to apply for asylum seems to have been implemented. This year, Frontex will also start, together with European and international partners, the development of a special THB training module for European law-enforcement officers. The aim of this training module is to raise awareness and harmonise standards of practice in this area. An officer, who

---

[142] Council Regulation 863/2007 [2007] OJ L199 Art. 6(10).

[143] See website Frontex, News Releases, 'Frontex Head Calls for More Powers to Detect and Prevent Human Trafficking', 18 October 2010 <http://www.frontex.europa.eu/newsroom/news_releases/art77.html> accessed 15 March 2011.

[144] Ibid.

received the training, should be able to deal with victims and potential victims of THB.

Part IV
External Relations

4.1 Introduction

The last field in which counter measures on THB for labour exploitation are and can be taken is the field of external relations. One of the root causes of THB is the inequality of living standards both between and within States in different parts of the world. Part III showed that a lack of legal migration opportunities further contributes to the THB problem. People are more likely to take disproportionate risks and become vulnerable to illegal practices when they have a limited number of legal migration options. In order to effectively combat THB, the EU must therefore strengthen its cooperation with third countries to prevent irregular migration, to facilitate legal migration, and to fight THB by addressing its other root causes, in both countries of origin and countries of destination.[145]

4.2 The Action Oriented Paper [146]

This non-binding instrument provides several suggestions for the implementation of the external dimension and includes concrete steps to help realise them. The aim of the Action Oriented Paper (AOP) is to 'strengthen the commitment and coordinated action of the EU and the Member States to prevent and fight all forms of THB.'[147] This will be done in partnership with third countries, regions and organisations at the international level. It is intended to promote a proactive rather than a reactive approach and is based on the recognition that an integrated, multidisciplinary approach is needed.[148] The AOP discusses victim protection only briefly, but also includes information on how to mobilise society to combat THB.[149]

---

[145] C. Rijken and R. Römkens, 'Trafficking for Sexual Purposes as a Globalized Shadow Economy: Human Security as the Tool to Facilitate a Human Rights Based Approach' in R. Letschert and J. van Dijk, *The New Faces of Victimhood. Globalization, Transnational Crimes and Victim Rights* (Springer 2011) pp. 73–98.

[146] Council of the European Union, *Action Oriented Paper on strengthening the EU External Dimension on Action Against Trafficking in Human Beings* (2009 11450/5/09 REV 5).

[147] Ibid, at 10.

[148] Ibid.

[149] C. Rijken and E. de Volder, 'The European Union's Struggle to Realize a Human Rights-Based Approach to Trafficking in Human Beings: A call on the EU to Take THB-Sensitive Action in Relevant Areas of Law' (2009) Connecticut Journal of International Law, Volume 25, No. 1, p. 76.

4.3 European Neighbourhood Policy[150]

The European Neighbourhood Policy (ENP) was launched at the Thessalonica European Council in May 2003. It was established in order to create more coherence in the EU approach towards third countries in the immediate geographical vicinity of the EU.[151] The development of the ENP was a transpillar process in which the Commission has taken the lead.

Action Plans are important instruments provided for in the ENP, which address economic, political, and security-related issues.[152] The ENP mandates the composition of Country Reports, in which the external policy of a country is assessed with respect to various issues. In the ENP Country Reports, a separate Justice and Home Affairs section deals with organised crime and specifically addresses THB.[153]

A condition for cooperation with third countries and a goal of the ENP is the protection of human rights. [154] Addressing THB through ENP-related initiatives, thus, would both contribute to accomplishment of the underlying goals of the ENP, and would serve as an indicator of further cooperation between the EU and third countries.[155] THB has been explicitly mentioned, in particular, in the Action Plans for THB victims' countries of origin.[156] Also important, further contributions in the fight against THB are related to areas such as organised crime reduction and improving equality between men and women in order to reduce the vulnerability of women. Gender equality is

---

[150] Communication from the Commission to the European Parliament and the Council: Implementation of the European Neighbourhood Policy in 2008, COM 188/3 at 6-7 (23 April 2009).

[151] M. Cremona, *The European Neighbourhood Policy: More than a Partnership? Developments in EU External Relations Law* (Oxford University Press 2008), p. 244.

[152] E. Johansson-Nogués, 'The EU and its Neighbourhood: An Overview' in K. Weber, M.E. Smith, and M. Baun, *Governing Europe's New Neighborhood: Partners or Periphery?* (Manchester University Press 2007), p. 21.

[153] Communication from the Commission to the European Parliament and the Council: Implementation of the European Neighbourhood Policy in 2008, COM 188/3 at 6–7 (23 April 2009).

[154] Communication from the Commission, European Neighbourhood Policy: Strategy Paper, COM 373 final (12 May 2004).

[155] C. Rijken, 'The External Dimension of EU Policy on Trafficking in Human Beings' (2011) in M. Cremona, J. Monar and S. Poli (eds), *The External Dimension of the Area of Freedom, Security and Justice* (Peter Lang-P.I.E. forthcoming 2011); C. Rijken and E. de Volder, 'The European Union's Struggle to Realize a Human Rights-Based Approach to Trafficking in Human Beings: A call on the EU to Take THB-Sensitive Action in Relevant Areas of Law' (2009) Connecticut Journal of International Law, Volume 25, No. 1, p. 76.

[156] See for example the EU/Moldavia Action Plan and the EU/Ukraine Action Plan.

addressed both generally, and specifically in relation to THB, in the Action Plans.[157]

4.4 The Ouagadougou Action Plan[158]

Development policy directly addresses some of the root causes of THB. This has also been recognised in the Ouagadougou Action Plan to Combat THB (Action Plan), and the Communication on Policy Priorities in the Fight Against Illegal Migration. The Action Plan advocates a comprehensive regional and international approach.[159] The Action Plan is comprised of a list of recommendations and political commitments made by the EU to individual African States. This document must be seen as a starting point for new initiatives because it involves cooperation between the EU and African States on important THB-related issues.[160]

4.5 Joint Africa-EU Declaration on Migration and Development[161]

African and EU States have also adopted the Joint Africa-EU Declaration on Migration and Development. The language of this Declaration is occasionally a bit stronger and the cooperative actions are more concrete than those of the Action Plan mentioned above. For example, the Joint Africa-EU Declaration reaffirms that all EU and African countries have a duty to cooperate fully in the prevention and control of illegal and irregular migration.[162] The Declaration has resulted in the establishment of the Migration Information and Management Centre in Mali, which was inaugurated on 6 October 2008, and which is financed by the EU. This pilot project aims to enhance Mali's capacity to deal with migration issues in partnership with Europe and with its neighbouring countries. It has been set up to fight irregular migration through job counselling for would-be and returned migrants. This initiative can be seen

---

[157] C. Rijken, 'The External Dimension of EU Policy on Trafficking in Human Beings' (2011) in M. Cremona, J. Monar and S. Poli (eds), *The External Dimension of the Area of Freedom, Security and Justice* (Peter Lang-P.I.E. forthcoming 2011).

[158] Commission of the African Union, Ouagadougou Action Plan to Combat Trafficking in Human Beings, Especially Women and Children, as Adopted by the Ministerial Conference on Migration and Development (22–23 November 2006) and Communication from the Commission on Policy Priorities in the Fight Against Illegal Immigration of Third-Country Nationals, COM 402 final at 4–5 (19 July 2006).

[159] Ibid, at 3–5.

[160] C. Rijken and E. de Volder, 'The European Union's Struggle to Realize a Human Rights-Based Approach to Trafficking in Human Beings: A call on the EU to Take THB-Sensitive Action in Relevant Areas of Law' (2009) Connecticut Journal of International Law, Volume 25, No. 1, p. 77.

[161] Commission of the African Union, Joint Africa-EU Declaration on Migration and Development, Tripoli (22–23 November 2006).

[162] Ibid, p. 2.

as a means to better prevent and control irregular migration, to Europe in particular, thereby frustrating the activities of smugglers and traffickers.[163] Unfortunately, no evaluation reports on this initiative can be found.

[163] C. Rijken, 'The External Dimension of EU Policy on Trafficking in Human Beings' (2011) in M. Cremona, J. Monar and S. Poli (eds), *The External Dimension of the Area of Freedom, Security and Justice* (Peter Lang-P.I.E. forthcoming 2011).

Part V
Conclusion

Given this overview, it can be concluded that the EU is particularly active in the combating of THB, including THB for labour exploitation. It does provide contributions from various angles. However, the contributions seem not to be concerted and there are challenges for improvement. Once the EU can link together these fields and the activities in these fields in a coherent way, with the human rights perspective as the focus point, then it will indeed be promoting a human rights-based approach to THB. The EU does have the ingredients; now it is up to them to use these ingredients in such a way that the comprehensive approach becomes a reality.

Chapter 7
Challenges and Pitfalls in Combating Trafficking in Human Beings for Labour Exploitation

Conny Rijken[1]

Introduction

Over the last couple of years, there has been an increased focus on trafficking in human beings (THB) for labour exploitation. The project 'Combating THB for labour exploitation' adds to this focus. The current chapter is mainly based on the research conducted in the five countries that participated in the project and the chapter on the EU legal framework on THB for labour exploitation, the results of which are included in this book. What can be learned from this research is that the increased focus has not yet watered down through all the levels that are involved in combating THB for labour exploitation. More than ten years after the adoption of the internationally agreed definition in the Palermo Protocol, much remains unclear in relation to the actual definition; the new actors involved in combating this form of THB are still not familiar with their new roles and tasks; and NGOs providing victim support still mainly focus on THB for sexual exploitation and female victims. This means that there is still room for improvement, and this chapter helps to identify where improvements can be made. It reflects on the main issues raised by the research conducted in the five countries, and focuses on how the EU is dealing with these issues. A more specific analysis of the countries and detailed recommendations can be found in the separate chapters. The overall aim of the project, and consequently of this chapter, is to contribute to a comprehensive human rights based approach to THB for labour exploitation. In parallel with the individual country chapters, this chapter is divided into three major parts; the legal framework, national and international cooperation, and victim protection and assistance, followed by the recommendations.

---

[1] Conny Rijken is Associate Professor at Tilburg Law School, European and International Public Law Department and research fellow at INTERVICT (International Victimology Institute Tilburg). She was project coordinator of the project 'Improving the investigation and prosecution of THB for labour exploitation. Identifying problems and best practices' (short title: Combating THB for Labour Exploitation) funded by the European Commission (JLS/2009/ISEC/AG/176).

Part I
The legal framework

1.1. The definition: Focus on trafficking instead of exploitation

In all the States included in this project, the definition of THB for labour exploitation is based on the Palermo Protocol, but this does not mean that it is clear which cases meet the conditions of the protocol. In 2000, it was considered a great breakthrough when an international definition of THB was agreed upon.[2] This definition was included in Article 3 of the so-called Palermo Protocol, which is a protocol to the UN Convention against Transnational Organised Crime (UNCTOC or the Convention). Consequently, in the Palermo Protocol, THB must have a transnational character and must be conducted as an organised crime. To that end, Article 4 of the Palermo Protocol states that: 'This Protocol shall apply ... to the prevention, investigation and prosecution of the offences established in accordance with Article 5 of this Protocol, where those offences are transnational in nature and involve an organised criminal group, as well as to the protection of victims of such offences.'[3] The question that followed was whether the elements of transnational nature and organised crime were elements of the definition of THB. The UN Office on Drugs and Crime gave some guidance on the interpretation of the Convention and its protocols in 2004, and although it restated that these elements were required for the Convention to apply, it also stated that elements of a transnational nature and organised crime should not be posed as elements in the definition of THB in national laws.[4] When

[2] According to Article 3 trafficking in persons shall mean the recruitment, transportation, transfer, harbouring or receipt of persons, by means of the threat or use of force or other forms of coercion, of abduction, of fraud, of deception, of the abuse of power or of a position of vulnerability or of the giving or receiving of payments or benefits to achieve the consent of a person having control over another person, for the purpose of exploitation.

[3] According to Article 37 of the UNCTOC, the protocol should be interpreted together with the Convention, although Article 34 of the same protocol denies the requirements of transnational and organised crime for a number of offences criminalised in the UNCTOC.

[4] UN Office on Drugs and Crime, Legislative Guides for the Implementation of the United Nations Convention Against Transnational Organised Crime and the Protocols thereto, New York 2004, p. 10-11 "It must be strongly emphasised that, while offences must involve transnationality and organised criminal groups for the Convention and its international cooperation provisions to apply, neither of these must be made elements of the domestic offence (Art. 34, Para. 2)." In addition, more specifically in relation to THB pp. 258-259. "Notwithstanding the comment in Paragraph 23 about the Convention dealing only with situations having an element of transnationality or organised crime, it will be noted that the relevant provisions of the Convention and the Protocol must be reviewed carefully. The text of the provisions is relatively broad." 25. "It is important for drafters of legislation to note that the provisions relating to the involvement of

looking at the definition in Article 3 of the Palermo Protocol, we see that neither of these two elements has been explicitly included as such in the definition, but that the transnational aspect seems to have especially influenced the definition in the sense that an element of movement is included in it. This is one of the reasons that we are now lumbered with a complicated definition which includes acts (recruitment, transportation, transfer, harbouring or receipt) and means (use of force or other forms of coercion, abduction, fraud, the abuse of power or of a position of vulnerability, etc.) for the purpose of exploitation, which are difficult to unravel.

A primary difficulty is the function of 'exploitation' in the definition. The question is whether using the terminology of THB for labour exploitation has not made the whole debate needlessly complicated. Related terms such as forced labour, or slavery (-like practices) were already being used, and these terms do indeed focus on the primary issue, namely, exploitation itself (see below). Adding the phrase 'trafficking in human beings' leads attention away from exploitation and seems to include movement. In addition, the fact that the existence of an *aim* to exploit is sufficient to qualify as a case of THB without the need of the *actual* exploitation taking place, contributes to the effect that focus is more on forced recruitment. What can be drawn from the country reports is that the States are creative in defining the element of trafficking in the sense that in most of the countries under research the acts are broadly interpreted.

A second difficulty in relation to the definition is that the 'means' relate to the act and not to the exploitation, although exploitation seems to imply an involuntariness as well, especially considering the specification of exploitation given in the Palermo Protocol. Looking at the second phrase of Article 3(1), *'exploitation shall include at a minimum .... forced labour, slavery or practices similar to slavery....'*, in these forms of exploitation, a form of coercion or involuntariness is clearly present. For THB in these forms of exploitation, a double requirement of force applies. However, exploitation as such does not necessarily involve involuntariness or force. The exploitation can, for instance, also exist in bad living conditions, bad working conditions, long working hours, etc. This also follows from the national researches in this project, where in some countries the violation of labour laws is sufficient to qualify as exploitation, thus not requiring a 'means' or involuntariness. However, one has to keep in mind that the existence of exploitation does not necessarily mean that THB for labour exploitation exists, as for the existence of THB an act and force are also required.

---

transnationality and organised crime do not always apply." "... the Convention provides that legislators must not incorporate elements concerning transnationality or an organised criminal group into domestic offence provisions."... "In the case of trafficking in persons, domestic offences should apply even where transnationality and the involvement of organised criminal groups do not exist."

A third related problem is that a further definition of exploitation is lacking in the Palermo Protocol, the EU Framework Decision[5], the newly adopted Directive, and at national level. The States under research do indeed have a difficulty with the definition of exploitation. In Austria and Romania for instance, THB for non-sexual exploitative purposes only relates to labour exploitation and does not include slavery or slavery like practices for which separate provisions have been adopted. Acts that are taken into account in Austria to determine whether a case is indeed exploitation include: the oppression of vital interests, disproportionality between service and reward, major part of the payment is taken ruthlessly, no or little payment, working hours are excessive, working conditions are unacceptable. These elements stem from case law in relation to sexual exploitation. In the Netherlands, it has been explicitly left to the judiciary to further define exploitation. In October 2009, the Supreme Court declared that case law developed in relation to sexual exploitation should apply *mutatis mutandis* in cases of labour exploitation to explain the elements 'abuse of authority arising from the actual state of affairs' or 'the abuse of a vulnerable position'.[6] The Supreme Court declared that if these elements are fulfilled, the person finds him- or herself in an exploitative position, thereby using means as a relevant factor for the existence of exploitation (or exploitative position). In Romania, there is a very broad definition of labour exploitation, namely, that violations of legal rules on working conditions, wages, health and security do constitute exploitation. In Spain, such acts do qualify as a crime under criminal labour law, namely, labour exploitation itself. In the latter case, if this was preceded by a trafficking act it constitutes the crime of THB for labour exploitation. As said, the fact that all three elements need to be fulfilled to qualify as a crime of THB draws attention away from the most objectionable part of the crime, namely, the exploitation.

In addition to the lack of a definition of exploitation, the explanation given in the second phrase of Article 3(1), referring to forced labour and slavery (-like practices), does not bring us any further in understanding the content of exploitation, as mentioned above.

Within international law, these acts have long been defined and, although limited, have actually been used. The ILO adopted a definition of forced labour in 1930 stating that forced or compulsory labour[7]:

> *shall mean all work or service which is exacted from any person under the menace of any penalty and for which the said person has not offered himself voluntarily.*

[5] 2002/629/JHA Council Framework Decision of 19 July 2002 on combating Trafficking in Human Beings, [2002] OJ L203.

[6] Supreme Court of the Netherlands, 27 October 2009, LJN: BI7097.

[7] Article 2(1) Convention Concerning Forced or Compulsory labour (ILO no. 29), 39 UNTS 55, 1930.

Slavery is defined in the slavery convention of 1926 as[8]:

> *the status or condition of a person over whom any or all of the powers attaching to the right of ownership are exercised*

For slavery-like practices, we have to refer to the additional convention of 1957 where the following acts are considered as slavery-like practices: debt bondage, serfdom, giving in marriage on payment, transfer of women, wife inheritance, and selling or giving away of a child for exploitation.[9] When looking at this terminology, without going into it in detail, the question that arises is what is the added value of using the term THB instead of the terms forced labour or slavery (-like practices) as were used in the past.[10] Within the ILO, expertise is built on when a case must be considered as one of forced labour, and this expertise can be used for the interpretation of THB for labour exploitation as well.[11] However, what then is the benefit of qualifying a situation as THB when forced labour is at stake?[12] It cannot be denied that the effect of the Palermo Protocol is impressive, with 143 parties signing up to it and harmonisation of the offence all over the world. Regardless of the comments made above, the definition adopted in the protocol has been used at regional[13] and national levels to draw implementation laws. A further and maybe even more important harmonising effect comes from the monitoring mechanism of the US Department of State, in its yearly Trafficking in Persons Report.[14] One criterion in the minimum standards of the Trafficking Victims Protection Act, which is the framework for evaluating national laws and policies, is whether the State has prohibited severe forms of trafficking in its national legislation. Although not formally included in the minimum standards, the Department of State monitors whether a State complies with the obligations in the Palermo Protocol. In one decade, more has been achieved than in the preceding century in which a number of international documents on trafficking as well as on slavery and forced labour were adopted, since these

---

[8] Article 1(1), Slavery Convention of 1926, 25 September 1926, 60 LNTS 253.

[9] Article 1, Supplementary Convention on the Abolition of Slavery, the Slave Trade, and Institutions and Practices Similar to Slavery, 7 September 1956, 226 UNTS 3.

[10] See on this matter J.C. Hathaway, 'The Human Rights Quagmire of "Human Trafficking"' and A.T. Gallagher, 'Human Rights and Human Trafficking: Quagmire or Firm Ground? A Response to James Hathaway' (2008/2009) Va.J.Int'L, 19, 1 and 4.

[11] See e.g. <http://www.ilo.org/sapfl/Informationresources/ILOPublications/lang--en/docName--WCMS_081991/index.htm>.

[12] Valuable research on this question has been conducted by Klara Skrivankova, Between decent work and forced labour: examining the continuum of exploitation, November 2010, Joseph Rowntree Foundation.

[13] Examples of the regional levels can be found in the EU Directive on Preventing and Combating Trafficking in Human Beings and the Protection of Victims, 2011 and the Council of Europe Convention on Action against Trafficking in Human Beings, 2005,.

[14] Available at: <http://www.state.gov/g/tip/rls/tiprpt/2010/142744.htm>.

documents lacked implementation at a national level. Furthermore, the Palermo Protocol revived the debate on the use of the old terminology. It is noteworthy to mention that recently in the UK and Ireland new provisions prohibiting forced labour have been adopted, apart from the criminalisation of THB. Despite these positive effects, the fact is that the definition adopted in the Palermo Protocol has driven attention away from actual exploitation, and there is a serious need to further explain when a situation must be qualified as exploitation.

An addition to the problems indicated above is the difficulty of overlap with other crimes. Serbia, mainly as a transit country, reports a problematic overlap with human smuggling, because when the presumed trafficking is intercepted at the border the exploitation has not yet taken place, making it difficult to prove the intent of exploitation on the part of the suspect. In Austria, there is an overlap with the provision of the exploitation of foreigners, which does not qualify as THB although this act most likely includes the three elements of THB. In Romania, there is an overlap of THB with the provisions for labour exploitation, leading to a paradoxical situation where in cases of THB where actual exploitation has not yet taken place, higher penalties are given than in cases of labour exploitation because these are often dealt with under labour law. Apart from the new provision adopted in December 2010 implementing the EU Framework Decision on THB, Spain does have a section on Criminal Labour Law that determines when a violation of labour laws constitutes a criminal act. Furthermore, although it does not use the term THB, it is clear that there is an overlap.

Why is it important to determine whether a situation qualifies as THB for labour exploitation? The following reasons will answer this question. First, because victims of THB are often granted special protection, often including a reflection period and a temporary residence permit. If an exploitative situation is not considered as THB, the person is not considered to be a victim of THB and thus cannot apply for special protection. Second, if a case is 'only' dealt with under labour law, the penalties are often less severe and the offence is considered to be less serious.

A final question that has arisen in the research is whether sexual exploitation and labour exploitation can actually be dealt with in one definition, as in the Palermo Protocol, since the nature of these crimes differs considerably, especially when prostitution is not considered as legal labour. It would be beyond the scope of this research to answer all these questions or deal with the difficulties raised, but it is clear that further clarification on these matters is needed. If not, then instances of THB will not be considered as such, which might have major consequences for the victims of this type of crime who are then not treated appropriately.

1.2. Risk of extending the scope of THB

Although in the Dutch criminal code the wording of the Palermo Protocol and consequently the EU Framework Decision on THB has been chosen, since the Supreme Court case in October 2009, judges have reinterpreted the provision more lenient and now apply it even in cases that are normally not considered as trafficking cases, such as the fraudulent purchasing of cell phone contracts.[15] This risk is also apparent in the situation in Romania, where the mere violation of labour laws and social laws can be considered as THB for labour exploitation. The same applies to the newly adopted provision on THB in Spain. In the latter case, a violation of labour laws qualifies as exploitation in cases where a profit is made. As far as we know, there have been no cases in Romania or Spain where the mere violation of labour laws actually led to a conviction of THB for labour exploitation. In the cases that were studied in these countries, there was always a form of force and involuntariness present and not merely the violation of labour laws. If the range of the provision is extended to a standard that is not normally considered as THB, this might also have negative consequences for the awareness of THB and the erosion of the crime. It is perfectly possible that in the end people will not consider THB to be a severe crime, which will diminish all the efforts that have been made to put THB on the (political) agenda. Consequently, police and prosecution services will be less inclined to investigate and prosecute cases of THB, and we therefore need to take action to prevent this from happening.

1.3. How to define labour exploitation: using home country or host country standards as a point of reference

When further considering the definition of labour exploitation, the question of which standards apply when deciding whether labour conditions are exploitative or not must be answered. It is well known that major differences in labour conditions exist in different countries, even within the EU. According to Eurostat, as of July 2010, the highest minimum wage was recorded in Luxembourg (EUR 1,725 per month) and the lowest in Bulgaria and Romania (EUR 123 and EUR 137 respectively). When taking the situation in the home country as a starting point, it would be highly attractive for companies in Luxembourg to hire personnel from Bulgaria or Romania and apply the standard on wages from those countries. That would have negative consequences for the labour market in Luxembourg, as well as leading to exploitative situations since the standard of living is much more expensive in Luxembourg than in Bulgaria or Romania. To avoid such situations and to prevent social dumping, the EU adopted some harmonising measures to further facilitate the free movement of workers and services and the freedom of establishment. With regard to workers, the host country

[15] See M. Heemskerk and C. Rijken, 'Combating Trafficking in Human Beings for Labour Exploitation in the Netherlands', Chapter 2 and L. van Krimpen, 'The interpretation and implementation of labour exploitation in Dutch case law', Chapter 11 in this book.

principle applies, which means that workers from other EU MSs must be treated in the same way as the host country's nationals. For self-employed persons, the principle of freedom to provide services applies, which means that self-employed persons can determine their own standards. With regard to posted workers, the situation is more complicated, since a combination of the two applies.[16] One can easily imagine that there is an incentive to attract self-employed persons, as no standard is prescribed for this group, but which creates a risk of bogus self-employment. Furthermore, the EU Court of Justice (CoJ) case law on posted workers (Laval,[17] Commission v. Luxembourg,[18] Rüffert)[19], the Court gave prevalence to the freedom to provide services and to establishment at the expense of workers' rights and social security, and gave, for instance, a restrictive interpretation of Article 3(10) of the posting directive in the case of the Commission v. Luxembourg, limiting the possibilities to impose extra protective measures for posted workers in Luxembourg.

How then does this relate to combating THB for labour exploitation? First, the legal framework shows that it is often not a black and white situation to determine the legal position of a person at work in the EU, and to determine which labour standards apply. Second, by limiting the possibilities to restrict, for example, the freedom to provide services, the EU draws the boundaries of this freedom. By doing so, it implicitly restricts national autonomy as to how to give substance to the term exploitation. In the Netherlands, for instance, the Supreme Court decided that Dutch standards should be taken into account when deciding whether a situation is exploitative or not. However, taking into consideration the fact that certain EU citizens may work in the Netherlands based on the freedom to provide services (i.e. self-employed persons and posted workers), the question arises whether the ruling of the Dutch Supreme Court must be interpreted in the sense that the legal framework for Dutch self-employed persons also applies for self-employed persons from other EU MSs, meaning that they are free to apply labour conditions and wages.[20] The rulings of the CoJ mentioned above seem to prohibit another understanding. Considering the substantial differences in minimum wages and costs of living in the different EU Member States as mentioned above, it is questionable whether this is desirable, and whether this does not make persons from certain (low income) EU countries vulnerable to exploitation in other (high income) EU countries. To tackle this problem, the Spanish authors propose the

[16] For further elaboration, see A. Middelburg and C. Rijken, 'The EU Legal Framework on Combating Trafficking in Human Beings for Labour Exploitation', Chapter 6 in this book.

[17] *Laval v. Svenska Byggnadsarbetareförbundet*, Case C-341/05, E.C.R. I-11767 [2007].

[18] *Commission v. Luxembourg*, Case C-319/06, E.C.R. I-04323 [2008].

[19] *Rüffert v. Land Niedersachsen*, Case C-346/06, E.C.R. I-01989 [2008].

[20] In 2001, the CoJ ruled on a case where the freedom to provide services was invoked by self-employed prostitutes from the Czech Republic and other countries. The Court then ruled that if this was possible for own nationals it must be possible for other EU citizens and citizens from states with whom the EU has concluded association agreements with as well, *Jany and others*, C-268/99, 20.11.2001, Jur 2001, P. I-8615.

adoption of host country standards in all cases, regardless of the way in which a person is employed. They even go a step further in proposing a financial penalty if local standards are not adhered to. From a social perspective, this would be a good idea; however, it would most likely run counter to the freedom to provide services as it is interpreted by the CoJ.

1.4. Rebalancing freedoms and social policy within the EU

As long as the difference in minimum wages remains within the EU, there will be an incentive for people to migrate.[21] In order to have a more competitive labour market in which the fundamental rights of workers are guaranteed, it is worth considering whether it is achievable and desirable to strive for European minimum standards. In relation to working conditions, we could say that this is the case and a lot has already been achieved,[22] however, in relation to wages, this seems to be less realistic, at least in the short-term, given the considerable differences between States as indicated above.

As mentioned earlier, the liberalisation of the labour market within the EU does have its downside. The application of the free movement of workers and services without a solid policy on labour conditions and measures against social dumping make certain groups more vulnerable to exploitative practices. Posted workers and those working as bogus self-employers need special attention. Posted workers (non-self-employed service providers), are only subject to the labour standards of the host State with regard to the so-called core provisions: maximum work periods and minimum rest periods; minimum paid annual holidays; minimum rates of pay, health, safety and hygiene at work; equal treatment of men and women; and other non-discrimination provisions.[23] The cases mentioned above in which the CoJ has decided in favour of the free movement of services and freedom of establishment have been widely discussed and criticised. The main critics were concerned about the effects of these cases on the right to collective action and to conclude collective agreements, although the effects on labour rights and on social dumping have received some attention as well. At the EU level, these concerns have found fertile ground. The realisation at EU level of the erosion of political and social support for market integration and the lack of attention to the creation of a

---

[21] See for instance: C. Giulietti, *Is the Minimum Wage a Pull Factor for Immigrants?* (IZA 9 Institute for the Study of Labour, discussion paper series No. 5410, December 2010); J. Cremers, *In search of Cheap Labour in Europe, Working and Living Conditions of Posted Workers* (European Institute for Construction labour Research, CLR Studies 6, Brussels 2011).

[22] For instance, directive on working conditions for temporary workers directive 2008/104/EC, on part-time work directive 97/81/EC, on equal treatment directive 2000/78/EC, on working hours directive 2003/88/EC but also Regulation 593/2008, the Rome I regulation, for instance, in Article 8.

[23] Article 3(1) Posting Directive, Directive 96/71.

single market for *all* EU citizens, has led to the adoption of a new aim for the single market, namely, a social market economy.[24] To that end, a new strategy for the single market has been drafted by Maria Monti on which the European Commission has adopted a communication for a highly competitive social market economy.[25] Proposals 29 and 30 especially relate to our concerns here. According to proposal 29, the Commission will conduct an in-depth analysis of the social impact of all proposed legislation concerning the single market. It explicitly refers to the Charter on Fundamental Rights and the strategy for the effective implementation of this Charter.[26] Furthermore, the Commission intends to adopt a new legislative proposal aimed at improving the implementation of the posting directive, especially focussing on fundamental social rights (proposal 30). To give further body to Europe's social policy, the EU, through the Treaty of Lisbon, expanded its competences in this field. Article 4 of the Treaty on the Functioning of the EU (TFEU) now states that the EU has a shared competence in relation to social policy for the aspects defined in the Treaty. With regard to the other aspects, it will retain its complementary competence and it may take initiatives to ensure coordination of MSs' social policies.[27] This means that we have to look into the specific articles of the TFEU to find out whether the EU is competent to adopt measures that might affect social policy, including working conditions. When doing so, Article 153 TFEU is most important as it relates to the working environment to protect workers' health and safety, working conditions, social security and the social protection of workers, the protection of workers after the termination of employment contract, conditions for employment for Third Country Nationals, equality, combating social exclusion, etc. With regard to working conditions and the social protection of workers, harmonisation is excluded, meaning that the EU cannot adopt harmonising measures on these issues. However, under Letter b of Paragraph 2, this prohibition seems to be somewhat limited by allowing Member States to adopt minimum requirements for the gradual implementation of the rules. Even with this exception, the powers of the EU to adopt legislative measures in relation to working conditions and the social protection of workers are limited. It is not unlikely that further development of EU policy on this matter will take place along non-legislative lines, for instance, through the open method of coordination or through the adoption of soft law instruments.[28]

---

[24] Article 3(3) TFEU.

[25] COM(2010)608 fin. 11.11.2010, Communication from the Commission to the European Parliament, the Council, the Economic and Social Committee and the Committee of the Regions, *Towards a Single Market Act. For a highly competitive social market economy, 50 proposals for improving our work, business and exchanges with one another.*

[26] Charter of Fundamental Rights of the EU, *OJ* C 364, 18.12.2000.

[27] Article 5 TFEU.

[28] The OMC provides a framework for cooperation between the member states whose national policies can be directed towards certain common objectives. Under this intergovernmental method, the member states are evaluated by one another, with the Commission's role being limited to surveillance. Further on the OMC, L. Senden, The

A more social policy within the EU, including the labour market, could develop conditions for the application of the freedoms in such a way that they prevent exploitation, instead of a fully unrestricted application of the freedoms which might contribute to the vulnerability of workers. Although it is welcomed that the social face of the internal market will be an explicit strategy for the EU in the years to come, the contribution of it to the prevention of THB for labour exploitation remains to be seen.

Another incentive for a more social policy will be generated from the Charter of Fundamental Rights of the EU. First of all, Article 5 includes the prohibition of slavery and forced labour as well as THB. The freedom to choose an occupation and the right to engage in work is guaranteed in Article 15, in which it is stated that Third Country Nationals (TCN) who are allowed to work in the EU are entitled to working conditions equivalent to those of the citizens of the EU. Furthermore, Chapter VI on Solidarity includes some important rights for workers such as fair and just working conditions (Article 31), the prohibition of child labour (Article 32), and social security and social assistance (Article 34). Although there are some serious limitations to the application of the Charter, namely, that it only applies to Member States to the extent that they are implementing Union law,[29] and provisions of the Charter cannot be invoked against the UK and Poland,[30] it is an important step forward that these rights are considered as fundamental, that the CoJ is competent to rule on these rights, and that the institutions are also bound to these rights.[31]

OMC and its patch in the European regulatory and constitutional landscape, EUI Working Papers RSCAS 2010/61 Robert Schuman Centre for Advanced Studies.

[29] Article 51(1) Charter of Fundamental Rights of the EU.

[30] Protocol 30 to the TFEU.

[31] Article 51(1) Charter of Fundamental Rights of the EU.

Part II
National and international cooperation in combating trafficking in human beings for labour exploitation

2.1. Increased cooperation at the national level

2.1.1. New actors in combating THB for labour exploitation

What has been reported by all the country rapporteurs is the involvement of new actors in the field of combating THB. Especially labour services or inspectorates and entities related thereto have now become involved or given a specific role to identify cases of THB for labour exploitation. It largely depends on national structures as to whether this is centralised in one organisation (such as is the case in Serbia and Romania) or whether it is divided between separate organisational structures with different tasks (such as in the Netherlands), more de-centrally conducted (as in Spain), or a combination of these (as in Austria).

What all the countries do have in common is that addressing issues of THB is new for these organisations and that it requires creating awareness of exploitative situations. The parties involved are often not familiar with criminal law and they lack investigative powers. From the participating countries, the Netherlands is the only one that indeed has a special investigative service for social affairs. In most countries, specialised units at police level, and sometimes also at prosecution level, do exist. Most of them receive regular training on THB. However, in Romania, the specific section dealing with THB is specialised in organised crime.

Besides limited awareness about THB for labour exploitation, unfamiliarity with criminal law, lack of investigative powers, and the complexity of the definition of THB often leads to confusion for the relevant parties as to when a certain situation should be perceived as THB. For these reasons, THB situations may not be recognised as such. Furthermore, the actors involved often see only part of the THB activities, making it difficult for them to recognise (potential) cases of THB. In addition, the perception still exists that labour exploitation is less serious than sexual exploitation, resulting in the fact that parties do not act on indicators of THB for labour exploitation. Furthermore, parties that may come across indicators of THB may be under the impression that THB lies outside their mandate, and will not act on the detected indicators.

In the Netherlands, where the monitoring of labour laws is divided over many divisions, it is difficult to identify cases of exploitation because the information reaches the inspectors in a fragmented way. Indicators of THB are more difficult to identify in these cases. If data collected is not stored and analysed centrally, indicators of THB will not be discovered. However, even in cases where such a centralised structure is in place, such as the EMM (expertise centre on human smuggling and human trafficking) in the Netherlands, this is no guarantee that indicators and thus instances of THB and victims of THB will be identified. Furthermore, if inspections are being held, inspectors visit those branches that are at risk of violating labour laws and they have items prepared that they have to focus on. In such a regime, it is difficult to look for indicators of THB.

2.1.2. Lack of information exchange between the various actors

All countries have reported problems involving cooperation between the various actors, and especially in relation to the information exchange between those actors. These problems and the ensuing rationales derived from the country reports are discussed below.

In most countries, information exchange between the various actors is not legally formalised, or is formalised in a fragmented way such as is the case in Austria. In Serbia, it is reported that the cooperation is to a large extent dependent on personal contacts between people from the inspectorate and the police, which must be considered as a weak point. In the national strategy to combat THB, provisions on cooperation and information exchange are adopted, but this strategy has not been implemented yet in Serbia. The same applies for Romania and Spain. In the 2006 Romania national action plan, provisions were adopted for enhanced cooperation and information exchange with a broad number of actors, including transporters, taxi companies, construction companies, etc. In Spain, the integrated plan to combat THB was adopted, including the strengthening of cooperation, but mainly within the police and between the police and NGOs. The Galicia protocol, in addition, includes a model agreement that should be used for cooperation between the police and the labour inspectorate. Finally, in Spain, the working group on THB will draft a national action plan. The integrated plan and the protocol have been in force since 2009 and 2010 respectively and it is too early to draw conclusions as to their effectiveness.

In many countries, the inspectorates have an obligation to report criminal offences to the police for further investigation. To that end, inspectors need to be able to recognise indicators of THB and therefore awareness raising and training is needed to create sensitivity for indicators of THB for labour exploitation. Some countries also reported a kind of competition between authorities as to who is best equipped to deal with cases of THB. Those institutions and organisations that have been involved in the identification and combating of THB for a longer period sometimes have the idea that they are the ones with the best training and competency to combat THB and they do not want to share information, as is reported in Austria. In this way, a conflict of interests might arise. A related problem indicated in all the countries was the lack of feedback once information was shared with other authorities (often by labour inspectorates to law enforcement officers). Consequently, the providing actors did not have information on the relevance of the information they had transmitted, nor did they know if and how their information was used. Here, also, a change in mentality would be required. Regulations on data protection are another reason for the lack of information sharing. The legal aspects of data protection are dealt with below.

2.1.3. Intensified cooperation and data protection at national level

The question of the role of data protection in information exchange (or lack thereof) is important to address since many of the researchers in their reports point out that there is a need in practice for intensified cooperation between all actors involved.

Organisations related to labour inspections, municipalities, trade unions and the like, are now also involved in combating THB and especially in the early identification of it. Cooperation between all the actors involved gives rise to important questions on data protection, especially when a suspect has not yet been identified. For instance, the aim of information collected by municipalities relating to housing regulations, fire safety, etc is not, or not primarily, for combating of labour exploitation. Exchange of this information might be problematic, especially if the limited information available to the municipalities does not qualify as a clear indication of THB but only when combined with other information it might be an indication for the existence of a case of THB. If the information is indeed a clear indication of THB, then usually there is legal ground to share information with law enforcement authorities.

Furthermore, the data protection regimes and rules for transmission of collected data by the various actors are often different. In the Romania report, it is suggested that more institutions and organisations must help to identify THB for labour exploitation at an early stage. One can, for instance, think about the transport sector, taxi drivers, schools, health care workers. Some of these are restricted from sharing information based on their duty of professional confidentiality. Furthermore, the police often fall within a separate regime governing the dissemination of information.

In the Netherlands, in order to facilitate enhanced cooperation between the actors, a programmatic approach has been developed.[32] Within this approach, measures to combat THB are developed from a local, regional, national and an international level, and aspects of an administrative, criminal and international nature are considered. Within such an approach, information exchange is even more complicated since additional actors are involved in the early identification of THB for labour exploitation, such as municipalities, tax authorities, investigation departments, NGOs and trade unions. In order to facilitate cooperation between all these actors, covenants are established. It is the aim that data protection is taken into account in these covenants. However, as highlighted by the Dutch report as well as the evaluation of the

[32] For further elaboration, see Chapter 2 on the Netherlands.

Dutch Act on data protection,[33] such covenants are not easy to establish. The evaluation has identified that some five steps need to be taken to safely exchange information.[34] Furthermore, it has been established that in cases where there is a common goal within the covenant that is considered to be of primary importance (combating crime or the protection of vulnerable persons), cooperation and information exchange will take place regardless of the data protection burdens.[35]

The question that arises is whether the rules on data protection are too complex and if they limit information exchange, or if it all comes down to attitude and whether data protection legislation is used by the actors as a reason not to exchange information. When looking into the specific regulations and acts, it seems that there is leeway for information exchange. For instance, in the Protection Personal Data Act (Wet Bescherming Persoonsgegevens, BPG) in the Netherlands, provisions are created for the dissemination of data for law enforcement purposes.[36] Investigation of possible suspects of THB for labour exploitation seems to fit this purpose. However, further research into the rules on data protection in relation to THB for labour exploitation as well as into the question whether and to what extent the programmatic approach is transposable to other States is required.

Enhanced information exchange also raises more fundamental questions. First, established data protection principles should be upheld. Second, when actors with many different functions in society exchange information, the roles of these actors might be mixed up and the division of powers might be at stake when the judiciary uses information collected by the executing powers and risks blurring legal boundaries. This is not necessarily problematic as long as it is conducted in a transparent way, based on legal provisions and is independently monitored, and as long as the concerned person has the possibility for legal redress. Third, the risk of data mining and phishing increases in cases of large-scale information exchange without sufficient monitoring. Fourth, a general problem in relation to data protection, both at a national and EU level, is the issue of false-identities and the lack of quality in

---

[33] H.B. Winter et al. *Wat niet weet wat niet deert. Evaluatieonderzoek naar de werking van de Wet Bescherming Persoonsgegevens in de Praktijk* (WODC 2008) [evaluation research Dutch Act on data protection].

[34] These are 1) determine the tasks of the organisations involved and their interest in information exchange in relation to these tasks, 2) determine the aims of information exchange, 3) determine the legal frameworks that apply for the different organisations and which information can be exchanged by each organisation, 4) determine which organisations can exchange with which, and what information can be exchanged, and under what conditions can this information be exchanged, 5) determine who is responsible for the information exchange. Then maybe a sixth step is to lay down all these findings in a covenant. Evaluation research Dutch Act on data protection, pp. 122-124.

[35] Evaluation research Dutch Act on data protection, p. 131.

[36] Dutch Report, section Act for the Protection of Personal Data.

respect of the data itself. Fifth, and last, in relation to THB, one has to be aware that profiling in criminal law should focus on the perpetrators and that this is not different in cases of THB. What easily happens is the profiling of the victims, with the ultimate aim of getting testimonies and finding the perpetrators. However, the profiling of the victims can be harmful to the victims, breaches their privacy, is stigmatising and is an investment of energy in the wrong place. The focus should rather be on the perpetrator than on the victim. All of these aspects need to be taken into account as well when considering enhanced information exchange.

2.1.4. Intensified cooperation and data protection at EU level

When aiming at intensified cooperation to combat THB for labour exploitation, this must not be limited to the national level but must be applied on an international level as well. Similar to the national levels, the need for further and enhanced information exchange is also felt at EU level. This is, for instance, reflected in the high number of databases that have been established or will be established in the near future. An overview, given by the European Commission last year, of database usage in the areas of criminal law and migration law shows that there are at least 18 databases.[37] It is hard to control who may access these databases and what the information retrieved from these databases is used for.[38] The proliferation of so many databases does raise a number of questions: how can the reliability of the information be secured, how can it be guaranteed that the information is not used for purposes other than what it was collected for, how can the data be adequately protected, and how can data subjects have access to justice in case of (presumed) violations of their rights. Despite the directive and the framework decision on data protection that are often referred to in the documents on which the databases are established, an overall framework on the rights of data subjects is absent. In general, they are referred to their national system for redress.[39]

When addressing an integrated approach to THB in which all relevant actors take responsibility, broad information exchange in the phase before a suspect is identified might be needed. However, this can only be done when certain conditions are fulfilled. This mainly refers to the rules on data protection, the aim for which the information was collected (purpose limitation), the possibilities for redress, and the principle of proportionality. The current organisation, both at a national and EU level, does not meet these conditions.

---

[37] Memo/10/349 Brussels, 20 July 2010, on EU information management instruments.

[38] Geyer gives an insight into these problems when listing all the different authorities accessing the various databases in: Geyer, "Taking stock: databases and systems of information exchange in the Area of Freedom, Security and Justice", (2008) Challenge Liberty and Security, Research Paper no. 9.

[39] C. Rijken, 'Rebalancing Security and Justice. Fundamental rights protection in police and judicial cooperation in criminal matters' (2010) CML Rev.

2.2. International cooperation

Over the last two decades, Justice and Home affairs, later renamed Police and Judicial Cooperation in Criminal Matters, and now, since Lisbon, included in the new title of the Area of Freedom, Security and Justice, has expanded and developed into a mature field of law within the EU with its own dynamics.[40] Cooperation within the EU has been facilitated to a large extent by a number of framework decisions, the adoption of the principle of mutual recognition and the principle of availability. It would go beyond the scope of this chapter to discuss the entire legal framework, but it can be said that in cases where cooperation with other EU countries is needed, the authorities do profit from these developments, including in cases of THB for labour exploitation. However, this does not mean that cooperation problems within the EU are resolved, nor that cooperation outside the EU is problematic. The case discussed in Chapter 1 on Austria gives a positive example of cooperation with Romania, where there was direct contact between the authorities, and solutions were found easily. A less positive example can be found in one of the case studies discussed in Chapter 2 on the Netherlands, where the request for a hearing through video conferencing with Portugal caused a serious delay in the proceedings because Portugal was technically not equipped for video conferencing and they failed to inform the investigative judge about this. It can be concluded that cultural differences and (a lack of) willingness, still plays an important role when cooperation is required, often based on a lack of trust. Outside the EU but within the Council of Europe (CoE) territory, cooperation in general takes place based on the CoE Conventions on Extradition and Mutual Legal Assistance and its protocols. The second protocol to the mutual legal assistance convention is of particular importance since it adopted a large number of the far-reaching provisions included in the EU Convention on Mutual Assistance. As follows from Chapter 4 on Serbia, the only country in this project outside of the EU, cooperation takes place most often on a regional level with States where an agreement has already been established. In cases of THB in general, an important legal basis for cooperation is to be found in the mother convention of the Palermo Protocol, namely, the Convention on Transnational Organised Crime. Article 16 deals with extradition, Article 17 with the transfer of sentenced persons, and Article 18 with mutual legal assistance. The latter is a very lengthy one, including spontaneous information exchange and hearings by video conferencing. In accordance with Article 19, joint investigative bodies may be established. Article 1, Paragraph 2 of the Palermo Protocol states that the provisions of UNCTOC apply *mutatis mutandis* to the protocol unless indicated otherwise. This means that in the absence of other legal instruments, the provisions in the

---

[40] See especially Section 2 of A. Middelburg and C. Rijken, 'The EU Legal Framework on Combating Trafficking in Human Beings for Labour Exploitation', Chapter 6 in this book.

Convention are a solid basis for cooperation in THB cases between States that are party to both the convention and the protocol.

From the country reports, it follows that liaison officers are easily used when cooperation is sought with other countries. They often know the situation in the other country and can more easily identify the appropriate person to cooperate with. Especially in States that are considered less reliable, liaison officers are particularly valuable in identifying the right person and preventing information given to foreign officers from being forwarded to suspects.

2.2.1. *The role of European agencies in combating THB for labour exploitation*

As mentioned in many other reports and studies, European agencies, especially Europol and Eurojust, are not used to their full potential. This is not different in cases of THB for labour exploitation. Although the functioning of these agencies was not specifically researched in this project, many have indicated that Europol and Eurojust are just below the radar of investigative officers and therefore are often not actively approached in cases of THB for labour exploitation. This attitude seems to be based on a reluctance to use these agencies, because the actors think that to do so would be too time consuming. However, Romania reported positive experiences with Europol as well. This concerned a case in which minor gipsy boys were trafficked to the UK for the purpose of forced begging. The cooperation with Europol in this case was very satisfactory. When looking at the broad set of instruments available to law enforcement officers for cooperation in criminal matters, one might indeed question what Europol and Eurojust can add. As mentioned in the contribution by van Dijk and Vonk in this book, the fact that these organisations can look at the whole chain of the trafficking process, from recruitment to exploitation, and provide an insight into the modus operandi, is indeed a benefit. Even stronger, one can say that with the ruling of the European Court of Human Rights in the Rantsev case, in which not only Cyprus but also Russia was convicted for violating procedural obligations under Article 4 ECHR, the latter by not investigating the process of recruitment of Ms. Rantseva on its territory, the need to have Europol involved in trafficking cases is more pressing.[41]

The role of Eurojust is often mentioned in cases where more than two States are involved in an investigation and prosecution, and in relation to the establishment of joint investigation teams (JITs). Although the impression is that Eurojust is used more easily, especially because it is technically well equipped to hold large meetings with many countries, it is not used frequently in cases of THB for labour exploitation in the States under research.

However, the benefit of both agencies is often described and recognised, especially by those who do use the services of these organisations. Although

[41] *Rantsev v. Cyprus and Russia*, ECtHR (Application no. 25965/04) [2010] paras 307-309.

earlier recommendations that Europol and Eurojust must be used more frequently are important, it is more interesting to know why there is a reluctance to use them in some States, and why so many law enforcement officers do not use the resources that are available. More fundamental research on these aspects would be valuable.

2.2.2. Frontex; a new actor on the playing field?

When considering THB in general, and for labour exploitation in particular, special attention must be paid to Frontex.[42] Frontex is the acronym of Frontiere Extérieures, a body that was established to secure the external borders of the EU. Its main task is to coordinate cooperation and to assist Member States in the management of the EU's external borders. It also assists Member States in implementing operational aspects of external border management, including the return of Third Country Nationals who are illegally present in a Member State.[43] In this way, Frontex is linked to the prevention of illegal migration. It must be stressed that THB must not be confused with illegal migration, and that the debate on trafficking is often troubled when considering the illegal status of many victims of trafficking. This fact is too often used as an argument for more restrictive migration laws. However, in this chapter, the opposite will be advocated, namely, that THB is worse off with restrictive migration laws and that a more social and humane migration policy is needed in an integrated approach to THB. With these remarks in mind, one must understand the possible role of Frontex, namely, as an agency guaranteeing the right to seek asylum and, if possible, identifying people at risk of THB or potential victims of THB, and to look for the perpetrators. If Frontex is aware that it can play this role, it must be given the tools to perform this task.

In the past, Frontex has been criticised, especially in relation to the HERA operations they conducted on request and in cooperation with Spain.[44]

---

[42] Established on 1 May 2005, based on Regulation 2007/2004 of 26 October 2004 [2004] OJ L349/1, 25.11.2004. Currently a proposal is tabled to amend the regulation, 24.2.2010, COM(2010)61 Proposal for a regulation of the European Parliament and the Council amending Council Regulation (EC) No 2007/2004 establishing a European Agency for the Management of Operational Cooperation at the External Borders of the member states of the European Union (FRONTEX). The adoption of this amended regulation is planned in June 2011. The amendment was considered necessary based on two evaluations of FRONTEX; an internal one COM(2008)67 fin, 13.2.2008 and an external one by COWI, *Frontex External evaluation of the European Agency for the Management of Operational Cooperation at the External Borders of the Member States of the European Union, Final Report*, January 2009.

[43] Consideration 5 Regulation 2007/2004.

[44] See F. Manrique López, F.J. Arrieta Idiakez and F.Manrique Rojo, 'Combating Trafficking in Human Beings for Labour Exploitation in Spain', Chapter 5 in this book.

In Chapter 5 on Spain, reference is made to the HERA operations, which must be regarded as joint operations that were established in conformity with Article 3, Regulation 2007/2004. These joint operations (in which Spain, Italy, Portugal and Finland participated) were coordinated by Frontex and took place in the territorial waters of various African States to prevent illegal migrants from trying to reach the Spanish Canary Islands, by preventing them from leaving the territorial waters of the African States. When these migrants were intercepted, they were 'accompanied' by Frontex back to the mainland of the African States and handed over to the authorities of those countries. They were prevented from applying for asylum, and they could not appeal the decision to refuse entry, if such a decision had been made at all. From the perspective of combating THB for labour exploitation, and given the fact that trafficking (and smuggling) is often orchestrated in the home and transit countries, it is not inconceivable that in this way people (potential victims of THB) are once again placed in a situation that makes them vulnerable to exploitation, or are even handed to smugglers who might in fact be traffickers.

Criticisms of these operations seem to have been heard, and an adjustment to the policy saw the establishment of Rapid Border Intervention Teams (Rabits). Rabits were established for the first time in October 2010 when Greece faced a huge influx of migrants from Turkey.[45]

Following comments from the UNHCR, as well as evaluations from Frontex, a proposal to amend the regulation establishing Frontex (regulation 2007/2004) was tabled, including many positive references to fundamental rights and international protection, especially the right to seek asylum and the principle of non-refoulement.[46]

[45] It is estimated that some 40,000 migrants entered Greece's territory illegally in the 10 months preceding the operation. Also Chapter 6 on the European legal framework.

[46] COM(2010)61 Proposal for a regulation of the European Parliament and the Council amending Council Regulation (EC) No 2007/2004 establishing a European Agency for the Management of Operational Cooperation at the External Borders of the Member States of the European Union (FRONTEX).

Part III
Victim protection and assistance

3.1. When is a person to be considered a victim of THB?

From the interviews and limited research conducted into the victims of THB for labour exploitation, the impression arises that there is a difference in the needs of victims of labour exploitation compared to the victims of sexual exploitation. Chapter 4 on Serbia, and specifically the research conducted by the authors on male victims, provides valuable information. Although testimonies are difficult to acquire, in labour exploitation cases many victims either do not see that the employer did anything wrong (they thought it was logical that they were treated differently to host country colleagues) or they feel loyal to the employer. Furthermore, the only thing many victims want is to find new work. Often, victims are afraid their illegal status will be exposed when criminal proceedings for THB are lodged, and that this would jeopardise their possibilities for future work.

Linked to these findings is the observation that victims do not consider themselves to be victims, a fact that was reported by most of the countries. The explanation given for this is that male victims think of victims as being passive and helpless women, and they do not see themselves in this description. This perception is also present in police officers, prosecutors and judges, for instance. The example given in the Austria case study provides a good example. In that case, the victim was very assertive and spoke German fluently. This did not fit with the picture of victims of THB that the judges had in mind. The question whether this is indeed specific to victims of THB for labour exploitation must be answered in the negative, since victims of THB for sexual exploitation often do not consider themselves as victims in the first place either.

Because of the complexity of labour relations within the EU, where people can work as a worker, posted worker or self-employer, with all different legal regimes, it is difficult to draw a clear distinction between illegal workers and people using their rights achieved within the EU. In addition, although illegal workers are, of course, not *per se* exploited, their illegal status is an indication of their vulnerability for exploitation. Furthermore, this might raise some ethical questions as well. If a worker from a host country works overtime voluntarily, sometimes without being paid, why would we not consider this as exploitation, while in the case of a foreign worker we might (at least in some countries) consider this as exploitation or even THB for labour exploitation. Do we, in these cases, negatively discriminate against our own nationals, or is the threshold for foreign workers too low? Furthermore, is the consent of a foreign worker considered different to the consent of a local worker? Moreover, if this is the case, would this be a matter of paternalism *vis-à-vis* the foreign workers?

The question behind these questions and thoughts is when does a person qualify as a victim and who determines if that a person is a victim? In the whole debate on trafficking in human beings, these questions are often not addressed, although they do have huge implications not only on the systems of referral and assistance, but also on the policy framework for THB as a whole. The qualification of a victim depends largely on the point of reference one takes. A person can be considered a victim of a crime once the crime is indeed proven by the judiciary. One might say that a person cannot be a victim of THB when the crime has not been proven by the judiciary. However, what if the suspect is not convicted for THB because the prosecutor made a fatal error in the proceedings following which the judge could only dismiss the case? The person against whom the trafficking took place is no less a victim because of the dismissal, but the THB in that case has not been proven by the judiciary.
A different picture can be drawn when considering a victim from a health care or relief aid perspective. Then the question of whether a conviction for THB has been declared is of less importance, and relief or health care is not limited to the victims of the cases in which a prosecution or conviction has taken place.

There seems to be a discrepancy between the qualification of people as victims, and how victims perceive themselves. Research indicates that people move to other countries for work to improve their living conditions or those of their relatives.[47] They simply think it is justified that they do not receive the same rights as the workers from the host country. When irregularities are identified, they sometimes want to continue working for the employer in any event, or they want to continue working because they think they will be paid the money that the employer owes them. Some want to go back to their own country as soon as possible, while others only want help in finding another job or in achieving legal status. Although a bit premature to conclude, it seems that fear of the trafficker seems to be of less influence to the victims of labour exploitation than those of sexual exploitation.

Furthermore, it can be concluded that the percentage of male victims is higher in cases of THB for labour exploitation than in cases of THB for sexual exploitation. This gives rise to other problems such as a lack of capacity for male victims in shelters, or the fact that assistance and care is predominantly focussed on female victims of sexual exploitation. These problems are highlighted in all reports and are therefore of specific importance. In addition, male victims are more often punished for migration offences (for instance the illegal crossing of a border) than female victims. In Serbia, victims of THB for labour exploitation staying illegally are isolated with the aim of expelling them,

---

[47] A. Arya, S. Roy, 'When Poor Women Migrate' in S. Arya and A. Roy, *Poverty, Gender and Migration* (New Delhi: Sage Publications 2006); S. Sassen, *Globalisation and its discontents. Essays on the new mobility of people and money* (New York: W.W. Norton & Company 1998); C. Rijken and R. Römkens, 'Trafficking for Sexual Purposes as a Globalised Shadow Economy: Human Security as the Tool to Facilitate a Human Rights Based Approach' in R. Letschert and J. van Dijk, *The New Faces of Victimhood. Globalisation, Transnational Crimes and Victim Rights* (Springer 2011) pp. 73-98.

while if they have the necessary documents they will not be allowed into a 'shelter'.

3.2. Recognition and referral

The comments made above tie into the more general problem of the recognition and referral of victims of THB for labour exploitation, or actually the non-recognition and non-referral. The reasons for this, gathered from the research conducted in this project, will be elaborated on below.

When focussing on the recognition of victims, we have to take into account the differences in labour relations as mentioned before. For a labour inspector, it is not easy to determine whether a person is working legally because of all these possibilities. Furthermore, it also depends on the country a person originates from since, for instance, in the Netherlands different rules apply for people from Romania and Bulgaria (who cannot be employed as workers on the same footing as other EU citizens). A comparable situation exists in Austria. Therefore, the inspector has to check on the nationality, the legal status and the actual situation at the workplace, especially in cases of self-employment to find out whether it is a case of illegal employment or bogus self-employment, which might be an indication of exploitation. If the inspector is capable of establishing irregularities, which is not an easy task, then the second step is to identify whether it is an indication of THB for labour exploitation or any other violation of labour laws. In Romania, for instance, such an irregularity will easily qualify as a case of THB for labour exploitation, but in Spain it might be considered a violation of criminal labour law.

Another factor of non-recognition and non-referral is the fact that the new actors have to build their levels of expertise in order to be able to recognise THB for labour exploitation. Labour inspectors are used to dealing with irregularities under labour law, and in many cases this might be an efficient way of dealing with such irregularities, especially when considering the long procedures in criminal cases as has been discussed in the case of Spain.

A third important factor is the fact that often it is only the police that can offer a reflection period or apply for a residence permit for a victim of THB. If victims are identified by, for instance, the labour inspectorate, the latter has to ask the police to apply for a reflection period. In many cases, the police are not familiar with the case and then the labour inspectorate has to convince the police that they have to take action.

Furthermore, in some countries, the Netherlands and Spain, following Article 10 of the CoE Convention on action against THB, only trained and prepared police officers are allowed to contact the victims and to interview them. In the Netherlands, victims sometimes have to wait two weeks before they have their first contact with certified police officers. Meanwhile the victim is not entitled to the reflection period and there is a high risk that they will go back to the trafficker because they cannot wait so long for the authorities to act.

Serbia is a positive exception to this practice in that the police do play a central role. In Serbia, victim indication is completed at the central level by the Central Agency. The Agency makes the indication and also completes the request/application for the reflection period and the temporary residence permit. In some cases, of course, they are dependent on information from the police for such a request or application, but in the end it is the Agency that is the responsible authority. This seems to make sense since the police are not the only authority that victims of THB go to (if they go at all), and it is more likely that NGOs are approached by victims. Although there are many problems with the implementation of this system in Serbia, its wider application is worth considering. Another interesting point was described in the Chapter on Spain, where a body of experts reports on the status of victims to law enforcement authorities.

3.3. Increased possibilities for participation and compensation

Many of the researchers indicated an increase in opportunities for victims of THB to participate in and receive compensation from criminal proceedings. Most authors describe an increase in opportunities to make a civil claim in criminal proceedings. Compensation from the State is, however, much more difficult to obtain. In most cases, you need to be a citizen of the State, although a legal stay based on a residence permit might also suffice, as suggested by the Spanish authors. These increased possibilities are welcomed and can be seen as a positive effect of harmonising measures at EU level.[48] However, it is also concluded that in most of the countries the provisions for victim participation and compensation need to be improved.

3.4. Clash between migration law and criminal law

The fact that victims of THB for sexual exploitation are usually considered as illegal immigrants rather than as victims of crime and are therefore expelled from the country instead of helped and assisted, has been reported in the past on various occasions.[49] The side effect of these practices is that with expulsion, criminal evidence is also expelled from the country, which is a difficulty one has to deal with in criminal procedures. It is then, however, striking to see that the same practices do still exist in relation to THB for labour exploitation. An example of this practice is the expulsion of Romanian asparagus-cutters from Dutch territory when they were found in locked and unsafe rooms on the farmer's premises.[50] They were expelled even before the reflection period was offered to them. They were simply considered to be illegal migrants rather

---

[48] Especially Directive on compensation to victims of Crime, [2004] OJ L261.

[49] C. Rijken, *Trafficking in Persons, Prosecution from a European Perspective* (Asser Press 2003) pp. 204-207, 227.

[50] J. van der Leun, '(EU) Migration policy and labour exploitation', Chapter 8 in this book.

than possible victims of THB. This practice is also reported by Spain and Austria. It is rather shocking that not much has been learned from the lessons of cases of THB for sexual exploitation in this regard

3.5. De-link criminal law and assistance to victims

Following comments on the THB framework decision, especially relating to the limited scope of the framework decision, it has been revised and a directive has been adopted.[51] In its title, the directive explicitly mentions the protection of victims of THB, apart from addressing the prevention and prosecution of the crime. As discussed more elaborately in Chapter 6 on the EU legal framework to combat THB for labour exploitation, the directive includes specific and concrete provisions for victim protection and assistance. With regard to the condition of cooperation with law enforcement authorities before protection and assistance can be obtained, it is a further incentive to MSs to implement and apply Article 12, Paragraph 6 of the Council of Europe Convention on Action against THB. This Article stipulates that 'Each Party shall adopt such legislative or other measures as may be necessary to ensure that assistance to a victim is not made conditional on his or her willingness to act as a witness'. The explanatory note to this Paragraph is slightly broader stating that 'The drafters wish to make it clear that under Article 12(6) of the Convention, assistance is not conditional upon a victim's agreement to cooperate with competent authorities in investigations and criminal proceedings'. Thus, in the explanatory note, assistance cannot be made conditional to *cooperation,* which is broader than the text of Paragraph 6 itself which states that it cannot be made conditional to the willingness to *act as a witness*. Be it as it may, it is clear that the drafters of the convention had the intention to de-link criminal law and assistance to victims to some extent, and that this has now been adopted at an EU level as well, fortunately in its broader understanding by stating that assistance and support cannot be made conditional to the *cooperation* of the victim with the authorities. These provisions all relate to the assistance offered to victims; it does not refer to the granting of a residence permit. It is still considered a step too far to prohibit the granting of a residence permit conditional on cooperation, which is practiced in most countries.[52]

---

[51] 21 March 2011, A. Middelburg, C. Rijken, 'The EU Legal Framework on Combating Trafficking in Human Beings for Labour Exploitation', Chapter 6 in this book.

[52] See also point 169 of the explanatory note to the Council of Europe Convention stating that 'Some Parties may decide – as allowed by Article 14 – to grant residence permits only to victims who cooperate with the authorities. Nevertheless, Paragraph 6 of Article 12 provides that each Party shall adopt such legislative or other measures as may be necessary to ensure that assistance to a victim is not made conditional on his or her willingness to act as a witness.'

3.6. Role of the victim in cases of THB for labour exploitation

Several States mention the dependency on victims in criminal proceedings. In comparison to THB for sexual exploitation, THB for labour exploitation does create opportunities to be less dependent on the cooperation and testimonies of victims. By its nature, the sex industry is an illegal or semi-legal business (except in the Netherlands where part of the sector is legalised) operating in the criminal sphere. This creates limited possibilities for States to regulate or monitor activities, since a State cannot regulate illegal activities.[53] This is different from labour exploitation since this concerns legal activities that are performed in a criminal way. By regulating the labour market and, especially, labour conditions, governments have an instrument with which to objectify what is considered as labour exploitation and when such a case must be considered as THB for labour exploitation. By monitoring these regulations, the monitoring authorities (labour inspectorates, trade unions, social investigative authorities, treasury, etc) can collect evidence in cases of THB for labour exploitation. In this way, the prosecution can be less dependent on the testimonies of victims in cases of THB for labour exploitation.

[53] Although there are possibilities to regulate semi-legal businesses not through the government but by means of self-regulation. See on this matter G. Vermeulen (ed), *EU Quality Standards in Support of the Fight against Trafficking in Human Beings and Sexual Exploitation of Children* (Antwerp, Maklu 2007).

Part IV
Recommendations

In the first decade after the adoption of the Palermo Protocol, THB was mainly associated with sexual exploitation. It is only more recently that the debate on how to understand the Palermo Protocol definition in relation to labour exploitation has started, and it is now included on the agenda more often. It can be said that it has even revived and given new impetus to the debate on phenomena that were adopted in conventions long ago, but which were not applied on a large scale, such as the concepts of forced labour and slavery (-like practices). Although there is reason to be optimistic, a lot remains to be done before a human rights based approach to THB is realised, and the EU can play an important role in this. Apart from the recommendations made on a State level in the separate chapters, the following overall recommendations can be made.

As follows from this chapter, as well as the debate on the definition of the Palermo Protocol and its relation with concepts such as slavery (-like practices) and forced labour and the difficulties to define exploitation, there is a need for further clarification and harmonisation. The new directive, when it has been implemented, will create advanced opportunities, especially in relation to the EU CoJ which will become fully competent in this area. It would be good if national judges in the future use their competence to ask for preliminary rulings in order to obtain greater clarity on how the terminology used in the definition must be explained and interpreted. In this way, the CoJ can play an important role in the more unambiguous and harmonised use of the terminology.

Somehow related to this problem, and as has been explained above, cases of THB are difficult to identify, especially because indicators of THB are often revealed in a fragmented manner. Only when these fragments are brought together can a possible case of THB be identified. However, there is a need for the early identification of possible cases of THB and thus for the need to also recognise that the fragments might in and of themselves not be recognised as indicators of THB for labour exploitation. It would be helpful if, on an EU level, a list of indicators specific to THB for labour exploitation were developed, to be used union wide for the early identification of THB for labour exploitation.[54] These indicators can have a double function: on the one hand they can function to identify (possible) cases of THB when controlling workplaces and living standards, and on the other they can be used by

[54] These should build upon indicators already identified in other forums such as the ILO (2009) Operational indicators of trafficking in human beings: Results from a Delphi survey implemented by the ILO and the European Commission, 2009 also ILO (2004), Human Trafficking and Forced Labour Exploitation: Guidelines for Legislators and Law Enforcement.

employers, employment agencies and housing companies as identifiers of situations that need to be avoided. In this way, they can provide actors with guidance for positive action.

As stated above, the identification of indicators of THB is often only possible when different fragments of information are brought together and combined. In order to bring this information together, information needs to be shared among various actors. To this end, more sophisticated ways of information exchange, both at national and European levels are required. However, this raises questions on data protection that relate not only to purpose limitation, and the principle of proportionality, but also questions as to the division of powers. When developing structures for enhanced information sharing, these and other data protection principles need to be taken into account. Furthermore, it seems that data protection rules are often used as a shield to avoid data sharing, while in many legal acts, rules have been included for exchange of data for law enforcement purposes. In general, a distinction is made between the exchange of intelligence (general information not necessarily linked to a specific case of a specific person) and law enforcement information (information linked to a specific case or a specific person, the suspect). The rules on the exchange of intelligence as well as law enforcement information need further study in relation to THB for labour exploitation. The programmatic approach as developed in the Netherlands can serve as an example of a structure in which such information exchange can take place. However, the data protection principles developed within the Council of Europe and adopted in the EU instruments, and especially the principles of purpose limitation and proportionality, need to taken into account at all times.

More generally, with regard to cooperation between States, it is noted that Europol and Eurojust are still not considered as being obvious opportunities for cooperation, but are still considered as being somewhat exotic forms of cooperation that are time consuming and difficult. Further research focussing on the reasons behind this reluctance to use Europol and Eurojust, can give insight and guidance for future improvement.

As has been discussed on various occasions, economic inequalities around the world are the main reason for the existence of migration streams. Although a more equal division of wealth is an aim to strive for, practice shows a different direction. Worldwide, the gap between rich and poor is increasing, and the expertise of global economists is required to identify possibilities to turn this tide. From a more legal perspective, and given the reality of migration streams, actions can be taken on the management of migration streams. When linking this to THB for labour exploitation in the EU, we see that working opportunities and increased opportunities to earn money (legally or not) are reasons to migrate within and to Europe. When focussing on migration to the EU, it must be concluded that up until now the EU has followed a very restrictive migration policy for Third Country Nationals (TCN), in which the advantages of migration for the EU were leading. This, for instance, is reflected in the adoption of a directive allowing entrance to the EU for highly qualified TCN. In order to increase opportunities for TCN, to improve their living conditions and to prevent them resorting to the illegal forms of residency and work that makes them vulnerable to exploitation, the EU should adopt a more social and generous migration policy that also includes non-highly qualified TCN. In creating more possibilities for those who want to improve their living conditions and those of their relatives, in the end the EU might as well contribute to the ultimate cause of the existence of migration as well as the existence of THB, namely, economic inequality in the world. It is therefore welcomed that the EU has now tabled a proposal for a directive for seasonal workers, which indeed includes the aim of contributing to the improvement of living standards in the home country of those workers.

Victim protection and assistance is another aspect of THB receiving increased attention also at an EU level. In the EU framework decision, little reference was made to victim protection, but in the new Directive it is one of the three main items. As can be read in Chapter 6 on the EU legal framework, concrete measures for protection during criminal proceedings and assistance to victims of trafficking have been adopted and must be implemented in the 27 Member States. Following the Council of Europe Convention on Action Against THB, it has been stated that assistance should not be made dependent on the willingness of the victim to cooperate in criminal proceedings. Although these are steps in the right direction, important difficulties remain as can be read in the various chapters in this book. One of these difficulties is the identification of (possible) victims. As stated above it largely depends on the point of view one takes whether a person can be qualified as a trafficking victim. With the exception of Serbia, in all the States under research, law enforcement authorities play a central role in the identification of victims and in the application of measures for protection and assistance. When looking at the various institutions, organisations and actors that can and do report victims to either the police or other organisations dealing with victim registration and support, it is a serious limitation to only give law enforcement a central role in the application of residence status or access to assistance regulations. In addition, victims often hesitate to go to the police for various reasons, such as, bad experiences with police in their home countries, fear their illegal status will be exposed, fear of losing a job and being expelled from the country, etc. This provides reasons for considering different structures for victim identification. To this end, more research is required on how applications for reflection periods and residence permits can be completed by organisations that specialise in victim assistance. The case of Serbia in which such a central organisation (the Agency) has been established might serve as an example. As can be learned from the Chapter on Serbia, the Agency does not function optimally and its structure can be improved. However, despite these comments, it would still be more logical if victim assistance organisations play a more central role in the identification of, protection of, and assistance given to victims of THB. Then, of course, immigration services must make their own assessment when considering applications of THB victims.

Because THB for labour exploitation, in contrast to THB for sexual exploitation, occurs most often in legalised sectors, it creates opportunities for regulation and monitoring. In most countries, this regulation and monitoring already takes place, but this can be shaped in a way that is more sensitive to indicators of THB. The involvement of the many actors that are concerned in controlling businesses, such as municipalities, tax authorities, food inspectorates, labour inspectorates, trade unions, etc can provide (part of the) evidence needed to identify the existence of THB for labour exploitation, and create opportunities for law enforcement to be less dependent on the testimonies of victims in cases of THB for labour exploitation. As the participation of victims in criminal proceedings or the giving of testimonies is often a cause of secondary victimisation, the use of information from other actors in criminal proceedings should be fully exploited. It might be helpful to standardise the involvement of other actors in criminal proceedings when cases of THB for labour exploitation are at stake. It would be helpful for victims if these proceedings were less dependent on their testimonies.

As follows from the country-based research, there seems to be a difference between the needs of victims of THB for labour exploitation and THB for sexual exploitation, which relates to a gender perspective. However, further research into the needs of victims of THB for labour exploitation is required to draw more far-reaching conclusions. What can be concluded at this stage is that the assistance to THB victims is mainly focussed on victims of sexual exploitation and on female victims. In all the countries under research, a lack of measures tailored to victims of THB for labour exploitation as well as a lack of protective measures, including shelters, for male victims is reported. Awareness raising on these issues, as well as positive action, is needed. Furthermore, it has been reported that in relation to THB for labour exploitation, victims are more easily considered as illegal migrants instead of as victims and are expelled from the territory or even put in detention centres. Again, awareness raising and positive action is required. It is to be regretted that in this regard no lessons have been learned from earlier experiences in relation to THB for sexual exploitation.

Finally, in relation to victim protection, the debate on this is made difficult by the fact that it is sometimes easy to conclude that a person is a victim of THB for labour exploitation, rather than a worker whose labour rights have been violated. This, of course, is largely related to the problems indicated here in relation to defining the crime. In order to help people who are exploited and might be the victims of THB for labour exploitation, it is better to consider them as people seeking assistance. A broad spectrum of assistance and protective measures must then be available, which the person seeking assistance can use as they need.[55] To achieve this, one must, however, be well

[55] To that end, the author in other publications has suggested the adoption a Victim Assistance and Protection Package (VAPP) from which the victim can choose what they need. C. Rijken, 'A Human Rights Based Approach to Trafficking in Human Beings'

aware of their legal position and labour rights. The agency of workers within the EU and outside the EU is an important aspect in the human rights based approach to THB for labour exploitation. To that end, information campaigns on working in the EU, including campaigns on labour rights, must be established. The trade unions (including the ETUC and ITUC) can play an important role in this. In this way, traffickers and employers with bad intentions will regress.

(2009) Security and Human Rights, Volume 20. issue 3 and C. Rijken and D. Koster at <http://papers.ssrn.com/sol3/papers.cfm?abstract_id=1135108 >.

Chapter 8
(EU) Migration Policy and Labour Exploitation

Joanne van der Leun[1]

I. Introduction

All economies have an informal segment in which many, though not exclusively, migrants without the formal permission to work find employment. Irregular labour has become a fact of life in advanced economies (Van der Leun & Kloosterman 2006). According to the global city-literature, economic globalisation has not only resulted in a highly mobile class of high skilled workers, but also brought the third world to cities across nations (Sassen 2006). Yet, over the recent years a new way of looking at this type of labour, or at least at excesses in the informal economy seems to prevail, stemming from the rapidly increasing international attention for trafficking in human beings (further called THB). The workers involved (who might also be labelled 'victims', although the term is problematic as will be explained below) are not necessarily irregular immigrants, but a common means of pressure in the case of cross-border THB is using the illegal residence or irregular labour status of a migrant worker and the persons fear for deportation. The present chapter therefore focuses on migrants who work irregularly/ illegally. The terms are used interchangeably and refer to being employed without formal permission to do so in the country of employment.[2]

For a long time the default way of responding to irregular labour which had been detected was sanctioning the employer through either a warning or a fine and attempting to expel the workers. A punitive perspective prevailed and concerns over uncontrolled migration dominated. Workers were rarely viewed as potential victims of human trafficking, based on the human rights perspective. These ways of framing issues as issues of migration control perfectly illustrates a dilemma between migration control and combating THB which is often not recognised and which is the subject of this chapter.

Departing from this dilemma, which is not specific for the Netherlands, the present chapter will focus on the interplay between migration policy in the EU and in the Member States and the combat against THB as far as it concerns labour exploitation. It will demonstrate that it is often unclear what happens in practice when professionals in Western European economies come across people who can either be seen as 'victims' of labour exploitation or as

[1] Prof.dr. JP van der Leun is professor of Criminology at Leiden Law School. She expresses her thanks to Leida Castillejo who held the interviews when writing her Master Thesis, see Castillejo 2010.

[2] For a thorough discussion of terms see Schrover et al 2008. In the Netherlands the term 'illegal' is often used, whereas internationally the term 'irregular' is increasingly used.

perpetrators of immigration law (these two perspectives will be summarised as protective versus punitive respectively).

The chapter is organised as follows: in the remainder of the present section I will briefly refer to definitions of trafficking, in section 2 the context of controlling migration will be outlined. Section 3 deals specifically with the position of irregular workers in receiving societies, whereas section 4 zooms in on what has come to be known as labour exploitation. In section 5 the crucial dilemma will be depicted: the dilemma between a punitive and a protective approach. It will be maintained that this dilemma is often not explicitly recognised, leaving the question open as to what happens at the level of implementation. The remainder of the chapter aims at finding out how implementation practices in the Netherlands and Belgium take shape, given the existence of this dilemma. First some general hypotheses will be formulated on the basis of more general theoretical literature (section 6) after which the result of interviews with key figures in the field will add some flesh to the bones (section 7).

As the research is exploratory and limited in scale and scope, firm conclusions cannot be drawn yet, but the first results confirm the idea that whereas migration control and anti-trafficking policies are commonly depicted as reinforcing each other, this does not have to be the case. This chapter uses the case of the Netherlands as an example of a country where on the one hand human trafficking is actively combated, and on the other hand the government policy with respect to combating irregular residence and illegal work is fierce (Van der Leun 2003, Triandafyllidou 2010). Therefore, the interplay and potential conflict between a punitive and a protective perspective is expected to come to the fore stronger than elsewhere. Yet, it is certainly not unique for the Netherlands or the low countries (including Belgium where one of the interviews was held).

Definitions

Even though similar definitions of human trafficking are applied in many countries, based on the United Nations Convention against Transnational Organised Crime 2000 (Palermo Convention) there are still differences in how different countries interpret this definition of human trafficking in national legislation (BNRM 2007). The definition leaves room for different interpretation, which is not surprising for a definition which is the result of an international compromise (Rijken & Koster 2008). It therefore should be seen as the lowest common denominator. Pressuring an individual to move from one place to another against his/her will is a common occurrence in the act of human trafficking. This also includes pressuring individuals to carry out certain services against their will as a way to introduce them into trade to achieve profitable gains (UNODC 2010). To a certain extent, the suspect and victim have motivations to engage in THB. It is a high-profit and low risk crime, which does not require a huge capital investment (Carroll 2009, Bales 2000). This motivates criminals in need of cash with little to no risk of getting caught by authorities to engage in the act of THB. Reliable statistics are not available (Tyldum 2010). Figures may be inflated to aid or promote governmental anti-trafficking policies and advocacy of anti-trafficking NGOs. According to UNODC, globally, human trafficking is an estimated US$ 32 billion illegal industry and third to illegal drugs and arms smuggling[3].

Most trafficked persons become 'victims' of THB out of the will to have a better life for themselves and their families. They often come from developing countries with relatively poor economical conditions and are looking to make a better life in countries with better economic perspectives. Although this is true, individuals can also fall victim to traffickers in their home countries. They are for several reasons vulnerable candidates that will buy into the false promises of better jobs, higher wages or interesting lives offered to them by their traffickers (Bales 2000).

Human trafficking in general has received ample international attention over the past two decades. Renewed interest in the international arena was influenced by developments regarding unwanted migration in the 1980s and 1990s, as many victims of human trafficking turned out to be immigrants with an irregular status or individuals who otherwise find themselves in a vulnerable position (Wijers and Lap-Chew 1999, Bruckert and Parent 2002). For a long time the focus has been on the sex industry, other forms of exploitation are so far under-researched.

These other forms are called labour exploitation, socio-economic exploitation or modern slavery. In the Netherlands – with a regulated sex sector the term 'other forms of exploitation' is often preferred, as according to many people sex work is also labour, albeit a particular form of labour. In line with international publications the choice is made to use the term labour exploitation.

II. The context of controlling migration

In Europe today, the right to free movement and residence is one of the most visible rights conferred to EU citizens (European Commission 2008). European citizens enjoy the right to move across the Union in order to pursue opportunities such as work, relationships and education. Third country nationals however, do not have these rights. All Member States of the European Union (EU) are affected by international migration from third countries which they aim to control. Therefore, they have agreed to develop a common immigration policy at EU level. The European Commission has made proposals for developing this policy, many of which have now become EU legislation. The main objective is to try and manage migration flows by a coordinated and concerted approach.

There is a certain level of ambiguity at stake, however, because Europe needs workers, but many citizens (and voters) worry about integration, societal

[3] <http://www.unodc.org/southasia/en/topics/frontpage/2009/preventin-of-human-trafficking.html> accessed March 2011.

changes and employment and oppose ongoing immigration. Moreover, Nation States try to stop illegal or irregular migration and illegal work, although it is also recognised that the EU needs flexibility and migrants in certain sectors and regions in order to deal with its economic and demographic needs. And this labour may also be situated in the informal economy. In 1999, the leaders of the EU set out the elements for a common EU immigration policy at the 1999 European Council in Tampere, Finland. The approach agreed in Tampere in 1999 was confirmed in 2004 with the adoption of The Hague programme, which sets the objectives for strengthening freedom, security and justice in the EU for the period 2005-2010. Apart from that, all Nation States still pursue their own goals with their national immigration control measures as well as internal controls (Van der Leun and Ilies 2011).

In spite of restrictive immigration policies which have been in place since the 1970s in most Member States, large numbers of legal migrants including asylum-seekers and illegal migrants have continued to come to the EU. Taking advantage of persons seeking a better life, smuggling and trafficking networks have taken hold across the EU and this even seemed to have been stimulated by restrictive policies. This situation meant that considerable resources have been mobilised to fight illegal migration and to target traffickers and smugglers and criminal infrastructures behind irregular migration, whilst at the same time the demand for irregular or illegal labour continued.

III. The category of illegal or irregular workers

The term 'irregular immigration' is relatively modern, as are national laws on entry, exit and residence. Yet, restrictions on movement are anything but a recent invention. Before the era of strong nation States, cities used to decide who were the wanted and the unwanted. These decisions were often related to issues such as employment, poverty, and public disorder (Lucassen 1996, Schrover et al. 2008). The construction of irregularity is directly related to State control and State sovereignty (Abraham and Van Schendel 2005). Yet, what States consider as legitimate (legal), might not fully coincide with what individuals consider as such (ibidem). Transnational movements of people are irregular because they defy the norms and formal authority, while in the participants' view they can be acceptable, even licit.

Thus, the irregularity of residence comes into effect when that person interacts with the authorities of the host State, which categorise him as sojourning 'irregularly' (Guild, 2004: 16). From the perspective of the State, people categorised as irregular are 'offenders of immigration laws' and do not have to right to reside on the host State's territory (Kostakopoulou 2004: 42). Irregularity, much like citizenship, is a political identity, a juridical status that entails a social relation to the State (De Genova 2002: 422, cf. Engbersen 2001). The sociologist De Genova (2002) has coined the term deportability, which refers to the way that irregularity is lived, namely the permanent fear for the possibility of being removed from the territory of the Nation State, which renders irregular migrants vulnerable. It should be noted that it is not deportation per se, but the threat that this may occur. The essential differentiation between the undocumented immigrants and legal residents is the former's fundamentally different position within national legal systems: they always face the risk of expulsion and (temporary) imprisonment (van der Leun and Kloosterman 2006: 60).

Besides entry and residence, work is another source of migrant illegality, and employment is the backbone of many of the theories on irregular immigration (van der Leun, 2003: 35). Irregular labour migration dominates most discourses on irregular immigration throughout. Irregular employment exists not just because poor and desperate people wish to improve their living conditions. Businesses in receiving countries need cheap labour input while private homeowners welcome the domestic workers that otherwise they might not afford. The most important asset of the undocumented migrants is their cheap, exploitable labour. It must be noted however, that illegal labour can also be done by individuals with legal residence rights. They can for instance work fully or partially off the books, and they can be work as bogus self-employed persons.

Because irregular migrants have almost no other long-term survival strategy than irregular employment, their role in Europe's informal sectors has been thoroughly assessed by scholars and policy-makers. For instance, estimates place the average of undeclared work at 11%–16% of EU's GDP, with Bulgaria, Greece, Hungary and Slovenia have registering the highest rates at 25%–40% of GDP (EIRO 2005). Irregular migrants even sustain certain economic sectors in Member States. In Italy for instance, undocumented workers are a substantial labour input for the industrial sector, while in the Netherlands, irregular labour is what makes horticulture a competitive sector (van der Leun & Kloosterman 2006: 59). Estimates show that one third of the motorways of France were built by irregular workers and about one one-third of all automobile production in France has been done by irregular workers (Bade 2003: 22). It is clear that irregular immigration is theoretically unwanted by the destination and transit societies (governments would not publicly state whether irregular migrants might be somehow economically beneficial to the economy, or that they should be granted a set of rights). Thus, at least certain types of irregular labour are in many cases silently accepted.

IV. Labour exploitation

Many cases of labour exploitation are found on the cross roads of irregular labour and THB. As said above, following implementation of international, pan-European and European legislation, the crime of human trafficking not only encompasses activities in the sex industry, but also human trafficking for labour exploitation. The official definitions have expanded to also include the crime of forcing others into work in other – generally legal – sectors and industries. Based on international agreements, human trafficking for labour exploitation in the Netherlands is punishable under Criminal Law since 2005. Combating human trafficking has become a policy priority and several government agencies have been established or their task have been broadened in order to combat these 'new' forms too. A specialised Centre of Expertise (EMM), the Bureau National Rapporteur (BNRM) and the Social Intelligence and Investigation Service (SIOD) have been established and expanded in order to encourage an active approach and a Human Trafficking Task Force has been set up. Yet, so far only a limited number of cases have been brought before court and the policies in this field are still to be developed further (BNRM 2010).[4]

This chapter addresses the multitude of different forms of exploitative labour outside the sex industry in the Netherlands. It must be realised that not all unacceptable working conditions constitute labour exploitation (Van der Leun & Vervoorn 2004, Boot & Smit 2007). There is a thin line between a substandard employer and a human trafficker who exploits others (De Jonge van Ellemeet 2007). Coster van Voorhout (2007) rightly depicts (potential) labour exploitation as a continuum, with substandard labour as a minimum situation of exploitation, and slavery on the far end as the most aggravated circumstance. In slightly different terms, Skrivankova (2010) also suggests thinking in terms of a continuum in stead of framing all violations of labour laws as exploitation. The approach to outlaw forced labour within the anti-trafficking laws has been more prominent in the past fifteen years, reflecting the increasing concern of the international community about THB. A criminal offence of trafficking in human beings for the purpose of forced labour was introduced into criminal legislation in a number countries (Skrivankova 2010, Van Dijk & Ungureanu 2010).

Scale and dark number

Although it would appear on the basis of law enforcement data that human trafficking for labour exploitation does not happen on a large scale, this is doubtful. At least 2.45 million people world wide are currently believed to be in forced labour resulting from human trafficking (ILO 2009). In the Netherlands, the national rapporteur BNRM collects and checks relevant data nationwide. Some years ago, this organisation compiled 119 concrete cases of potential labour exploitation of which so far only a few have been brought before court and even less have been recognised by judges as labour exploitation. Although many estimates may be unreliable, still the 'dark number' is supposed to be sizable (BNRM 2007).

The information available suggests that trafficked persons form a diverse and complex category including both males and females. It is also found that legal routes of entry are not immune to trafficking and worker exploitation. Trafficked migrants are found in a broad range of sectors, including agriculture, construction, cleaning, nursing and domestic work. These industries tend to be

[4] Also L. van Krimpen, 'The interpretation and implementation of labour exploitation in Dutch case law', Chapter 11 in this book.

characterised by '3D' work – dangerous, difficult and dirty – and they typically involve low pay and low skill levels, requiring large numbers of flexible, seasonal workers. Trafficking tends to occur in sectors that use sub-contracting chains in which many migrant workers are employed (BNRM 2007, 2009) Similar outcomes have been found in the UK (Dowling, Moreton and Wright 2007.

V. The crucial dilemma: which legal perspective prevails when?

Trafficking for labour exploitation is a complex phenomenon requiring responses from a variety of intersecting legal fields: criminal justice, human rights, migration, and labour law. States have responsibilities to meet international standards in each of these areas. How the intersections interact or should interact, however, is less clear. As far as publications mention this, it is usually associated with a lack of knowledge as the main impediment to effective policy making (Coster-van Voorhout 2007).

Under different labels, (potential) labour exploitation of migrant workers does come to the fore in a different – and rather separate- strand of literature: publications on unwanted or irregular migration and migration control. Yet, this literature refers to illegal labour under unfavourable conditions rather than to trafficking or other criminal activities or intentions. Immigrant workers are primarily seen as active agents who try to better themselves (van der Leun 2003). In this literature, for obvious reasons, potential victims who are residing and/or working legally in another country fall outside the scope.

Ethnographic migration research in the Netherlands also uncovered evidence of the misuse of the position of vulnerability of irregular migrant workers. Intermediaries and employers sometimes derive unfair benefit from the illegality of the working situation for instance by withholding payments and by limiting working hours in order to make individuals dependent. In this regard, labour exploitation appears to be a reality for many irregular immigrants in the Netherlands (see also Garces and Doomernik 2006) as in other European countries (for a summary see Coster van Voorhout 2007). However, victims often do not identify themselves as such and for several reasons seldom take action. Irregular migrants in particular fear being detected and expelled from the country and have very little trust that they will receive help from the authorities.

Given the rather separate research traditions of trafficking research and migration research it is not surprising that the crucial dilemma in combating labour exploitation is rarely systematically addressed in existing studies: whether a potential victim of labour exploitation is perceived as such in practice or if he or she is rather seen as perpetrator of immigration laws (and/or labour regularisations) and therefore apprehended and if possible expelled (cf. Pieters 2006).

The analysis here is that a more structural problem lies underneath: the search for labour exploitation involves two legal perspectives that do not necessarily go well together, summarised here as the punitive and the protective perspective. Subsequently two very different policy domains are involved: on the one hand organisations dealing with crimes, such as in the Netherlands the general police and the social fraud inspectorate SIOD, or on the other hand those dealing with infringements of immigration law and labour regulations, such as the labour inspectorate and the immigration service. When a person is seen as a potential victim of trafficking a rights based protective perspective prevails, when a person is seen as a perpetrator of – for instance immigration law - the punitive perspective dominates.

It must be noted that the punitive perspective is not the same as a criminal law based approach. This depends on the question whether controlling agencies show more interest in employers who exploit workers or rather in workers who do not meet certain conditions. As Anderson and Rogaly (2009;4) conclude for the UK: 'A simple immigration control approach does nothing to reduce exploitation as unscrupulous employers simply take on new workers and exploit them in turn.' Therefore, the term punitive approach is here applied to those situations in which potentially exploited individuals are in one way or another punished, be it on the basis of criminal or on administrative law. When potentially exploited individuals are seen as potential victims, the term protective perspective is applied.

In fact, the opposition between two legal perspectives already became evident during the negotiations of the UN Palermo Protocol which has been of paramount importance in addressing human trafficking. Despite academic outcries for a 'holistic' approach, the gap between what is often called a law enforcement approach and a protective or human rights approach has not been bridged (Krieg 2009). Even from the very beginning of EU efforts to combat irregular immigration more effectively, measures to counter human trafficking were seen as an integral part of the policy area of migration control, but the question how the two approaches should go together at the level of implementation has been surrounded by silence (Krieg 2009: 787).

The same holds for national policy measures in the Netherlands. In recent policy papers on irregular migration it is maintained that combating human trafficking reinforces tackling illegal employment and vice versa by sharing information between the agencies involved. It does not become clear how this should take place. In a more critical vein Coster van Voorhout (2007) notices that the authorities involved in dealing with labour exploitation all work independently. According to her, the major problem in prosecuting human trafficking for labour exploitation is the scattering of information (a lack of centralisation and linking of information). The latter source underscores the difficulties in identifying potential victims, but hardly acknowledges the more fundamental issue of two potentially conflicting legal perspectives and policy traditions.

As far as this potential conflict of perspectives is addressed in the wider more theoretical literature, the dominant view seems to be that a criminal law or punitive approach increasingly dominates, in line with a trend of 'crimmigration' or 'securitisation' (Stumpf 2006, Huysmans 2000, Miller 2005, Bigo 2002 and many others). Migration issues are increasingly framed as criminal ones and migration policies often blend in with criminal law. Yet, one of the problems of this more critical theoretical literature is that the discussions rely heavily on speech acts and (political, policy and media) discourses, thereby overlooking complex and often ambiguous practices at policy recipient level. Even the outcome of a criminal law approach, for instance, can still imply different priorities depending on who is seen as potential perpetrator: the employer who may exploit workers or the worker who may be exploited (see above, cf. Van der Leun 2010). In order to deal with these complexities and to move beyond these broad discourses it is crucial to delve into implementation in practice or laws in action rather than sticking to the laws in the books and broad discourses. Looking at implementation of policies in practice is crucial, as it is where representatives of the State encounter real people in stead of rather abstract administrative categories and at which actors have to look for pragmatic answers to concrete situations and dilemmas which can no longer be ignored (Lipsky 1980, Hasenfeld 1983).

VI. Policy decisions: expectations based on the literature

When taking into account implementation or law in action, the question becomes: how do two legal perspectives on human trafficking for labour exploitation, the punitive and the protective perspective, shape responses to labour exploitation in practice and how can different responses, if these are found, be explained?

Social policy analysis has long ago abandoned the idea that implementation is only an administrative follow-on to top-down policy making and policy formulation. Rather, implementation should be seen as an integral and continuous part of the political policy process, involving bargaining between those seeking to put policy into effect and semi-autonomous actors upon whom action depends (Barrett and Hill 1984, Barrett 2004). In different domains, these actors turned out to have competing interests and divergent values. Moreover, they work in organisations with their own logics, ethics and their own systems of accountability. This, together with the vast literature on so-called 'street-level bureaucrats' (see, for example, Lipsky 1980; Hasenfeld 1983), explored the nature of discretionary power – or scope for action – in organisational settings. In addition there are theories on 'styles' of regulation and the embeddedness of these styles, including ideas on responsive regulation (Mascini and Van Wijk 2009). Research on the police more specifically has long acknowledged the role that informal norms and values associated with the rank and file culture play in shaping everyday decisions and practices of the police (Banton 1964, Holdaway 1983 and many others). Recently Loftus has argued that despite rather fundamental changes within the police force, these classical findings are still relevant (Loftus 2010).

One of the consistent findings of the policy literature is that in general in the absence of clear policy rules, discretion is often being used by front-line professionals either to develop 'coping mechanisms' or to negotiate policy modification in action. As in this specific case, the conflicting legal perspectives (punitive and protective) do not offer clear policy rules when dealing with a specific case of potential labour exploitation in practice, we expect modifications to take place at the street level. It is not clear beforehand how and in which direction these modifications will take place. In fact, conflicting trends can be derived from the different bodies of literature.

1) Based on the crimmigration and securitisation literature it is to be expected that the punitive perspective will prevail across all organisations and sectors. In practice this would make it more likely that irregular workers are seen as potential perpetrators rather than as victims of labour exploitation.
2) On the other hand, as both national and European approaches to human trafficking clearly state that a human rights approach should come first, and as this has become a policy priority in the Netherlands over the last few years, we could also expect the search for potential victims to come first across all organisations and sectors.
3) Based on competing interests of different organisations and their workers, different work ethics and possibly also a lack of knowledge about other perspectives, we can thirdly expect that outcomes vary highly across sectors and organisations.

In sum, existing studies and theories lead to ambiguous and sometimes even conflicting expectations. The present exploration is based on a large number of personal conversations at meetings and conferences, desk research and 10 additional interviews with key informants in the field in the Netherlands and Belgium, held in the first half of 2010. Although the study is limited in scope and the hypotheses are heuristic devices rather than testable hypotheses, this chapter aims at providing a highly needed insight in the situation 'on the ground.'

VII. Policy decisions in practice

The interviews which were held support that both the Netherlands and Belgium have put increasing attention to tackling the problem of forced labour or labour exploitation. Belgium was an early mover, but the Netherlands and its professionals working in the field to combat human trafficking are rapidly becoming more aware of the problem and vast resources have been put into it over the years, according to respondents.

Both human trafficking for the purposes of forced labour and irregular migration are complex issues professionals are working to find solutions for on a daily basis. However, most of them claim this is not an easy task because forced labour and irregular migration are hidden problems. According to one of the respondents, economic exploitation as it is known in Belgium is nowadays more difficult to trace due to more professional networks and obscure strategies. Also, victims of THB for the purposes of forced labour do not usually view themselves as victims of THB and therefore do not denounce it to the authorities. In Belgium and the Netherlands it is often through informants that labour inspection agencies or supporting NGOs come across cases of forced labour. Irregular migrants and their support groups are unlikely to report forced labour cases to authorities out of fear of getting arrested and deported themselves. The SIOD in the Netherlands is currently developing a risk model to overcome this problem (Bogaerts et al. 2010).

During the interviews and the study of policy documents it became clear that there exists a certain distance between the debate on THB and the one on irregular migration. Professionals who work for anti-trafficking agencies often stress the finding that not all victims of labour exploitation are migrants or irregular migrants. This is true, but it is not unlikely that non-migrant victims are more likely to come to the fore and as a result that the dark number among migrants is much higher. In documents on illegal labour, on the other hand, the possibility that THB is going on behind the scenes is rarely mentioned. Illegally employed migrants are than primarily seen as perpetrators of migration laws and persons who should be subject to deportation. The same distance was also found in the interviews. The main outcome was *not* that in practice professionals appear to be struggling with the dilemma of punitiveness versus protection. They rather think within one of framework and tend to downplay the other.

The interviews with key informants, therefore, mostly point into the direction of the third hypothesis: every organisations has its own way of looking at violations they come across. This can be from the perspective of detecting THB. In that case, respondents feel they have made progress over the years in recognizing labour exploitation. They now have relatively good instruments such as lists of indicators and information sheets and awareness has risen. This is not the same as saying that these lists are easily applied, though. One respondents says: 'Of course there are discussions on the situations we come across. Experience and a professional's gut feeling are also important.' Another respondent agrees: 'It is a matter of are we looking at the right signals? And evidence in legislation is very helpful in that respect.'

Other organisations however, have a different way of assessing situations. As one respondent notices: 'There still is a highly biased view on the part of the foreigners police and border patrol. They rather see an illegal immigrant as somebody who breaks the law. Being an illegal immigrant is not a crime, but forging documents or having false documents is a crime, so they go after that.' Another respondent spoke to a foreign labour inspector who says very openly: 'it is not my job to look at victims, I look at breaches of labour laws.' Regular police officers are in many cases also not trained to ask the right questions, according to two respondents. They rather ask for identification papers than for signals of exploitation. Police officers are also the ones who have their doubts about too many rights for alleged victims, because they fear this might act as a magnet for irregular migrants and foster fraud. They tend to see migrants who work irregularly primarily as calculating individuals who are looking for every opportunity to stay and not as people deserving protection.

Most professionals in the field who are involved in the THB policies we spoke to, think the policies can be made more effective by providing better information, by raising awareness and by intensifying the co-operation between different agencies, only few stress that the dilemma lies much deeper and see a tension between a punitive migration control and a protective victim-based approach.

The examples above make it plausible that especially illegal immigrants are often not identified, recognised and treated as potential victims of forced labour. Most respondents agree that this still is likely to be the case, although they note a change for the better. Some respondents seem to be reluctant to link THB to irregular migration too strongly. They have very vague ideas about illegal labour in general and seem to give very little thought to the fact that illegal labour can also be consented labour and they focus on excesses. THB professionals also appear to neglect the fact that an indicator that is not an indicator of trafficking can still be one of labour rights violation and hence require interventions by different parties, other than deportation. They tend to think solely in terms of victims of THB and have a blind spot for other issues in the lowest segment of the labour market. Or as Sirkankova (2010: 9) states: 'The influence of the anti-trafficking discourse in the area of forced labour has resulted in the use, or sometimes overuse, of the word victim'.

VIII. Conclusions

The starting point of this chapter was the tension between the punitive and the protective response to potential THB outside the sex industry. A central question was if this tension also came to the fore in practices of implementation.

Although we have to be careful because of the small scale and scope of the study, outcomes of the interviews offered most support for the third hypothesis based on existing theories: that based on competing interests of different organisations and their workers, different work ethics and possibly also a lack of knowledge about other perspectives, varying outcomes were expected across sectors and organisations was largely corroborated. On the basis of the present research, we can go a step further and conclude that organisations seem to be divided between those looking at labour issues and migration control on the one hand and those aiming at combating THB on the other.

Bridging the gap is still a long way to go. Most commentators in the existing literature as well as many respondents seem to agree that this dilemma is largely a matter of awareness. According to them, this would change if people would start asking the right questions and looking at the right indicators. Based on the present chapter that seems to be an optimistic view. Awareness is important, but it does not appear to be the whole story.

In general, of course, it will be beneficial if professionals become more aware of what their local situations regarding irregular migration and THB for the purposes of forced labour are. Also, in terms of irregular migration and THB, professionals should distinguish what indicators suggest when a person is a victim of THB and which indicators suggest that a person is an illegally employed worker. Having a solid distinction between the concepts and their indicators, it will deliver more tools to tackle exploitation more accurately and effectively as well as efficiently. In addition, intensive cooperation between different agencies is important.

Yet, as the tension lie deeper, the problems also appear to be more fundamental than these remedies suggest. This becomes clearer when we think through the most extreme possible situations. In theory, if the punitive approach would fully dominate, the down side would be that migration control would always prevail and THB for labour exploitation would never be detected. If, on the other hand, the protective perspective would prevail, all labour exploitation would be seen as potential THB and would be framed as being associated with crime, if not organised crime. Labour which violates labour regulations would also be, indirectly and paradoxically, criminalised in line with the crimmigration thesis.

In fact, Skrivankova, when writing about the UK, warns for the second situation. She provides a valuable analysis, pointing to the pitfalls of this approach. In response she argues in favour of disregarding the whole concept of illegality, which is a far-reaching proposal of which the outcomes are unforeseeable. Moreover, it does not sound realistic in the present societal and political climate in most of Europe. After all, recent EU proposals for sanctions against employers of irregular migrants once again largely ignore the need to address exploitation or to consider protection aspects instead of only focusing on punishing those aspects related to illegal employment.

Both extreme situations are however not found in practice. The outcomes of the exploratory research suggest that both approaches largely follow their own course. Although this is hardly ever problematised, neither in the literature, nor in practice the outcome is also unfavourable. The result, after all, is that it is highly contingent if an irregular migrant worker who is detected falls under one framework or the other. This, in turn, results in a severe inequality: some irregular migrant workers will be recognised as victims and receive protection up to the level that even criminal activities are not necessarily held against them (the so-called non punishment principle), others are seen as law violators, maybe even perpetrators because they work in bad situations, even when they have not committed a single crime. If the Netherlands, in the near future, takes the step of bringing illegal residence under Criminal Law and defining it as a criminal offence, just as Italy has already done, the gap may even be widened further (van der Leun 2010).[5]

This unequal treatment, which is to a certain extent based on contingency, will continue to exist as long as anti trafficking policies and migration control follow their own course without truly taking into account the implications for the other perspective and without a clear political choice is being made. The current THB approach focuses on a small number of the most severe cases and tries to solve them through the criminal justice system which builds on victim-based thinking. The embeddedness within a much wider informal economy in which many irregular workers are employed is ignored.

Fighting labour exploitation more structurally may include rethinking migration control policies and labour market policies accordingly by, for instance, recognizing the labour market demand for work which is now done in the informal economy and by providing temporary work permits to immigrants for certain economic sectors where the demand is high. It also may require viewing workers as active agents rather than as passive victims. Lodging complaints against employers who exploit workers should be made possible for workers despite a lack of legal (employment) status and they should be supported by institutions through which they can claim their rights. Without political will, however, this cannot be achieved and the fight against THB will remain a partial fight with extremely different positions for those with and without rights.

[5] Although Dutch law already offers indirect options for bringing illegal residence under Criminal Law, the message of de jure criminalisation can be expected to be powerful and to foster fears among illegally working or residing individuals.

References

I. Abraham and W. van Schendel, 'Introduction: The making of illicitness' in W. van Schendel and I. Abraham (eds), *Illicit flows and criminal things. States, borders and the other side of globalization* (Bloomington: Indiana University Press 2005) pp. 1-37.

B. Anderson and B. Rogaly, *Forced Labour and Migration to the UK. Study prepared by COMPAS in collaboration with the Trades Union Congress* (IMG, 2009).

J-K. Bade, 'Legal and Illegal Immigration into Europe: Experiences and Challenges' (2003) Ortelius-lecture Wassenaar: NIAS.

K. Bales, *Disposable People: New Slavery in the Global Economy* (Berkeley: University of California Press 1999).

M. Banton, *The Policeman in the Community* (London: Tavistock 1964).

S. Barret and M. Hill. 'Policy, Bargaining and Structure in Implementation Theory: Towards an Integrated Perspective' (1984) Policy and Politics, 12, 3, pp. 219–40.

S.M. Barrett, 'Implementation studies: time for a Revival? Personal reflections on 20 Years of implementation studies' (2004) Public Administration, Vol. 82, No. 2, pp. 249–262.

D. Bigo, 'Security and Immigration: Toward a Critique of the Governmentality of Unease' (1984) Alternatives, 27(1) (supplement) pp. 63–92.

BNRM, *Mensenhandel* (Den Haag: Bureau Rapporteur Mensenhandel 2007 and subsequent yearly reports).

A. Bogaerts, P. Plooij & R. Zoetekouw, 'De bestrijding van arbeidsuitbuiting - Werkwijzen en bevindingen van de SIOD' (2010) JV, nr. 7, pp. 68- 80.

M. Boot and M. Smit, 'Het begrip mensenhandel in de Nederlandse context. Achtergronden en reikwijdte' (2007) Justitiële Verkenningen, jaargang 33, nr. 7, pp. 10-22.

C. Bruckert & C. Parent, *Trafficking in human beings and organised crime: a literature review* (Ottawa: Royal Canadian Mounted Police 1984).

L. Castillejo, *Victims of Forced Labour: The Dilemma of Human Trafficking Victim vs. Illegal Immigrant in the Netherlands & Belgium* (Master thesis Leiden Law School, Criminology 2010).

S. Carroll, 'More men victims of human trafficking' (2010) Houston Chronicle <http://www.chron.com/disp/story.mpl/special/immigration/6514945.html> accessed 3 April 2010

J.C. van Voorhout, 'Human Trafficking for Labour Exploitation: Interpreting the Crime' (2007) Utrecht Law Review, Vol. 3, No. 2, pp. 44-69.

H. De Jonge van Ellemeet, 'Slecht werkgeverschap of "moderne slavernij". Handhaving van een nader af te bakenen verbod' (2007) *Justitiële Verkenningen*, jaargang 33, nr. 7, pp. 107- 119.

N.P. De Genova, 'Migrant Illegality and Deportability in Everyday Life' (2002) Annual Review of Anthropology, 31, pp. 419 447.

S. Dowling, K. Moreton and L. Wright, *Trafficking for the purposes of labour exploitation: A literature review* (Home Office Online Report 10/07) <http://www.homeoffice.gov.uk/rds/pdfs07/rdsolr1007.pdf> accessed March 2010.

EIRO, 'Industrial relations and undeclared work' (2005) EIRO thematic feature, available at <www.eurofound.europa.eu/pubdocs/2005/135/en/1/ef05135en.pdf>

G.B.M. Engbersen, 'The unanticipated consequences of panopticon Europe: residence strategies of illegal immigrants' in V. Guiraudon, V & C. Joppke (eds), *Controlling a New Migration World* (London: Routledge 2001) pp. 222-246.

European Commission. 'The Directive on the right of EU citizens to move and reside freely in the European Union / The Commission issues report on the application of the Directive' (2008) Memo/08/778.

E. Guild, 'Who is an Irregular Migrant?' in B. Bogusz, R. Cholewinski, A. Cygan, E. Szyszcak (eds), *Irregular Migration and Human Rights: theoretical, European and International Perspectives* (Leiden: Martinus Nijhoff Publishers 2003) pp. 3-28.

B. Garcés-Mascareñas, J. Doomernik, *Exploratory study on trafficking and labour exploitation among west African immigrants in the Netherlands.* (Amsterdam: IMES/ University of Amsterdam 2006).

Y. Hasenfeld, *Human Service Organizations* (USA: Prentice- Hall Inc. 1982)

S. Holdaway, *Inside the British police. A force at work* (Oxford: Blackwell 1983)

J. Huysmans, 'The European Union and the Securitization of Migration' (2000) Journal of Common Market Studies, Vol. 38, No. 5, pp. 751-777.

ILO/ International Labour Organisation, *Forced Labour* <http:// www.ilo.org/global/Themes/Forced_Labour/lang--en/index.htm> accessed March 2010.

D. Kostakopoulou, 'Irregular Migration and Migration Theory: Making State Authorisation Less relevant' in B. Bogusz, R. Cholewinski, A. Cygan, E. Szyszcak (eds), *Irregular Migration and Human Rights: theoretical, European and International Perspectives* (Leiden: Martinus Nijhoff Publishers 2004) pp. 41-57,

S.H. Krieg, 'Trafficking in Human Beings: The EU Approach between Border Control, Law Enforcement and Human Rights' (2009) European Law Journal, Vol. 15, Issue 6, pp. 775-790.

F. Laczko, *Human trafficking: the need for better data* (Migration Information Source, Migration Policy Institute, Washington DC 2002).

M. Lipsky, *Street-level Bureaucracy; Dilemmas of the Individual in Public Services.* (New York: Russel Sage Foundation 1983).

B. Loftus, 'Police occupational culture: classic themes, altered times' (2010) Policing and Society, 20: 1, pp. 1 - 20.

L. Lucassen, *Zigeuner. Die Geschichte eines polizeilichen Ordnungsbegriffes in Deutschland 1700-1945.* (Köln: Böhlau-Verlag 1996).

P. Mascini and E. van Wijk, 'Responsive Regulation at the Dutch Food and Commodity Authority. An Empirical Assessment of Assumptions Underlying the Theory' (2009) Regulation and Governance, 3, pp. 27-47.

T. Miller, 'Blurring the boundaries between immigration and crime control after September 11th' (2005) Boston College Third World Law Journal, 25, pp. 81–124.

B. Pieters, 'Dutch Criminal and Administrative Law Concerning Trafficking in and Smuggling of Human Beings: The blurred Legal Position of Smuggled and Trafficked Persons: Victims, Instigators or Illegals?' in E. Guild and P. Minderhoud (eds), *Immigration and Criminal Law in the European Union: The Legal Measures and Social Consequences of Criminal Law in Member States on Trafficking and Smuggling in Human Beings* (Leiden: Martinus Nijhof Publishers 2006).

R. Plant, *Forced Labour and Human Trafficking: The Challenges Ahead* (International Labour Organization (ILO)) <http://www.ilo.org/sapfl/Informationresources/Speeches/langen/WCMS_097002/index.html> accessed 2 June 2010.

C. Rijken and D. Koster, 'Human Rights Based Approach to Trafficking in Human Beings' (2008) Theory and Practice, available at SSRN <http://ssrn.com/abstract=1135108>.

C. Sassen, *Cities in a world economy.* (Pine Forge Press 2006).

M. Schrover, J-P. van der Leun, L. Lucassen, C. Quispel, *Illegal Migration and Gender in a Global and Historical Perspective* (Amsterdam: Amsterdam University Press 2008).

K. Skrivankova, *Between decent work and forced labour: examining the continuum of exploitation* (Joseph Rowntree Foundation 2010).

J. Stumpf, 'The Crimmigration Crisis: Immigrants, Crime, and Sovereign Power' (2006) American University Law Review, Vol. 56, pp. 367-419,

A. Triandafyllidou, *Irregular Migration in Europe. Myths and realities* (Farnham, Burlington: Ashgate 2010).

G. Tyldum, 'Limitations in Research on Human Trafficking' (2010) International Migration, Vol. 48 (5), pp. 1-13.

J. van der Leun, *Crimmigratie* (Oratie Universiteit Leiden December 2010).

J. van der Leun and L. Vervoorn, *Slavernij-achtige uitbuiting in Nederland Een inventariserende literatuurstudie in het kader van de uitbreiding van de strafbaarstelling van mensenhandel* (Den Haag: BJU 2004).

J.P. van der Leun, and R.C. Kloosterman, 'Going Underground: Immigration Policy Changes and Shifts in Modes of Provision of Undocumented Immigrants in the Netherlands'(2006) Tijdschrift voor Economische en Sociale Geografie, Vol 97, No 1, pp. 59-68.

J.P. van der Leun, M. Ilies, 'Undocumented Migration. An Explanatory Framework' in M. Martiniello and J. Rath (eds), *IMISCOE textbooks on Migration, part II* (Amsterdam, AUP, forthcoming 2011).

F. van Dijk and R. Ungureanu, *Labour exploitation in Europe* (The Hague, SZW 2010).

M. Wijers and L. Lap Chew, *Trafficking in women forced labor and slavery-like practices in marriage domestic labour and prostitution* (Utrecht: Stichting Tegen Vrouwenhandel 1999).

Chapter 9
The European efforts in combating human trafficking for the purpose of labour exploitation; on milestones, migration, Member States and mutual assistance

F.H. van Dijk
P.A. Vonk[1]

'Ill-treatment of a servant by his master will be subject to a fine. Everyone entering the Netherlands as a slave becomes a free man automatically. The number of poor people and refugees, looking for a better future, is high'.[2] The French philosopher and author Denis Diderot (1713-1784) was in full appreciation of Dutch society during a visit: the country was wealthy, the level of wages was high, there was hardly any theft and even books, subject to a ban elsewhere, could be legally purchased. On the other hand, the aristocrat also became acquainted with some nasty habits of the Dutch: he experienced some rude behaviour, a horrifying low sense of fashion and awful beer (which was drunk way in excess by the locals), and besides that he did not notice any attractive women.

Denis Diderot was definitely not the last being interested in social relations. Regarding the combat of human trafficking for the purpose of labour exploitation, a number of European milestones and important national developments can be noted. In this article light is shed on the necessity for better cooperation between Member States of the European Union (EU), seen in the light of future global developments and the European labour market.

In the first decade of the 21st century the public have been confronted with several expressions of art, where the exploitation of persons has revealed itself as a rewarding subject. Some startling exhibitions have been showing the victims of exploitation and their social environment.[3] In another visual art form, more and more commercial cinematographic works have been devoted to illegal stay, illegal migration and the victims of exploitation.[4] There are also

---

[1] F.H. van Dijk: advisor on the combating of human trafficking, working at the Sociale Inlichtingen- en Opsporingsdienst (Social Security Intelligence and Investigation Service), part of the Ministry of Social Affairs and Employment; Member of the Group of Experts on Trafficking in Human Beings, European Commission.
P.A. Vonk: lawyer, working at the Sociale Inlichtingen- en Opsporingsdienst (Social Security Intelligence and Investigation Service), part of the Ministry of Social Affairs and Employment; seconded to Europol at the end of 2010.
[2] D. Diderot, *Over Holland; een journalistieke reis 1773-1774* (Amsterdam 1994) p. 85.
[3] D. Popa, *Not Natascha*, (London 2009); K. Chernush, *Bought and sold* (Arlington 2009); R. Dallaporta, O. Millot, *Domestic slavery* (Lausanne 2009); N.J. Roy, M. Pearl, *Traffik* (New York 2008); Helen Bamber Foundation, *The Journey* (London 2007).
[4] Ph. Lioret, *Welcome* (France 2009); C. Fukunaga, *Sin nombre* (Mexico, USA 2009);A.K. Olesen, *Lille soldat* (Denmark 2008); L. Cantet, *Entre les murs* (France 2008); M.

films about minors, the hard life on the streets and child prostitution.[5] Traditionally, the focus in the billion dollar film industry in Hollywood and Europe used to be more on the sexual exploitation of women and girls.[6]

Regarding the demand side, for years the ongoing discussion has been about the involvement of the clients of prostitutes. But the same members of the public are not always aware of running the risk of becoming involved in a criminal pattern of exploitation when making use of cheap services for private purposes, such as home improvements, gardening, painting or domestic services. One might also wonder whether people, while enjoying the broadcasting of global mega sports events, such as the football World Cup (South Africa 2010) and the Olympic Games (China 2008), realise that labourers could have fallen prey to harsh working conditions, long working days, low pay and degrading living conditions, all in order to comply with strict deadlines when finishing the required building activities on time – while this is also common knowledge. In India, where the Commonwealth Games were held in October 2010, there is hardly any social security system or mandatory registration of employees.

The purpose of exploitation

Power, status and coalition, but also submission, abuse of power and the protection of the weakest are social elements in a society of chimpanzees. Hierarchy and clear lines of authority empower the privileges of a few, as well as the discrimination and exploitation of those that are lower in the social order.[7]

Comparable dynamics are also known in our human society. The exploitation of a person is the core of human trafficking, as defined in international law and criminalised in national laws. The following elements of this definition can be identified: recruitment, transportation, transfer, harbouring or receipt of a person as *activities*; force, deception, abduction, coercion, fraud,

---

Kreutzpaintner, *Trade* (USA 2007); A. Salomonwitz, *Kurz davor ist es passiert* (Austria 2006); B. Turner, *Human cargo* (USA 2004)); L. Moodysson, *Lilja 4-ever* (Sweden 2002);S. Frears, *Dirty pretty things* (UK 2002).

[5] G. Jacobson, A. Ezroni, *Redlight* (2009); D. Boyle, L. Shandan, *Slumdog millionaire* (USA 2008); P. Gurung, *Nabarsijeki Jhari* (Nepal 2006); I. Fíla, *König der Diebe* (Slovakia 2004); D. Illiadis, *Hardcore* (Greece 2004); F. Gallenberger, *Schatten der Zeit* (Germany 2004); F. Meirelles, *Cidade de deus* (Brazil 2002).

[6] P. Morrel, *Taken* (USA 2008); D. Barnhart jr., *China dolls* (USA 2008); C. Duguay, *Human trafficking* (France 2005); D. Yates, *Sex traffic* (USA 2004); S. Soderbergh, *Traffic* (USA 2000); J. Schumacher, *8MM* (USA 1999); P.T. Anderson, *Boogie nights* (USA 1997); P. Schrader, *Hardcore* (USA 1979); J. d'Amato, *La via della prostituzione* (Italy 1978); M. Scorcese, *Taxi Driver* (USA 1976).

[7] F. de Waal, *Our inner ape* (New York 2005) pp. 43-88.

threats, abuse of power, or a position of vulnerability as a *means*; exploitation, such as forced labour or the removal of organs, as a *purpose*.[8]

Human trafficking is a serious crime, violating basic human rights and the right to decide on one's own; free will is denied, individual social capital is exploited and, in some cases, the situation is not all that far-removed from historic slavery: violating human dignity, physical integrity and personal freedom. The economic factor, the financial profit, is in practically all cases the guiding principle for the unscrupulous perpetrators: many cases are known that have even caused the death of victims. The population groups at risk consist of vulnerable people in society, such as irregular migrants, regular migrants, minors, women, unemployed, and people with several social problems (homelessness, poverty, debts, ill-health). In contrast to human trafficking is human smuggling, where the smuggled persons are facilitated with illegal border crossing and/or travel for a fee. Smuggled persons can nonetheless become victims of exploitation too, especially when they try to find a source of income after arriving in the country of destination. Human trafficking is also a remarkably less studied subject.

One might divide human trafficking into five subtypes, as people can be exploited for sexual services, for 'regular' labour or services (also called 'forced labour'), for the harvesting of organs (or tissues, blood products or human cells such as female ovaries), for forced begging, and for forced criminal behaviour (such as petty crimes, fraud, drug smuggling and theft).

Historic slavery concerns the individual labour force as private ownership, as a provision that can be bought or sold and thus legally penalising any escape; although having been abolished worldwide, this still occurs in countries based on ethno-cultural traditions and upheld by the government. Recently, Niger was found guilty of enabling a situation of slavery.[9] The differences with ancient slavery practices are nowadays not only the absence of legal ownership, but also the very high profits, the very low purchase costs, the short-term relationships, the surplus of potential slaves, the slaves' disposable nature and the unimportance of ethnic differences.[10] Labour exploitation in the modern sense, also called modern slavery, shows an abuse of the labour force by the creation of multiple dependency by means of physical and psychological threats and maltreatment, the strong curtailment of the freedom of movement, or coercion in different forms. Labour exploitation, or forced labour, is anyway very difficult to discover and to prove. The methods and techniques

---

[8] Directive on preventing and combating trafficking in human beings and protecting victims, repealing Framework Decision 2002/629/JHA, Art. 2 (adopted by the Council on 21 March 2011); Council of Europe Convention on action against trafficking in human beings, (16 May 2005) art. 4.; Protocol to prevent, suppress and punish trafficking in persons especially women and children, supplementing the United Nations Convention against transnational organized crime (15 November 2000), Palermo Protocol, Art. 3.

[9] *Hadijatou Mani Koraou v. Republic of Niger*, ECW/CCJ/JUD/06/08 (27 October 2008).

[10] K. Bales, *Disposable people; new slavery in the global economy* (Berkeley 1999) pp. 1-33.

used to bring people (registered and unregistered employees, housekeepers, au pairs and even relatives) into a situation of total dependency demonstrate very refined cruelty, all in order to exploit someone's social capital. The personal accounts illustrate modern slavery and slavery-like practices across the world, and provide an insight into ill-treatment by European employers, violation of labour relations, domestic servitude and a hostile perception of foreigners in general.[11] By its nature, domestic servitude is a sector very vulnerable to social isolation and exploitation.[12]

Human trafficking is often referred to as 'the fastest growing criminal industry in the world' and is assumed to have 'epidemic proportions'. A cautious estimate years ago was that at least some 12.3 million people were victims of forced labour worldwide, of whom 9.8 million exploited by private actors and 2.4 million due to human trafficking. Even in industrialised countries an estimated 23 percent were victims of non-sexual, economic exploitation already.[13]

But there are typologies in society that lead to a discussion on the concept and definition of human trafficking and the purpose of exploitation. For instance, there is some confusion as to the terminology of prostitution and human trafficking: in eight European countries prostitution is a legalised or regulated economic sector (Austria, Germany, Greece, Hungary, Latvia, the Netherlands, Switzerland and Turkey) and thus containing an element of formal labour, other European countries outlawed the act of engaging in sexual activity in exchange for money (such as Albania, Croatia, Romania, Russia, and Slovenia), while others allow prostitution itself but prohibit most forms of procuring such as operating brothels, facilitating the prostitution of another, deriving financial gain from the prostitution of another, and soliciting or loitering (such as Belgium, Bulgaria, the Czech Republic, Finland, France, Ireland, Italy, Poland, Portugal, Slovakia, Spain, and the United Kingdom). To discourage human trafficking Iceland, Norway and Sweden have adopted an approach by penalizing the making use of prostitutes' services as a measure to combat human trafficking; according to some, this does not approach

---

[11] N. Kampusch, *3096 Tage* (Berlin 2010) pp. 35-223; F. Oum'Hamed, *De uitverkorene; een importbruid acht jaar lang in Nederland* (Amsterdam 2009) pp. 15-204; G. Wallraf, *Aus der schönen neuen Welt*, Cologne (2009) pp. 7-311; E.B. Skinner, *A crime so monstrous; face-to-face with modern-day slavery* (New York 2008) pp. 63-104; M. Slattery, 'The journey of an orphan' in J. Sage, L. Kasten (ed), *Enslaved; true stories of modern day slavery* (Basingstoke 2006) pp. 11-38; A. Bak, 'Beyond Abeeda', *ib.*, pp. 39-60; S. Juma, 'Out of Egypt: a lifeline via email for an enslaved au pair in Cairo', *ib.*, pp. 177-205; A.N. Ould Yessa, 'Amazing Grace: a slave owner's awakening in Mauritania', *ib.*, pp. 205-230; F. Bok, *Escape from slavery; the true story of my ten years in captivity and my journey to freedom in America* (New York 2003) pp. 13-252; M. Nazer, *Slave; my true story* (London 2003) pp. 212-262; G. Wallraff, *Ganz Unten* (Cologne 1985) pp. 14-312.

[12] OSCE, *Unprotected work, invisible exploitation: trafficking for the purpose of domestic servitude* (Vienna 2010) pp. 13-29.

[13] ILO, *Eine globale Allianz gegen Zwangsarbeit* (Geneva 2005) pp. 11-17.

prostitution as a sector where people must be able to earn a living of their own free will from a women's rights perspective. Then, subjected to discussions about hidden exploitation are certain religious groups (some of which are well known and have millions of followers, such as famous actors), characterized by social isolation and managed by a system of far-reaching dependence, discipline and punishment with supposed forced labour of their devotees. Another discussion is the use of minors for military forces or armed groups; while this is well known in several African and Asiatic countries and Colombia (and autobiographic reports from the Sudan and Sierra Leone[14]), Western countries such as Belgium, Canada, Germany, the United Kingdom and the United States still have legal possibilities to recruit minors.[15] It was only at the end of 2009 that the Netherlands changed its law, meaning that 17-year old minors can only be trained with permission from their parents, but not used for military operations. Yet another group are children born from commercial surrogate mothers (like the Belgian/Dutch cases of the babies Donna and Jayden, born in 2005 and 2007 respectively); buying a newborn baby abroad is like human trafficking, and it is useful to realise that the supply of adoptive children is decreasing which will probably influence illegal adoption. State-organised birth programmes and child adoption aimed at ethnic minorities, lower social classes and political adversaries were known only a few decades ago in Argentina, Australia, the Czech Republic and Spain, among others. Again another discussion reflects on the way in which tens of thousands of young footballers are transferred to European clubs also brings to mind a sense of trafficking, especially since UEFA introduced the so-called Home-grown Rule which states that a fixed number of players have to be trained by clubs for three years, thus enabling clubs to chase talented teenagers. This type of exploitation in sport is definitely not limited to camel jockeys in the Near East. Finally, even some convictions fuel discussions about the interpretation and application of the legal definition: recent cases in the Netherlands led to convictions of human trafficking having forced women to subscribe to telephone cards.[16]

Shifting environment

The process of exploitation by abusing one's labour or services takes place in a hidden part of the national economy, often referred to as 'the informal economy'. For a good understanding of the combination 'informal' and 'economy' it is important to realise that during the last few decades a few nouns have been fortified with different adjectives, while the same socio-

---

[14] E. Jal, *War child; a child soldier's story* (London 2009) pp. 3-260; I. Beah, *A long way gone: memoirs of a boy soldier* (New York 2007) pp. 5-226.
[15] Child Soldiers, *Child Soldiers Global Report 2008* (London 2008) pp. 389-407.
[16] District Court of Haarlem, 8 December 2010, LJN BO8985; District Court of Dordrecht, 20 April 2010, LJN BM 1743.

economic phenomenon was meant. Words such as *economy, labour, work* or *sector* can and could be found to be associated with *informal, alternative, black, clandestine, community, criminal, dual, fraudulent, hidden, invisible, irregular, non-official, occult, other, parallel, precarious, second, subterranean, supplementary, underground, unobserved, unofficial, unorganised, unrecorded, unregulated,* and so forth. To avoid diversity and confusion, in this study we will use 'informal' in connection with 'economy', a combination first introduced in 1972 while discussing African urban poverty.[17] There are various definitions of an informal economy, but in essence 'informal activities' do not hinge on the character of the final product, but on the manner in which it is produced and exchanged; whereas 'criminal activities specialise in the production of goods and services socially defined as illicit. The boundaries will therefore vary and move substantially in various contexts, since the informal economy does not result from the intrinsic characteristics of activities but from the social definition of state intervention.[18] It goes without saying that nothing can be said with certainty about the size of the informal economy, or for the evasion of official registration. The average size, in the year 2000 as a percentage of the Gross National Income (GNI), was estimated at 41 % in developing countries, 38 % in transition countries and 18 % in OECD countries.[19] The informal economy is often accompanied by corruption: across the world corruption levels are perceived as having increased during the last three years; within the EU this is experienced by 73 % of the persons asked. The top three most corrupt institutions that were reported are political parties 80 % (was 71 % in 2004), parliament and the legislature 61 % (was 59 %) and the police 59 % (was 57 %).[20]

The year 2010 also saw grim repercussions of an economic crisis with unprecedented global dimensions. The Millennium Declaration set 2015 as the target date for achieving the goals to halve extreme poverty in all its forms worldwide since 1990. In spite of certain advances, an estimated 55 million to 90 million more people will be living in extreme poverty than anticipated before the crisis, also influencing education and health care in poor regions. Likewise, the encouraging trend in the eradication of hunger since the early 1990s was reversed, largely due to higher food prices in 2008, whereas promised assistance increased to the highest dollar figure ever recorded: $119.8

[17] ILO, *Employment, income and equality: a strategy for increasing productive unemployment in Kenya* (Geneva 1972).

[18] R. Kloosterman, J. van der Leun, J. Rath, *Over grenzen; immigranten en de informele economie* (Amsterdam 1997) pp. 16-27; M. Castells, A. Portes, 'World underneath: the origins, dynamics, and effects of the informal economy' in A. Portes, M. Castells, L.A. Benton (ed), *The informal economy; studies in advanced and less developed countries* (Baltimore 1989) pp. 11-37.

[19] F. Schneider, *Size and measurement of the informal economy in 110 countries around the world* (Linz 2002) pp. 44-45.

[20] TI, *Global corruption barometer 2010* (Berlin 2011) pp. 2-9.

billion.[21] The loss of income for developing countries, due to the economic crisis, is compounded by food prices that are still relatively high in the local markets of many poor countries. As a result, poor households have been forced to eat fewer meals and less nutritious food, to cut back on health and education expenses, and to sell their assets. The number of undernourished people in the world is estimated to have reached 925 million in 2010 - higher than before the food and economic crises, and higher than forty years ago.[22]

The world population is calculated to increase from 6,892 billion in 2010 to 8,108 billion in 2025 and 9,485 billion in 2050. In 1950, the elderly support ratio was 12 working-age people for every elderly person in the world; by 2010, this ratio had declined to nine, with the largest decline occurring in more developed countries (the lowest being in Japan, Italy, and Germany - at three). By 2050, the ratio for the world is predicted to decline to 4, and Japan will have the lowest ratio of only one working-age adult per elderly person. The elderly support ratio will be below 5 in more than half of the world's countries.[23] So the population growth does require an equal increase in global food production, already leading to the anticipation of developed countries leasing vast estates with millions of agricultural hectares, such as Saudi Arabia in Ethiopia, China in Congo, the United Arab Emirates in Sudan, and South Korea in Madagascar. This type of international strategic anticipation is increasingly seen. Continued industrialisation has led to growing demands and an increase in prices worldwide, such as for 17 minerals that are indispensable for the mass production of electronic equipment and motor vehicles. The Chinese share of the world production of some of these strategic minerals is already 95 %, while global demand will double over the next 25 years.[24]

The unfair division of opportunities already leads to migration, as migration is caused by expectations of better income, obtaining health security and increased prospects for descendants. About 740 million people are internal migrants, and from the 200 million international migrants more then 5 million have entered the developed countries. About 50 million people stay in their new environment illegally. Two-thirds of the world's refugees are to be found in developing countries, and nearly 80 per cent of asylum applications in the industrialised world are lodged in Europe, representing a 7 per cent increase over 2008. Regarding the labour market there is hardly any doubt that industrialised countries in the next 40 years will be confronted with a decrease in the labour population, whereas in poorer countries a population growth by more than one third is expected.[25]

---

[21] UN, *The Millenium development goals report 2009* (New York 2009) pp. 4-7; 48-52.
[22] FAO, *The state of food insecurity in the world; addressing food insecurity in protracted crisis* (Rome 2010) pp. 8-11.
[23] PRB, *2010 world population data sheet* (Washington DC 2010) pp. 2-17.
[24] HCSS, *Scarcity of minerals; a strategic security issue* (The Hague 2010) pp. 9-15; 81-88.
[25] UNHCR, *Global report 2009; new threats, new challenges* (Geneva 2010) pp. 17-18; 110; 301-305; UNHCR, *2008 Global trends: refugees, asylum-seekers, internally displaced and stateless persons* (Geneva 2009) pp. 2-21; UNDP, *Human Development Report 2009;*

The legal and illegal migration movements worldwide have a huge impact, not only on Mediterranean islands such as Lampedusa and Agathonissi or in the economically attractive regions, but also resulting in social changes in the poorer regions. Many countries where labour migrants come from see a flow of money sent home. In China labour migrants are no longer pitiful, since shortages in skilled labour have caused a drift to Western China of enterprises and labourers, recently leading to an increase in loans and an improvement in labour conditions. One out of every ten Filipinos is said to work abroad, especially in Saudi Arabia, Qatar and the United Arab Emirates: the men usually as seafarers or bricklayers, the women as nurses or domestic servants. Apart from financial prosperity and better opportunities in education, as a result there is also a risk of a social imbalance as many children grow up without (one of their) parents, love affairs develop abroad and in traditional, male-centred cultures the remaining men do not take over the caring duties.

In North-Western Europe from about the 1950s relations on the labour market became standardised due to organisational economic changes, the evolving structure of the family, and the power of the nation state. The economic security and stability which had been achieved by the working population then encountered shifting environmental conditions, such as the growth in self-employment, the rising grey zone containing neither employees nor self-employed people, and female participation.[26]

On a macro-economic level the supply of the European market rose at the start of this millennium, as analysed in Austria, Denmark, Ireland and the Netherlands, due to the labour participation of women, more specifically married women with children. This is the result of a growing level of education and a need for higher salaries, leading to two-income families. The demand side showed the need for a more flexible organisation of labour, such as a reduction in standard hours and the expansion of part-time labour.[27]

The participation of women on the European labour market rose from 48.5 % in 1960 to 52.4 % in 2000. Taking the dynamics of migration and differences between Member States into account, some economic sectors illustrate the participation of female migrant workers, such as domestic servitude, health care, restaurants and education. This feminisation of labour migration which has seen an increasing demand for female migrant workers often resulting in discrimination and unequal treatment in comparison with male labourers go hand in hand.[28]

---

overcoming barriers (New York 2009) pp. 1-20; 71-112; UNDP, *Annual Report 2009; living up to commitments* (New York 2009) pp. 3-29.

[26] S. Deakin, 'The evolution of the employment relationship' in P. Auer, B. Gazier (ed), *The future of work, employment and social protection – the dynamics of change and the protection of workers* (Geneva 2002) pp. 191-205.

[27] G. Bosch, 'Working time: from redistribution to modernization' in P. Auer (ed), *Changing labour markets in Europe; the role of institutions and policies* (Geneva 2001) pp. 55-115.

[28] OSCE, *Guide on gender-sensitive labour migration policies* (Vienna 2009) pp. 13-26.

It is clear that in the EU people were, are and will be exploited by their labour or services being abused. A problem is that the term 'trafficking' seems to imply a movement, while the purpose always has to be exploitation - not necessarily implying a movement. It goes without saying that these victims do not have to be illegal from outside the EU; having a closer look at the differences in minimum wages between Member States can be revealing. They vary widely within the Union, from € 123 in Bulgaria to € 1,683 in Luxembourg. Twenty of the EU's 27 Member States (Belgium, Bulgaria, the Czech Republic, Estonia, Hungary, Ireland, Greece, Spain, France, Latvia, Lithuania, Luxembourg, Malta, the Netherlands, Poland, Portugal, Romania, Slovakia, Slovenia, and the United Kingdom) and two Candidate Member States (Croatia and Turkey) have national legislation setting a minimum wage by statute or by national intersectoral agreement.[29] There are also huge differences in wealth between European regions, up to seven times wealthier than the poorest region of Bulgaria. In 2010 the average yearly income in the Netherlands was € 20,753, in the United Kingdom it was € 24,625 and in Denmark € 25,113, compared to Bulgaria € 1,714, Romania € 1,987, Latvia € 3,939 and Lithuania € 4,086. If we further compare the Netherlands with Latvia a difference can be noticed in the field of the working population (69.3 % against 26.7 %, respectively) and the risk of fall into poverty (11 % against 21%).[30]

One of the factors that eventually lead to exploitation is the actual recruitment. Much more than a few migrants who have fallen prey to unscrupulous recruitment agents have shown a dependency on intermediaries that are not part of their own social and reliable network, and neither are official job placement agencies.[31] In general, trafficking and labour exploitation used to seem less likely to occur with existing established migration routes, support for labour standards, accompanying knowledge, official contacts and so forth, all to exclude the isolation in which migrant workers find themselves.[32] But now the situation occurs that people have migrated legally and become exploited nonetheless. One of the problems for the current 27 Member States is the synchronisation of systems of labour regulation on the international and national level. In the European context the labour force as well as the systems of regulation are concerned primarily with the free movement of workers and services, and additionally with other forms of regulation that shape Europe's labour market; these can conflict with the objectives associated with national labour market regulation, where employment protection and industrial relations are the chief concerns. This all shows the attraction towards the

---

[29] Eurostat, *Minimum wage statistics* (Luxembourg 2010).

[30] Eurostat, *Combating poverty and social exclusion; a statistical portait of the European Union 2010* (Luxembourg 2010) pp. 15-62.

[31] B. Andrees, 'Combating criminal activities in the recruitment of migrant workers' in C. Kuptsch (ed), *Merchants of labour* (Geneva 2006) pp. 175-183.

[32] M. Cunneen, 'Strategies to combat forced labour in the context of migration' in C. Kuptsch (ed), *Merchants of labour* (Geneva 2006) pp. 185-189.

West-European labour markets for citizens from Member States that recently joined the EU. In prostitution, the nationalities of sex workers from these new EU-countries are already in the majority and are widely represented within the European Union (Romania 12 %, Bulgaria 8 % and Russia 9 % - in 2006 Russia, Ukraine and Romania were dominant).[33]

The employment rates for those with high skill levels across the EU as a whole is 83.9 %, that for medium skill levels is 70.6 %, and that for low skill levels is 48.1 %. Nearly one third of Europe's population aged 25-64, around 77 million people, have no or low formal qualifications and only one quarter have high level qualifications. In 2010 there were 22.9 million unemployed people in the EU, including more than 5 million young people; in this decade, some 80 million job opportunities are expected to emerge, including almost 7 million new additional jobs.[34]

Focus on labour exploitation

The year 2010, devoted by the European Commission to the international combating of poverty and social exclusion, without any doubt can be considered to be of the highest importance with regard to the international fight against trafficking in human beings. On the 7th of January 2010, the European Court of Human Rights (ECtHR) delivered its verdict in the case of Rantsev versus Cyprus and Russia[35], a second milestone after the case of Siliadin versus France in 2005.[36] The decision of Rantsev clarified that the Member States of the European Union must take significant action in order to meet their obligation to secure to all those within their jurisdiction the right to be free from the threat of enslavement, servitude and forced labour and to live in dignity, thus giving a new interpretation to article 4 of the ECHR by – in contrast to Siliadin - not considering it to be necessary to identify whether this has been a case of slavery, servitude, or forced and compulsory labour.[37] Supported by earlier international rulings emphasising the rights and position of victims, this can also be considered to be at variance with a more traditional approach, primarily focusing on the prosecution of the perpetrators. In addition, the case of Rantsev also showed that a comprehensive approach, encompassing all aspects of prevention, protection and prosecution is essential

---

[33] TAMPEP, *Sex work in Europe; a mapping of the prostitution scene in 25 European countries* (Amsterdam 2009) pp. 14-33.

[34] EC/NSNJ, *New skills for new jobs: a report by the Expert Group on New Skills for New Jobs prepared for the European Commission* (Brussels 2010) pp. 8-18.

[35] *Rantsev v. Cyprus and Russia*, Chamber Judgment, Application No. 25965/04 (7 January 2010).

[36] *Siliadin v. France*, Chamber Judgment, Application No. 73316/01 (26 October 2005).

[37] M. Boot, 'Artikel 4 EVRM en de aanpak van mensenhandel' (2010) NTM/NCM-Bulletin, 35, pp. 501-519; Rantsev, para 282.

in securing effective State action against trafficking in human beings.[38] Following the case of Rantsev, there are more cases of human trafficking for purposes other than sexual services pending before the ECtHR.[39]

Other important developments in 2010 were, amongst others, the launching by the European Commission of the draft for a new Directive on human trafficking, repealing the Framework Decision from 2002 and stressing the position and rights of victims of human trafficking; the appointment of an anti-trafficking coordinator in the EU; the development of a system of independent National Rapporteurs, or equivalent mechanisms, to ensure cooperation; and the establishment of an EU website dedicated to human trafficking. Other relevant developments were, amongst others, the publication of the RighT Guide, a tool developed to put policies and measures, meant for fighting human trafficking, on trial against the framework of human rights; contributions to the problem of data collection, such as the MONTRASEC demo and initiatives by the International Centre for Migration Policy Development (ICMPD); the establishment of E-Notes Observatory, as a partnership between several NGOs; and the first international seminar on the operational side of combating labour exploitation called LABOREX10, organised by the Dutch Sociale Inlichtingen- en Opsporingsdienst (SIOD; Social Security Intelligence and Investigation Service) and Romanian colleagues, where 100 experts from 23 European countries met.

In 2010 some Member States adjusted their national legislation with regard to combating human trafficking, such as Poland. For some other Member States 2010 was very important in the light of the very first convictions for a certain type of human trafficking as well; in the Netherlands five convictions for human trafficking for the purpose of labour exploitation saw the light of day (these cases concerned exploitation in, so to say, a 'classical' labour relationship between employer and employee). Of these five verdicts one concerned the exploitation of employees in a Chinese restaurant, one Indonesians working in a food processing factory, one labourers from India working at a market, one Bulgarian cleaning activities in a coffee shop, and one was related to Polish mushroom pickers.[40] In 2011 a sixth conviction concerned people from Surinam being misled in order to obtain a residence permit and having to work in the construction industry in return.[41] These

[38] Group of Experts on Trafficking in Human Beings, *Opinion nr. 6: on the decision of the European Court of Human Rights in the case of Rantsev v. Cyprus and Russia* (Brussels 22 June 2010), para 14.

[39] *Elisabeth Kawogo v. United Kingdom*, Application No. 56921/09; *C.N. v. United Kingdom*, Application No. 4239/08; *Liliyana Sashkova and others v. Italy and Bulgaria*, Application No. 40020/03.

[40] Respectively Court of Appeal Den Bosch, 19 February 2010, LJN BL5492; District Court of The Hague, 3 May 2010, LJN BM3374; District Court of The Hague, 12 May 2010, LJN BM4291; District Court of Utrecht, 5 October 2010, LJN BO2835; District Court of Roermond, 26 October 2010, LJN BO3022.

[41] District Court of The Hague, 11 February 2011, LJN BP4006.

were all preceded by a judgment by the Supreme Court of 27 October 2009 that gave direction to the interpretation of a paragraph in the Criminal Code.[42]

Looking at domestic servitude there was a case in 2007 which was also the very first Dutch conviction for human trafficking for a purpose other than sexual exploitation. A couple from India exploited three countrymen who had to work under degrading circumstances, characterised by low pay, no privacy, having to lodge at the couple's home, not having their own passports at their disposal, and being subjected to physical violence, all leading to the death of a 2-year old eventually.[43] Only weeks before the judgment by the Supreme Court, a Higher Court had ruled in the case of a professional social worker who had taken care of a woman with mental problems and had taken her into his home; the Court not only considered the fact that there had been sexual abuse, but also the fact that he had forced her to do on the housework.[44] These two verdicts, together with one concerning a mentally handicapped person[45], show the development of the interpretation of exploitation in labour or services in the Netherlands.[46] This and other relevant Dutch case law is meticulously analysed in this volume by Ms L. van Krimpen.

An important development is the increasing focus on human trafficking for the purpose of labour exploitation. This criminal act not only conflicts with international standards of human rights and the national constitutions of EU Member States, it also conflicts profoundly with basic principles of national systems of social security, developed to protect employees against dependence on and the arbitrariness of an employer. Given this complexity of the crime, counter-trafficking measures should be derived not only from criminal law, but from a wider approach such as labour law, migration law, external relations and development policy.[47] But in the end, criminals always have to be stopped by effective law enforcement operations.

Every year an authoritative American report assesses the countries' efforts across the world regarding the elimination of trafficking in human beings, by

[42] Supreme Court, HR 08/03894 27 October 2009, LJN BI7079; HR 08/03895, 27 October 2009, LJN BI7099.

[43] District Court of The Hague, 14 december 2007, LJN BC1195 and BC1761 and BC0775.

[44] Court of Appeal of Leeuwarden, 6 October 2009, LJN BJ9385.

[45] District Court of Utrecht, 17 June 2008, LJN BD7426.

[46] S. Lestrade, W. ten Kate, 'De strafbaarstelling van "overige uitbuiting" binnen mensenhandel' (2009) NJCM-Bulletin, 34, pp. 852-870.

[47] C. Rijken, E. de Volder, 'The European Union's struggle to realize a human rights-based approach to trafficking in human beings' (2010) in Connecticut Journal of International Law, 25, pp. 49-79; J. Coster van Voorhout, *Human trafficking for the purpose of labour exploitation; a framework for implementation of the crime of human trafficking for labour exploitation as defined in the European Council Framework Decision in EU countries* (Utrecht 2009) pp. 131-146.

[48] Department of State, *Trafficking in Person report 2010* (Washington DC 2010) pp. 51, 58-338.

using so-called 'tier placements'. Except for Iceland, all countries in North-West Europe in 2010 had the highest ranking of fully complying with minimum standards (tier 1). In East-Europe most countries had a score of tier 2 (as well as Portugal, Switzerland and Turkey), whereas the ranking tier 1 was only given to Bosnia Herzegovina, Croatia, the Czech Republic, Lithuania, Poland and Slovenia. Serious worries were related to Azerbaijan, Malta, Moldova and Russia (tier 2 watch list).[48]

The last two decades Europe is characterised by an increasing transnational crime; crime can be regarded transnational when a certain level of organisation is needed to commit the crime, when it affects the interests of more than one State, when the involvement of more States aggravates the problems involved in prosecuting transnational crime, and when effective solutions are sought beyond national borders.[49] From the end of the eighties international organised crime was not limited anymore, because of the fall of Soviet Union and East-European totalitarian regimes, the liberalisation of China, the implementation of the Schengen Agreement and the expansion of the European Union (in 2011 27 Member States, four Candidate Countries and five potential candidate Countries). In Europe criminal groups, especially from Russia, Bulgaria and Albania, expanded rapidly and focussed on car theft, weapons, cigarettes, drugs, malversations on the (Russian) energy market and last but not least on the trade in human beings, either for the Western and Near Eastern sex markets or for the labour market. Some even speak about a revival of slavery, due to these criminal dynamics of the world's economic market. The strict regulations towards international migration have not been very helpful to prevent and fight these crimes.[50]

The most active organised crime groups involved in trafficking in human beings in the EU are Bulgarian, Nigerian and Romanian. Groups from other Balkan countries, China, Moldova, Russia, Turkey, Ukraine and Vietnam are also frequently reported. Albanian groups tend to exploit victims trafficked by other groups. The trafficking of women for sexual exploitation is stabilising, while trafficking for forced labour is increasing, mainly in the construction, drug production and begging sectors. Intelligence indicates increasing trafficking in children destined for illegal labour – including domestic slavery – or sexual exploitation. Romanian organised groups of Roma ethnicity dominate trafficking in children.[51]

Focusing on human trafficking for the purpose of labour exploitation, one cannot solely rely on one or some indicators. Victims hardly see themselves as victim. In order to identify a criminal scheme or a victim of human trafficking for the purpose of labour exploitation, it might seem tempting to evaluate the

---

[49] C. Rijken, *Trafficking in persons; prosecution from a European perspective*, (The Hague 2003) pp. 19-52

[50] M. Glenny, *McMafia, Seriously organised crime* (London 2008) pp. 33-59; 118-141; L. Napoleoni, *Rogue economics; capitalism's new reality* (New York 2008) pp. 137-155.

[51] Europol, *OCTA 2009* (The Hague 2010) pp. 20-21.

residential stay of a supposed victim (illegal status) as an important factor, or the employer's initiative that eventually leads to a pattern of exploitation, or the presence of physical violence and threats, or not having identity documents at one's disposal (withdrawn by the employer). Every case stands on its own merits, having its own complexity and dynamics. As labour exploitation takes place on the labour market, the criminal scheme of labour exploitation has connections with other acknowledged international fraud schemes, such as undeclared work, money laundering, the use of forged identity documents, the trade in tax and social insurance numbers, abusing the local authority registration system, and the abuse of E-101 forms on secondments. It must be recognised that labour exploitation is hardly or is never 'caught in the act'. This also has implications for the coordination and exchange of information for the purpose of criminal analysis - especially with regard to the piling up of different social misdemeanours such as reported undeclared labour, reported illegal employment, paying below minimum wages, the violation of labour conditions, the violation of maximum working hours, and other (police) data such as violations of immigration law, and acts of violence or threats. Other misunderstandings are, for instance, that huge groups of victims are expected, or organised criminal groups have to be involved exclusively.[52]

There are some legal differences between European countries when looking at combating labour exploitation, as this volume shows in the case of Austria, the Netherlands, Romania, Serbia and Spain. These differences are definitely not limited to these five countries: for instance, in Norway and the Netherlands the use of certain means of coercion is a standard element of the offence of human trafficking, whereas in Belgium the use of coercion is an aggravating circumstance. Other legal differences can be found, for instance, relating to preparing a criminal act, facilitating exploitation and the level of penalties. There are also some lacunae, such as in the United Kingdom where prosecution is only possible when a victim is trafficked into the country, and not within. In some countries the crime of human trafficking is found in the Criminal Code beneath the chapter 'crimes against personal freedom' (such as the Netherlands), in other countries in 'crimes against human dignity' (such as Belgium). An independent national rapporteur is present in only four of the 27 Member States (Belgium, Finland, the Netherlands and Portugal[53]), generally considered to be of vital importance in order to successfully combat human trafficking for the purpose of labour exploitation; the Dutch Rapporteur issues an annual comprehensive overview with policy recommendations.[54] But also

[52] F.H. van Dijk, R.N. Ungureanu, *Labour exploitation in Europe; a practical guide with operational observations and recommendations on European inspection, investigation and prosecution of labour exploitation* (The Hague 2010) pp. 62-63.

[53] G. Vermeulen, N. Paterson, *The MONTRASEC demo; a bench-mark for member state and EU automated data collection and reporting on trafficking in human beings and sexual exploitation of children* (Antwerp 2010) pp. 58-61.

[54] NRM, *Mensenhandel; achtste rapportage* (The Hague 2010); NRM, *Mensenhandel; zevende rapportage* (The Hague 2009).

the number of convictions for human trafficking for the purpose of labour exploitation differs a great deal. In 2010 in most European countries there were no convictions at all, from Ireland to Cyprus. In contrast, in Belgium the number of prosecutions for human trafficking for the purpose of labour exploitation is considerably high: in 2009 173 and in 2008 202, with the registered number of victims being 76 in 2009 and 124 in 2008.[55] In Norway one conviction can be noted (a case where British citizens were the victims)[56], whereas in Finland the only case so far has resulted in the conviction of one of the defendants for facilitating an illegal entry.[57] In the Netherlands, as said, five convictions are registered in 2010 (all pertaining to non-EU citizens as victims), and other convictions are known from Italy and the United Kingdom. But the scope of who can be victimised seems to vary too: in France, according to the Supreme Court, students working as an obligatory part of their education can be considered as victim of labour exploitation.[58] Anyway, there are still many cases to be brought before the courts, as the investigation phase has ended successfully, for instance in Cyprus concerning 103 Romanian labourers in the construction industry, or in the Czech Republic concerning Romanians on an asparagus farm and in a slaughterhouse.[59]

The low self-identification, the identification by competent authorities, the invisibility, and the recognition of position and rights of victims of human trafficking for the purpose of labour exploitation remain problematic.[60] This also stresses the importance of looking at the labour relationship itself, or the supposed labour relationship also when it takes place within a family or another social structure. Labour contracts are meant to record the relationship between employer and employee with regard to authority, labour, wages and labour conditions. The oldest known individual labour contracts stem from about 2000 B.C., in times when Mesopotamian royal codexes proclaimed social regulations such as the legal protection of widows, minimum wages per economic sector, remission of debts, public work for the poor (paid with food rations) and special adapted work for handicapped people.[61]

By examining the labour relation itself, a better understanding is possible of the existing grey zone between exploitation according to criminal standards,

---

[55] CGKR, *Mensenhandel -smokkel; in een schijn van wettelijkheid, Jaarverslag 2009* (Brussels 2010) pp. 46-48.

[56] Jaeren District Court: The Public Prosecution Authority vs Daniel D., Case no. 08-069332MED-JARE, 4 July 2008.

[57] Vantaa Court of Appeal R 07/1363, 13 July 2007; FNR THB, *Report 2010; Trafficking in human beings, phenomena related to it, and implementation of the rights of human trafficking victims in Finland* (Helsinki 2010) pp. 136-139.

[58] Cour de Cassation, 20 March 2003, no. 02-81453.

[59] F.H. van Dijk, R.N. Ungureanu, *op.cit.*, pp. 99-116.

[60] BlinN, *Uitbuiting in andere sectoren dan de seksindustrie* (Amsterdam 2010) pp. 36-43; G. Vaz Cabral, *La traite des êtres humains; réalités de l'esclavage contemporain* (Paris 2006) pp. 128-152.

[61] F.H. van Dijk, *Sociale zekerheid: ouder dan de weg naar Rome* (Zutphen 2001) pp. 47-63.

and an employer acting unlawfully with regard to labour standards. At least in the Netherlands this is an important issue since article 273f – not coincidentally the longest article in the whole Criminal Code – leaves this interpretation to the judges; the Civil Code only prescribes that an employer and an employee ought to behave as a good employer and a good employee.[62] A Court of Appeal in the Netherlands recently ruled in the case of an accountant who had fallen victim to the burn-out syndrome and who eventually had to rely on the Disablement Act. In his work (for 22 years) the man had usually systematically worked a considerable amount of overtime for half of the year, up to 60 hours (possibly even 80) instead of the official 40 hours a week. These were not properly registered and not compensated because they were regarded as being part of the job. The Court of Appeal considered that this not only conflicted with the Working Hours Act, but held the employer responsible for the physical damage as well as for not implementing measures to avoid stress from work that exceeds a person's natural physical or mental capabilities.[63]

With regard to labour exploitation, a group easily overlooked is children. Children pertain to a different legal framework as they are extremely vulnerable. But children are still put to work, although it is acknowledged that economic exploitation is hazardous or interferes with the child's education, or is harmful to the child's health or physical, mental, spiritual, moral or social development.[64] Recent operations to fight child labour are Cascades (Burkina Faso, 25-27 October 2010, 177 children in gold mining quarries, 11 suspects arrested) and Bia (Côte d'Ivoire, 18-19 June 2009, 54 children on cacao and palm plantations, eight suspects arrested) by Interpol.[65] Across the world there are 218 million child labourers, dropping slowly from 246 million at the end of the previous century – mostly in agriculture and to clear a family debt. Roughly 2.5 million children are economically active in developed countries. The rate of injury per hour worked appears to be nearly twice as high for children and adolescents as for adults. The 12-year minimum age for light work dominates in the Americas and in Africa, while it is more common in Europe to allow 13 or 14-year-old children to perform light work.[66]

In 2010 the Netherlands, with 16.7 million inhabitants, had a labour market with a relatively low unemployment rate of 4.8 % out of a professional population of 7.4 million. That year also showed the highest number of immigrants ever (149,800) due to the increasing number of migrants from EU countries.[67] Poverty, according to four criteria, is gradually increasing: the

---

[62] Article 7:611 Civil Code.

[63] Court of Appeal Den Bosch, 25 August 2009, LJN BK0617.

[64] Convention of the rights of the child, article 32 (20 November 1989).

[65] Interpol media release, 5 November 2010; Interpol media release, 3 August 2009.

[66] Stop Child Labour, *Child Labour* (Dublin 2008) pp. 2-3; ILO/Cornell Univ, *Child labour in Europe* (Geneva 2005) p. 2; ILO, *Child labour: targeting the intolerable* (Geneva 1998) pp. 24-25.

[67] CBS, *Totaalbeeld arbeidsmarkt* (Den Haag 20 January 2011); CBS, Press release 9 February 2010.

number of households and persons living in low budget conditions was 453,000 and 971,000 respectively (living on basic needs 315,000 and 684,000). This growth especially touched children and non-Western immigrants.[68]
In the Netherlands many administrative and criminal bodies are cooperating in combating human trafficking for the purpose of labour exploitation. Inspections are carried out by the Labour Inspectorate (on minimum wages, working hours, labour conditions and illegal employment), the police (on illegal aliens) and the border patrol (on migration). Criminal investigation is executed by the SIOD and the police. The border patrol, moreover, investigate human smuggling. Then there are a number of institutions in charge of information exchange and analysis, such as the Expertisecentrum Mensenhandel en Mensensmokkel (EMM), translated as the Expertise Centre for Human Trafficking and Human Smuggling. In 2008 a high-level National Taskforce was established by the Minister of Justice.

The number of victims in 2009 was 909, of whom 56 were in agriculture, 48 in other sectors, 16 in domestic servitude, 14 in the construction industry, 13 in the food processing industry, 6 in catering, and 1 in the cleaning industry (and the remaining in the sex industry); in 2008 the figure was 826, of whom 29 had worked outside the sex industry, 7 in catering, 6 in domestic servitude and 3 in the cleaning industry.[69]

There are signals that the system of protection shows imperfections. There is a call for a more balanced protective regime for victims of human trafficking in the Netherlands and, according to some reports, the victims of trafficking in human beings are found in Dutch detention centres for illegal aliens, but even there they are not recognised as victims of a serious crime and are therefore not provided with their rights concerning specific arrangements, support etc.[70] There is an arrangement for victims of human trafficking, the so-called B9-Regulation, which was recently expanded and named after the relevant chapter of the Aliens Act Implementation Guidelines 2000, giving the possibility of access to EU nationals as well as illegal aliens from outside the Union.[71]

The Netherlands, one of the countries with a well-developed system of social security, can also provide a specialised investigation service in this field. The SIOD, founded on 1 January 2002 and operating with a staff of 300, combats the misuse of social legislation and benefits. SIOD's investigation of major and complex fraud imparts a new dimension to the Ministry of Social Affairs and Employment's endeavours in combating misuse. The operations

---

[68] SCP/CBS, *Armoedesignalement 2010* (The Hague 2011) pp. 9-12.

[69] CoMensha, *Jaarverslag 2009* (Amersfoort 2010) pp. 5-9; CoMensha, *Jaarverslag 2008* (Amersfoort 2009) pp. 4-10.

[70] ACVZ, *De mens beschermd en de handel bestreden; een advies over een evnewichtig beschermingsregime voor slachtoffers van mensenhandel* (Den Haag 2009) pp. 67-71; BlinN, *Uitgebuit en in de bak; slachtoffers van mensenhandel in vreemdelingendetentie* (Amsterdam 2009) pp. 51-55.

[71] B9 regulation, Chapter B9 Aliens Act Implementation Guidelines, 22 Dec. 2010.

also contribute to the retention of society's support for social security and the focus on human trafficking for the purpose of labour exploitation; labour market fraud schemes, such as organised labour by (illegal) aliens from outside the EU without working permits and/or benefit recipients 'forgetting' to mention additional income; E 101-fraud schemes; fraud schemes with reintegration and European funding subsidies; and combinations of labour market fraud, benefit fraud, contributions fraud, and tax fraud.

The year before the introduction of article 273f in the Criminal Code, SIOD launched a project called *Labyrint*. It focused on West-African criminal networks in social security and provided an insight into the shadowy world of illegal migrants being exploited by employers and facilitators. Those labourers who hired a legal identity only received one third of the actual wages, or had to pay € 100 a month for their identity papers and a bank account, € 500 for sole registration at a temporary employment agency, and € 180-250 for sleeping on a bed or couch. In one investigation the director of a temporary employment agency paid € 150 a week to the labourers; in his administration more than 35 per cent of the identity papers turned out to be forged.[72] Another project from the SIOD and partners was called *Flock*, focusing on Chinese organised crime groups active in massage parlours and nail studios.

As said, SIOD has sent several criminal investigations, focusing on human trafficking for the purpose of labour exploitation, to the public prosecutor. The numbers are increasing: six criminal files in 2010 (three in the economic sector of catering, one in the construction and building industry, one in the food processing industry, and one in the cleaning industry) and two in 2009 (the food processing industry, massage parlours). Besides, on 1 January 2011 seven criminal investigations were operational. In the light of the ongoing process of specialisation in combating human trafficking for the purpose of labour exploitation these numbers still seem relatively modest.

Another interesting case has not yet been brought before the courts, and it took place in the early hours of 10 August 2010 when a strawberry grower was arrested, who was suspected of the labour exploitation of foreign seasonal workers, document forgery and embezzling part of workers' salaries. The suspected employer was remanded in custody for seven days. Two neighbours who had allowed the building of primitive housing for the seasonal workers were detained on suspicion of being accessories to labour exploitation. The strawberry grower is suspected of having abused the services of East European seasonal workers by housing them in substandard accommodation and having them work long hours, from sunrise to sundown, for six days a week for a salary which was a fraction of the promised hourly wage. Sanctions were imposed for (in the employer's opinion) poor performance and a portion of the salary was withheld as compensation for the meagre accommodation. The seasonal workers were instructed on what to say if a supervisory authority

72 SIOD, *Beleidsdocument Labyrint; onderzoek naar West-Afrikaanse criminele netwerken in de sociale zekerheid* (The Hague 2005) pp. 9-10.

visited the company. By falsifying employment contracts and timesheets, the employer was able to circumvent, for years, the legal minimum wage, the appropriate employees' salary and care allowance, and he evaded social security premiums and taxes. During the raid, thanks in part to the use of a helicopter, 43 East Europeans (41 Slovaks and 2 Poles, mostly students) were discovered in quarters on neighbouring properties. The shelters were not visible from the public road. The housing was illegal, primitive and lacked adequate sanitary facilities. None of the workers had identity papers because they had been seized by the employer.[73]

International cooperation and Europol

The lack of effective international cooperation in the field of combating human trafficking is generally acknowledged. One might say that the legislation and the legal tools are not the problem, it is more the lacking application thereof. The European Commission has repeatedly pointed to the gap between policy and policy measures, and the operational side.[74]

Internal security can not be achieved in isolation from the rest of the world, and it is therefore important to ensure coherence and complementarity between the internal and external aspects of EU security. With common external borders, smuggling and other cross-border illegal activity must be targeted at European level. Efficient control of the EU's external borders is thus crucial for the area of free movement. The objective of the European Commission is to strengthen security through border management. Member States should by the end of 2011 start developing common risk analyses. This should involve all relevant authorities with a security role, including police, border guards and customs authorities who identify hot spots and multiple and cross-cutting threats at external borders. These analyses should complement the yearly report by the Commission on cross-border crimes with joint contributions from Frontex and Europol.[75]

Nevertheless, international cooperation faces a huge amount of serious problems, pitfalls and thresholds to conquer. In 2010 the 27 Member States represented more than 500 million inhabitants, 23 official different languages (and, in addition, a multitude of minority languages which have official status within the Member States), 15 different currencies apart from the Euro, 74,000 kilometres of sea borders, the Schengen travel area, various judicial systems, strict data protection systems, a lack of points of contact or networks, insufficient resources and capacity, and the cultural differences between national law enforcement agencies. However, the groups of traffickers are not always highly organized and sophisticated criminal professionals, as can be seen,

---

[73] Press release by the National Prosecutors Office, 13 August 2010.

[74] COM/2010/493 (15 October 2010); COM/2008/657 (17 October 2008); EU plan on best practices, standards and procedures for combating and preventing trafficking in human beings (9 December 2005).

[75] COM (2010)673 (22 November 2010).

for instance, in China or Nigeria; in certain other cases they seem more informally network-based, operating from a shared cultural background, which requires a different approach to law enforcement.

The case of Rantsev has already been introduced as an international milestone, from a human rights' point of view. But it has also turned out to be an important illustration of failing international cooperation with regard to human trafficking. In the Rantsev case mutual assistance between Cyprus and Russia brought about many difficulties. The Court referred to the importance of bilateral and multilateral cooperation, as it is provided in the Palermo Protocol.[76] Parties shall take or strengthen measures, including through bilateral or multilateral cooperation, to alleviate the factors that make persons, especially women and children, vulnerable to trafficking, such as poverty, underdevelopment and the lack of equal opportunity.[77]

The Court observed that both Cyprus and Russia are parties to the Mutual Assistance Convention and have, in addition, concluded a bilateral Legal Assistance Treaty.[78] These instruments set out a clear procedure for assistance. The Prosecutor General of the Russian Federation provided an unsollicited undertaking that Russia would assist in any request for legal assistance by Cyprus aimed at the collection of further evidence. However, there is no evidence that the Cypriot authorities sought any legal assistance from Russia in the context of their investigation. In the circumstances, the Court considered the Cypriot authorities' refusal to make a legal assistance request to obtain the testimony of the two Russian women who worked with Ms Rantseva, the victim, at the cabaret facility particularly unfortunate given the value of such testimony in helping to clarify matters which were central to the investigation. These testimonies could clarify whether Ms Rantseva was sexually exploited in Cyprus. Therefore the Court considered that there had been a violation of the procedural obligations under Article 2 of the Convention as the Cypriot authorities failed to conduct an effective investigation into Ms Rantseva's death.[79] The Court did not consider that Article 2 of the Convention requires Member States' criminal laws to provide for universal jurisdiction in cases involving the death of one of their nationals. The applicant argued that the Russian authorities should have proceeded to interview the two women, notwithstanding the absence of any request from the Cypriot authorities. However, the Court recalled that the responsibility for investigating Ms Rantseva's death lay with Cyprus. In the absence of a legal assistance request, the Russian authorities were not required under Article 2 to secure the evidence themselves. In conclusion, the Court found that there had been no

[76] Palermo protocol art. 9.

[77] *Rantsev*, para 154.

[78] European Convention on Mutual Assistance in Criminal Matters, CETS No.: 030, 20 April 1959 (Mutual assistance convention).

[79] *Rantsev*, paras 241 and 242.

violation of the procedural obligations of Article 2 by the Russian Federation.[80]

On the other hand, the Court considered there has been a violation by the Russian authorities of their procedural obligation under article 4 to investigate alleged trafficking in human beings.[81] The Court observes that the Russian authorities undertook no investigation into how and where ms Rantseva was recruited, having occurred on Russian territory.[82] The Court reiterates that trafficking is a problem which is often not confined to the domestic arena. When a person is trafficked from one State to another, trafficking offences may occur in the State of origin, any State of transit and the State of destination. Relevant evidence and witnesses may be located in all States. Although the Palermo Protocol is silent on the question of jurisdiction, the Anti-Trafficking Convention explicitly requires each Member State to establish jurisdiction over any trafficking offence committed in its territory.[83] Such an approach is, in the Court's view, only logical in light of the general obligation, incumbent on all States under Article 4 of the Convention to investigate alleged trafficking offences. In addition to the obligation to conduct a domestic investigation into events occurring on their own territories, Member States are also subject to a duty in cross-border trafficking cases to cooperate effectively with the relevant authorities of other States concerned in the investigation of events which occurred outside their territories.[84]

In the field of international information exchange different European initiatives have taken place. In 2005 the Treaty of Prüm was signed in which Belgium, Germany, the Netherlands, Luxembourg, France, Spain and Austria agreed on an intensified effort to combat organised crime[85] and has now been adopted in a Decision, thus now applying throughout the EU. Designated contact points of the law enforcement agencies in the Member States will have mutual access to each other's DNA, fingerprint and vehicle registration information systems. Another such an initiative is the Swedish Framework Decision (also called the Swedish initiative) aimed at speeding up information exchange between law enforcement authorities.[86] It applies to information that

[80] Paras 244, 245 and 24.7

[81] Para 309.

[82] Para 308.

[83] The Council of Europe Convention on action against Trafficking in Human Beings, 16 May 2005 (Anti-Trafficking Convention).

[84] Rantsev, paras 172 and 289.

[85] Convention between the Kingdom of Belgium, the Federal Republic of Germany, the Kingdom of Spain, the French Republic, the Grand Duchy of Luxembourg, the Kingdom of the Netherlands and the Republic of Austria on the stepping up of cross-border cooperation, particularly in combating terrorism, cross-border crime and illegal migration, CE 10900/05, 27 May 2005 (Prüm Treaty).

[86] Council Framework Decision on simplifying the exchange of information and intelligence between law enforcement authorities of the Member States of the European

is already available with the law enforcement authorities, and all information they may obtain without using measures of compulsion. It does not regulate the exchange of information for the purpose of evidence in criminal proceedings. These developments are stepped up with the Lisbon Treaty with regards to the combat of transnational criminality, enforcing the combat of crimes such as human trafficking and stressing the position of international organisations such as Europol and Eurojust.[87] The relevant EU legal framework regarding human trafficking is described meticulously in this volume by Ms A. Middelburg and Mrs C. Rijken.
Interpol is the world's largest international police organisation with 188 member countries. Created in 1923, it facilitates cross-border police co-operation and supports and assists all organisations, authorities and services whose mission is to prevent or combat international crime. Its headquarters are located in Lyon.

Europol is the European Law Enforcement Agency which aims to improve the effectiveness and co–operation of the competent authorities in the Member States in preventing and combating terrorism, unlawful drug trafficking and other serious forms of organised crime. Europol is not a police force with executive forces, but supporting Member States primarily. Human trafficking is one of the priority areas for Europol. Europol, located in The Hague, has 620 employees and is accountable at the EU level to the Council of Ministers for Justice and Home Affairs. The Council is responsible for the main control and guidance functions of Europol Europol has a Management Board which is composed of one representative of each Member State and the European Commission. Each member has one vote. The Management Board discusses a wide range of Europol issues which relate to current activities and future developments, such as annual reports on Europol's activities and budgetary and staffing implications.[88]

The establishment of a European Police Office (Europol) was decided in 1992.[89] The principle of the establishment of a European Police Office, responsible for combating international drug trafficking and organised crime, was adopted after a proposal by the German chancellor, Helmut Kohl.[90] Europol came into being with the establishment of a 'Drugs Unit'.[91] In the Treaty of Amsterdam it was laid down that Europol could ask the Member

Union, 2006/960/JHA, 18 December 2006 (Swedish Framework Decision or the Swedish initiative).

[87] G.J.M. Corstens, 'De strafrechtspleging na "Lissabon"' (2010) Trema, 9, pp. 378-387.

[88] Europol Council Decision, article 37.

[89] Treaty on European Union of 7 February 1992 (Maastricht Treaty).

[90] Proposal at the Luxembourg European Council, 28 and 29 June 1991.

[91] Maastricht European Council, CE 10900/05, 9 and 10 December 1991.

States to conduct investigations and, in general, to wield more extensive operational powers than it does at present.[92]

Eurojust was established as a result of a decision taken by the European Council of Tampere, held in October 1999.[93] The European Council held a special meeting dedicated to the creation of an area of freedom, security and justice in the European Union; this would be achieved by concentrating on establishing a more uniform immigration and asylum policy based on solidarity and on the reinforcement of the fight against transborder crime by consolidating the cooperation among authorities.

Europol was further established in 1995, but because of the slowness of the ratification procedures, it did not enter into force until July 1999.[94] The Europol Convention has been the subject of a number of amendments enshrined in three protocols which entered into force after a lengthy process of ratification. Europol's powers are thus limited to dealing with offences committed on an international scale, such as drug trafficking, illegal immigration, trafficking in human beings, radioactive substances or motor vehicles, money laundering, counterfeiting and terrorism. By a unanimous decision, the Council of Ministers may extend Europol's jurisdiction to other offences not included in the list, thus ranging from drug trafficking to terrorism. Consequently, replacing the Convention by a Decision would make any further necessary amendments somewhat easier; this happened with the Europol Council Decision of 2009.[95]

Europol's competence covers organised crime, terrorism and other forms of serious crime as listed in the Annex affecting two or more Member States. Trafficking in human beings and facilitated illegal immigration are listed in the Annex as forms of serious crime which Europol is competent to deal with. Other forms of serious crime that are listed are, e.g., unlawful drug trafficking, illegal money-laundering activities, illicit trade in human organs and tissue, and motor vehicle crime. The following definition of illegal immigrant smuggling is provided: activities intended deliberately to facilitate, for financial gain, the entry into, residence or employment in the territory of the Member States, contrary to the rules and conditions applicable in the Member States. The definition of human trafficking follows the Palermo Protocol.[96]

To facilitate international cooperation the Europol Decision makes it possible to have contacts with non-EU States, other EU bodies and international organisations. The Council Decision provides guidelines and conditions as to how the exchange of information should take place, together

[92] Treaty of Amsterdam amending the treaty on European Union, the treaties establishing the European communities and certain related acts, C 340, 2 October 1997 (Treaty of Amsterdam).

[93] Conclusions of the Tampere European Council (15 and 16 October 1999).

[94] Europol Convention, C 316, 26 July 1995.

[95] Council Decision 2009/371 establishing the European Police Office (Europol).

[96] Council Decision, 2009/371, Art. 4 and Annex.

with complementing Council Acts.[97] Data protection and the security of data are two of the main items which are taken into consideration. To realise operational cooperation with Europol and the Member States, Europol has operational agreements with the following non-EU States, EU Bodies and international organisations: Australia, Canada, Croatia, Iceland, Norway, Switzerland, the United States of America, Eurojust and Interpol. These agreements are based more on an operational, rather than on a policy level. To realise good cooperation with other partners, Europol has strategic agreements with the following non-EU States, EU bodies and international organisations: Albania, Bosnia & Herzegovina, Colombia, the Former Yugoslav Republic of Macedonia, Moldova, Russia, Turkey, Republic of Serbia, Montenegro, Ukraine, the European Central Bank, the European Commission, the European Monitoring Centre for Drugs and Drug Addiction, the European Anti-Fraud Office (OLAF), Frontex, CEPOL, SitCen, the World Customs Organization and the United Nations Office on Drugs and Crime.[98]

In the field of combating trafficking in human beings Europol has the following objectives: to enable the information exchange of criminal data between Member states by the national units that are in connection with Europol; to notify the competent authorities of the Member States of information concerning them and of any connections identified between criminal offences; to collect, store, process, analyse and exchange information and intelligence; to prepare threat assessments, strategic analyses and general situation reports[99]. Especially the strategic analyses provide new tools to the Member States as they might be unfamiliar with analytical products traditionally.

The units from the Member States or Third States and other organisations at Europol are an important part when it comes to international information exchange. These national units, to which at least one liaison officer shall be seconded, is the only liaison body between Europol and the competent authorities of the Member States.[100] Europol also has strict rules on data protection and data security. Europol and the Member States have a shared responsibility for this protection.[101]

---

[97] Council Decision 2009/936/JHA adopting the implementing rules for Europol analysis work files, 30 November 2009; Council Decision 2009/968/JHA adopting the rules on the confidentiality of Europol information, 30 November 2009; Council Decision 2009/934/JHA adopting the implementing rules governing Europol's relations with partners, including the exchange of personal data and classified information, 30 November 2009; Council Decision 2009/935/JHA determining the list of third States and organisations with which Europol shall conclude agreements, 30 November 2009; Decision of the Management Board of Europol laying down the rules concerning access to Europol documents, 8 July 2009.

[98] Council Decision, 2009/371 Art. 22 and 23.

[99] Council Decision, 2009/371 Art. 5.

[100] Council Decision, 2009/371 Art. 8(2).

[101] Council Decision, 2009/371 Art. 28 and 29.

Europol makes use of Analysis Work Files (AWF) in which it may store, modify, and use data concerning criminal offences in respect of which it is competent. These AWFs may contain data on different categories of persons, such as suspects, witnesses, and victims.[102] The data from the file are held in files by Europol as long as this is necessary for the performance of its tasks. There will be a review no later than three years after the input of the data.[103] In general, the AWF concept is submitted to discussions of possible reconstruction.

AWF *Phoenix* is such an AWF, primarily focusing on trafficking in human beings. AWF Phoenix opened in June 2007 and is supported by 22 EU Member States and three Third States. This support does not include automatically that all relevant data is shared with AWF Phoenix, and therefore running the risk that criminal phenomena are restricted to the boundaries of those European countries that do deliver contributions. AWF Phoenix works with different priority areas, each having its specific focus: human trafficking by organised crime groups originating from Nigeria, China, Romania, Bulgaria and Hungary; one on labour exploitation; and one on child trafficking. Especially for the facilitated illegal immigration Europol has an AWF called *Checkpoint,* and for the combat of child sexual abuse an AWF called *Twins.* The aim of AWF Phoenix is to support live investigations into trafficking in human beings. This support consists of expertise and knowledge, the organisation of operational meetings between Europol, the concerned Member States' law enforcement and judicial authorities, the provision of a communication platform for information exchange (information systems), a network of liaison officers and operational partners, a mobile office, on the spot assistance and the provision of operational analysis support. Sometimes the support consists of merely logistical support, such as support concerning IT problems, language problems or the organising of an operational meeting.

In 2000 a proposal was made to provide for specific forms of mutual agreements, *like* a Joint Investigation Team (JIT).[104] The competent authorities of the Member States may set up a JIT for a specific purpose and for a limited period of time. Any Member State concerned with the investigation of offences with a cross-border dimension may request the setting up of a JIT. The composition of the team will consist of law enforcement officers, prosecutors and judges and other relevant personnel. The team will be led by a person from the State in which the JIT operates. Although the members of the team may originate from various jurisdictions, they are to carry out their duties in accordance with the national law of the territory where the investigation is taking place.

The JIT concept presents advantages of increased cooperation and coordination. The provisions allow for investigations to be carried out in the

[102] Council Decision, 2009/371 Art. 14.

[103] Council Decision, 2009/371 Art. 20.

[104] EU Convention on Mutual Assistance (2000) Art. 13.

Member State of operation by seconded members and introduce the possibility for seconded members stationed abroad with the team to request investigative measures from their competent national authorities without the need for any further requests under the traditional mutual legal assistance regime. Such requests shall be considered as if they were put forward on national territory within a national investigation.

Europol can participate in JITs and play an important role in facilitating investigations.[105] An example of a successful JIT is Operation *Golf*, which is a cooperation between police forces from the UK and Romania, in tackling a specific Romanian Roma organised criminal network, specialised in trafficking in and exploiting children from one of the poorest and most disadvantaged communities in Europe. The JIT has been supported by Europol, Eurojust, the UK Crown Prosecution Service and the Romanian Prosecutors Office. The UK investigation by Operation *Golf* has led to the arrest of 126 individuals. The offences included: trafficking human beings into the UK, money laundering, benefit fraud, child neglect, perverting the course of justice, theft and the handling of stolen goods. The court cases resulting therefrom are currently ongoing. Several of the 1107 trafficked children have been placed in police protection or hospitalised for treatment.[106]

In the field of human trafficking for the purpose of labour exploitation Europol has detected patterns from Ireland and the UK to Sweden, and from Romania and Kosovo to Finland. Another successful operation was the Italian-Polish operation *Terra Promessa* in 2006, an operation where Europol did not partipate from the beginning: five labour camps near Foggia, Orta Nova, and Ceriniola were raided, freeing 113 Polish workers and the perpetrators were arrested, including recruiters, guards, organisers and camp managers. Investigations revealed that the workers had been recruited through advertisements in Polish newspapers and websites promising good wages for picking fruit and vegetables in Italy. In reality, they worked for little or no payment and were physically abused. They were housed in shacks without water or electricity and armed men stood watch so that no one escaped; such accommodation has often been compared in the press with concentration camps from the Second World War. The investigation was commenced after reports that 13 Poles who came to work in Puglia had disappeared; officials believe that they were murdered.[107]

[105] Council Decision, 2009/371 Art. 6.

[106] MPS Bulletin no. 1998, 12 October 2010; Europol presss release, 20 October 2010.

[107] OSCE, *A summary of challenges facing legal responses to human trafficking for labour exploitation in the OSCE region* (Vienna 2006) p. 36.

Conclusion

The modern world is characterised by an unequal distribution of opportunities, being a major driving factor for the movement of people. Regarding the labour market it is quite likely that in the next decades industrialised countries will be confronted with a decrease of the labour population, whereas in poorer countries a population growth by more than one third is expected. But also inside the EU migration will be influenced by existing differences in minimum wages and further disappearance of internal borders. So the foreseen increase in food prices worldwide and the demographic changes in Europe will influence human trafficking for the purpose of labour exploitation, a severe crime conflicting with international standards of human rights, national constitutions and basic principles of national systems of social security.

Within the scope of human trafficking for the purpose of labour exploitation the year 2010 was in many ways a milestone: the Rantsev case, numerous policy developments within the EU and the first five convictions in the Netherlands. But the Rantsev case also stressed the importance of international cooperation. Realising that human trafficking for the purpose of labour exploitation affects all Member States, be it as a country of origin, transfer, or destination, an insufficient international cooperation and mutal assistance as integrated part of the whole approach is dangerous. It gives way to unscrupulous employers and middlemen, flourishing in the informal economy, whose only criminal interest is financial profits by abusing cheap labour and market opportunities.

The existing gap between international and national legislation and the operational side has been pointed out more often. Europol, having as two main tasks the exchange of information and data analysis, but not having executive forces, provides a tool to improve international cooperation and mutual assistance. But many Member States are still reluctant to use Europol to its full potential, having their own channels for international information exchange or prefering to keep criminal investigations on a national level. Thus the picture of European human trafficking for the purpose of labour exploitation will remain unclear as a whole, indicating that it is not addressed sufficiently and conflicting profoundly with the approach focusing on the investigation and prosecution of perpetrators, as well as the protection, support and rehabilitation of victims.

Chapter 10
A Trade Union Perspective on Combating Trafficking and Forced Labour in Europe

Jeroen Beirnaert[1]

While slavery has been outlawed for over 200 years, in 2005, the International Labour Office did ground-breaking research showing that 12.3 million workers are still in forced labour today.[2] The fact that forced labour is present in most if not all countries has been corroborated by growing evidence ever since. Human trafficking for forced labour is a contemporary incarnation of the transatlantic slave trade. This paper will illustrate how the emergence of trafficking and forced labour is an unfortunate sign of our times, how government interventions to date have been ineffective and even detrimental to the rights of victims and how labour market measures are key to turning the tide.

Labour exploitation

Whereas 'trafficking for labour exploitation' is a commonly used term, the specialised UN agency for labour standards has in its entire history never defined 'labour exploitation'. Arguably all of its 189 Conventions and the almost 100 years of their legal interpretation, have in fact been a continuous effort to define what constitutes labour exploitation, an interpretation that indeed needs constant revising and updating to respond to changing realities. In practice, it is difficult to draw a clear line separating exploitation as a violation of labour rights from forced labour or human trafficking specifically. In some European countries, a narrow definition is used while in others the concept of trafficking for labour exploitation is broader. The problem hampers identification in practice and creates legal insecurity for workers.

To overcome these problems, the ILO produced a set of indicators to identify forced labour in practice as an end result of a trafficking process. Later, in cooperation with the European Commission, they were further refined in a European context often referred to as the Delphi methodology.[3] A combination of indicators constitutes a probability of a case of forced labour.

---

[1] Jeroen Beirnaert, Project Coordinator at the International Trade Union Confederation; the text contains elements of a speech given at a conference on the occasion of the fourth EU Anti-Trafficking Day entitled Towards a multidisciplinary approach to prevention of trafficking in human beings, prosecution of traffickers and protection of victims?, Brussels, 18-19 October 2010.

[2] ILO, *Global Report under the Follow-up to the ILO Declaration on Fundamental Principles and Rights at Work: A Global Alliance against Forced Labour* (Geneva 2005).

[3] ILO Special Action Programme to Combat Forced Labour, *Indicators of trafficking of adults for labour exploitation* (28 October, 2009) <http://www.ilo.org/global/topics/forced-labour/WCMS_105884/lang--en/index.htm> accessed 28 February 2011.

Indicators include debt bondage, retention of identity documents, withholding and non-payment of wages, deception or false promises, financial penalties, denunciation to the authorities and threats of deportation, and restrictions on freedom of movement.

The indicators illustrate the thinking behind argumentation to see trafficking and forced labour along a continuum of labour exploitation that ranges from decent work to forced labour[4], and to see protection from any form of exploitation along the continuum as a way to interrupt the process leading to forced labour, preventing future abuse.[5] Trafficking for forced labour cannot be seen nor addressed as an isolated problem, as it is an accumulation of serious human rights violations. [6] In terms of Core Labour Standards[7] only, workers in forced labour suffer from discrimination, their residence status is likely to affect their human right to freedom of association and collective bargaining and in some cases they might even be under age. Other rights violations are likely to include non- or late payment of wages, salaries below the minimum wage, violations of health and safety prescriptions, social security entitlements, etc. All these elements are different facets of trafficking for labour exploitation. Forced labour is also a process more than a static relationship. Workers do not become forced labourers overnight, but are gradually, increasingly coerced. 'The vulnerability of migrants often increases over time as they are under pressure to repay their debts, or as they have been subjected to immigration controls and extortion from criminal networks. Moreover, employers often 'test' the resistance of workers before they squeeze them into more exploitative situations. One could think of this process as an ever narrowing labyrinth where the decision-making power of the worker is surrendered in the end.'[8] Many migrants are deceived by false promises of employment abroad by middlemen, agents, or informal or criminal networks. To pay the recruitment fee, they are forced to take on loans from family, friends, or their recruiter and future employer. Upon arrival, after deduction of inflated costs of food, accommodation and other essentials, the salary left over

---

[4] K. Skrivankova, *Between Decent Work and Forced Labour: Examining the Continuum of Exploitation* (Joseph Rowntree Foundation Programme Paper, York 2010).

[5] OSCE/ODIHR, *Compensation for Trafficked and Exploited Persons in the OSCE Region* (Warsaw 2008); J. Lam and K. Skrivankova, 'Opportunities and Obstacles: Ensuring Access to Compensation for Trafficked Persons in the UK' (London 2008) Anti-Slavery International.

[6] K. Skrivankova, *Between Decent Work and Forced Labour: Examining the Continuum of Exploitation* (Joseph Rowntree Foundation Programme Paper, York 2010).

[7] ILO Core Labour Standards: 1949 Right to Organise and Collective Bargaining Convention No. 98, 1930 Forced Labour Convention No. 29, 1957 Abolition of Forced Labour Convention No. 105, 1951 Equal Remuneration Convention No. 100, 1958 Discrimination (Employment and Occupation) Convention No. 111, 1973 Minimum Age Convention No. 138, 1999 Prohibition and Immediate Elimination of the Worst Forms of Child Labour Convention No. 182.

[8] B. Andrees, *Forced Labour and Trafficking in Europe: How People are Trapped in, Live through and Come out* (Working paper ILO, Geneva, 2008) p. 22.

is not nearly enough to save money to repay the loan, let alone to send remittances home as many had been planning to do from the outset. These abusive practices keep migrants bonded to their employer and force them to keep working for the same, under unilaterally enforced conditions. Workers ending up in forced labour are not necessarily undocumented or irregular workers. Many enter the country legally with a work permit or were country nationals from the outset.

The fact that workers are trafficked into forced labour in our mainstream economic sectors bring us inevitably to the debate on the under-regulated global labour market and the current state of protection of workers' rights. In past decades we have witnessed a transition from social dialogue and industrial relations to increasingly individual, informal and precarious work and labour relations. Deregulation of labour markets and the reduction of social protection as a strategy to increase competitiveness in the global economy has deformalised the employment relationship. This trend of casualisation, informalisation and individualisation of labour and employment relationships has created the setting which now appears to be a breeding ground for all kinds of abuse, including the extreme of forced labour and trafficking. With many trade unions still developing strategies to appropriately address this reality, it leaves many workers without proper protection.

In 2006, the British TUC's independent Policy Studies Institute produced a report on the effect of 30 years of deregulation of the UK labour market. It indicates the emergence of extreme vulnerability amongst numerous groups, including nationals and migrant workers, subject to labour exploitation, abuse and criminality.[9] 'If taken seriously, steps will need to be taken to address the systemic features that have led to such vulnerability. Respect of labour standards is central to an effective response and a failure to respect standards for all workers would lead to continued unfair competition between employers.'[10]

Forced labour

Freedom from forced labour is a human right and a 'fundamental right at work'. The 1930 ILO Convention No 29 banning forced labour now enjoys almost universal ratification with a few marked exceptions such as China, the US and Canada.[11] Workers in forced labour are not free to leave their job under the menace of a penalty, in other words, they are coerced. The most

---

[9] M. Hudson, *The Hidden One-in-Five – Winning a Fair Deal for Britain's Vulnerable Workers* (TUC Publications, London 2006).

[10] OSCE/ODIHR, *Report on Civil Society Meeting* (Warsaw 24 April 2007) 'The NRM approach to trafficking and its application to trafficking for labour exploitation', p. 11.

[11] ILO Lex, Database of International labour Standards <http://www.ilo.org/ilolex/english/ newratframeE.htm> accessed 8 March 2011.

widespread but probably least known form of coercion is the practice of debt bondage where workers are indebted to their employer, or their (transnational) recruiter as explained above. Other coercive mechanisms are restrictions on the freedom of movement due to physical confinement, abuse of precarious residence status and threats of deportation, which is very often perceived as a limitation on the freedom of movement. These more subtle forms of forced labour are being suffered by many more than one may expect in industrialised countries. Indeed, some so-called human rights champions are now confronted with the fact that their societies are not immune to slavery and slavery-like practices.[12]

A quick tour around the world allows highlighting some of the diverse forced labour issues today. The Federation of Trade Unions – Burma[13] reports consistent and widespread use of forced labour of civilians in public works by the military regime. Thousands face hard labour, with no remuneration and with total disregard of their human dignity. The workers need to bring their own materials and food and are subject to beatings, sexual assault and murder. Often, the summoned men are the only family breadwinner. Their absence deprives entire families of any source of income during weeks. In Uzbekistan, as a remnant of the centralised market economy under Soviet times, the Government systematically mobilises both school-aged children and adults to work in the annual cotton harvest by putting up quota for each region. In addition to the forcible nature of the work, the conditions are exploitative, harmful and sometimes life threatening. In North Korea and China prisoners are forced to work. Indigenous peoples on remote farms in the Paraguayan Chaco or in the Amazon forest in Brazil are working in debt bondage because the Government lacks the institutional capacity or the local presence to protect them. Abductions or forced subscription into armies take place in Uganda, Sudan, Chad, etc. The list of contemporary forced labour is far too long.[14] Traditional slavery even still persists in some countries in Western Africa. On 27 October 2008, the Community Court of Justice of the Economic

---

[12] 'Time and realities may have changed but the core essence of slavery persists in modern economies.' *Report of the Special Rapporteur on contemporary forms of slavery, including its causes and consequences* (Gulnara Shahinian 2009) United Nations Human Rights Council, 12th Session and 2010, Human Rights Council, 15th Session; P. Belser and M. de Cock, *ILO Minimum Estimate of Forced Labour in the World* (ILO, Geneva 2005); ILO, *Eradication of forced labour* (General Survey concerning the Forced Labour Convention 1930), *Report III* (Part 1B) (96th International Labour Conference 2007).

[13] The Federation of Trade Unions-Burma (FTUB) was formed in 1991 by exiled workers and students who had participated in the 8 August 1988 people's uprising. Their offices are based in Thailand. In Burma, they work in clandestine and dangerous circumstances. <www.ftub.org> accessed 8 March 2011.

[14] ILO, *Report III (1A) - Report of the Committee of Experts on the Application of Conventions and Recommendations* <http://www.ilo.org/wcmsp5/groups/public/---ed_norm/---relconf/documents/meetingdocument/wcms_151556.pdf> accessed 8 March 2011; also see earlier reports of the ILO CEACR.

Community of West African States (ECOWAS) found Niger in breach of its own laws and international obligations to protect its citizens from slavery.[15] This may cause one to think that forced labour is always exacted by the State or agencies of a State and confined to developing countries, but while numbers of workers in traditional slavery and forced labour exacted by States have significantly diminished as a consequence of centuries of abolitionist movement and antislavery legislation, new practices of forced labour have arisen, and more subtle and difficult to discover forms of coercion have appeared. Of the 12.3 million in forced labour, 9.8 million are found in the private industry.[16] 'Research confirms the ingenuity of unscrupulous employers in coming up with a variety of ways that they can effectively control and manipulate a person in order to take advantage of their unpaid services, in ways that are powerfully coercive, yet difficult to prove.'[17]

Forced labour vs. human trafficking

Forced labour is not identical to human trafficking, but in both cases, trade unions relate to labour standards. Trafficking in human beings is a violation of labour rights with as a key component coercion, also the key component to identify forced labour. The employment relationship is more relevant than the nature or even the legitimacy of the activity undertaken under coercion per se, be it harvesting, domestic work, prostitution or begging, done by either a child or an adult. Seeing human trafficking for labour exploitation as a subset of forced labour allows concentrating on the real problem, the exploitation of workers, and avoids conflation with smuggling or illegal migration.[18] However, not all workers in forced labour have been trafficked, and not all trafficking victims are in forced labour in a strict sense. Only where internal or cross-border movement of workers into forced labour and recruitment by an

[15] *Dame Hadijatou Mani Koraou v la République du Niger* [2008] Community Court of Justice Economic Community of Western African States (ECOWAS) <http:// www .unhcr.org/refworld/docid/491168d42.html> accessed 2 March 2010; Jeroen Beirnaert, 'West-African court slavery judgement' (2009) International union rights, Vol. 16 Issue 2.

[16] P. Belser, M. de Cock, F. Mehran, *Minimum Estimate of Forced Labour in the World* (ILO,Geneva 2005).

[17] F. David, 'Labour Trafficking' (2010) Research and Policy Series nr 108, Australian Institute of Criminology, Canberra, p. 13.

[18] TUC EUIRD, *Tackling trafficking through workers' rights: TUC response to the January 2006 Home Office consultation* (London, 2006) < http://www.tuc.org.uk/international/ tuc-11911-f0.pdf > accessed 1 March 2011.

intermediary are combined, forced labour and human trafficking overlap.[19] In industrialised countries including Europe, however, the ILO estimated that out of 360,000 forced labour victims, three out of four were trafficked.[20]

On the ground, the ITUC has over the past years seen an alarming increase in reports of trafficking from European national affiliates. The Dutch trade union FNV Bondgenoten reported trafficking and economic exploitation of forty persons working in appalling conditions on an asparagus farm in Someren and said that this case of exploitation was by no means an exception and that Polish workers in the Netherlands are exploited and treated as slaves.[21] It also published an article on Polish women strawberry pickers sanctioned €250 when using the toilet or having visitors in the weekend outside fixed 'consultation hours'.[22] The French CGT was deplored the situation of Romanian and Polish women workers hired to harvest asparagus and strawberries in the Alsace region. Women, citizens of the EU, were paid about 18 Euros per month and housed in buildings that reportedly looked like caves. They reported 'inhumane' and 'slave like' working conditions.[23] Reports come from Swedish and Finnish unions of extreme exploitation of migrants in agriculture and construction.[24] Major abuse of Asian workers in forestry and

---

[19] B. Andrees and P. Belser (ed), *Forced labour: coercion and exploitation in the private economy* (ILO, Geneva 2009) p. 180.

[20] P. Belser, M. de Cock, F. Mehran, *Minimum Estimate of Forced Labour in the World* (ILO, Geneva 2005).

[21] E. van der Goot, 'Aanhouding voor uitbuiting Roemeense werknemers' (21 January 2010) <http://www.fnvbondgenoten.nl/nieuws/acties_en_campagnes/gewoon_goed_werk/nieuws/34070_aanhouding_voor_uitbuiting/> accessed 8 March 2011.

[22] W. Balthussen, '"Wilde" staking aardbeienpluksters Ooirschot: Vijf dagen staken voor vier dubbeltjes per uur en respect' in De Zaaier (12 October 2009) <http://www.srada.nl/nl/Media/10-2009.pdf> accessed 28 February 2011.

[23] Le Point.fr, 'Récolte de fraises et d'asperges : un cas "d'esclavagisme" en Alsace' (29 May 2009)<http://www.lepoint.fr/actualites-societe/2009-05-29/recolte-de-fraises-et-d-asperges-un-cas-d-esclavagisme-en-alsace/920/0/347739> accessed 28 February 2011.

[24] P. Bardh, 'Bäruppköp are shirking from their responsibilities', Aftonbladet (26 August 2010), <http://www.lo.se/home/lo/home.nsf/unidView/1F8FF420303D9C54C125778B0031197C> accessed 8 March 2011; YLE News, 'Thai Berry Pickers Face Bleak Working Conditions in Finland' (19 September 2010) <http://www.cawinfo.org/2010/09/thai-berry-pickers-face-bleak-working-conditions-in-finland/> accessed 8 March 2011; Helsingin Sanomat Finland, 'Trafficking in human beings often hidden away' <http://www.flarenetwork.org/learn/europe/article/finland_trafficking_in_humans_often_hidden_away.htm> accessed 8 March 2011.

construction have been reported in eastern Europe[25], while Belgians colleagues have reported forced labour of domestic workers and in meat processing, etc.[26]

Increasingly, patterns of exploitation in Europe amount to what activists call modern-day slavery, but also to what the ILO's independent Committee of Experts[27] has legally qualified as forced labour in the sense of ILO Convention 29, ratified by all EU Member States. The Convention was originally developed to eradicate atrocities of governments in overseas colonies as from the 1930s. If today, in 2011, independent legal experts indicate that emerging forms of labour exploitation technically amount to the same level, it shows the seriousness of the situation and the urgency of the need to better protect workers in our economies against modern slavery.[28]

Criminal and social justice

Early policy interventions to combat trafficking did not take labour-market dynamics, mechanism or institutions into account to address what was then seen as a pure organised crime with no links to the mainstream economy.[29] Despite the evident increase in cases of labour trafficking, indicating the adverse effects and the ineffectiveness of policy interventions, many European countries still primarily see human trafficking in a criminal justice framework. Criminal justice brings with it an approach of saving victims from perpetrators without acknowledging these workers as active agents on the labour market. To be effective, measures should focus on empowering workers and making them less vulnerable by better social inclusion and by offering effective

[25] M. Křížková and M. Čaněk Czech state forestry and exploitation of migrant workers (22 February 2011) <http://migrationonline.cz/e-library/?x=2278267> accessed 4 March 2011; BWI Connect 'Migrant Workers Exploited in the Czech Republic' (28 February 2011) <http://connect.bwint.org/?p=147> accessed 8 March 2011.

[26] ACV Voeding en Diensten, 'Wij willen de vleessector niet overleveren aan koppelbazen! Het loopt fout in het vlees', ACV Nieuwsflash (January 2010) <http://acv-voeding-diensten.acv-online.be/Images/2010%20-%20januari%20vlees_def_nl_web_tcm47-212999.pdf> accessed 1 March 2011; P. Stalpaert and A. Kiekens, 'Bindende arbeidsregels voor huispersoneel', (December 2010) <http://www.acw.be/index.php?option=com_content&view=article&id=3224:bindende-arbeidsregels-voor-huispersoneel&catid=126&Itemid=503> accessed 8 March 2011.

[27] ILO Committee of Experts on the Application of Conventions and Recommendations.

[28] ILO, *Eradication of forced labour* (General Survey concerning the Forced Labour Convention 1930); *Report III* (Part 1B) (96th International Labour Conference 2007).

[29] B. Andrees and P. Belser (ed), *Forced Labour: Coercion and Exploitation in the Private Economy* (ILO, Geneva 2009) p. 107.

mechanisms for support and redress before people end up in forced labour.[30] The scourge is rooted in a socio-economic context and needs an urgent and long overdue integrated approach involving all relevant stakeholders to tackle it. The preventive potential of strengthening labour regulation to prevent exploitation seems to still be structurally ignored.

Governments have instead opted to strongly link combating trafficking with migration regulation. While the ILO estimated in 2008 that out of 191 million migrants worldwide, 95 million left their origin country directly in search of better work[31], again labour market mechanisms and institutions have been largely left out. As a result, rigid and restrictive migration policies not adequately addressing real labour shortages on national labour markets have caused much migration to be illegal, abusive and exploitative.[32] Especially where migrant workers' residence status is tied to employment, it has generated a tool for exploitation and trafficking. Concerns have been expressed by the American Federation of Labour and the Canadian Labour Congress regarding their respective governments' temporary workers' scheme. [33] The European Trade Union Confederation (ETUC) has consistently indicated the shortcomings of EU migration policy. For example, the ETUC stated that 'the European institutions sent yet another signal that the EU prioritises repressive migration policy over clear policies against labour exploitation' when introducing the Employers' Sanction Directive.[34] In April 2007, the ETUC stated that: 'Protecting the rights of irregular migrant workers and opening up legal channels for economic migration are important ways to prevent trafficking in human beings. It will reduce the recourse of potential migrants to unofficial intermediaries, and will thereby reduce the risk that they fall victim

---

[30] F. David, *Labour Trafficking* (Research and Policy Series nr 108, Australian Institute of Criminology, Canberra 2010) p. 13; B. Andrees, 'Strengthening Labour market Governance' in B. Andrees and P. Belser (ed), *Forced Labour: Coercion and Exploitation in the Private Economy* (ILO, Geneva 2009) p. 123.

[31] ILO Estimate source ILO Migrants, 2005.

[32] I. Awad, *The global economic crisis and migrant workers: Impact and Response* (International Migration Programme, ILO, Geneva 2009).

[33] American Federation of Labour – Congress of Industrial Organizations (AFL-CIO), New Orleans Workers' Center for Racial Justice (NOWCRJ), Centro de los Derechos del Migrante (CDM) and the Solidarity Center, 'Joint Response to the US Department of State, Office to Monitor and Combat Trafficking in Persons' (G/TIP) Request for Information for the 2010 Trafficking in Persons Report (Public Notice 6921) , Washington D.C, 2010 <http://www.ituc-csi.org/afl-cio-submits-comments-to-the .html> accessed 14 March 2011; Canadian Labour Congress, 'Temporary Foreign Workers and ILO Convention 105 on Forced Labour' (10 August 2010), <http://www.canadianlabour.ca/news-room/publications/temporary-foreign-workers-and-ilo-convention-105-forced-labour> accessed 8 March 2011.

[34] Directive 2009/52/EC of the European Parliament and of the Council of 18 June 2009 providing for minimum standards on sanctions and measures against employers of illegally staying third-country nationals; ETUC, Sanctions against employers of irregular migrants: ETUC deplores a toothless and counterproductive instrument <http:// www.etuc.org/a/5801> accessed 28 February 2011.

to criminal organisations that enjoy enormous profit by trafficking human beings for labour or sexual exploitation.'[35] Where large numbers of undocumented migrants were working in a vacuum, trade unions have supported regularisation campaigns, e.g. in Spain and Belgium. The Irish Congress of Trade Unions (ICTU) actively campaigned for the rights of migrants who have become undocumented for reasons beyond their control to have an opportunity to get back into the system. 'Failure to provide a solution for undocumented migrant workers benefits no one but abusive and exploitative employers'.[36] Such major amnesty campaigns are not needed when better migration regulation is put in place. [37] This shows the urgent need to structurally involve social partners and labour institutions more in the development of migration policies.

In many countries, policies to combat human trafficking still target the illegal movement of workers at the expense of leaving the exploitation suffered ignored, thus not effectively protecting people from forced labour and trafficking. Workers are being identified as perpetrators of administrative migration regulations rather than workers who have had their human rights violated. Migrant workers are being stigmatised and migration criminalised whereas exploitation should be criminalised and exploiters punished. In addition, protection of victims of trafficking is mostly conditional, and there is the structural problem with identification of workers trafficked for labour exploitation. As a result, after coming into contact with authorities, exploited migrants are likely to be deported without compensation for any abuse suffered. To better address cases of extreme abuse, unions in the UK and Ireland have joined campaigns to make forced labour a penal offence in its own right, regardless of the migration or transportation element of the Palermo protocol definition of human trafficking.[38] This allows using existing

---

[35] ETUC, PICUM, Solidar, *Joint comments of ETUC, PICUM and Solidar on expected commission proposals to fight 'illegal' employment and exploitative working conditions* (26 April 2007) <http://www.etuc.org/a/4325> accessed 14 March 2011.

[36] 'MRCI and ICTU Welcome Long-Awaited Scheme for Undocumented Migrant Workers' (13 September 2009) <http://www.atlanticphilanthropies.org/news/mrci-and-ictu-welcome-long-awaited-scheme-undocumented-migrant-workers> accessed 28 February 2011.

[37] For more information on the role of trade unions with regard to migrant workers, see: ILO ACTRAV, Bureau for Workers' Activities, In search of Decent Work – Migrant workers' rights: Am manual for trade unionists, ILO, Geneva, 2008 <http:// www .ilo.org/global/publications/books/WCMS_120113/lang--en/index.htm> accessed 8 March 2011.

[38] Protocol to Prevent, Suppress and Punish Trafficking in Persons Especially Women and Children, supplementing the United Nations Convention against Transnational Organized Crime, 2000; MRCI, *Forced Labour: the case for criminalisation* (Policy Paper

protection mechanisms for victims of trafficking to protect workers in forced labour and is a first and very welcome improvement of the existing anti-trafficking legislation in these countries.

As part of the criminal justice approach to combating trafficking, now often security or intelligence bodies such as police are entrusted with the competence to control workplaces to identify trafficked workers. As these institutions do not have a mandate to protect workers, many support organisations deplore the adverse effect: '... Police raids to tackle labour exploitation have so far been counterproductive in terms of protection of the exploited.'[39]

To combat modern-day slavery, we need to fight against inequality and for decent work, strengthen labour market regulations and institutions and implement a rights-based migration policy. Any other measures are doomed to be ineffective. [40] The OSCE (a security body) Special Representative for Combating Trafficking said earlier this year: 'To prevent and fight against trafficking in human beings means to promote decent work, to build societies free from the cancer of organised crime and corruption, based on the principles of non-discrimination and the rule of law, and inspired by the ideal of social justice, in which human rights and fundamental freedoms can really flourish.'[41]

A global trade in cheap and docile labour

Globalisation has accentuated the unevenness of development between countries, increased the visibility of wealth in developed countries and facilitated transportation. Poverty, underdevelopment and the lack of decent work forces people to migrate at any cost oblivious of risks involved. This generates a ready supply of migrant workers. [42] At the same time there is a growing demand for cheap labour to fill up the '3D' jobs.[43] Local workers are unwilling to take up these posts for the conditions offered, and migration regulation usually does not allow large numbers of low skilled workers to enter

---

2010)<http://www.mrci.ie/media/File/MRCI%20PP%20Forced%20Labour.%20The %20Case% 20for%20Criminalization.pdf> accessed 8 March 2011.

[39] OSCE/ODIHR, *Report on Civil Society Meeting* (Warsaw 2007) 'The NRM approach to trafficking and its application to trafficking for labour exploitation', p. 15.

[40] B. Andrees, 'Strengthening Labour market Governance' in Beate Andrees and Patrick Belser (ed), *Forced labour: coercion and exploitation in the private economy* (ILO, Geneva 2009) p. 127.

[41] OSCE Special Representative and Co-ordinator for Combating Trafficking in Human Beings, Maria Grazia Giammarinaro, press statement on the occasion of International Day for Social Justice (20 February 2011) <http://www.osce.org/cthb/75678> accessed 28 February 2011.

[42] N. Misra, *The Push and Pull of Globalisation: How the Global Economy Makes Migrant Workers Vulnerable to Exploitation* (Policy Brief, Solidarity Centre, Washington 2007).

[43] Referring to Dirty, Dangerous and Difficult.

the country legally. This combination is being exploited by unscrupulous middlemen, agents, smugglers and traffickers. Exploiting and trafficking workers is a high-profit and low-risk criminal activity. Migrant workers' possibilities to denounce their situation are limited due to language ability, limited knowledge of rights or capacity to access rights, tenuous migration situations, family obligation, etc.[44] Unscrupulous employers can make huge profits by under- or non-payment of wages, taxes and social security contributions.[45] The United Nations Office on Drugs and Crime states that human trafficking is the third biggest crime business after the drugs and arms trade.[46] In its Global Report on Forced Labour of 2009, the ILO came up with a yearly 'cost of coercion', i.e., the illicit profits produced in one year by trafficked persons, of 32 billion USD.[47]

This trend has not missed its effect on the recruitment industry. Since the 80s, public employment agencies have lost their monopoly throughout Europe. Established private employment agencies have since mainly been focusing on national workers only, leaving a business opportunity to cater for the huge demand for cheaper migrant labour. The lucrative market brought a proliferation of all kinds of recruiters and middlemen while national regulation for this booming industry in many European countries is still not adapted to this new reality. Thus, much of the recruitment is uncontrolled.[48]

Demand is creating the market for this criminal business. As consumers we are all indirectly responsible for what we buy, and there is definitely an urgent need for consumer awareness towards unrealistically priced goods suggesting exploitation in the supply chain. Employers, however, are directly responsible for their workers. To address the demand for cheap labour by businesses, there is a logical need to discourage exploitation by making it less profitable and

---

[44] F. David, *Labour Trafficking* (Research and Policy Series nr 108, Australian Institute of Criminology, Canberra 2010) p. 13.

[45] B. Andrees, 'Strengthening Labour market Governance' in Beate Andrees and Patrick Belser (ed), *Forced labour: coercion and exploitation in the private economy* (ILO, Geneva 2009) p. 106.

[46] P. Arlacchi, *Under-Secretary-General Director-General to the International Seminar on Trafficking in Human Beings* (Brasilia 28-29 November 2000) <http://www.unodc.org/unodc/en/about-unodc/speeches/speech_2000-11-28_1.html > accessed 8 March 2011.

[47] Including under market rate wages, overcharging of accommodation, food and other items, underpayment of overtime, as well as costs related to the recruitment process, including fees to agents, inflated travel costs and other charges, ILO, *The Cost of Coercion* (Global Report under the Follow-up to the ILO Declaration on Fundamental Principles and Rights at Work, Geneva 2009) <http://www.ilo.org/wcmsp5/groups/public/---ed_norm/---relconf/documents/meetingdocument/wcms_106230.pdf> accessed 28 February 2011.

[48] B. Andrees, *Forced Labour and Trafficking in Europe: How People are Trapped in, Live through and Come out* (Working paper, ILO, Geneva 2008).

increasing the risks involved. Empowering workers will force employers to increase wages and working standards and make the exploitation less profitable, while strengthening labour market regulations, monitoring and sanctions will increase the risks.[49] Crime prevention is, amongst other things, premised on understanding the opportunities for offending, the likely risk of offending and factors that impact on vulnerability.[50]

An interesting novel trade union strategy to discourage demand in combination with monitoring standards and raising consumer awareness has been developed by the Committee on Workers' Capital (CWC). This international labour union network for responsible investment of workers' capital works to educate union pension trustees on responsible investment issues. The CWC recently launched a thematic campaign to develop strategies to divert investment of workers' capital in business using forced labour in the supply chain.[51]

Reducing profits, raising the risks and reducing vulnerability

The best defence against traffickers is to make the business less profitable, raise the risks and empower workers to denounce and act against exploitation.[52]

To raise the risks, governments need to improve labour market regulation, monitoring and institutions. Labour inspectorates need to be strengthened and equipped with the necessary tools to be more effective and need guaranteed access to workplaces. In the exceptional case of employment in private homes of domestic workers, security personnel, gardeners etc., a specific solution needs to be developed to reconcile the human rights of the workers with the right to privacy of the people living on the premises and the inviolability of private homes. In some countries labour inspectorates have direct access to private homes, in others special divisions have been established within the labour inspectorate with particular competence.[53] Trade unions can also play an important role in making labour inspection more effective and inform the labour inspectorate to investigate workplaces where they suspect severe exploitation.

---

[49] B. Andrees, *Forced Labour and Trafficking in Europe: How People are Trapped in, Live through and Come out* (Working paper, ILO, Geneva 2008) p. 33.

[50] F. David, *Labour Trafficking* (Research and Policy Series nr 108, Australian Institute of Criminology, Canberra 2010).

[51] A joint initiative of the ITUC, the Global Union Federations (GUFs) and the Trade Union Advisory Committee to the OECD (TUAC); CWC, *Investing in Decent Work: The Case for Investor Action on Forced Labour* (Briefing Paper) and CWC, *Case studies of investor action on forced labour* (Briefing Paper Nr 2, Vancouver, Canada 2010).

[52] B. Andrees, *Forced Labour and Trafficking in Europe: How People are Trapped in, Live through and Come out* (Working paper, ILO, Geneva 2008) p. 33.

[53] For an overview of government, employer and trade union positions on this particular issue, see: International Labour Conference, 100th Session, 2011, ILO Report IV(2A), Decent work for domestic workers; Fourth item on the agenda ILC.100/IV/2A

Profit is being made by deception of workers and through charging excessive recruitment fees to workers. Therefore, regulation of the recruitment sector is essential. The ILO adopted in 1997 the Private Employment Agencies Convention No. 181 and its accompanying Recommendation No. 188 containing a set of rules to be respected in the sector: agencies should not charge fees to workers, but to employers; inform migrant workers, as far as possible in their own language or in a language with which they are familiar, of the nature of the position offered and the applicable terms and conditions of employment; consult with unions and adopt appropriate measures to avoid exploitation; and there should be sanctions, supervision of labour inspection and investigation of cases of violations.[54]

The role of trade unions

Strong, independent, democratic and effective trade unions guarantee the eradication of exploitation at work. The persistence of forced labour in today's world of work therefore shows that the trade union movement needs increased support and less legal obstacles to organise vulnerable workers, but also that it faces a number of challenges which go to the heart of the movement. As trade union density is decreasing across Europe, trade unions need to strengthen their democratic base to make their voices heard by governments and employers and prioritise organising to render their organisations more inclusive and representative. Democratic representativeness is the unique strength of the trade union movement and the reason why trade unions are essential in guaranteeing sustainable peace on the work floor and outside. Trade unions need to face up to this major challenge and adopt novel structures and organising strategies to protect vulnerable workers. European trade unions' reluctance to organise can be linked to their trade union tradition and the socio-economic context in which trade unions have developed. Compared to trade unions in the U.S. or from an Anglo-Saxon culture, organising workers is not always the first priority of European trade unions.[55] American trade unions have traditionally been forced to organise to strengthen their ranks, as labour market regulations and industrial relation systems have traditionally been less trade union-friendly on the other side of the Atlantic. European trade unions have enjoyed a strong social dialogue and an acknowledged role in society which has had a direct influence on their membership. However, the social dialogue in European countries has also

[54] M.N.J. van der Linden, *Trafficking for Forced Labour, How to Monitor the Recruitment of Migrant Workers* (ILO, Geneva 2006) p. 30.

[55] PICUM, *Ten ways to Protect Undocumented Migrant Workers* (Brussels 2005) <http://picum.org/picum.org/uploads/file_/PICUM_Ten_Ways_to_Protect_Undocumented_Migrant_Workers.pdf> accessed 14 March 2011.

been gradually degrading and is consistently under attack. In that sense, organising should again become a priority for European trade unions as well.

The challenge for trade unions to regain the lost terrain and represent 'all' workers is easy to spell out. In practice, however, it has proved to be hard to overcome. To protect people from the most extreme forms of exploitation in particular, the focus needs to be on workers in low-paid employment at risk of discrimination, poverty and social exclusion. The most vulnerable workers are not found in workplaces with trade union presence, but isolated in private homes or remote rural areas. Traditional trade union structures face several obstacles to reach these workers. In addition to legal obstacles to the right to organise, migrant workers have a multitude of linguistic, cultural and political backgrounds demanding tailored organising approaches which can put limited

resources under pressure. Language barriers are often a first important hurdle to overcome. As organisers are mostly local workers with a strong connection to their union, they are often limited to come in contact with migrant workers, and no union will have the resources to accompany all its organisers with a full-time interpreter. Numerous pilot projects have been looking into developing novel approaches to better reach out and integrate the most vulnerable workers, some of which have been successful. For example, when a particularly important migrant workers community is identified, unions can hire organisers from within this group to meet and discuss with them outside working hours. Another possible approach are partnerships between unions in origin and destination countries with, e.g., an exchange of staff. In countries of origin, a foreign officer can offer an inside perspective on the labour market of destination, rights, training possibilities, realities and risks. In the country of destination, an officer with the same language and culture as the immigrants can inform workers of the role of a trade union and how it can empower them and increase their bargaining power.[56]

Outreach and organising offer great potential for cooperation between unions and other organisations working for the rights and interests of a specific group. Over the past two years, the ITUC has been working with Anti-Slavery International and its European constituency of specialised anti-trafficking (traditionally women's rights organisations) and migrants' rights NGOs and the Churches Commission for Migrants in Europe with its network of faith-based service organisations for victims of trafficking and migrants in general. The information coming from trade unions and the specific protection that trade unions offer for people at the workplace is an added value to the work of these NGOs and their members while their community meetings offer an excellent opportunity for trade unions to explain

[56] For more examples of trade union outreach to migrant workers, see: ILO ACTRAV, Bureau for Workers' Activities, In search of Decent Work – Migrant workers' rights: A manual for trade unionists, ILO, Geneva, 2008 <http://www.ilo.org/ global/ publications /books/WCMS_120113/lang--en/index.htm> accessed 8 March 2011.

their role and the benefits attached to joining a union.[57] Sometimes, trade unions carry a bad legacy from trade unions in their origin country generating distrust from migrant workers towards unions in their country of destination. Community groups or faith-based organisations may be able to generate the necessary trust needed to overcome reluctance to approach unions.

An excellent example of cooperation is provided by the Migrants Rights Centre Ireland (MRCI) and the Irish trade unions. MRCI has a drop-in centre for migrants who need support. Many of the issues raised by people who enter their office had to do with workplace rights and exploitation. Hence, the MRCI decided to support migrant workers in different groups according to the economic sector of activity, de facto organising domestic, restaurant and mushroom workers. To address their labour issues, the MRCI and the groups approached the Irish trade union SIPTU.[58] Some of the migrant workers support groups are now affiliated to the trade union.

Apart from certain communities, trade unions can obviously also target specific sectors or regions. The Italian Federation of Agriculture and Food Workers (FLAI) organised a major campaign on migrant farm workers' conditions in Puglia. Union activists went around in rural areas to talk to more than 5,000 labourers harvesting tomatoes and inform them about labour rights. Instead of 46 euro for a 6.5 hour working day, people received a 3-euro wage per 300 kilo basket forcing them to work 14 hours a day for a pittance.[59]

Trade union bilateral partnerships on migrant workers can include portable membership. It is based on the principle that any worker, member of the trade union in the country of origin, would automatically be entitled to services of the trade union in the destination country. This has become a reality on an international level in several sectors for unions affiliated to, e.g., IUF, BWI or UNI.[60] This is a major step in the right direction. However, it is clear that there are significant limitations, as migrant workers do not always end up working in the same sector. There are numerous bilateral agreements on portable membership, however, between national trade union centres offering wider coverage.

The fact that domestic work is often not covered by labour legislation makes that domestic workers are mostly still informal workers in an unregulated sector. The majority of domestic workers are migrants and

---

[57] ITUC and ASI, *Never Work Alone, Trade Unions and NGOs Joining Forced to Combat Forced Labour and Trafficking* (ITUC and Anti-Slavery International, Brussels 2011).

[58] Services, Industrial, Professional and Technical Union

[59] 'Oro rosso, campagna nazionale di CGIL e FLAI. A Stornara dibattito sui 'immigrati e media' con i giornalisti de L´Espresso e de l´Unità' (09 August 2009) <http://www.cgilfoggia.it/news/default.asp?id=2225> accessed 8 March 2011.

[60] Trade unions in food and agriculture, construction and forestry and services respectively.

women, leaving them open to double or even triple discrimination. For various obvious reasons domestic workers, the majority of whom are women, are particularly vulnerable to forced labour. Working and sometimes also residing in private homes isolates them, and it is therefore relatively easy for their employer to intentionally confine them to their workplace. Here also, targeted responses are needed from trade unions to organise these workers.[61] Since 2005, trade unions, self-organised domestic workers organisations, as well as NGOs providing services and assistance to domestic workers formed a global network.[62] The main message of this consortium is the urgent need to recognise domestic work as work to be better regulated as a form of employment. Since then, the Global Unions[63] used their position on the ILO Governing Body to include a discussion on standard setting on Decent Work for Domestic Workers on the agenda of the International Labour Conference in 2010. There is an important role to be played for trade unions to ensure that the instrument adopted at the ILC session in 2011 becomes a strong and effective tool to ensure better protection of domestic workers.[64] Better regulation of the sector will improve representation in and protection from trade unions.

States' obligations in human rights protection

Governments have the obligation to respect, protect and fulfil human rights of people within their jurisdiction.[65] Governments are thus responsible for developing adequate regulation, implementing action plans and effective monitoring to eradicate forced labour and trafficking. Again, the obligation to protect people from contemporary slavery is embedded in a wider range of States' human rights obligations.[66] In the discussion on how labour rights relate to human rights, it is acknowledged that labour rights are human rights and that it is impossible to protect civil and political rights without upholding labour rights and vice versa.[67] 'Like civil and political rights, economic, social

---

[61] ITUC, *Decent work, decent life for domestic workers* (Action Guide, Brussels 2010).

[62] ETUC, *Out of the Shadows: organising and protecting migrant workers in Europe: the role of trade unions* (2005) <www.etuc.org/a/2809 accessed 14 March 2011>; IUF and IRENE *Respect and Rights, Protection for domestic/household workers!* (Geneva 2008).

[63] International Trade Union Confederation, Global Union Federations, Trade Union Advisory Committee to the OECD.

[64] International Labour Conference, 100th Session, 2011, ILO Report IV(2A), Decent work for domestic workers, fourth item on the agenda ILC.100/IV/2A.

[65] A. Eide, *The Right to Adequate Food as a Human Right* (Report prepared, UN Doc E/CN.4/Sub.2/1987/23) p. 19. This typology of states' obligations has been accepted beyond the right to food. See e.g. Olivier De Schutter, *International Human Rights Law, Cases, Materials, Commentary* (Cambridge 2010).

[66] Office of the High Commissioner for Human Rights, *Principles and Guidelines for a Human Rights Approach to Poverty Reduction Strategies* (2005) paras 47-8.

[67] Vienna Declaration and programme of Action adopted at the World Conference on Human Rights, Vienna, 1993, I, 5, 'All human rights are universal, indivisible and

and cultural rights impose three different types of obligations on States: the obligations to respect, protect and fulfil. Failure to perform one of these three obligations constitutes a violation of such rights. The obligation to respect requires States to refrain from interfering with the enjoyment of economic, social and cultural rights. The obligation to protect requires States to prevent violations of such rights by third parties. Thus, the failure to ensure that private employers comply with basic labour standards may amount to a violation of rights at work or the right to just and favourable conditions of work. The obligation to fulfil requires States to take appropriate legislative, administrative, budgetary, judicial and other measures towards the full realisation of such rights.'[68]

To be more effective in rights protection, governments can involve other stakeholders such as social partners in policy and strategy development and implementation. Trade unions are organisations of workers defending the rights and interests of workers and an important instrument to combat any kind of labour exploitation. Trade unions face the intrinsic duty to fight abuse anywhere, as it undermines decent work everywhere.

Social dialogue and collective bargaining

Social dialogue is the right of workers to present their views, defend their interests and engage in discussions to negotiate work-related matters with employers and authorities. Collective bargaining is the right of employees to talk as a group with their employer to try to agree on matters such as pay and working conditions. Social partners can make use of sector-specific labour market mechanisms and approaches and their direct contact with workers and their families to address specific problems which make migrant workers vulnerable to human trafficking.

Working with trade unions and employers' organisations in traditional social dialogue requires formal representation. This again shows the importance of regulating informal work and, e.g., a proper domestic workers' convention of the ILO.[69] The new convention should amongst other things

---

interdependent and interrelated. The international community must treat human rights globally in a fair and equal manner, on the same footing, and with the same emphasis'.

[68] The Maastricht Guidelines on Violations of Economic, Social and Cultural Rights (1997), adopted by a group of academic experts meeting in Maastricht 22-26 January 1997, para 6.

[69] See: ILO, Report IV (2A) - Decent work for domestic workers Report IV(1) was sent out to ILO constituents for their feedback in August 2010. Report IV(2A) contains the essential points of the replies received from governments and from employers' and workers' organization, as well as the Office commentary. On this basis, the Office prepared Report IV(2B) which contains a revised proposed Convention and

facilitate the establishment of social dialogue between workers and employers to agree on terms and conditions themselves. Self-organisation still is the most effective way to rule out abuse or exploitation in any economic sector or area of activity.

In the recruitment industry, the International Confederation of Private Employment Agencies CIETT, which covers the main recruitment businesses such as Manpower, Adecco, Kelly Services and Randstad, and UNI Global Union, the global trade union umbrella for trade unions in the services sector, have concluded a memorandum of understanding to create partnership and a global social dialogue to achieve fair conditions for the temporary agency work industry. Both parties committed to the promotion and respect of the principles outlined in ILO Convention 181 and the accompanying Recommendation. This is a strong message that workers and business have a shared interest in increased regularisation and monitoring of the recruitment industry.[70] In 2010 Global Unions expressed their concern about the increased use of temporary work agencies replacing permanent, open-ended and direct employment as a mechanism used by businesses to avoid their social responsibility as an employer, bypass labour legislation and weaken collective bargaining.[71]

In the UK, the Ethical Trading Initiative (ETI) is a multi-stakeholder initiative where business and unions are represented. Following the tragic death of 21 Chinese cockle pickers in Morecambe Bay[72], the ETI organised discussions which ultimately led to the adoption of the Gangmasters Licensing Act[73] in 2005 and the establishment of the Gangmasters Licensing Authority (GLA) developing and promoting standards for best practice in the supply and use of temporary labour and licensing and monitoring labour providers in agricultural, horticultural and shellfish industries.[74] The GLA was welcomed by suppliers themselves stating that increased monitoring helped them maintain

---

Recommendation, and which will serve as a basis for the discussion at the 100th Session of the International Labour Conference., <https://www.ilo.org/wcmsp5/groups/public/---ed_norm/---relconf/documents/meetingdocument/wcms_151864.pdf> accessed 8 March 2011.

[70] Memorandum of Understanding between CIETT Corporate Members & UNI Global Union on Temporary agancy Work, 24 October 2008, San Diego <http://www.uniglobalunion.org/apps/iportal.nsf/3100172b0315a124c125717d005dd9bb/513a7b55742a39eec125755100579d2a/$FILE/MoU-UNI-CiettCMC-En.pdf> accessed 1 March 2011.

[71] Global Unions, 'Global Unions adopt principles on temporary agency work and call for good, secure jobs for all' <http://www.global-unions.org/global-unions-adopt-principles-on.html> accessed 14 March 2011.

[72] BBC News, 'Tide kills 18 cockle pickers' (6 February 2004) <http://news.bbc.co.uk/2/hi/uk_news/england/lancashire/3464203.stm> accessed 08 March 2011.

[73] The Gangmasters (Licensing) Act 2004 (Commencement No. 2) Order 2005.

[74] The GLA Board consists of representative members of the associated industries as well as Trades Union Congress (TUC) and Unite the Union.Website GLA <http://www.gla.gov.uk/> accessed 8 March 2011.

business and avoid unfair competition by unscrupulous agents.[75] Trade unions in the UK are therefore campaigning for a broader competence of the GLA to cover more sectors.

Awareness raising

Trade unions not only have a role to play in informing vulnerable workers of their rights; a lot of work remains to be done in informing their membership about the reality of trafficking in Europe and involving their membership in the fight against it. Trade unions in transport and logistics have done a lot of work in their sector. Awareness raising campaigns for workers on busses, trains, ferries and airports have sensitised and trained workers to be better equipped to identify possible cases of trafficking and providing contact numbers for follow-up, etc. The International Transport Workers' Federation organised such a campaign in 2006 on the occasion of the football World Cup in Germany. The workers showed prevention and awareness raising videos, put up posters and distributed leaflets to a targeted audience of travellers.[76] Unions in hotels and the tourism industry have undertaken similar campaigns. However, they are mostly oriented towards awareness-raising about sexual exploitation and child abuse, and are not thus far targeted towards the protection of other hotel staff such as maids or the workers in the restaurant. Such industry campaigns have a lot of potential to address and prevent forced labour in targeted sectors.

Racism and xenophobia allow labour exploitation to flourish among excluded migrants. Trade union activities should at all times include activities to combat racism, xenophobia and other types of discrimination, and promote social inclusion. Trade unions need to educate their activists of the fact that any unequal treatment suffered by either a local or a migrant worker undermines the labour standards on their national labour market in general, including their own. Demagogic politics often abuse migrant workers as scapegoats to blame for the loss of jobs, but migrant workers are attractive

[75] A. Geddes, S. Scott and K. Bang Nielsen, *Gangmasters Licensing Aurhority, Evaluation Study, Baseline Report* (Public Services Academy, University of Sheffield 2007); Gangmasters Licensing Authority, *The journey to licensing, The experience of implementing a voluntary code of practice in the UK agricultural industry (2004-2006)* (Temporary Labour Working Group, London 2006).

[76] ETF/ITF, 2006 World Cup: 'No to Forced Prostitution and Human Trafficking' (01 July 2006) <http://www.itfglobal.org/campaigns/traffickingstate.cfm > accessed 1 March 2011.

alternatives for national workers to employers, only because of their vulnerability to exploitation.[77]

Monitoring

Governments should monitor labour standards through effective inspection services, but in countries with well-developed labour inspection systems, employers tend to transfer the risk to subcontractors making the employment relationship less transparent. This can be done by subcontracting to bogus or 'letterbox' companies that claim to be based abroad, bogus self-employment of workers, etc. [78] The Belgian union ACV-CSC Food and Services has urged their government to take action proposing a system of joint liability, licensing and registration of subcontractors, more effective control and strengthening of labour inspection, effective prosecution, and more consultation with social partners in an effort to particularly address the extreme exploitation in the meat processing industry.[79] A similar campaign is run by the European Federation of Building and Woodworkers.[80]

The most effective way to monitor labour standards is by workers themselves. Monitoring labour standards in workplaces is a traditional role of trade unions, but also for trade unions, it has been and remains a challenge to ensure compliance of business throughout international supply chains. In an effort to better monitor compliance in global supply chains of multinational enterprises, international industry federations have developed the equivalent of a collective bargaining agreement on a multi-national level called an 'International Framework Agreement' to be concluded between a multinational company and one or several international industry federations.[81]

To quote just one example, the International Textile, Garment and Leather Workers' Federation (ITGLWF) has signed an international framework agreement with Inditex, the world's second largest retailer grouping brands such as Zara, Pull & Bear, Massimo Dutti and Bershka. The agreement covers the entire supply chain and places the rights of workers to unionise and bargain collectively with their employer at the heart of efforts to secure sustainable

---

[77] M. Merlino and J. Parkin, *Irregular Migration in Europe EU policies and the Fundamental Rights Gap* (Centre for European Policy Studies, Brussels 2011) p. 15.

[78] B. Andrees, 'Strengthening Labour market Governance' in Beate Andrees and Patrick Belser (ed), *Forced labour: coercion and exploitation in the private economy* (ILO, Geneva 2009) p. 89.

[79] ACV Voeding en Diensten, 'Wij willen de vleessector niet overleveren aan koppelbazen! Het loopt fout in het vlees', ACV Nieuwsflash (January 2010) <http://acv-voeding-diensten.acv-online.be/Images/2010%20-%20januari%20vlees_def_nl_web_tcm47-212999.pdf> accessed 1 March 2011.

[80] EFBWW press release 'Illicit Work in construction – Asbestos in our daily life: Europe must act' (March 2010) <http://www.gmb.org.uk /PDF/EFBWW%20Press%20release %20March %202010.pdf> accessed 14 March 2011.

[81] For a list of all International Framework Agreements', see the Global Unions website <http://www.global-unions.org/framework-agreements.html> accessed 8 March 2011.

compliance to key labour standards by suppliers to Inditex. Inditex's Code of Conduct for External Manufacturers and Suppliers underpins the agreement, which outlaws forced labour (and, e.g., specifically bans the retention of residence documents) and harsh and inhumane treatment throughout the Inditex supply chain. No subcontracting is allowed without prior written consent of Inditex, and suppliers are responsible for subcontractor compliance. Monitoring is being done jointly by Inditex and ITGLWF, and irregular policing through snap shot audits is replaced by constant internal factory monitoring by those who know the enterprise best: management and workers.[82]

Redress

Means to redress trafficking and forced labour in the framework of criminal justice show serious limitations and do not adequately guarantee the right to compensation. For vulnerable workers it is often difficult to seek redress through civil or criminal procedures. Many end up unprotected and deported if their abuse is not legally identified as forced labour or human trafficking. Labour courts, mediation and collective action may offer pragmatic avenues for legal redress and compensation along the continuum of exploitation.[83] Migrants are entitled to all labour rights attached to their employment regardless of status including payment of minimum wage, non-discrimination, payment of damages for workplace accidents or health problems caused by the employment, etc.[84] Labour courts may be more accessible with lower fees, and the mechanisms for compensation for damages following breaches of labour law may be much faster and chances of effective compensation being paid to the worker are generally significantly higher. Standardised scales may be in place to quantify damages to be paid for certain breaches of labour law.

Cases of issues and violations of rights at the workplace are preferable settled through negotiation or mediation. Trade unions offer an interlocutor that can bring issues to the attention of the employer with the objective to come to an agreement without putting the individuals at risk. Especially when workers have a precarious or irregular residence status, they still enjoy the human right to organise, join a union and bargain collectively to claim their

---

[82] International Framework Agreement between Industria de Diseño Textil, S.A. (Inditex S.A.) and the International Textile, Garment and Leather Workers' Federation (ITGLWF) on Standards throughout the Inditex Supply Chain <http://www .itglwf.org /lang/en/global-framework-agreements.html> accessed 8 March 2011.

[83] B. Andrees, 'Strengthening Labour market Governance' in B. Andrees and P. Belser (ed), *Forced labour: coercion and exploitation in the private economy* (ILO, Geneva 2009) p. 123.

[84] ILO Convention No. 97 on Migrant Workers.

human rights at work. Effective compensation is a right for trafficked workers and the emerging good practice of trade unions to obtain effective compensation for trafficked workers through labour courts or other means illustrates their important role.

Trade unions with community-based organisations can guide and help organise industrial or collective action, a very effective tool to pressure employers to settle cases and prevent future abuse. 'Compensation awards arrived at by way of voluntary or mediated agreement or which are instituted through a third party (e.g., a trade union in collective action or a labour inspectorate) may have a greater chance of being pursued successfully and paid as well as having a less traumatising effect on the trafficked person.'[85] The MRCI -SIPTU collaborative project to improve and strengthen the organisation of mushroom workers in Ireland, brought mushroom workers together, built and developed leadership and empowered workers to take collective action to ensure that their rights at the workplace are respected. It resulted in the transfer of hundreds of thousands of euros in unpaid wages to the mainly migrant women mushroom workers and a 'Registered Employment Agreement'[86] setting out terms and conditions, rates of pay, holiday entitlements and sick pay for the industry. In the first case mentioned of the 40 asparagus pickers in Someren in the Netherlands, the Dutch trade union FNV negotiated € 115,000 in back wages for the workers involved.[87]

Trade unions can also offer legal assistance and can usually represent workers in front of labour courts, even when the worker was or is an irregular migrant who no longer resides in the country. Migr.Ar is a support centre run by the German trade union Ver.di offering services for undocumented workers. Migrant workers in need of assistance or support are being referred within a network of specialised support organisations. In case of employment-related questions or of violations of labour rights, undocumented workers are referred to the legal service of the German national trade union DGB for advice, mediation or legal representation in front of a labour court.[88]

Despite the clear added value that the involvement of trade unions would bring to the effective protection of workers against forced labour, they are still consistently ignored in anti-trafficking strategies. Where they exist, trade unions should, e.g., be integrated in National Referral Mechanisms (NRMs).[89] NRMs were conceived by the OSCE in 2004, but already in 2007 they stated: 'The NRM was not developed with the kinds of assistance provision needed

---

[85] OSCE/ODIHR, *Compensation for Trafficked and Exploited Persons in the OSCE Region* (Warsaw 2008).

[86] Irish Collective Agreement which has been registered with the Labour Court.

[87] W. Balthussen, '"Wilde" staking aardbeienpluksters Ooirschot: Vijf dagen staken voor vier dubbeltjes per uur en respect' in De Zaaier (12 October 2009) <http://www . srada.nl/nl/Media/10-2009.pdf> accessed 28 February 2011.

[88] Website Migr.Ar.<http://besondere-dienste.hamburg.verdi.de/themen/migrar>accessed 28 February 2011.

[89] OSCE/ODIHR, *National Referral Mechanisms: Joining Efforts to Protect the Rights of Trafficked Persons. A practical Handbook* (Warsaw 2004).

in the context of labour exploitation and in this regard the NRM requires updating.'[90]

Conclusion

It is about time that European governments start realising that human trafficking and modern forms of forced labour are not marginal phenomena but a significant problem in our society, rooted in the contemporary socio-economic context of globalisation, deregulation and migration. Moreover, major industries such as construction, agriculture and textile in our national economies depend on cheap migrant labour, but governments refuse to take the responsibility for the protection of their human rights. Any strategies to combat trafficking and forced labour should be embedded in comprehensive governmental policies with a focus on rights-based migration regulations, poverty reduction and development in countries of origin, regulation of private employment agencies, guarantees for freedom of association and collective bargaining for all, end responsibility of employers and anti-discrimination campaigns. European countries need stronger labour regulation, more effective labour inspection and monitoring and strengthened labour institutions. The policy approach to combating trafficking needs to shift from a reactionary and curative to a more proactive and anticipative one putting more emphasis on prevention. Workers need to be empowered and given support and assistance before they reach the point of ending in forced labour.

The key word for a comprehensive approach is multi-stakeholder cooperation respecting the respective roles, mandates and possibilities of each. There needs to be close cooperation between government with all relevant ministries, labour inspectorate, police, social partners and civil society at large. Trade unions themselves have a large responsibility to organise more workers, especially the most vulnerable such as migrants and domestic workers. Workers' solidarity in times of globalisation is a must and should be truly international and inclusive. Business has the responsibility to operate within the legal framework set up by government or through social dialogue, and there is no better means to monitor compliance than through engaging with organised workers themselves in workplaces throughout supply chains.

This paper shows that there is a huge and massively underused potential in combating trafficking through labour market measures. In the introduction, the ECOWAS Court ruling was mentioned convicting Niger of not doing enough to protect its citizens from slavery. Indeed, States have the human-rights obligation to protect workers under their jurisdiction and should take all

---

[90] OSCE/ODIHR, *Report on Civil Society Meeting* (Warsaw 24 April 2007), 'The NRM approach to trafficking and its application to trafficking for labour exploitation', p. 16.

reasonable measures to prevent the violation of rights of individuals. The alarming rise of forced labour practices in Europe in the mainstream economy shows that measures taken by European governments to date have not been effective. Since almost a decade, activists have been calling for better labour-market based measures as an essential part of the fight against trafficking and modern-day slavery. If European governments continue to refuse to structurally improve the protection of especially migrant workers, they continue to violate their human-rights obligations for not doing what could reasonably be expected, with workers suffering from the absence of State protection against human trafficking, forced labour and contemporary slavery as a result.

Chapter 11
The Interpretation and Implementation of Labour Exploitation in Dutch case law

Linda van Krimpen[1]

Introduction

As in international definitions, human trafficking in the Dutch legislation is not limited to exploitation in the sex industry, but also includes labour exploitation and forced organ removal. When the current human trafficking article entered into force in the Netherlands on 1 January 2005, the Dutch legislator left the further interpretation of the scope of the description of the offence to legal practice.[2] This was relevant, in particular, for case law on labour exploitation, as this type of human trafficking had not previously been criminalised as such in the Netherlands.

Six years after the current Dutch definition of human trafficking for labour exploitation came into force, the interpretation of the scope of the definition by the judiciary is beginning to take shape. This chapter seeks to analyse Dutch case law in cases of trafficking for labour exploitation. The central question is how the legal definition of human trafficking for the purpose of labour exploitation has so far been interpreted by Dutch courts. Special attention will be paid to some recent judgments on 'new' types of exploitation by forced services.

After a brief discussion of the definition of the offence in Dutch legislation, the interpretation in case law of each of the elements of the offence will be discussed. A very important ruling by the Dutch Supreme Court will be discussed more elaborately, as this judgment has had a great impact on the interpretation by the judiciary. In section 3, new types of exploitation by forced services will be discussed, as well as the developments in the way these types of exploitation are qualified by the judiciary. This contribution concludes with some general remarks.

Interpretation and application of the legal definition by the judiciary

The current definition of human trafficking in Article 273f paragraph 1 of the Dutch Criminal Code literally reflects – inter alia – the UN Palermo

---

[1] Linda van Krimpen LL.M works as a researcher at the Bureau of the Dutch Rapporteur on Trafficking in Human Beings.

[2] NRM, *Trafficking in Human Beings. Seventh Report of the National Rapporteur* (BNRM 2009) p. 494.

Protocol.[3] According to subsection 1 of the article, recruiting, transporting, moving, accommodating or sheltering a person by force, violence or other act, with the intention of exploiting that person, constitutes trafficking in human beings. As in the UN Palermo Protocol and in the EU Framework Decision on combating trafficking in human beings[4], the legal definition consists of three elements: act, means and intention of exploitation. In addition to the means 'force', 'violence' and 'other act', the provision also refers to 'threat of violence or other act', 'extortion', 'fraud', 'deception', 'the misuse of authority arising from the actual state of affairs', 'the misuse of a vulnerable position', and 'giving or receiving remuneration or benefits in order to obtain the consent of a person who has control over this other person'.[5] Apart from sexual exploitation, exploitation encompasses at least forced or compulsory labour or services, slavery and practices similar to slavery or servitude.[6] As prostitution is considered labour in the Netherlands, in practice a distinction is made between 'sexual exploitation' (in prostitution), 'exploitation for organ removal', and 'other forms of exploitation'.[7] The latter encompasses exploitation in all sectors except for the prostitution sector. For the readability of this paper, the international term 'labour exploitation' will be used, meaning all types of exploitation outside the sex industry and apart from forced organ removal.

Apart from the implementation of the UN Palermo Protocol and the EU Framework Decision, Article 273f also replaced the former Article 250a of the Dutch Criminal Code. The definition of human trafficking in that provision was partly different from the international definition implemented in subsection 1. Nevertheless, all behaviour falling within the scope of Article 273f constitutes human trafficking. In some subsections, the definition is somewhat broader than the international definition.

Aside from subsection 1, charges are often brought under subsection 4 of Article 273f as well in cases of labour exploitation.[8] This subsection covers any

---

[3] UN Protocol to Prevent, Suppress and Punish Trafficking in Persons, Especially Women and Children, Supplementing the United Nations Convention against Transnational Organised Crime, 2000. The UN Palermo Protocol entered into force on 23 September 2005 (Bulletin of Treaties 2001, 130).

[4] EU Framework Decision on Combating Trafficking in Human Beings, 19 July 2002, 2002/629/JHA. The EU Framework Decision is about to be repealed by the proposed EU Directive on Preventing and Combating Trafficking in Human Beings, and Protecting Victims. At the time of writing, the directive had not yet come into force.

[5] The (non-official) English translation of Article 273f of the Dutch Criminal Code can be found at <http://english.bnrm.nl/legislation/> accessed 24 February 2011.

[6] Article 273f (2) of the Dutch Criminal Code.

[7] NRM, *Trafficking in Human Beings. Seventh Report of the National Rapporteur* (BNRM 2009) p. 478.

[8] Article 273f (1) (4) reads: 'the person who forces or induces another person by the means referred to under 1 to make himself/herself available for performing work or services or making his/her organs available or takes any action in the circumstances referred to under 1 which he knows or may reasonably be expected to know will result in that other person making himself/herself available for performing labour or services or making his/her organs available'.

act that causes the other person to be in a situation where he or she makes him or herself available[9] for performing labour or services.

Prosecutions for human trafficking for labour exploitation were slow to take off in the Netherlands after 2005. The number of convictions for this type of exploitation was even lower. In the first five years after the criminalisation, twelve different cases[10] of labour exploitation were dealt with in court, of which only four led to convictions for labour exploitation. The judgments indicated that neither producing convincing evidence, nor weighing the facts and circumstances in cases of labour exploitation was straightforward.[11]
The first – and so far only – judgment in a case of labour exploitation by the Supreme Court, on 27 October 2009, has led to a change in perception by the courts.

Act

Proving the first element of human trafficking for labour exploitation has not constituted many difficulties in court. The definition includes cross border trafficking as well as internal trafficking. In almost all prosecuted cases, victims were somehow internally moved at a certain point. Even transporting someone from the workplace to his home constitutes an act as described in the human trafficking article.
Moreover, Article 273f paragraph 1(4) of the Dutch Criminal Code, in which the person who forces or induces another person by one of the means to make himself/herself available for performing work or services is criminalised, does not require an act. Nevertheless, behaviour falling under the description of this subparagraph constitutes human trafficking.[12]

Means

In the first five years after the criminalisation of labour exploitation, only cases in which severe means of coercion were used, such as force or violence, led to convictions for labour exploitation. The first case of labour exploitation that led to a conviction for human trafficking is the 'Mehak case'.[13] In this case, three Indian people were exploited as domestic servants by a married couple from India. The victims came to the Netherlands with the help of the

---

[9] H.M. Van Maurik, 'Titel XVIII Misdrijven tegen de persoonlijke vrijheid' in C.P.M. Cleiren and M.J.M. Verpalen, *Strafrecht Tekst & Commentaar* (Kluwer 2010) p. 1244.

[10] In most cases, several suspects were prosecuted. The total number of suspects in the twelve cases is 36.

[11] The judgments are described elaborately in NRM, *Trafficking in Human Beings. Seventh Report of the National Rapporteur* (BNRM 2009) pp. 494–521.

[12] Subsection 4 is an implementation of the former Article 250a (1) (1) of the Dutch Criminal Code.

[13] The Hague District Court, 14 December 2007, LJN: BC1195 and LJN: BC1761. The case also led to convictions for human trafficking in appeal, and is currently pending before the Supreme Court.

exploiters, and were entirely dependent on them. The victims were subjected to physical violence. The physical violence could be proven by statements of the victims and a forensic report by a doctor.

Misuse of a vulnerable position

Apart from severe means of coercion, the legal definition also contains 'soft' means, such as deception and misuse of a vulnerable position. The means of coercion most often charged is misuse of a vulnerable position. The line taken in case law is that the combination of illegal residence, a poor economic position and inability to speak the Dutch language create a vulnerable position.[14] However, during the early years after criminalisation, the judiciary was divided on the interpretation of the terminology *misuse* of this vulnerable position.[15] In the case 'Cannabis cultivation – Fleurtop' where illegally residing Bulgarian people had to cut the tops off cannabis plants under poor working conditions, the court found that there was coercion through misuse of their vulnerable position because the suspects were aware of that position and took advantage of that position to derive benefit.[16] However, in another case, the 'Chinese restaurant case' in which illegal Chinese workers were employed in a restaurant, the court ruled that in order to prove misuse of a vulnerable position, a certain initiative and positive act by the perpetrators is presumed, by which they consciously misuse the weaker or vulnerable position of the victims.[17] This criterion on initiative and positive action was adopted by other judges in later cases involving labour exploitation[18], resulting in acquittals, as it was hard to prove such an element.

Interpretation of 'misuse of a vulnerable position' by the Supreme Court

By ruling on the interpretation of the means 'misuse of a vulnerable position', the Supreme Court ended the differences in interpretation of this means by different courts.

The case concerned the presumed exploitation of Chinese workers living illegally in the Netherlands. The workers had themselves approached the restaurant, asking for work. The restaurant owner agreed to take them on. The Chinese were subsequently put to work under poor conditions. Both the

---

[14] NRM, *Trafficking in Human Beings. Seventh Report of the National Rapporteur* (BNRM 2009) p. 496.

[15] L. van Krimpen, 'Mensenhandel en arbeidsuitbuiting. Recente ontwikkelingen in de jurisprudentie' in *Justitiële Verkenningen* (2010) p. 58.

[16] The Hague District Court, 21 November 2006, LJN: AZ2707.

[17] Den Bosch Court of Appeal, 30 January 2008, LJN: BA0145 and LJN: BA0141.

[18] I.e. Zwolle District Court, 29 April 2008, LJN: BD0860, Almelo District Court, 10 April 2009, LJN: BI0944.

District Court and the Court of Appeal judged that human trafficking could not be proven because the workers had approached the restaurant themselves. Because of that, the Appeal Court found, it could not be proven that the suspects had consciously misused the vulnerable position of the Chinese by taking them in and housing them. The Court of Appeal upheld the judgment of the District Court that a presumption of misuse of a vulnerable position requires a certain initiative and positive action on the part of the perpetrator. The vulnerable position should be consciously misused, according to the Court of Appeal.

The legal question before the Supreme Court first of all concerned the definition of the elements 'misuse of authority arising from the actual state of affairs' and 'misuse of a vulnerable position' contained in the charges.[19] The Supreme Court[20] ruled that to prove 'misuse', it is sufficient to show conditional intent on the part of the suspect with respect to those circumstances or the vulnerable position. Consequently, there is no need for conscious misuse. Neither is it essential that the victim has been put into the exploitative situation by the employer. To prove misuse of a vulnerable position, for example, it is enough that the perpetrator recognises the vulnerable position and takes advantage of this position. With this ruling, the Supreme Court deemed the Appeal Court's requirement of initiative or a positive action on the part of the suspect not to be an independent requirement.

The explanation by the Supreme Court on the element of misuse of a vulnerable position had a major impact on the judgments following the Supreme Court decision. By following the explanation of the Supreme Court, labour exploitation cases with the charge of misuse of a vulnerable position resulted in convictions for the first time, whereas in the first five years after the criminalisation of labour exploitation, only cases with charges of severe (violent) means of coercion led to convictions.

(Intention of) exploitation

In addition to sexual exploitation, exploitation encompasses at least forced or compulsory labour or services, slavery and practices similar to slavery or servitude.[21] These types of exploitation are not limited to certain sectors. The explanatory report cited, as an example of exploitation, an extremely long working week for disproportionately low pay in poor working conditions.[22] In

[19] In this paper only the 'misuse of a vulnerable position' will be discussed.

[20] Supreme Court, 27 October 2009, LJN: BI7099408. This case is also described in NRM, *Trafficking in Human Beings. Eighth Report of the National Rapporteur* (BNRM, 2010) pp. 85–86.

[21] Article 273f (2) of the Dutch Criminal Code.

[22] Parliamentary Documents II 2003/04, 29 291, no. 3, p. 18.

the case of exploitation, fundamental rights such as physical integrity, personal freedom or human dignity are at stake.[23]

Determining that victims had been exploited, and consequently, that fundamental rights had been infringed, appeared not to be an easy task. The standard was set rather high during the first five years after the criminalisation. The judgments confirmed that Article 273f only pertained to excessive misuse in relation to work. What prosecutors and judges seemed to grapple with most, was exactly how excessive the facts and circumstances needed to be, in order for them to qualify as a trafficking case.

Interpretation of (intention of) exploitation by the Supreme Court

In the case about the presumed exploitation of Chinese workers in a restaurant, the Supreme Court in its judgment of 27 October 2009 also gave its view on the element (intention of) exploitation. It was proven that the Chinese were put to work on an average of eleven to thirteen hours a day, six days a week, for a wage far below the minimum wage.[24] They slept a number of workers to a bedroom. The Court of Appeal found that in this case, there was no question of exploitation, deciding that although the situation was socially undesirable it had not been shown that the working conditions were in themselves bad.

The Public Prosecutor at the Supreme Court was of the opinion that the Court of Appeal had failed to give adequate reasons for its finding that there was no exploitation. The Supreme Court judged that it is impossible to give a general definition of exploitation, as it depends heavily on the circumstances of the case. In a case like the present one however, relevant factors include the nature and duration of the work, the restrictions imposed on the individuals concerned and the economic benefit to the employer. In addition, the generally accepted standards in Dutch society should be adopted as the framework of reference for weighing these factors. The Supreme Court added that, in order to meet the definition of the offence, there is no requirement for the victims to be actually exploited. The intention of exploitation is enough to arrive at a conviction. This taken into account, the Supreme Court judged that the Appeal Court's decision – without further reasoning – that there was no situation of exploitation, was incomprehensible, given the court's finding that some victims worked eleven to thirteen hours a day just for room and board and others for a monthly income of €450 and €800, that they had no more than five days off a month and that they had to share their bedroom with others.[25]

[23] Korvinus et al., 'Mensenhandel: het begrip uitbuiting in art. 273a Sr.' in Trema (2006) pp. 286–290.

[24] They earned €500–€800 per month, which is between €1.50 and €3 an hour.

[25] See also NRM, *Trafficking in Human Beings. Eighth Report of the National Rapporteur* (BNRM 2010) p. 86.

The case was referred back to the Court of Appeal in Den Bosch. Subsequently, the Appeal Court convicted one of the two suspects on the charge of human trafficking.[26]

Exploitation within a professional setting v. personal setting

Before the Supreme Court ruling, eight out of twelve cases of presumed labour exploitation led to acquittals. These cases had in common that, in most instances, the labour took place in a professional setting such as factories, a restaurant, a massage parlour and a cleaning company.

In a case about Indian men performing heavy labour in a tofu factory and living under poor circumstances, the court described the situation as socially undesirable but judged there was no intention of exploitation, ruling that the circumstances were insufficiently serious to be described as violations of fundamental rights.[27] Nevertheless, the court proved that the workers, who were living in the Netherlands illegally, performed work which was onerous by Dutch standards, for long hours, six days a week and for a pay of only €800 a month. The workers were accommodated with eight people in one dwelling and some had to share a bed. Even though these circumstances were socially undesirable, the court found that the situation was not excessive, and could consequently not come to a conviction.[28]

The four cases that resulted in convictions for labour exploitation in the period before the Supreme Court ruling had in common that the exploitation took place within a personal setting; three cases were about domestic servitude, and in another case the victim was exploited in crime as she was forced to smuggle drugs for the suspect. In three of the convicted cases, violence was used against the victim(s). Another aspect the cases had in common was that the victims lived with their exploiters during (part of) the exploitative period. Lestrade and Ten Kate argued that with these convictions, the Dutch judge passed over exploitation in the form of forced labour or services, by only convicting for the most flagrant form of exploitation, namely servitude.[29]

With the Supreme Court's explanation of (the intention of) exploitation in the Chinese restaurant case, it seems that more clarification is given to the distinction between bad labour circumstances and exploitation. Eight cases of exploitation within a professional setting were prosecuted after the Supreme Court ruling. The sectors in which the charged exploitation took place were restaurants (two cases), agriculture (two cases), construction (two cases), food

[26] Den Bosch Court of Appeal, 17 September 2010, LJN BN7215. A third suspect was convicted for human trafficking earlier that year: Den Bosch Court of Appeal, 19 February 2010, LJN: BL5492.

[27] Zwolle District Court, 29 April 2008, LJN: BD0860, LJN: BD0846 and LJN: BD0857.

[28] The public prosecution service has appealed the ruling.

[29] S. Lestrade and W. ten Kate, 'De strafbaarstelling van 'overige uitbuiting' binnen mensenhandel' in NJCM-Bulletin 34/8 (2009) p. 866.

processing (one case) and the market (one case). The cases had some characteristics in common. First of all, in seven cases the employees/victims were housed by the employers/perpetrators. The accommodation was, in all cases, very basic and, in some cases, far below Dutch standards with large numbers of people sleeping in small rooms in dangerous and very unhygienic circumstances. In all cases, the victims were in a vulnerable position either because they were illegal immigrants or because they worked illegally as a consequence of lacking the required work permits. Whereas before the Supreme Court ruling, cases of presumed labour exploitation within a professional setting did not lead to convictions for labour exploitation, six out of eight cases that were prosecuted after the Supreme Court decision did lead to convictions.

'New' types of forced services

Apart from the increase in prosecutions and convictions for exploitation within sectors of the formal economy, another development in case law after the Supreme Court ruling is becoming visible. This development concerns rather 'new' types of forced services as exploitation. A characteristic in these cases is that the services are only performed over a short period of time, sometimes only once. The victims in all these prosecuted cases were young, mostly female, Dutch nationals. In some instances, the services performed by the victims were criminal activities. In the next subsections, case law with regard to these 'new' types of exploitation will be discussed. A distinction is made between criminal exploitation and exploitation by forced subscribing to phone contracts.

Criminal exploitation by forced drug smuggling

Although not explicitly criminalised as human trafficking, criminal exploitation can fall within the scope of the Dutch trafficking article.[30] The conduct that compels a victim to commit a criminal offence can be defined as human trafficking if all elements of the definition of the offence are met.[31] *Before* the Supreme Court ruling, three cases of criminal exploitation had been prosecuted. Two were about alleged exploitation in hemp factories. In these two cases, human trafficking could not be proven. The third case of criminal

---

[30] For an elaborate description of criminal exploitation and non-punishment of victims, see NRM, *Trafficking in Human Beings. Seventh Report of the National Rapporteur* (BNRM 2009) Chapter 6.

[31] By contrast with the Netherlands, in Belgium for instance, criminal exploitation is explicitly mentioned as a form of human trafficking in the criminal law (Article 433 quinquies, (1) (5) Criminal Code. Moreover, in Article 2 (3) of the proposed EU Directive on Preventing and Combating Trafficking in Human beings, and Protecting Victims, 'the exploitation of criminal activities' is included in the definition of exploitation.

exploitation was about a young woman who was forced to smuggle cocaine from Curacao to the Netherlands. In order to have her smuggle the drugs, the suspect raped her and threatened her severely. This case led to the first conviction for criminal exploitation.[32]

Two of the labour exploitation cases that were prosecuted *after* the Supreme Court ruling were cases in which the suspects were charged with criminal exploitation. The two cases concerned forced drug smuggling.

Moroccan drug smuggling case

In the first case, the court acquitted the suspects of the charged criminal exploitation.[33] In this case, two minors and three young adult women had been incited to smuggle drugs from Morocco to the Netherlands. Although The Hague District Court came to the conclusion that 'misuse of a vulnerable position' of two of the girls could be proven, as the suspects knew of this vulnerable position and had asked if there were 'dumb' girls who could smuggle drugs, the court concluded that the 'intention of exploitation' could not be proven. With regard to this element, the court attached great importance to the fact that two of the girls cancelled a drugs transport, without far-reaching consequences. Apparently, according to the court, they had the opportunity to withdraw from the situation.

An interesting aspect is the court's view on the means 'misuse of a vulnerable position' with respect to a third victim. This woman was in a vulnerable position because she was mentally impaired, according to the court. However, it could not be proven that the suspects knew about the mental impairment, and therefore, about the vulnerable position of the woman. Because this could not be proven, conditional intent to the misuse of a vulnerable position could not be proven. A parallel is drawn with the Supreme Court decision in the Chinese restaurant case, although not explicitly.

Suriname drug smuggling case

Unlike the aforementioned case, the same District Court was able to reach a conviction in another case of criminal exploitation one month later.[34] In this case, young women had been incited to smuggle drugs from Suriname to the Netherlands. The recruiter of one of the two women who was incited to smuggle drugs had a remarkable case history. The suspect had been in prison for a few months because he was suspected of sexually exploiting this girl in prostitution. Finally, he was acquitted of sexual exploitation. However, once the suspect was at liberty, he blamed the girl for lost income during the period he was in prison. He ordered her to smuggle drugs for him so she could make

[32] Haarlem District Court, 22 April 2009, LJN: BI3519.
[33] The Hague District Court, 17 February 2010, LJN: BL4298 and LJN: BL4279. The judgments of the other two suspects have not been published.
[34] The Hague District Court, 18 March 2010, LJN: BL8022.

up for this. The District Court proved the criminal exploitation of the girl. It is remarkable that in proving the criminal exploitation, the court took into consideration that the victim had been brought into prostitution by the suspect, even though the suspect was acquitted from sexual exploitation of the same victim in another judgment.[35]
According to the charges, there was also another victim who was forced to smuggle drugs for the suspect. This victim had asked the suspect about the drug smuggling herself, and she was aware of the advantages and disadvantages of the smuggling, according to the court. Besides, unlike the first victim, this woman was not in a situation that restricted her freedom of choice in such a way that she had no other option than to agree to the request of the suspect to smuggle the drugs. From this, the court derived that there was no situation of exploitation of the second victim.

Exploitation by forced subscribing to phone contracts

In the 'Suriname drug smuggling case' discussed above, the suspect was also charged with another type of exploitation, namely, he was accused of exploiting the two women by forcing them to subscribe to a number of phone contracts, after which they had to give the phones to the suspect. Subsequently, the phones were sold and the women were left with high debts because of the phone contracts. The Prosecutor in this case defined these facts as forced labour or services as described in paragraph 1 subsection 4 of the human trafficking article.[36] With regard to this charge, the court judged that the suspect had pressed the women to subscribe to the phone contracts. However, this did not qualify as exploitation, as fundamental rights had not been grossly violated, according to the court. With regard to the phone contracts, the court declared the suspect guilty of fraud.

Phone contracts case II

One month later, a similar case about forced subscription to phone contracts did lead to a conviction for human trafficking.[37] In this case, the suspect had forced several young women to subscribe to phone contracts and to hand over the phones.

[35] The Hague District Court, 26 June 2009, unpublished.
[36] Art. 273f (1) (4) of the Criminal Code: 'Any person who forces or induces another person by the means referred to under (a) to make himself/herself available for performing work or services or making his/her organs available or takes any action in the circumstances referred to under (a) which he knows or may reasonably be expected to know will result in that other person making himself/herself available for performing labour or services or making his/her organs available; shall be guilty of trafficking in human beings [...]'
[37] Dordrecht District Court, 20 April 2010, LJN: BM1743.

The Dordrecht District Court first considered that from the explanatory report to Article 273a[38], it would seem that trafficking always includes a form of exploitation. With the criminalisation of human trafficking, the interest of the individual is the first matter of importance. This interest concerns the preservation of his or her physical and mental integrity and personal freedom. Although '(the intention of) exploitation' is not explicitly mentioned as an element in subsection 4 of Article 273f (1), this element is required in order to come to a conviction for human trafficking. This, according to the court, derives from the preceding grounds.

Secondly, in order to decide whether there was (the intention of) exploitation, it is relevant if the will of the victims was affected by the suspects in such a way, that they had no free choice in subscribing to the phone contracts, or that they had no reasonable option other than to act the way the suspects wanted them to act.[39] With regard to ten of the women who had subscribed to phone contracts for the suspects, the court judged that human trafficking could not be proven because the will of these women was not affected by the suspects in such a way that they had no free choice than to subscribe to the phone contracts. As the women still had the option not to subscribe to the phone contracts, (the intention of) exploitation could not be proven, leading to acquittals for human trafficking. The suspects were convicted for fraud.

However, as regards two other women, the court came to another conclusion. Initially, these two women refused subscribing to the phone contracts because they knew that other women had run into problems due to the phone contracts. After their refusal to subscribe to the phone contracts, the suspects intimidated the two women by saying that they knew all about the problems one of these women had with her parents, and that they knew where the women lived. The suspects also told them that they would never see their parents again. Because of these threats, the court judged that the suspects had intentionally put these women in a position in which they reasonably had no other option than to subscribe to the phone contracts. Subsequently, human trafficking was proven.

Phone contracts case III

In a third case about phone contracts, a young woman and her boyfriend were charged with human trafficking as well.[40] They had asked several youngsters to do promotional work. As in the aforementioned cases, these youngsters had to subscribe to phone contracts and give the phones to the suspects. The victims would receive a free phone as a reward for their 'promotional work'. Just as in the two cases mentioned above, the suspects were charged under Article 273f

---

[38] Article 273a of the Dutch Criminal Code was later renumbered to Article 273f.

[39] This argumentation is similar to the reasoning of the courts in the cases of criminal exploitation through smuggling drugs, as discussed in section 3.1.

[40] Haarlem District Court, 8 December 2010, LJN: BO8985.

(1) (4) of the Criminal Code. Unlike the Dordrecht District Court in 'Phone contracts case II', the Haarlem District Court in 'Phone contracts case III' ruled that the element '(intention of) exploitation' was not an element of subsection 4, and therefore, exploitation, or the intention of exploitation was not required in order to fulfil the definition of the offence. In order to reach a conviction for this type of trafficking, it was sufficient to prove that the suspect had induced the victims with one of the means – in this case 'deception' – to make themselves available for performing labour or services, according to the Haarlem District Court. In the present case, this could be proven, resulting in a conviction for human trafficking.

Despite the conviction for human trafficking, the court stated in its grounds for sentencing that although the offences declared proven qualified as human trafficking, the facts did rather remind of a form of fraud. This term (fraud) did better fit common parlance and the public perception of the facts of this case, according to the court.

The interpretation and application of forced services ex. Article 273f 1 (4)

In each of the four cases discussed in this section, charges were brought under Article 273f 1 (4) of the Dutch Criminal Code. This subsection covers any act that causes the other person to be in a situation where he or she makes him or herself available for performing labour or services. As such, this constitutes human trafficking.

Case law confirms that even though criminal exploitation is not explicitly criminalised in the Dutch human trafficking article, it can fall within its scope. Furthermore, the broad definition of human trafficking in the Dutch legislation seems to allow the inclusion of other new types of exploitation, such as exploitation by forced subscribing to a phone contract.

Exploitation as element of subsection 4

The element (intention of) exploitation is not included in the text of subsection 4. However, in three of the four judgments discussed above, the courts decided that although '(the intention of) exploitation' is not explicitly mentioned as an element in this subsection, this element is required in order to come to a conviction for human trafficking.

In 'Phone contracts case III', the court argued that (intention of) exploitation is *not* an element of subsection 4, and therefore this does not have to be proven. As a consequence, the court came to a conviction for human trafficking by proving that the suspects deceived the victims, which resulted in the victims making themselves available for performing services. However, it can be argued that in most situations of deception, it is the deceiver's objective to make his/her victim do something for him/her. The following example[41] makes this clear: someone orders food in a restaurant, making the waitress believe that he will pay for the food. However, he runs away after having eaten his dinner without paying for the meal. In this example, the customer has deceived the waitress, which caused her to make herself available for performing services. Defining this as human trafficking ex. Article 273f (1) (4) seems to overstep the mark, and it remains to be seen if the legislator had this in mind when drafting subsection 4. It would mean that almost every case of deception or swindle could be defined as human trafficking. That does not seem to be in compliance with the severity of the crime of human trafficking. As the court argued in 'Phone contracts case III', the facts do rather remind of a form of fraud.

Relevant factors for defining a situation as exploitation

In contrast to the 'Phone contracts case III', in the other three cases discussed in this section, the courts argued that (the intention of) exploitation is required in order to come to a conviction for human trafficking. The question about whether or not (the intention of) exploitation is an element of subsection 4 has not been asked of the Supreme Court in the Chinese restaurant case. Nevertheless, when looking into the assessment of the element (intention of) exploitation, the Supreme Court ruled that relevant factors include the nature and duration of the work, the restrictions they impose on the individuals concerned and the economic benefit to the employer. These factors were not explicitly applied in the cases of 'new' types of forced services as discussed in this section. Instead, a decisive factor in the judgments was whether the victims had the opportunity to withdraw from the exploitative situation. Only cases in which the freedom of choice of the victim was severely restricted, resulting in a situation in which they had no other option than to agree to committing the crime, led to convictions for Article 273f (1) (4).

Although the impossibility of withdrawing from the situation is an important factor to be considered when deciding whether or not the victim has been exploited,[42] it remains to be seen why the factors formulated by the Supreme Court are not explicitly taken into consideration by lower courts in cases of exploitation by forced services as discussed in this section. One would think that in these cases too, the court could look into the nature and duration of the work or services, the restrictions they imposed on the individuals concerned and the economic benefit to the employer, in this case exploiter. By only taking into consideration the impossibility to withdraw from the

[41] This example is taken from: M. Alink and J. Wiarda, 'Materieelrechtelijke aspecten van mensenhandel in het Nederlands strafrecht' in D. De Prins et al., *Preadviezen 2010* (BJU 2010) p. 226.

[42] NRM, *Trafficking in Human Beings. Seventh Report of the National Rapporteur* (BNRM 2009) p. 498.

situation, the bar might be set too low, with the risk of erosion of the human trafficking definition.[43]

Conclusion

The central question of this paper is how the legal definition of human trafficking, for the purpose of labour exploitation, is interpreted in Dutch case law. When studying case law before and after the Supreme Court decision, it is clear that this ruling has had a major impact on the interpretation and the perception of labour exploitation by the judiciary. The standards of the Supreme Court about 'misuse of a vulnerable position' and 'intention of exploitation' are visible in the judgments. In most cases, these standards have been applied explicitly, with a reference to the Supreme Court ruling.

Whereas before the Supreme Court ruling, only cases of exploitation within a personal setting led to convictions, after the Supreme Court decision, six cases of exploitation within a professional setting led to convictions for labour exploitation. Furthermore, the number of prosecutions after October 2009 doubled in one year to 24 cases by the end of 2010. Also, the number of convictions increased considerably, from four to thirteen convictions.[44]

Among the cases prosecuted after the Supreme Court decision are some 'new' types of exploitation, where victims are forced to perform services for the exploiter. Case law confirms that even though these new types of forced services are not explicitly criminalised in the Dutch human trafficking article, they can be brought within the scope of Article 273f (1) (4). Whether or not the (intention of) exploitation should be taken into account when qualifying facts fall within the scope of subsection 4, is not completely clarified yet.

A decisive factor in the judgments on forced services, as discussed in this paper, has been whether the victims had the opportunity to withdraw from the exploitative situation. Although this is an important factor to be considered when deciding whether or not the victim has been exploited, it remains to be seen why the factors formulated by the Supreme Court are not explicitly taken into consideration by lower courts in cases of forced services.

Whereas case law during the first five years after the criminalisation of labour exploitation confirmed that Article 273f only pertained to excessive misuse in relation to work, this standard seems to be different in last year's case law on forced services. As the requirements for a situation of exploitation by forced services to qualify as human trafficking have not yet taken definite shape in Dutch case law, it seems that in some cases the standard might be set too low, with the risk of erosion of the human trafficking definition. As a matter of

[43] See also: Korvinus et al. 'Mensenhandel: het begrip uitbuiting in art. 273a Sr.' in Trema (2006) pp. 286–290; C. Rijken, 'Challenges and Pitfalls in Combating Trafficking in Human Beings for Labour Exploitation', Chapter 7 in this book.

[44] The total number of convictions is higher, as in several cases there was more than one suspect.

legal certainty, it would be desirable to have these issues decided upon in case law, preferably by the Supreme Court.

Annex 1

List of participants in the project

Austria
Julia Planitzer and Helmut Sax
Ludwig Boltzmann Institute of Human Rights
Group on Women's Rights, Child Rights and Human Trafficking Vienna

The Netherlands
Marijn Heemskerk and Conny Rijken
European and International Law Department
Tilburg Law School
Tilburg University

Romania
George Cristinel Zaharia
PhD candidate on Human Trafficking, Bucharest University, Romania
Assistant Professor, Craiova University, Romania
Judge at District Court in Drobeta – Turnu Severin, Romania

Serbia
Sanja Ćopić and Vesna Nikolić-Ristanović
Vesna Nikolić-Ristanović, Victimology Society of Serbia Faculty of Special Education and Rehabilitation, University of Belgrade.
Sanja Ćopić, Victimology Society of Serbia and Institute for Criminological and Sociological Research in Belgrade.

Spain
Fernando Manrique López and Francisco Javier Arrieta Idiakez
Law Faculty
University of Deusto
Fernando Manrique Rojo
Lawyer specialised in labour law in Bilbao.

EU Legal Framework
Annemarie Middelburg and Conny Rijken
European and International Law Department
Tilburg Law School
Tilburg University

Experts in the project
Floris van Dijk
Senior adviser Dutch Social Security Intelligence and Investigation Service (SIOD) The Hague

Bärbel Uhl
Chair of the EU experts Group on THB, Germany

External experts in the expert meeting:
Joanna Goodey
Head of Department Freedoms and Justice,
EU Fundamental Rights Agency
Vienna

Warner ten Kate
National public prosecutor on THB in the Netherlands
National Office of the National Prosecution Service, Zwolle

Gert Vermeulen
Professor criminology and criminal law Ghent University and extraordinary professor evidence law, Maastricht University